ECOFEMINISM

Ecofeminism

Women, Culture, Nature

Edited by Karen J. Warren

with editorial assistance from Nisvan Erkal

INDIANA UNIVERSITY PRESS

Bloomington and Indianapolis

The paper used in this publication
meets the minimum requirements of American National Standard
for Information Sciences—Permanence of Paper
for Printed Library Materials,
ANSI Z39.48-1984.

Manufactured in the United States of America

Library of Congress Cataloging-in-Publication Data

Ecofeminism: women, culture, nature / edited by Karen J.
Warren with editorial assistance from
Nisvan Erkal.
p.   cm.
Includes index.
ISBN 978-0-253-33031-4 (cloth : alk. paper) — ISBN 978-0-253-21057-9
(pbk. : alk. paper)
1. Ecofeminism.   I. Warren, Karen, date.   II. Erkal, Nisvan.
HQ1233.E23   1997
305.42'01—dc20   96-28481

3   4   5   6   7   12   11   10   09   08   07

To the memory of Petra Kelly

Contents

Introduction   xi
   Karen J. Warren

PART I
Taking Empirical Data Seriously

One: Taking Empirical Data Seriously:
An Ecofeminist Philosophical Perspective   3
   Karen J. Warren

Two: Ecofeminism through an
Anticolonial Framework   21
   Andy Smith

Three: Women of Color, Environmental Justice,
and Ecofeminism   38
   Dorceta E. Taylor

Four: Women's Knowledge as Expert Knowledge:
Indian Women and Ecodevelopment   82
   Deane Curtin

Five: Epistemic Responsibility and the Inuit of
Canada's Eastern Arctic: An Ecofeminist Appraisal   99
   Douglas J. Buege

Six: Women and Power   112
   Petra Kelly

Seven: Learning to Live with Differences:
The Challenge of Ecofeminist Community   120
   Judith Plant

Eight: "The Earth Is the Indian's Mother,
Nhãndecy"   140
   Eliane Potiguara
   (Translated by Leland Robert Guyer; edited by Karen J. Warren)

PART II
Interdisciplinary Perspectives

Nine: Leisure: Celebration and
Resistance in the Ecofeminist Quilt   155
   Karen M. Fox

Contents

viii

Ten: Ecofeminism and Work   176
Robert Alan Sessions

Eleven: Ecofeminism and Children   193
Ruthanne Kurth-Schai

Twelve: Ecofeminism and Meaning   213
Susan Griffin

Thirteen: Ecofeminist Literary Criticism   227
Gretchen T. Legler

Fourteen: Rhetoric, Rape, and Ecowarfare
in the Persian Gulf   239
Adrienne Elizabeth Christiansen

Fifteen: The Nature of Race: Discourses of Racial
Difference in Ecofeminism   260
Noël Sturgeon

Sixteen: Ecofeminism in Kenya:
A Chemical Engineer's Perspective   279
Joseph R. Loer

Seventeen: Keeping the Soil in Good Heart: Women
Weeders, the Environment, and Ecofeminism   290
Candice Bradley

Eighteen: Remediating Development through an
Ecofeminist Lens   300
Betty Wells and Danielle Wirth

Nineteen: Scientific Ecology and Ecological
Feminism: The Potential for Dialogue   314
Catherine Zabinski

PART III

Philosophical Perspectives

Twenty: Androcentrism and Anthropocentrism:
Parallels and Politics   327
Val Plumwood

Twenty-one: Revaluing Nature   356
Lori Gruen

Twenty-two: Self and Community in
Environmental Ethics   375
Wendy Donner

Twenty-three: Kant and Ecofeminism   390
Holyn Wilson

Twenty-four: Women-Animals-Machines:
A Grammar for a Wittgensteinian Ecofeminism   412
Wendy Lee-Lampshire

Contents

Twenty-five: Radical Nonduality in
Ecofeminist Philosophy 425
    Charlene Spretnak

Contributors 437

Index 441

Introduction

Karen J. Warren

During the past ten years, several journals, anthologies, and single-authored books have been published on ecological feminism, or "ecofeminism." Ecological feminism is the position that there are important connections between how one treats women, people of color, and the underclass on one hand and how one treats the nonhuman natural environment on the other. Of these various publications, none has provided a multidisciplinary perspective on topics in ecofeminist scholarship. What this volume does is just that: it provides a critical examination of ecofeminism from a variety of cross-cultural and multidisciplinary perspectives. As such, it is an important addition to the literature on ecofeminism.

The book is divided into three parts. Part I, "Taking Empirical Data Seriously," explores real-life, experiential concerns which have motivated ecofeminism as a grassroots, women-initiated movement around the globe. Part II, "Interdisciplinary Perspectives," presents the works of scholars in a variety of academic disciplines and vocational fields (e.g., anthropology, biology, chemical engineering, communication studies, education, environmental studies, literature, political science, recreation and leisure studies, sociology) on the application or appropriateness of ecofeminism to their research and to the peoples whose lives are touched by it. Part III, "Philosophical Perspectives," provides a critical examination of ecofeminism from professional philosophers on topics which range from the expected (e.g., challenges of ecofeminist philosophy to mainstream Western thought) to the unexpected (e.g., ecofeminism and Wittgenstein and Kant). Together these three parts provide a balanced cross-cultural lens through which to begin to access the potential strengths and weaknesses of ecofeminism as a political movement and theoretical position.

In part I, the first essay, by the editor, Karen J. Warren, looks at such topics as trees and forests, water, food production, toxins, the United States military, environmental racism, classism and ageism, and language to motivate an ecofeminist analysis of environmental problems and solutions. Warren argues that any development project or environmental philosophy which fails to take seriously the connections between these issues and women will be grossly inadequate.

In the second essay, Andy Smith, Cherokee woman and member of Women of All Red Nations, discusses environmentalism and ecofeminism through an anticolonial perspective. She argues that any ecofeminist practice and theory which fails to reject any of its colonial underpinnings will be unacceptable.

Dorceta E. Taylor, in her essay, "Women of Color, Environmental Justice, and Ecofeminism," provides a brief description of the development of the environmental justice movement and the emerging role of women of color in this movement. She examines the critical relationship between women of color, environmental justice activism, and ecofeminism.

Deane Curtin, in "Women's Knowledge as Expert Knowledge: Indian Women and Ecodevelopment," considers women's agricultural practices as a way of highlighting women's environmental expertise. Curtin's claim is that Third World women's knowledge of the environment is often dismissed in ecodevelopment programs, even though no sustainable development will occur until women's instinctive practices and ways of knowing are accorded the conceptually central places they deserve.

In Douglas J. Buege's essay, "Epistemic Responsibility and the Inuit of Canada's Eastern Arctic: An Ecofeminist Appraisal," Buege argues that an ecofeminist perspective on Inuit knowledge may prove to offer insight into some of the problems attendant on a failure to appreciate indigenous technical and cultural knowledge—knowledge which is a political, cultural, and ecological construct.

The essay "Women and Power," written by the late co-founder of the Green party in Germany and active environmentalist Petra Kelly, is about feminism as a movement to alleviate women's powerlessness and about women of the Green movement working together with men on issues such as ecology and disarmament. Like all ecofeminist accounts, it involves a critique of the basic structure of male dominant hierarchies. This essay is reprinted from Kelly's posthumously published book, *Thinking Green*; Kelly had agreed to write a new piece for this volume but was unable to do so before her untimely death.

Bioregionalist ecofeminist Judith Plant, in her essay, "Learning to Live with Differences: The Challenge of Ecofeminist Community," argues that Western civilization appears to be blind to the sensitive web of relationships and differences that constitute the natural world and to humankind as part of this web. Such myopia has been revealed by the First Peoples of North America and increasingly reinforced by scientists, ecologists, feminists, radical theologians, and others. Plant's essay discusses this alienation from nature and each other and, with a host of concrete examples, points the way toward ecofeminist community building as a strategy for healing the delicate balance of relationships that make life possible.

Eliane Potiguara, a Brazilian member of Women's Group for Indigenous Education (Grumin), in a pamphlet containing the essay that appears in this volume, "The Earth Is the Indian's Mother, Nhãndecy," summarizes "the efforts of brother and sister Indians seeking their goal to convey their support of education officials, indigenous health care givers, and urban professors to help in the understanding of the social, political, and economic reasons that have caused the oppression and social and racial discrimination that have always encroached upon them and the natural world." I met Potiguara in 1992 at the Seminar on Ecofeminism held in conjunction with the United Nations Earth Summit in Rio de Janerio, and her perspective is crucial to ecofeminists attempting to conceive a theory and practice which is neither ethnocentric nor colonialist in its foundations or implications.

In part II, Karen M. Fox's essay, "Leisure: Celebration and Resistance in the Ecofeminist Quilt," explores the relevant concepts of leisure and how they relate to an ecofeminist framework. Fox argues that leisure is a significant component of women's lives and must be properly understood and incorporated into ecofeminism as part of an understanding of the social fabric that helps maintain health, survival, and connection to nature.

In a complementary essay, "Ecofeminism and Work," philosopher Robert Sessions shows how and why work must be seen as a central idea and issue for any ecological perspective; in particular, he shows how work and ecological feminism are intertwined. Sessions argues that without an understanding of work or substantial changes in our work system, the sexism and naturism (i.e., unjustified exploitation of the nonhuman environment) built into contemporary ways of life are unresolvable.

In a novel addition to the scope of ecofeminist literature, educator Ruthanne Kurth-Schai argues in "Ecofeminism and Children" that the inclusion of children's perspectives and issues within ecofeminist dialogue and activism is potentially liberating for both children and ecofeminism. Kurth-Schai argues that the inclusion of children in ecofeminist analysis deepens the significance and impact of the ecofeminist movement.

Ecofeminist writer and poet Susan Griffin contributes a new piece, "Ecofeminism and Meaning," to this volume. In it she argues that what is critical in the emergence of ecofeminism is not only the addition of ecology to feminism; it is also the introduction of various approaches, viewpoints, starting points, and perspectives which affect the meaning, language, and significance of ecofeminist discourse.

Creative writer and English scholar Gretchen T. Legler argues in her essay, "Ecofeminist Literary Criticism," that ecofeminist literary theory is a critical tool that allows for the reinterpretation and revaluation of so-called canonical nature literature. Legler claims that perhaps the most important way ecofeminist literary critics can engage in the process of revisioning human relationships with the natural world is by raising awareness about a whole range of alternative stories about landscape and the natural world that have been ignored as merely "nature writing."

Adrienne Christiansen's essay, "Rhetoric, Rape, and Ecowarfare in the Persian Gulf," focuses on the 1991 Persian Gulf War debates that took place in the United States Congress. She argues that the Persian Gulf War is uniquely suited to show the importance of ecofeminist concerns about women, war, sexual aggression, and the environment. It also shows how the expectations of contemporary political discourse maintain traditional Western and patriarchal relationships among these concerns.

In "The Nature of Race: Discourses of Racial Difference in Ecofeminism," political scientist Noël Sturgeon argues that ecofeminism inherits a legacy of discourses about racial difference which need to be critically examined, including a binary conception of race and a valorization of Native American women as the "ultimate ecofeminists." Sturgeon suggests two intertwined approaches, each of which is intended to provide a basis for effective coalitions between ecofeminism and the environmental justice movement.

Joseph R. Loer's essay, "Ecofeminism in Kenya: A Chemical Engineer's Perspective," stems from his work with the United States Peace Corps as a water engineer. Loer utilizes ecofeminism to examine means to improve current uses of science and technology, especially in Third World development projects.

Anthropologist Candice Bradley, in "Keeping the Soil in Good Heart: Women Weeders, the Environment, and Ecofeminism," describes how both women weeders and weeds are historically misunderstood through a nineteenth-century world view in which man dominates nature. She offers an ecofeminist analysis of women weeders and weeds as a corrective to this outdated view.

Naturalist Danielle Wirth and sociologist Betty Wells collaborate on "Remediating Development through an Ecofeminist Lens." Their essay focuses on three missing pieces in conventional development practice—nature, local culture, and women and other oppressed peoples—and offers ecological feminism as a counterbalance to today's dominant world view. The strategy suggested for remediating development is an ecofeminist perspective by which practitioners can redress concrete local situations brought about by inappropriate and disrespectful development, especially First World development.

In "Scientific Ecology and Ecological Feminism: The Potential for Dialogue," biologist Catherine Zabinski argues that scientific ecology and ecofeminism have a common purpose of understanding nature and our social constructs of nature. Zabinski's claim is that the promise for a dialogue between these two disparate fields lies in recognizing their overlapping goals.

Ecofeminist philosopher Val Plumwood opens part III with her essay, "Androcentrism and Anthropocentrism: Parallels and Politics." While making only a few explicit references to ecofeminism, Plumwood argues that the sophisticated understanding of androcentrism which has emerged from ecofeminism and feminism can help resolve some problems with the key concept of anthropocentrism, problems which threaten the foundations of environmental philosophy.

Philosopher Lori Gruen continues the ecofeminist philosophical critique of dominant Western anthropocentric accounts of human–nonhuman relationships in her essay, "Revaluing Nature." Gruen uses an ecofeminist perspective to answer two basic questions: How do we justify our moral claims about human interactions with nature? And does this justification provide motivating reasons for acting morally toward nature? She argues that an ecofeminist answer to these questions should not be grounded in traditional objectivist notions of intrinsic value. Rather, a conceptualization of values which focuses on chosen communities, direct experience, and inclusivity is a starting point from which to build an ecofeminist moral theory that does not leave one in a relativist abyss.

Wendy Donner's critical essay, "Self and Community in Environmental Ethics," takes up questions that arise from the tendency of some proponents of ecofeminism to repudiate or undervalue such human capacities as reason, autonomy, and a strong sense of self. Donner argues that these capacities need to be appropriately valued by ecofeminist and feminist theories if either is to provide an adequate environmental perspective.

A groundbreaking essay by philosopher Holyn Wilson, "Kant and Ecofeminism," argues that Kant's theory of human nature and his methodology of teleological judgment are relevant to ecofeminism and environmental philosophy. The essay challenges familiar positions espoused by feminist and environmental philosophers who find Kant's philosophy to be in opposition to women and animals and thus to a conception of humans as ecological beings.

Philosopher Wendy Lee-Lampshire argues in "Women-Animals-Machines: A Grammar for a Wittgensteinian Ecofeminism" that the later work of Ludwig Wittgenstein provides a useful point for grounding an ecofeminist standpoint. Her argument focuses particularly on Wittgenstein's remarks concerning the application of psychological attributes to nonhumans.

In the final piece, "Radical Nonduality in Ecofeminist Philosophy," Charlene Spretnak suggests that ecofeminism's longstanding critique of dualistic thinking in the West prepares the way for an opening that challenges various prejudices of both modern and constructivist philosophy. She concludes that ecofeminism allows for a consideration of the cross-cultural, experiential evidence for unitive dimensions of being.

As editor of this volume, I hope that the reader will find in these pages a plethora of new perspectives on ecofeminist theory and practice—ones which help to undergird the power and promise of ecofeminism. If you do, the book will have accomplished its main objective.

This book would not have been possible without the contributions of many people and institutions. First and foremost I would like to thank Joan Catapano, Assistant Director of Indiana University Press, for her enthusiastic and unwavering support of this project since its inception. I would also like to thank my academic institution, Macalester College, for its continued support of my scholarship in ecological feminism. In addition, there are many friends I would like to thank: my conversational partners at my favorite writing place, Costello's Espresso Bar in Eagan, Minnesota; friends Fran Dunne, Mark Jones, and Bruce Nordstrom; my mother, Marge Bails, and my daughter, Cortney Warren; my student research assistant, Nisvan Erkal; and the Macalester Philosophy Department administrative assistant Barbara Wells-Howe. Each has contributed time, energy, and emotional support for which I am deeply grateful. I thank all of you.

PART I:
TAKING EMPIRICAL
DATA SERIOUSLY

One

Taking Empirical
Data Seriously

An Ecofeminist
Philosophical Perspective

Karen J. Warren

Trees, forests, and deforestation. Water, drought, and desertification. Food production, poverty, and toxic wastes. Environmental destruction and women. And women? What do these environmental issues have to do with women?[1]

According to ecological feminists ("ecofeminists"), important connections exist between the treatment of women, people of color, and the underclass on one hand and the treatment of nonhuman nature on the other. Ecological feminists claim that any feminism, environmentalism, or environmental ethic which fails to take these connections seriously is grossly inadequate.[2] Establishing the nature of these connections, particularly what I call women-nature connections, and determining which are potentially liberating for both women and nonhuman nature is a major project of ecofeminist philosophy.[3]

In this chapter I focus on empirical women-nature connections. I suggest that from an ecofeminist philosophical perspective, it is important for all of us interested in finding solutions to the problems of environmental destruction and the unjustified subordination of women and other subdominant groups to take these connections seriously. By doing so, I hope to motivate and establish the practical significance of ecofeminist philosophy.[4]

Feminism and Feminist Issues

As I understand feminism, it is a movement committed to the elimination of male-gender power and privilege, or sexism. Despite differences among feminists, all feminists agree that sexism exists, is wrong, and ought to be changed. But while feminism was initially conceived as a movement to end sexist oppression, academic feminists have come to see that liberation of women cannot be achieved until *all* women are liberated from the multiple oppressions that structure our gendered identities: women of color from racism, poor women from classism, lesbian women from heterosexism, young and older women from ageism, Jewish women from anti-Semitism, women of the South from ethnocentrism. Thus feminism is intrinsically a movement to end racism, classism, heterosexism, ageism, anti-Semitism, ethnocentrism.

Something is a feminist issue if an understanding of it helps one understand the oppression or subordination of women. Issues involving equal rights, comparable pay for comparable work, and day-care centers are feminist because understanding them sheds light on the subordination of women. Racism, classism, ableism, anti-Semitism raise feminist issues because understanding them helps one understand the subordination of women. According to ecofeminists, trees, water, animals, toxics, and nature language are feminist issues because understanding them helps one understand the status and plight of women cross-culturally. At least, that's what I hope to suggest in this chapter.

Ecofeminism

Just as there is not one feminism, there is not one ecofeminism or one ecofeminist philosophy. Ecological feminism has roots in the wide variety of feminisms (e.g., liberal feminism, Marxist feminism, radical and socialist feminisms, black and Third World feminisms). What makes ecofeminism distinct is its insistence that nonhuman nature and naturism (i.e., the unjustified domination of nature) are feminist issues. Ecofeminist philosophy extends familiar feminist critiques of social isms of domination (e.g., sexism, racism, classism, heterosexism, ageism, anti-Semitism) to nature (i.e., naturism). According to ecofeminists, nature is a feminist issue. In fact, an understanding of the overlapping and intersecting nature of isms of domination is so important to feminism, science, and local community life that I have found it helpful to visualize ecofeminist philosophy as the intersection of three spheres at * in the drawing on the facing page. According to this way of visualizing ecofeminist philosophy, it arises out of and builds on the mutually supportive insights of feminism, of science, development and technology, and of local perspectives. Ecofeminist philosophy brings all the tools of feminist philosophy to bear on issues which are at *. Those contributions which fall outside * would not be distinctively ecofeminist philosophy.

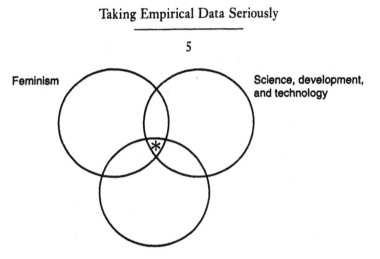

Feminism

Science, development, and technology

Native / indigenous / local perspectives

Trees, Forests, Forestry

Consider next why nature is a feminist issue. This will show why ecofeminist philosophers take empirical data on women-nature connections very seriously.

In 1974, twenty-seven women of Reni in northern India took simple but effective action to stop tree felling. They threatened to hug the trees if the lumberjacks attempted to fell them. The women's protest, known as the Chipko (Hindi for "to embrace" or "hug") movement, saved 12,000 square kilometers of sensitive watershed.[5] This grassroots, nonviolent, women-initiated movement also gave visibility to two basic complaints of local women: commercial felling by contractors damages a large number of unfelled trees, and the teak and eucalyptus monoculture plantations are replacing valuable indigenous forests.[6]

The Chipko movement is ostensibly about saving trees, especially indigenous forests.[7] But it is also about important women-nature connections: trees and forests are inextricably connected to rural and household economies governed by women, especially in Third World countries, so tree shortages are about women, too. As a result of First World development decisions in India, multiculture species of trees have been replaced by monocultural species, primarily eucalyptus. But eucalyptus is very unpopular among local women.[8] The reasons why local women dislike eucalyptus plantations show four crucial respects in which trees, forests, and forestry are a feminist issue, i.e., how understanding the empirical connections between women and trees improves one's understanding of the subordination of women.

First, in developing countries women are more dependent than men on tree and forest products.[9] Trees provide five essential elements in these household economies: food, fuel, fodder, products for the home (including building materials, household utensils, gardens, dyes, medicines), and income.[10]

Second, women are the primary sufferers of environmental degradation and forest resource depletion.[11] This is because it is women who must walk farther for fuelwood and fodder and who must carry it all back themselves (e.g., without the help of animals). According to one estimate, women in New Delhi walk an average of ten kilometers every three or four days for an average of seven hours each time just to obtain firewood.[12] As more and more men seek employment in towns and cities, women must carry out men's former jobs plus the laborious tasks of collecting and processing forest products on degraded soils. It is women whom the reduced availability of forest products used as a source of income leaves without income-producing alternatives. And it is the household technology needs of women which new development projects have failed to adequately address.

Third, women face customs, taboos, and legal and time constraints that men do not face. For example, among the Ibo, men own timber trees and women control the use of food trees; women cannot inherit economic trees, although they have a right to be maintained from the proceeds of trees owned by their parents.[13]

Fourth, trees, forests, and forestry are a feminist issue for conceptual reasons: some key assumptions of orthodox forestry are male-biased. Consider three such assumptions.

One assumption of orthodox forestry is that the outsider knows best: the outsider has the requisite technical expertise to solve the problem of the lack of trees in Third World countries. But this assumption is false or problematic. It is the insider most inside the culture—the Chipko women of India, for example—who are the experts, who have what feminist foresters call indigenous technical knowledge (ITK) and feminist philosophers call epistemic privilege around forestry production.[14] Because local women are the primary users of forest commodities in most developing countries, Louise P. Fortmann and Sally K. Fairfax state that their "day-to-day, hands-on involvement with forestry goes far beyond that of many professionally trained foresters."[15] Women in a Sierra Leone village were able to identify thirty-one products from nearby bushes and trees, whereas men could identify only eight.[16] Women's ITK grows out of their daily felt and lived experiences as managers of trees and tree products.

A second assumption of orthodox forestry is that activities which fall outside the boundaries of commercial fiber production are of lesser importance.[17] Yet these activities are precisely those which women engage in on a daily basis. Conceptually, the seeming invisibility of what women do accounts for the mistaken assumption that management and production policies of orthodox forestry are not gender-biased. It also explains why, as

Fortmann and Fairfax report, many foresters "literally do not see trees that are used as hedgerows or living fence poles; trees that provide materials for basketry, dyes, medicines, or decorations; trees that provide sites for honey barrels; trees that provide shade; or trees that provide human food."[18] And because these foresters literally do not see these multiple uses of trees, they also often do not see a lot more, e.g., that multiculture tree species are useful, that men and women may have very different uses for the same tree or may use different trees for different purposes. This inability to see women's contributions has been called a "patriarchal conceptual trap" of orthodox forestry.[19]

A third assumption of orthodox forestry is that it usually is better to have large-scale production using a small number of tree species than small-scale, community-based forestry using a wide variety of species. The Chipko movement challenges this assumption.[20] Since small-scale production reflects local priorities, involves multiple uses of many species of trees, and is responsive to the social reality of women's importance in agriculture and forest production, to threaten small-scale production is to threaten the livelihood and well-being of women.

Water

Without doubt, then, trees, forests, and forestry are ecofeminist issues. Let us next consider other empirical examples.[21]

Only 8 percent of the world's water supply is fresh or potable.[22] Millions of humans have difficulty getting the water necessary for their survival, about five liters a day. In more than half of the so-called developing countries, less than 50 percent of the population has a source of potable water or facilities for sewage disposal. The World Health Organization estimates that approximately 85 percent of all sickness and disease in countries in the southern hemisphere is attributable to inadequate water or sanitation and as many as 25 million deaths a year are due to water-related illnesses. Some fifteen million children die every year before they are five years old; four million of them die from diarrhea and associated water-related diseases.[23]

In the southern hemisphere, women and children perform most of the water-collection work.[24] Because of natural resource depletion, women also must walk further for water (e.g., one to fifteen kilometers daily through rough terrain in Uttarakhand, India). Since it is typically women and children who perform the water-collection work, it is women and children who experience disproportionately higher health risks in the presence of unsanitary water. Each year millions of people, predominantly women, are affected by major illnesses acquired while drawing water—300 million people with malaria, 20–30 million with river blindness, and 270 million with elephantiasis.[25] Drinking water is often drawn from public bathing and laundering places, and the same places frequently are used as public toilets.[26]

Contaminated water is not just a problem of countries of the southern hemisphere. In 1980, the United States produced 125 billion pounds of hazardous waste, enough to fill approximately 3,000 Love Canals. In the mid-1970s, 90 percent of hazardous wastes were being disposed of improperly. "These wastes have contributed to groundwater contamination on a local basis in all parts of the nation and on a regional basis in some heavily populated and industrialized areas," the *New York Times* reported in 1980, adding that the U.S. House Subcommittee on Environment, Energy, and Natural Resources listed 250 dump sites that "present a great potential threat to drinking water supplies."[27] Groundwater is the drinking water source for nearly half of the population of the United States.[28] Yet, according to 1991 estimates, one in six persons in the United States drinks water contaminated by lead, a known cause of I.Q. impairment in children. Water, then, is an ecofeminist issue.

Food and Farming

It is estimated that women farmers grow at least 59 percent of the world's food, perhaps as much as 80 percent. Between one-third and one-half of the agricultural laborers in the Third World are women. Yet the gender division of labor typically puts men in charge of cash crops while the women manage food crops. Women in Africa produce more than 70 percent of Africa's food, typically without tractors, oxen, or even plows.[29] According to Mayra Buvinic and Sally Yadelman,

> As a rule, women farmers work longer hours, have fewer assets and lower incomes than men farmers do, and have almost as many dependents to support. The disparity is not due to lack of education or competence. Women farmers are poorer because their access to credit is limited. Without credit they cannot acquire productive assets, such as cattle, fertilizer or improved seeds, to improve the productivity of their labor.[30]

Consider the root crop cassava. Cassava is critically important in parts of Africa in times of scarcity. Women do 70 to 80 percent of the growing and harvesting of cassava and 100 percent of the processing, which includes washing out the natural cyanide found in it (a process which takes eighteen five-hour days). Little money has been devoted to research on cassava or on the development of technologies that would increase the productivity of women farmers and the demand and price of cassava.[31]

Women's agricultural roles are many. Women are farm owners and farm managers (with major decision-making responsibilities about production and most agricultural tasks), farm partners (who share responsibility for agricultural production, typically with another household member), farm workers (unpaid family laborers), and wage laborers (who work for a daily wage or are paid by output).[32] Historically, a failure to realize the extent of women's contribution to agriculture (e.g., by First World development policies and practices) has contributed to the "invisibility of women" in all aspects of agricultural work (e.g., in plowing, planting, caring for livestock, harvesting, weeding, processing and the storing of crops).[33]

Technologies

Often the technologies exported from northern to southern countries only exacerbate the problem of tree, water, and food shortages for women. In forestry, men are the primary recipients of training in urban pulp and commodity production plants, and are the major decision makers about forest management, even though local women often know more about trees than local men or outsiders. In agriculture, men are the primary recipients of training and access to machines, tractors, plows, and irrigation systems, even though women are the major food producers. In water systems, men are the primary recipients of training in the construction and use of water pumps, wells, filtering systems, and faucets, even though women are responsible for water collection and distribution.

Here is a striking example of a so-called appropriate technology, i.e., a small-scale, simple, inexpensive, intermediate technology made from local materials and labor, which is totally inappropriate for women in Africa:

> In Africa where sunshine is abundant but oil, coal and wood are scarce and expensive, a solar stove should really mean utmost happiness to women—or so some eager development theoreticians thought. Field tests then showed what every experienced expert [or local woman] could have predicted: in the African bush, meals are prepared in the morning or in the evening when the sun has not yet risen or has already set. Furthermore: which cook wants to stand in the scorching sun? Finally: the nightly fire also has a group and therefore social function.[34]

"Appropriate technology," when developed and carried out by men and women who lack a basic understanding of women's lives and work, results in the creation not only of solar stoves for women who cook before dawn and after dusk but also of maize shellers which take longer to do the job than women do when shelling themselves and pedal-driven grinding mills in areas where women are forbidden to sit astride.[35] Technology is an ecofeminist issue.

Toxins

While neither sex is naturally more resistant to toxic agents, and resistance often appears to depend on the substance in question,[36] there is strong evidence for the existence of gender-related differences in reactions to environmental toxic substances. Persistent toxic chemicals, largely because of their ability to cross the placenta, to bioaccumulate, and to occur as mixtures, pose serious health threats disproportionately to infants, mothers, and the elderly.

The household is an important locus of environmental health hazards for women.[37] Woman-headed households are a growing worldwide phenomenon, making up over 20 percent of all households in Africa, the developed regions, Latin America, and the Caribbean.[38] Edward Calabrese and Michael Dorsey state that "most workplace health standards tend to be based on criteria derived from the assessment of how *men* have responded in the historical past to pollutants."[39] Toxins are a gender issue; they are also a race and class issue.

Environmental Racism

In the United States, Native American women face unique health risks because of the presence of uranium mining on or near reservations. (The uranium is used for nuclear energy.) According to Lance Hughes, director of Native Americans for a Clean Environment, the Navajo, Zuni, Laguna, Cheyenne, Arapahoe, Utes, and Cree all report health problems from uranium mining on their land.[40] According to one report,

A survey of households and hospitals on the Pine Ridge Reservation in South Dakota revealed that in one month in 1979, 38 percent of the pregnant women on the reservation suffered miscarriages, compared to the normal rate of between 10 and 20 percent. . . . [There were] extremely high rates of cleft palate and other birth defects, as well as hepatitis, jaundice, and serious diarrhea. Health officials confirmed that their reservation had higher than average rates of bone and gynecological cancers.[41]

Navajo Indians are the primary work force in the mining of uranium in the United States. According to a 1986 report, "Toxics and Minority Communities," by the Center for Third World Organizing in Oakland, California, two million tons of radioactive uranium trailings have been dumped on Native American lands. Reservations of the Kaibab Paiutes (northern Arizona) and other tribes across the United States are targeted sites for hazardous waste incinerators, disposal, and storage facilities.[42] Many tribes, states the *Christian Science Monitor*, "faced with unemployment rates of 80 percent or higher, are desperate for both jobs and capital."[43]

The issues facing women and men of color raise serious concerns about environmental racism. In 1987 the United Church of Christ Commission for Racial Justice did a study entitled "Toxic Waste and Race in the United States."[44] The study concluded that race is a major factor in the location of hazardous waste in the United States: three out of every five African and Hispanic Americans (more than 15 million of the nation's 26 million African Americans, and over 8 million of the 15 million Hispanics) and over half of all Asian Pacific Islanders and American Indians live in communities with one or more uncontrolled toxic waste sites. Seventy-five percent of residents in the rural Southwest, mostly Hispanic, drink pesticide-contaminated water. The nation's largest hazardous-waste landfill, receiving toxins from forty-five states, is in Emelle, Alabama, which is 79.9 percent African American. Probably the greatest concentration of hazardous waste sites in the United States is on the predominantly African American and Hispanic South Side of Chicago. In Houston, Texas, six of eight municipal incinerators and all five city landfills are located in predominantly African American neighborhoods.[45]

There are hundreds of grassroots environmental organizations and actions initiated by women and low-income minorities throughout the world. As Cynthia Hamilton claims,

Women often play a primary role in community action because it is about things they know best. They also tend to use organizing strategies and methods that are the antithesis of those of the traditional environmental movement. Minority women in several urban areas [of the United States] have found themselves part of a new radical core of environmental activists, motivated by the irrationalities of capital-intensive growth. These individuals are responding not to "nature" in the abstract but to their homes and the health of their children. . . . Women are more likely to take on these issues than men precisely because the home has been defined as a woman's domain.[46]

Environmental racism is an ecofeminist issue.

Environmental Ageism: Children

As Hamilton suggests, the health of children is also a feminist environmental issue. The federal Centers for Disease Control in Atlanta document that lead poisoning endangers the health of nearly eight million inner-city, largely African American and Hispanic children. Countless more live with crumbling asbestos in housing projects and schools.[47] In the United States, over 700,000 inner-city children are suffering from lead poisoning (and the learning disabilities which result); 50 percent of them are African, Hispanic, and Asian American.[48] In the United States, the National Resources Defence Council estimates that more than half of the lifetime risk of cancer associated with pesticides on fruit is incurred before age six.[49] Reproductive organ cancer among Navajo teenagers is seventeen times the national average.

Furthermore, women and children are seriously affected by poverty. In the United States, 78 percent of all people living in poverty are women or children under the age of eighteen. In Australia, the proportion is 75 percent. Worldwide, the largest poverty group is women-headed households.[50] The three elements which make up the major part of Third World disasters are deforestation, desertification, and soil erosion. The rural poor, a disproportionate number of whom are women and children, are the primary victims of these disasters. The living conditions of women, people of color, the poor, and children, then, are an ecofeminist issue.

Sexist-Naturist Language

Many philosophers (e.g., Wittgenstein) have argued that the language we use mirrors and reflects our conception of ourselves and our world. When language is sexist or naturist, it mirrors and reflects conceptions of women and nonhuman nature as inferior to, having less prestige or status than, that which is identified as male, masculine, or "human" (i.e., male).

The language used to describe women, nature, and nuclear weaponry often is sexist and naturist. Women are described in animal terms as pets, cows, sows, foxes, chicks, serpents, bitches, beavers, old bats, old hens, mother hens, pussycats, cats, cheetahs, birdbrains, and harebrains. Animalizing or naturalizing women in a (patriarchal) culture where animals are seen as inferior to humans (men) thereby reinforces and authorizes women's inferior status. Similarly, language which feminizes nature in a (patriarchal) culture where women are viewed as subordinate and inferior reinforces and authorizes the domination of nature: "Mother Nature" is raped, mastered, conquered, mined; her secrets are "penetrated" and her "womb" is to be put into service of the "man of science." Virgin timber is felled, cut down; fertile soil is tilled, and land that lies "fallow" is "barren," useless. The exploitation of nature and animals is justified by feminizing them; the exploitation of women is justified by naturalizing them.

In a startling essay called "Sex and Death in the Rational World of Defense Intellectuals," Carol Cohn describes how sexist-naturist language pervades nuclear parlance. Nuclear missiles are in "silos" on "farms." That part of the submarine where twenty-four multiple warhead nuclear missiles are lined up, ready for launching, is called "the Christmas tree farm." BAMBI is the acronym developed for an early version of an antiballistic missile system (for Ballistic Missile Boost Intercept). Cohn describes a linguistic world of vertical erector launchers, thrust-to-weight ratios, soft laydowns, deep penetration, penetration aids (familiarly known as "penaids": devices that help bombers or missiles get past the "enemy's" defensive systems), and "the comparative advantages of protracted versus spasm attacks"—or what one military advisor to the National Security Council called "releasing 70 to 80 percent of our megatonnage in one orgasmic whump." It is a world where missiles are "patted" like pets (how can pets be harmful?), where India's explosion of a nuclear bomb is spoken of as "losing her virginity," and where New Zealand's refusal to allow nuclear arms or nuclear-powered warships into its ports is described as "nuclear virginity."[51] Such sexist-naturist language creates, reinforces, and justifies nuclear weapons as a kind of sexual dominance.

Lest one suppose that use of such language is a philosophical oxymoron, consider the language used routinely by philosophers to describe that which "we" value most: reason. Since Aristotle, reason, or rationality, has been taken not only as the hallmark of humanness (allegedly, humans alone are rational animals) but also as what makes humans superior to (some) other humans and to nonhuman animals and nature. Yet, as Vance Cope-Kasten shows in an article entitled "A Portrait of Dominating Rationality," domination metaphors and sexist language pervade philosophical descriptions of reason, rationality, and good reasoning: good reasoners knock down arguments; they tear, rip, chew, cut them up, attack them, try to beat, destroy, or annihilate them, preferably by "nailing them to the wall." Good arguers are sharp, incisive, cutting, relentless, intimidating, brutal. Those not good at giving arguments are wimpy, touchy, quarrelsome, irritable, nagging. Good arguments have a thrust to them; they are compelling, binding, air-tight, steel-trap, knock-down, dynamite, smashing and devastating bits of reasoning which lay things out and pin them down, overcoming any resistance. Bad arguments are described in metaphors of the dominated and powerless: they "fall flat on their face," are limp, lame, soft, fuzzy, silly, and "full of holes."[52]

So even if in some sense the concepts of reason and rationality are gender-neutral, certainly historically both their distribution and characterization have been gender-biased and nature-biased: women and animals are less rational or nonrational (respectively), and "bad reasoning" is described in sexist and domination metaphors. Therefore, sexist-naturist language is an ecofeminist issue.

Taking Empirical Data Seriously

The empirical and linguistic data provided by ecofeminism are significant philosophically. These data suggest (1) the historical and causal significance of ways in which environmental destruction disproportionately affects women and children; (2) the epistemological significance of the "invisibility of women," especially of what women know (e.g., about trees), for policies which affect both women's livelihood and ecological sustainability; (3) the methodological significance of omitting, neglecting, or overlooking issues about gender, race, class, and age in framing environmental policies and theories; (4) the conceptual significance of mainstream assumptions, e.g., about rationality and the environment, which may inadvertently, unconsciously, and unintentionally sanction or perpetuate environmental activities, with disproportionately adverse effects on women, children, people of color, and the poor; (5) the political and practical significance of women-initiated protests and grassroots organizing activities for both women and the natural environment; (6) the ethical significance of empirical data for theories and theorizing about women, people of color, children, and nature; (7) the theoretical significance of ecofeminist insights for any politics, policy, or philosophy; and (8) the linguistic and symbolic significance of language used to conceptualize and describe women and nonhuman nature.

I hope these remarks will motivate and establish the need for feminists, environmentalists, philosophers—indeed, all of us—to think deeply about empirical connections between women and nature, and also between people of color, children, the poor, and nature. I also hope they will suggest why, from an ecofeminist philosophical perspective, one should take this sort of empirical data very seriously.

Notes

1. This essay was given at a conference on Human Values and the Environment in October 1992 at the University of Wisconsin-Madison and appeared in the Proceedings of that conference, published by the University of Wisconsin-Madison. An expanded version appears as chap. 1 in my forthcoming book, *Quilting Feminist Philosophies* (Boulder: Westview Press). Sections of the essay have also appeared in "Toward an Ecofeminist Ethic," *Studies in the Humanities* 15, no. 2 (December 1988): 140–56, and "Women, Nature, and Technology: An Ecofeminist Philosophical Perspective," *Research in Philosophy and Technology*, Special Issue on Technology and Feminism (1993).

2. For a selected bibliography of ecofeminist literature, see Carol J. Adams and Karen J. Warren, "Feminism and the Environment: A Selected Bibliography," *Newsletter on Feminism and Philosophy* (American Philosophical Association, Fall 1991): 148–57.

3. For a discussion of a variety of women-nature connections, see Karen J. Warren, "Feminism and the Environment: An Overview of the Issues," *Newsletter on Feminism and Philosophy* (American Philosophical Association, Fall 1991): 108–16.

4. Two caveats are in order. First, the examples offered here provide only a glimpse of the range and diversity of contemporary women-nature issues which motivate, document, and inspire ecofeminism as a political movement and set of theoretical positions. These examples also provide only a pigeonhole view of the sorts of philosophically significant things one could say about empirical women-nature connections. Second, although my focus is on women, I do not intend to suggest that men are not affected by these issues or that all men are affected in similar ways (any more than I intend to suggest that all women are affected in similar ways). I intend that the empirical considerations offered here to be read as just that: empirical considerations that illustrate and motivate the need to take seriously women-nature connections. This is true even if, as I believe, these connections also illustrate the need to take seriously other connections (e.g., connections between nature and old persons/young persons, race/ethnicity).

5. This discussion of the Chipko movement as an ecofeminist concern is taken from my article "Toward an Ecofeminist Ethic" (see n.1).

6. See *The State of India's Environment: 1984-1985, The Second Citizens' Report* (New Delhi: Center for Science and Environment, 1985), 94. The Chipko movement is especially noteworthy for its distinctively ecological sensitivity. This is clearly seen in the slogan of the movement, which points out that the main products of the forests are not timber or resin, but "soil, water, and oxygen"; cited in Jayanta Bandyopadhyay and Vandana Shiva, "Chipko: Rekindling India's Forest Culture," *Ecologist* 17, no. 1 (1987): 35. According to Bandyopadhyay and Shiva,

> The new concern to save and protect forests through Chipko satyagraha did not arise from resentment against further encroachment on the people's access to forest resources. It arose from the alarming signals of rapid ecological destabilisation in the hills. . . . It has now evolved to the demand for ecological rehabilitation. Since the Chipko movement is based upon the perception of forests in their ecological context, it exposes the social and ecological costs of short-term growth-oriented forest management.

For an excellent discussion of the Chipko movement and its effectiveness as a resistance strategy to what Shiva calls Western maldevelopment (First World development policies and practices aimed primarily at increasing productivity, capital accumulation, and the commercialization of Third World economies for surplus and profit), see Vandana Shiva, *Staying Alive: Women, Ecology and Development* (London: Zed Books, 1988).

7. India is losing 1.3 million hectares of forests a year, nearly eight times the annual rate admitted by forest departments. Wood shortages are great and wood prices are high (*The State of India's Environment,* 49).

8. The replacement of natural forests in India with eucalyptus plantations has been justified on the grounds of increased productivity. But the productivity is in the area of pulpwood only:

What has been called the "Eucalyptus controversy" is in reality a conflict of paradigms, between an ecological approach to forestry on the one hand, and a reductionist, partisan approach which only responds to industrial requirements on the other. While the former views natural forests and many indigenous tree species more productive than eucalyptus, the reverse is true according to the paradigm of Commercial Forestry. The scientific conflict is in fact an economic conflict over *which* needs and *whose* needs are important. (*The State of India's Environment*, 33)

9. See *Restoring the Balance: Women and Forest Resources* (Rome: Food and Culture Organization and Swedish International Development Authority, 1987), 4.

10. Ibid., 104.

11. Louise Fortmann and Dianne Rocheleau, "Women and Agroforestry: Four Myths and Three Case Studies," *Agroforestry Systems* 9, no. 2 (1985): 37.

12. Marilyn Waring, *If Women Counted: A New Feminist Economics* (New York: Harper and Row, 1988), 263.

13. Louise P. Fortmann and Sally K. Fairfax, "American Forestry Professionalism in the Third World: Some Preliminary Observations on Effects," in *Women Creating Wealth: Transforming Economic Development*, Selected Papers and Speeches from the Association of Women in Development Conference (Washington, D.C., 1988), 107. Fortmann and Fairfax take their information from S. N. C. Obi, *The Law of Property* (London: Butterworths, 1963), 97.

14. See, e.g., Fortmann and Fairfax, "American Forestry Professionalism"; Fortmann and Rocheleau, "Women and Agroforestry"; *Linking Energy with Survival: A Guide to Energy, Environment, and Rural Women's Work* (Geneva: International Labor Office, 1987); *Restoring the Balance*; Irene Tinker, "Women and Energy: Program Implications," Equity Policy Center, Washington, D.C., 1980; *Women and the World Conservation Strategy* (Gland: International Union for the Conservancy of Nature, 1987).

15. Fortmann and Fairfax, "American Forestry Professionalism," 105.

16. Marilyn Hoskins, "Observations on Indigenous and Modern Agroforestry Activities in West Africa," in *Problems of Agroforestry* (University of Freiburg, 1982); cited in Fortmann and Fairfax, 105.

17. See Fortmann and Fairfax, 106.

18. Ibid.

19. This term is used by Elizabeth Dodson Gray, *Patriarchy as a Conceptual Trap* (Wellesley, Mass.: Roundtable Press, 1982).

20. In developing countries, women, as heads of households, have become increasingly involved in nontraditional roles in both agriculture and forestry.

21. Unlike the preceding discussion of women and trees, the data in this section are given without critical commentary. The philosophical and feminist significance of the data will be given generically at the end.

22. Waring, *If Women Counted*, 258.

23. See ibid., 257, and Lloyd Timberlake and Laura Thomas, *When The Bough Breaks: Our Children, Our Environment* (London; Earthscan, 1990), 128. According to Waring, half of these children could be saved if they had access to safe drinking water.

24. Small-scale studies in Asia and Africa indicate that women and girls spend on average five to seventeen hours per week collecting and carrying water (e.g., in Africa: 17.5 hours in Senegal, 5.5 hours in rural areas of Botswana, and 43.5 hours on northern farms in Ghana; in Asia: 7 hours in the Baroda region of India, 1.5–4.9 hours in Nepal villages depending on the ages of the girls, and 3.5 hours in Pakistan). See *The World's Women, 1970–1990: Trends and Statistics* (New York: United Nations, 1991), 75.

25. Ann Olson and Joni Seager, *Women in the World: An International Atlas* (New York: Simon and Schuster, 1986), sec. 25.

26. The war in the Persian Gulf drew attention to and exacerbated the problem of unpotable water. "The Tigris River has been used as a well, as a bathing place, and, increasingly, as a latrine," according to Richard Reid of the United Nation's Children's Fund (*Minneapolis Star/Tribune*, March 2, 1991, 11A). Reid worries about the "burning urgency to make sure that kids and pregnant women do not fall victim to" this environmental disaster.

27. *New York Times*, September 20, 1980, 45; cited in Nicholas Freudenberg and Ellen Zalzberg, "From Grassroots Activism to Political Power: Women Organizing against Environmental Hazards," in *Double Exposure*, ed. Wendy Chavkin (New York: Monthly Review Press, 1984), 253.

28. Waring, ibid., 259.

29. Jane Perlez, "Inequalities Plague African Women," *Minneapolis Star/Tribune*, March 4, 1991, 4A.

30. Mayra Buvinic and Sally Yudelman, *Women, Poverty and Progress in the Third World* (New York: Foreign Policy Association, 1989), 24.

31. Ibid., 30. According to Buvinic and Yudelman, cassava illustrates four issues critical to understanding women's role in agriculture: the extent of women's participation in food production and their contributions to food security; the heavy demands farming places on women's time and labor; the willingness of women to grow crops which have little or no economic payoff but enable poor families to eat during periods of food scarcity; and the general tendency to assign fewer resources to crops grown by women.

32. Buvinic and Yudelman, 24–26.

33. See *Handbook on Women in Africa*, United Nations Economic Commission for Africa, 1975. Cited in *The World's Women: 1970–1990*, 17.

34. Helmut Mylenbusch, "Appropriate Technology—Fashionable Term, Practical Necessity, or New Social Philosophy?" *Development and Cooperation* 3 (1979): 18.

35. Cited in Karl, ibid., 90.

36. See *Health Risks*, 318.

37. In "The Home Is the Workplace: Hazards, Stress, and Pollutants in the Household" (in *Double Exposure*, 219–24), Harriet Rosenberg claims that a rigid sexual division of labor in the household contributes to significant health and safety hazards for women who work in the home. (The data are based on United States households.) Health hazards exist in most home cleaning products (e.g., drain and oven cleaners containing lye, toilet bowl and window cleaners containing ammonia, scouring powders, chlorine bleach, disinfectants, detergents, furniture polishes) and in appliances (e.g., gas stoves which emit carbon monoxide, radiation leakage from microwave ovens, fluorescent lights). Furthermore, according to Rosenberg, the average household has about 250 chemicals which, if ingested, could send a child to the hospital. And the home has a full range of problematic substances (e.g., lead, asbestos, PCBs, formaldehyde) used in household construction and insulation as well as insecticides, pesticides, and herbicides used outdoors.

38. *The World's Women*, 17.

39. Edward Calabrese and Michael Dorsey, *Healthy Living in an Unhealthy World* (New York: Simon and Schuster, 1984), 3.

40. Lance Hughes, "American Indians and the Energy Crisis: Interview with Lance Hughes," *Race, Poverty, and the Environment* 2, no. 2 (Summer 1992): 5, 17.

41. Freudenberg and Zalzberg, 249.

42. On July 4, 1990, the *Minneapolis Star/Tribune* reported that members of the Kaibab Paiute reservation in northern Arizona were negotiating to bring about 70,000 tons of hazardous waste each year to the Kaibab Paiute reservation. An incinerator would burn the waste, and the ash would be buried on tribal land. The Paiutes stand to reap $1 million a year from the waste-burning operation. The Kaibab Paiutes and other tribes are torn between accepting the economic gains and giving up the integrity of their land and traditional ways.

43. *Christian Science Monitor*, February 14, 1991, 18.

44. "Toxic Waste and Race in the United States: A National Report on the Racial and Socioeconomic Characteristics of Communities with Hazardous Waste Sites," 1987, Commission for Racial Justice, United Church of Christ, 105 Madison Avenue, New York, NY 10016.

45. Mainstream media attention within the United States and Canada to what is called environmental racism was the topic of an important groundbreaking essay in 1970 by Nathan Hare, "Black Ecology." Hare argued that environmental problems are different for black Americans, since black and white environments differ in degree and nature. Hare presented alarming empirical data. There is a greater degree of all varieties of pollutants in the black ghetto (e.g., smoke, soot, dust, fly ash, fumes, gases, stench, carbon monoxide) and a heavier preponderance of rats and cockroaches (disease-spreading rodents and insects). Blacks are exposed to more harmful and diverse sorts of environmental handicaps: black Americans suffer disproportionately the effects of overcrowding (e.g., increased noise levels, loss of individual space, greater probability of hearing loss, more exposure to unsanitary debris), polluted housing (e.g., three out

of ten units are without hot water, toilet, or bath), lack of "climate control" (e.g., of temperature and humidity) contributing to a higher proportional incidence of communicable diseases (e.g., pneumonia and influenza), shorter life expectancy, and poor nutrition during pregnancy. Hare argued that some of these ecological differentials between blacks and whites were due to racism.

46. Cynthia Hamilton, "Women, Home, and Community," *woman of power*, no. 20 (Spring 1991): 43.

47. There are four specific areas in which children are physically more vulnerable than adults: food and water, home, schools, outdoor play areas. Furthermore, characteristics unique to children, especially poor children and children of color, make them particularly vulnerable to environmental hazards. Poor children are more likely to live in neighborhoods with environmental hazards; poor families lack the financial resources to remove hazards from their home or purchase alternative, nonhazardous products; poor children are less likely to have access to health care for treatment; the families of poor children often lack the necessary political clout to insist on the cleanup of hazards in the neighborhood. In homes and schools, hazardous products (e.g., cleaning products) and exposure to lead, radon, asbestos, and indoor air pollution (e.g., tobacco smoke, formaldehyde found in some carpeting, wallboard, and insulation) are particularly harmful to children, since the same amount of exposure is believed to produce higher concentrations in the smaller bodies of children than in adults. Outdoors, pesticides, harmful sun exposure, air pollution, and play in unsafe areas can result in serious health conditions in children (e.g., breathing certain kinds of asbestos fibers can increase the chance of developing chronic diseases; ground-level, ozone-caused air pollution can cause respiratory problems, such as shortness of breath and coughing). See Dana Hughes, "What's Gotten into Our Children," published 1990 by Children Now, 10951 West Pico Boulevard, Los Angeles, CA 90064.

48. Hamilton, "Women, Home, and Community," 42.

49. Hughes, "What's Gotten into Our Children," 6.

50. Olson and Seager, *Women in the World*, 114.

51. Carol Cohn, "Sex and Death in the Rational World of Defense Intellectuals," in *Exposing Nuclear Fallacies*, ed. Diana E. H. Russell (New York: Pergamon Press, 1989), 133–37.

52. Vance Cope-Kasten, "A Portrait of Dominating Rationality," *Newsletter on Feminism and Philosophy* (American Philosophical Association, March 1989): 29–34. Of course, suggesting the significance of these empirical connections and defending their significance are two different activities. I have suggested elsewhere (Warren, "Feminism and Ecology: Making Connections," *Environmental Ethics* 9, no. 3 [Winter 1987]: 3–20; "The Power and the Promise of Ecological Feminism," *Environmental Ethics* 12, no. 2 [Winter 1990]: 125–46) that one main source of the philosophical significance of empirical women-nature connections is conceptual: it is traceable to oppressive patriarchal conceptual frameworks and the behaviors they sanction. An oppressive conceptual framework is characterized by five features: (1) value-hierarchical thinking, i.e.,

"up–down" thinking which attributes greater value to that which is higher or "up" than to that which is lower or "down;" (2) value dualisms, i.e., disjunctive pairs in which the disjuncts are seen as exclusive (rather than inclusive) and oppositional (rather than complementary); (3) power-over conceptions of power; (4) conceptions of privilege which serve to maintain and justify the dominance of those who are "up" over those who are "down"; and (5) a logic of domination, i.e., a structure of argumentation which provides the moral justification of subordination, viz., that superiority justifies subordination. It is the last condition, the logic of domination, which is conceptually fundamental. Without it, difference would just be glorious diversity. With it, difference becomes grounds for domination and subordination, inferiorization and marginalization. Bona fide and respected cultural diversity or cultural pluralism in any system whose basic relationships are structured by a logic of domination is not possible. We must all oppose the way this logic of domination has functioned historically within different cultural contexts to justify the domination of groups deemed inferior—women, people of color, Jews, gays and lesbians, the differently abled. An ecofeminist philosophical perspective on empirical women-nature connections extends this sort of feminist critique of oppressive conceptual frameworks, and the behaviors of domination they give rise to, to nonhuman nature. Making visible oppressive conceptual frameworks and the logic of domination which undergirds them, wherever and whenever they occur, is a central project of ecofeminist philosophy.

Two

Ecofeminism through an Anticolonial Framework

Andy Smith

Barbara Smith articulates a feminist politics that challenges all forms of social domination: "Feminism is the political theory and practice that struggles to free all women: women of color, working-class women, poor women, disabled women, lesbians, old women—as well as white, economically privileged, heterosexual women. Anything less than this vision of total freedom is not feminism, but merely female self-aggrandizement."[1] Ynestra King extends this analysis to include the domination of nature prevalent in mainstream Western society: "[Ecofeminism's] challenge of social domination extends beyond sex to social domination of all kinds, because the domination of sex, race, and class and the domination of nature are mutually reinforcing."[2]

The term *ecofeminism* may seem to imply that ecofeminists are concerned only about the oppression of women and the oppression of earth. But, as Karen J. Warren argues, "Because all feminists do or must oppose the logic of domination which keeps oppressive conceptual frameworks in place, all feminists must also oppose any isms of domination that are maintained and justified by that logic of domination."[3]

Many ecofeminist theorists argue that there is no primary form of oppression, as all oppressions are related and reinforce each other. However, depending on one's position in society, there is often one form of oppression that seems most pressing in one's everyday life. For instance, King's statement that "domination of woman was the original domination in human society, from which all other hierarchies—of rank, class, and political

21

power—flow"[4] suggests that, for her, sexism is the most pressing form of oppression.

For Native American women, sexism oppression often seems secondary to colonial oppression. As Lorelei Means states,

> We are American Indian women, in that order. We are oppressed, first and foremost, as American Indians, as peoples colonized by the United States of America, not as women. As Indians, we can never forget that. Our survival, the survival of every one of us—man, woman and child—as Indians depends on it. Decolonization is the agenda, the whole agenda, and until it is accomplished, it is the only agenda that counts for American Indians.[5]

Many Native women completely dismiss feminism in light of colonization.[6] I do not necessarily see one oppression as more important than others. However, most Native women probably feel the impact of colonization on our everyday lives more than other forms of oppression.

One reason why colonization seems to be the primary issue for Native women is that most forms of oppression did not exist in most Native societies prior to colonization.[7] As Paula Gunn Allen and Annette Jaimes have shown, prior to colonization, Indian societies were not male dominated. Women served as spiritual, political, and military leaders. Many societies were matrilineal and matrilocal. Violence against women and children was unheard of. Although there existed at division of labor between women and men, women's labor and men's labor were accorded similar status. Environmental destruction also did not exist in Indian societies. As Winona LaDuke states,

> Traditionally, American Indian women were never subordinate to men. Or vice versa, for that matter. What native societies have always been about is achieving balance in all things, gender relations no less than any other. Nobody needs to tell us how to do it. We've had that all worked out for thousands for years. And, left to our own devices, that's exactly how we'd be living right now.[8]

With colonization begins the domination of women and the domination of nature. As Allen argues, subjugating Indian women was critical in our colonizers' efforts to subjugate Indian societies as a whole: "The assault on the system of woman power requires the replacing of a peaceful, nonpunitive, nonauthoritarian social system wherein women wield power by making social life easy and gentle with one based on child terrorization, male dominance and submission of women to male authority."[9]

Other women, particularly white women, may not experience colonization as a primary form of oppression to the degree that Native women do. However, I do believe it is essential that ecofeminist theory more seriously grapple with the issues of colonization, particularly the colonization of Native lands, in its analysis of oppression.

One reason why this is necessary is because Native lands are the site of the most environmental destruction that takes place in this country. About 60 percent of the energy resources (i.e., coal, oil, uranium) in this country are on Indian land.[10] In addition, 100 percent of uranium production takes place on or near Indian land.[11] In the areas where there is uranium mining, such as Four Corners and the Black Hills, Indian people face skyrocketing incidents of radiation poisoning and birth defects.[12] Many Navajo traditionalists are speculating that the "mystery virus" that is afflicting people in Arizona may be related to the uranium tailings left by mining companies. They think that the uranium has poisoned rats in the area.[13] Children growing up in this area are developing ovarian and testicular cancers at fifteen times the national average.[14] Indian women on Pine Ridge experience a miscarriage rate six times higher than the national average.[15]

Native reservations are often targeted for toxic waste dumps, since companies do not have to meet the same EPA standards that they do on other lands.[16] Over fifty reservations have been targeted for waste dumps.[17] In addition, military and nuclear testing takes place on Native lands. For instance, there have been at least 650 nuclear explosions on Shoshone land at the Nevada test site. Fifty percent of the underground tests have leaked radiation into the atmosphere.[18]

At the historic People of Color Environmental Summit held in October 1991 in Washington, D.C., Native people from across the country reported the environmental destruction taking place on Indian lands through resource development. The Yakima people in Washington State stated that nuclear wastes coming from the Hanford nuclear reactor had been placed in such unstable containers that they were now leaking, and they believed that their underground water was contaminated. They said it would cost $150 billion to clean up these wastes,[19] and plans were being made to relocate the wastes to a repository on Yucca Mountain, where the Shoshone live, at a cost of $3.25 billion. Yucca Mountain is on an active volcanic zone. Kiloton bombs are also exploded nearby, thus increasing the risks of radioactive leakage.[20]

The Inuit of Canada reported that NATO war exercises had been wreaking environmental havoc where they live. The 8,000 low-level flights that had already taken place over Inuit land had created so much noise from sonic booms that it had disrupted the wildlife and impaired the hearing of the Inuit. Furthermore, oil falling from the jets had poisoned the water supply.

The Shoshone reported that low-level flying also takes place over their land. One man was killed when his horse threw him because it was frightened by the noise of the jets. They reported that the flying had been scheduled to take place over the cattle range until the Humane Society interceded, saying this would be inhumane treatment of the cattle. Consequently, the war exercises were redirected to take place over Indian people instead.

The delegates all reported that they were having an exceedingly difficult time in getting the U.S. government to acknowledge the effects of radiation on their people, despite the obvious and widespread effects in the region. If the United States recognizes one case of radioactive poisoning, it will have to recognize thousands.[21]

Because Native people suffer the brunt of environmental destruction, it is incumbent upon ecofeminist theorists to analyze colonization as a fundamental aspect of the domination of nature. This is true not just because we should all be concerned about the welfare of Native people but also because what befalls Native people will eventually affect everyone. Radiation will not stay nicely packaged on Indian land; it will eventually affect all of the land.

As a case in point, Jessie DeerInWater of Native Americans for Clean Environment was one of the organizers of the campaign to stop the Kerr-McGee uranium processing plant in Oklahoma. Kerr-McGee was eventually closed down, although it has not cleaned up its nuclear waste from the plant. In her campaign, DeerInWater discovered that Kerr-McGee was using radioactive wastes to make fertilizer. The Nuclear Regulatory Commission has allowed Kerr-McGee to use this fertilizer on 15,000 acres of hayfields in Oklahoma, where cattle are grazed and then sold on the open market. The only health study conducted on the cattle revealed that 10 percent had cancerous growths. This was deemed "normal." There have been no studies on the long-term effects of this fertilizer on either the hay or the cattle. The cattle can be sold without notifying consumers that they have been fed on hay fertilized with nuclear wastes. In addition, bales of hay usually sell for $25–$30 per bale, while Kerr-McGee bales sell for $5 and thus undercut the market on hay bales. One of Kerr-McGee's customers is Brahm's, an ice cream franchise in Oklahoma. Kerr-McGee has also donated the hay to the Larry Jones Ministries' Save the Children program. It has been delivered to drought-ridden areas all over the country so that Kerr-McGee can take a tax write-off. Thus it is not only Native people who may be affected by radiation poisoning.[22]

Another example is the proposed plan to relocate nuclear wastes to Yucca Mountain, already described. If this plan is approved, the proposed repository on Yucca Mountain would receive nuclear wastes from throughout the nation. Only five states would not be impacted by the transportation of high-level radioactive wastes. With up to 4,000 shipments of radioactive waste crossing the nation annually, trucking industry statistics reveal that up to fifty accidents per year could occur during the thirty-year period that nuclear waste would stream in to Yucca Mountain.[23]

Ecofeminist theorists, particularly those living in the Americas, also must take seriously Native struggles, simply because they are living on Indian land. Many Native people sense that feminists struggle to make a better life for themselves at the expense of Native people. They do not see feminists acknowledging that their feminist conferences, feminist discussion groups, and so forth all take place on land for which Indian people were murdered. Even if social relationships are ordered on a more egalitarian basis in this society, it does not change the fact that Native societies have been destroyed and continue to be destroyed to maintain this society. While white feminists can see how they have been oppressed by men, they do not see how privileged they are just to be living on the Natives' land. They are not necessarily willing to give back the land they live on to Indian people. As Pam Colorado states,

> it seems to me the feminist agenda is basically one of rearranging social relations within the society which is occupying our land and utilizing our resources for its own benefit. Nothing I've encountered in feminist theory addresses the fact of our colonization, or the wrongness of white women's stake in it. To the contrary, there seems to be a presumption among feminist writers that the colonization of Native America will, even should, continue permanently. At least there's no indication that any feminist theorist has actively advocated pulling out of Indian Country, should a "transformation of social relations" actually occur. Instead, feminists appear to share a presumption in common with the patriarchs they oppose, that they have some sort of inalienable right to simply go on occupying our land and exploiting our resources for as long as they like. Hence, I can only conclude that . . . feminism is essentially a Euro-supremacist ideology and is therefore quite imperialist in its implications.[24]

The inability to fully embrace an anticolonialist ideology is the major stumbling block in developing alliances between Native people and members of the mainstream environmental movement and the feminist movement.

For instance, in "Deep Ecology and Ecofeminism," Michael Zimmerman argues in favor of eradicating the dualism between humans and nature: "Only by recognizing that humanity is no more, but also no less, important than all other things on Earth can we learn to dwell on the planet within limits that would allow other species to flourish."[25] However, deep ecologists and other environmental theorists are often not consistent in applying this theory in practice. For instance, sentiments that have been expressed in *Earth First!* journal include that "the AIDS virus may be Gaia's tailor-made answer to human overpopulation" and that famine should take its course in Africa to stem overpopulation.[26] Such sentiments reinforce, rather than negate the duality between humans and nature, because they imply that humans are not part of nature and that their destruction would not also mean environmental destruction. Saving people should be as important as saving trees. In addition, it is noteworthy that the people that are targeted as expendable (victims of AIDS and Africans in the foregoing example) are people of color or Third World people who have the least institutional power or access to resources in society.

While these may be extreme examples, I often hear sentiments expressed to the effect that the world would be much better off if people just died or that the world needs to cleanse itself of people. Again, this sentiment assumes that people are not part of the world. To even make such a comment indicates that one has to be in a fairly privileged position in society where one is not faced with death on a regular basis. It also assumes that all people are equally responsible for massive environmental destruction, rather than facing the fact that it is people in positions of institutional power who are killing the earth and the people who are more marginalized to further their economic interests. It is racist and imperialist to look at the people who are dying now from environmental degradation (generally people of color and poor people) and say that it is a good thing that the earth is cleansing itself.

Another example in which the environmentalist movement did not adopt a consistent anticolonialist ideology is when it organized to stop drilling in the Arctic Wildlife Refuge mandated in the proposed 1991 Johnson-Wallop bill. This bill was of major concern to the Gwich'in people of Alaska, since oil drilling would destroy the 40 percent of the caribou which they depend upon for survival. It would also destroy, in particular, the calving areas so that the caribou would not be able to reproduce.

While it was a positive step that environmental organizations opposed this legislation, they also supported a compromise bill (the Wirth bill) that would provide incentives for oil drilling in the lower forty-eight states. Since a large percentage of oil reserves are on Indian land, such legislation would have continued to jeopardize Native people. When the Sierra Club was confronted on its position at the People of Color Environmental Summit in October 1991, club president Michael Fischer denied that the club supported the bill, even though his support for the bill was in print.[27] The Alaska Coalition (a coalition of environmental organizations of which the Sierra Club is a member) supported the bill because "we had to take a little bad . . . with all the good" and because "on sovereign Indian lands [as compared to Alaska Native lands] only Indians themselves have the authority and responsibility to make the decision [to drill for oil]."[28] This statement completely ignores the fact that it is not Indian people per se who make the decisions about oil on their land; it is the tribal governments, who are often under the control of business interests, who make these decisions. If the energy resources on Indian land were really under the control of Indian people, then Indian people would be the richest people in this country. In fact, they are the poorest people in the country, with a life expectancy of forty-four years for men and forty-seven for women.[29] Fortunately, neither bill passed.

Another example illustrating colonialist attitudes in the environmental and feminist movements is the increasingly popular concept of "population control." According to the Population Institute, "Burgeoning population is the single greatest threat to the health of the planet."[30] According to the Sierra Club, lack of population control is the cause of infant mortality, famine, poverty, noise pollution, global warming, and most forms of environmental damage: "If we don't act now to stabilize the human population, then the death factor will act for us. Disease, famine and war will eventually stop the inexorable expansion of our masses."[31] Planned Parenthood echoes that population control contributes "to the process of socioeconomic development and to family health, particularly in countries where rapid population growth hinders development efforts."[32]

But as Betsy Hartmann points out, population issues serve to disguise the real causes of environmental destruction:

> dominant economic systems which squander natural and human resources in the drive for short-term profits; and the displacement of peasant farmers and indigenous peoples by agribusiness, timber, mining and energy firms. Ignored also is the role of international lending institutions, war and arms production, and the wasteful consumption patterns of industrialized countries and wealthy elites the world over in creating and exacerbating environmental destruction.[33]

I would argue that colonization and not overpopulation is the cause of poverty in the Third World. Land which formerly supported local subsistence has been appropriated by imperialist countries to produce export crops for the First World. Since much of the land is going to produce export crops rather than crops to meet local needs, people in the Third World find themselves increasingly relying upon imports. The money they spend on imports is more than they make from selling export crops. Consequently, they find themselves in spiraling debt. To maintain these systems of economic inequality, the United States and other colonial powers provide covert and overt support to military regimes to crush popular uprisings. I would argue that is the cause of war, not overpopulation as the Sierra Club would have us believe.

"Overpopulation" is a natural consequence of colonization, since families in colonized lands need as many workers as possible to meet their financial responsibilities. In Bangladesh, boys at age ten are producing more than they consume and by age fifteen have repaid their parents' investment in their upbringing.[34] Consequently, under conditions of colonization, it is in the economic interest of Third World women to have more children in order to raise more export crops. Until the broader social, economic, and political problems are addressed, it will not be in the best interest of the poor to have fewer children.

The average American consumes three hundred times more energy than the average Bangladeshi.[35] The United States constitutes 4 percent of the world's population and consumes 30 percent of its resources. It follows that population control efforts should be directed toward the United States. In fact, some organizations, such as Population-Environment Balance, have argued that the United States is overpopulated. Their solution is to restrict immigration into the United States because it adds "to the United States' rapid population growth (now over three million per year) which already threatens our environment's health" and burdens the taxpayer through "increased funding obligations in AFDC, Medicare, Food Stamps, School Lunch, Unemployment Compensation, [etc.]."[36]

It would seem logical that if U.S. immigrants are poor enough to be on food stamps, then they are probably not the people who are expending most of the energy resources in this country. It would seem we need population control to be directed toward the richest groups in this country. Furthermore, if the United States would stop supporting totalitarian regimes in other countries in order to promote its economic and political interests, we might find that fewer people will need to immigrate.

Again, environmental (and many feminist) organizations blame Third World women and women of color in the United States for all the world's ills, charging that they are having too many babies. It is seen as critical that women of color restrict their births by any means necessary. White middle-class women have been organizing around issues of reproductive freedom, and they have often framed their struggle in terms of "choice" (i.e., they are prochoice). However, when President Bill Clinton reversed the Mexico City policy so that the United States would reinstate funding to organizations that perform abortions as a method of family planning, he stated that his motivation was to "stabilize the world's population," not to increase choices for women. Women of color, in fact, do not get choices regarding our reproductive health. In the efforts to stabilize our population, we are constantly subjected to unsafe drug testing or forced sterilization.

Before Norplant devices were introduced in the United States, nearly one-half million women in Indonesia had been inserted with these devices, often without counseling on their possible side effects (which include menstrual irregularity, nausea, and nervousness). No long-term studies on the effects had been conducted. Many of the women were not told that the devices needed to be removed after five years to avoid an increased risk of ectopic pregnancy.[37] Some 3,500 women in India were implanted with Norplant 2 without being warned about possible side effects or screened to determine if they were suitable candidates. The devices were eventually removed from use owing to concerns about "teratogenicity and carcinogenicity." But in both cases, women who wanted the implant removed had great difficulty finding doctors who would remove them.[38] (Similarly, in the United States many doctors can insert the devices but few know how to remove them.)

Poor women and women of color in the United States are singled out as likely candidates for the devices. State legislatures have been considering bills which would give women on public assistance bonuses if they used them. In California, a black single mother charged with child abuse was given the "choice" of using Norplant or being sentenced to four years in prison. The *Philadelphia Inquirer* ran an editorial suggesting that Norplant could be a useful tool in "reducing the underclass."[39] Every woman I know who is on AFDC has received a call from her caseworker insisting that she go on Norplant and has been advised that there are no side effects to Norplant.[40] I also know that many women who go into Indian health services for contraceptive counseling are often given Depo-Provera or Norplant without being told what they are or even told that other forms of contraception exist.

Population control efforts resulted in 42 percent of Indian women being involuntarily sterilized by 1974.[41] One woman I know went into Indian health services not long ago for back surgery and doctors took out her uterus instead. When I asked members of the Sierra Club's subcommittee on population control if they thought this issue could give rise to increasing forced sterilization, they informed me that sterilization abuse does not exist.

Even feminist organizations seldom analyze this issue in terms of racism and imperialism. While they think white women should have reproductive choices, they feel women of color do not know what's good for them and are in need of the contraception that white women feel will most effectively restrict their population. For instance, at one local feminist health center, a white health worker was pushing Norplant specifically on young women of color without informing them of side effects or screening them to see if they were appropriate candidates. But we often hear, even among feminists, that teen pregnancy, particularly among women of color, is so critical a problem that it is essentially all right to jeopardize a young woman's health just as long as she does not have a baby.

I do not see that teen pregnancy is, in itself, a problem. The problem is the society in which teens become pregnant. Prior to colonization, Indian women had children at an early age, but this was not a problem. They did not have to worry about having children as a result of rape. Since the entire tribe took responsibility for raising the child, the responsibility did not fall solely on the mother and hence she could do whatever she wanted to do. If teens today had society's support behind them when raising children so that they could continue on with school if they wanted to, if there was no social stigma to teen pregnancy, if violence against women and sexism were eradicated so that teens were able to have more choices about how they expressed their sexuality, if safe contraception was readily available, if this country prioritized health care instead of the military budget, then teen pregnancy would not be a problem. Scapegoating teen pregnancy as the cause of all society's evils disguises the broader problems of social inequality. The struggle for reproductive rights is incomplete without an antiracist, anticolonialist analysis.

I have discussed why it is essential for ecofeminist theory to more fully analyze sexism and environmental destruction in terms of colonization. In particular, I have discussed why Native rights have to be on the ecofeminist agenda. I would now like to discuss the process by which ecofeminists can be more inclusive of Native women's struggles.

Environmentalist, ecofeminist thinkers pay tribute to Native people and their ability to live harmoniously with nature. As Judith Plant states, "The shift from the western theological tradition of the hierarchical chain of being to an earth-based spirituality begins the healing of the split between spirit and matter. For ecofeminist spirituality, like the traditions of Native Americans and other tribal peoples, sees the spiritual as alive in us, where spirit and matter, mind and body, are all part of the same living organism."[42]

However, ecofeminist thinkers do not adequately discuss the material conditions in which Indian people live, how these conditions affect non-Indians, and what strategies we can employ to stop the genocide of Indian people and end the destructive forms of resource development on Indian land. Rather, they use Indian people as inspirational symbols for the environmental movement. Ecofeminists quote Native people, but they seldom take the time to develop relationships with Indian communities to struggle along with us.

There are many examples of this in ecofeminist literature. For instance, Sally Abbott writes that she went on a Native American vision quest.[43] She does not question the imperialism of appropriating Native traditions for her own benefit.[44] It is notable that this vision question did not inspire her to become involved in Indian issues. Once she took what she wanted from us, she felt no need to give anything back. Rather, she was inspired to become a vegetarian. She concludes that "early" people (with whom she categorizes Native people) felt guilty about killing animals and their rituals arose to propitiate this guilt. She perpetuates the stereotype that Native people are "early" people and not contemporary people who face contemporary problems. One would not describe white people as "early" people. Why are Natives "early" people when they are alive today and not extinct?

However, mainstream society portrays Indians as people who had a romantic past, but people who have no place in modern society.

Abbott also brings Christian assumptions into her analysis by presuming that "guilt" is even meaningful in discussing Native cultures. In fact, in my experience, Native spiritual traditions do not rest on individual guilt but rather on the collective responsibility we all have to remember that we are connected to all of creation. Abbott's answer to all the guilt Native people feel is "enlightened secularism" through the liberation of animals that "could heal the false division of body and soul." It is not my experience that the body/soul dichotomy is a problem for Native people, and it is certainly not the case that Native societies are based on large-scale subjugation of animals.

Carol B. Christ talks at length about Native spirituality.[45] One source she quotes is Lynn Andrews's *Flight of the Seventh Moon*, which has been denounced by most Native people as a thoroughly exploitative and inaccurate rendition of Native spirituality. It appears that Christ has no real ongoing relationship with Indian communities from which to derive her inspiration. Her perceptions of Native reality are not grounded in the present-day lived struggles of Native people but in her (mis)perceptions of Native spirituality based on books.

Ecofeminist thinkers often appropriate Native culture to advance their claims. I have discussed elsewhere the problems of Native cultural appropriation.[46] I think that these white ecofeminist theorists, besides being imperialist when they appropriate Native traditions, also do themselves a disservice.

In my view, mainstream society has very little understanding of spirituality. Our individualist, capitalist society tends to destroy our sense of meaningful connectedness with nature, with all creatures and all people, and to replace these relationships with commodities. Instead of looking for joy in our relationships, we look for joy at the shopping center and what we can buy for ourselves. In mainstream Christianity, we also buy prepackaged spirituality. We go to church once a week and forget about God the rest of the week; we listen to preachers who give us simple solutions to complex problems; we buy books that explain what our spirituality should be. This has little to do with spirituality because spirituality *is* one's life. Spirituality is not something one reads about or something one gets at a certain place at a certain day of the week. It is living one's life with the understanding that one is intimately connected to all of creation, all forces seen and unseen.

Thus for Native people, spirituality is most clearly seen in our everyday struggles for survival. It is not seen in a Lynn Andrews book. It is an integral part of struggle against genocide. It is what holds us together against the forces of oppression. Many non-Natives, particularly white people, often sense a spiritual void in their religious traditions and look to Native people for spirituality. Ecofeminists look to Native spirituality to help connect them with the earth. Unfortunately, when they appropriate Native spirituality out of its context, when they seek Indian spirituality in a book or a $300 sweat lodge, they are treating Native spirituality as a commodity. What they are receiving has nothing to do with spirituality. Only by becoming unconditional, faithful allies with Native people in their struggles against genocide will non-Native people ever understand anything about Native spirituality. As Chrystos writes in her poem "Shame On" about Indian spiritual exploitation,

America is starving to death for spiritual meaning.
It's the price you pay for taking everything.
It's the price you pay for buying everything.
It's the price you pay for loving your stuff more than life.
Everything goes on without you.
You can't hear the grass breathe because you're too busy talking about being an
    Indian holy woman 200 years ago.
The wind won't talk to you because you're always right, even when you don't
    know what you're talking about.
We've been polite for 500 years and you still don't get it.
Take nothing you cannot return.
Give to others; give more.
Walk quietly, do what needs to be done.
Give thanks for your life; respect all beings.
Simple, and it doesn't cost a penny.[47]

To incorporate the struggles of Native women, I suggest that ecofeminist theorists more adequately discuss another dualism: the dualism between theory and action, between academics and community activism. There seems to be a division of labor between ecofeminists who have opportunities to publish their theories or teach at universities and those who are more directly active in community organizing. I am not suggesting that many academic theorists are not also active in their communities. However, I am suggesting that since only 3 percent of Native women will ever attend college and Native people experience an 85 percent high school dropout rate, it is likely that Native women's voices will not be heard in mainstream ecofeminist discourse.

I also think that many academic feminists think that "scholarly work" should be seen as separate from activism. For instance, Karen Lehrman argues: "Volunteering in a battered-women's shelter or rape crisis center may be deeply significant for both students and society. But should this be part of an undergraduate education? Students have only four years to learn the things a liberal education can offer—and the rest of their lives to put that knowledge to use."[48] Such an attitude is not helpful to Native women who, in the presence of impending genocide, do not have time for feminists who sit around and theorize and write books all day. We need people to be actively involved in our struggle now.

I believe many academic ecofeminists and ecofeminist theorists are concerned about integrating ecofeminist theory and action. However, I think ecofeminists (and feminists in general) need to further explore how we can integrate the two more effectively. Ecofeminist theorists should not be content to see their writing or their university teaching as activism and be content to let others do the grassroots work. The reason is that it is the academic feminists who become famous feminist theorists while community-based women have no access to the academy or publishing (particularly women of color and poor women) and their work goes unrecognized. Academic feminists and feminist theorists who have access to publishing should take the lead in questioning this hierarchy.

These are a few of my thoughts on how we can challenge this hierarchy. If an ecofeminist is well known on the lecture circuit, she can bring some community-based women with her and let them speak with her at speaking engagements. White women in particular often have the luxury of visiting poor communities; then they return and make a name for themselves by talking about the oppressed women they have met. Perhaps they could instead fund these women to speak for themselves. Perhaps they could transcribe these women's stories for publication and give the money from these sales back to the communities. I think also that the theories that ecofeminists write should be more closely tied with specific actions that we can take to further ecofeminist goals.

On that note, I would like to conclude by listing suggestions for action that the organization I belong to, Women of All Red Nations, distributes. Since we are a Chicago-based organization, some of these actions are centered in Illinois. Although these issues are just a few of the ones around which Native people are organizing, I hope they will challenge readers to begin to become involved as partners with Native people in the struggle against all forms of domination.

1. Oppose geothermal development on Mauna Loa volcano, sacred site to Native Hawaiians. Oppose the proposed nuclear testing on Native Hawaiians. Contact Pele Defense Fund, P.O. Box 404, Volcano, HI 96785, 808-935-1663 for more info.
2. Send letters to the University of Arizona and the Roman Catholic Church asking them to stop their plans to construct an observatory (called the Columbus Project, appropriately enough) on Big Seated Mountain, a sacred site of the San Carlos Apache Indians. Contact Pope John Paul II, c/o Archbishop Agostino Cacciavil-

lan, Apostolic Nuncia Ture, 339 Massachusetts Ave., NW, Washington, DC 20008 or University of Arizona, Dr. Manuel Pacheco, President, University of Arizona, Tucson, AZ 85721, 202-621-1514. For more info, contact Apache Survival Coalition, P.O. Box 11814, Tucson, AZ 85734.

3. Write a letter to the World Bank urging it not to fund dam projects on Indian lands. In James Bay, Quebec, hydroelectric reservoirs have already submerged the hunting and trapping grounds of the James Bay Cree, the Naskapi, and the Eastern Inuit. Contact the James Bay and Northern Wilderness Task Force, c/o Solidarity Foundation, 30 W. 52d St., New York, NY 10019, for more info.

4. Oppose medical experimentation on American Indians. For more info, contact Traditional Dena'ina Tribe, P.O. Box 143, Sterling, Alaska 99669, 907-262-5403, or Native American Women's Health Education Resource Center, P.O. Box 572, Lake Andes, SD 57356-0572, 605-487-7072.

5. Help free Indian political prisoners. Write to President Clinton and ask for executive clemency for Leonard Peltier, who is serving two life sentences for crimes he did not commit (the FBI fabricated the evidence against him). Sign and distribute petitions to free Norma Jean Croy, who is serving a life sentence for shooting an officer even though she was unarmed at the time. Her brother, who actually shot the officer, was not prosecuted for reasons of self-defense. Contact WARN at 4511 N. Hermitage, Chicago, IL 60640, for more info.

6. Stop the spiritual and cultural exploitation of Indian people by refusing to buy anything considered spiritual or sacred to Native peoples. Oppose the use of Indians as mascots for sports teams. For a partial list of so-called Indian spiritual leaders who have been exposed as fraudulent, contact WARN at 4511 N. Hermitage, Chicago, IL 60640.

Notes

1. Barbara Smith, "Racism and Women's Studies," *But Some of Us Are Brave* (Old Westbury: Feminist Press, 1982), p. 49.

2. Ynestra King, "The Ecology of Feminism and the Feminism of Ecology," in *Healing the Wounds* (Philadelphia: New Society, 1989), p. 20.

3. Karen J. Warren, "A Feminist Philosophical Perspective on Ecofeminist Spiritualities," in *Ecofeminism and the Sacred*, ed. Carol J. Adams (New York: Crossroads, 1993).

4. King, "Ecology of Feminism," p. 25.

5. Lorelei DeCora Means, quoted in M. Annette Jaimes, "American Indian Women: At the Center of Indigenous Resistance in Contemporary North America," in *State of Native America* (Boston: South End Press, 1992), p. 314.

6. See Jaimes, "American Indian Women," pp. 311–37.

7. Some thinkers argue that there was environmental destruction and patriarchal oppression in most Native societies. Riane Eisler in "The Gaia Tradition and the Partnership Future" (in *Healing the Wounds*, p. 32) argues that we must approach tribal societies with caution since they "have all too often been blindly [*sic*] destructive of their environment. . . . there are Western and non-Western peasant and nomadic cultures that have overgrazed and overcultivated land, decimated forests . . . and killed off animals needlessly and indifferently" and "have been as barbarous as the most 'civilized' Roman emperors or the most 'spiritual' Christian inquisitors." What this analysis is based on is not clear. What tribal societies is she referring to that have authored the same kind of mass environmental destruction that is endemic in mainstream Western society? She regurgitates the tired notions that tribal people in general are savages without seeing any need to justify or explain this statement. While no society is perfect, her article does not address the fact that most Native societies in the United States were far more peaceful and socially just than their European counterparts. I think the reason thinkers such as Eisler claim that Native people were in fact savage and disrespectful to the environment is to suggest that Native people are not "innocent" victims of genocide, and consequently white people do not have to feel quite so guilty about the privileges they currently enjoy on the backs of Native people.

8. Quoted in Jaimes, "American Indian Women," p. 318.

9. Paula Gunn Allen, *The Sacred Hoop*, (Boston: Beacon Press, 1986), p. 40.

10. Ward Churchill, *Marxism and Native Americans* (Boston: South End Press, 1983).

11. Ward Churchill, "The Political Economy of Radioactive Colonialism," in *State of Native America*, p. 242.

12. See Ward Churchill, "Radioactive Colonization," *Struggle for the Land* (Monroe, ME: Common Courage Press), pp. 261–328.

13. John Flynn, "How Many Legs Do the Rats Have?" *Smoke Signals*, July 1993, p. 1.

14. Valerie Tallman, "The Toxic Waste of Indian Lives," *Covert Action* 17 (Spring 1992), p. 17.

15. Lakota Harden, *Black Hills PAHA SAPA Report*, August–September 1980, p. 15.

16. One reason why Indian lands are targeted for various forms of environmental destruction is that many tribal government leaders are supported by the U.S. government and thus serve the interests of big business rather than the interests of Native people at large. This process began with the Indian Reorganization Act of 1934 in which traditional forms of indigenous government were

supplanted in favor of a tribal council structure modeled after corporate boards. The U.S. government or corporations fund those candidates who sell Native lands for energy resource development. See Rebecca Robbins, "Self-Determination and Subordination: The Past, Present, and Future of American Indian Governance," *State of Native America*, pp. 87–122. In effect, tribal governments are similar to colonial governments in the Third World.

17. Conger Beasely, "Dances with Garbage," *E Magazine*, November–December 1991, p. 40.

18. Valerie Tallman, "Tribes Speak Out on Toxic Assault," *Lakota Times*, December 18, 1991.

19. Tallman, "Toxic Waste of Indian Lives," p. 18.

20. Tallman, "Tribes Speak Out on Toxic Assault."

21. This information is from oral testimony at the 1991 People of Color Environmental Summit.

22. Jessie DeerInWater, "The War against Nuclear Waste Disposal," *Sojourner*, June 1992, p. 15.

23. Tallman, "Toxic Assault on Indian Land."

24. Pam Colorado, quoted in *State of Native America*, p. 332.

25. Michael Zimmerman, "Deep Ecology and Ecofeminism," in *Reweaving the World* (San Francisco: Sierra Club, 1990), p. 140.

26. Quoted in Starhawk, "Feminist Earth-Based Spirituality and Ecofeminism," in *Healing the Wounds*, p. 179.

27. See the Carrying Capacity Network's *Clearinghouse Bulletin* 1, no. 3 (June 1991), p. 1.

28. Michael Matz, letter to Women of All Red Nations, December 3, 1991.

29. Churchill, *Struggle for the Land*, p. 55.

30. 1991 Annual Report, Population Institute.

31. "Population Stabilization: The Real Solution," Sierra Club pamphlet.

32. Mission and Policy Statements, Planned Parenthood, 1984.

33. Betsy Hartmann, "Population Control as Foreign Policy," *Covert Action*, no. 39 (Winter 1991–92), p. 27.

34. *New Internationalist*, October 1987, p. 9.

35. Ibid.

36. *Clearinghouse Bulletin* 1, no. 3 (June 1991), p. 6.

37. Hartmann, "Population Control as Foreign Policy," pp. 29–30.

38. Ammu Joseph, "India's Population Bomb," *Ms.* 3, no. 3 (Nov./Dec. 1992), p. 12.

39. Gretchen Long, "Norplant: A Victory, Not a Panacea for Poverty," *National Lawyers Guild Practitioner* 50, no. 1, p. 11.

40. This includes women I know on a social basis and women I have worked with through my rape crisis center, Women of All Red Nations (WARN), and other women's organizations.

41. Women of All Red Nations Report, 1978.

42. Judith Plant, in *Healing the Wounds*, p. 113.

43. Sally Abbott, "The Origins of God in the Blood of the Lamb," in *Healing the Wounds*, p. 35.

44. See Andy Smith, "For All Those Who Were Indian in a Former Life," *Ms.*, November–December 1991.

45. Carol B. Christ, "Rethinking Technology and Nature," in *Healing the Wounds*.

46. See n. 44.

47. Chrystos, "Shame On," *Dream On* (Vancouver: Press Gang Publishers, 1991), 100–101.

48. Karen Lehrman, "Off-Course," *Mother Jones*, September–October 1993, p. 50.

Three

Women of Color, Environmental Justice, and Ecofeminism

Dorceta E. Taylor

People of color have brought the issues of environmental racism, environmental equity, environmental justice, environmental blackmail, and toxic terrorism to the forefront of the environmental debate in recent years.[1] Until people of color made these issues commonplace in environmental circles, the terms, the concepts they embody, and the questions arising from them were not used, explored, or asked by traditional, well-established environmental groups, deep ecologists, social ecologists, bioregionalists, ecofeminists, or Greens. Environmental activists (even the more radical ones and those who were critical of traditional environmental activism) ignored or paid little attention to the processes, practices, and policies that led to grave inequities, to charges of environmental racism, and to a call for environmental justice. For a long time environmentalists did not recognize that certain issues and activities had disproportionate negative impacts on communities of color; if they were aware of the impacts, they paid no attention to them. This occurred because many in the environmental movement failed to perceive and define issues affecting communities of color as environmental issues, did not consider people of color to be part of the constituency they served, or did not see themselves engaging in environmental dialogues and struggles with such communities. If and when they considered people of color, these people were an afterthought deserving only marginal consideration. Many environmentalists were too concerned with other issues to move issues affecting primarily people of color to the top of their agendas.[2]

Women of color have been at the forefront of the struggle to bring attention to the issues that are devastating minority communities—issues such as hazardous waste disposal; exposure to toxins; occupational health and safety; lead poisoning, cancers, and other health issues; housing; pollution; and environmental contamination. Their communities, some of the most degraded environments in this country, are the repositories of the waste products of capitalist production and excessive consumption. As a result, they have been in the vanguard of the struggle for environmental justice; they are founders of environmental groups, grassroots activists, researchers, conference organizers, workshop leaders, lobbyists, and campaign and community organizers. But do these activists consider themselves ecofeminists? Do they adopt an ecofeminist perspective in their campaigns? Can an ecofeminist perspective help them attain their short- and long-term goals? To answer these questions, we must first understand more about the environmental justice movement, its goals, what it has accomplished, the role of women of color in it, the way in which women of color define their environmental activism, and the differences and similarities between women-of-color environmental activists and ecofeminists.

The Environmental Justice Movement

The publication of Rachel Carson's *Silent Spring* in 1962 led to an immense public outcry against pollution. This outrage sparked a mass mobilization drive that resulted in cleaner air, rivers, and lakes for many Americans. In the euphoria over the new environmental consciousness sweeping the country, the growing political power of the reenergized environmental movement, and the readily discernible environmental gains, most people failed to notice that pollution cleanup did not necessarily reach minority inner-city communities.[3] For example, in Washington, D.C., while the Potomac River was cleaned up to enhance tourism and recreation, the Anacostia River, which runs through one of the city's African-American communities, was not cleaned up. This neglect of African-American and other communities led to declining air and water quality, increased toxic exposure, increased health risks, and a declining quality of life.[4] Furthermore, some of the undesirable wastes that were removed from other communities to make them clean were dumped in poor minority communities.

Although the environmental movement emerged as a successful mass movement by the 1970s, it was a movement in which few people of color participated.[5] Since then there has been a change in the attitudes of people of color toward environmental issues nationwide. Many minority commu-

Table 1. Constituencies Served by Environmental Groups, 1992

Constituency Served*	Environmental Justice Organizations (%)	Traditional Environmental Organizations (%)
African-American	18	
Latino/Latina	11	
Native American	17	
Asian-American	11	
Multiracial	43	
Predominantly people of color		5
Predominantly white		11
Don't know		84
Total	100	100

*Based on a 1992 survey of 76 environmental justice and 61 trational organizations. Adapted from Environmental Careers Organization, *Beyond the Green: Redefining and Diversifying the Environmental Movement* (1992), pp. 47, 72–74.

nities are mobilizing around environmental issues and are participating in the environmental debates and agenda setting of the present and future (see table 1).

The most dramatic change in levels of participation occurred during the late 1980s with the emergence of the environmental justice movement, a radical, multiracial, grassroots environmental and social justice movement.[6] This rapidly growing sector of the environmental movement is made up of thousands of grassroots environmental groups nationwide.[7] These groups have varying levels of collaboration with each other and coordination among themselves. Environmental justice activists come from an assortment of racial and social class backgrounds; they are African, Latino, Asian, Native, and white activists from various social class backgrounds. Such a sociodemographic profile is unique in the environmental movement. Prior to the emergence of the environmental justice movement, the members of all the other sectors of the environmental movement were primarily white and middle class. Even the most radical environmental groups lacked racial and social class diversity among their leadership, staff, volunteers, and membership.

Environmental justice can be described as the fourth stage of the environmental movement. Each stage has had profound effects on the growth and public participation, direction, power, nature, and effectiveness of the movement.[8] Environmental justice marks a radical departure from the traditional ways of perceiving, defining, organizing around, fighting, and discussing environmental issues; it challenges some of the most fundamental tenets of environmentalism that have been around since the 1890s. It questions some of the basic postulates, values, and themes underlying the kinds of environmentalism characteristic of organizations such as the Sierra Club, the Audubon Society, the Appalachian Mountain Club, the Izaak Walton League, the Nature Conservancy, and the National Wildlife Federation, which are concerned primarily with wildlife, mountaineering, forest preservation, and hunting and fishing. It also challenges the types of environmentalism that arose in the sixties and seventies. The orientation of groups formed in this period ranged from radical, direct-action-oriented groups such as Greenpeace[9] and Earth First!, which focused their attention primarily on whales, nuclear disarmament, and forest preservation, to legal, technocratic, and lobbyist-oriented groups such as the Natural Resources Defense Council and the Environmental Defense Fund, which focused on environmental laws and policies.

Several factors contributed to the emergence of the environmental justice stage of the movement and to the growing participation of people of color in environmental issues. First, many communities and individuals were astounded when they discovered that they were exposed to toxins and other environmental hazards. Environmental disasters in white communities such as Love Canal (New York), Stringfellow Acid Pits (California), and Lapari Landfill (New Jersey) and in people-of-color communities such as Texarkana (Texas), Triana (Alabama), and Institute (West Virginia); policy decisions that resulted in the siting of enormous landfill facilities in Warren County (North Carolina) and Emelle (Alabama); the concentration of highly polluting industries and facilities along Cancer Alley (Baton Rouge to New Orleans, Louisiana) and Chemical Valley (West Virginia)—all these factors spawned a whole new breed of environmental activists.[10] In addition, the struggles of the United Farm Workers and the deliberate targeting of minority and low-income communities such as South Central Los Angeles and Kettleman City (California), Atgeld Gardens and Robbins (Illinois), Flint and Detroit (Michigan), Alsen (Louisiana), and Native American lands to make them the repositories of hazardous wastes or the sites of noxious facilities (landfills, incinerators, nuclear waste storage complexes) stimulated an unprecedented level of environmental activism in minority communities.[11]

Principles of Environmental Justice

The environmental justice movement fights the most vicious and pervasive kinds of inequalities in the country, including inequalities or discrimination based on race, gender, and class. By making justice a central organizing theme, the environmental justice movement has been able to attract a membership that is far more diverse and representative of the general population than any of the other sectors of the environmental movement. The movement focuses on themes of fairness, justice, distribution of environmental impacts, and sharing the costs of environmental impacts as a way of linking the struggles for equality and as a way of mobilizing communitywide coalitions built across race, ethnic, and class lines and between interest groups.

Members of the environmental justice movement speak of justice as it is related to the notions of equity, impartiality or equality, sharing, and partnership. A distinction is made between two kinds of justice: distributive justice, i.e., the ways in which members of a society properly distribute the benefits and burdens of social cooperation, the just or fair principles of distribution in society, or who should get what; and corrective, commutative, or retributive justice, i.e., a concern with the way individuals are treated during a social transaction.[12] The environmental justice movement is concerned with distributive justice as it relates to identifying past injustices and remedial action. It is also concerned with corrective justice because the relationships that citizens and the government have, or the relationships citizens and corporations have, can be seen as forms of social transactions (a social contract). The deliberate placement of wastes or noxious facilities in communities or the poisoning of the soil, air, and water with chemicals because of the residents' race, socioeconomic status, or perceived inability to oppose the sitings can be viewed as a breach of the social contract. Environmental justice activists are pushing for corporations to be held responsible for their actions and penalized for harming people. Fairness and justice are issues that all can agree on as ones which are important in building a desirable society;[13] therefore they are ideas around which one can build broad coalitions.

The principles of environmental justice upon which this movement is based was clearly articulated on October 27, 1991, by delegates attending the First National People of Color Environmental Leadership Summit. Delegates agreed on and adopted seventeen guiding principles that have since been adopted throughout the environmental justice movement. These principles state that environmental justice:

1. Affirms the sacredness of Mother Earth, ecological unity, and the interdependence of all species, and the right to be free from ecological destruction.
2. Demands that public policy be based on mutual respect and justice for all peoples, free from any form of discrimination or bias.
3. Mandates the right to ethical, balanced, and responsible uses of land and renewable resources in the interest of a sustainable planet for humans and other living things.
4. Calls for universal protection from nuclear testing and the ex-

traction, production, and disposal of toxic/hazardous wastes and poisons that threaten the fundamental right to clean air, land, water, and food.

5. Affirms the fundamental right to political, economic, cultural, and environmental self-determination of all peoples.

6. Demands the cessation of the production of all toxins, hazardous wastes, and radioactive materials and that all past and current producers be held strictly accountable to the people for detoxification and the containment at the point of production.

7. Demands the right to participate as equal partners at every level of decision making, including needs assessment, planning, implementation, enforcement, and evaluation.

8. Affirms the right of all workers to a safe and healthy work environment, without being forced to choose between an unsafe livelihood and unemployment. It also affirms the right of those who work at home to be free from environmental hazards.

9. Protects the right of victims of environmental injustice to receive full compensation and reparations for damages as well as quality health care.

10. Considers governmental acts of environmental injustice a violation of international law, the Universal Declaration on Human Rights, and the United Nations Convention on Genocide.

11. Must recognize a special legal and natural relationship of Native peoples and the U.S. government through treaties, agreements, compacts, and covenants affirming sovereignty and self-determination.

12. Affirms the need for urban and rural ecological policies to clean up and rebuild our cities and rural areas in balance with nature, honoring the cultural integrity of all our communities and providing fair access for all to the full range of resources.

13. Calls for the strict enforcement of principles of informed consent and a halt to the testing of experimental reproductive and medical procedures and vaccinations on people of color.

14. Opposes the destructive operations of multinational corporations.

15. Opposes military occupation, repression, and exploitation of lands, peoples, and cultures and other life forms.

16. Calls for the education of present and future generations to emphasize social and environmental issues, based on our experience and an appreciation of diverse cultural perspectives.

17. Requires that we, as individuals, make personal choices to consume as little of Mother Earth's resources and to produce as little waste as possible, and that we make conscious decisions to

challenge and reprioritize our lifestyles to ensure the health of the natural world for present and future generations.

Research and Evidence

Research played a key role in the growth of the environmental justice movement. Where research did not exist to substantiate claims being made by grassroots environmental groups, people of color and other activists conducted research that validated the claims. The findings of some of the more important studies are summarized in table 2.

In addition to these studies, others document the questionable and dishonest tactics that many corporations use to ensure that their facilities are located in people-of-color communities.[14] Once these corporations become established in communities that subsequently become poisoned, a new corporate strategy emerges—houses and stores are boarded up, bought out (at bargain prices), and relocated and former residents are sworn to a lifetime of silence about their experiences. Despite the efforts of activists such as Janice Dickerson and Ernestine Johnson of Revelletown, that has been the story in African-American communities such as Revelletown and Morrisonville, Louisiana.[15] (Morrisonville, one of the oldest African-American communities in this country, was formed by freed slaves; it does not exist anymore because the residents were not relocated together and the community dissolved.)[16]

The courts and the Environmental Protection Agency (EPA) have promulgated policies and instituted procedures that have severe discriminatory effects on people of color. Gelobter (1992) has demonstrated how the Clean Air Act has a discriminatory effect on the poor and people of color, while Moses (1993) argues that because farmworkers (the only group of workers in this situation) are not covered by occupational safety and health laws, child labor laws, or laws giving them the right to organize, they are severely mistreated on the job and suffer detrimental health consequences.

The EPA is not averse to ignoring some of its own guidelines when it comes to choosing sites for noxious facilities. In Warren County, North Carolina, a predominantly African-American community, the EPA gave permission to build a landfill to store PCB-laced soil (polychlorinated biphenyls) in an area where the soil was highly permeable, with only small amounts of clay present and where the water table was only seven feet below the bottom of the landfill.[17] The EPA's guidelines stipulate that a landfill must be at least fifty feet above the groundwater and that such sites must be located where there are thick, relatively impermeable formations, such as large-area clay pans.[18]

Even when the evidence clearly points to discrimination, people of color have a difficult time proving in court that they are being discriminated

Table 2. Research Findings on the Locations and Effects of
Waste Facilities

Author, Study, Year	Findings
U.S. General Accounting Office, *Siting of Hazardous Waste Landfills*, 1983	In the southeastern United States a disproportionate number of waste dumps were placed in African-American communities
Urban Environment Conference, *Environmental Cancer*, 1985	Documents links between cancer, race, and poverty
Urban Environment Conference, *Taking Back Our Health*, 1985	People of color have higher rates of occupational injury because they have the most dangerous jobs
	Presents case studies of communities of color (such as Triana, Alabama) that have been poisoned by toxic chemicals
	Presents case studies of labor, social, and environmental justice campaigns
Center for Third World Organizing, *Toxics and Minority Communities*, 1986	People-of-color communities are more exposed to toxics than white communities
United Church of Christ, *Toxic Waste and Race*, 1987	In Chicago, Los Angeles, Atlanta, St. Louis, and other cities, most of the hazardous facilities and uncontrolled toxic waste sites are located in zip code areas that are predominantly African-American and Latino
	Most of the largest, most hazardous waste facilities are located in African-American communities
R. Bullard, *Dumping in Dixie*, 1990	Presents case studies of landfill and incinerator sitings and community opposition to these facilities
	A disproportionate number of landfills and incinerators are placed in African-American communities in the five southern cities and rural areas studied (Emelle, Alabama; Alsen, Louisiana; West Dallas and Houston, Texas; and Institute, West Virginia)
E. Mann, *L.A.'s Lethal Air*, 1991	People of color live in areas of Los Angeles that are most severely impacted by air pollution
B. Bryant and P. Mohai, *Race and the Incidence of Environmental Hazards*, 1992 (anthology; authors cited in findings)	People of color live in communities with lower air quality; the environmental laws regulating air have a discriminatory effect (Michael Gelobter)

(Table 2 continued on next page)

Table 2. (*continued*)

Author, Study, Year	Findings
B. Bryant and P. Mohai, *Race and the Incidence of Environmental Hazards*, 1992 (anthology; authors cited in findings)	Farmworkers in the U.S. (most of whom are Latinos) and in Latin America toil under inhumane conditions and suffer severe health impacts (Ivette Perfecto)
	Minority anglers who engage in subsistence fishing consume large amounts of toxic fish (Patrick C. West et al.)
	Native American communities are being poisoned by uranium tailings (W. Paul Robinson)
	African-American workers have more dangerous jobs and sustain more severe job-related injuries than whites (Beverly H. Wright)
	African-American communities have a disproportionate number of incinerators (Harvey White)
Cohen, *Chicago Reporter*, 1992	In Chicago, fly (illegal) dumping occurs in wards that are predominantly African-American and Latino
	Incinerators and waste dumps are located in predominantly African-American and Latino zip code areas
R. Bullard, *Confronting Environmental Racism*, 1993 (anthology; authors cited in findings)	African-American and Latino children are more likely than other children to suffer lead poisoning (Janet Phoenix)
	Farmworkers work under inhumane conditions and suffer severe health impacts arising from exposure to pesticides (Marion Moses)
	Native American communities are being targeted for hazardous waste facilities by companies wanting to circumvent state regulations (Robert Bullard)
	A disproportionate number of incinerators and landfills are placed in communities of color (Robert Collin and William Harris)

against. For instance, in cases involving the siting of facilities, it is not enough to prove that the pattern of siting is discriminatory; one has to prove that the responsible party intended to discriminate at the time of establishing the facility. Lavelle and Coyle (1992) document how difficult it is to prove discrimination in this context. Even in the case of Houston, where six out of the seven waste dumps in the city were placed in African-American communities, Linda Bullard was unable to win her case.[19] The judge argued that she failed to prove discriminatory intent in the granting of the permit. Despite these results, activists continue to press the claim of environmental racism.[20]

Marianne Lavelle and Marcia Coyle's study, "Unequal Protection: The Racial Divide in Environmental Law," provides an extensive analysis of the discriminatory impacts of environmental laws and policies. The study examined how the actions of the EPA (particularly during the Superfund process) discriminate against people of color. Lavelle and Coyle found that:

- The Environmental Protection Agency, under Title VI, has a responsibility to ensure nondiscrimination in the use of pollution control funds, but early in the history of the agency, a decision was made not to emphasize the agency's civil rights enforcement responsibilities.[21]
- Contaminated sites in many urban areas where people of color live were less likely to be recognized as Superfund sites than sites in other communities. Although communities like the predominantly African-American Atgeld Gardens (the "Toxic Donut," as residents call it) have fifty toxic sites in a six-by-six-mile area, the Hazard Ranking System[22] does not take into account the combined effect of each of these sites on the 10,000 residents. The sites are evaluated and ranked separately. Despite criticisms, the EPA has been reluctant to change the system.
- The Hazard Ranking System is biased in such a way that sites in rural areas are more likely to be placed on the National Priorities List than other sites. This is particularly true of rural sites that get their water from wells, which are more likely to be placed on the list than urban sites with city water supplies.
- It takes 20 percent longer to evaluate sites in minority communities to determine if they should be placed on the list than it does to evaluate sites in white communities.
- Once sites are placed on the list, it takes longer to clean up sites in communities of color than in white communities—an average of about 9.5 years in white communities and 13.1 years in communities of color.

- There is a difference in the type of cleanup options chosen for communities of color and white communities. While 45 percent of the sites in white communities were contained and 55 percent treated, 52 percent of the sites in communities of color were contained and only 48 percent treated.
- There were significant differences between the fines levied against companies violating the Resource Conservation and Recovery Act in communities of color and in white communities. Penalties averaged $55,318 in communities of color and $335,556 in white communities. That is, corporations know that, on average, it is about six times more expensive to violate waste laws in white communities than in communities of color.
- If the decision is made to relocate communities, it takes longer to relocate communities of color and residents of these communities are paid less than residents in white communities in similar circumstances.

Before research findings linked race and poverty to the increased likelihood of being exposed to environmental hazards and risks on the job and at home, to having environmental health problems, and to reduced access to clean air, water, and outdoor recreational experiences, such phrases as *environmental discrimination, environmental equity, environmental racism,* and *environmental blackmail* were not used in the environmental movement or were dismissed as unfounded, unnecessary, or unrealistic. Although most environmentalists still misunderstand these terms and bristle at their use, the preceding discussion demonstrates that an understanding of these terms is crucial and that the current trends are abhorrent and unacceptable.

Increased Communication

Research and increased communication helped communities to realize that their problems were not isolated. Shared outrage and newfound solidarity then motivated people to act. People weren't only objecting to and organizing against chronic exposures in the home, but they started to question exposures on the job. The Urban Environment Health Conference (1985), the University of Michigan Conference on Race and the Incidence of Environmental Hazards (1990), the First National People of Color Environmental Leadership Summit (1991), and the Southern Organizing Committee's Conference (1992) were important milestones, because they provided the forum for people to discuss exposures to environmental hazards on the job and at home. These conferences highlighted the fact that poor people and people of color were being forced to choose between their sources of income and their health and safety.[23]

A side effect of the discussions of health and safety risks on the job and at home was the opening up of discussions on issues of environmental blackmail. Many communities which remained silent or did not question the nature of the jobs provided when companies manufacturing dangerous products moved into town or when landfills, incinerators, or other toxic dumps were placed in their neighborhoods have now become wary enough to question these job opportunities and in many instances to reject them (as in the case of South Central Los Angeles, Atgeld Gardens, and Kettleman City).

An Alternative to NIMBYism

Environmental justice activists did not simply respond to the conditions existing in their communities; they responded to threats to other communities and to the growing presence and strength of NIMBYism ("not in my backyard" campaigns). Environmental justice supporters saw a problem with NIMBYism. It was a movement that said "not in my backyard" without questioning or caring about whose backyard the problem ended up in. The environmental justice activists looked at the relationship between class, race, power, control, money, and the exposure to environmental hazards and saw that increasing numbers of undesirable facilities and land uses were being foisted on communities of color after they were successfully blocked in other communities. It was becoming increasingly clear that because of the narrow, self-interested approach of NIMBYism, people of color were subject to greater risks because they were perceived as being incapable of mobilizing the political opposition necessary to block unwanted facilities.[24] Consequently, environmental justice activists insisted that instead of merely shifting the production facilities, the end products, and the wastes around, as a society we should examine feasible ways of halting production, reducing consumption, and substituting harmful chemicals with safe or less harmful alternatives. They urged people to examine the inequities and injustices of the current system and embark on a strategy to make the system more equitable and just in the future. So in addition to asking "why in my backyard?" they insisted that such hazards should not be located in anyone's backyard.

Herein lies a key distinction between the environmental justice movement, NIMBYism, and the traditional, well-established sectors of the environmental movement. The individuals in the environmental justice movement perceive past and present injustice in the distribution of environmental risks, hazards, and burdens; they see a trend toward increasing inequities in the way the harmful effects of industrial production are distributed in the population. That is, people of color and the poor have been bearing more of the brunt of these harmful effects, and if the current trends continue, they will bear an increasing share of these risks and hazards in the future. They ask members of this society to come to grips with the consequences of increased production, consumption, and waste generation. How can society reduce its levels of production, consumption, and waste generation? If current production and consumption levels continue, how will the society deal with the question of which groups are put at risk? Why should certain groups be put at risk and not others? Is it fair to continue past practices of putting some at risk and not others? If not, how will risks be shared in the future?

Redefining What Is Considered "Environmental"

Another factor that has contributed to increased environmental justice activism among people of color is the redefinition of which issues are considered "environmental" and which are appropriate for environmentalists to spend time on. A combination of political strategies and research helped to successfully challenge the traditional definition of the environment and the narrow frameworks of mainstream and radical environmental discourse.[25] People of color have infused issues of power, domination, racism, discrimination, distribution of risks and benefits, and inequality and justice into the debate. Lack of housing for the poor and homeless, hazardous working conditions, cancers, and other health effects arising from environmental causes are but a few of the issues that environmental justice activists have brought into the environmental debate when other environmentalists did not consider them to be environmental issues or paid little attention to them. In addition, the environmental justice movement has helped to focus attention on issues like toxic contamination and exposure to toxic chemicals—environmental issues that are affecting large sectors of the population.

A 1988 survey of 248 staff members of environmental organizations (environmental justice groups were not included in the survey) showed that they spent most of their resources on fish and wildlife protection, forest and park management and land stewardship, and other closely related issues. Table 3 shows that although some groups spent money on toxic and hazardous waste management issues, these organizations really dealt with a narrow range of issues.

The results of a 1992 survey presented in table 4 tell a different story. The table shows that the sixty-one traditional, non-justice-oriented environmental organizations surveyed have expanded their agendas somewhat but still spend most of their time on wildlife, forest management, and conservation issues. They are far less likely to work on issues such as housing, public health, occupational safety and health, hazardous wastes, incineration, human and civil rights, and environmental justice than the seventy-

Table 3. Allocation of Program Resources by Traditional
Environmental Organizations, 1988

Program Type	Resources Spent (%)
Fish and wildlife management and protection	19
National forests, parks, and public lands management	12
Private land preservation and stewardship	11
Toxic, hazardous, and solid waste management	8
Protection of waterways (rivers, lakes, coasts)	7
Water quality	6
Urban and rural land-use planning	4
Wilderness	4
Agriculture	4
Air quality	3
Economic, sustainable development	3
Marine conservation	3
Energy conservation and facility regulation	2
Zoological or botanical gardens	1
Mining law and regulation	1
Nuclear power or weapons	1
Population control	0
Other	11

Adapted from Donald Snow (1992), *Inside the Environmental Movement: Meeting the Leadership Challenge*, Washington, D.C.: Island Press, p. 55.

six justice-oriented environmental groups surveyed. None of the traditional groups worked on issues such as housing, garbage, Native water rights, labor organizing, and military toxics. On the other hand, very low percentages of environmental justice groups worked on issues such as conservation and depletion of the ozone layer.

Environmental justice activists argue that when certain environmental issues affected primarily people of color, there was a tendency to claim that the issue was not environmental, therefore not worthy of or suitable for discussion by environmentalists. A case in point involves the struggles of the United Farm Workers to stop companies from spraying pesticides on workers, to document job-related illnesses (such as increased incidences of birth defects), to be protected under the Occupational Safety and Health Act, and to have employers provide toilets and water in the fields. These struggles were not widely supported by environmentalists, who saw these

Table 4. Issues Addressed by 61 Traditional and 76 Environmental
Justice Organizations

Issue Type	Traditional Environmental Organizations (%)	Environmental Justice Organizations (%)
Conservation, wildlife, natural areas	45	4
Toxic substances	39	39
Water pollution	26	33
Municipal solid waste management landfills	24	17
Air pollution	21	9
Energy	19	3
Agriculture	16	5
Hazardous wastes	15	32
Land use planning	13	21
Environmental education	21	11
Recycling	13	14
Resource management	13	–
Water resource planning	10	14
Transportation	8	–
Growth management	8	–
Urban environment	6	3
Incinerators	6	26
Public health	5	13
Occupational health and safety	3	21
Nuclear waste, nuclear power	3	–
Hunting, fishing, game	3	3
Noise pollution	3	–
Population and family planning	3	3
Ozone destruction	3	–
Emergency response, planning and preparedness	2	–
Household or neighborhood pests	2	4
Environmental impacts of war	2	–
Human rights, civil rights	2	16
Environmental racism, environmental justice	2	8

(Table 4 continued on next page)

Table 4. (*continued*)

Issue Type	Traditional Environmental Organizations (%)	Environmental Justice Organizations (%)
Housing	–	19
Litter, garbage in neighborhood	–	9
Native land, water, fishing rights	–	8
Farmworker organizing	–	4
Military/toxics	–	4
Employment, training	3	16
Youth recreation and development	–	8
Substance abuse	–	7
Developing countries' issues	–	5
Worker/labor rights	–	5
Immigration	–	4
Voting	–	3
Leadership development	5	–

Adapted from Environmental Careers Organization, *Beyond the Green: Redefining and Diversifying the Environmental Movement* (1992), pp. 44–45, 71–72.

issues as labor and health issues, not environmental issues. Yet when there was an outbreak of Mediterranean fruit flies and the State of California decided to spray malathion to stop the spread of the flies (i.e., in areas where white residents lived), there was a huge outcry from many in the environmental community as well as other citizens outraged at the spraying. The issue of malathion spraying was then transformed into an environmental issue, and claims of risks and potential birth defects became credible (claims that could be made because of the availability of data gathered on Latina farmworkers).[26] Another aspect of this spraying that environmentalists and most of the public failed to notice was its discriminatory nature. Environmental justice activists argue that the pattern of spraying was discriminatory: residents in a Latino neighborhood claimed their neighborhood was sprayed more often than white neighborhoods.[27]

Similarly, the case involving Asian-American women who work in Silicon Valley and have reproductive and other health problems has been perceived as a labor and health issue. Consequently, the plight of these women has received scant attention in environmental circles. However, environmental justice activist Pam Tau Lee and others consider the problems the Asian-American women face as environmental problems and are collaborating with labor groups on the issue. Lead poisoning is another case in point. When gasoline contained lead and the potential for lead poisoning was widespread, there were high levels of public concern over lead. Now, with lead removed from gasoline, African-American and Latino children are most at risk for exposure to high levels of lead,[28] and lead is no longer a high-priority issue for many environmental groups.

People of color have pointed to such narrow, often inflexible definitions as types of discourses that have an exclusionary or marginalizing effect on people who do not share the same perceptions, experiences, and world view as those from the dominant, most powerful environmental organizations. There is strong resistance to new ideas, new definitions, and new kinds of discourses from these organizations.[29] Because people of color define the environment more broadly, look at the disproportionate effects of hazards on race, gender, age, and social class, and take innovative alternative approaches to solving environmental problems, they are often excluded from crucial environmental dialogues.

Alternative Focus

Recognizing that a narrow definition limits the discussion and the approach to problem solving, environmental groups of color are attempting to change the way environmental issues are looked at. They see people-of-color communities, urban and poor rural, as environments worthy of attention and understanding. This is in contrast to other sectors of the environmental movement that focus primarily on wildlife habitats or wildlands as the environments for which they seek health and sustainability. The ethnic minority environmental groups see the human environment as being intricately linked to the physical environment, and they believe the health of one depends on the health of the other.[30] Therefore, if the human environment is poisoned or has been targeted to be poisoned, if there are no opportunities for economic survival or nutritional sustenance, or if there are no possibilities to be sheltered, then these human environmental issues have to be dealt with before, or in conjunction with, other kinds of environmental issues. This is not an attempt to make humans dominant over the rest of nature; it is a way to say that humans, particularly people of color who have been ignored or thought of as expendable by many capitalists and environmentalists, are a part of the ecosystem. It is a way of bringing people of color back into the equation. People of color want to stop the destruction of the earth, not dominate it. This position was clearly articulated in discussions and in the principles of environmental justice adopted at the First National People of Color Environmental Leadership Summit, already listed.

Environmental justice activists are critical of the tendency to compart-

mentalize and fragment ideas and knowledge of the environment, environmental problem definition, and problem resolution. Such fragmentation
has contributed to the neglect of minority communities. These activists
do not partition the environment and discuss it in separate spheres. They
do not separate the home sphere from the work sphere, the leisure/recrea-
tion/outdoor sphere from the religious/spiritual or political sphere. These
spheres are all linked when they define a problem or fight or resolve issues.
This occurs because people of color often live, work, play, and worship
in the same environment or community setting. A definition of environment that requires the individual to focus on forest or wilderness protection without any consideration of health, occupational safety, or recreation
is not an option for people of color. In the communities from which they
hail, one cannot attempt to improve any aspect of environmental quality
without trying to improve the human quality of life and vice versa.

This vision is more holistic than the disjointed approach taken by most
environmentalists. Although basic ecological principles and the rhetoric of
most environmental groups advocate a holistic approach to dealing with
environmental issues, in practice many environmentalists think about the
environment in fragmented ways. Environmental justice activists are striving to be more holistic in their approach to environmental activism. Other
sectors of the movement, such as deep ecology and ecofeminism, also advocate a holistic approach to environmental activism.[31]

Building Alliances

The alliances that were important in the civil rights movement have also
become important in the environmental justice movement. People of color
have embarked on this quest for environmental justice in close partnership
with religious institutions. For example, the Commission for Racial Justice of the United Church of Christ has emerged as a major player in this
movement through its involvement in the Warren County campaign, its
production of the *Toxic Wastes and Race* document (1987), and its cospon-
sorship of the 1991 People of Color Environmental Leadership Summit.
In addition, there is a strong alliance with labor and occupational health
and safety groups. This being the case, issues that other environmentalists
would consider outside their domain are issues that environmental justice
activists focus on.

Civil and Environmental Rights

In 1962, Carson (*Silent Spring*) presented a chilling documentation of the
effects of pesticide production and use. In addition to reevaluating the use
of pesticides, she argued that individuals had a right to be protected from

poisons applied by others to the environment and that they should have a right to legal redress when this right is violated. Thirty years later, environmental justice groups are making a similar argument about harm and redress. They argue that individuals have a right to safe jobs, housing, and environments. They say that civil rights cannot be separated from environmental rights and environmental justice.[32] That is, when people of color are forced to live with disproportionate numbers of solid waste dumps, incinerators, and toxic production facilities in their backyards and to take hazardous jobs, and when the patterns of siting dangerous facilities have been shown to be discriminatory, then people's civil rights have been violated. They don't just fight for an end to toxic exposures; they link this fight to increased opportunities for safer jobs, improved health, and safer communities.

Political Strategies

People of color have not only brought the notions of civil rights and environmental rights to the forefront of the environmental debate; they have also reintroduced civil rights strategies as a means of accomplishing their goals. Grassroots demonstrations, toxic marches, civil disobedience, mass arrests, lawsuits, community organizing and education, crafting legislation, and skillful use of the media are some of the more successful strategies being used.[33] Table 5 compares traditional and environmental justice political strategies. As one can see, environmental justice groups are using radical and revolutionary direct-action strategies in combination with more mainstream and institutional tactics, such as filing lawsuits. It is striking how much public education, research, and community organizing these groups engage in. In contrast, the traditional and well-established environmental organizations rely on radical, direct-action political strategies.

Some activists involved in these campaigns had little or no knowledge of environmental issues or had little training in political activism and civil disobedience when they started their first campaigns, yet they were willing to advocate environmental causes. For example, in South Central Los Angeles, African-American women such as Shilela Cannon (of Concerned Citizens of South Central Los Angeles) and Latinas such as Juana Gutierrez (of Mothers of East Los Angeles) fought hard to stop an incinerator from being placed in their neighborhood. In another example, African-American women such as Dollie Burwell, along with men and children, stood and lay in front of trucks in Warren County, North Carolina, to prevent them from taking toxics to the dump.[34] Scenes like these have been repeated all over the country, with people of various racial and ethnic groups participating.

Environmental justice groups are critical of industry and the way in

Table 5. Activist Strategies Used by Traditional and Environmental
Justice Organizations

Strategy Type	Traditional Environmental Organizations (%)	Environmental Justice Organizations (%)
Public education	85	92
Research and report writing	63	82
Organize community/constituency	55	74
Media outreach	50	64
Technical/assistance	48	62
Training	52	57
Community development	27	52
Protesting existing or future facilities	21	43
Lobbying	48	40
Litigation	37	34
Legal assistance	21	31
Negotiating with polluting facilities	19	31
Civil disobedience	2	19
Advocacy	19	14
Conferences, workshops, camps	5	8
Cultural awareness	–	4
Fundraising, endowment building	2	4
Networking	2	4
Land acquisition	11	–
Protest government action, inaction	3	–
Monitoring	3	–
Product packaging	2	–

Adapted from Environmental Careers Organization, *Beyond the Green: Redefining and Diversifying the Environmental Movement* (1992), pp. 46, 73.

which industrial activities affect minority communities, but they also criticize environmentalists for ignoring the conditions in minority communities and for the way in which environmental agendas are set. Consequently,
they have embarked on a strategy to isolate the most powerful and influen-
tial environmental organizations and scutinize them publicly. This strategy
has left these high-profile environmental groups groping for responses to
questions relating to the racial composition of their membership, work-

force, and boards; their hiring practices; and their past and present actions and agenda. People of color have also demonstrated that alliances of progressive environmentalists, policymakers, religious organizations, social service organizations, academics, and labor can make for a vibrant and healthy movement; the numerous conferences, workshops, and research projects that have resulted from these alliances have enhanced the growth of the movement. People of color have used the spiritual, intellectual, and political energies and the talents of activists to identify the needs of their communities and to chart a course of action to meet these needs.

Women of Color and the
Environmental Movement

The role of women of color in the environmental justice movement cannot be understated. In no other sector of the environmental movement (not even in the more progressive or radical sectors) can one find such high percentages of women of color occupying positions as founders and leaders of organizations, workshop and conference organizers, researchers, strategists, lawyers, academics, policymakers, community organizers, and environmental educators. As table 6 shows, 49% of 205 people-of-color environmental justice groups had women as founders, presidents, or chief contact persons. In twenty-two of the thirty-nine jurisdictions listed, more than 50 percent of the groups had women leaders. A similar analysis in Malaspina et al. (1993) shows that 59 percent of the environmental justice groups profiled were led by women, many of whom were women of color. Similarly, about 48 percent of the delegates attending the People of Color Environmental Leadership Summit were women of color.[35] Table 7 shows that much lower percentages of the women are listed as occupying leadership positions in the traditional, mainly mainstream, predominantly white organizations.

Ecofeminism

There is no question that ecofeminists broke new ground when they began arguing that the capitalist exploitation of resources was connected to the degradation of nature and women. They introduced a feminist perspective to traditional ways of perceiving and relating to the environment that was badly needed. This type of critique, long ignored in a male-dominated movement, opened up the discourse and expanded the environmental debates to some extent. However, despite the ecofeminists' success in getting gender issues and alternative critiques of the capitalist, patriarchal system into the environmental dialogue, they, like other environmentalists, have done little to bring the issues of central concern to women of color (and

Table 6. Gender and Leadership in Environmental Groups of Color

Jurisdiction	No. of Groups	% with Women Leaders
Alabama	3	33
Alaska	2	0
Arizona	5	40
Arkansas	1	0
California	30	57
Colorado	4	67
District of Columbia	8	50
Florida	2	100
Georgia	4	75
Idaho	3	33
Illinois	4	75
Kansas	2	50
Louisiana	4	75
Maine	1	0
Maryland	3	67
Michigan	1	0
Minnesota	1	0
Mississippi	3	100
Missouri	2	50
Montana	3	100
Nebraska	3	0
Nevada	6	17
New Jersey	3	67
New Mexico	21	48
New York	7	14
North Carolina	9	67
Ohio	7	57
Oklahoma	8	50
Oregon	4	0
Pennsylvania	2	100
Rhode Island	1	100
South Dakota	3	67
Tennessee	2	100
Texas	18	50

(Table 6 continued on next page)

Table 6. (*continued*)

Jurisdiction	No. of Groups	% with Women Leaders
Virginia	3	100
Washington	8	13
Wisconsin	9	22
Puerto Rico	4	25
Quebec, Canada	1	100
Total (or average)	205	(49)

Source: *People of Color Environmental Groups Directory* (1992).

Table 7. Gender and Leadership in Traditional Environmental Organizations

Jurisdiction	No. of Groups	Leadership Positions	
		Total	% Women
Alabama	13	55	22
Alaska	13	86	40
Arizona	14	82	17
Arkansas	6	16	6
California	66	429	31
Colorado	27	128	25
Connecticut	16	77	32
Delaware	12	47	19
District of Columbia	122	922	33
Florida	31	141	30
Georgia	19	96	29
Hawaii	12	55	31
Idaho	9	50	8
Illinois	31	163	21
Indiana	15	83	25
International Organizations	12	71	23
Iowa	20	96	29
Kansas	12	55	29
Kentucky	13	35	20
Louisiana	10	41	20
Maine	16	57	19
Maryland	39	288	27

(*Table 7 continued on next page*)

Table 7. *(continued)*

Jurisdiction	No. of Groups	Leadership Positions	
		Total	% Women
Massachusetts	27	143	35
Michigan	17	67	25
Minnesota	26	137	25
Mississippi	5	14	29
Missouri	15	59	32
Montana	21	147	22
Nebraska	10	46	24
Nevada	5	16	31
New Hampshire	17	86	26
New Jersey	15	77	18
New Mexico	9	28	18
New York	55	404	34
North Carolina	17	77	13
North Dakota	5	21	10
Ohio	23	118	16
Oklahoma	11	36	26
Oregon	24	117	19
Pennsylvania	34	230	16
Puerto Rico	3	20	15
Rhode Island	7	53	42
South Carolina	12	55	18
South Dakota	10	38	16
Tennessee	17	64	22
Texas	25	138	19
Utah	8	29	28
Vermont	12	62	40
Virgin Islands	3	11	36
Virginia	24	307	24
Washington	54	249	32
West Virginia	11	47	23
Wisconsin	22	138	15
Wyoming	11	41	34
Total (or average)	1083	6148	(27)

Sources: *Conservation Directory* (1993) and *Gale Environmental Sourcebook* (1992).

men of color) to the forefront of the environmental dialogue in a consistent and earnest way or to make such issues a central part of their agenda. Although some ecofeminists are making an effort to increase their awareness and deal with issues of immediate concern to women of color, there is still much to be done to ameliorate the situation. This part of the chapter explores differences and similarities between women-of-color environmental justice activists and ecofeminists. It also discusses changes that will have to occur within ecofeminism if it is to become more attractive to environmental justice activists of color.

Ecofeminists match the racial and socioeconomic profiles of traditional environmentalists, that is, they are predominantly white and middle class. However, they differ significantly from members of traditional environmental groups when it comes to the role of women. While males control the discourse (formulating theories and policies and setting agendas) and leadership positions in most of the traditional and well-established sectors of the environmental movement, in ecofeminism women define the movement and the theories, control and disseminate ideas, and craft political strategies. The white women who consider themselves ecofeminists have founded, defined, and shaped a movement that reflects their perceptions of reality, their experiences, and their cultural heritage.

Consequently, it does not come as a surprise to most women of color that as it is currently conceived, ecofeminism does not adequately consider the experiences of women of color; neither does it fully understand or accept the differences between white women and women of color. According to ecofeminist scholars, there are four types of feminism—liberal, Marxist, radical, and socialist—and two kinds of ecofeminism arising from them: radical ecofeminism and socialist ecofeminism. Of the two kinds, radical ecofeminism is the more common.[36] While some feminists, including Simone de Beauvoir, repudiate the women-nature connection, claiming that such arguments have a negative impact on women,[37] radical ecofeminists affirm the women-nature connection.[38] Some womanists also associate the domination and destruction of nature with the abuse of black women's bodies.[39] The typology laid out by ecofeminists is not very helpful in trying to understand the lives, experiences, and activism of women of color; it doesn't even recognize womanism or any of the other kinds of feminism with which women of color strongly identify.[40]

Although African-American women and other women of color have repeatedly argued that the foregoing formulation does not adequately reflect their experiences, ecofeminists still adhere to it. There is a slight glimmer of hope that change is possible. A few ecofeminists have started making references to many feminisms and ecofeminisms, but even these ecofeminists do not attempt to make fundamental changes in the definition.[41] As long as this basic definition remains intact, women of color will not be lulled into thinking there has been fundamental change and will continue to raise questions about typologies and definitions.

Race and Domination

One reality that ecofeminists continue to miss is that women of color cannot simply aim their criticisms at patriarchy or at men and cannot seek liberation only for themselves. The political activism of women of color in the environmental justice movement is very complex. These women of color will agree that they are fighting gender issues (e.g., toxics invading the home and workplace and threatening their lives, health, reproduction, and families), but they will also argue that they are fighting much more than that. Their fight is also about racial and sexual discrimination, inequality, civil rights, and labor rights. The feminist and ecofeminist framework laid out by scholars fails to capture this complexity or the uniqueness of women-of-color environmental justice activism. Male domination and the institutions of patriarchy are major components of the ecofeminist critique of society. While ecofeminists perceive that they are dominated by white men and seek to eliminate patriarchal barriers, women of color perceive their inequality differently. They are dominated not only by white men but also by men of color and by white women. In addition, they work closely with men of color who are also dominated by white men. So while ecofeminists perceive a unidirectional form of domination (in which females do not dominate and in which their dominator is not dominated), women of color perceive sexual domination differently. The domination is multidirectional, and both males and females are dominated or are dominators. Therefore gender equality for women of color means something quite different from what it means for white women. While both white women and women of color have some commonality in the fact that both groups are oppressed by men, women of color have to deal with oppression from women, too.[42] Whereas there is much discussion in ecofeminist writings about opposite-sex oppression, there is a distinct reluctance to discuss same-sex oppression.

Racial and Sexual Equality

Women of color do not fight for sexual equality without fighting for racial equality.[43] Their inequality and oppression won't end until they are equal in both respects. Whereas fighting for racial equality is an option for white women (though it should not be for anyone), this option does not exist for women of color. If and when white women fight for racial equality, it definitely assumes less importance than the fight for gender equality.

While ecofeminists are critical of Marx's dominance theory, arguing that domination stems not only from money and class but from gender relations also,[44] most do not include racial domination as a part of the critique. Environmental justice activists would add racism and colonization to any critique of dominance.[45] Although some ecofeminists argue that ecofeminism is concerned with gender, race, and class, their statements cannot be generalized to ecofeminist writings.[46] It is true that in the last year or two, more ecofeminist books and articles mention race and class, but these still account for a small portion of the ecofeminist writings. In pre-1990 writings, discussions of race and class are not common. The ecofeminist anthologies are particularly striking in their limited or nonexistent coverage of these issues. In one of the major anthologies of 1993, Gaard's *Ecofeminism: Women, Animals, Nature,* animals feature more prominently than discussions of race, class, or women of color despite a mention in the introduction that such issues were the concern of ecofeminism.

Given that women of color are struggling for gender and racial equality in the context of a newly emerging social movement, it makes sense for them to try to achieve this goal along with men of color. Women of color cannot gain racial equality if men of color do not. As a result, most of the language of the environmental justice campaigns is structured around racial equality.[47] Women of color do not support the dominator society world view. They do not see an alternative society where patriarchy (men dominating women) continues to be pervasive or where patriarchy is replaced by matriarchy (women dominating men). They envision a society wherein women and men work closely with each other. In such a society, neither gender nor race would be associated with inferiority or superiority.[48]

The absence of large numbers of environmental justice campaigns based solely or primarily on gender equality is no denial of the importance of the issue; it is the result of a strategy to mobilize a broad and effective coalition to help people and communities survive. In many instances, the struggles in which environmental justice groups are engaged are about survival. The language is about survival because it tells about life and death struggles. Consequently the language of gender equality is embedded in the language of survival.

Social Class

Another dimension of women-of-color activism is class. Women of color will not attain equality until there is a fundamental restructuring of the society and systems of production, industrialization, and capitalism that make some people wealthy and some poor. Most of the issues being discussed affect the poor, and in many instances the group most ravaged by environmental degradation comprises poor, minority females and their children. Environmental justice campaigns therefore strive for better con-

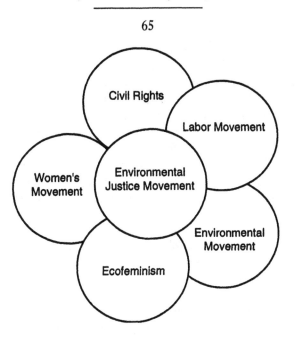

Figure 1. The relationship between environmental
justice and other social movements.

ditions for the working and lower classes, at the same time that they strive for racial and gender equality.[49] Whereas ecofeminists recognize the degradation of nature and link it with the degradation and devaluation of women, women and men of color point to the degradation of nature, then to the accelerated degradation and exploitation of nature in their communities in the United States and in developing countries, and argue that such degradation has a racial and class basis, too.

Social and Environmental Justice Activism

Compared with feminism and ecofeminism, movements in which the gender dimension dwarfs the other dimensions of the struggle, the environmental justice movement wages a struggle which is more balanced, with race, gender, and class forming the basic elements. The movement incorporates aspects of civil rights, feminism, ecofeminism, environment, and labor (see figure 1). So defined, women-of-color environmental justice activism is not just feminism or ecofeminism; it is broader and more complex than either of these movements.

Women of color participate in a movement that has developed language, strategies, and work that are different from those of all the movements from which it is drawn. It is a multiple-foci movement that straddles the domains of all the social movements mentioned. This contrasts with the narrower foci of ecofeminism and radical feminism.[50] The environmental justice movement has multiple foci because it is a grassroots movement that remains accountable to its constituents. While some groups are working on toxics, others are working on sovereignty issues, community gardens, the nutritional status of poor women and children, occupational health and safety, and housing, to name a few.

As a matter of fact, some women of color in the environmental justice movement see themselves as social justice activists; they do not use any environmental, feminist, or ecofeminist labels to describe themselves.[51] This is evident not only from the way their campaigns are structured and articulated but also from their writings. The term *ecofeminism* is not used to describe who they are or the ideological basis of their claims. Among ecofeminists, the term *ecofeminism* is an explicit descriptor; the terminology, the ideology, is influenced by this body of thought identified with ecofeminism.

The activism of women of color does not fit neatly into either of the two tenets of ecofeminism. These women incorporate aspects of radical and socialist ecofeminism, but they also endorse perceptions and ideas that are at odds with beliefs espoused by both of these canons. They are critical of technological developments that have harmful effects on people, and they are aware that technology has a detrimental effect on women's reproduction; but a focus on gender does not constitute the total of their critique.[52] (See table 2 for other dimensions of their critique.) They criticize technologies that harm people of color in developed and developing countries, and race, gender, class, and other types of oppression and domination form the basis of the critique, not gender alone.

Spirituality and Goddess Worship

Spirituality is an important part of ecofeminism.[53] The same is true for people-of-color environmental justice groups, in which spirituality is encouraged and there is a strong connection to religious institutions. However, the similarities between women-of-color environmental justice activism and radical ecofeminism ends there. Radical ecofeminists are critical of the worship of a father god or transcendental god; they worship goddesses, claiming that the replacement of goddesses with a transcendental god was linked to the rise of patriarchy, male dominance, wars, and the devaluation and destruction of nature. The rise of male dominance, they say, resulted in the subordination and devaluation of female cultures and power, the linkage of women and nature, and the devaluation of both.[54] These beliefs have been challenged by ecofeminists and nonecofeminists alike who argue that the evidence presented to support these claims is weak and questionable.[55]

Women of color in the environmental justice movement express their spirituality in a multiplicity of ways. Religious observances range from worship of the transcendental God to observance of Far Eastern religious rites or the traditional ceremonies and rites of Native Americans. Because people in the environmental justice movement see diversity as strength, there is tolerance and respect for the diverse sources from which people draw their spirituality and energies. At the First National People of Color Environmental Leadership Summit, for instance, this diversity was drawn on throughout the summit to help people share unique features of their culture and as a way to form common spiritual bonds that all could understand.

One example is worth sharing. Native American delegates from Alaska organized a march on the Capitol to register their complaints on drilling in the Alaska National Wildlife Refuge. They told summit delegates of their plans and said that "if the spirit moves you, we would appreciate your support on this march." It was amazing that the delegates, who had been in session till the wee hours of the morning, had rested a few hours, and had been back in session for over three hours that day without a break, all got up and moved silently to the door to participate in this march (which meant forfeiting their lunch hour). The Alaskan delegation asked that the march be a silent march led by an elder female spiritual healer and the only sound should be one drumbeat played to a rhythm signifying our connection to the earth and to each other. Again this occurred without protest despite the traditions in other people-of-color cultures that have singing or chanting as an integral part of protest marches. It was an amazing march that reinforced the tone of the conference, whose aim was to focus delegates and observers to utilize their intellectual, political, cultural, and spiritual energies to work together.

As mentioned, women-of-color environmental justice activists work quite closely with religious institutions (churches adhering to the notion of a father god). In fact, some of the key people of color in the environmental justice movement are pastors, such as the Reverend Ben Chavis and Pat Bryant. Reverend Jesse Jackson, another high-profile minister, has lent his support to the movement. Such alliances would be problematic for ecofeminists.

The Struggles of Women of Color

Although some radical environmentalists such as ecofeminists have operated with broad definitions of the environment, they have not paid enough attention to the ways in which the issues they explore have disproportionate impacts on people of color. While they have identified ways in which capitalist policies and practices have had a disproportionate effect on women (and have chided men—particularly radical male environmentalists—for not recognizing this),[56] they have been slow in recognizing that the negative impacts do not affect all women equally. As the foregoing discussion shows, the devastation in communities of color is generally far more severe than what is occurring in white communities. It is time for ecofeminists to increase their awareness of these problems and their commitment to work with women of color to improve conditions.

Ecofeminists can increase their awareness of these struggles and work with women of color without being domineering or imperialistic. They should resist the urge to impose a totalizing discourse or co-opt and shape what they see to their own liking, theories, typologies, images, and interpretations of reality. There is a tendency for movements, even the most progressive ones, to develop totalizing discourses that may exclude others from participating, or to try to impose unity, a common will or voice, on adherents; deviations are not tolerated.[57] For example, one cannot help but notice the dogmatic, totalizing language in Gaard's *Ecofeminism: Women, Animals, Nature.* Slayton's 1992 article, "The Failure of the United States Greens to Root in Fertile Soil," chronicles the detrimental effects that totalizing, exclusionary language and intolerance and disrespect for differences have had on the Greens. If ecofeminists want to expand the reach and influence of ecofeminism and make it accessible to a broader range of women, they should pay more attention to ecofeminism to see where such totalizing discourses might arise or are arising.

Movements also have a tendency to co-opt or envelop others.[58] There is a temptation for closely related movements such as feminism, ecofeminism, and the environmental movement to look at the environmental justice movement and try to claim it as a part of their domain. As figure 1 shows, the movement overlaps with several movements but doesn't fit into any. Feminists may look at the environmental justice movement and say it is a feminist movement, or ecofeminists may look at it and say it is an ecofeminist movement, and environmentalists may do the same. But this is not entirely true. In the same way that feminists, ecofeminists, and environmentalists took time to develop and define their movements, environmental justice activists will do the same. It is important for people of color to define themselves and not be defined by others. Ecofeminists should resist the urge to define what they see going on in the environmental justice movement in the existing framework of ecofeminism.[59] Definitions are an important part of empowerment, and women of color in the environmental justice movement will define themselves and their activism in due course.

A definition that interprets women-of-color activism only within the existing framework of ecofeminism and not in a more appropriate framework is totalizing and imperialistic.

In the past, ecofeminism, like other sectors of the environmental movement, did not pay much attention to the environmental struggles of women of color in the United States. Today women-of-color environmental justice activists still receive only marginal recognition from ecofeminists; only a few ecofeminists recognize and discuss their works, struggles, or accomplishments.[60] Ecofeminists seemed more aware of the struggles of women in developing countries (like the Chipko movement) than of the struggles of women of color close by. Ecofeminists should continue to heighten their awareness and support the struggles of women in developing countries, but they should not ignore the plight of women of color in the United States. Many other environmentalists have done so in the past and continue to do so, because it is easier to bypass the problems of the inner city and poor rural areas to tackle similar problems in distant lands. Here is an opportunity for ecofeminists to cultivate closer relationships with women of color in the United States.

Ecofeminists insist (and rightfully so) that they will belong only to a movement in which their ideas, needs, problems, concerns, politics, culture, and perceptions are of central interest. They argue that they don't want to be made marginal or irrelevant. Women of color feel the same—as long as their interests, needs, ideas, problems, and concerns are of marginal consideration or if they are made to feel irrelevant, then they will not belong to such a movement. The challenge, therefore, for ecofeminists is to increase their awareness of issues devastating communities of color, explore ways of developing understanding and mutually respectful working relationships, and be open to changes that will come from such alliances. Most important, they have to resist the urge to take over.

Theory, Politics, and Activism

While ecofeminists focus a lot of attention on theoretical discussions (discussions which are relevant and necessary to the building of a strong and effective movement), women-of-color environmental justice activists have to focus on theory and practice with a heavy emphasis on practice. Time is not on their side; they cannot afford to theorize in splendid isolation while the death and devastation continue. The devastation they face is real. For instance, if one walks down Calle Evelina ("Street of Death") in South Tucson with Marie Sosa, who has had a double mastectomy, she will point out the thirty or so homes on the street where someone is ill with or has died of TCE (trichloroethylene)-related cancer.[61] Hazel Johnson and the residents of Atgeld Gardens on the South Side of Chicago can cite similar cases. Other stories can be told along Cancer Alley, in Chemical Valley, and all over the country.

Although there are some women of color who consider themselves ecofeminists, the formulation, control, and dissemination of ecofeminist beliefs, practices, and ideas are firmly under the control of white women. White women are the dominant, driving force behind ecofeminism. Women-of-color environmental justice activists who have had prominent and varied roles in the environmental justice movement will wonder if there would be space to empower themselves and grow as they have in the environmental justice movement or if they would be relegated to roles in the supporting casts. Could they be the lawyers trying to build cases for environmental racism, the researchers, academics, theoreticians, philosophers, activists, organizers, or educators? Could they worship as they please, eat what they want, structure their political opposition in ways that are different from what has become the norm in ecofeminism? Given the realities of little recognition of their work and lack of understanding of their oppression and politics, they would be justified in wondering if ecofeminism would be an improvement over working within the framework of environmental justice.

If women of color could have fit their activism within the framework of one of these three already existing movements (ecofeminism, feminism, and other sectors of the environmental movement), they would have done so. Precisely because of the complexity and uniqueness of the issues women of color fight and their approach to tackling these issues, there wasn't a perfect fit with any of these movements. If there had been, there wouldn't have been a need for the environmental justice movement and the movement wouldn't have grown so rapidly. The best strategy for women of color is to work within a movement that overlays several other important social movements, and to build bridges with people from these closely related movements.

Notes

1. Although the issues raised here could and should be discussed and applied in a larger context, this essay focuses on environmental activism in the United States. It is beyond the essay's scope to discuss women of color worldwide and their relationship to ecofeminism. Therefore the terms *women of color* and *people of color* here refer specifically to African-Americans, Latinos and Latinas, Na-

tive Americans, Asian-Americans, and other ethnic minority groups in the United States.

2. See Mitchell, 1980: 44–45, 1979: 16–55; Hohn, 1976; Van Ardsol et al., 1965: 144–63; Kellert, 1984: 209–28; Kellert and Westerfelt, 1983; Kreger, 1973: 30–34; Dorceta Taylor, 1989: 175–205; Ostheimer and Ritt, 1976; Crenson, 1971; LaHart, 1978; Giles, 1957: 488–99; Hershey and Hill, 1978: 339–58; Horvat, 1974; Commoner, 1971: 207–208; Lowe & Pinhey, 1982: 114–128; Lowe et al., 1980: 423–45; Buttel and Flinn, 1978: 445; Van Liere and Dunlap, 1980: 191–97; Buttel, 1987: 465–88; Dunlap and Catton, 1979: 243–73; Geisler et al., 1977: 241–49; Dolin, 1988: 17–21; Nash, 1982; Paehlke, 1989: 4–22; Fox, 1985; Devall and Sessions, 1985; Fleming, 1972; Russell, 1968; Pepper, 1986; Bramwell, 1989; Pursell, 1973; Allaby, 1989.

3. See Gelobter, 1992; Hamilton, 1990; Mann, 1991.

4. See Mann, 1991; Commission for Racial Justice, 1987; Bullard, 1990; *EPA Journal*, 1992; *Environmental Action*, 1990.

5. See Paehlke, 1989: 14–22; Fox, 1985: 103–47; Devall, 1970: 123–26; Mohai, 1991, 1985; Dorceta Taylor, 1989: 175–205; Harry et al., 1969: 246–54; Buttel and Flinn, 1974; Hendee et al., 1968; Faich and Gale, 1971: 270–87; Morrison et al., 1972: 259–79; Lowe et. al., 1980: 423–45.

6. Although whites are involved in the environmental justice movement, this chapter focuses on the efforts of people of color in the United States to develop a movement that comes from the perspective of people of color.

7. See CCHW, 1991: 2; Lester, 1989; Suro, 1989: 18; Collette, 1987: 44–45; Bullard, 1992, 1991.

8. See D. Taylor, 1992, for a detailed discussion of the four stages in the evolution of the environmental movement and the various sectors of the environmental movement.

9. Greenpeace has been more responsive to the criticisms of environmental justice groups and people of color than any other major environmental organization or any of the radical groups or sectors. Greenpeace has done extensive work on toxics and hazardous wastes, has worked extensively with people-of-color communities, and has demonstrated that its members understand that in working with these communities, they need to act as partners rather than superiors.

10. For detailed information on these and other sites, see *Race and the Incidence of Environmental Hazards: A Time for Discourse* (1992), ed. B. Bryant and P. Mohai; Bullard, 1993, 1990; R. Bullard, *Toxic Struggles: The Theory and Practice of Environmental Justice* (1993); R. Hofrichter, ed., *What Works: Local Solutions to Toxic Pollution* (1993).

11. See Cerrel Associates, 1984; Trimble, 1988; Blumberg and Gottlieb, 1989; Mles, 1991; Moses, 1993: 161–78; Geldicks, 1993; Robinson, 1992: 153–62; White, 1992: 126–39; Bullard, 1990; Cohen, 1992; Mann, 1991; Perfecto, 1992: 177–203; *National Law Journal*, 1992; LaBalme, 1988: 23–30; Bailey et al., 1993: 107–22.

12. See Rawls, 1971; Nozick, 1975; Abercrombie et al., 1984; Cook, 1989: 205; Kuper and Kuper, 1989; Eckhoff, 1974; Greenberg, 1981; Lerner and Lerner, 1981.

13. Rawls, 1971.

14. See LaBalme, 1988, and Bailey et al., 1993.

15. Warden and Hirsch, 1990.

16. O'Byrne, 1990.

17. PCBs had been dumped illegally on back roads covering a large area of North Carolina. After considering several options, a decision was made to remove the contaminated soil and place it in a landfill to be built in Warren County, the county with the largest African-American population in the state.

18. LaBalme, 1988: 23–30.

19. Bean v. Southwestern Waste Management Corp., 482 F. Supp. 673 (S.D. Tex. 1979).

20. Lavelle and Coyle, 1992.

21. Under mounting criticisms from environmental justice organizations and increasing publicity generated by Lavelle and Coyle's study, the EPA has decided to look into its civil rights mission and take a case to court (*New York Times*, December 1993).

22. In deciding whether a site should be designated a Superfund site, contaminated areas are evaluated to see if they are eligible to be placed on the National Priorities List (NPL). The EPA has developed a numerical rating scheme known as the Hazard Ranking System (HRS) to determine eligibility. The HRS considers seven factors: the relative hazard to public health or the environment, taking into account the population at risk; the hazardous potential of the substances at the site; the potential for contamination of drinking water supplies; direct contact with or destruction of sensitive ecosystems; damage to natural resources that may affect the human food chain; ambient air pollution; and preparedness of the state involved to assume its share (typically 10 percent) of the total costs and responsibilities for the cleanup. Sites receiving 28.5 or more on a scale of 1–100 are placed on the NPL. Sites on the NPL are eligible for Superfund monies (Mazmanian and Morell, 1992: 31; Wolf, 1988: 237).

23. See the Urban Environment Conference's *Taking Back Our Health*, 1985; *Environmental Cancer*, 1985; First National People of Color Environmental Leadership Summit, 1991.

24. Cerrel Associates, 1984; Trimble, 1988; Blumberg and Gottlieb, 1989; Miles, 1991.

25. Brough, 1990: 5–7; *Environmental Action*, 1990; Pena and Gallegos, 1992: 141–60; D. Taylor, 1992: 28–54, 224–30.

26. Dishman, 1993; Moses, 1993: 161–78; Perfecto, 1992: 177–203, 247–50; Steinhart, 1991: 18–20; United Farm Workers, "Wrath of Grapes," 1986; "No Grapes," 1993; Weir and Schapiro, 1981.

27. Steinhart, 1991: 18–20.

28. Phoenix, 1993: 77–92; Agency for Toxic Substances Disease Registry, 1988.

29. Foucault, 1969, 1966.

30. See Christ, 1990: 58–69; Griffin, 1978; Sanchez, 1993: 207–228.

31. See Swimme, 1990: 15–22; Christ, 1990: 58–69; Griffin, 1990; 1978; Eisler, 1990: 23–34.

32. Environmental justice activists argue that people have a right to clean air, water, housing, safe jobs, etc. That is, they have a right to be assured of their basic environmental needs.

33. Foucault (1980) argues that because power is decentered and changes from one moment to the next, an appropriate response calls for a decentered political struggle, with a plurality of resistance. People of color are using a plurality of strategies in a decentered political struggle.

34. LaBalme, 1988: 23–30.

35. National People of Color Environmental Leadership Summit, Summary Report of Delegate Registrations, October 15, 1991.

36. See Merchant, 1990: 100–105; 1989; Spretnak, 1990: 3–14, 1982; King, 1990: 106–21. See also the following works for descriptions of feminism and eco-feminism: V. Taylor and Whittier, 1992: 104–29; Freeman, 1975; Gelb and Palley, 1982; Hole and Levine, 1971, Evans, 1979; Jaggar and Struhl, 1978; Ferree and Miller, 1985; V. Taylor 1989; Warren, 1993: 119–32, 1992; Reuther, 1993: 13–23, 1992; O'Laughlin, 1993: 146–66; Gruen, 1993: 60–90; Rose, 1993: 149–67; Daly, 1990; Griffin, 1978. For discussion and critiques of ecofeminism, see Biehl, 1991; Cuomo, 1992: 351–63; O'Laughlin, 1993: 146–66.

37. Beauvoir, 1952.

38. See Daly, 1990; Griffin, 1978; Merchant, 1990: 100–105; Rose, 1993: 149–67; Warren, 1993: 119–32; Gaard, 1993 (several essays).

39. See Williams, 1993: 24–29; Riley, 1993: 191–204; hooks and West, 1991: 153.

40. Although not all women of color express their feminism in identical ways or experience identical forms of oppression, they share many experiences. They are constantly discriminated against because of their race and gender, and because they are often poor, their environments are quite degraded.

41. See Warren, 1993: 119–32, and Gruen, 1993: 60–90.

42. See King, 1990: 106–21; Quinby, 1990: 122–27; Spivak, 1987: 89; O'Laughlin, 1993: 146–166; Cuomo, 1992: 351–63; Riley, 1993: 191–204.

43. See Riley, 1993: 191–204, and Lourde, 1983.

44. See Spretnak, 1990: 3–14; Hartmann, 1976.

45. Fanon (1963) argues that colonization is a form of dominance not discussed by Marx. Blauner (1972: 53–81) argues that African-Americans are in a state of internal colonization. In addition, many people in developing countries have been colonized, and this affects their experiences and their world views.

46. See Warren, 1993: 119–32; Gaard, 1993: 1–12.

47. This development could be at odds with the assertion that any ecofeminist ethic must have an explicit gender analysis. See Dinnerstein, 1989: 192–200; Warren, 1990: 125–46; Davion, forthcoming.

48. See Eisler, 1990: 23–34.

49. Working-class white women find the environmental justice movement quite attractive and participate in it, too. The environmental justice movement must be saying something about class that these women are not hearing from other sectors of the environmental movement.

50. See MacKinnon, 1987, 1982: 515–44, and Quinby, 1990: 122–27.

51. See Nelson, 1990: 173–88; Biehl, 1991; O'Laughlin, 1993: 146–66.

52. See Hynes, 1989; Merchant, 1990: 100–105, 1989; Razak, 1990: 165–72; Kheel, 1990: 128–37; Nelson, 1990: 173–88; Raymond, 1988; Diamond, 1990, 201–10; Wyden, 1984.

53. See Warren, 1993: 119–32.

54. See King, 1990: 106–21; Zimmerman, 1990: 138–54; Abbott, 1990: 35–40; Keller, 1990: 41–51; Eisler, 1990: 20–34, 1987; Merchant, 1990: 100–105; Stone, 1976; Sjöö and Mor, 1987; Starhawk, 1979; Spretnak, 1981.

55. See Lahar, 1993: 91–117; Sanchez, 1993: 207–28; Reuther, 1993: 13–23; Cuomo, 1992: 351–63; Biehl, 1991.

56. See Doubiago, 1989: 40–44, and Salleh, 1992.

57. See Quinby, 1990: 122–27; Foucault, 1980, 1978, 1969, 1966; Slayton, 1992: 83–117; Hawkins, 1988: 86–87; Hoexter, 1988: 106–118; Cuomo, 1992: 351–63.

58. See O'Laughlin, 1993: 146–66.

59. See Biehl, 1991.

60. For example, King, 1990: 106–21; Quinby, 122–27; Nelson, 1990: 173–89; Hamilton, 1990: 215–22; Warren, 1993: 119–32, 1992; O'Laughlin, 1993: 146–66.

61. Lavelle and Coyle, 1992.

References

Abbott, Sally (1990), "The Origins of God in the Blood of the Lamb," in *Reweaving the World: The Emergence of Ecofeminism*, ed. Irene Diamond and Gloria Feman Orenstein, San Francisco: Sierra Club Books.

Abercrombie, Nicholas, Stephen Hill, and Bryan S. Turner (1984), *Dictionary of Sociology*, New York: Penguin.

Allaby, Michael (1989), *Dictionary of the Environment*, New York: New York University Press.

Beauvoir, Simone de (1952), *The Second Sex*, New York: Knopf.

Biehl, Janet (1991), *Rethinking Ecofeminist Politics*, Boston: South End Press.

Blauner, Robert (1972), *Racial Oppression in America*, New York: Harper and Row.

Blumberg, Louis, and Robert Gottlieb (1989), *War on Waste: Can America Win Its Battle with Garbage?* Covelo, Calif.: Island Press.

Bramwell, Anna (1989), *Ecology in the 20th Century: A History*, New Haven: Yale University Press.

Bullard, Robert (1993), ed., *Confronting Environmental Racism: Voices from the Grassroots*, Boston: South End Press.

—— (1992), "Environmental Blackmail in Minority Communities," in *Race and the Incidence of Environmental Hazards*, ed. Bunyan Bryant and Paul Mohai, Boulder: Westview Press.

—— (1991), "Environmental Justice for All," *EnviroAction*, Environmental News Digest for the National Wildlife Federation, November.

—— (1990), *Dumping on Dixie: Race, Class and Environmental Quality*, Boulder: Westview Press.

Buttel, Frederick H. (1987), "New Directions in Environmental Sociology," *Annual Review of Sociology*, vol. 13.

——, and W. L. Flinn (1978), "Social Class and Mass Environmental Beliefs: A Reconsideration," *Environment and Behavior*, vol. 10: 433–450.

—— (1974), "The Structure and Support for the Environmental Movement, 1968–70" *Rural Sociology*, vol. 39, #1: 56–69.

Carson, Rachel (1962), *Silent Spring*, Boston: Houghton Mifflin.

CCHW (Citizen's Clearinghouse for Hazardous Wastes, 1991), *Everyone's Backyard*, vol. 9, no. 5: 2.

Cerrel Associates (1984), "Political Difficulties Facing Waste-to-Energy Conversion Plant Siting," in J. Stephen Powell, *Waste-to-Energy Technical Information Series*, chap. 3a, California Waste Management Board, Los Angeles.

Christ, Carol P. (1990), "Rethinking Theology and Nature," in *Reweaving the World*, ed. Diamond and Orenstein.

Collette, Will (1987), "Institutions: Citizens Clearinghouse for Hazardous Wastes," *Environment*, vol. 29, no. 9.

Commission for Racial Justice (1987), *Toxic Wastes and Race in the United States: A National Report on the Racial and Socioeconomic Characteristics of Communities with Hazardous Waste Sites*, United Church of Christ, New York.

Commoner, Barry B. (1971), *Closing Circle: Nature, Man and Technology*, New York: Knopf.

Conservation Directory (1993), Washington, D.C.: National Wildlife Federation.

Cook, Karen S. (1989), "Distributive Justice," in *The Social Science Encyclopedia*, ed. Adam Kuper and Jessica Kuper, New York: Routledge.

Crenson, M. A. (1971), *The Un-Politics of Air Pollution*, Baltimore: Johns Hopkins University Press.

Cuomo, Christine J. (1992), "Unraveling the Problems in Ecofeminism," *Environmental Ethics*, vol. 14, no. 4.

Daly, Mary (1990), *Gyn/Ecology: The Metaethics of Radical Feminism*, Boston: Beacon Press.

Devall, Bill, and George Sessions (1985), *Deep Ecology: Living as if Nature Mattered*, Salt Lake City: Gibbs Smith.

Devall, W. B. (1970), "Conservation: An Upper-Middle Class Social Movement: A Replication," *Journal of Leisure Research*, vol. 2, no. 2: 123–26.

Diamond, Irene (1990), "Babies, Heroic Experts, and a Poisoned Earth," in *Reweaving the World*, ed. Diamond and Orenstein.

Dolin, Eric J. (1988), "Black Americans' Attitudes toward Wildlife," *Journal of Environmental Education*, vol. 20, no. 1.

Doubiago, S. (1989), "Mama Coyote Talks to the Boys," in Judith Plant, ed., *Healing the Wounds: The Promise of Ecofeminism*, Philadelphia: New Society Publishers.

Dunlap, R. E., and W. R. Catton, Jr. (1979), "Environmental Sociology," *Annual Review of Sociology*, vol. 5.

Eckhoff, T. (1974), *Justice: Its Determinants in Social Interaction*, Rotterdam: Rotterdam University Press.

Eisler, Riane (1990), "The Gaia Tradition and the Partnership Future: An Ecofeminist Manifesto" in *Reweaving the World*, ed. Diamond and Orenstein.

Environmental Action (1990). Special issue entitled "Beyond White Environmentalism," vol. 22, no. 1.

Environmental Cancer: Causes, Victims and Solutions (1985), Washington, D.C., Urban Environment Conference.

EPA Journal (1992). Special issue entitled "Environmental Protection—Has It Been Fair?" vol. 18, no. 1.

Evans, Sarah (1979), *Personal Politics*, New York: Vintage.

Faich, Ronald G., and Richard P. Gale (1971), "The Environmental Movement: From Recreation to Politics," *Pacific Sociological Review*, vol. 14, no. 2: 270–87.

Fanon, Frantz (1963), *The Wretched of the Earth*, New York: Grove Press.

Ferree, Myra Marx, and Frederick D. Miller (1985), *Controversy and Coalition: The New Feminist Movement*, Boston: Twayne.

Fleming (1972), "Roots of the New Conservation Movement," *Perspectives in American History*, vol. 6.

Foucault, Michel (1980), *Power/Knowledge: Selected Interviews and Other Writings, 1972–1977*, New York: Pantheon.

—— (1978), *The History of Sexuality*, vol. 1., New York: Pantheon.

—— (1969), *The Archeology of Knowledge*, London: Tavistock.

—— (1966), *The Order of Things, An Archeology of the Human Sciences*, London: Tavistock.

Fox, Stephen (1985), *The American Conservation Movement: John Muir and His Legacy*, Madison: University of Wisconsin Press.

Freeman, Jo (1975), *The Politics of Women's Liberation*, New York: David McKay.

Gaard, Greta (1993), ed., *Ecofeminism: Women, Animals, Nature*, Philadelphia: Temple University Press.

Gale Environmental Sourcebook (1992), Detroit: Gale Research, Inc.

Geisler, C. C., O. B. Martison, and E. A. Wilkening (1977), "Outdoor Recreation and Environmental Concern: A Re-Study," *Rural Sociology*, vol. 42, no. 2.

Gelb, Joyce, and Marian L. Palley (1982), *Women and Public Policy*, Princeton: Princeton University Press.

Gelobter, Michael (1992), "Toward a Model of Environmental Discrimination: How Environmental Laws Discriminate against Low-Income and Minority Communities," *Race and the Incidence of Environmental Hazards*, ed. Bryant and Mohai.

Giles, R. H., Jr. (1957), "The Conservation Knowledge of Virginia School Pupils," Proceedings of the Twenty-Fourth North American Wildlife Conference, Release no. 59-4 of the Virginia Cooperative Wildlife Research Unit, Blacksburg, Virginia.

Greenberg, J. (1981), "The Justice of Distributing Scarce and Abundant Resources," in M. J. Lerner and S. C. Lerner, eds., *The Justice Motive in Social Behavior*, New York: Plenum Press.

Griffin, Susan (1990), "Curves Along the Road," in *Reweaving the World*, ed. Diamond and Orenstein.

—— (1978), *Woman and Nature: The Roaring Inside Her*, New York: Harper and Row.

Gruen, Lori (1993), "Re-Valuing Nature," in *An Applied Ethics Reader*, ed. Earl R. Winkler and Jerrold R. Coombs, Oxford: Blackwell.

Hamilton, Cynthia (1990), "Women, Home and Community: The Struggle in an Urban Environment," in *Reweaving the World*, ed. Diamond and Orenstein.

Harry, J., R. Gale, and J. Hendee (1969), "Conservation: An Upper-Middle-Class Social Movement," *Journal of Leisure Research*, vol. 1, no. 2: 255–61.

Hartmann, Heidi (1976), "Capitalism, Patriarchy, and Job Segregation by Sex," *Signs*, vol. 1, no. 3: 137–55, 159–61, 164–68.

Hawkins, Howard (1988), "The Potential of the Green Movement," *New Politics*, vol. 5.

Hendee, J. C., W. R. Catton, L. D. Marlow, and C. F. Brockman (1968), "Wilderness Users in the Pacific Northwest—Their Characteristics, Values, and Management Preferences," U.S. Department of Agriculture, Forest Service Research Paper PNW-61, Forest Range Experiment Station, Portland, Ore.

Hershey, M. R., and D. B. Hill (1978), "Is Pollution 'a White Thing'? Racial Differences in Pre-adults' Attitudes," *Public Opinion Quarterly*, vol. 41, no. 2, 439.

Hoexter, Michael (1988), "It's Not Easy Being Green," *New Politics*, vol. 5.

Hohn, C. F. (1976), "A Human-Ecological Approach to the Reality and Perception of Air Pollution: The Los Angeles Case," *Pacific Sociological Review*, vol. 19, no. 1.

Hole, Judith, and Ellen Levine (1971), *Rebirth of Feminism*, New York: Quadrangle.

hooks, bell, and Cornel West. *Breaking Bread: Insurgent Black Intellectual Life*. Boston: South End Press, 1991.

Horvat, R. E. (1974), "Fifth and Eighth Grade Student Orientation towards the Environment and Environmental Problems," Ph.D. dissertation, University of Wisconsin, Madison.

Hynes, H. Patricia (1989), *The Recurrent Silent Spring*, New York: Pergamon.

Jaggar, Alison M., and Paula R. Struhl (1978), *Feminist Framework*, New York: McGraw-Hill.

Keller, Mara L. (1990), "The Eleusinian Mysteries: Ancient Nature Religion of Demeter and Persephone," in *Reweaving the World*, ed. Diamond and Orenstein.

Kellert, S. R. (1984), "Urban American Perceptions of Animals and the Natural Environment," *Urban Ecology*, vol. 8: 209–28.

Kellert, S. R., and M. O. Westerfelt (1983), *Children's Attitudes, Knowledge, and Behaviors toward Animals*, Washington, D.C.: Government Printing Office.

Kheel, Marti (1990), "Ecofeminism and Deep Ecology: Reflections on Identity and Difference," in *Reweaving the World*, ed. Diamond and Orenstein.

King, Ynestra (1990), "Healing the Wounds: Feminism, Ecology, and the Nature/Culture Dualism," in *Reweaving the World*, ed. Diamond and Orenstein.

Kreger, Janet (1973), "Ecology and Black Student Opinion," *Journal of Environmental Education*, vol. 4, no. 3: 30–34.

Kuper, Adam, and Jessica Kuper (1989), *The Social Science Encyclopedia*, New York: Routledge.

LaBalme, Jenny (1988), "Dumping on Warren County," in *Environmental Politics: Lessons from the Grassroots*, ed. Bob Hall, Durham, N.C.: Institute for Southern Studies.

LaHart, D. E. (1978), "The Influence of Knowledge on Young People's Perceptions about Wildlife," final project report to the National Wildlife Federation, College of Education, Florida State University.

Lerner, M. J., and S. C. Lerner (1981), eds., *The Justice Motive in Social Behavior*, New York.

Lester, S. V. (1989), personal communication, Citizens Clearinghouse for Hazardous Wastes, Arlington, VA, September 25, 1989.

Lowe, G. D., T. K. Pinhey, and M. D. Grimes (1980), "Public Support for Environmental Protection: New Evidence from National Surveys," *Pacific Sociological Review*, vol. 23 (October).

MacKinnon, Catharine (1987), *Feminism Unmodified*, Cambridge: Harvard University Press.

—— (1982), "Feminism, Marxism, Method, and the State: An Agenda for Theory," *Signs*, vol. 7.

Malaspina, Mark, Kristin Schafer, and Richard Wiles (1993), eds., *What Works: Local Solutions to Toxic Pollution*, Washington, D.C.: The Environmental Exchange.

Mann, Eric (1991), *L.A.'s Lethal Air: New Strategies for Policy, Organizing, and Action*, Los Angeles: Labor/Community Watchdog Strategy Center.

Mazmanian, Daniel, and David Morell (1992), *Beyond Superfailure: America's Toxics Policy for the 1990s*, Boulder: Westview Press.

Merchant, Carolyn (1990), "Ecofeminism and Feminist Theory," in *Reweaving the World*, ed. Diamond and Orenstein.

—— (1989), *Ecological Revolutions: Nature, Gender, and Science in New England*, Chapel Hill: University of North Carolina Press.

Mitchell, Robert C. (1980), *Public Opinion on Environmental Issues: Results of a National Public Opinion Survey*, CEQ, DOA, DOE, and the EPA, Washington, D.C.: Government Printing Office.

—— (1979), "National Environmental Lobbies and the Apparent Illogic of Collective Action," in *Collective Decision Making*, ed. C. Russell, Baltimore: Johns Hopkins University Press.

Mohai, Paul (1991), "Black Environmentalism," *Social Science Quarterly*, vol. 71, no. 4: 744–65.

—— (1985), "Public Concern and Elite Involvement in Environmental Conservation Issues," *Social Science Quarterly*, vol. 55, no. 4: 820–38.

Monroe, Arthur (1990), "Lead Poisoning Still Strikes Inner City Youth," *Race, Poverty and the Environment*, vol. 1, no. 3: 1, 17–18.

Morrison, Denton E., K. E. Hornback, and W. K. Warner (1972), "The Environmental Movement: Some Preliminary Observations and Predictions," in W. Burch, Jr. et al., eds., *Social Behavior, Natural Resources and the Environment*, New York: Harper and Row.

Nash, Roderick (1982), *Wilderness and the American Mind*, 3d ed., New Haven: Yale University Press.

National People of Color Environmental Leadership Summit Program Guide, 1991, Washington, D.C.

Nelson, Lin (1990), "The Place of a Woman in Polluted Places," in *Reweaving the World*, ed. Diamond and Orenstein.

Nozick, Robert (1975), *Anarchy, State and Utopia*, Oxford: Blackwell.

Ostheimer, J. M., and L. G. Ritt (1976), *Environment, Energy and Black Americans*, Beverly Hills: Sage.

Paehlke, Robert (1989), *Environmentalism and the Future of Progressive Politics*, New Haven: Yale University Press.

Pepper, David (1986), *The Roots of Modern Environmentalism*, London: Croom & Helm.

Perfecto, Ivette (1992), "Pesticide Exposure of Farm Workers and the International Connection," in *Race and the Incidence of Environmental Hazards*, ed. Bryant and Mohai.

Pursell, Carroll, ed. (1973), *From Conservation to Ecology: The Development of Environmental Concern*, New York: Crowell.

Quinby, Lee (1990), "Ecofeminism and the Politics of Resistance," in *Reweaving the World*, ed. Diamond and Orenstein.

Rawls, John (1971), *A Theory of Justice*, Cambridge: Harvard University Press.

Raymond, Janice (1988), "In the Matter of Baby M—Rejudged," *Reproductive and Genetic Engineering*, vol. 1, no. 1.

Razak, Arisika (1990), "Toward a Womanist Analysis of Birth," in *Reweaving the World*, ed. Diamond and Orenstein.

"The Regulatory Thickets of Environmental Racism" (1993), *New York Times*, December 19, section IV, page 5.

Robinson, W. Paul (1992), "Uranium Production and Its Effects on Navajo Communities along the Rio Puerco in Western New Mexico," in *Race and the Incidence of Environmental Hazards*, ed. Bryant and Mohai.

Ruether, Rosemary Radford (1993), *Sexism and God-Talk: Toward a Feminist Theology*, Boston: Beacon Press.

Russell, Franklin (1968), "The Vermont Prophet: George Perkins Marsh," *Horizon*, vol. 10, no. 3.

Salleh, Ariel (1992), "The Ecofeminism/Deep Ecology Debate," *Environmental Ethics*, vol. 14, no. 3.

Sjöö, Monica, and Barbara Mor (1987), *The Great Cosmic Mother: Rediscovering the Religion of the Earth*, San Francisco: Harper and Row.

Slayton, Christa D. (1992), "The Failure of the United States Greens to Root in Fertile Soil," in *Research in Social Movements, Conflicts and Change*, supplement 2, Mathias Finger, volume editor, Greenwich, Conn.: JAI.

Spivak, Gayatri C. (1987), "Feminism and Critical Theory," in *In Other Worlds:*

Essays in Cultural Politics, ed. Gayatri C. Spivak, New York: Routledge & Kegan Paul.

Spretnak, Charlene (1990), "Ecofeminism: Our Roots and Flowering," in *Reweaving the World*, ed. Diamond and Orenstein.

Starhawk (1979), *The Spiral Dance: A Rebirth of the Ancient Religion of the Great Goddess*, San Francisco: Harper and Row, 1979.

Stone, Merlin (1976), *When God Was a Woman*, New York: Harcourt Brace Jovanovich.

Suman, Daniel (1990), "Fighting LULUs: Effective Community Organizing," *Race, Poverty and the Environment*, vol. 1, no. 2: 6.

Suro, R. (1989), "Grass Roots Groups Show Power Battling Pollution Close to Home," *New York Times*, July 2; section A1.

Swimme, Brian (1990), "How to Heal a Lobotomy," in *Reweaving the World*, ed. Diamond and Orenstein.

Taking Back Our Health, An Institute on Surviving the Toxics Threat to Minority Communities (1985), Urban Environmental Conference, Washington, D.C.

Taylor, Dorceta E. (1992), "Can the Environmental Movement Attract and Maintain the Support of Minorities?" in *Race and the Incidence of Environmental Hazards*, ed. Bryant and Mohai.

—— (1989), "Blacks and the Environment: Toward an Explanation of the Concern and Action Gap between Blacks and Whites," *Environment and Behavior*, vol. 21, no. 2: 175–205.

—— (1982), "Contemporary Opinions concerning Environmental Issues," Department of Geography and Environmental Studies, Northeastern Illinois University.

Taylor, Verta (1989), "The Future of Feminism," in *Feminist Frontiers II*, ed. Laurel Richardson and Verta Taylor, New York: Random House.

——, and Nancy Whittier (1992), "Collective Identity in Social Movement Communities: Lesbian Feminist Mobilization," in *Frontiers in Social Movement Theory*, ed. Aldon Morris and Carol M. Mueller, New Haven: Yale University Press.

Trimble, Lillie C. (1988), "What Do Citizens Want in Siting of Waste Management Facilities?" *Risk Analysis*, vol. 8, no. 3.

Van Ardsol, Maurice D., Jr., George Sabagh, and Francesca Alexander (1965), "Reality and the Perception of Environmental Hazards," *Journal of Health and Human Behavior*, vol. 5: 144–53.

Van Liere, K. D., and Riley Dunlap (1980), "The Social Bases of Environmental Concern: A Review of Hypothesis, Explanations, and Empirical Evidence," *Public Opinion Quarterly*, vol. 44, no. 2: 181–97.

Warren, Karen J. (1993), "A Feminist Philosophical Perspective on Ecofeminist Spiritualities," in *Ecofeminism and the Sacred*, ed. Carol J. Adams, New York: Continuum.

—— (1990), "The Power and Promise of Ecological Feminism," *Environmental Ethics*, vol. 12, no. 2.

——, and Nancy Tuana (1992), eds., *APA Newsletter on Feminism and Philosophy*, special issue entitled "Feminism and the Environment," vol. 91, no. 1.

Weir, David, and Mark Schapiro (1981), *The Circle of Poison: Pesticides and People in a Hungry World*, San Francisco: Institute for Food and Development Policy.

White, Harvey (1992), "Hazardous Waste Incineration and Minority Communities," in *Race and the Incidence of Environmental Hazards*, ed. Bryant and Mohai.

Wyden, P. (1984), *Day One: Before Hiroshima and After*, New York: Simon and Schuster.

Zimmerman, Michael E. (1990), "Deep Ecology and Feminism: The Emerging Dialogue," in *Reweaving the World*, ed. Diamond and Orenstein.

Four

Women's Knowledge as Expert Knowledge
Indian Women and Ecodevelopment

Deane Curtin

An Indian scholar gave this description of the daily lives of village women in her country:

> While they work on an average many more hours than their men, they eat much less. When there is little food, it is the woman who has to go without. . . . She works in the fields, looks after the children, comes home and prepares the family meal and then has to be available for her man whenever she is required. . . . rural women endure childbirth after childbirth which drains them of physical energy and destroys their health. They have little or no access to health care and such facilities as there are are pitifully inadequate. In any militant struggle that they, or their men, have been involved in, they are the ones who are most vulnerable to police and state repression. They suffer violence and abuse within their own homes. Yet little is known of their condition. (Butalia, 132–33)

Reading this, one could easily conclude that there is little hope for rural women's development in the so-called Third World, much less for an approach to ecodevelopment based on their distinctive practices. Real ecodevelopment cannot be sustained, however, unless distinctively women's practices and ways of knowing are granted the conceptually central places they deserve.

Yet this is exactly the problem: how *can* we generalize about women's ecological practices to the point that their roles become recognizable without thereby sacrificing the enormous diversity of their lives? In India, for example, dalit (untouchable) women suffer the worst effects of the caste system, while tribal (adivasi) women come from cultures that have traditionally been outside the caste system, and often fare better. Some tribes have matrilineal social structures. Western feminists have learned how easy it is for race and class biases to slip into their generalizing about the conditions of Western women. There is always a tension between recognition of common problems and maintaining recognition of diversity. The attempt to make visible the conditions of Third World women and their diverse relationships to the land is surely much more risky.

Not to enter into this hazardous territory, however, risks something even greater: that the lives of women will continue to occupy conceptually marginal places. It made good sense to well-intended development experts, for example, that women in a sunny continent like Africa could benefit from solar stoves.[1] Experts' ignorance of what women know, however, caused them to ignore the fact that women are not likely to cook in the heat of the day; nor are they often able to cook during the valuable daylight hours, given the other demands that claim their time. When we consider that we are fast approaching the day when 80 percent of the world's women will live in the Third World, it becomes an urgent task for feminists to think about how women's lives can become more visible while minimizing the conceptual biases of race, class, and caste.

Fortunately, the attempt to represent the diversity of Third World women's lives, as well as their common themes, is now an international project. It has sometimes been charged that feminism is a First World phenomenon that is inappropriately projected onto the Third World. This is an important and complex issue that deserves careful attention. Two comments must suffice here. First, there is no doubt that the so-called second wave of feminism was originally a predominantly northern, white, middle-class phenomenon. However, international feminism is evolving toward pluralistic perspectives that include relations between First and Third Worlds, as well as relations between race, class, caste, and gender. Second, there are, in fact, development perspectives that arise from the lives of Third World women. In India, for example, these include the famed Chipko movement, the feminist journal *Manushi*, and Kali for Women, which publishes important feminist development books in association with Zed Books. To dismiss feminism as a First World perspective denies that there are self-identified Third World feminists.

I am interested in exploring an approach to women's environmental practices and ways of knowing that does not resort to abstractions about the inherent natures of women and the environment. We have seen in recent years how self-defeating it is to draw on traditional images of the earth as female. Such images only tend to reinforce stereotypes of "man" as the builder of culture out of nature. "Woman" is left to clean up the mess (see Murphy).

The approach I propose is nonessentialist.[2] That is, while women are not essentially more "natural," closer to nature, than men and nature is no more female than male, the actual practices typically demanded of women involve mediation between culture and nature. We see this particularly in the material lives of Third World women farmers.

I focus mainly on rural women in India, though I hope my brief references to other contexts make it clear that Third World women's stories have connecting themes. One connecting theme, entirely apart from whether their communities have issues in common, is that women face a common threat from the outside: the attempt of misguided, if sometimes well-intended, agencies who seek to "develop" without appreciating what women tend to know about the environment.[3] There are some resources for generalization, that is, in the very fact that diverse cultures are facing a common threat.

Women's Practices/Women's Knowledge

Vandana Shiva gives a contemporary example of the contrast between typically women's and men's agriculture and agricultural knowledge. Traditionally, she says, "the backyard of each rural home was a nursery, and each peasant woman the sylviculturalist. The invisible, decentred agroforestry model was significant because the humblest of species and the smallest of people could participate in it." This plant diversity, along with the mixture of private and public treestands, provides "food and fodder, fertilizer and pesticide, fuel and small timber."

In masculinist development projects, this knowledge is replaced by the "reductionist mind" of outside experts who do not understand the multiple uses of traditional plantings, nor their uses in Indian culture. Shiva says:

> The experts decided that indigenous knowledge was worthless and "unscientific," and proceeded to destroy the diversity of indigenous species by replacing them with row after row of eucalyptus seedlings in polythene bags, in government nurseries. Nature's locally available seeds were laid waste; people's locally available knowledge and energies were laid waste. With imported seeds and expertise came the import of loans and debt and the export of wood, soils—and people. Trees, as a living resource, maintaining the life of the soil and water and of local people, were replaced by trees whose dead wood went straight to a pulp factory hundreds of miles away. (Shiva 1988, 79)

The eucalyptus is valuable as a cash crop because it grows fast and straight, putting most of its energy into wood pulp instead of into branches and leafy matter. But it is also an ecological disaster whose impact is felt particularly by women. Its lack of leaves and small branches means there is very little to return to the land to conserve moisture and fertility; nor does it provide wood for housing. The fact that it grows quickly means that it places heavy demand on water supplies. In arid regions the demand on water and its lack of contribution to humus, which maintains soil moisture, have contributed directly to the oppression of women who must walk farther and farther each year to obtain drinking water.

The eucalyptus has become a symbol for the many ways in which women's ecological knowledge is marginalized. When cash crops drive out traditional crops that return nitrogen to the soil without expensive inorganic fertilizers (crops like pulses), this is a gender bias. When herbicides kill grasses that are used to make baskets and mats, grasses that are defined by outside experts as worthless, this is a gender bias. When plants are genetically engineered to produce only cash value, thereby reducing by-products that go to fuel and fodder, this is gender bias. When so-called undeveloped lands to which everyone has access are privatized and dedicated to plant monoculture, this is gender bias.

Technological innovations, such as irrigation and plant monoculture, are typical of men's agriculture. The impact of these and other Green Revolution techniques has often been devastating for women. The scarcity of water in the Third World reveals much. Though 73 percent of the world's water use is dedicated to irrigation, only 20–30 percent gets to its destination. Such waste has a tragic impact on women's lives. Women are still overwhelmingly responsible for collecting water for drinking and cooking. Yet in India 23,000 villages are without drinking water due to deforestation and irrigation. Seventy percent of the ground water that is available is polluted (Dankelman and Davidson, 21 and 33). Water collection increasingly demands women's time. The need to carry water over greater distances affects women's health, particularly the health of girls whose bodies are still developing.

The experiences of Chipko women in the Himalayan foothills are justly celebrated. Their experiences with the effects of technology were typical. The modern Chipko movement began as a response to flooding due to deforestation in the mountains above Chipko villages. The response to deforestation varied by gender. Men were drawn to wage-labor jobs in the forestry industry. Women were drawn to reforestation, since their concerns were different. These include the entire cycle of concerns that depend on forests, from adequate water supplies to fuel and fodder and sources of traditional medicines. A healthy ecosystem is a necessity for the safety of children and for the possibility of future generations. When villagers were asked about which trees should be planted as part of a reforestation plan, the men immediately chose fruit trees. The women responded: "The men would take the fruits and sell them by the roadside. The cash will only go to buy liquor and tobacco. We women prefer fuel and fodder trees" (Dankelman and Davidson, 50–51).[4]

We can see that social forestry is a feminist issue. Tree hugging by Chipko women is more than the simple attempt to save trees from logging companies. It is a distinctively feminist political act growing out of typically women's knowledge of the forest. The circling of trees can be understood as representing the broad circle of concerns that women understand. Trees mean water for Chipko women. Trees mean safety from flooding. Forests, not simply plant monoculture, mean food, fodder, building materials, and medicines. Hugging trees is as much a defense of culture and future generations as it is a defense of nature.

Consider, as well, the issue of intellectual property rights debated at the Rio Summit and embodied in the GATT and NAFTA agreements. The government of the United States and First World medical technology corporations demanded the right to financial reward for medicines derived from the Third World's biological diversity. Yet, whereas medical science has examined less than one percent of these resources for potential medical benefit, indigenous women's medical knowledge has developed over forty centuries. Women's medical knowledge is a vast storehouse of expertise, yet it goes unrecognized because of the biases of modern science against traditional, indigenous forms of knowledge. The debate over whether northern science should gain its financial reward remains immune to the rights of indigenous women. Epistemic biases like this cannot be addressed simply by adding a new fact to the dominant paradigm of masculinized knowledge. Women's knowledge is not valued when it challenges the paradigm.

Development theory has progressed from what can only be described as racist and sexist beginnings.[5] Nevertheless, contemporary programs that are advertised as profamily often remain antiwoman. Masculinity and the culture of high technology are connected through the division of labor. Men's cultural status tends to increase under the influence of technology, while women's status tends to decrease. Young men, in particular, can insist on becoming "modern," often wearing Western clothes and sporting Western electronic goods. Women are expected to maintain traditional values and dress (Mies 1988, 138)

Many international agents—even the World Bank—now include women's issues in their programs. Yet programs directed at the male "head of household" are conceptually flawed when they assume equity and identity of interests within the family. Because equity is rare, these programs pull the family apart. The effort to involve Third World communities in international markets through introduction of technologies to produce cash crops is one example. This tends to cause dual economies, with men working in the for-profit sector while women continue with traditional agriculture to meet the needs of the family. Such programs rarely improve the lives of women and children.

Taking Women's Practices Seriously

This tendency of traditional development schemes to elevate men while further marginalizing women depends on a familiar set of normative categories. These prioritize mind over body, reason over feeling, and theory over practice. In the case of women's agricultural knowledge, however, the most powerful tool for marginalization is the nature/culture distinction. While the distinction varies widely within indigenous cultures, a common theme across cultures is their need to respond to the demands of masculinist models of development. The masculine bias in these dualisms favors the "modern," scientific, rational, global, and high-tech over the traditional, small-scale, and low-tech. Men are constructed by these dualisms as independent, autonomous, and rational; women are constructed as dependent or interdependent. Men's agriculture, which can hardly be understood as anything but a practical activity, is nevertheless represented as a "theoretical practice," that is, as an applied science. Women's expert knowledge of soil, climate, and seeds is marginalized as anecdotal; it is often dismissed as mere "wives' tales."

Patriarchal cultures tend to locate women's practices on the border between nature and culture. These involve caring for others, e.g., mothering, cooking, health care, and certain kinds of simple, traditional agricultural labor that are low paid or unpaid, such as weeding and tending to livestock. Women's work is the everyday work of translation between the needs of the environment and the needs of the human community.

Such depictions of a woman's "proper" role create a dilemma: while such labor is often experienced by women as an oppressive demand, the environment and the human community cannot survive without it. Children's health and safety depend on regular access to clean water. Traditional medicine and agriculture depend on the biodiversity of an environment that can supply medicines as well as fuel, fodder, and food. Caring labor holds together the family and the environment and is inherently interested in future generations. Third World development, therefore, is a feminist project. Its success requires the revaluation of women's caring labor.

The issue, then, is how an epistemology can be constructed that is faithful to what Third World women know as well as to the ways in which they know. First, some clarifications. In emphasizing gender bias in the construction of what is counted as knowledge, I am speaking about the construction of gender categories, not about particular individuals. While gender does have a powerful hold on individuals, there are other forces that intersect in the individual as well, including race, caste, class, and religion. This means that some men are nonsexist despite sexist constructions of gender; some women are implicated in the destruction of the environment even though women's praxis involves caring. Consequently, my argument is that recognition of gender is a necessary condition—not a sufficient condition—for sustainable development.

Furthermore, it would be a mistake to look to the traditional philosophical distinction between propositional (the belief that a proposition is true) and nonpropositional attitudes to clarify the distinction between men's and women's ways of knowing. I would say, rather, that such forms of knowledge are constructed by gendered categories as propositional or nonpropositional to the disadvantage of both. As medicine has been masculinized, for example, it has been important to construct medical knowledge as propositional (abstract, theoretical) despite the evident hands-on expertise required by the skilled surgeon. Cooking, a clear case of a hands-on epistemic practice, is diminished if it is reduced simply to knowing how.

This brief overview of the construction of gendered agricultural knowledge leads me, instead, to focus on practices as a way of getting at a reconstructed conception of women's agricultural labor. Practices, as I understand them, are much more than sets of individual actions. They are fundamental ways of categorizing, experiencing, and valuing the world. In turn, the requirements of a practice generate distinctive forms of knowledge. Mothering, for example, is a practice that generates its own epistemology (Ruddick).[6] There are also epistemologies of cooking (Curtin and Heldke, section 3) and land cultivation. Epistemic attitudes derive from doings. If women have been assigned agricultural tasks throughout history and knowledge derives from the requirements of a particular kind of practice, should we not expect to find that women have been responsible for the advances required by that practice? If women have been located at the intersection of the environment and those practices that sustain the community, such as mothering, health care, and care for the land, would we not expect them to be sources of traditional knowledge on these matters? Simply put, attention to practices has a better chance of capturing "thoughtful actions" like traditional farming than philosophical distinctions between propositional and nonpropositional attitudes.

A sympathetic and accurate portrayal of women's actual involvement in agricultural production might begin with some revisionist history. In a review of anthropological and mythological sources, Autumn Stanley says, "From the earliest times until at least the horticultural period . . . women were largely responsible for the gathering, processing, storing, and eventually for the cultivation of plant foods." In contrast to the hunter-gatherer myth, according to which man-the-hunter provides most of the food, anthropological evidence indicates that until recent times 60–80 percent of food was provided by women. While both women and men must have been involved in food gathering, "females' gathering would be different from males'—more highly motivated, and more of a 'social role' from the start in that females were usually gathering for one or more offspring as well as for themselves. Females . . . would thus be more likely to innovate and improve" (Stanley, 290).

Women have been farmers for more than forty centuries. Given the assumption that "the workers invented their tools," Stanley says that it makes sense to assume that women were responsible for

> (1) food-gathering inventions such as the digging stick, the carrying sling or bag, the reaping knife or sickle, and other knives; (2) food processing inventions such as the mortar and pestle or pounder, winnowing methods, grain-roasting tray, querns . . . , washing to remove grit, detoxification . . . , and some forms of cooking . . . and (3) food-storage inventions such as baskets, clay-lined storage pits, drying and smoking of food, and preservation with honey. (Stanley, 293–94)

Stanley also argues that women were responsible for domestication of wheat, rice, maize, barley, oats, sorghum, millet, and rye. These cereals still provide 75 percent of all human food energy. The same pattern can be found in the development of traditional medicines. Still today, women are responsible for 80 percent of the world's medical care (Kheel).

We should not expect to find women's expert knowledge at work everywhere in the contemporary world. The ancient patterns of women's knowledge have been distorted and disrupted. Women struggle to invent and reinvent forms of knowledge that are appropriate to their complex situations as mothers, wives, traditional farmers, health care workers, and last line of environmental defense. If their indigenous knowledge of the sustainable ecological community has often been destroyed by maldevelopment, women are still invested by their daily practices in the reinvention of such knowledge. That women are dedicated to saving and restoring their knowledge is shown in the many organizations worldwide that are doing just that, organizations such as Chipko in India, Development Alternatives with Women for a New Era (DAWN) based in Brazil, the Third World Network in Malaysia, the Green Belt movement in Kenya, and Women of All Red Nations (WARN) in Chicago.

The work of these organizations demonstrates it would be a mistake to think that women's knowledge is backward-looking, that it is antitechnology or antiprogress. In fact, if Stanley is correct, women have been responsible for most technological innovation. Women can hardly afford to be against progress if it is genuinely life-nurturing progress.

This historical account of women's agricultural labor undercuts the typical reductionist accounts of the relation between nature and culture. Women are often pressed in two ways by this distinction. The first claims that nature ought to be preserved museumlike, free from human interaction. This mistake has caused some Third World countries to remove indigenous people from their traditional lands to create American-style national parks. The second version claims that nature is only here for human manipulation and consumption, one cause of the tragedies I have discussed. Both are forms of the myth that man lives apart from nature. Because of their traditional practices, women are typically well positioned to know that ecodevelopment inevitably changes nature and that changes that constitute real progress must be measured against the welfare of whole communities and future generations.

What, then, is distinctive about women's ecological knowledge? Based on the cases previously considered, I offer several generalizations. Since we are talking of constructions of gender, we need to keep in mind that these are, indeed, generalizations, not universal rules. No set of generalizations can capture the complexity of women's lives.

Because women have been charged with many kinds of caring labor, *women's knowledge is relational.* Women tend to locate knowledge in the concrete, relational space between individuals, not in the abstraction of isolated, autonomous individuals. The relations that define community are broader than the human community. They include the entire ecological community, *this* place.

Women's knowledge is inherently collaborative. It is the project of the whole ecological community that is engaged by caring practices. A familiar example of this is home cooking. We tend not to think of cooking as an epistemic practice that has its own rules and procedures. Yet sharing family and community culinary traditions is a perfect example of a collaborative epistemic community. A less familiar example is sharing seeds over generations of women farmers. Such patient development of ecological knowledge reflects the complexity of local ecosystems. Within a single valley, women often plant dozens of genetically different strains of a single crop to take advantage of subtle changes in growing conditions.

Women's knowledge is also transparently situated, not abstract and rule-bound. To form an opinion, women need to know the life histories of the people and contexts they are speaking about. Concretely, we have seen this often means that what the outsider dismisses as waste has value within a context, for example, grasses at the edges of a field or commons areas used by an entire village.

Women's knowledge is temporal. If it grows out of actual contexts and histories, it is also future-directed. As those who have been defined in terms of their responsibility for children and future generations, women cannot help but test their knowledge against a criterion of sustainability. Women's knowledge is knowledge that operates not only in the spaces between individuals but also in the times between generations.

Finally, *women's knowledge is bodily knowledge.* Because cultural dualisms have defined women in terms of the body and nature, women tend to cultivate knowledge that integrates head and hand. Their knowledge consists more in "thoughtful ways of doing" than in "ways of thinking about."

We can understand why it is easy to miss women's knowledge and thereby to abuse it. To those who look for knowledge as a decisive intervention from above, a self-confident declaration, women's relational knowledge can appear indecisive. It appears to the outsider as what Plato would have called "accidentally true belief" rather than knowledge. Women often have difficulty saying what they know about *all* situations. Growing out of practices that cannot escape their temporality, women's knowledge has the appearance to outsiders of being qualified or tentative. One task required by the revaluation of caring labor is to value this apparent tentativeness as a positive quality. Since women's knowledge is marked by its group collaboration, for example, we should expect that Third World women's knowledge is expressed through the group rather than through the individual.

Because knowledge varies in relation to different forms of practice, moving between forms of knowledge involves what María Lugones calls "world-travelling" (see Lugones). Her term is useful because it emphasizes that entire worlds must be traversed for communication to occur. If we assume, for example, that the epistemic world of the outsider, the (male) scientific expert, is the standard against which all others are measured, it is impossible to cross over into the world of hands-on expertise that is characteristic of women's ecological knowledge.

Since we are talking about different worlds of discourse, each having its own standards for knowledge and success, there is an important distinction between those who function as insiders to the practice and those who come to it as outsiders. The rules of the practice are, by definition, known to the insiders, those who engage in the practice. To outsiders, it may appear there is no knowledge at all. The outsider, particularly when motivated by conceptual biases, can easily dismiss the real inside knowledge that motivates and sustains the practice as mere superstition or old wives' tales. Gender-biased development programs, therefore, are not always reducible to simple malice. It may well be that from another "world" the insider's knowledge is not or cannot be revealed. The work of those concerned with the lives of Third World women is a matter of devising strategies for making these forms of practice and knowledge visible.

While the insider's knowledge may be initially invisible to the outsider, that does not mean it lacks power. If it is true that "real knowledge is history that comes from below" (Rose, 162), then we must learn to recognize the intersection of forces in tribal or dalit women that makes their forms of knowledge conceptually central to the task of reconstructing caring labor. In the "lowest of the low," in those who must care for others without being cared for themselves, there is a praxis that is the key to sustainable development. Those who are marginalized and charged with responsibility for caring labor cannot fail to know the lives of those who marginalize them. The converse is not true. The master need not know the servant. Simply stated, because of their caring practices, Third World women of low caste and class know things that others—including outside development experts—do not know.

Poor Third World women cannot even pretend to escape the temporal reality of life that is demanded by caring labor. They do not have secretaries to reschedule appointments; they do not have servants to whom work can be delegated when they are tired or busy. Meals must come with predictable regularity, therefore food and fuel must be gathered *now*. Need for medical care is unpredictable; the need is immediate and cannot wait.

Women cannot afford the illusion that it is possible to escape time and place. This is one reason for calling typically women's knowledge expert knowledge. Caring labor produces transparent knowledge; such knowledge is superior just because it is transparent, situated between nature and culture. Survival depends on it.

In contrast, there is delusion in constructions of life that claim to be free of time and place. While men are inevitably dependent on many forms of caring labor, they have the power to construct the self-serving myth of themselves as independent, autonomous, and atemporal. Patriarchal constructions work to bolster this delusive self-construction.

Liberated from patriarchal distortions, caring contexts are potentially those in which women and men can experience themselves as citizens in a broadly ecological community. This space, which is normally an ambiguous borderland, neither fully culture nor fully nature, can become a context in which the dualistic opposition between culture and nature is transformed. While caring contexts are defined oppressively, that is, they can be reconstructed as small-scale contexts in which citizenship for women and men is defined in relation to an environment that can produce safe food and water, sustainable fuels, and health care that works toward the well-being of this and future generations.

Though much can be said about the practical consequences of the approach I have developed here, I will mention only one. There is the tendency to assume that one aspect of development must come first. It has been argued, for example, that the development of the head of household should come first or that race or class must take precedence. A nonreductionist perspective indicates that race, caste, class, and other issues are intricately woven into a quilt whose patterns vary subtly. I believe women's issues in development should not be delayed for the sake of solidarity with another group. From the beginning, women need the resource of other women in groups whose purpose is to articulate their distinctive concerns. This is required not only because of the character of women's knowledge as collaborative, but simply for the safety of women who risk much by speaking out alone. If development is to be truly dialogical, then all aspects of development must move together. Dialogue can only take place among dialogical equals.

Several years ago I visited several tribal villages in a remote section of Orissa state in India.[7] The area had been logged off twenty years ago. People face all-too-typical problems of bonded labor, access to land, alcohol abuse among the men, and illiteracy, which makes it difficult to communicate with those outside experts who have an impact on their lives.

I was invited to meet with people of one village to hear their concerns. For the first hour I listened to a confident young man, dressed in Western clothing, talk about how much his leadership had accomplished for the village. Then a middle-aged woman, dressed traditionally, was asked to speak. Her name was Ujal Khillo; she came from a dalit family. She began tentatively, saying she had become tired of her life and decided to do something to help herself and her village. A carpentry training program was offered by the local development office, and she decided to enroll. This overt act of independence embarrassed her husband, and he appeared the next day threatening to beat her. She would not be deterred and told him that if he beat her again, she would report him to the police. The shock was enough to send him back down the road to his village.

Training complete, she went to the local bank to apply for a small loan the government made available to tradespeople for tools. The banker noted that she was a woman; women weren't carpenters, so she was not eligible for a loan. She refused to leave his office until he agreed to visit her village to observe her skills for himself. He came, saw, and agreed to authorize the loan.

Told to mark the loan forms with an X, she refused, saying she knew how to sign her name. That was impossible, he said; tribals are illiterate. After a further standoff, the banker relented and she finally signed her name. She then became the first certified woman carpenter in her area. Her husband, by the way, accepted his wife's accomplishments and appeared to be proud of her.

I tell the story of this courageous woman because, as a carpenter making wooden furniture and children's toys for her village in an area that has been decimated by deforestation, she works in that ambiguous borderland between injured nature and a dysfunctional society. In her caring labor and her refusal to be dismissed rest hope for a genuinely ecological community.

Notes

This chapter was presented originally at the International Development Ethics Association (IDEA) meeting in Tegucigalpa, Honduras, June 1992. I appreciate the support of many colleagues in this extraordinary organization, particularly Natalie Dandakar.

1. I owe this example to Kristin Cashman, Center for Indigenous Knowledge for Agriculture and Rural Development, Iowa State University.

2. Though I will not develop the point here, the approach I propose is sympathetic to Amartya Sen's proposal that development be understood not in terms of rights or basic needs but in terms of "capabilities to function." Sen regards development as a moral, not simply an economic, enterprise. See, for example, Sen, and Nussbaum and Sen. (Works cited are listed in the bibliography at the end of the notes.)

3. In Curtin 1995 I describe the universalism of developmentalist attitudes. Part of what allows for generalization is precisely the fact that such attitudes seek to make the entire world conform to a single model.

4. The demonstrated effectiveness of women's projects that involve caring labor cannot be doubted. In a ten-year study of trees planted and cared for by Chipko women, it was found that their survival rate had increased from 10 percent to the 80–90 percent range (Dankelman and Davidson, 50). Similar statistics on women's reforestation projects can be found for other locations in India and in the Green Belt movement in Kenya.

5. Ester Boserup, for example, has documented the impact of colonial attitudes on development practices in Africa. Her work serves as an example of how sexist (and racist) categories have affected the concept of development historically. Prior to the arrival of European culture, men's traditional activities in Africa were tree felling, hunting, and war. All were curbed by Europeans. Forcibly deprived of their traditional roles, African males were left with little to do; thus arose the Western stereotype of the "lazy African male." African women were responsible for most agricultural work and food gathering. Development might have begun, therefore, with women's traditional knowledge. However, because of the European bias that farming is men's work, most European efforts were addressed solely to men (Boserup, 19 and 55). Such biases certify masculine knowledge as official—they also certify indigenous men as ignorant—while challenging and marginalizing traditionally women's knowledge.

6. This chapter takes its inspiration from feminist standpoint theory (see Hartsock 1983a), which argues that there are typically women's ways of categorizing, experiencing, and valuing the world. Hilary Rose has said that "feminist epistemology derives from women's lived experience, centred on the domains of interconnectedness and affectual rationality. It emphasizes holism and harmonious relationships with nature, which is why feminism has links with that other major social movement of our time, ecology" (Rose, 162–63). A feminist standpoint

values and organizes the world precisely through a revaluation of those practices that sexist categories marginalize, practices that are pushed to the periphery of what has counted as important. Thus, like the meal that miraculously appears on the table every night and only becomes important when it is not there, these practices are often invisible to those who benefit from them.

7. The program was offered by WIDA (Integrated Rural Development of Weaker-Sections in India). My appreciation to Dr. K. Rajaratnam, director of the program, and to Sasi Prabha, director of women's programs, for assistance in helping me to understand WIDA's programs.

Bibliography

Ahmad, Zubeida, and Martha Loutfi. *Women Workers in Rural Development*. Geneva: International Labor Office, 1985.

Bhati, J. B., and D. V. Singh. "Women's Contribution to Agricultural Economy in Hill Regions of North-West India." *Economic and Political Weekly* 22, no. 17 (1987): WS 7-11.

Bhatt, Radha. "Lakshmi Ashram: A Gandhian Perspective in the Himalayan Foothills." In *Healing the Wounds: The Promise of Ecofeminism*, ed. Judith Plant. Philadelphia: New Society, 1989.

Boserup, Ester. *Women's Role in Economic Development*. London: Allen and Unwin, 1970.

Brydon, Lynne, and Sylvia Chant. *Women in the Third World: Gender Issues in Rural and Urban Areas*. New Brunswick, N.J.: Rutgers University Press, 1989.

Butalia, Urvashi. "Indian Women and the New Movement." *Women's Studies International Forum* 8, no. 2 (1985): 131-33.

Cashman, Kristin. "Systems of Knowledge as Systems of Domination: The Limitations of Established Meaning." *Agriculture and Human Values* (Winter–Spring 1991): 49-58.

Chabousson, F. "How Pesticides Increase Pests." *Ecologist* 16, no. 1 (1986): 29-36.

Charlton, Sue Ellen. *Women in Third World Development*. Boulder: Westview, 1984.

The Chipko Message. Silyara, Tehri-Garhwal: Chipko Information Center, 1987.

Clairmonte, F. F., and J. L. Cavanagh, eds. "Third World Debt: The Approaching Holocaust," *Economic and Political Weekly* 21.

"The Concept and Practice of Regenerative Agriculture." In *The Rural Poor*. Madras: Association for the Rural Poor, 1989.

Curtin, Deane. "Dogen, Deep Ecology and the Ecological Self." *Environmental Ethics* 16, no. 2 (1994): 195-213.

———. "Making Peace with the Earth: Indigenous Agriculture and the Green Revolution." *Environmental Ethics* 17, no. 1 (Spring 1995): 59-74.

———. "Toward an Ecological Ethic of Care." *Hypatia* 6, no. 1 (1991): 61-74.

———, and Lisa Heldke, eds. *Cooking, Eating, Thinking: Transformative Philosophies of Food*. Bloomington: Indiana University Press, 1992.

Dankelman, Irene, and Joan Davidson, eds. *Women and Environment in the Third World*. London: Earthscan, 1988.

Doyle, Joseph. *Altered Harvest*. New York: Viking, 1985.

D'Souza, Corinne Kumar. "A New Movement, a New Hope: East Wind, West Wind, and the Wind from the South." In *Healing the Wounds*, ed. Plant.

Ehrenreich, Barbara, and Deirdre English. *For Her Own Good: 150 Years of Experts' Advice to Women*. New York: Anchor/Doubleday, 1979.

Forbes, Geraldine H. "Caged Tigers: 'First Wave' Feminists in India." *Women's Studies International Forum* 5, no. 6 (1982): 525–36.

Geertz, Clifford. *Agricultural Innovation: The Process of Ecological Change in Indonesia*. Berkeley: University of California Press, 1963.

Harding, Sandra. *The Science Question in Feminism*. Ithaca, N.Y.: Cornell University Press, 1986.

Hartsock, Nancy. "The Feminist Standpoint: Developing the Ground for a Specifically Feminist Historical Materialism." In *Discovering Reality*, ed. Sandra Harding and Merrill Hintikka. London: D. Reidel, 1983a, 283–310.

Hartsock, Nancy. *Money, Sex, and Power*. New York: Longman, 1983b.

Howard, A. *An Agricultural Testament*. London: Oxford University Press, 1940.

Hyams, E. *Soil and Civilization*. London: Thames and Hudson, 1952.

ILO. *Rural Development and Women in Asia*. Geneva: International Labor Office, 1982.

Jacobson, Doranne. "Studying the Changing Roles of Women in Rural India." *Signs* 8, no. 1 (1982): 132–37.

Jain, Devaki. *Women's Quest for Power*. Sahibabad: Vikas, 1980.

Jayawardena, Kumari. *Feminism and Nationalism in the Third World*. London: Zed, 1986.

Jeffery, Patricia. *Frogs in a Well: Indian Women in Purdah*. London: Zed, 1979.

Kenney, M. *Bio-technology: The University-Industrial Complex*. New Haven: Yale University Press, 1986.

Kheel, Marti. "From Healing Herbs to Deadly Drugs: Western Medicine's War against the Natural World." In *Healing the Wounds*, ed. Plant.

Kishwar, Madhu, and Ruth Vanita, eds. *In Search of Answers: Indian Women's Voices from Manushi*. London: Zed, 1984.

Lappé, Frances Moore, and Joseph Collins. *Food First*. London: Abacus, 1980.

Lee, R. B., and I. de Vore, eds. *Man, the Hunter*. Chicago: Aldine, 1968.

Lugones, María. "Playfulness, 'World-Travelling,' and Loving Perception." *Hypatia* 2, no. 2 (1987): 3–18.

Mazumdar, Vina. "From Research to Policy: Rural Women in India." *Studies in Family Planning* 10, nos. 11–12 (1979): 353–58.

Michelwait, Donald, Mary Ann Riegelman, and Charles Sweet, eds. *Women in Rural Development*. Boulder: Westview, 1976.

Mies, Maria. "Class Struggles and Women's Struggles in Rural India." In *Women: The Last Colony*, ed. Maria Mies, Veronika Bennholdt-Thomsen, and Claudia von Werlhof. London: Zed, 1988.

Mies, Maria. "The Dynamics of the Sexual Division of Labor and Integration of Rural Women into the World Market." In *Women and Development*, ed. Lourdes Benería. New York: Praeger, 1982, 1–28.

Mies, Maria. *Patriarchy and Accumulation on a World Scale*. London: Zed Books, 1986.

Mitchell, Juliet, and Ann Oakley, eds. *What Is Feminism?* New York: Pantheon, 1986.

Mohanty, Chandra Talpade. "Cartographies of Struggle: Third World Women and the Politics of Feminism." In *Third World Women and the Politics of Feminism*, ed. Chandra Talpade Mohanty, Ann Russo, and Lourdes Torres. Bloomington: Indiana University Press, 1991.

Mohanty, Chandra Talpade. "Under Western Eyes: Feminist Scholarship and Colonial Discourses." In *Third World Women and the Politics of Feminism*, ed. Mohanty et al.

Morgan, D. *Merchants of Grain*. New York: Viking, 1979.

Murphy, Patrick D. "Sex-Typing the Planet: Gaia Imagery and the Problem of Subverting Patriarchy." *Environmental Ethics* 10, no. 2 (1988): 155–68.

Nelson, Nici. *Why Has Development Neglected Rural Women? A Review of the South Asian Literature*. Oxford: Pergamon, 1979.

Nussbaum, Martha, and Amartya Sen. "Internal Criticism and Indian Rationalist Traditions." In *Relativism: Interpretation and Confrontation*. Notre Dame: University of Notre Dame Press, 1989.

Omari, C. K. "Traditional African Land Ethics." In *Ethics of Environment and Development: Global Challenge, International Response*, ed. Ronald J. Engel and Joan Gibb Engel. Tucson: University of Arizona Press, 1990.

Omo-Fadaka, Jimoh. "Communalism: The Moral Factor in African Development." In *Ethics of Environment and Development*, ed. Engel and Engel.

Palmer, Ingrid. "New Official Ideas on Women and Development." *Bulletin* (Institute of Development Studies, University of Sussex) 10, no. 3 (1979): 42–52.

Philipose, Pamela. "Women Act: Women and Environmental Protection in India." In *Healing the Wounds*, ed. Plant.

Pietilä, Hilkka. "Women as an Alternative Culture Here and Now." *Development* 4 (1984).

Pietilä, Hilkka. "The Daughters of the Earth: Women's Culture as a Basis for Sustainable Development." In *Ethics of Environment and Development*, ed. Engel and Engel.

Posey, D. A. "Indigenous Ecological Knowledge and Development of the Amazon." In *The Dilemma of Amazonian Development*, ed. E. F. Moran. Boulder: Westview, 1983.

Rogers, Barbara. *The Domestication of Women: Discrimination in Developing Societies*. London: Tavistock, 1980.

Rose, Hilary. "Women's Work, Women's Knowledge." In *What Is Feminism?* ed. Mitchell and Oakley.

Ruddick, Sara. *Maternal Thinking: Toward a Politics of Peace*. New York: Ballantine, 1989.

Salleh, Ariel. "Living with Nature: Reciprocity or Control?" In *Ethics of Environment and Development*, ed. Engel and Engel.

Saradamoni, K. "Labour, Land and Rice Production: Women's Involvement in Three States." *Economic and Political Weekly* 22, no. 17 (1987): WS 2–6.

Satchel, J. E. *Earthworm Ecology*. London: Chapman and Hall, 1983.

Sen, Amartya. "Rights and Capabilities." In *Resources, Values and Development*. Cambridge: Harvard University Press, 1984.

Shiva, Vandana. *Staying Alive: Women, Ecology and Development*. London: Zed Books, 1988.

Shiva, Vandana. *The Violence of the Green Revolution: Third World Agriculture, Ecology and Politics*. London and Penang: Zed and Third World Network, 1991.

Stanley, Autumn. "Daughters of Isis, Daughters of Demeter: When Women Sowed and Reaped." In *Women, Technology and Innovation*, ed. Joan Rothschild. New York: Pergamon, 1982.

Trinh T. Minh-ha. *Woman, Native, Other*. Bloomington: Indiana University Press, 1989.

Venkatramani, S. H. "Female Infanticide: Born to Die." *India Today*, June 15, 1986.

Voelker, J. A. *Report of the Improvement of Indian Agriculture*. London: Eyre and Spottiswode, 1893.

Waerness, Kari. "On the Rationality of Caring." In *Patriarchy in a Welfare Society*, ed. H. Holter. Bergen: University of Bergen Press, 1984.

Warren, Karen J. "The Power and Promise of Ecological Feminism." *Environmental Ethics* 12 (Summer 1990): 125–46.

Warren, Karen J. "Towards a Feminist Peace Politics." *Journal for Peace and Justice Studies* 3, no. 1 (1991).

Warren, Karen J. "Toward an Ecofeminist Ethic." *Studies in the Humanities* 15 (1988): 140–56.

Winant, Terry. "The Feminist Standpoint: A Matter of Knowledge." *Hypatia* 2, no. 1 (1987).

Wolfe, E. *Beyond the Green Revolution*. World Watch Paper no. 73. Washington: World Watch, 1986.

Five

Epistemic Responsibility
and the Inuit of
Canada's Eastern Arctic
An Ecofeminist Appraisal

Douglas J. Buege

Anthropologist and social philosopher Hugh Brody begins his book *The People's Land* with an anecdote concerning a planeload of white men—*Qallunaat* in the Inuit language, Inuktitut—landing at an Arctic settlement in eastern Canada where he was working. Air traffic is a rare enough occurrence for word of these visitors to circulate rapidly throughout the Inuit community. Brody spent a half-hour with these nine males who were looking for information concerning Arctic fishing conditions. In this brief time, he writes,

> they quizzed me about how the Eskimos fished for Arctic char near the settlement. I reminisced about a few fishing trips but my knowledge of the subject was scanty. I repeatedly suggested that they talk to some of the local hunters who were at home because of the bad weather. A meeting with the best informants could easily be arranged, and I assured them that these [Inuit] hunters would be very interested to hear what they [the whites] had to say about char fisheries in other places. No, they said, their time was too short. But, I pointed out, their time here had been extended by the weather. . . . In the High Arctic, summer evenings last all night, no one feels bound to go to bed at any particular time and they could talk as long as they liked. No, they said, they had been invited to visit the home of one of the whites in the settlement; that night they would not have time for any prolonged discussion. (Brody 1975, 2–3)

Indeed, the white fishing enthusiasts spent the night at the other white man's house, apparently favoring cocktails and white companionship to the information they claimed to desire, information that would have been best supplied by the Inuit fisherpeople. The Inuit experts were slighted and knew that these visitors did not value their knowledge.

This story provides an example of how Inuit knowledge is ignored even when such knowledge is easily obtained and invaluable to the seekers of such knowledge, in this case, white men. Now I would like to consider another example that illustrates a much more insidious consequence of disregarding indigenous people's knowledge, a consequence that may not be as obvious as the consequences involved in the first example.

Going back to 1955, various groups have protested the hunting of seals by dwellers of various northern regions. In this same time, the Inuit were moved, by market forces, to expand their hunting of ringed seals. The price for ringed sealskins increased from less than a dollar (Canadian) per skin in 1960 to $15 per skin in 1975 to $25-30 in the early 1980s, making seal hunting a lucrative activity (Wenzel 1985). Harvesting ringed seals came to be a preferable alternative to wage labor as a source of income for the Inuit, who were becoming increasingly reliant upon nontraditional goods and services.[1]

The values of European-Americans who protested the killing of harp and hooded seals came to have an impact upon the Inuit, who were supposedly not a target of these protesters. In 1982, the European Economic Community approved a ban on many sealskin goods, effectively crippling the market for Inuit-harvested furs.[2] A representative of the International Fund for Animal Welfare defended the collapse of the sealskin market by arguing that his organization would not have a problem with Inuit hunting if the Inuit hunted in the same way they did "five hundred years ago."[3] In effect, the Inuit people are caught in the double bind that Marilyn Frye (1983) describes: they can live their traditional lifestyles and be subject to the colonial activities of people and governments, or they can accept Western ways while abandoning their traditional practices. Either way, this choice is imposed upon them by outsiders to their culture, people who see the need to impose their morality upon the Inuit. At the same time, these outsiders do not hold themselves to this morality; their "technologies of colonization" have improved greatly in the past five hundred years.

The European Economic Community, pressured by the animal rights movement, failed to consult the Inuit concerning the legislation that would prove detrimental to the Inuit economy. As in the fishing example, Inuit knowledge was ignored, but this time the Inuit were the people most adversely affected. While the EEC is relatively stable in the face of economic adversity, the Inuit economy is less stable because it is smaller and is greatly influenced by forces beyond Inuit control. It is only fair to include the Inuit in deliberation of actions that affect them.

Both these examples illustrate problems with intercultural communications of knowledge. An ecofeminist perspective on Inuit knowledge may prove to offer insight into some of the problems evident in these examples; this is what I attempt to do in this chapter. I conceive of Inuit knowledge as a political, cultural, and ecological knowledge, in accord with many feminist and ecofeminist projects (Code 1987 and 1991; Jaggar 1989; Warren 1990; Cheney 1989; Buege 1992).

Karen J. Warren's ecofeminist philosophy reconceptualizes theory as theory-in-progress; her metaphorical ecofeminist quilt is stitched from a collection of individual ecofeminist narratives that combine to create ecoeminist theory (Warren 1990). Each patch of the quilt is informed by three areas: feminism; science, development, and technology; and local and indigenous knowledge (Warren 1992). The present work offers direction in creating patches for this quilt representing narratives of Inuit cultural groups. Warren maintains that patches for the ecofeminist quilt must meet certain boundary conditions. In this chapter, I am further explicating Warren's first boundary condition: "nothing gets on the quilt which is naturist, sexist, racist, classist, and so forth" (Warren 1990, 141). Inuit ways of life need to be represented in ecofeminist theory, but European-American perceptions of the Inuit must be examined in order to prevent these perceptions from being racist, classist, or sexist. I maintain that the Inuit are subject to treatment that is not commonly understood as, yet is, racist, sexist, and classist.

"Primitive" Ideologies

In this section, I will discuss some central issues involved in including indigenous peoples' knowledge in ecofeminist theory. I think it is reasonable to say that before non-Inuit people can understand any Arctic cultural groups, we (non-Inuit) must examine how our perceptions of these people are already structured. We have preconceived notions of what life is like for dwellers of the Arctic. We also have misconceptions of what the Arctic is as a physical environment.[4] It would go against our core beliefs for those of us involved in ecofeminism to ignore misconceptions that may make our theory problematic.

In the 1920s, filmmaker Robert Joseph Flaherty made and released the documentary *Nanook of the North*. This silent film was a box-office smash in the United States, Canada, and Europe. Flaherty described his intentions in making the movie: "I wanted to show the Innuit. And I wanted to show them, not from the civilized point of view, but as they saw themselves, as 'we the people' " (quoted in Griffith 1953). Despite Flaherty's intentions, people were drawn to the exotic culture of the "Eskimos"[5] depicted in the film and romanticized a lifestyle that was so incredibly different from the day-to-day existence they experienced in Cleveland, Paris, or wherever. Visions of Nanook standing on the ice in caribou skins thrusting a spear mesmerized audiences and invited them to fantasize about life in the Arctic. This film did not present Nanook and his kin as political, intellectual beings; it portrayed them as savages with subsistence lifestyles, emphasizing the severity of such existence. Audiences, stunned by the harsh environmental conditions, could not avoid being awed by this severity. I contend that many of the perceptions of Nanook's culture this film fostered are still alive today, more than seventy years after Nanook himself starved to death.

Marianna Torgovnick discusses perceptions of peoples such as the Inuit in her book *Gone Primitive*. She explains how the idea of primitive cultures elicits many widely held preconceptions:

> Primitives are like children. . . . Primitives are our untamed selves, our id forces—libidinous, irrational, violent, dangerous. Primitives are mystics, in tune with nature, part of its harmonies. Primitives are free. Primitives exist at the "lowest cultural levels"; we occupy the "highest," in the metaphors of stratification and hierarchy commonly used [by some anthropologists]. (Torgovnick 1990, 8)

She argues that these conceptions of primitive people do not arise out of a knowledge of these people; instead, such ideologies are created by outsiders, European-Americans, in order to shape the Inuit and other groups into something we desire. Perhaps we are thrilled by the idea of savages living in a severe climate under the harshest of social and economic conditions. If that is what we desire, that may be how we view the Inuit.[6]

Our conceptions of indigenous people are not merely descriptive; they also carry normative force. When I visited Baffin Island, NWT, in 1988, I was taken aback by the acned teenage Inuit wearing acid-washed blue jeans and leather bomber jackets, playing video games. I didn't want the Inuit to be like people back home in Wisconsin. I wanted them to be rugged, dressed in the native garb I had come to expect. My vision of what it means to be Inuit involved my deciding what an Inuit *should* be. Such ideas, when expressed, tend to undermine the self-determination of the Inuit people. They also expose prejudices that I have, prejudices that should not be included in ecofeminist theory, even though ecofeminists do acknowledge the inevitability of these prejudices, given our social history.

One particularly potent ideology concerning indigenous peoples is the idea of the "ecologically noble savage."[7] We are led to believe that the Inuit are particularly ecologically responsible people, that they are in harmony with their natural environments. But such a viewpoint cannot stand up to the scrutiny it deserves. The Inuit took to guns and ammunition, steel pots and tools, Skidoos and television, very quickly. Many are willing to exploit the natural resources on their land holdings. The North Slope Inupiat of Alaska have taken strong prodevelopment stances, prompted by the possibility of gaining economically from the sale of oil from their land (Eathorne 1991). The conception of the ecologically noble savage is challenged by much evidence, yet seems to be maintained.

One problem with the ideology of the ecologically noble Inuit is that it leads us to expect a certain type of behavior from the Inuit, a behavior that they do not live up to and that often proves damaging to their cultural integrity. To expect the Inuit to return to their traditional hunting ways is to impose our values upon them, values that we obviously do not hold as strongly toward our own societies. Since ecofeminists cannot knowingly perpetuate sexism, racism, or classism, we cannot expect the Inuit to abandon their Skidoos and motorboats, along with all the other "luxuries" of a market economy, so that *they* live up to *our* expectations.

A more significant problem that stems from viewing the Inuit as primitive is that such a perspective comprehends the Inuit as children, as people who need to be taken care of in this modern world, a world to which they are quite foreign yet with which we European-Americans believe we are quite well acquainted.[8] The result of this view is that we find a need to minister to their religious, political, educational, and economic needs. Thus the Inuit tend to become reliant upon the systems we set up to benefit them, creating a self-perpetuating cycle of dependence which seems to confirm our original ideas of the primitive as child. In effect, the ideology of the primitive serves as a seemingly irrefutable rationalization for patriarchy.

Warren maintains that any theory that is considered ecofeminist must be antiracist, anticlassist, and antisexist (it rejects "all other 'isms' of social domination as well") (Warren 1990, 141). Ecofeminism must also be antiprimitivist. An awareness of primitivism is important for ecofeminist theory concerning the Inuit, as well as many other cultural groups that have traditionally been stereotyped as primitive.

Responsible Knowing

In an earlier paper, I developed a theory of knowledge based upon the feminist work of Lorraine Code designated "responsible knowing" (Buege 1992). I connected this theory with environmentalism to create the ecofeminist position I call environmentally responsible knowing. Responsible knowing focuses upon individual people as knowers who have a responsibility to obtain and use knowledge in activities in which they participate and are accountable for that knowledge. There are five points to responsible knowing: knowers, emotions, understanding, normative realism, and community. It is not my project to argue that the Inuit are environmentally responsible knowers; to do so would negate a project that I find most important, using ongoing dialogue to determine knowers' environmental responsibilities. I will have more to say about this later. I now turn to discuss these five points and show ways in which they relate to the Inuit living in their Arctic environment.

Knowers

Traditionally, theories of knowledge have failed to emphasize the importance of individual knowers; the view of responsible knowing places the knower central to the examination of knowledge claims. Knowers know in particular contexts. Thus time, place, culture, and environment all shape how knowers structure their perceptions of the world. Inuit knowers are heavily influenced by their Arctic environments and their social structures. Their knowledge is also affected by colonial actions of European-Americans. The EEC, in its sealskin moratorium, failed to take contextual issues of the Inuit into account.

In environmentally responsible knowing, individuals become more environmentally responsible by developing relationships with their environments. Relationships are not simple one-way relations but are interactive ways of knowing. Caroline Whitbeck argues that the self/other opposition which is commonly used to define relationships is inadequate (Whitbeck 1989). Instead, I endorse Whitbeck's mutual realization, a view that holds that reciprocity is a fundamental part of relationships. Responsible knowing is demonstrated by information, often in the form of narrative, that illustrates a mutually beneficial relationship between knowers and their environments.

Emotions

Responsible knowing takes emotions as central to cognitive practice. Emotions are an essential component of oppressed people's knowledge of the world; they "enrich [their] knowledge of the nature of that oppression," according to feminist philosopher Uma Narayan (1988). When Brody discusses the Qallunaat fishermen, he mentions how the Inuit fisherpeople felt slighted by the attitudes of these whites. This emotional response is significant because it shows that the Inuit involved were affected by the white men's impertinence, even though they might not be able to offer a verbal account of their experience. Their emotional response may be quite complex: they might blame themselves for being less than accommodating, feel their way of life is less important, feel powerless to react, feel anger toward the Qallunaat that they do not want to express. All these emotional reactions are important in understanding the larger picture of Inuit perceptions of their world.

Understanding

Understanding is a complex way of knowing. It involves creating a holistic picture of many individual facts and processes as they relate to one another. Understanding one's natural environment involves knowing how activities impact upon that environment and how one can live in that environment sustainably. A well-developed knower-environment relationship is characteristic of an understanding of one's environment. Narrative can illustrate one's understanding of one's environment.

Minnie Aodla Freeman combines her understandings of her environment and her experience of colonialism:

> Inuit never went out into the ocean without testing their kayak first, Inuit never put up their igloo without examining the location, Inuit did not go into action without weighing the total situation first. The plane arrives, the government or industry officials step out and out comes a new situation. Often, even today, no letters, no phone calls, no information. Are *Qallunaat* always so unthinking, unfeeling and so rash? (Aodla Freeman 1980)

This narrative does more than simply point out the rudeness Aodla Freeman experiences with Qallunaat; it also exhibits an understanding of how Inuit and Qallunaat are, and how they relate to one another. Her words carry much more information because she invests these words with her personal perspective as a woman and an Inuit who has lived among Qallunaat for over half of her life.

Normative Realism

The condition of normative realism simply means that we should work to understand the world as it is and not how we may want it to be. I have already brought up one example where it is important to strive for normative realism. Recall what I said about viewing the Inuit as primitive or as ecologically noble savages. Both are ways that we might want to see the Inuit, but these perspectives are not empirically justified.[9] At all times, we must take account of the perspective from which we view the world and work to understand how the world really operates.

The Inuit are in a situation where their survival depends upon a commitment to normative realism. They need to understand how to maintain their own traditions while coexisting with First World colonialism. To stop environmental projects they challenge, they must know how to argue their cases with the Canadian government and through the media. They must understand much about white culture just to preserve their own culture. Allootook Ippellie (1981) emphasizes the importance of normative realism when he writes, "It would be far better and more appropriate to grant power to those whose lives and the environment they live and depend on is being threatened."

Community

Environmentally responsible knowers do not operate in a vacuum; they share their knowledge with others. The community is an important structure for gathering and transmitting knowledge to future generations and outside peoples. The importance of individuals interacting in the community is such that interaction promotes honesty among individuals and development of language and ethical concepts.

Language is a key device for maintaining community. It is interesting how Inuktitut captures much information that assists in maintaining social ties. For example, place names often offer a depiction of the location. A place English speakers call Baker Lake the Inuit call Qamanituaq, which translates to "where the river widens into a lake" (Pelly 1991). Such descriptive naming promotes the sharing of travel itineraries, aiding Inuit in traveling vast stretches of land accurately. Indeed, the ability to travel in the Arctic depends upon learning how to navigate from experienced elders.

Colonialism threatens the traditional social structure of the Inuit, thus affecting their conveyance of traditional knowledge. Peter Inukpuk reports of this problem: "Many of our young people are losing the ability to live off the land, and in this future situation, we will all live on welfare, strangers in the land of our forefathers" (quoted in Smith 1984). Education, speaking English, and the increased availability of affordable Western goods all contribute to the acculturation of younger people. Paradoxically, the young Inuit are more likely to learn Western ways that help them understand how to maintain Inuit autonomy but, at the same time, these Inuit risk losing touch with their own culture.

Inuit Knowledge

My criticism of the ideology of the ecologically noble savage does not entail viewing Inuit as environmentally destructive, as typical Americans or Europeans are. Certainly the Inuit people have gathered an incredible amount of information about their environments. One consequence of developing an environmentally responsible knowledge of one's environment is that such knowledge gives one an expertise in dealing with issues concerning that environment. In the case of the eastern Canadian Arctic, the Inuit people have the most expertise in dealing with their surroundings because they have lived there for a very long time and their knowledge of the land is more extensive than that of any other group. If we agree with Cheney's (1989) claims concerning the ecofeminist ideal of "bioregional narrative," then we must recognize that the Inuit have a relationship to their environment that makes them authorities concerning that environment; they are experts concerning their Arctic bioregions. This expertise must be taken seriously when making decisions and policies that may be important to the Inuit.

But one goal of this chapter has been to show that the environmental situation of the Inuit is linked to political, social, and cultural views that are continually ignored by non-Inuit. This situation is also linked to science. Recall that patches of Warren's ecofeminist quilt are informed by indigenous peoples' sciences, as well as by Western science. Aodla Freeman recalls that scientists were quite important members of the Inuit community at one time:

> There were many Inuit natural scientists who acquired their knowledge from their own observations and by purely wanting to understand their total surroundings, whether animals, snow and ice, people or land. Today, to me it is questionable if those Inuit scientists are still around. Probably not many are, because for the last twenty years or so Inuit have not really passed on their knowledge to their children. (1980, 5)

She offers an ecofeminist criticism of colonialism by showing that Qallunaat are successfully eroding Inuit systems of knowledge by imposing their own scientific rationale upon the Inuit. The disappearance of these traditional natural scientists coincides with the invasion of Western science and economics. One possible result of this invasion is the loss of the Inuit lifestyles through erosion of the social and epistemological ties that bind kinship groups and communities.

Are the Inuit environmentally responsible knowers? This is a difficult question to answer simply. I believe that in the past, before contact with Qallunaat, they certainly were. Their lifestyle was sustainable, intimately linked with the natural environment, yet not overtly disruptive of that environment. This was a time when the Inuit's knowledge of their own natural science was pervasive.

Today, conditions are quite different for the Inuit. Thanks to colonialism, Inuit lives are in a state of flux. Environmental responsibility is connected to all aspects of Inuit lifestyles. If the Inuit become a dependent culture that occupies government-owned lands, then I doubt that they can be environmentally responsible people. In other words, the power of colonialism is pernicious enough to rob a people of their most important qualities, their responsibility and their relationships. Some Inuit may certainly be able to maintain environmentally responsible relationships to the land and its occupants; others will lose these connections as they become acculturated.

If the Inuit can obtain a high degree of autonomy over their lands and their culture, then I believe that the Inuit as a group will have the basis for maintaining the intimate relationships with their environment. The Nunavut agreement, which divides the Northwest Territories into two provinces, one being the 136,000-square-mile Nunavut, is one step toward the Inuit's attaining of this autonomy.[10] But Nunavut is not without problems; even though the Inuit will have jurisdiction of their land, they will hold mineral rights to only 20 percent or so of that land. The issue of mineral rights should be of concern to ecofeminists, because the profits from the sale of minerals, gas, and oil from these lands will probably not be distributed equitably. Extraction of these resources will not necessarily be environmentally sound. Ecofeminists should realize the necessity of addressing Inuit issues with some urgency.

I claimed that one goal of this chapter was to provide some direction in creating an Inuit patch for Warren's ecofeminist quilt. One reason I do not offer an actual patch is that Inuit women's voices have been strikingly underrepresented in the works I have read; thus the feminist input is insufficient to inform an Inuit patch. Aodla Freeman stands out as a rare spokesperson for Inuit women. This lack of representation of women is due only in part to what I perceive as the patriarchal nature of Inuit culture.[11] I do not think traditional cultural roles (men as hunters and women as garment makers, cooks, and processors of furs and skins) sufficiently explain present-day gender inequalities. Non-Inuit anthropologists, missionaries, teachers, politicians, and traders are all responsible for contributing to gender inequality and to the perceptions of such inequality by non-Inuit. Thus I call for Inuit women's voices to be heard and for all those people concerned to promote this project.

One reason I think that Inuit women's voices are underrepresented in the literature I have studied is that the Inuit have not been affected by the colonial powers of European-Americans as long as groups such as Native Americans have been. The Inuit, for economic and geographical reasons, do not have access to literature and the television media that other groups have. In some ways, the Inuit remain relatively isolated from European-American ways of life (or, more accurately, European-Americans remain ignorant of the existence of the Inuit). The Inuit are currently being exposed to more aspects of European-American culture than in the past; this exposure will increase dramatically once the extraction of vast oil, natural gas, and mineral reserves in the Arctic becomes economically feasible.

I referred earlier to ongoing dialogue as one project that I would like this work to inspire; I will conclude with comments concerning dialogue. Inuit are no longer isolated from European-Americans; thus European-Americans cannot remain isolated from the Inuit and their concerns.

Ecofeminist theory recognizes that Inuit knowledge is intricately entwined with environmental, scientific, economic, and cultural issues. I believe that dialogue between cultures is essential for construction of an adequate ecofeminist quilt. Especially important in this dialogue are the Inuit voices, female and male, that can contribute to an understanding of their daily lives and experiences. We must remember that the Inuit people are going through incredible changes. Aodla Freeman asks us to empathize with her people: "How many of us can go from extreme hot to cold conditions within a few minutes? There is bound to be some very painful change within our body. The changes the Inuit have gone through are similar to that example" (1980, 33).

Notes

I would like to give my fondest thanks to Dr. Helen Hoy, Dr. Karen J. Warren, Veronica Weadock, Yvonne Holl, Jason Demeny, David Rothenberg, David Buege, Beth Jelinek, the staff of the Historical Society Library at the University of Wisconsin, and the people of Broughton Island and Pangnirtung, NWT, for making this work possible.

1. It is important to note that hunting, a traditional activity, is far preferential to wage labor. In part this is because traditional activities are more fulfilling and essential to cultural survival than the wage positions that are commonly ser-vices rendered to non-Inuit people. Hunting is an activity of an *inummariit*—which translates into English as "real eskimo."

2. "Anti-Sealing Lobby Severely Hurting Inuit Hunters," *Native Perspective* 2, no. 7 (1977), 8.

3. Daniel Morast is credited with offering this argument. See Wenzel (1985, 84). Wenzel offers a plethora of such statements from various proponents of animal welfare and environmentalism.

4. See Brody (1975) for an in-depth discussion of the connection between images of the land and of the people. On page 81, he comments, "The great social and intellectual distance between Whites and Eskimos is emphasized in the minds of Whites by the harshness of the Arctic and the intimate closeness of Eskimo life with the land: the harsher the environment, the closer to nature must be the people who are able to inhabit it."

5. Inuit people prefer *Inuit* to *Eskimo*. Thus I employ quote marks to denote some-one else's use of the term *Eskimo*, which is often seen as pejorative.

6. Ideologies of primitivism involve what Marilyn Frye (1983) sees as a distinc-tion between arrogant and loving perception, a distinction that Karen J. Warren (1990) invokes in her ecofeminist work. Frye, speaking of arrogant perception, writes, "How one sees another and how one expects the other to behave are in

tight interdependence, and how one expects another to behave is a large factor in determining how the other does behave" (1983, 67).

7. See Redford (1991) for an extended discussion of the ideas discussed here.

8. The arrogance that we have of ourselves as experts on surviving in the modern world are exemplified by former U.S. President Bush's infatuation with the creation of a "new world order," quite obviously an order that denies the self-determination of almost all peoples on the planet, including many citizens of First World countries as well as all Third and Fourth World peoples.

9. For a discussion of the importance of empirical data to ecofeminism, see Warren (1992, 1993, and forthcoming).

10. For a good presentation of Nunavut, see Bell (1992).

11. Throughout my work with the Inuit I have puzzled over the question of whether traditional Inuit culture was as patriarchal as many theorists would argue. Indeed, the prevalence of female infanticide, if what I have read is accurate, is one way that traditional culture was patriarchal. On the other hand, it is not clear to me that issues of power were delineated primarily by gender. There certainly was a labor division according to gender, but this does not prove patriarchy. Certainly the contemporary situation of Inuit culture, what can be called without equivocation patriarchal, is greatly influenced by non-Inuit patriarchy. The predominance of European-American men as traders, travelers, politicians, etc., has heavily influenced Inuit patriarchy itself, as well as our perceptions of Inuit "patriarchy."

References

Aodla Freeman, M. 1980. "Living in Two Hells," *Inuit Today* 8 (October), 32–35.

Bell, J. 1992. "Nunavut: The Quiet Revolution," *Arctic Circle* (January–February), 12–21.

Brody, H. 1975. *The People's Land: Eskimos and Whites in the Eastern Arctic*, Middlesex, England: Penguin Books.

Buege, D. 1992. "Epistemic Responsibility to the Natural: Toward a Feminist Epistemology for Environmental Ethics," APA *Newsletter on Feminism and Philosophy* 91 (Spring), 73–78.

Cheney, J. 1989. "Postmodern Environmental Ethics: Ethics as Bioregional Narrative," *Environmental Ethics* 11, 117–34.

Code, L. 1987. *Epistemic Responsibility*, Hanover, N.H.: University Press of New England.

———. 1991. *What Can She Know? Feminist Theory and the Construction of Knowledge*, Ithaca: Cornell University Press.

Eathorne, R. 1991. "Fade to Black: The Untold Story in the ANWR Battle," *Buzzworm: The Environmental Journal* 3 (July–August), 34–35.

Frye, M. 1983. *The Politics of Reality*, Freedom, Calif.: Crossing Press.

Griffith, R. 1953. *The World of Robert Flaherty*, Westport, Conn.: Greenwood Press.

Ippellie, A. 1981. Editorial, *Inuit Today* 9 (July–August), 4–5.

Jaggar, A. 1989. "Love and Knowledge: Emotion in Feminist Epistemology," in A. Garry and M. Pearsall, eds., *Women, Knowledge, and Reality*, Boston: Unwin Hyman.

Narayan, U. 1988. "Working Together across Differences: Some Considerations of Emotions and Political Practice," *Hypatia* 3, no. 2, 31–47.

Pelly, D. 1991. "How Inuit Find Their Way in the Trackless Arctic," *Canadian Geographic* 3 (August–September), 58–64.

Redford, K. 1991. "The Ecologically Noble Savage," *Cultural Survival Quarterly* 15, 46–48.

Smith, E. 1984. "Inuit of the Canadian Eastern Arctic," *Cultural Survival Quarterly* 8, no. 3, 32–37.

Torgovnick, M. 1990. *Gone Primitive: Savage Intellects, Modern Lives*, Chicago: University of Chicago Press.

Warren, K. 1988. "Toward an Ecofeminist Ethic," *Studies in the Humanities* 15, 140–56.

———. 1990. "The Power and the Promise of Ecological Feminism," *Environmental Ethics* 12, no. 2, 125–46.

———. 1992. "Taking Empirical Data Seriously: An Ecofeminist Philosophical Perspective," *Human Values and the Environment*, Madison: Institute for Environmental Studies at the University of Wisconsin-Madison, 32–40.

———. 1993. "Women, Nature, and Technology: An Ecofeminist Philosophical Perspective," *Research in Philosophy and Technology*, special issue on technology and feminism, guest editor, Joan Rothschild.

———. Forthcoming. *Quilting Feminist Philosophies*, Boulder: Westview Press.

Wenzel, G. 1985. "Marooned in a Blizzard of Contradictions: Inuit and the Anti-Sealing Movement," *Etudes/Inuit/Studies* 9, 75–91.

Whitbeck, C. 1989. "A Different Reality: Feminist Ontology," in Ann Garry and Marilyn Pearsall, eds., *Women, Knowledge, and Reality*, Boston: Unwin Hyman, 51–76.

Six

Women and Power

Petra Kelly

> True emancipation begins neither at the polls nor in the
> courts. It begins in women's soul.
>
> —Emma Goldman[1]

As a teenager growing up into a young woman, I was enraged when I saw how women have been obliterated from the pages of history and the pages of the Bible. Women were subordinated and dependent on men for their realization and value, always needing men as their path to fulfillment. I began to read Rosa Luxemburg's writings, particularly her prison diaries, and to search through biographies of Alexandra Kollontai, George Sand, Emma Goldman, Helen Keller, and other women who have put their very special stamp on history but have been mostly ignored by male historians and male scholars. I set out to rediscover these brave women. I never had much respect for Marx, Engels, and all the other dogmatic macho men who theorized and philosophized about the working classes and capital while, at the same time, discriminating against their wives and children and leading the lives of "academic *pashas*," always being rejuvenated by their wives and mistresses. They couldn't even cook or clean or sew or take care of themselves. They always needed women for their most basic needs.

Men's domination of women is deep and systemic, and it is accepted around the world by most men and many women as "natural," as something that somehow cannot be changed. But norms of human behavior do change. Because the oppression of women is so deeply embedded in our societies and our psyches, it continues to be invisible, even to those who are working to overcome other forms of injustice. Feminism is considered by many people to be one aspect of social justice, but to me it is a principle in and of itself. To rid the world of nuclear weapons and poverty, we must end racism and sexism. As long as white males hold all of the social and economic power, women and people of color will continue to be discriminated against, and poverty and the military mentality will continue unabated.

We cannot just analyze structures of domination and oppression. We must also practice disobedience in our own lives, starting by disobeying all systems of male domination.

The system in which men have more value and more social and economic power than women is found throughout the world—East and West, North and South. Women suffer both from structural oppression and from individual men. Too many movements for social justice accept the assumptions of male dominance and ignore the oppression of women, but patriarchy pervades both our political and our personal lives. Feminism rejects all forms of male dominance and affirms the value of women's lives and experiences. It recognizes that no pattern of domination is necessary and seeks to liberate women and men from the structures of dominance that characterize patriarchy.

Many women are beginning to reject the existing systems and styles of male politics. Whether at Greenham Common, Comiso, Australia, Belau, protecting the Himalayan forests, or working for peace in Eastern Europe, women have been stirred to action. Motivated to act on our own, not only as mothers and nurturers but also as leaders in a changing world, we must stand up as women and become elected to political and economic offices throughout the world, so we can change the policies and structures from those of death to those of life. We do not need to abrogate our positive, feminist principles of loving, caring, showing emotions, and nurturing. Every individual has both feminine and masculine qualities. We should not relieve men of their responsibility to transform themselves, to develop caring human qualities and become responsible for child care, housework, and all other essential support work. We will never be able to reclaim the earth if men do not give up their privileges and share these basic tasks with women. Children are not just the responsibility of their mothers.

The scientific revolution of the seventeenth century contained in it the seeds of today's oppressive technologies. If we trace the myths and metaphors associated with the conquest of nature, we will realize how much we are under the sway of masculine institutions and ideologies. Masculine technology and patriarchal values have prevailed in Auschwitz, Dresden, Hiroshima, Nagasaki, Vietnam, Iran, Iraq, Afghanistan, and many other parts of the world. The ultimate result of unchecked, terminal patriarchy will be ecological catastrophe or nuclear holocaust.

Feminism is about alleviating women's powerlessness. Women must share half the earth and half the sky, on our own terms and with our own self-determined values. Feminism seeks to redefine our very modes of existence and to transform nonviolently the structures of male dominance. I am not saying that women are inherently better than men. Overturning patriarchy does not mean replacing men's dominance with women's dominance. That would merely maintain the patriarchal pattern of dominance.

We need to transform the pattern itself. The work of feminist women and profeminist men is to liberate everyone from a system that is oppressive to women and restrictive to men, and to restore balance and harmony between women and men and between masculine and feminine values in society and within each of us. Feminists working in the peace and ecology movements are sometimes viewed as kind, nurturing earth mothers, but that is too comfortable a stereotype. We are not meek and we are not weak. We are angry—on our own behalf, for our sisters and children who suffer, and for the entire planet—and we are determined to protect life on Earth.

Green women work together with men on issues like ecology and disarmament. But we must also assert women's oppression as a central concern, for our experience is that men do not take women's oppression as seriously as other causes. There is a clear and profound relationship between militarism, environmental degradation, and sexism. Any commitment to social justice and nonviolence that does not address the structures of male domination of women is incomplete. We will work with our Green brothers, but we will not be subservient to them. They must demonstrate their willingness to give up the privileges of membership in the male caste.

There is a saying: where power is, women are not. Women must be willing to be powerful. Because we bear scars from the ways men have used their power over us, women often want no part of power. To a certain extent, this is good sense. Patriarchal power has brought us acid rain, global warming, military states, and countless cases of private suffering. We have all seen men whose power has caused them to lose all sense of reality, decency, and imagination, and we are right to fear such power. But playing an active part in society, on an equal footing with men, does not mean adopting the old thought patterns and strategies of the patriarchal world. It means putting our own ideas of an emancipatory society into practice. Rather than emulating Margaret Thatcher and others who loyally adapt themselves to male values of hierarchy, we must find our own definitions of power that reflect women's values and women's experience. Jean Baker Miller points out how women, though closed out of male dominions of power, experience great power in the daily work of nurturing others.[2] This is not power *over* others, but power *with* others, the kind of shared power that has to replace patriarchal power.

Women in the Green movement are committed to fighting the big wars—the destruction of nature, imperial politics, militarism, and the like. But we are just as determined to end the little wars that take place against women every day, often invisibly. Women's suffering seems so normal and is so pervasive that it is scarcely noticed. These restrictions, degradations, and acts of violence are so embedded in our societies that they appear natural, but they are not natural. The system of which these are a part has been constructed over centuries by laws and through institutions that were de-

veloped by men and excluded women. We want to end these forms of oppression by doing away with the power and mentality that produced and
maintains them.

There are many structures of domination—nation over nation, class
over class, race over race, humans over nature. But domination of women
by men is a constant feature within every other aspect of oppression. Male
dominance is typical of other patterns of domination across all cultural
divides. It is the basis of the systems of politics that have brought the world
to its present, extreme state. It is the pattern that connects acts of individual rape with the ecological rape of our planet.

In *Sisterhood Is Global*, Robin Morgan describes the daily war against
women:

> While women represent half the global population and one-third of the labor
> force, they receive only one-tenth of the world income and own less than one
> percent of world property. They also are responsible for two-thirds of all work-
> ing hours. . . . Not only are females most of the poor, the starving, and the illit-
> erate, but women and children constitute more than 90 percent of all refugee
> populations. Women outlive men in most cultures and therefore *are* the elderly
> of the world, as well as being the primary caretakers of the elderly. . . . In indus-
> trialized countries, women still are paid only one-half to three-quarters of what
> men earn at the same jobs, still are ghettoized into lower-paying, "female-inten-
> sive" job categories, and still are the last hired and the first fired.[3]

Just as patriarchy is global, so too is sisterhood. The most pernicious of
all patriarchal tactics is to keep women divided. We feminists in Europe
and North America have been so occupied with our own struggles that we
have neglected our solidarity with women's struggles in other parts of the
world. Today, and perhaps throughout history, indigenous women's movements have mobilized to defend human life and nature. Women of the
Chipko movement are defending the forests in India. In Belau, women are
demanding nuclear-free constitutions. Women have been instrumental
in the democratic movements in the Philippines, South Africa, Central
America, and among indigenous peoples everywhere. In the Middle East,
Israeli and Palestinian feminists have maintained a dialogue toward peace
based on the recognition of their common experience as women. It is essential that we work with and learn from our sisters throughout the world.
Feminist women and profeminist men must recognize the particular urgency of women's struggles in the Third World. Over the last thirty-five
years, the gap between rich and poor nations has widened. As the poor
become poorer, women, being the poorest of the poor, suffer the most
acutely. When one considers women as a single worldwide caste, it is not
difficult to see that, despite some progress, our situation remains dire.

Third World women are oppressed both by national and international injustices and by family systems that give husbands, fathers, and brothers absolute priority. Even where economic development benefits poor families, it is often of no benefit to poor women, for inequality and exploitation exist within families as well as between them. The unfair sexual distribution of power, resources, and responsibilities is legitimized by ancient traditions, socialized into women's own attitudes, enshrined in law, and enforced when necessary by male violence.

Women constitute the largest group of landless laborers in the world. Though they do much of the work in most agricultural regions, because land ownership is generally the domain of men, women have even less security than male tenants or employees. In many places, a woman may be evicted by her husband upon divorce or by her husband's male relatives upon his death. Membership in cooperatives is often restricted to men. While cash crop programs boost men's incomes, women are called upon to help with the extra work, while their own food crops are shifted to more distant or less fertile plots. Agricultural extension services are staffed almost exclusively by men and addressed to helping men.

Industrial development and urbanization have worsened an already unjust division of labor between women and men. Factory production wipes out domestic handicrafts businesses on which women depend, but women are at a disadvantage competing with men for factory jobs because their educational qualifications are lower and they are more likely to be raising children. Two-thirds of the world's illiterate are women. In Nairobi, half the working women earn less than a poverty wage, compared to 20 percent of the men. Studies in both developed and developing countries reveal that men enjoy more free time than women. A survey in Zaire assessed that men did only 30 percent of the amount of work women do. In most of Africa and Asia, women work, on average, sixteen-hour days, jeopardizing their own health and that of their children.

Besides housework and child care, many heavy chores are universally relegated to women. For Masai women of Kenya's Rift Valley, fetching up to fifty pounds of water at a time can take up to five hours a day. Gathering a similar weight of wood for cooking may be a two-hour job, and much longer in areas of extensive deforestation. The notorious "double day," in which women work as a full unit of economic production and also do all the unpaid housework and child care, is spreading in agrarian societies as well as in industrial ones. It is one of the longest lasting of women's oppressions.

Throughout the Third World, women are dispossessed, overlooked, and overworked. The examples given here barely scratch the surface. We who live in industrialized countries must challenge the sexism of our own countries' programs of international development aid. Legal discriminations must be removed, and women must have equal access to the benefits of these programs. To those who say it is not up to us in the industrialized world to tell those in the Third World how to live, I agree. Let it be up to those societies to determine their own courses. But let *everyone* be included, not only the men.

Courageous women in the ecology, human rights, and feminist movements in the Third World have taught me about the link between the violation of nature and the violation and marginalization of women. Meeting aboriginal women in Australia, women in the alternative movements in India, and feminist ecologists around the globe, I have seen how ecofeminists in the Third World are deeply challenging many concepts the West has defended until now. Indian physicist Vandana Shiva describes how Western science ignores or excludes certain bodies of knowledge while elevating itself. This arrogance, she tells us, constitutes a great threat to our planet.

> While Third World women have privileged access to survival expertise, their knowledge is inclusive, not exclusive. The ecological categories with which they think and act can become the categories of liberation for all, for men as well as for women, for West as well as the non-West, and for the human as well as the non-human elements of the earth.[4]

Many Greens, including myself, have been inspired by the work of nonviolent men like Mahatma Gandhi, Martin Luther King, Jr., and Cesar Chavez. We know far less about contributions to nonviolence by women like Dorothy Day, Rosa Parks, and the women in the recent nonviolent revolutions in Eastern Europe. Invisibility of women is a familiar pattern of male dominance, even within otherwise progressive movements. Much of the effectiveness of nonviolent resistance in awakening people's consciences derives from the willingness of those practicing it to accept suffering. But because women's suffering is taken for granted, in the eyes of the media and the general public the work of nonviolent women is less noteworthy and carries less virtue than that of men. Media coverage of the women at Greenham Common, for example, who endured great hardship camping out during one of England's harshest winters to protest American militarism, concentrated not on what they were doing or why, but on their families who were "left behind to cope" without them.

Women's power arouses great hostility in the male-dominated media. As a woman active and visible in politics, I experience this often. In the early 1980s, when I was a speaker for the Green party in Parliament, a reporter asked in an interview what was wrong with me, an intelligent, clever, attractive, and unmarried young woman, that would cause me to be involved in politics, a realm he clearly considered the exclusive province of men. (Perhaps he thought I was looking for a husband.) I turned and walked out. The women present—the staff, the studio's cleaning women—supported me, but the reporter, to this day, has never understood why I left the interview. In 1985, *Penthouse* published a degrading pornographic cartoon of me; I brought suit against them.

Incidents like these should not surprise anyone. The media, for the most part, perpetuate double standards and sexist stereotypes: women are sex toys for men; women's lives count less than those of men; women who assert their independence and power are in some way defective. Freedom of the press is one of the most important freedoms, and it must never be curtailed. But protection from sexism must also be recognized as a full human right. I do not believe that freedom of the press includes the right to sell sexist images of women to the general public.

As women assert ourselves, we face the question of whether we should seek access to every male arena of power, even at the price of giving up feminist principles. My own feeling is that we cannot forsake women's liberation by accepting a patriarchal interpretation of equality. We must work from our own values and elevate their influence to those of men. It cannot be part of feminist logic to seek access to all professions, no matter how inhumane. In Germany this question has been focused on the issue of women's conscription into the military. Under the cloak of equality, men in the federal government have moved to pass legislation calling for conscription of women. It is ridiculous that the equality we want is possible in the military but not in other sectors of society. I do not want to see women stand equal with our brothers, fathers, and husbands in nuclear command centers, on battlefronts, or in meeting rooms where the deaths of thousands are planned. As one woman working for peace said, "To establish more equal relations between the sexes, rather than training women to kill, let men learn to nurture life." For centuries, we have been locked out of power in male-dominated societies. We should not now allow ourselves to be cynically manipulated by men who wish to exploit our legitimate needs and aspirations by granting us power on their terms to serve their ends. We must work for ends consistent with feminist values. There should not be women in the military. Take the men out.

Because the world's governments are unable to sustain and guarantee peace, the women at Greenham Common formed a living chain around a military weapons base. I call upon women everywhere, young and old, to form a chain around the world, to resist those who say war is inevitable, and to love only those men who are willing to speak out against the violence. We all need to join together—women uncorrupted by male power and men opposed to violence who wish to break out of the rigid patriarchal institutions.

Throughout history, male-led social movements have always been mere exchanges of power, while the basic structure of dominant hierarchies has remained. The liberation of women and men from the bonds of patriarchy is essential to the work of building a peaceful, just, and ecological society. I often hear people arguing about the world's many evils and which should be the first confronted. This fragmentary approach is itself part of the problem, reflecting the linear, hierarchical nature of patriarchal thinking that fails to grasp the complexity of living systems. What is needed is a perspective that integrates the many problems we face and approaches them holistically. Working toward such a future begins by living now in accord with what we seek to bring forth.

Notes

This chapter is reprinted from *Thinking Green!* by Petra K. Kelly, 1994, with permission from Parallax Press, Berkeley, California.

1. Emma Goldman, "The Tragedy of Woman's Emancipation," in *The Traffic in Women and Other Essays on Feminism* (Albion, Calif.: Times Change Press, 1970), 14.

2. Jean Baker Miller, *Toward a New Psychology of Women*, 2d ed. (Boston: Beacon Press, 1986).

3. Robin Morgan, "Planetary Feminism: The Politics of the 21st Century," in *Sisterhood Is Global* (Garden City: Doubleday, 1984), 1–2.

4. Vandana Shiva, *Staying Alive: Women, Ecology and Development* (London: Zed Books, 1989), 244.

Seven

Learning to Live
with Differences

*The Challenge of
Ecofeminist Community*

Judith Plant

A recent article by Jim Nollman, who writes about interspecies communication, retells a story from the Kalahari desert. According to the !Kung, who have survived in this harsh environment for a very long time, it was only around the middle of this century that lions ever attacked their tribespeople. The !Kung tell of a life before four-wheel-drive vehicles, rifles, and massive cattle ranching that revolved around the waterhole, the vital center that many ferocious creatures—including humans—shared. Despite ongoing instances of tribespeople's being carried off into the bush, mauled, trampled, or impaled by just about every species living in their ecosystem, nowhere in their entire oral history is there a single account of a !Kung ever being attacked by a lion. The lions drank at night and the people during the day. Though the glowing eyes of the lions could be seen just beyond the cooking fires, humans and lions lived side by side in mutual respect. With the coming of ranching, however, and the subsequent simplification of the ecosystem, the delicate balance of life became disrupted. The !Kung, hired by ranchers to kill lions which threaten the loitering cattle at the waterhole, have themselves now been attacked and killed by the lions.

This story from the Kalahari desert reflects the history of Western civilization's relationship with nature. Fear and alienation replace mutual trust and coexistence, over and over again. And in the end, we humans lose every relationship we have depended on for our very lives. There's an irony about this culture of estrangement. While it gives the impression of being totally in control in its relations with nature, it is, from an ecosystem point of

120

view, wielding disproportionate power, totally out of control. This chapter takes a look at Western civilization and how we might do something about healing these relationships.

There are many philosophers and thinkers more learned than I who could tell exactly why and how ecofeminism as a body of thought has emerged among the many strands of feminism which exist today. What I bring to this work is the committed belief that humanity must turn toward ecocommunity: the creation of vibrant and sustainable human communities, a way of being in this world that reflects a respect and love for all of life and has these sentiments as fundamental ethics. Practically speaking, this means learning to live with all the differences that are inherent and indeed necessary for humanity's survival and for healthy and stable ecosystems. For in the natural world, good health is sustained by a tolerance of diversity, and stability is a result of ongoing mutual aid between and among species. Thus the notion of interdependence.

This ideal of ecocommunity must be feminist because if it is anything less I believe we will simply repeat the same destructive patterns of the past in which someone is always better than or more deserving than someone else. Perhaps the most essential feature of ecofeminist thought is that all oppressions—whether men over women, First World over Third World, north over south, white over black, adults over children, human beings over other species, society over nature—have their roots in common. The basis of power-over, of domination of one over the other, comes from a philosophical belief that has rationalized exploitation on such a massive scale that we now not only have extinguished other species but have also placed our own species on a trajectory toward self-destruction. This philosophy that undermines the present dominating worldview puts "man" (i.e., not woman) at the top—or second to the top, second only to God the Father. It is a hierarchical structure that repeats itself over and over again, in political and economic organizations, in religious institutions, and in our most intimate relationships.

But more on this later. I offer this preamble to give two key reference points for the remainder of my remarks: on one hand, the notion of power-over, of separation and alienation—what we are all up against—and, on the other, the positive and hopeful possibility of community rooted in a love of life.

Early in the spring of 1991 the people of the coast of British Columbia had their first bittersweet taste of the hoopla to come in 1992, the year that would mark the five hundredth anniversary of the coming of Christopher Columbus to the "New World." The second-largest sailing vessel in the world, a Spanish ship, docked at the harbors in the Strait of Georgia—Vancouver, Victoria, and Nanaimo. The strait is dotted with islands, and not surprisingly, many have Spanish names: Gabriola, Valdez, Cortes. It made quite a stir, this impressive ship crewed by more than three hundred sailors. The mayors, the dignitaries, the yacht clubs, used this event to remind the people of the story of the settlement, i.e., the colonization, of this land and its peoples. Of course the native peoples were invited—the Squamish, the Ahousat, the Nuuh-Chah-Nuulth, the Nanaimo, the Haida. But not one of them came.

Five hundred years ago these tall ships were most often welcomed by the many different cultures up and down both coasts of what was at that time known to some inhabitants as Turtle Island. Today, one Indian leader in Canada has publicly said of the newly arrived Europeans, "We should have killed you all." For the five centuries have brought total annihilation of some tribes; sickness and demoralization have seriously weakened most others. The land has been scarred and abused—as have been the original peoples. For those of us who know this story, there is only deep sadness and shame—not celebration—in this anniversary of centuries of violence.

The Europeans left the Old World in a desperate attempt to find a New World, a new beginning, away from the tyranny and repression of the Old. Some of our ancestors came with high ideals, visions of better ways of doing things. After all, what they left behind was far from utopia. What they didn't realize was that they brought the Old World with them—in their attitudes and values.

There is much scholarly work being done in the United States and Canada that is revealing how the U.S. Constitution, through Benjamin Franklin and Tom Paine, was very much influenced by the Iroquois, or Haudenosaunee, form of democracy. According to Iroquois history, their peoples worked out a system of democracy only after a long period of violence and turmoil. Their system constantly brings decisions back to the people; the leaders are chosen and, if necessary, recalled by the clan mothers. Leaders have no force of arms to demand that the people obey them. Instead, leadership is by example, for life, and leaders belong to the people. How is it, then, that what we have today in the United States and in other nations of European origins is a social and political system that supports the continued oppression of native peoples; continues to rape and abuse women; allows the incredible wealth of a few while many, including children, go to bed cold and hungry; and, stunningly, has raped and abused the land, the "home of the free and the land of the brave"?

I'm no expert on the cultures of the original peoples, but over and over again, whether the voice is Iroquois or Haida, Tsimshian or Mohawk, the message the Indian people have been trying to get us nonnative people to hear for five hundred years is that human beings must honor and respect the land. This is what the Iroquois mean, for example, when they talk about the natural law. While we may listen to this message, it's difficult for our ears to hear because, while the words might even be the same, the attitudes are often completely opposite. Western civilization might believe that the earth is a divine creation, but it also believes that it is only matter, created solely for the material use of people.

This difference in attitude is reflected in the native and nonnative approach to hunting. Nonnative people believe they have the right to hunt, to take an animal from the forest. The Gitskan and Wetsuwet'en people in northern British Columbia, however, believe that if they properly prepare themselves through prayer and fasting, an animal will *give itself* to the hunters. Nonnative people believe in *taking*—that the gifts of the natural world are there principally for our benefit; native people believe that they are given to us only if due respect is shown.

Lacking any cultural and spiritual connection with the land, nonnative society assumes the so-called democratic right of the individual—"It's my right as a free citizen to take a deer from the forest." Rights, however, are doled out by centralized governments and not everybody has access to them. And who is taking responsibility for the deer? Another centralized authority, at best, that has no real relationship with the deer. This idea of "rights" actually serves to keep us separated from each other and the land. Handed down in a linear fashion for those who can afford them or whose gender or color is acceptable, rights carry with them few, if any, responsibilities or means of accountability.

The Americans have also appropriated symbols from the original peoples. Again, their meanings have been totally skewed. In Iroquois mythology, the Great Peacemaker insisted that, as a symbol of peace, the Iroquois dig a hole beneath a large white pine tree with four roots in the four directions. In the hole, the people were told to place all their weapons of war. The white pine became known as the Tree of Peace. An eagle was placed on top of the tree to be ever-vigilant. The way in which the eagle was appropriated is revealing. The Americans used the eagle more as a symbol of power-over; it appears more fierce than wise, to have more to do with dominating others than with keeping peace and harmony among themselves.

I would like to suggest that just as our "forefathers" were unable to hear about humankind's place in nature from the First Peoples they met five hundred years ago on the shores of Turtle Island, they also couldn't hear when the Iroquois talked about the power of women in their system. After all, our earliest forefathers, or their predecessors, had witnessed and perhaps even participated in the burning, hanging, and torturing of one to nine million people—80 percent of them women, once and for all putting women in their place. In fact, the practice of killing "witches" was part of the attitudes and values that were transplanted to the New World.

The newcomers' world view was built on the notion of a hierarchy—the

Great Chain of Being—that had men second only to God, with women, other peoples (i.e., dark-skinned ones), and other creatures closest to the earth and therefore to the devil. It's no wonder they couldn't hear the First Peoples. In the eyes of the Europeans, no matter how liberal, the original peoples of Turtle Island were not seen as their intellectual, moral, or spiritual equals. In the newcomers' worldview, these people were part of the wilderness, too close to the earth and therefore too close to the devil. In fact, the original peoples of this vast continent had to be eliminated, one way or another, so that the real mission of the Europeans—the domination of the land for profit—could proceed unfettered.

Had the Europeans possessed the wherewithal to truly hear the peoples of Turtle Island—notably the Haudenesaunee on the eastern seaboard—they might really have found a New World. But coexistence with other peoples, living side by side in peace and friendship, was not a priority; nor was such a view even possible. For the newcomers just didn't have a philosophy that would allow for such mutuality and respect for differences. Instead, this European philosophical perspective—driven by the notion that there's only one right way to do things and locked into its inherent self-interest—has given us today a system of government and a way of being in the world that is self-centered, twisted, distorted, and very seriously out of balance. From an ecofeminist point of view, the newcomers saw through typically but tragically blindered glasses.

The great-great-great grandchildren of the Haudenosaunee, the Mohawk people at Oka in Quebec, in the summer of 1990, said no to a golf course proposed for construction on their traditional, sacred land. They stood up for their cultural convictions and, as most know, the Canadian army was sent in to set the record straight. These same people who carry the story of the Peacemaker, whose democracy places women at the center of its society, were brought to their knees on nationwide television. A more loathsome example of the failure of Western civilization to appreciate and live with differences was, at the time, difficult to imagine.

A year later, in a manipulative ploy by the federal government, the Mohawks were "given an opportunity" to change the way their leaders are chosen, so that the government would, ostensibly, be able to deal with their land claims. (Do you smell a rat?) In the summer of 1991, the Mohawks were forced to *vote* on whether or not to keep their *consensus-based* decision-making process. The irony is typical of modern society. It is a case of being damned if you do and damned if you don't—once again refusing to acknowledge that any other system, though different, has any validity. The federal government's strategy, of course, is an attempt to weaken the people by dividing them. An older Mohawk woman, driving away from the voting station, expressed the essence of Canada's "democratic process" well. "They forced us to," she said. Forcing "democracy" on a consensual people reveals how little the "democratic process" can be trusted to deal fairly with ethnic and cultural differences.

Also in Quebec is another sovereignty issue of a different order. Gaining popular and political support is the issue of Quebec's economic and political separation from Canada. While this case might sound like a decentralist's dream come true, in reality it is made possible by the enormous economic potential of the second stage of the James Bay hydroelectric power project—perhaps one of the largest dam projects in the world. What is really at issue, in spite of the rhetoric of community and culture that touches the hearts and minds of once-oppressed French-speaking people, is the vast amount of electric power that Quebec will make available to transnational corporations—aluminum transnationals like Reynolds—investing in its province and electricity sales to the United States. By being independent, Quebec hopes it can avoid federal environmental assessments and ignore the massive damage to native people and ecosystems. And in the full-blown plan, more than hydroelectricity is involved. The James Bay scheme is part of an enormous and diabolical plan to divert freshwater from dozens of northern Canadian rivers, then pump that water through a network of dams, canals, and rivers to the Great Lakes, across the southern Canadian prairies and south across the border to the midwestern and southwestern states. And who loses? The Cree and the Inuit people and all their relations—the caribou and the elk and others—who have lived on and loved this land since time immemorial. And what gives other people the idea that they have the right to enact such enormous ecosystem disturbance? The patriarchy, with its hierarchical viewpoint that sees some persons as more deserving and better than others, must surely have deluded itself to now become godlike, endowing itself with such mighty powers.

There's Nothing New in the New World Order

So it continues today—this Old World notion that there is only one right way to do things and all others must succumb or be wiped out. Today this attitude has perhaps reached its pinnacle of absurdity with the "New World Order." Power-over is the order of the day. And if nation-states don't have the economic clout to wield such power (as do Japan and Germany), then military might and a vast arsenal of deadly weapons will suffice. So it was that George Bush planned to enable the United States to continue to play with the powerful, in spite of a failing economy, by ensuring that less powerful nations do things the "right" way—all in the service of the transnational corporations. The goal of this unholy alliance of corporate policemen and megacorporations is complete control of the global economic and political order.

Thus what has logically evolved since the Haudenosaunee and the new-comers talked democracy and the newcomers couldn't hear crucial parts of the message is a system based on tyranny, self-interest, profit, and rampant exploitation. Any regard for the well-being of humanity is, at best, secondary. For today's so-called democratic governments and institutions do not work for the well-being of people and place. Today's political leaders have become the handmaidens of not just corporations, or even multinational corporations, but of transnational corporations. Corporations that, by definition, are from no place or nation.

In Canada, the move toward free trade—the so-called level playing field demanded by the transnationals—is systematically proceeding. Vast forests are being handed over to Japanese firms to pulp or, in the case of the cottonwood forests of northern British Columbia, made into disposable chopsticks for the international market. In Alberta, an area of public land almost the size of Great Britain has been leased to twelve firms. Two Japanese-controlled companies secured leased rights to tracts covering 15 percent of the province. Much of this so-called economic development is hugely underwritten by eager governments doling out millions of dollars of taxpayers' money to ensure the success of the industry—the destruction of vast "places"—and thus making the area desirable for the transnationals.

As many learned people have said, if the planet is sick, so are the people. Western civilization's blindness to the sensitive web of relations and differences that constitutes the natural world (and humankind as a part of that), as seen so clearly by the First Peoples and increasingly reinforced by scientists, ecologists, radical theologists, and others, cannot continue. At the current rate of extinction of species, the next five hundred years of our inhabitation of the planet will wipe out *all* differences, different species of flora and fauna, and, if the New World Order takes hold, different cultures and societies of people. Is this what we want to leave for future generations?

Ecofeminism—A Response to
Fear and Alienation

Ursula LeGuin, in "Women/Wilderness" from *Healing the Wounds*, encapsulates the attitude brought from the Old World to Turtle Island, an attitude which continues to propel this society: "Civilized Man says: I am Self, I am Master, all the rest is other—outside, below, underneath, subservient. I own, I use, I explore, I exploit, I control. What I do is what matters. What I want is what matter is for. I am that I am, and the rest is women and the wilderness, to be used as I see fit." With God, and his righthand *Man*, at the "center of the universe"—conceived of as the hierarchical Chain of Being—there is no room for anyone or anything else in the driver's seat. Thus decisions made from this lofty position reflect only him—a lonely and isolated character, dissociated from all the rest of life by his own self-importance.

There are always consequences to decisions—sometimes quite different in the short term than in the long term. So, in the immediate, man might gain power and prestige from exploitation of women or nature; in the long term what may well be revealed is that he has bitten the hand that feeds him. And this is just what is being seen today as a growing number of people are waking up to the fact that everything is connected and that there are profound consequences to human behavior, particularly oppressive and exploitative activities which threaten nature's natural economy, that delicate balance of relationships that makes life possible.

Today the voices of many native and nonnative people are responding to the New World Order and the oppression and violence that underlie it. Among the many strands of thought and action helping to uncover the lies and half-baked truths of Western civilization is ecofeminism. Susan Griffin, a leading ecofeminist writer, peace activist, and poet, insists with the might of a passionate pen that we stop deluding ourselves, that we stop defending this civilization that has shaped our minds and which is now destroying the earth:

> We say there is no way to see his dying as separate from her living, or what he had done to her, or what part of her he had used. We say if you change the course of this river you change the shape of the whole place. And we say that what she did then could not be separated from what she held sacred in herself, what she had felt when he did that to her, what we hold sacred to ourselves, what we feel we could not go on without, and we say if this river leaves this place, nothing will grow and the mountain will crumble away, and we say what he did to her could not be separated from the way that he looked at her, and what he felt was right to do to her, and what they do to us, we say, shapes how they see us. That once the trees are cut down, the water will wash the mountain away and the river be heavy with mud, and there will be a flood. And we say that what he did to her he did to all of us. And that one act cannot be separated from another. And had he seen more clearly, we say, he might have predicted his own death. How if the trees grew on the hillside there would be no flood. And you cannot divert this river. We say look how the water flows from this place and returns as rainfall, everything returns, we say, and one thing follows another, there are limits, we say, on what can be done and everything moves. We are all part of this motion, we say, and the way of the river is sacred, and this grove of trees is sacred, and we ourselves, we tell you, are sacred.

If only Griffin's words could be more widely heard and understood, the elk, the caribou, the Inuit and the Cree, and all the rest of the sacred life of James Bay could be spared.

Such a call as Griffin's goes beyond the feminist notion that demands equal rights with men. As Ynestra King, ecofeminist and peace activist, has so aptly said, "we are not interested in an equal slice of a rotten pie." In fact, it is more an ecofeminist strategy to resist participation in this man's world. And there are many gentle, peaceful, and loving men among us. Ecofeminists do not stand alone in some isolated ecofeminist camp. Rather, we find ourselves in the company of peoples who are organically rooted to place. For what Griffin calls sacred is also sacred to the First Peoples—the Haudenosaunee and others. It is what is life-giving, its value inherent in the natural laws. As Linda Hogan of the Chickasaw people writes,

Daughters, the women are speaking.
They arrive
over the wise distances
on perfect feet.

The women are speaking. Again, Ursula LeGuin:

Those who were identified as having nothing to say, as sweet silence or monkey chatterers, those who were identified with Nature, which listens, as against Man, who speaks—those people are speaking. They speak for themselves and for the other people, the others who have been silent, or silenced, or unheard, the animals, the trees, the rivers, the rocks. And what they say is: We are sacred.

Speaking for what has been abused in today's corporate empire has required claiming our history—whether the story of the oppression of women, or the definition of what it has meant to be a "man," or the violent domination of other, nonwhite people, or the callous disregard for the well-being of other species. It's a murky and painful past, as native persons will tell you as they recount, for instance, the mental, physical, and sexual abuse sometimes suffered at the hands of priests in residential schools. Women are continually revealing their abuse, most recently at the hands of society's other priests—the medical and psychiatric doctors, 10 percent of whom, in the United States, are estimated to have sexually abused their female patients. And, increasingly, men are speaking up about how images and the experience of, for example, militarism, have distorted their own sense of self. And who can speak for the many species that have become extinct, which no human power, no matter how great, can bring back?

Some say that it was the gradual process of the Industrial Revolution that cemented Western culture's determination to dominate nature, that to alter the landscape to such a vast extent required a view of the world that justified subduing and conquering nature and all that was associated with it. There is also the theory that underlying this male-dominated society is a terrible fear of death: that this inevitable fact of life can somehow be denied. Respecting that which is life-giving—for example, the ability of women's bodies to bring forth life—must also mean recognizing and accepting the other side of life-giving, i.e., death. But if nature can be conquered there is a higher order than life-giving—the victory over death.

Western civilization sees life in either/or, self/other, mind/body dualities. From that lonely and isolated position, all other aspects of life are separated one from the other. In the same way, people have been separated from each other by viewing differences in either/or terms, where one is better than, or more deserving than, the other. This view doesn't recognize or value the fact that life is a mutual affair, that there are consequences that move in circles, not in hierarchical straight lines.

There can be no doubt that today the "New World" is rationalized by this hierarchical, either/or world view. Surely this point need not be labored? One need only watch the "news," or as Sonia Johnson calls it, "the olds," to see the same old story—men and, increasingly, women behaving like these men, in the dry-cleaned uniform of the establishment, authoritatively telling us what they want us to hear. And Western civilization isn't working for most people—women *and* men, though each plays a different part—and it certainly isn't benefiting nonhumans! How can such a widespread social system continue to be so blind to the fact that its own life depends on the integrity and well-being of the whole? And what can be done about this situation? These are some of the questions to which ecofeminism is responding.

Connecting feminism with ecology is an eye opener for many who might otherwise not have been able to hear either issue. Taking the feminist critique of human relationships and putting it side by side with an analysis of human and nonhuman relationships, showing that both women and the earth have been regarded as the object of a self-interested few, is making a lot of sense to a lot of people. Men—our brothers, fathers, lovers, and friends—need not be the enemy. Though they have been groomed since early childhood to become the enactors of this power-over society, they began life in the arms of women and, as little boys, they undoubtedly loved the freedom of the outdoors, were thrilled at the sight of a nest of baby birds, for instance, or ecstatic with fresh-fallen snow. It breaks many a young boy's heart to find out that the slingshot he so innocently plays with actually kills the little bird. Male human beings have the capacity to have compassion for life, but they will have to struggle long and hard to overcome their own upbringing. More and more men are embracing ecofeminism because they see the depth of the analysis and realize that in shedding the privileges of a male-dominated culture they do more than create equal rights for all, that this great effort may actually save the earth and the life it supports.

It is true that women have been socialized in a way that allows them to experience compassion. This experience is, however, often skewed by the subordinate, deferential position given to women that somehow loads the responsibility of caring for others with guilt and anxiety. For this compassion that women have been allowed does not carry with it any power to make decisions. Because of this distorted situation, caring often becomes entangled with personal frustrations over feelings of powerlessness and lack of self-esteem, leading to an inability to take responsibility.

Western civilization has separated us, women from men, humanity from the rest of life. It is no wonder that our psyches are filled with fear, because in some way, whether female or male, we are out of touch with our origins.

In a powerful essay, "Invoking the Grove," in *Healing the Wounds*, Deena Metzger suggests that it is no accident that we are looking for an earth-based sensibility precisely at the same time as men are assuming more nurturing roles in society and questioning their once lofty positions. As men's experiences radically alter, so do women's, as we begin to assume responsibility for nurturing and structuring the world. Deena believes that as we change the essential patterns of our life, which were once based on exclusivity, distinction, and separation, it will enable a higher consciousness and the possibility of an ecological perspective in practice. The tree, Deena feels, is an essential symbol.

> The tree sends its roots down into the center of the earth and sends its branches up into the sky. Going down into the center of the earth means descending into the infinity of the unconscious which is as deep, far, and profound as the heavens, the ends of the galaxies. . . . The tree teaches us that the spiritual world and the material world are the same. The tree is always potentially burning. The yule log, the burning bush, the candelabra are symbolic of the transformation of the living tree into the fire of spirit. So the tree speaks to us about reconciliation, about bringing the opposites together. The tree and the grove are not only important in themselves but in what they point toward, what they stretch up toward, what they descend to, what they symbolize. When we cut down the literal tree, when we cut down the essential oxygen in order to feed cattle for McDonald's hamburgers, we cut down everything, all of culture and all of spirit.

Where I live, the magnificent old growth of the temperate rainforest is being clear-cut to the point where there is very little left, in spite of the relentless persistence of activists in just about every small community in the province. One need not go to the rainforests of Brazil to see this abuse of nature in the name of profit. In both the north and the south, the destruction of these rainforests means that many species of flora and fauna will also be destroyed and this will ultimately affect the well-being of Earth's natural economy—the delicate balance achieved by evolution over millennia that now supports a huge number of diverse species.

The attitude that prevails, that of the Old World and now the New World Order, is not just simply unfair to other cultures, women, and other species. By setting one class, gender, and species above the others, we are alienating ourselves from our ecological reality. We do not come from the heavens; nor will we return to the heavens. Our origins are in the earth beneath our feet, in the living and dying that is our organic reality. This arrogant smokescreen of patriarchy—where some are deemed better than, or more deserving than, others—allows us to deny this most basic fact of life. Indeed, this separating attitude enables us to rape, to kill, to exploit.

Western civilization, then, has no idea how to value and live with differences. Nature, this culture has it, is "out there," waiting for the hand of humanity: in the case of forests, so-called virgin stands of timber waiting to be "harvested." In the myopic Western view, the once-diverse forest ecosystems are replaced by single-species replanting, which won't recreate forests at all. Instead "tree farms" replace forests, to grow "stems" for the insatiable appetite of single-industry economies. But this view, intent on destroying diversity with its determination to control life, also has meant loneliness and deep despair for humankind.

Clear-Cutting Rainforests
Isn't All That's Going On

What we never hear about on the all-important "news" is how much gentleness there is in the world today. There is never a lead story that begins, "Today, love was alive and well in the little town of Tranquillity, where the folks celebrated once again the coming of the longest day. People came from far and wide, bringing with them such fabulously wonderful differences that everyone grew in stature and understanding." Or "Today, in the southwest of the great subcontinent of India, local people successfully resisted the richest corporation in all the land. In a protest called 'pluck and plant,' industrial eucalyptus trees were plucked from the ground and replaced with trees that could be of use to their community." And this last story is a true one.

No, the "news" is the "olds," as Sonia aptly describes it: the same old story. Yet there are many, many wonderful true stories of people changing things for the better. Perhaps "the world" will never hear about these stories in the "mass" media, for these stories of hope are particular, for the most part, to a place and the people who live there. And today they have mostly to do with finding a way of transcending the old system of exploitation and moving toward the creation of truly sustainable communities.

There is a movement in North America, on Turtle Island, that is gaining momentum because it speaks to something that many are already practicing. And drawing on nature's designs, this movement has a lot to do with learning to live with differences. As Earth First! activist Dave Foreman describes it, "If diversity is good for an ecosystem, it's good for a social movement." So it is with bioregionalism. Though an awkward and unappealing term at first sight, bioregionalism is a theory and practice that promises to radically change the world so that all of life may survive. Indeed, it is a way of life that is both new in its consciousness and old in that humanity has lived in harmony with nature before. Bioregionalism calls for human society to be more closely related to nature (hence "bio") and to be more conscious of its locale, or regions, or life-place (thus "bioregion"). It responds to a recognition that we are floundering without an adequate overall philosophy of life to guide our action toward a sane alternative. It is a proposal to ground human cultures within natural systems, to get to know one's place intimately in order to fit human communities to the earth, not distort the earth to our demands.

Stephanie Mills, a longtime environmental activist, in *Whatever Happened To Ecology?* puts it this way:

> Being bioregionalists means that we believe that civilization itself is destroying the biosphere and that neither resignation nor reform is the correct response. We believe that the lethal ecological disturbances of our time, perpetrated by humans, have social causes and demand the creation, or re-creation, of social forms shaped by ecology. In short, we try to pose a sustainable alternative. We try to work in local and particular ways to create a culture reverent enough to seek harmony with nature, and we ourselves try to live on that basis.

So, what does bioregionalism mean for women? As feminists we have learned, through painful experience, to ask this question of any movement that promises a better world. It is so often the case that political theories promoting a better world do nothing to improve the day-to-day reality of most women. In fact, many new ideologies when put into practice merely shift the power to some other group (of men) while oppression remains unaltered and society continues to have the same assumptions about woman's place.

One of the strategies of bioregional organizing is to turn our attention toward home and community, instead of primarily focusing on the world away from home. This echoes the sentiment once passed on to me at a conference on regional development by a native Indian leader, in response to my question about what nonnative people could do in the midst of the havoc we had created. She said, "Find a place and stay there. We can't work things out with you when you don't stay put." In other words, stay home.

As women, of course, we must be very careful with a movement that idealizes home. For home has been anything but a place of liberation for us. To be different, home needs to be newly understood, revalued, and redefined. We have to put our own house in order. Without healthy relations with each other, we will not have the understanding or capability to have healthy relations with the natural world.

In redefining and reconsidering this idea of "home" we see that the closer we get to where we live, regionally and in our communities, the more real power women—indeed, all of us—have on a day-to-day basis. Since we are seeking an ecologically sustainable way of life, let's look at the word *ecology*. It comes from the Greek *oikos*, meaning "home," clearly an indication that home means much more than the nuclear family. As it is in the natural world, where all life is interrelated, teeming with diversity and complexities, so it is with everyday human life. Here is the scene of what social thinker Murray Bookchin calls social ecology. Because at home people really have a measure of control over the creation of new values and the consequences of political decisions are actually felt, our homes, in this broader sense, have the potential to be the centers of real change. This stands in marked contrast to so-called political changes of centralized governments where one is left wondering if anything has really changed at all and what the "trickle-down" effect of such promises will make in the daily lives of ordinary people.

The bioregional method involves our dealing with issues related to this newly defined image of home. When bioregionalists from my part of the world talk about the Ministry of Forests' cut-and-run mentality, they are speaking from their hearts from their own experience. For clear-cutting the watershed, the vital artery that supports the "ecocommunity" in which one lives, stirs the emotions and the intellect together in a powerful expression. To be an environmentalist thus takes on a deep personal meaning and commitment.

It is because of this personal connection with political decisions and actions that the bioregional process helps people to see that what is valued personally is the same as what is valued politically. This seems common sense enough but, as many have experienced in political activism (in the alternative politics of the Left in the 1960s, for instance), there has been a blind spot in seeing this relationship. So exploitative behavior in the market was viewed as unrelated to exploitative behavior interpersonally. The connection between personal values and political ones was missed. It was because of this blind spot, or inability to make this connection once again, that many women broke away from Left politics.

Even in the movements for progressive social and political change, remnants of the thinking of the Old World have remained. Feminist analysis, however, enables us to reflect critically on where we have been in a holistic way. We have no time left to remain blind to the truth that the personal and the political are intimately connected. That is why it is essential that the bioregional movement, the move toward ecocommunity, must be feminist. For without feminism, we will not have the consciousness to truly bring us to the better world humanity must have if our species is to survive.

The ecofeminist contribution to the bioregional movement, however, goes beyond critical analysis. For ecofeminism also offers a vision and a process, a means and ends all in one. How we go about our decision making is as important as the decision itself.

Feminist bioregional organizing is inclusive; it embraces differences. The basic premises are that culturally defined sex roles which value one over the other are destructive to people and that this attitude has the same roots as our separation from the natural world, which sees nature as resources there for human exploitation. Bioregionalism is attempting to rebuild human and natural community, and we know that it is nonadaptive to repeat the separated and alienated social organization of the past and present. There is room for men in this process, men who are willing to cultivate gentleness, caring, and cooperation, and this movement must have the leadership of women.

How can humans meet their requirements and live healthy lives? What would an ecologically sustainable human community be like? It is in dealing with these questions through the real stories of place that ecofeminists can find a way to practice what we're thinking. It is a hard pill to swallow for some, but it is nevertheless the case that though brush fires may sometimes be put out, simply doing battle with the corporate establishment will not create the kind of world that will bring back the sacred grove, will not put humankind in harmony with itself and the natural world. In fact, not only do we need to take on the transnationals in the protection of our watersheds; we must also create and maintain the process of developing a home, in the broader, community sense of the word.

Examples of Living with Differences

There is no blueprint for what a bioregional community is supposed to look like, for each community will be different according to its particular ecosystem and depending on the capabilities and numbers of people and the degree of organization. But there are many examples of communities working together for a better world, each as different as the people and place from which they emerge. Like so many stories of women who have made contributions to social change movements, the progress toward truly sustainable human community is a song that largely remains unsung. For these are not heroic stories of war; nor do they glorify the world's political stage. These unique stories of place, though, inspire like no others. And no one community has all the answers. To begin with, here is a story from my own experience.

Several years ago, to kill the invasive plant knapweed, the Ministry of Highways decided to spray roadsides with the herbicide Tordon all through the watershed where I and many others lived. The area is a favorite picking place for saskatoons and other wild foods currently harvested by the native people and others, including, of course, the nonhuman life. Spraying the area would have put an end to this food gathering and would have threatened the browsing animals' health—a classic example of how ecosystems are simplified. The ministry announced its intention with only a few days' advance notice. The local people quickly organized and said no to this plan, offering instead to handpick the area of its "weeds." I'm sure the government never imagined that we would ever be successful, but it placated us and agreed to give us the same amount of money for handpicking as it would have spent spraying the area. In truth, we had no idea what we were up against. We only knew what we didn't want—Tordon in our watershed. It turns out that knapweed grows on a two-year cycle, that the plant has an incredibly long tap root, making it very difficult to pull out once the soil dries up in the summer, and that every year trucks and cars bring more seeds into the area. What our commitment to no Tordon meant to this little community was that every Saturday during the spring and early summer— for years—clusters of people, young and old, with homemade digging sticks, could be seen by the roadside baling up loads of knapweed into burn barrels. Showing up, year after year, was a test of strength. Our resolve to each other and the place grew as a result.

From quite a different community on the eastern coast of Turtle Island comes an exciting and innovative economic strategy that dares to print its own money. The story has several parts but begins with a restaurant in Great Barrington, Massachusetts. Susan Witt, who works with the E. F. Schumacher Society and is administrator of SHARE—the Self Help Association for a Regional Economy—was one of the facilitators of this daring scheme and she tells the story.

When our local Deli—a restaurant well-loved by many people in town, with community bulletin boards there, young college students, construction workers, the vacation home people, all meeting there and having their meals—when news came that the Deli had to move its location because its lease was running out, and the bank had turned down their application for a loan, there was community support to help do something about it. Frank, the owner of the Deli, came to SHARE and we suggested that he issue his own currency—Deli Dollars—and sell them to his customers in order to raise the capital he needed to renovate the new spot. He had tried to raise the money at the local bank and, although the bankers ate at the Deli on a regular basis, nonetheless his figures didn't work out on paper, in part because he kept his prices low and just worked long hours, so they didn't compute. But in the community mind they did compute because everyone knew that Frank wouldn't go bad on the loan, he'd just work harder. . . .

What he did was to presell meals to his customers. He sold a ten-dollar Deli Dollar for nine dollars in October to be redeemable at the new business, once it was renovated, for ten dollars worth of sandwiches. . . . There was just terrific, enthusiastic response. The contractors found it was a great Christmas present for their crew members—they gave away a whole slew of them. One even showed up in the collection plate for the local Congregational Church because the Minister was known to have regular breakfasts at the Deli. . . . In one month Frank raised $5,000. . . . The customers liked being part of helping Frank move. They felt, in a way, that they were beating the system because they were helping to find a way of keeping the Deli in town through their own efforts.

This same organization—SHARE—has helped others who were encouraged by the success of Deli Dollars to print their own money. So, in the same community, local farmers have issued "Berkshire Farm Preserve Notes," which carry the slogan "In Farms We Trust" instead of the federal reserve message "In God We Trust" and a cabbage head instead of the head of George Washington! These Berkshire Farm Preserve Notes helped farmers get through the long winter months when there is little or no income from their market gardens. Customers spend these notes during the summer months. But the local currency does more than simply give economic relief. By valuing their own community, investors can see, touch, and feel the effects of their money in their own community. Gradually the loans that people make begin to work into the investors' own social and cultural life. The produce at the local farm becomes identified with the lenders, with their friends, and with their way of life. What begins as a simple financial arrangement turns out to have cultural consequences that go way beyond moneylending. Investing in one's own community is a way of valuing differences at home and, in so doing, enriching the fabric of everyone's life.

Springing up in many places are strategies to regain control of our food supply. As many of us have no doubt experienced, shopping for food in supermarkets can leave us feeling powerless and alienated, not to mention concerned about the quality of the food itself. Near where I live is a creative gardening strategy that involves people who are otherwise living on the streets and farms that are otherwise abandoned. With a little organization and commitment, local people have come together as a collective to rent farms owned by absentee landlords. The local welfare agency has then been convinced to pay rent money that is normally due the street people directly to these farm renters, and the street people—who often know quite a bit about how to keep up a farm—are growing magnificent gardens, which produce much more than they can use. The logical extension has been a food bank in the town, and sometimes there is so much surplus that during summer months they can set up at the Saturday market. Many of these once-demoralized and homeless people have been involved with these farms for over ten years. And the outreach continues to grow.

Other grassroots food systems involve local people supporting a collective of people who will guarantee so much fresh produce throughout the summer for a modest amount of money up front. For about $350, one such group promises eight pounds of food a week for a twenty-five-week season. With about twenty commitments, two full-time gardeners can be kept employed at work they love, and lots of people are guaranteed a high-quality, nonalienated food supply.

These food strategies are doubly good. First, they demonstrate that people can choose to overcome the petty differences that may exist in local communities to support one another's initiatives. And second, they help ensure that our food supply itself is not simplified to the danger point by overreliance on transnational supermarkets or distant monocropping agribusiness.

Again, from my neck-of-the-woods, come some very innovative forestry strategies that make the transnationals look ridiculously outdated and cumbersome. This is a simple story about a man who has made a good living from a 136-acre tree farm for over forty years. When you walk through his "forest" you don't see great cut-blocks or burned-over rubble as you do wherever a transnational has laid claim to the trees. Merv Wilkinson, in his late seventies, is still healthy and strong enough to maintain his woodlot, too. His trees have not just provided pulp for the pulp mill down the road. No, his market is much more diverse. He cuts fence posts, Christmas trees, and log-house building material as well as timber for dimension lumber—anything that his place can provide to a ready market. He has logged-over his place eight times, but you would never know this to see it. Now the transnationals can't claim this. Their strategy is to cut down everything and then replant with only one marketable species, which results in simplification of the ecosystem. Merv's forestry strategy is just the opposite. Because his approach is more in tune with what is actually going on in nature in his woodlot, he nurtures young trees where they occur naturally.

Out of the forestry situation in British Columbia, several other innovative strategies have emerged. For instance, the Eagle clan of the Gitskan and Wetsuwet'en, the original people in an area of northern British Columbia who have lived there for upwards of ten thousand years, have a five-hundred-year forestry plan! They have always used the trees, and they believe that with the wisdom of cultural hindsight they can continue to live in harmony with the forests. This does not mean no logging. In fact, they believe they can participate in the forest economy of British Columbia. Sometimes nonnative people, not being able to fully understand just exactly how the native people intend to do this, resist supporting native land claims. But the better strategy for nonnative people is simple. Native people are literally a part of the place they call home. They aren't going anywhere—unlike the big corporations. While we may all have a lot to learn about sustainable forestry, the Gitskan and Wetsuwet'en's ethic is bound to be much healthier because it comes from a culture that believes the trees are sacred and whose children will be there to inherit the consequences of decisions made today. And if nonnative people take up the idea of staying put, then all of us who care about the forests will be living side by side and will work it out. Surely this is a far better option than having control rest in some corporate office thousands of miles away?

The last example that I want to share is more of a process than an event, though it began as a conference which was attempting to deal with the polarization of jobs versus the environment promoted by the public relations firms of the transnationals. More and more communities are being divided by threats from government and industry to local people's economic security—their pay checks. Environmentalists and native people are often held responsible because of their questioning of the jurisdiction over, and ethical use of, the land. The challenge of the conference was to bring together those who were being pitted against each other, and this included people who had given up trying to talk with one another, including native leaders, regional labor people from the International Woodworkers of America and Fisherman's Union, grassroots environmentalists, far-sighted academics, elected and nonelected political party people, and ordinary, nonaligned citizens. In the conference's opening address by George Watts, spokesperson for the Nuu-Chah-Nuulth people on whose land we were meeting, he touched the hearts and minds of us all. He said that he would never dream of leaving his "real" security—his family, his people, and his place—for higher wages somewhere else, and he was hoping others were having the same idea.

Over the few days that we were together, sitting around conference tables looking our differences squarely in the face, it became apparent that we were asking ourselves to do more than just elect the right politicians. This business of working together meant overcoming our own fears; it meant letting go of enough of our own often tightly held points of view so that we might all work together. This meant, for nonnative people, for instance, that we had to get firmly behind native land claims, which in turn ultimately meant dealing with our own racism. And native people were being asked once again to trust white people, in spite of years of abuse. Politicians were being asked to be accountable to the local people, no matter what their party lines, and to realize that centralized policies frequently don't make sense. Environmentalists were being asked to go beyond preservationism, to see the land as something we need to learn to use with sensitivity, not with abuse.

On a deep level, we were exploring whether we could trust each other. Could we open up our hearts and minds and find some way to allow each other our "piece of the truth," or were the differences simply too enormous to reach a consensus? At some point, many realized that what we were asking of ourselves was whether we cared enough about the places and people we love to transcend the fear of difference and its hierarchical solutions—the personal baggage inherited from Western culture—so that we all might move beyond self-righteousness and self-interest? Without embracing diversity, the various organizations and factions would continue to be limited to single-issue struggles. But by building common ground, this coalition could do more than fight corporate forestry practices, for example. Rooted in the familiar territory of place, it could begin to create a community in which our differences could work together for the common well-being of both people and place. After all, this is nature's pattern: diversity is the sign of a healthy and stable ecosystem.

The message of the First Peoples to the Europeans five hundred years ago was to recognize that human beings have a place in the natural world and that this place, like all of life, is sacred. Native people, if we listen, are still saying this. And now ecofeminists are speaking for all that has been denied this sacred reality, in order that Western civilization may move beyond its isolated and destructive way of being and in so doing not repeat the same old order. The old order, with its fear of difference and its desperate need to control the world, cannot possibly be the world view that will enable humanity to find its place in nature.

The good news is that in pockets of resistance and renewal, things *are* changing. People are shaking their heads, awakening to the consciousness of a constantly changing, ever-evolving world, of which humankind is a part. No longer can we bear to live apart, above and separate from such truth. Coming home to our place in nature means learning to live with the infinite differences that make life possible. Our real security in this universe that is always in motion cannot possibly come from rigid and fixed views. Real security must lie in a commitment to that which sustains us—like George Watts' security of family, people, and place. With roots firmly placed, what joys there must be in contemplating this astounding miracle of life that is ever unfolding. Out of the dark ages of fear and power-over there is emerging a way of being for humanity which we can barely comprehend but to which we are attracted like bees to honey. The trail is uphill, and the load is heavy. Take heart in each small step along the way.

Eight

"The Earth Is the Indian's Mother, Nhãndecy"

Eliane Potiguara
Translated by Leland Robert Guyer;
edited by Karen J. Warren

In the proposal by GRUMIN (Grupo Mulher-Educação Indígena, or Women's Group for Indigenous Education), the work directed toward village-based education is unique in its contribution to the indigenous movement's struggle to reclaim its history, its culture, even its identity within the regions where the process of colonization has been most destructive. It is also unique in its work to preserve those cultures as yet untouched.

In this reconstructive effort, education and health emerge as the pillars of the work to be done. It is perfectly realistic in that it is in step with the consciousness-raising process of indigenous peoples toward the defense of their land rights, their environment of which they are courageous defenders and, in the end, their lives. For this to happen, it is not enough that the Indian be aware of his or her problems in terms of the reality of the encroaching society. The encroaching society must also become aware that the Indian is not a quaint or incapable being. Throughout the last five centuries, circumstances have forced Indians to be warriors in defense of their people and their lands in the longest war in the world's memory.

By publishing the pamphlet from which this chapter is edited, GRUMIN aspires only to summarize the efforts of brother and sister Indians seeking their goal to convey their support of education officials, indigenous health care givers, and urban professors to help in the understanding of the social, political and economic reasons that have caused the oppression and social and racial discrimination that have always encroached upon them and the natural world.

The Indigenous Population: Who Are We?

Science continues to study the origins of primitive peoples. What we already know, however, is that Indians inhabited America for many centuries prior to the European invasion.

Before 1500, Brazilian Indians numbered five million, forming nine hundred indigenous nations. The extermination wrought by the invaders reduced the population to the current level of little more than 200,000, forming 180 nations and speaking 120 languages.

The capitalist economic model transformed the indigenous way of life as the Indian encountered the notions of the accumulation of wealth, products, metals, currency, and private property. They succumbed to this for the most part, transforming their customs and traditions in the same way as, for example, the Iroquois in the United States, whose matriarchal system ceased to exist.[1]

In the new society, as men accumulated money and goods, they became the proprietors of wealth, which their names and surnames guaranteed. Previously honored and respected, women and their families went to work for the holders of money—an acquaintance, a brother, even the husband. Indigenous cultures are rich. Nevertheless, the white people's attempts to acculturate them to serve their own needs puts the purity of their customs at risk. If we were allowed to continue to exist in our traditional ways, we would forever have stories as beautiful as the ones which follow, as told by the Amazonian Toyucas.

Possessing its own beliefs, mythology, customs and traditions, the Toyuca tribe was part of the indigenous nations long before Brazil ever existed. Today the Toyuca tribe is reasonably conservative, in the sense that it conserves its culture. We celebrate nature, manioc and fish. We observe *Dabucuri*, a festival in which we gather fish and fruit to offer to our relatives. It is a traditional festival for which we make *caxiri*, a drink prepared from grated manioc. A woman prepares the drink. She chews the manioc and then spits into a bowl, believing that the process fortifies the cairi and helps ferment the drink. Without *caxiri* the festival is not lively. We smoke natural *sorocaba* tobacco which we form into a long, thick rolled cigar which must remain lit throughout the night. We do not smoke the way city dwellers do. We smoke seldom and only in rituals. *Epadu* is a plant that must not disappear. Used only in our rituals, it helps enhance the ideas of our elders, our shamans and our thinkers. This plant helps us communicate with the spirits. Our parents and grandparents also use it as a stimulant on long journeys to ward off hunger.

We pray for the health of nature, for the phenomenal power of the rains and of lightning, and we pray to the God of Summer. It is our thinker who prays for us, and if I also wish to pray I must be near him.

Indigenous Participation

Up until now Indians have been warriors in a struggle for their life. Today, as a consequence of this struggle, we have a constitution that was written in recognition of their historical rights. Nevertheless, a lot of work must still be done to guarantee these rights. Toward this end, Indians are publicizing their rights on television, in newspapers, on radio, and in conferences held at schools, universities, and union halls.

Others have gone to international congresses at the United Nations where they have denounced the grand governmental projects that have assaulted our ecology, attacked our social structure, and upset the ecosystem.

In local assemblies or regional conferences held in our villages we have discussed the problems affecting Indians. Our leaders demand discussion of these problems with the government. We have won many battles, each one the result of the heightened awareness of indigenous people.

Customs and Traditions

Food and drink prepared by women and children permeate dances, festivals, and music. The people celebrate their harvests, the rain, the sun, the birds, and an endless number of natural phenomena in their festivals.

The community makes its day-to-day utensils. These include baskets, hammocks or sleeping nets, weaving, individual or collective home construction, and the production of canoes, adornments, and feathered crafts.

The division of labor in the areas of weaving, painting, and tattooing varies from village to village. Some allow men to paint; in others painting is the exclusive domain of the women. The paints, derived from the genipap and annatto trees, are used on the occasion of festivals, wars, death, and sickness.

Kinship forms the social and political organizations of the indigenous communities, with some variation from group to group. Some people, the Marubo as an example, divide themselves into clans, and the ancestry of each clan is matrilineal, that is, based on the ancestry of the mother.

The *pajés*, or shamans, care for the sick. They are the tribe's wise old men who know secret herbal cures and invoke the protection of the spirits through ritual.

Before the arrival of the Europeans, the tribal council would gather the wisest and most experienced of the collective. The Europeans introduced the "little despotic king" concept of subregional tribal chief.

Indigenous Society

Indigenous society has five key features. First, barter, not money, is the basis for the exchange of staple foodstuffs and objects of necessity. Second, indigenous society is classless. Since the collective is the basis of land and produce, there are neither rich people nor poor people. Third, indigenous society is communal. Labor is communal. Having no basis in power, relations between parents and children, husbands and wives, etc. are harmonious, and cooperative effort and mutual solidarity are everywhere present. Fourth, Indians do not accumulate material goods. They produce only that which they need to survive. Lastly, indigenous society is different from the encroaching society in customs, traditions, history, economy, social politics, and religion.

Misunderstanding and Prejudice

When the Portuguese came to the land that is now called Brazil they did not understand indigenous life and society. The letters to Portugal sent by Pero Vaz de Caminha to Aspilcueta Navarro reflect misunderstanding and ignorance about the realities of indigenous people. Following are quotations which show this misunderstanding and prejudice: "Everything about them reveals a culture of the most abject backwardness." "They were deceitful, disloyal, untrustworthy and, in a word, barbarous." "This Indian language is the only one along the length of the Brazilian coast. Lacking the three phonemes F, L and R, it follows that the Indians have neither Faith, Law nor Royalty, and for this reason they exist in a state of chaos and anarchy."

When the Spanish encountered indigenous civilization they raised doubt as to whether the Indian belonged to the human race. They came to consider the Indian as *casi mono*, "nearly monkeys." European morality, troubled by the religious notion of sin in the Indian settlements, brought in the Jesuits to dress the Indian women in white from head to toe. In Gorotire, a missionary interpreted indigenous culture as having absurd customs.

"Indians are synonymous with the past." In what may appear to be nothing more than harmless jokes there hides a legacy of prejudice that the colonists have nurtured through the centuries. Its intent is to destroy indigenous culture with misinformation. It is an oppressor's game where we find an attempted sense of humor in quips such as the following: "Indians know that if there's nothing else to eat, at least they've got their whistles." "Those lazy Indians just won't work." "Indians are drunken, thieving savages." "He's an Indian, but at least he's clean." "The Indian's a relic from the past." "How did the Indians live?" (as if they were not alive today). The year 1759 marks the official beginning of paternalism toward the Indian: Francisco Xavier, brother of the Marquis of Pombal and responsible for the expulsion of the Jesuits from Brazil, created the office of "Director of Indians" in response to the inherent savagery and manifest ignorance of the Indian.

"Indians wear no clothes. They're depraved; they're indecent." There are seven cardinal concepts about indigenous peoples:

1. Indians are minors, lazy and incompetent.
2. Blacks are slum dwellers, marginal.
3. Rural workers are people without land rights; they are lunch pailers, low-paid manual laborers.
4. Women are inferior and incompetent.
5. Children are ignorant.
6. Elders are obsolete, useless as workers.
7. The disabled are crippled and incompetent.

The exercise of these concepts by the elite and the powerful has done violence against human beings, especially indigenous peoples. They allege that the masses have limited education, then turn around and deny them education. Ignoring these problems and devaluing its very self, Brazilian society perpetuates its prejudicial underpinnings. It adopts a holier-than-thou attitude toward others and ultimately within its own arena. It is repressive and misinformed about health and nutrition. All of this reveals a feature of our educational system that is distinctly out of touch.

The prejudice of a whole era and centuries of paternalism have had powerful effects. The Indian cultures have been decimated, leaving virtually no mark upon the register of history.

Education and the Indigenous Family

The education of the indigenous child is very wise and simple. Children accompany their parents in their daily tasks, such as hunting, working in the field, preparing food and drink, producing arts and crafts, and participating in festivals and dances. In this way the child learns from an early age to be independent and enjoy working. This relationship does not allow violence or repression to intrude. It develops a link with the collective sentiment for the earth, a feeling of solidarity, the lifestyle and experience of the parents, grandparents, and extended family, and leads to a natural and healthful education of all children and young people.

Brazil Was Not Discovered; Brazil Was Invaded

People oppressed and discriminated against throughout the world, including those in Africa, Asia, Latin America, Central America, and Australia, have suffered centuries of subordination, inflicted upon them by European domination. During the fifteenth and sixteenth centuries in Brazil, the colonizers enslaved indigenous people. However, Indians refused to accept this slavery and many of them, such as the Guarani in the south of Brazil, would throw their wives, elders, and children from cliff tops prior to killing themselves. This was a comprehensible manner of protest.

The Indians would never accept subordination, racism, or violence against their people in their own land. They would never work hours of forced labor on behalf of the invaders whose culture, language, and lives were different from their own. Yet from the perspective of the colonizer of that era, indigenous resistance, struggle, dignity, and culture were synonymous with indolence and incompetence.[2]

Despite resistance to forced labor, slavery of the indigenous people was imposed by force of arms, and many deaths resulted. Sadly, the history of Brazil does not recognize this. At the same time, there are hundreds of books and documents that tell of the heroic deeds of the colonial explorers and pioneers, the work of the Jesuits and the first regional governors. History is written to mark the trajectory of human lives and truth. Employing these factors, we would have a history that gave birth to the Brazilian people: whites, mestizos, blacks, and the Indians who were already here.

In 130 years, two million Guarani Indians from the basins of the Paraná, the Paraguay, and the Uruguay rivers were killed or enslaved. We know that in a single year Indians harvested two thousand tons of the invaders' cotton and that, through the eyes of slavery, Indians watched over a million head of cattle in the Guara region.

The colonial explorers and pioneers, about whom history records glorious deeds, were nothing more than large paramilitary bands engaged in the capture and enslavement of Indians. Every manner of degenerate who had come to the New World or to Brazil formed these Indian hunting parties.

After illness, massacres, and the inhuman treatment of slavery eliminated 90 percent of the Indian population, the enslavement of blacks began in Brazil. Indians no longer served a function. They were "indolent and incompetent," according to the Portuguese.

The differences between indigenous society and the encroaching society can be represented by the following table:

Indigenous Society	Encroaching Society
1. Sense of collective land holding	1. Private property
2. Economy of subsistence	2. Economy of acquisition
3. Egalitarian society	3. Discriminatory society
4. Barter system	4. Cash-based system
5. Respect for life and environment	5. Predatory behavior

146

The Northeastern Indians:
Five Hundred Years of Resistance

The invasion of Brazil began in the northeast and moved eastward along the coast. For this reason the Indians of this region suffered the most. With a coalition of several tribes, the Tamoio Confederation waged the best-known armed conflict.

With lies and treachery the Portuguese defeated but did not subjugate these tribes. They preferred death to slavery, and for this reason the Tupinambá Kaete, Goiataká, Aymoré, and Tomiminó exist only in our memory.

Through all this the surviving Indians of the northeast and east assimilated the colonial culture. Many lost their native language, adopted mud and wattle construction for their homes, and began wearing clothing as they worked. In addition, many adopted the colonial economic system of work for pay.

Even the fashions, customs, and cherished dances, symbols of indigenous origins, sustained change as a consequence of the acculturation process, suffered for nearly five centuries in which the people confronted the Portuguese, the Dutch, the French, and the *sertanejos*.[3] Throughout these centuries they also confronted pressures to stop being Indian: the missions with their religious instruction, the Pombaline emancipation, the scorn and prejudice of the sertanejos and, today, the capitalist society.

Despite these pressures, they remain united with the same conviction: they continue being Indians with a powerful sense of solidarity, founded upon the beliefs that explain nature, their origins, and a common destiny that unifies them as a people. From this they derive their organization as well as their political and cultural work toward the restoration of their traditions, the reaffirmation of their ethnic identity, and the recovery of their lands. This is the struggle of the Potiguara, of the Kukuru, of the Fulni-ô of the Pankakaru, of the Tupiniquim, of the Xocó, and of others.

Against this backdrop they confront multinational corporations that covet their lands and natural resources, as well as local plantation owners, lumber companies, even gold miners, not to mention our traditional politicians.

The Twentieth Century

Nowadays the invasions of our lands by large landholders, the constant threats to indigenous families by gunmen, the huge mining, hydroelectric, highway, and lumber concerns are responsible for death, violence, and aggression against indigenous people. Just as in the past, indigenous leaders still combat these invasions of their lands, these attacks upon Mother Nature, this violence against their people. They are our twentieth-century warriors.

Going beyond the examples through history of social and racial prejudice against Indians, we can now demonstrate the consequences of the behavior of the people in power. They possess national and foreign capital, control the means of production and retain all profits, possess advanced technology and do not extend its benefit to others, possess money but do not distribute its earnings, possess land for their private use, and possess firearms and use them to repress.

The colonizers have employed violence to subjugate indigenous people. In the following table, one can compare the differences between whites and Indians. These differences have determined the outcomes of each.

Whites	Indians
1. Superiority in firearms	1. Bows and arrows, spears, snares, and bolas
2. Ships and horses for transportation	2. Canoes and feet
3. Use of steel and other metals	3. Traditional crafts
4. Imposition of psychological, racial, intellectual, and religious sense of superiority	4. Misunderstood indigenous culture and traditions
5. Climate of violence, injustice, and hypocrisy	5. Climate of struggle and resistance against slavery

Other factors have also contributed to the annihilation of the indigenous society by the whites: biological devastation (illnesses, premature aging), economic devastation (forced Indian labor with no recourse), psychological devastation (the Indians' sense of inferiority), and social devastation (social maladjustment).

The social disintegration of indigenous peoples affects even more the acculturated indigenous communities and the displaced and marginalized Indians who live in the city, with the following results: illegal ghettos, deaths and suicides, rapes, massacres, alcoholism, insecurity, timidity, discouragement, and mental illness. The first contacts with white people brought the school-based concept to the village, an idea that had both positive and negative aspects, given the indigenous population's lifestyle.

Energy: A Challenge to Nature

"These lands belong to us now. You have twenty-four hours to clear out." The politics of development in Brazil evolved in the second half of the twentieth century. In 1964, the military government then in power, in an effort to transform a Third World country into a First World country overnight, put into action a development plan financed with foreign loans that we'll be paying off until who knows when. This resulted in the impoverishment of the entire Brazilian nation.

With the implementation of these grand projects, we have witnessed enormous assaults upon nature and the environment. The powers that be have flooded lands, poisoned rivers and seas, devastated whole regions, and spread sickness and ethnic and social disorder. Mercury and sugarcane waste products have contaminated the Indians' rivers, and their flora and fauna have died. The Indians have suffered the most from the authorities' neglect of their future and the disrespect with which they deal with their issues.

Development, yes. Massacre, no!

There are four types of energy available to us. First, there is hydroelectric energy. Dams built on large rivers generate energy for lights for factories, for cities, and so on. When they flood the areas behind the dams, cities, indigenous settlements, and riverbank populations must leave. The flora and fauna of the flooded areas die and decompose, and the results are diseases like malaria and leishmaniasis. More than ninety hydroelectric projects are planned in the Amazonian basin and in the south.

Second, there is mineral energy. Petroleum is the basis for this energy source. Gasoline and other thousands of derivatives (plastics, foam rubber, diesel fuel, kerosene, etc.) come from petroleum. The national petroleum conglomerate Petrobras is responsible for the exploration for and production of petroleum. In addition, there are other subsidiary concerns that operate refineries and conduct research (Shell, Esso, British Petroleum, Ida Mitsu, and Elf Equitaine).

Third, there is energy derived from the atom, from matter itself, nuclear energy. This source is highly controversial because it is a powerful and dangerous form of energy that, if it escapes, can contaminate the population with its radioactivity. A disaster of this type occurred in Goiânia, where many people died.

Finally, there are alternative sources of energy. One is energy derived from sugarcane. It appeared in response to the gasoline shortage. The Pro-Alcohol Program was created for the development of this source of energy. Now, tons of *vinhoto* (a sugarcane waste product) poison the rivers.

When the sugar refineries appeared, everything began to die. They drained the wetlands, and the black and green chameleon, the freshwater turtle and the cayman died off. The snakes also died. I remember them—the maracatifa, the salamanta-bois, the howling snake and the rattlesnake. The river fish. . . . What can I say? Today everything's polluted. The camurim, the saúna, the traira and the pitu are gone.

Our land used to give us everything: fruits and nuts like capi, mango, mangaba, guava, pine nuts, graviola, jack fruit, bananas, cana-caiana and pineapple. The sweet potato and the yam would grow to an immense size in the earth. With the sugarcane residue from the refineries, together with deforestation, the Potiguara lands diminished. Now we must rebuild what remains. It's a shame.

Brazilian society will respect Indians only when it recognizes them as a part of its own culture, language, and traditions. When Brazilian society, in a nonpaternalistic way, looks upon the Indian as a brother, as the head of a family, and not as an indigent but as a Brazilian in need like anyone else, then Indians will have respect. After all, they have the great fortune of nature and all the wealth that it encompasses.

What Should We Do?

If we want to undergo a social transformation in our country it is not enough to criticize. Besides criticizing, we must present solutions in pursuit of change. All the struggles undertaken up to now on behalf of indigenous peoples have been very valuable. We won a new constitution. Now we must find new ways to struggle, work programs, and suggestions to guarantee the rights we have established.

This is why we need the Organization of Indigenous Movements. The National Indigenous Union, other indigenous organizations, and legal counsel exist. The GRUMIN Project appeared as an offshoot to sensitize and strengthen and communicate the work that the women and children have been doing. This is how we'll get to where we're going. It is through unity that the prophecy will come true and indigenous people will survive, and it is through hard work and persistence that we will build unity.

We must suggest—no, demand—of the powers that be that we have a Program of Health, Education, and Agriculture, backed by state and municipal administrations. We can seek solutions with the Department of Education, Health, and Agriculture. Indigenous leadership has already opened lines of communication and has done a lot of work. We need to get moving.

But how? By organizing workers' groups within or outside the village by the labor that they perform. The groups would focus on five key areas:

1. The right to land and the observance of its boundaries. How do we guarantee these lands? Have an attorney. The National Indigenous Union has a nucleus of indigenous rights.
2. Education. We must be convincing when we say that we need a hearing on education—its professionalization and salary, research into the indigenous reality, teaching materials, school supplies, guarantees with respect to our culture, traditions, and language. School-based education in the villages is still unrealistic, despite best efforts. This kind of education has harmed our customs and indigenous languages, and therefore we need a radical change in this area.
3. Health. We must be convincing when we say that we need a hear-

ing on health—its professionalization and salary, medicines that don't conflict with indigenous culture, the restoration of natural medicine, and the use of hospitals only in extreme cases.

4. The organization of position papers and how to advance them. These papers can be done on each topic (education, health, agriculture, etc.).

5. To advance projects that solicit funds, we must establish work groups in legal terms, have bank accounts, and truly work with the community.

There are people, present, absent, and anonymous, who have contributed greatly to GRUMIN, or Women's Group for Indigenous Education. Some are present in the strength they've given, others in the critiques that have helped put this work together.

Our work was born in our consciousness, in the blood that runs in our veins, and in the struggle against all forms of oppression or discrimination. It's there, ready for our discussion.

We will continue our project because our scope is enormous. Earth, nature and Tupã have been witness to our spilled blood, our pain, and the prejudice indigenous people have suffered.

Few know our true history. Many of our grandparents have responded to distress with silence, which, as much as struggling and persistence, represents wisdom. With this wisdom they have passed to us, we must dive deeply into the depths of the rivers and the sea, climb mountains, and enter the heart of the forests and the cataracts, and feel the origins of indigenous people and struggle with and for them.

It is the deliverance and the conservation of our identity. Nature cannot be conserved if its guardians—the Indians—exist no more.

So, let us live!

Afterword

"A Prayer for the Liberation of Indigenous People"
To Marçal Tupã-Y (Guarani Chief Nhandewa, murdered in 1983)

Stop stripping my leaves and give me back my hoe.
Quit drowning my beliefs and chopping up my roots.
Cease tearing out my lungs and smothering my reason.
It's time to stop killing my songs and silencing my voice.
You cannot dry out the roots of those who possess seeds
Cast upon the earth to sprout.
You cannot extinguish the fertile memory of our grandparents—
Ancestral blood, rituals to remember.
No one clips our broad wings
For the sky is liberty,

And we have faith in finding it.
Pray for us, our Father Xamã,
That the evil forest spirit
Not create weakness, misery, and death in us.
Pray for us, our Mother Earth,
That these torn clothes
And that these evil men
Withdraw before the rattle of maracas.
Deliver us from sorrow, cane liquor, and strife,
Help unite our nations.
Enlighten our men, women, and children,
Obliterate ingratitude and envy among the strong.
Give us light, faith, and life in our healing ceremony,
Avoid, oh Tupã, violence and bloodshed.
In a sacred spot near the river's edge,
On full moon nights, oh Marçal, invoke
The spirits of the stones so we can dance the Toré
Bring the life force
To our shamans and our celebrations of the manioc
After we drink our chicha in faith.
Pray for us, our heavenly bird,
That jaguars, peccaries, crested cranes, and capybaras
Line our rivers Jurena, São Francisco, and Paraná,
Line the shores of the Atlantic.
After all, we are pacific.
Show us our way like the freshwater dolphin,
Illuminate our star for our future.
Help us play the magic flutes
To sing to you a song of offering
Or dance our ritual lamakó
Pray for us, our bird-Xamã,
In the northeast and in the south all morning.
In the Amazon wilds or in the heart of the backwoods woman.
Pray for us, macaws, armadillos, or speckled catfish,
Come to us,
Our god that we call Nhendiru!
Make happy our children
Who from Indian bellies will be reborn.
Give us hope each day
For all we wish is earth and peace
For our poor people—our wealthy children.

Notes

Editor's Note: I met Eliane Potiguara at an International Seminar on Ecofeminism, held in conjunction with the Earth Summit, in Rio de Janeiro, Brazil, during May 1992. I was impressed by her passion and commitment, her work in GRUMIN, and the pamphlet she wrote, *A Terra É A Mãe Do Índio*, translated here as "The Earth Is the Indian's Mother, Nhãndecy." With Potiguara's permission, Macalester College Professor of Spanish and Portuguese Leland Guyer translated the pamphlet and then I edited it to produce this essay-length version. Anyone interested in the Portuguese version may write Eliane Potiguara at GRUMIN, Rua da Quitanda, 185 s/503-CEP 20.091, Rio de Janeiro, Brasil; anyone interested in the English version may contact Leland Guyer at Macalester College, 1600 Grand Avenue, St. Paul, MN 55105. Eliane Potiguara dedicates this work "to Vo Maria de Lourdes, for her awareness; to Mother Elza, for her life; to my children, Moina, Tajira, and Potiguara, for their strength, and to the indigenous peoples of Brazil, for their claws and for their struggle."

1. Many indigenous societies continue to resist the influence of the encroaching capitalist society. An example of this are the Yanomami, who preserve their culture, customs, and traditions. There are 20,000 Yanomami Indians living in Amazonia, in the Surucucus Mountains. They have managed to resist the ever-present threats of the gold miners and mining companies attracted by the richness of their soil. They live as protectors of their environment, in a struggle for which their great leader David Yanomami won the Global 2000 award, conferred by the United Nations.

2. Ângelo Kretã, Chief Kaigang, was the first Indian to exercise politics in the country, believing that this would accrue positive results to the war Indians waged for their lands. Speaking as a councilman, he said: "Brazil was not discovered. It was invaded."

3. *Sertanejo* is the name given to those who live in the *sertão*, a harsh region of the northeastern part of Brazil, of sparse population and vegetation, beset by periodic and extended droughts, regularly followed by sudden and devastating floods. Curiously, the sertão is the locale of many of the most powerful social movements in the last two hundred years of Brazilian history. We also know the sertão as the inspiration of much of Brazil's recent literature and film. (Translator's note.)

PART II:

INTERDISCIPLINARY PERSPECTIVES

Nine

Leisure
Celebration and Resistance in the Ecofeminist Quilt

Karen M. Fox

While there is no single ecofeminism, all ecofeminists focus on the intimate connections between the lives of women and the ecological condition. Karen J. Warren (1990) provides a wonderful metaphor, the "quilt of ecological feminism," for theorizing and theory-building and provides minimal and necessary conditions for choosing "pieces" for inclusion within the "quilt of ecological feminism."[1] Building on this metaphor and Warren's minimal conditions for ecofeminist philosophy, I argue that leisure is an important segment of women's lives for connecting with nature and re-affirming themselves and their relationships with nature. Leisure becomes one of many possible "quilting stitches" for the quilt of ecological feminism.

The process of quilting uses specific needles called "betweens" to sew together the various layers (i.e., the design layer of pieces, the batting and the backing) of a quilt. The most important qualities of a quilting stitch are the evenness (the uniform size of all stitches), the regularity (the uniform distance between each stitch), and the tension, which creates the puffed appearance of the well-done quilt. When finished, the quilting stitch is either a barely visible portion of the quilt or a distinct stitch that accents the design of the pieces while holding together the various layers of the quilt.

Functioning much like a quilting stitch, leisure does and should play a vital role in the development of an overall pattern of the ecofeminist quilt. Time and experiences associated with leisure may be barely visible or central components of a woman's life, but there are often stitches connecting women with nature, healthy lifestyles, self-expression, and self-affirmation. Leisure is important when it is a regular and even part of a woman's life, when it creates excitement within a woman's daily routine, when it provides an escape from tension or stress, or when it supports momentary joy and relaxation. Leisure encompasses, at a minimum, enjoyment, relaxation, freedom of choice, and self-affirmation that may connect various layers or elements of a woman's life, including a relationship with the natural environment.

As I will show, a proper understanding of the nature and roles of leisure in the lives of women reveals that leisure is often a connecting stitch for women's experience with nonhuman nature and to a means of joyful resistance. Sometimes this connection, like a barely visible quilting stitch, is overlooked but still essential to the integrity of the piece.

The Phenomenon of Leisure

Leisure appears to be a phenomenon so simple that most people assume they know what it is and quickly answer questions about their leisure activities. Nonetheless, leisure is so complex that scholars cannot specifically identify and define it. Leisure scholars have wrestled with the definition and parameters of leisure for generations. Although many people perceive leisure as a luxury and expendable, its significance is reflected in a statement in the 1975 United Nations commissioned report on leisure throughout the world: "People cannot grow on the basis of physical sustenance alone; they need a cultural identity, a sense of social fulfilment, a regeneration of body and spirit which comes from various forms of recreation and leisure and makes their role one of growing importance on the world's agenda." Even in difficult and oppressive situations, leisure plays a role in sustaining life, as exemplified by the call of the Fraternidad de Mujeres Salvador for constructing new recreation centers as a vital element of rebuilding the country (Thomson, 1986).

Numerous terms are used to describe the parts or whole of the phenomenon: e.g., leisure, recreation, escapism, serious leisure, pastimes, idleness, celebrations, play, amusements, festivals, free time, sports, adventure recreation, and socials. All of these terms label the ways people relax, escape stressful situations, develop physical and mental skills, regenerate, connect with family and friends, even sustain cultural traditions in an enjoyable fashion. Each of these concepts describes a necessary but not sufficient component of leisure. Historically, leisure scholars have primarily conceived the leisure phenomenon as an activity, as not-work or free time, as freedom of choice, and as state of mind.[2]

Leisure as Activity

Leisure defined as an activity is deceptively simple. Immediately, examples of activities associated with leisure come to mind: jogging, soccer, swimming, mountain climbing, golfing, visiting a park or friends, attending a party, walking through the woods, watching a movie or television, and listening to music. However, these examples may not be as straightforward as they seem. For instance, jogging can be done for pleasure, health, or necessity (e.g., jogging with clients as part of one's business). Is the experience of a party still leisure if the woman is obligated to attend or prepare all the food? Does adding an overlay of leisure to a work activity (e.g., making crafts enjoyable or listening to music while cleaning) provide a means of oppressing women who are basically working?

Leisure as Not-Work or Free Time

One of the most common characterizations, among leisure scholars and public alike, is leisure as something that is not-work and occurs during free time. In research studies in North America (Shaw, 1990), both women and men describe a distinct difference between work and leisure and often look at work as mandatory, obligatory, and necessary for survival. In contrast, people pursue activities related to leisure during time not devoted to work, or free time.

The dichotomy between work and leisure and obligated and free time is problematic for many women. First, the dichotomy or duality supports a logic of domination which has been addressed by numerous feminist scholars.[3] Historically, both work and leisure have been described in terms of "virtue" and "goodness" which were associated with a ruling class or gender.[4] For example, leisure scholars refer to the writing of Plato and Aristotle as the basis for the virtues of leisure which were contextually relevant only to free men. The influence of Luther and Calvin are examples of the change in society which led to equating free time, idleness, and sin and extolling the virtues of a work ethic that was partially responsible for the exploitation of women and children (Goodale and Godbey, 1988).

Second, the definition and measurement of work are based on "work for financial remuneration," which leaves invisible the work that women perform outside the workplace. In recent years, leisure scholars have expanded the concept of obligated time to include the second shift to account for other kinds of necessary tasks or chores. However, this adjustment leaves intact the underlying duality and value assumptions of work and leisure.

In addition, the obligations and role responsibilities of daughter, wife, and mother pervade many women's entire lives, and therefore the tasks within the second shift cannot be neatly compartmentalized. Women often combine numerous activities with the responsibility of child care. Is it leisure, work, or child care to take one's daughters and sons to the park for an afternoon? Is it leisure, work, or child care to wash clothes along a river bank, talk with other women, and watch the children?

Third, many women express an ambivalence toward their own personal entitlement to leisure and find it difficult to pursue leisure instead of more productive and worthwhile activities or family-supporting tasks (Henderson and Bialeschki, 1991). Even when women perceive leisure as important and are able to pursue leisure because of time and financial resources, women, in contrast to men, often choose other activities that reflect their connection and commitment to family and community (Henderson and Bialeschki, 1991; Henderson, Stalnaker, and Taylor, 1988).

Finally, the dichotomy may most obscure the significance of leisure for women who are members of classes, races, and cultures where work, leisure, family interaction, and religious practices flow together in form, structure, and time; for them, the separation of concepts such as leisure and work becomes even more difficult. For instance, when a Central American woman visits the cemetery with her family on a Sunday afternoon, pays her respects to departed relatives, participates in family games, and cooks and serves the food for the midday picnic, are the events leisure, religious, or obligatory? Does the application of a specific definition or concept of leisure enhance the woman's quality of life or reinforce oppression? Does differentiation of the various threads clarify or confuse the issues—and based on what criteria?

Leisure as Free Choice

Previous research studies (Howe and Rancourt, 1990; Shaw, 1990) indicate the European–North American men and women alike indicate that freedom of choice is strongly correlated with the popular concept of leisure. The concept of choice is closely allied with free time, an essentialist concept of autonomous self, and access to resources such as finances and facilities. However, freedom of choice may be problematic, irrelevant, or gender-related for many women who find it difficult, if not impossible, to separate their multiple roles as mother, wife, daughter, professional, and volunteer. If this is the case in a European–North American context, the definition of leisure, the access to leisure, or both becomes more problematic across cultural differences.

In addition, freedom of choice is rooted in a tradition that perceives individual identity and self as an essentialist concept distinct from family and culture.[5] Anthropological studies and narratives of women from a variety of cultures (Anzaldua, 1990; Hall, 1984; Smith-Ayala, 1991) support an alternative concept of self enmeshed in societal and cultural patterns, which may make a concept of freedom of choice irrelevant or secondary to other values, such as connection, harmony, and love. These different, cultural perspectives may question the primacy of freedom of choice or give a very different contextual meaning to the phrase.

Leisure as State of Mind

Most recently, leisure is viewed as a sociopsychological reality bridging the social and psychological, subjective realities of participants (Neulinger, 1981, 1982, 1984; Kelly, 1982). This is often termed "leisure as a state of mind" that provides the qualitative aspect need to balance the concept of leisure as time and activity. The sociopsychological perspective on leisure combines theories and models from psychology about individual self-affirmation and realization with sociological perspectives of group interaction and influences. Although time and activity are present, they become secondary to the perception of free choice for the sake of an individual doing or experiencing.

The concept of self as it relates to leisure experience (the personal, subjective experiencing of leisure) provides a focus on the needs, desires, and benefits for an individual. Samdahl (1988) suggests that "self-expression may be the critical distinction between anomic free time and engaging leisure experience" and that "the deeper value of leisure, and the rationale for its continued study may lie in the dimension of self-expression." Samdahl (1992) found that this held true during the occurrence of common leisure occasions—those occasions characterized by informal social interactions interspersed throughout one's life. They occur in comfortable settings that allow the expression of one's true self to appear without fear of judgment or censure and are important because others accept and reaffirm one's true self. Rancourt (1986, 71) stated:

> In leisure people are concerned with self-realization, self-development, self-fulfilment, self-determination, self-expression and self-enhancement. To pursue the essence of self is "to leisure." To engage in the pursuit of self—to try to experience the innermost core of one's spirit—is to leisure. To simply or completely participate in an activity is not "leisuring" unless one is engaged in expressing and enhancing one's spirit—the very essence of who one is at any point in time. What is found to be central to one's essence, for the most part, will drive one's leisure experience or perceiving an experience to be leisure will depend on what is needed to most fully [experience] and explore the self.

Within the social perspective, Joseph Pieper (1963) links leisure with culture through divine worship, festivals, and celebrations. Pieper claims that

> culture depends for its very existence on leisure, and leisure, in its turn, is not possible unless it has a durable and living link with the cultus, with divine worship. . . . Culture . . . is the quintessence of all the natural goods of the world and of those gifts and qualities which, while belonging to man, lie beyond the immediate sphere of his needs and wants. (17–18)

The social-psychological perspective pulls together some differing frameworks related to leisure that can be observed and measured, leisure that can be experienced, and leisure as an element of culture. Although providing a more complex view of leisure, it still remains bound within a specific European–North American, predominantly male tradition with essentialist definitions.

These four conceptions of leisure, although flawed and incomplete, provide a starting point and have profoundly influenced the epistemology and praxis of leisure. In recent writings, most leisure scholars, as they struggle to delineate an adequate definition of leisure, underscore that these concepts are crucial to the phenomenon although inadequate to discuss the totality and complexity of leisure. Kelly (1991) argues that leisure is significant because of its complexity and may be more a struggle than a gift. Leisure may play an important part in the balance and rhythm of life. Leisure may be a process or action in structures, not fully a world of its own. It is not unlike a quilting stitch that accents, helping focus the eye upon the main pattern of women and nature on the quilt of ecological feminism. At times, leisure may be a barely visible stitch that provides the context for connection; at other times it is a distinct design and focus of women and nature.

Ecofeminism and Leisure

Leisure is a concern for ecological feminism because it is integral to a healthy and self-affirming lifestyle, provides a context for or connection with the natural environment for women, and may provide one more avenue for resisting domination and sustaining cultural traditions vital to the survival of nature, women, and other groups. It becomes important to understand and analyze women and the environment in terms of leisure because leisure is one important way women resist oppression joyfully. Leisure is much more than a luxury; it is essential for women's health and survival as well as for their connection to the natural environment. Therefore leisure philosophy or praxis that excludes or prevents women from participating fully in a leisure that is respectful and positive for both women and nature is also an important issue for ecofeminist philosophers. In what follows, I use the connection between women and the environment as inscribed by leisure and the tenets enunciated by Warren (1990) to discuss the significance of leisure philosophy and praxis to ecofeminist philosophy and theory.[6]

Women, Nature, and Leisure

Recent feminist scholarship in leisure studies has begun to make visible the masculine gender bias and seeks to include perspectives of European–North American women (Henderson, Bialeschki, Shaw, and Freysinger, 1989; Freysinger & Flannery, 1992; Shaw, 1990). In addition, a connection between humans and the environment was and is normally absent except in discussions about outdoor recreation. More research, analysis, and interpretation are necessary to address the naturist, sexist, and racist perspectives within leisure scholarship. A glimpse at the history of mountain climbing may demonstrate some of the issues. Although a connection between humans and the environment is implied in outdoor recreation, the environment may only provide the backdrop for humans (and mostly men) to test their strength, develop self-confidence, and achieve dominance.

Mountain climbing has been seen as an outdoor pursuit primarily restricted to upper-class European–North American men. Most accounts of mountain climbing have emphasized men "conquering" mountain tops while leaving invisible the role of guides and support people. However, an examination of journals kept by women mountain climbers (Pilley, 1935; Schaffer, 1990), stories published in club journals (Crawford, 1909), and biographies of women (Robertson, 1990; Smith, 1989) indicates that perspective is only part of the story of mountain climbing. As early as 1809, women were resisting cultural norms and expectations to climb mountains.[7] Between 1907 and 1940, 484 women became active members of the Alpine Club of Canada (*Canadian Alpine Journal*, 1907–40). In fact, Mrs. Elizabeth Parker of Winnipeg, Manitoba, was a cofounder of the Alpine Club of Canada (Wheeler, 1944) which was the first to admit women as regular members. The accounts written by women (Blum, 1980; Cameron, 1909; Crawford, 1909; Pilley, 1935; Schaffer, 1960) describe their own resistance to cultural norms about women, acknowledge the function and efforts of guides and support people, and speak often and passionately about connecting with the natural world. Mary E. Crawford (1909) wrote:

There is no recreation which, in all its aspects of surrounding and exercise, will bring about a quicker rejuvenation of worn out nerves, tired brains and flabby muscles than mountaineering. It is for women one of the new things under the sun and every fresh mountain is a new delight. . . . Diseases of the imagination cannot be discovered anywhere on a mountain side, where Nature asserts herself so grandly to the consciousness and with such insistence that the "ego" with its troubles sinks out of sight.

A history of mountain climbing based solely on accounts by men has left invisible the courage of women, their resistance and redefinition of societal norms related to gender roles, and their drive to connect with the natural environment for health, psychological, social, and spiritual benefits.

Multiple Roles, Relationships, and Leisure

The move to a more complex conception of leisure has major implications for the intersection of leisure, women, and nature. As mentioned, many women do not easily separate their multiple roles or choose leisure over commitments to family and society. This perspective may be attributed to the fact that there is no time or resources in many women's lives for leisure. Or it may be attributed to the fact that the definition of leisure does not include constructs of self defined by relationships and other connections.

Many leisure scholars build upon the early writings of philosophers such as Plato and Aristotle (Goodale and Godbey, 1988) to define the meaning and significance of leisure. Even within this tradition, a different concept of leisure might emerge if the writings of early women philosophers (Waithe, 1987, 1989) provided the starting point. Within the historical context of Greek and Roman society, the ideals of freedom may not have applied equally or symmetrically to women circumscribed by relationships and obligations. Many early women philosophers (Waithe and Harper, 1987), such as Theano II and Perictione II of the Pythagorean school, concentrated on the principle of *harmonia*. This concept was developed and explored within the contexts of marital fidelity, child rearing, parental piety, religious worship, and public demeanor appropriate for women. Notice how these contexts might lead scholars to address multiple roles and obligations for both women and men. If leisure philosophy included early women philosophers, leisure conceptual systems might include a focus on relationships or a concept of self situated within relationships and nature. Oliva de Sabuco (1888), a Spanish philosopher of the 1500s, connected leisure with the pursuit of health. Sabuco believed that imagination influenced health positively. She associated the development of imagination with leisure and stated that leisure should be varied and interspersed within an individual's life to avoid boredom and nurture health (Sabuco, 1888; Waithe, 1989)

Current leisure research on European–North American women (Freysinger, 1992; Henderson, Bialeschki, Shaw, and Freysinger, 1989) indicates that these women place a primary emphasis on relationships and social interaction. Freysinger and Flannery (1992) discovered through a qualitative research project that some women in the United States find leisure to provide the opportunity and space for affiliation with other women. Leisure therefore enhances family, friendships, and interactions with others. The women did not resist being wife, partner, or mother, but rather resisted being limited to these roles and the devaluation of these roles and themselves. Through leisure, these women sought to strengthen the relationships, provide role models for children, and develop and maintain friendships. Leisure that was self-determined allowed the women to become aware of and express themselves in new and different ways. In turn, such awareness and expression enabled these women to feel better about themselves and challenge or participate in other activities. In this sense, leisure was empowering—a means of resisting devaluation of self and determining new affirmations of themselves and their roles. By exploring other concepts and interpretations of leisure, we make visible how women contextualize leisure in different ways, operate within a world of multiple roles and obligations, resist oppression and gender-limiting traditions, connect with the natural environment, and develop gender-specific leisure strategies.

The Value of Difference

Expressions of cultural and ethnic identity may occur more frequently in domains of leisure, play, sport, and arts because of such characteristics as enjoyment, relaxation, and free choice. Preliminary results in a study of leisure and ethnic identity (Aguilar, 1990) discovered a link between ethnic identity and leisure participation. Eidheim (1969) found that expression of ethnic identity varied from one context or social situation to another. Cultural festivals, for example, are contexts where the expression of ethnicity and valued cultural characteristics are supported and reinforced. Within this context and relationships, cultural identity could be enhanced. On the other hand, wearing traditional clothing to an office may not be reinforced. Allison (1988) discovered that the rules for expressing cultural identity differed between public and private and instrumental and expressive purposes. Furthermore, the rules are negotiated both within and among ethnic groups.

Allison (1988) proposes that one approach to increasing pluralism within leisure is to begin focusing on the role, nature, and meaning of leisure within different cultural groups. Anthropological writings (e.g., Hall, 1984; Lakoff, 1987) would indicate that the basic concepts (i.e., time, freedom, space, activity) are perceived differently across cultural boundaries and often complicate the application of concepts and definitions across these boundaries. Welch (1991) would maintain that material interaction among people and species provides the only way to be ethical because it enhances our knowledge related to our perspectives and provides a counterpoint and reference. For instance, the role leisure plays in resisting societal standards of normality is visible only when one studies leisure and marginalized populations such as women and aboriginal cultures.

This lack of material interaction is especially relevant to the discussion of nature and leisure. Much has been written about the benefits of leisure for the individual or society, the requirements for achievement and social interaction, and the health and leisure connection (Compton and Iso-Ahola, 1994). It is rare to discover a piece about a relationship with nature outside a role as a backdrop, place to hold an event, or resource that contributes to the human recreational experience. Recent writings have looked more closely at spiritual benefits, which may include a place for nature. If leisure is a focus or connection with nature for women, it is crucial to examine this relationship and how it may be supported or inhibited by the philosophy and frameworks inherent in current leisure philosophy and practice. The gap in this area leaves the accomplishments and relationships of women with nature invisible (e.g., women mountain climbers or naturalists) and sustains barriers between women and nature.

Emerging Theory

Leisure scholars are searching, through research and scholarly dialogue, for a more complex and vital understanding of leisure theory and praxis. Ecofeminism reconceives theory as including emerging patterns of meaning from storytelling or first-person narratives about women and nature. Different patterns emerge from the voices of women and other groups not normally included in leisure philosophy and theory, and they are crucial in this time of exploration and development. For example, women resisting political and physical violence provide another association between leisure, resisting violence, and connecting with nature for health and wholeness.

The poetry of Julia Esquivel (1982), an exiled Guatemalan, pieces together themes of resistance, community, nature, and religious insights. The poetry of Esquivel is about the struggle of people to survive, endure oppression, find joy in the midst of struggle and pain, and eventually become free. Connected with the dream of freedom is the ability to sustain one's own identity and celebrate that identity and life. Therefore, within the struggle for life is a struggle for moments of celebration, enjoyment, and leisure. For many indigenous women that celebration includes a connection to the earth because of its ability to sustain life and provide sustenance and a connection to those people who had fallen in the struggle.

In her poem "When the Dawn Breaks," Esquivel touches on elements that will be present when the violence is ended and a new day, or "dawn," begins for the people of Guatemala. The poem is about El Quiche, an area in Guatemala with a history of violence and oppression of indigenous people and traditions. Esquival interweaves moments of relaxation and enjoyment with the need for retribution, atonement, and justice.

When the Dawn Breaks
Julia Esquivel

We must be up early to hasten the coming of dawn,
to behold even sooner the rising of the sun.
There in Bijolon the marimba will laugh,
because the boys
will be tickling her sides.
We will hear once again the song of the birds
greeting the new day
near the waterfall.
We must see the corn fields flower
in Salaquil Grande.
We will eat boxbol again
and climb up to Xeucalbitz,
where we once made soup from the jutes
gathered in the stream.
Near the fire we will hear the women laugh
as they throw tortillas on the hot comal.
We will return to Trapichito
and hear the fireworks
once again announce
the celebration of the Holy Mass,
the true mass where there will be bread and wine for everyone.
We must return to Parramos
and pick fresh watercress at the creek,
and while we eat, we will hear the murmur of the stream
recounting the secrets of those who sow the seed.
When the dawn breaks
everything will be different,
the children will know
the taste of real milk
and their parents can return to school;
those who left it as children in order not to die of hunger.
We will enter Chajul
without seeing any military police,
those from the army of the rich
who now obey the orders
of the uniformed gorillas.
We will return to the Ixcan
hand in hand with Mario Jujia
and we will kneel and kiss the ground

which safeguards the hearts of the martyrs of '75.
We will clasp the hand of the orphans,
and listen to the echo of the footsteps
of the beggars who followed the Star
and mocked Herod.
When the dawn breaks
we will recognize them by their walk.
However, to ensure the breaking of dawn,
we must tenderly care for this pregnancy,
we must hurry along,
we must act before sleep overtakes us and anticipate
the absurd plans of the uniformed gorillas.
The Nation's sky has become very dark,
but the light of day is near,
God will help those who arise early
and it will dawn all the sooner for them.
We will gather again round the fire,
and the small hands of the children
will never again be ice-cold.
The tapeworms will no longer eat at
the families of the poor,
when the dawn breaks.
The soldiers will no longer take the keys
to the cooperative;
the children's fear will vanish
because they will go to the school in the new parish.
When the dawn breaks,
widows will beget new families,
but for now we must arise early
in order to hasten the new day.
Then rifles will no longer bash in our teeth
trying to quiet our screams
and soldiers will never again take Chepe away
and dump his body near El Boqueron.
No longer will they step on us,
raping the young girls
and dancing with our women.
We will no longer sow
for them to eat;
they will no longer steal our animals
to gorge their bellies.
when the dawn breaks.
Soon now,
the soothsayers will begin
beating on their drums
at the Great Reunion of Momostenango,

and prayer and smoke
will rise above us all.
Now, those who killed
the favorites of the Great Grandmother
will get what they really deserve, for now the Great Judgment
will begin and we are going to do them in.
He who stands above the world
has already smelled the odor of their burned bodies
in his very nostrils.
Now, a great rage
will descend from the mountain
from whence our victory is finally coming!
"God raises up the poor from the mire."
The powerful will fall flat on their faces,
those who cried will laugh satisfied,
and everything will return to what it was before.
When the dawn breaks.

Esquivel works with a sense of anticipation for a celebration, for freedom and for retribution. Leisure becomes the setting and celebration (e.g., marimbas, tickling her sides, fireworks). The relationship between humans and the natural environment surfaces within the poem as places to go (e.g, near the waterfall, gathered in a stream, light of day), the origin of the people of El Quiche (e.g., favorites of Great Grandmother), the connection to people who have died (e.g., the ground which safeguards), and the traditions of the past (e.g., secrets of those who sow the seed). Her poetry makes clear that all of these are relevant and necessary for surviving the violence and celebrating life.

One might overlook the significance and power of the context of leisure in two of Alice Walker's (1988) short stories, "Blue" and "Everything Is a Human Being." Both stories explore how humans oppress and devalue other humans and species. It is important to notice that the initial encounters and context for contemplating the themes are leisure-centered. Walker encounters and communicates with a tree in a park, a horse named Blue during walks in the country, and a snake while gardening for relaxation. Walker moves from this beginning to discuss the results of distance between humans and between humans and other species.

And then, occasionally, when he [Blue] came up for apples, or I took apples to him, he looked at me. It was a look so piercing, so full of grief, a look so human, I almost laughed (I felt too sad to cry) to think there are people who do not know that animals suffer. People like me who have forgotten, and daily forget, all that animals try to tell us. "Everything you do to us will happen to you; we are your teachers, as you are ours. We are one lesson" is essentially it, I think. There are those who never once have even considered animals' rights: those who have been taught that animals actually want to be used and abused by us, as small children "love" to be frightened, or women "love" to be mutilated and raped . . . (7–8)

Within a leisure context, Walker is able to interact with Blue, contemplate the meaning of the relationship and Blue's life, and lead us into a political discussion about how we treat each other and animals.

Inclusivity and Social Responsibility

The quilt of ecological feminism emerges from the voices and designs of women, indigenous people, and others who have been marginalized, and the pieces on the quilt are those that express a respectful connection between nature and women. Many of these pieces are highlighted by leisure practices and contexts. As we add pieces to the quilt, it is important to examine how leisure has been used to oppress women and nature as well as how women use leisure to resist violence and oppression and celebrate life.

Beckers (1990a and b) examined how the government of Hitler used leisure to reinforce the values of the state and indoctrinate young people into a set of values. Dewer (1990) links the leisure activities within residential homes for aboriginal children from northern Canada to the attempts of the teachers and administrators to "civilize" and "acculturate" aboriginal children into white society. In some sense, the motto was "play and pray white and Christian." Some activities, such as sports for young aboriginal males, could later be correlated with a young man's rise in leadership. On the other hand, leisure activities for young girls reinforced a domesticity within the home inappropriate to aboriginal family patterns and behavior.

Leisure programming with specific services and activities implies an institutional structure, expert knowledge held by a professional, and direct provision of leisure to the client. Heron (1991) argues that this structure reflects the European-American technological and linear bias. As a culture becomes more institutionalized, it acquires rational and technical values and loses expressive and creative values. Whether it be the "sacred time" of some cultures or "womantime" for some women, a structured, linear, and programmed leisure may be inappropriate and destructive to specific cultural patterns of leisure. Rosenzweig (1983) suggests that workers have long "fought for control" over their own leisure because leisure has often been an arena of class struggle outside the workplace. Therefore organized, competitive team sports may take precedence over other informal activities and begin to change or create generational conflict based on the difference between competition values in sports and cooperative values of family and community.

Some leisure practices can be oppressive to women and nature alike. The increase in the number of people visiting natural areas has created impact problems for the environment and for people living near the environment (Hammitt and Cole, 1987). The rise in consumptive outdoor pursuits such as motorboating, snowmobiling, and driving off-road vehicles has damaged many fragile ecosystems. Ecotourism is growing in popularity even as local people are suffering and natural areas declining from the same activity.

Clarke and Critcher (1985) have demonstrated that leisure has become an integral part of the structure of capitalist society in terms of time allotment, financial expenditure, and economic market segments. Alan Thein Durning (1992) of the Worldwatch Institute questioned the morality and environmental consciousness of supporting shopping malls as a valued leisure activity. He notes that the mall-centered lifestyle "requires enormous and continuous inputs of the very commodities that are most damaging to the earth to produce." This consumption destroys natural habitats such as the rainforest in other parts of the world, demands and creates cheap labor pools especially of women, and seems never ending. Consumerism, no matter how tastefully trimmed with green, seems to be a recipe for ecological decline and the destruction of women and entire cultures.

Leisure programs and structures, far from being value neutral, have changed individual lives and interpersonal relationships and influenced cultural adaptation. Leisure must be taken seriously as an economic, cultural, sociological, and psychological force in the lives of women.

A reexamination of a self-leisure relationship (Gunter, 1987; Stebbins, 1982; Kleiber et al., 1986) may be particularly relevant to women and marginalized groups. The narratives of women who emigrate from Central America to Canada experience mental and physical health challenges ranging from depression to weight gain to isolation. They encounter difficulties accessing recreation because what is acceptable and supported in their country of origin does not exist in Canada; they do not have the time, finances, or transportation necessary to attend; the recreation requires a separation from the family; and leisure is considered unimportant in relation to work and family obligations by both the host government and the women themselves. Thus Yeo and Yeo's (1981) conclusion that the real danger lies in "underpoliticizing leisure" is highly relevant to women and leaves them without access to leisure, good health, and positive relationships. Like the barely visible quilting stitch, it becomes noticeable when it unravels and the quilt or woman' s life no longer holds together.

Reconceiving Humans and Human Ethical Behavior

Leisure is often the context for maintaining mental and physical health, expressing oneself, making friends, creating positive communities, and celebrating life. Play, intimately related to leisure and recreation, is the basis, for development of children and all cultures, including some animal cultures, use play to educate and connect with their young (Piers, 1972). However, as demonstrated in this chapter, leisure can promote a variety of values that include oppression, exclusion, and violence. If we do not pay careful attention to both the positive and negative influences of the structure, organization, and implementation of leisure, we risk oppressing others and doing violence to ourselves, others, and nature. Therefore it is important and relevant to ecofeminism to carefully examine the phenomenon of leisure.

McAvoy (1990) and Dustin (1990) wrote an initial framework for an environmental ethic for leisure and recreation professionals. They advocated choosing activities that are less consumptive and more respectful toward natural environments. This initial step needs to be pursued and needs to include gender-specific patterns of women's leisure, the role of natural environments in people's mental and physical health, and the differences across cultures in terms of relationships among humans and between humans and the natural environment.

Leisure informs ecofeminist philosophy and theory about a vital component of our lives. Although there is no one, adequate definition of leisure, the different concepts and perspectives provide us with valuable clues to the significance of leisure. On the other hand, each of these perspectives needs to be carefully evaluated for its sensitivity toward women and nature. If we overlook the function of leisure, even with all its attendant flaws and gaps, we risk losing a vital force within women's lives—a force that helps them regenerate, maintain mental and physical health, express themselves, resist oppression, and connect with the natural environment.

Leisure plays a significant role in the lives of women and supports their connection with nature. However, a more complete understanding of leisure is important for the health and survival of women and their connection to the natural world; it needs further examination relevant to the tenets of ecological feminism. It is essential that we understand the more subtle patterns, interconnections, and differences if we are to give full significance to and support of women's leisure styles that are respectful and connected to the natural world.

The quilting stitch is sewn with needles called "betweens." So, leisure often occurs "between" activities, times, and experiences or within other structures and life elements (e.g., leisure at work). Leisure accents the pattern or design of the quilt of a woman's life. By bringing into focus or increasing the tension at specific stitches, the "puffs" can become more noticeable, especially when leisure involves a connection with nature or joyful resistance. Ecological feminism must take seriously leisure for women because it is a vital component of the health and well-being of women. It provides a means of self-determination, a connection with the natural environment and others, an inspiration for creativity and self-expression, and a potential for a more respectful connection with the natural environment.

For many women, leisure is intimately connected with relationships of sharing, trust, communicating, caring, and common action. Leisure is who they are as well as how they feel. As Kelly (1991, 9) states, "leisure is real action in the real world, action that may connect or alienate us from our selves and from others." It is not simple to define or nourish leisure, and for many it is not easy to capture even a moment of leisure. But its potential makes it worth the struggle. For many women, leisure is a quilting stitch that provides connection and accents patterns of community, development, self-affirmation, and respect of the natural environment. It is a way to be joyfully resistant and alive.

Notes

1. Warren (1990) created the metaphor of the "quilt of ecological feminism" to represent the conditions that would be included within an ecofeminist ethic. The necessary conditions, she writes, are "like the boundaries of a quilt or collage. They delimit the territory of the piece without dictating what the interior, the design, the actual pattern of the piece looks like. Because the actual design of the quilt emerges from the multiplicity of voices of women in a cross-cultural context, the design will change over time. It is not something static" (p. 139).

2. The leisure theories and concepts presented here represent those most commonly related to the discussion of ecofeminism and leisure. Each of them has inherent flaws related to cultural appropriateness; theory development in the fields of sociology, psychology, and so forth; and paradigm shifts. These theories and concepts are seen as part of the explanation of the phenomenon of leisure but are under current debate and revision within the leisure and recreation field.

3. Among the many feminist scholars who have discussed the problematic nature of dichotomies, hierarchical dualities, and a logic of domination are Warren (1990), Lugones (1991), Allison M. Jaggar (1991), John Shotter and Josephine Logan (1988), and Sharon Welch (1991).

4. Leisure scholars often categorize periods of history according to the dominant value related to work or leisure. For instance, leisure was highly valued in Greek society as it related to learning and virtue. Slaves and women performed work so that free men could pursue public and intellectual pursuits. The value of leisure declined after the Middle Ages, in part because of Calvin's and Luther's critique of the Catholic Church and the rise of the industrial state. In each case, either work or leisure was seen as the more valued state in opposition to the other. In addition, either pursuit was attributed to a particular class and level of privilege, which complicates the analysis.

5. *Self* is used in this discussion as it relates to the specific psychological and socio-logical theories of self used to support this concept of leisure. As such, it is a definition that is essentialist in nature. The critique and discussion of this concept of self is beyond the scope of this chapter.

6. For a complete discussion and detailed listing of the minimal conditions of eco-feminist philosophy, see Warren (1990).

7. In recent years, more biographies and autobiographies of women who have participated in adventure outdoor recreation have been published. These accounts indicate a very different ethic and perspective toward nature, the activities themselves, and the benefits derived from adventure outdoor recreation. There is still much analysis and interpretation necessary but it is obvious that many women were drawn to these activities as a means of connecting with nature.

References

Aguilar, T. E. (1990). The relationship of participation in ethnic leisure activity and strength of ethnic identity: Preliminary findings. *Proceedings of the Canadian Congress on Leisure Research*, May 9–12, 1990.

Allison, M. T. (1988). Breaking boundaries and barriers: Future directions in cross-cultural research. *Leisure Sciences* 10, 247–59.

Anzaldua, G., ed.. (1990). *Making face, making soul—Haciendo Caras: Creative and critical perspectives by women of color*. San Francisco: Aunt Lute Foundation.

Beckers, T. (1990a). Andries Sternheim and the study of leisure in the early critical theory. *Leisure Studies* 9, no. 3, 197–212.

———. (1990b). Leisure as oppression: Leisure policy and leisure science in a dangerous interlude. Keynote address for the Canadian Congress of Leisure Research. *Proceedings of the Canadian Congress on Leisure Research*, May 9–12, 1990.

Blum, A. (1980). *Annapurna: A woman's place*. San Francisco: Sierra Club.

Cameron, A.D. (1909). *The new north: An account of a woman's 1908 journey through Canada to the Arctic*. Lincoln: University of Nebraska Press.

Canadian Alpine Journal. (1907–40). Minutes of Summer Climbing Camps. Vol. 1–33.

Clarke, J., and Critcher, C. (1985). *The devil makes work: Leisure in capitalist Britain*. London: Macmillan.

Compton, D. M., and Iso-Ahola, S., eds.. (1994). *Leisure and mental health*. Park City, Utah: Family Development Resources.

Crawford, M. E. (1909). Mountain climbing for women. *Canadian Alpine Journal* 2, no. 1, 83–91.

Dawson, D. (1988). Social class in leisure: Reproduction and resistance. *Leisure Sciences* 10, 193–202.

Dewer, J. (1990). Presentation to the Faculty of Physical Education and Recreation Studies, University of Manitoba.

Durning, A. T. (1992). Shopping malls pose huge threat to this planet. *Winnipeg Free Press*, September 6.

Dustin, D. (1990). Looking inward to save the outdoors. *Parks and Recreation* 25, no. 9, 86–89.

Eidheim, H. (1969). When ethnic identity is a social stigma. In F. Barth, ed., *Ethnic groups and boundaries*. Boston: Little, Brown.

Esquivel, J. (1982). *Threatened with resurrection*. Elgin, Ill.: Brethren Press.

Freysinger, V. J., and Flannery, D. (1992). Women's leisure: Affiliation, self-determination, empowerment—and resistance? *Loisir et société/Society and Leisure*. 15, no. 1, 303–22.

Gonzalez, N. (1992). We are not conservationists. *Cultural Survival Quarterly* 16, no. 3, 43–46.

Goodale, T., & Godbey, G. (1988). *The evolution of leisure: Historical and philosophical perspectives*. State College, Pa.: Venture.

Gunter, B. G. (1987). The leisure experience: Selected properties. *Journal of Leisure Research* 19, no. 2, 115–30.

Hall, E. T. (1984). *The dance of life: The other dimension of time*. New York: Doubleday.

Hammitt, W. E., and Cole, D. N. (1987). *Wildland recreation: Ecology and management*. New York: Wiley.

Harrington, M. A. (1991). Time after work: Constraints on the leisure of working women. *Loisir et société/Society and Leisure* 14, no. 1, 115–32.

Henderson, K. A. (1989). Anatomy is not destiny: A feminist analysis of the scholarship on women's leisure. *Leisure Sciences* 12, 229–39.

——, and Bialeschki, M. D. (1991). A sense of entitlement to leisure as constraint and empowerment for women. *Leisure Sciences* 13, 51–65.

——, Bialeschki, M. D., Shaw, S. M., and Freysinger, V. J. (1989). *A leisure of one's own: A feminist perspective on women's leisure*. University Park, Pa.: Venture.

——, Stalnaker, D., and Taylor, G. (1988). The relationship between barriers to recreation and gender-role personality traits for women. *Journal of Leisure Research* 20, no. 1, 69–80.

Heron, R. P. (1991). The institutionalization of leisure: Cultural conflict and hegemony. *Loisir et société/Society and Leisure* 14, no. 1, 171–90.

Hollands, R. (1988). Leisure, work and working-class cultures: The case of leisure on the shop floor. In Cantelon, H., and Hollands, R., eds., *Leisure, Sport and Working-Class Cultures: Theory and History*. Toronto: Garamond, 17–40.

Howe, C. Z., and Rancourt, A. M. (1990). The importance of definitions of selected concepts for leisure inquiry. *Leisure Sciences* 12, 395–406.

Jaggar, A. M. (1991). Feminist ethics: Projects, problems, prospects. In C. Card, ed., *Feminist ethics*. Lawrence: University Press of Kansas.

Kelly, J. R. (1982). Leisure in later life: Roles and identities. In N. J. Osgood, ed., *Life after work: Retirement, leisure, recreation, and the elderly*. New York: Praeger, 268–94.

——. (1991). Counterpoints in the sociology of leisure. Paper presented at NRPA Research Symposium, Baltimore, October.

Kleiber, D., Larson, R., and Csikszentmihalyi, M. (1986). The experience of leisure in adolescence. *Journal of Leisure Research* 18, no. 3, 169–76.

Lakoff, G. (1987). *Women, fire, and dangerous things: What categories reveal about the mind*. Chicago: University of Chicago Press.

Lugones, M. C. (1991). On the logic of pluralist feminism. In C. Card, ed., *Feminist Ethics*. Lawrence: University Press of Kansas.

McAvoy, L. (1990). An environmental ethic for parks and recreation. *Parks and Recreation* 25, no. 9, 68–72.

Menchu, R. (1989). *I . . . Rigoberta Menchu: An Indian woman in Guatemala*. London: Verso Press.

Neulinger, J. (1981). *The psychology of leisure*. Springfield, Ill.: Charles Thomas.

———. (1982). Leisure lack and the quality of life: The broadening scope of the leisure professional. *Leisure Studies* 1, 53–63.

———. (1984). Key questions evoked by a state of mind conceptualization of leisure. *Loisir et Société/Society and Leisure* 7, no. 1, 25–36.

Pieper, J. (1963). *Leisure: The basis of culture*. New York: New American Library.

Piers, M. W., ed. (1972). *Play and development*. New York: Norton.

Pilley, D. (1935). *Climbing days*. London: Hogarth.

Rancourt, A. M. (1986). What is the role of leisure in the undergraduate park, recreation, and leisure curriculum? *SPRE Annual on Education* 1, 65–76.

Robertson, J. (1990). *The magnificent mountain women: Adventure in the Colorado Rockies*. Lincoln: University of Nebraska Press.

Rosenzweig, R. (1983). *Eight hours for what we will: Workers and leisure in an industrial city 1870–1920*. Cambridge: Cambridge University Press.

Sabuco, O. de (1888). *Obras*. Madrid: Ricado Fe.

Samdahl, D. M. (1988). A symbolic interactionist model of leisure: Theory and empirical support. *Leisure Sciences* 10, no. 1, 27–39.

———. (1992). Leisure in our lives: Exploring the common leisure occasion. *Journal of Leisure Research* 24, no. 1, 19–32.

Schaffer, M. T. S. (1990). *A hunter of peace*. Banff: Whyte Museum of the Canadian Rockies.

Shaw, S. M. (1985) The meaning of leisure in everyday life. *Leisure Sciences* 7, no. 1, 1–24.

———. (1990). Where has all the leisure gone? The distribution and redistribution of leisure. In Smale, B. J. A., ed, *Proceedings of the Canadian Congress on Leisure Research*, May 9–12, 1990, 1–4.

———. (1991). Research note: Women's leisure time—using time budget data to examine current trends and future predictions. *Leisure Studies* 10, no. 2, 171–81.

Shotter, J., and Logan J. (1988). The pervasiveness of patriarchy: On finding a different voice. In M. M. Gergen, ed., *Feminist thought and the structure of knowledge*. New York: New York University Press, 69–86.

Smith, C. (1989). *Off the beaten track: Women adventurers and mountaineers in western Canada*. Jasper, Alberta: Coyote.

Smith-Ayala, E. (1991). *The granddaughters of Ixmucane: Guatemalan women speak*. Toronto: Women's Press.

Stebbins, R. A. (1982). Serious leisure: A conceptual statement. *Pacific Sociological Review* 25, no. 2, 252–72.

Thomson, M. (1986). *Women of El Salvador: The price of freedom*. London: Zed Books.

Waithe, M. E., ed. (1987). *A history of women philosophers*. Vol. 1. Boston: Kluwer.

———. (1989). *A history of women philosophers*. Vol. 2. Boston: Kluwer.

——, and Harper, V. L. (1987). Late Pythagoreans: Theano II and Perictione II. In Waithe, M. E., ed., *A history of women philosophers*, vol. 1, 41-58.

Walker, A. (1988). *Selected writings 1973-1987*. New York: Harcourt Brace Jovanovich, 3-8, 139-52.

Warren, K. J. (1988). Critical thinking and feminism. *Informal Logic* X, no. 1, 31-42.

——. (1990). The power and the promise of ecological feminism. *Environmental Ethics* 12, no. 2, 125-46.

Wearing, B., and Wearing, S. (1988). "All in a day's leisure": Gender and the concept of leisure. *Leisure Studies* 7, no. 2, 11-123.

Welch, S. D. (1991). *A feminist ethic of risk*. Minneapolis: Fortress Press.

Wheeler, A. O. (1944). In memoriam: Elizabeth Parker. *Canadian Alpine Journal* 29, no. 1, 122-27.

Yeo, E., and Yeo, S., eds. (1981). *Popular culture and class conflict 1590-1914: Explorations in the history of labour and leisure*. Sussex: Harvester.

Ten

Ecofeminism and Work

Robert Alan Sessions

You can see the headlines almost daily, and they have come to echo a common fear and a way of thinking: "Spotted Owl vs. 20,000 Jobs," "Push for Wetlands Threatens Iowa Farms," "Ranchers Fight the Prairie Dog," "Brazilian Peasants Struggle against the Jungle," "Will Conservation Measures Eliminate Jobs?"[1] We are told we have to choose, and given this unhappy either/or situation, most Americans, probably usually reluctantly, side with humans against animals or plants or soil or an ecosystem. Many environmentalists contend the scales should tip the other way; but whichever side people take, conceptually and practically the die seems cast: we must choose *either* jobs *or* the environment.

Environmentalists, while growing in numbers, are a rather weak voice in this conflict. In America no politician could rise to national prominence who advocated reducing jobs or a no-growth economy in order to preserve or recreate a healthy environment. Our dominant economic paradigm is one where growth ("within certain limits," it is said) is an automatic good and development is the main fuel that stokes the fires of this growth. For most people the practical bottom line is jobs: developers take the raw materials of the earth, be it minerals or air, land or ideas, and turn them into jobs. In this value-added process, through human labor something of lesser value is turned into a product (or used to produce a product) of greater value. In the supercharged and too often unanalyzed system of values built into our economic reckoning, the revered bottom line dominates: things are valued for their contribution to the economy. From within this system we tend to think of economic values such as costs and benefits, profits and efficiency, instead of environmental values such as biodiversity, ecosystemic health, homeostasis or the inherent worth of natural beings.

Thus even when the "environment" in some sense wins, environmentalists find themselves in the awkward position of being perceived as against development and jobs, and hence perceived as being against the well-being of workers and their families.[2] The conceptual framework of jobs versus the environment is so widely used and is such a powerful ideological tool that clearheadedness about the issues involved is precluded and practical solutions that do more than create an uneasy truce or "pragmatic compromise" are as rare as members of an endangered species. Even most environmentally conscious people, who realize that industrial economies are the major source of environmental degradation in the modern world, still feel the pull of jobs against the environment; and although increasing numbers of people see that excesses such as consumerism, mindless technological use, and viewing growth economics as an automatic good must be ended if environmental health is to be preserved, few are able to extract themselves from the force of this framework of choice. I believe the reason this dualism is so powerful is that the peculiar jobs system found in the United States and other industrialized nations, and the economic and social systems of which it is a part, are the loci of many of the central values and conceptual frameworks of our culture. Without satisfactory conceptual and practical resolutions of the jobs/environment conflict, the outlook for convivial communities that include healthy natural environments is dim.

Jobs versus the Environment: A False
Dichotomy . . . and Dangerous Besides

Practically, our environmental destructiveness is absurd. In the pursuit of the good life our way of living and working destroys the very basis of the good life we seek.[3] For example, in Iowa, where I live, farmers for a century have been "mining" the soil in such a way that the "gold" (topsoil) literally has been washed to the sea. The tall grass prairie that covered Iowa for eons laid up two to six feet of rich topsoil, and in most places that legacy has been reduced to a few inches (in some areas only subsoil remains). Iowa farmers have always cared deeply about themselves, their families, and their offspring, and about the land that supports their lives. Yet they have become a part of a way of working that requires them to destroy the "ground of their being," the soil that sustains their livelihood and their lives. Iowa farms, like farms everywhere in industrialized societies, have, as Marx predicted nearly a century and a half ago, become industrialized. Wendell Berry calls this great transformation in farm culture the change from agri-culture to agri-business,[4] and agribusiness has the farm version of what I call the modern jobs system.

My Iowa illustration can help us see further dimensions of the practical and conceptual issues that underlie the jobs/environment conflict. The farming practices of Iowa farmers, especially since the rise of chemical farming after the Second World War, have sullied the waters farmers, their families, and their livestock drink (and, of course, drinking water for non-farmers has been poisoned as well). Many farmers[5] and their helpers and families have become ill from being near these "necessary ingredients" in this way of farming. Furthermore, in rural America, as in Third World countries everywhere,[6] women (and children), especially poor women and women of color, are harmed disproportionately to the rest of the population. Thus, as I shall argue in the next section, agricultural practices are feminist issues.

As farming has become increasingly mechanized, allowing one farmer today to do the work of 100 or more farmers a century ago, Iowa farmers are seeing their families and communities disintegrate.[7] And as the increasingly "irrelevant" (according to the values of agribusiness) children, women, and farm workers leave rural America in droves, they expand the potential work forces in cities where technological advances have decreased the number of jobs, especially production jobs, for urban dwellers. Thus the jobs system of agribusiness not only is responsible for the erosion of family farms, rural communities, and general rural well-being, as well as environmental degradation in rural America; it has also contributed to those same problems in towns and cities across the country.

Still further absurdities abound in this all-too-familiar story. In order to stay afloat in the current agricultural economy, farmers need to produce ever more crops.[8] They do this by pushing their land and livestock to their limits; they put more land into production; and, as an extension of the second strategy, farmers, behaving as corporations (which they usually are), buy each other out and gain the advantages of "economies of scale." As agriculture becomes increasingly "efficient" (according to this economic model) Iowa farms can reach 4,000 acres, and rural neighborhoods and the small towns that support farmers slip into oblivion as rural populations and economic activities decline.[9]

Consider briefly some features of this decline of rural culture.[10] Through increased mechanization American farm work has not become much less dangerous than it was a century ago, but it has become lonelier.[11] Instead of farming being a very social and communal activity as it was a century ago in America, or as it still is especially in societies with strong female peasant agriculture systems, most farming today is done in isolation. In pre-agribusiness times rural communities formed and thrived on shared needs, work, materials, and joys and sorrows. Today farmers increasingly are supported by their banks and machines rather than their neighbors and friends. In rural America solitariness is replacing the solidarity of old-style farm communities. Furthermore, farmers' families have become smaller and less close-knit as the locus of social life has shifted from home and neighborhood to area schools, towns, cities, and national cultural life (through electronic media especially). As farm work (like work throughout our economy) became industrialized, as farming became less centered in home economics and more tied to the marketplace, the new division of labor separated men's work from women's work, and children from parents. Fewer and fewer farm families work side by side at common and complementary labor; instead, increasingly the economic as well as the social and cultural activities of farm families are scattered and disintegrated.[12] The proverbial idyllic life of the American Jeffersonian yeoman farmer, a life of hard, honest, and convivial work done in close families and communities, insofar as it ever existed, is, for the most part, a relic of the past.[13] The cultural, social, and spiritual life of rural America has been transformed because of the new jobs system of agribusiness.

A parallel disintegration has occurred in the relationships between farmers and their land. While perhaps agriculture, as seen from a Paleolithic view of the earth as *magna mater*,[14] has always involved violation of the land (many Amerindians, e.g., believed that to plow is to violate the natural integrity of the land), in the Christian West agriculture, until the Industrial Revolution, at least came under the value system of "shepherding," of land as sacred trust, and therefore farm work was seen as a sacred activity.[15] With industrialization of agriculture, especially with the post-World War II move to agribusiness, the "sentimental" view of farming as a sacred trust disappeared from all except the necromantic movements "back to the land" during various decades of this century. In the agribusiness system, if one is to succeed in farming, land, animals, and people must be seen mainly or solely in terms of their economic values: as inputs and outputs, resources and commodities, not as Bessie or golden waves of grain. To use Marx's language, modern agribusiness has driven a wedge between the farm worker and the processes, means, and products of production. *His* land and animals, like *his* family and community (his "species existence"), increasingly are alienated from the farmer and he from them.

While obviously there is much more to be said about this complex and evolving jobs system of agribusiness, what I have discussed thus far should have made several things clear. First, given the agribusiness system of production, the disintegration of families and communities and the sexism inherent in modern farming are intimately connected with the environmental degradation found in contemporary farming practices. The underlying logic[16] of these practices precludes noneconomic values most farmers probably believe in: when a premium is put on economic growth, competition, and a reduction to "bottom line" values, the world becomes "despiritualized,"[17] other dimensions such as the joy of work or aesthetic values become secondary if not irrelevant, and even family and community life are valuable only insofar as they contribute to economic life as it is narrowly conceived in modern economic systems. However noble or desirable their ends, the means farmers "choose" (or were forced to accept in order to perform and keep their jobs, such as the heavy use of chemicals or cultivating highly erodable land) ultimately are contradictory to their goals. To their credit, many farmers realize that in farming, as in the rest of life, any ultimate distinction between means and ends is a mistake, and many farmers have tried and are trying to find alternative ways of working that do not destroy the environment or community and family. Some farmers have succeeded to some extent in their attempts to farm in ways that do not destroy their soil and their chosen ways of life, but the system is very large, very entrenched, and very powerful.

A second point that this example illustrates is that the modern jobs system, which pits jobs against the environment, is a recent invention. Other people at other times, and farmers within and outside of American agribusiness today, have made their livings in ways that did not generate the degree of alienation from people and land, nor the environmental degradation, that our modern agricultural jobs system tends to produce. Furthermore, the fact that this system is an invention, however intractable it might seem at the moment, can give us real hope: we could, if properly organized and clearheaded, create a different system. Before turning to the task of attempting to describe an environmentally and socially more satisfactory work system, I believe we will be better equipped to do so if we can comprehend how bizarre our modern jobs system actually is.

The Modern Jobs System: Environmentally, Socially, and Economically Dysfunctional

Karen J. Warren (1990) describes patriarchy as a dysfunctional system:

> In a *functional* system, the rules and roles tend to be clear, respectful, negotiable; they can be revised, negotiated, changed. Problems tend to be openly acknowledged and resolved. In a *dysfunctional* system, the rules tend to be confused and covert, rigid and unchanging. A high value tends to be placed on control; dysfunctional systems tend to display an exaggerated rationality and focus on rule-governed reason. . . . Dysfunctional systems are often maintained through systematic denial . . . [and] this denial need not be conscious, intentional, or malicious . . . furthermore, dysfunctional social systems often leave their members feeling powerless or helpless to make any significant changes. (125)

I would add that a dysfunctional system is marked by its inability to meet the real needs of those whom it is meant to serve—it is an inherently flawed system. Warren alludes to this striking feature (striking because even though a dysfunctional system fails over and over to deliver what it promises, people keep the system) when she says, "When patriarchy is understood as a dysfunctional system, this 'unmanageability' [patriarchy cannot 'manage its affairs equitably and justly'] can be seen for what it is—a predictable consequence of patriarchy" (129).

As a first attempt to comprehend the dysfunctionality of our jobs system, consider what Andre Gorz calls "compensatory consumption" (chap. 1). Each of us has practiced compensatory consumption. Some of us compensate for the pain of a conflict by eating some "sinful" food or drinking a soothing beverage. Others go shopping and compensate for a loss or some suffering with an item of clothing, a new record, or an automobile. Not all of our compensatory behavior is undesirable, of course, and by no means are we always compensating for what happens (or does not happen) on our jobs. Nevertheless, according to Gorz, a great deal of what people today compensate for is work related, whether from stress or lack of meaning on the job or from other problematic dimensions of their lives that are related to work. Furthermore, since much compensatory behavior is consumptive and therefore usually costs money, the amount of work we must do increases as we engage in further compensatory consumption. The circle of work and consumption comes full around and speeds up with every turn.

Add to this psycho-logic of work and compensatory consumption the huge motivational machinery of modern public relations,[18] which from the perspective of dysfunctionality plays the dual roles of the enabler and the tempter, and we have a powerful trap. If modern workers want to participate in the goods of their society and culture, they must do work that is to a great measure inherently unsatisfying of their real needs, and advertising tells them what they should want to meet those needs, even though what they thus come to want cannot do so. It seems that on the one hand advertisers do not want people actually to be satisfied; rather, they want people continually to have the insatiable desires of the modern economic myth and to buy their products. But on the other hand, it is crucial that compensatory consumers feel their wants are their own. How else could people believe they were "free" when they were acting like addicts in a dysfunctional system? (In her discussion of patriarchy as a dysfunctional system, Warren focuses on how such a set of beliefs is crucial for the overall system to operate.) Thus without this enabling belief structure ("consuming frees me to express and create myself"), people might begin to see how contrary to their real needs compensatory consumption really is.

Although both men and women in America practice compensatory consumption, not surprisingly women are the chief targets of advertisers. This happens, I believe, both because women have been given the support role—they are assigned to play "back up" (Illich calls this "shadow work")—and because women's exclusions from male sources of meaning and power have left them especially vulnerable to compensatory consumption. As a result of their supportive and secondary roles in this system, women not only buy most of the goods needed for running the household, but also are the main consumers of diets, plastic surgery, cosmetics, and other forms of personal feel-better consumption.

A second way to probe the dysfunctionality of our jobs system is to look at what leisure has become for us. In an essay in this volume (chapter 9), Karen Fox shows that the conception and practice of leisure can reveal a great deal about a culture's work. In our patriarchal jobs system, work that is typically done by women as supporters of men commonly is not viewed as real (paid) work at all but as "women's" (unpaid) work, thus giving men "freedom" from work called leisure, but leaving women's work and leisure in the shadows of unclarity. Leisure within this patriarchal system becomes a form of hegemony: since only men work, then only men need leisure because women never really work (and thus have to "work" while men are at leisure). In certain respects this changes when women join the jobs-for-pay part of our jobs system, but women often clearly are damned if they do work on paying jobs as well as if they do not: working women continue to do most of the shadow work (all the work needed to run a household and to keep the family's workers on the job) after their jobs are done, and often they still feel as if they are slighting the children (child care is "women's work," after all).

This system is not only dysfunctional for women, however; men, too, suffer from lack of real leisure. Fox argues that real leisure should not be defined and valued in terms of "freedom" from working; instead we should define it and gauge its worth in terms of caring relationships, play, and meaning (including self-expression). Many students of contemporary culture have noted that for all-too-many men as well as women, our leisure is more like putting salve on wounds than it is like play.[19]

Judith McGaw contends, in an article on the social history of modern work, that even though the modern jobs system is friendlier in many ways to men than to women, men also are wounded and stunted by it. McGaw believes that a major feature of industrialization was to change the geography of work from a situation where men and women both were "housebound," where they worked together in a home economics, to work done in "separate spheres" (men at the factory and women at home). She continues by saying that even though men's work done in their separate sphere was propped up by wages, relative to working at home, men suffered great loss: they lost the flexibility, interest, diversity, and craftsmanship of home work, and they gained industrial by-products such as boredom, alienation, and lack of opportunity to socialize and develop themselves. At the same time women, in their "inferior sphere" (which it was—and is—in terms of status, pay, respect, etc.), worked in highly relational ways on diverse tasks requiring advanced skills, and thus their personal and social strengths persisted while men's were weakened. McGaw makes the same point as

Warren concerning the contribution indigenous women could make if taken seriously instead of being dominated: if men (and women) could learn from what women still remember about working, communities, and nature, we would have the basis for much healthier communities (including nonhuman nature). And if Fox is correct that leisure should be based on caring relationships rather than on consumption and separation ("freedom"), women have a great deal to teach men about leisure.

Fox's greatest challenge, though, is to the work/leisure dichotomy itself. She points out that in many societies work and leisure were/are not separate. Both play time and work time were spent in social and playful ways,[20] thus cutting through our dichotomy of work and leisure. I will return to this suggestive point in the final section of this essay.

A third way to see the dysfunctionality of our jobs system is to think of how it distributes wealth. Adam Smith, surely a main architect of our current economic world, was a moral philosopher who, contrary to many advocates and opponents of capitalism, held no fancy for entrepreneurs. He granted mostly unlimited accumulation of wealth to capitalists in order that the poor be made better off; for Smith, the only virtue of unbridled material selfishness was as a means to the end of material betterment for ordinary people. Smith and the system he helped create gave a kind of promissory note: if you will be willing to put up with the hardships of work within industrial society, you will receive a substantial (and increasing?)[21] share of the wealth. For a short while in the United States and other industrialized societies, Smith's system seemed to work: access to good-paying jobs was fairly easy for "most" workers (except, of course, women, people of color, the handicapped, etc.) during several decades of this century. But with the onset of automation and the internationalization of the economy, the system's payoff on this promissory note was short-lived. Today fewer and fewer people in American and other industrialized societies have access, through jobs, to the ever-growing wealth produced. Thus at the heart of this system is an increasingly bizarre and unacceptable (even to Smith?) result: the central end toward which this system is a means is not being served. Seen through this lens, if Smith's jobs system was not dysfunctional from the outset, it has become dysfunctional even for white men. The chief way apologists for this system rationalize this fatal divergence from Smith's putative goal of improving "mankind's" lot is to change the goal: now what counts simply is the ever-increasing generation of wealth.

Does the fact that the modern jobs system is failing to meet the needs of its workers mean either that people lack the initiative and ingenuity to make things or that we are running out of work to be done? On the contrary, anyone who is half awake can see that we have tremendous work to be done (both in terms of importance and sheer volume) and that in every industrial society there are countless people ready and able to do that work. Not only is there the obvious infrastructure work of repairing and rebuilding roads, bridges, waterworks, and the like, but there is incalculable work needed to repair our natural and social environments: to rebuild our biotic and social communities, to raise our children well, etc. The problem is that this work falls outside the jobs system; it is not rewarded by those who control the wealth. Putting the issue in these terms shows finally what ails our way of working: we face a powerful crisis of values. A society as vastly wealthy as the United States that cannot manage to see that its children are safe, healthy, and well-educated and cannot provide its people with the basic amenities and securities of life has either an impoverished set of values, a sorry lack of imagination, or both.

Seen through the eyes of women, minorities, and social classes, our jobs system was dysfunctional from the beginning. For at the heart of the belief system that underlies and rationalizes this system is precisely what Warren sees as constitutive of patriarchy as a dysfunctional system: hierarchical thinking and the logic of dominataion. From the outset, women, people of color, and poor people have been disenfranchised from economic, social, and political power, as can be seen in the theoretical rationalizations of the system found in classical works such as Locke's *Second Treatise*, Smith's magnum opus, or the still-popular Social Darwinism, or if one looks at the realities of modern industrial societies.

Seen through the lens of ecofeminism, our jobs system and the larger economic-ideological-social-cultural system of which it is a part are patriarchal. According to Warren (1990), this patriarchy has five interrelated features:

> (1) *Value-hierarchical ("Up-Down") thinking*, which places higher value, status, or prestige on what is "Up" (men) or what is gender-identified with what is "Up" . . . than with what is "Down" (women) or what is gender-identified with what is "Down." . . . (2) *Value dualisms* . . . which organize reality into oppositional (rather than complementary) and exclusive (rather than inclusive) pairs. . . . (3) *Power-over conceptions of power*, which function to maintain relations of domination and subordination. (4) *Conceptions of privilege*, which function to maintain power-over relations of domination and subordination by "Ups" and "Downs." (5) *A logic of domination*, an argumentative structure that "justifies" the power and privilege of those who are "Up." (122–23)

These features simultaneously are sexist and naturist: these characteristics of "patriarchal conceptual frameworks . . . sanction the twin exploitations of women and nonhuman nature" (123). Thus, she argues, ecofeminism is a liberation movement that believes feminism should be ecological and ecology feminist."[22] This intimate link between women and nature is manifest in concrete reality. In another article, Warren (1992) gives a number of examples to show not only the linked domination of women and nature, but also that liberating women would enhance environmental relations and health.

Probably the quickest way to show a final central feature of our dysfunctional jobs system is to return to our farming example. We said that one of the central tragic ironies of contemporary farm life is that farmers in significant ways knowingly participate in the destruction of their ways of life and that this irony results from their seemingly unavoidable participation in the agribusiness model. To have a job farming, they seem to have to "choose" environmental destruction as a "natural" course of events. Town and city dwellers are caught in the same trap: the ways of life we have "chosen," wrapped as they are around our jobs system, predictably will also destroy the cultural and natural grounds upon which they are built.

We cannot continue this way. But to suggest that we consume less threatens people at a most vulnerable point: already in a mobile and rapidly changing society where traditional supports such as religion, a stable social and economic order, family continuity, and the like are disappearing or gone, to suggest that people give up on our jobs system and its concomitant consumerism is very threatening. Clearly such suggestions must be accompanied by viable alternatives, and it is to this more positive vision that we now turn.

Ecofeminism and Work: Toward a Functional Work System

Before modern economies and the Industrial Revolution, very little work was paid labor, and anthropologists tell us that in most small-scale societies people spent relatively little of their time doing what we might call "making a living" and much of their time "playing" (including socializing, preparing for and performing rituals, courting, making music, etc.).[23] Marshall Sahlins. e.g., estimates that even people living in harsh physical environments often spent less than three or four hours per day working. Equally significant, their work as well as their leisure time was richly social and often highly ritualized; thus the anthropological evidence from the past reinforces what Fox tells us about work and leisure in many nonindustrialized societies today.

Implicit in the anthropological descriptions of small-scale societies is that besides our basic material needs, humans need, in James Hillman's words, to love and be loved (Hillman, 37); we need a rich and caring social life. Feminists of every shade agree that healthy human relationships are at the heart of healthy communities; ecofeminists include both human and nonhuman dimensions in their descriptions of such communities. Allen Durning contends that consumerism fails of its own weight, both because the level and kinds of material consumption involved cannot be sustained and because consumerism cannot provide its most basic promise, happiness. During contends that empirical and philosophical studies indicate that happiness has far more to do with great quantities of leisure time and with a rich social life than it does with material abundance (or overabundance). While there are no formulas (nonessentialism) for how to structure more healthy communities, ecofeminists make a powerful argument that we must eliminate hierarchies of dominance from our systems and somehow dramatically reduce our consumption. I believe that if we were to make work more sociable and to create (once again) rich social lives, we would go a long ways toward meeting these goals.

Some might argue that good work would not get done if the workplace was too sociable, but all the discussions of and moves toward "democratic workplaces" and nonhierarchical structures in business and industry belie this view. Not only are sociality and good work (as opposed to being cogs in a machine) compatible, but in this age of "smart machines," when humans are needed mainly to do nonmechancial labor, even the captains of industry are coming to see that the former is a prerequisite of the latter.

A second dimension of our vision of functional, as opposed to dysfunctional, work is that work is as basic a human need as love.[24] Marx contended that people need to work to "create themselves"—to discover whom they are, to express themselves, to be recognized, to leave their marks, and so on. A major complaint about industrial work especially is that it reduces people to a state wherein their worth and work are gauged by the infamous "bottom line." Thus one change we must make in our work, whether paid or unpaid, is to render it more human, to create work that rewards and generates the flourishing of the finest human possibilities. This goal has been central to a wide variety of proposals to alter modern work; what ecofeminism has to offer our thinking about right livelihood (Buddhism) or unalienated labor (Marx) or new work (Bergmann) is the link between women and nature plus a strong emphasis on caring relationships in context.

Ecofeminists especially have helped us begin to see the gendered character of how people in the West, especially men, have been split off from nature. Nature/culture dualism informs our consciousness and is built into our behaviors and institutions. We are alienated from our bodies, from the nonhuman world, from each other, and from our work. The identification of women and nature as "other" is a central feature of our modern jobs system that shows up not only in continued lesser status and pay for women as compared to men, but also in the alienation of work: insofar as nature is an other seen merely as a resource base, we cannot have good work because we fail to appreciate the full range of values in what we work with, and because we therefore fail to develop our own full possibilities in the process.[25] The parallel to male/female relationships illustrates these two points powerfully: insofar as men treat women as lesser beings, men not only will fail to develop truly mutual and caring relationships with women but will not grow in fully human ways.

Max Oelschlaeger (1993) asks us to think in the following way about nature/culture dualism (and its concomitant, woman/man hierarchy) and its impact on men as well as on women and nature: as Western men have constructed their civilization on the denial of their own death and sexuality, they have built on a false assumption that men can control and transcend nature (death and sexuality). The denials upon which Western civilization rests not only devalue, degrade, and destroy women and nature, but they also give men a false sense of their own selves. The selves of Western men, seen through this lens, not only strive to conquer and control, but they ultimately are unhappy because they cannot know or satisfy their own desires.

Thus Oelschlaeger, a deep ecologist, as well as ecofeminists who for some time have been seeing the need to reconstruct Western civilization in similar dramatic ways, would likely agree that a good place to begin this reconstruction would be to eliminate the hierarchies of domination built into our practices and institutions. If our jobs system did not function to distinguish "real work" (paid labor) from "not really work" (unpaid labor) or different kinds of paid work from each other (women's work typically receives lower compensation and status both within job classifications and between), we would go a long way toward making our jobs system more humane, fulfilling, and just. Ending these value-hierarchical features of our jobs system would also help curtail people's consumption, for eliminating hierarchies of domination in our jobs system would reduce dramatically the insecurities for which people now compensate through unhealthy competition and consumption.

If our jobs system is a dysfunctional system, then what I am proposing is a liberation movement: a liberation from being addicts and enablers, dominators and subservients, in a dysfunctional system to living and working within a web of mutually caring relationships. If people are liberated from the vicious circles of work and consumption, they will be able to curb their appetites for the scarce resources of the earth. Furthermore, the dynamic of insecurity motivates people to lord it over those below: thus lower working class people lord it over the jobless, whites over blacks, men over women, etc., and most of us in industrial societies lord it over nature. To short-circuit this cycle by reducing and eliminating the insecurities generated by the jobs system and its accompanying consumerist motivators would be to reduce the need to feel superior or to dominate anything, including nature.

An objection to this vision of good work and environmental harmony is that perhaps such a vision made sense in a jobs-rich world, but with increasing international competition and the shrinking need for human labor because of automation, there are fewer and fewer jobs, especially good ones, to go around. This objection returns us to the central dysfunctionality of our jobs system: the modern jobs system no longer is (if it ever was) a satisfactory means to Adam Smith's most basic end, the distribution of wealth. With millions of people jobless and homeless, including many typical working-class and white-collar white men, the illusion is gone that the system works.

A significant reason people in American society engage in personally, socially, and environmentally dysfunctional behaviors such as compensatory consumption is time, time spent on the job or doing the shadow work required to maintain workers for the job. With significantly less time for relationships and for themselves than they need or want, those with jobs must compensate. But with machines able to do more and more of the work humans once did, workers now need only do uniquely or especially human tasks, and employers could pay them living wages for working fewer hours. The shorter hours movement got waylaid in the 1930s, and recently American workers have been working more hours each year.[26] This seems insane in a world of too few jobs, where many people love to work fewer hours and where that would mean they would be better workers the hours they were on the job. If people had more time for truly meaningful and caring relationships, for community-building activities—which anthropologists tell us are the heart of the convivial life in many small-scale societies—people would have less need to consume the earth and more need to spend time in and preserve healthy natural and social environments.

Notes

1. These headlines were taken from the *Des Moines Register* during 1992.

2. Sometimes, of course, the environment/jobs conflict is inflated or even wholly imaginary. Perhaps only 10,000 loggers will be out of work soon if the remaining 4 percent of the original virgin forests in Washington and Oregon are not put to the ax; or perhaps, as some environmentalists claim, the real threat to logging comes from the replacement of old-growth forests with tree farms that can be harvested by a few workers operating sophisticated machinery. Nevertheless, in many places the conflicts between jobs and the environment are very real.

3. Oelschlaeger says that "sustainability, whatever else that concept might entail, is a formal requirement for any definition of a good society." (1993, 20)

4. Berry focuses on the changes in culture that result from these profound changes in farming practices.

5. Fink and other feminist scholars point out that in America *farmer* usually refers to a man, while women are usually called "women farmers."

6. See Warren (1992) as well as Boserup, Monson, Creevey and Charleton.

7. Rural life in America has changed dramatically in the 125 years since the Industrial Revolution hit agriculture. Historians contend that the American Civil War was to a great extent about the transformation of American agricultural economics to industrial modes. Before this great transformation hit American agriculture, 95 percent of Americans lived and worked on farms. One hundred years later, 95 percent of them lived and worked in cities and towns, and by 1990 fewer than 2 percent lived and earned a living on farms. Thus the disintegration of rural communities, where in Iowa, for example, we are witnessing the disappearance of stores, banks, schools, and government offices from more and more small towns, is a continuation of a long industrialization of American agriculture. See Cochrane, Fink, Kramer, Sachs, Edwards et al., and Poincelot.

8. To understand the irony as well as absurdity of this situation, keep in mind that this is happening at the very same time that the overabundance of crops like corn, wheat, and soybeans keeps prices so low that farmers must be subsidized by government programs in order to stay in business, and at the very same time that many farmers in Iowa are idling land through yet other government programs.

9. Jane Smiley's recent novel paints a grim picture of what happens to people, their families, and communities when this "war" to own the largest farm occurs.

10. Please bear in mind that although there are differences between farm work and more common nonfarm jobs, most of what we find with farm work applies to other sectors of the economy as well.

11. Fink shows that in Iowa, e.g., while farm women are still essential to family farms, increasingly their contributions are made by working in town to bring home needed cash. The double irony is that in American agriculture today women (rather than men, predominantly) leave the farm to work in the cash economy, but that this move in significant ways marginalizes them as farmers. On the other hand, it would be interesting to discover the extent to which these women, so well described by McGaw (1982, 1989), carry their rich social culture to the workplaces which typically have been a source of depletion for men.

12. Unfortunately, as already suggested, as farms in developing countries become parts of industrial systems, and thus participate in cash economies, men tend to become more identified with farming and women become further depreciated. See Boserup, Creevey, Charleton, and especially Sachs. Also see the U.S. Commerce Department and the Iowa State Extension Service reports.

13. In rough historical terms McGaw and other social historians agree that patriarchy became worse with industrialization because of the creation of distinct, geographically and economically separated spheres; but none of them argue that this means preindustrial life was not patriarchal nor that it was easy for women or men.

14. See Oelschlaeger (1991), chaps. 1 and 2.

15. There is a large controversy concerning the extent to which Judaism and Christianity are "salvageable" as environmentally benign or friendly frameworks. However, even if one takes a negative position in this debate, the views of farming in Judaism and Christianity are environmentally more desirable than those that undergird agribusiness.

16. Note how this logic includes Warren's logic of domination (1987). To engage in the reductionism and control necessary for working in this way, nature and women must be reduced to lesser beings in order to be dominated.

17. The crucial idea here is Hegel's notion of the draining of value from the world to God, in "The Unhappy Consciousness" in his *Phenomenology of Spirit*. At the very least nature and women become valued only instrumentally. Many other values get downplayed or ignored, including possibly the "spirit" in a mystical sense.

18. Many of the works critical of consumer culture focus on these characteristics. See Ewing, Schiller, and Durning in particular.

19. Schor, e.g., contends that workers who watch television the most are those who work the most hours (Japanese and Americans). She also links, as does Fox, leisure and consumption: think of shopping as a favorite leisure-time activity of increasing numbers of Americans, but especially of women. But consider as well consuming nature activities such as the growing ecotourism industry or various adventures such as whitewater rafting or African safaris. None of these experiences/activities in itself is contrary to a healthy relationship with nature, but it becomes so when it is done from the impulse of compensation, of salving the wounds of work.

20. Besides the references Fox gives in her article, I would point especially to the work of anthropologists such as Lee, Sahlins, Diamond, Lee and DeVore, and Lévi-Strauss.

21. Thinkers like Marx and Proudhon, of course, believe that the system always was dysfunctional, because many people were excluded from the outset, because so many were disfigured in the process, and because it is theft.

22. Warren first makes her case for these connections in her 1987 article.

23. See Sahlins, Diamond, Lee, Lee and DeVore, and Lévi-Strauss. Much of what is suggested in this section is spelled out in greater detail in the third part of *Working in America*.

24. Many writers over the ages have made this point. See Sessions and Wortman, and especially the work of Hillman and Bergmann.

25. Palmer develops this point beautifully in a chapter called "The Woodcarver."

26. See Hunnicutt and Schor.

Works Cited

Agency for International Development. 1982. *Women in development*. Vols. 1 and 2. Washington, D.C.: Office of Women in Development, USAID.

Bergmann, Frithjof. 1992. The future of work. In Robert Sessions and Jack Wortman, eds., *Working in America*. Notre Dame, Ind.: University of Notre Dame Press, 11-27.

Berry, Wendell. 1977. *The unsettling of America*. San Francisco: Sierra Club.

Boserup, Esther. 1980. The position of women in economic production and in the household with special reference to Africa. In Clio Presveloa and Saskia Spijkers-Zwart, eds., *The household, women and agricultural development*. Wageningen: H. Veeman en Zonen, 11-16.

Charleton, Sue Ellen M. 1984. *Women in third world development*. Boulder: Westview.

Cochrane, Willard. 1979. *The development of American agriculture: A historical analysis*. Minneapolis: University of Minnesota Press.

Creevey, Lucy E. 1986. *Women farmers in Africa*. Syracuse: Syracuse University Press.

Diamond, Stanley. 1987. *In search of the primitive*. London: Transaction.

Durning, Allen. 1993. *How much is enough?* New York: Worldwatch Institute.

Edwards, Clive A., Rattan Lal, Patrick Madden, Robert H. Miller, and Gar House, eds. 1990. *Sustainable agricultural systems*. Ankeny, Iowa: Soil and Water Conservation Society.

Ehrenfeld, David. 1978. *The arrogance of humanism*. New York: Oxford University Press.

Ewen, Stuart. 1988. *All consuming images*. New York: Basic.

Fink, Deborah. 1986. *Open country, Iowa*. Albany: SUNY Press.

Gorz, Andre. 1989. *Critique of economic reason*. New York: Verso.

Hillman, James. 1983. *Inter/views*. New York: Harper and Row.

Hunnicut, Benjamin. 1988. *Work without end: Abandoning shorter hours for the right to work*. Philadelphia: Temple University Press.

Illich, Ivan. 1981. *Shadow work*. Boston: Boyars.

Iowa State Extension Service. 1985. The role of farm women in American history: Areas for additional research. *Agriculture and Human Values* 2 (1): 13-17.

Kramer, Mark. 1987. *Three farms*. Cambridge: Harvard University Press.

Lee, Dorothy. 1959. *Freedom and culture*. Englewood Cliffs, N.J.: Prentice-Hall.

Lee, Richard B., and Irven DeVore. 1968. *Man the hunter*. New York: Aldine.

Lévi-Strauss, Claude. 1966. *The savage mind*. Chicago: University of Chicago Press.

McGaw, Judith. 1989. No passive victims, no separate spheres: A feminist perspective on technology's history. In Stephen H. Cutcliffe and Robert C. Post, eds., *In context: History and the history of technology*. Bethlehem: Lehigh University Press, 172-91.

———. 1982. Women and the history of American technology. *Signs*, Summer: 798-828.

Monson, Jamie, and Marian Kalb, eds. 1985. *Women as food producers in developing countries*. Los Angeles: African Studies Center.

Oelschlaeger, Max. 1993. History, ecology and the denial of death: A re-reading of conservation, sexual personae, and the good society. *Journal of Social Philosophy* 24 (3):19-39.

———. 1991. *The idea of wilderness*. New Haven: Yale University Press.

Palmer, Parker. 1990. *The active life: A spirituality of work, creativity and caring*. San Francisco: Harper and Row.

Plant, Judith, ed. 1989. *Healing our wounds: The power of ecological feminism*. Boston: New Society.

Poincelot, Raymond. 1986. *Toward a more sustainable agriculture*. Westport, Conn.: AVI.

Sachs, Carolyn E. 1983. *The invisible farmers: Women in agricultural production*. Totowa, N.J.: Rowman and Allanheld.

Sahlins, Marshall. 1972. *Stone age economics*. New York: Aldine.

Schiller, Herbert. 1989. *Culture, Inc.* New York: Oxford University Press.

Schor, Juliet. 1991. *The overworked American: The unexpected decline of leisure*. New York: Basic.

Sessions, Robert, and Jack Wortman, eds. 1992. *Working in America*. Notre Dame, Ind.: University of Notre Dame Press.

Smiley, Jane. 1991. *A thousand acres*. New York: Ballantine.

U.S. Department of Commerce. 1983. *Lifetime earning estimates for men and women in the United States: 1979*. Current Population Reports. Series P-60. No. 144. Washington, D.C.: U.S. Government Printing Office.

Warren, Karen J. 1997. Taking emperical data seriously: An ecofeminist philosophical perspective. In this volume.

———. 1990. The power and the promise of ecological feminism. *Environmental Ethics* 12 (2): 125–46.

———. 1987. Feminism and ecology: Making connections. *Environmental Ethics* 9 (1): 3–20.

Eleven

Ecofeminism and Children

Ruthanne Kurth-Schai

Though the image of children as hope for the future is shared across cultures and continents, the experience of childhood as a time of innocence, security, self-worth, and contribution to family and community is a distant fantasy for most children. In the United States one of every five children is raised in poverty, one in six has no health insurance, one in five is at risk of becoming a teenage parent, one in three is chronically unserved or underserved in school, and growing numbers are homeless, abused, neglected, depressed, and disillusioned.[1] Throughout the world millions of children die each year of starvation and water-related diseases, while millions more survive in societies torn by political unrest only to watch as their families and communities disintegrate in the face of unimaginable hardship, dislocation, and death.[2]

Not as well documented, yet also of significant concern, is the sense of confusion, alienation, and despair experienced by many children in response to an emotional double bind characteristic of childhood in modern and postmodern societies. On one hand, children are asked far too soon to assume adult responsibilities that are not of their choosing (e.g., growing numbers of children care for themselves and younger siblings while parents are working, care for their own troubled parents, and must find their own food and shelter). On the other hand, children are systematically excluded from meaningful social and political participation (e.g., children cannot vote and are seldom allowed to participate in policy decisions affecting their lives; they have limited legal rights, and their opportunities to contribute are restricted largely to the private domain).[3]

Taken together, the above conditions indicate that children—similar to women, racial and ethnic minorities, the economically disadvantaged, the differently abled, and elements of nonhuman nature—are subjected to social oppression. Increasingly we live in an adult-centered, age-segregated world that better serves the political and economic interests of powerful adults than even the most basic survival needs of youth. Consequently, children are often denied appropriate care and attention, social participation, and respect.

For feminists, this presents an important challenge. Over the past decades, feminist theory and practice have become increasingly responsive to the multiple barriers affecting women's lives. Ecological feminists, in particular, have been instrumental in demonstrating the extent to which women's oppression and other systems of social injustice are mutually reinforcing. For this reason, ecofeminist philosophers contend that in order to effectively address women's concerns, feminism must be redefined as a movement to end *all* oppression.[4]

The oppression of children, however, has yet to assume an important position on either feminist or nonfeminist agendas. In the feminist struggle to conceptualize and to enact more just and compassionate human relationships, the voices of children still remain largely silent. As Barrie Thorne clarifies, "both feminist and traditional knowledge remain deeply and unreflectively centered around the experiences of adults. Our understanding of children tends to be filtered through adult perspectives and interests . . . their full lives, experiences, and agency obscured by adult standpoints."[5]

To the extent that ecofeminist philosophy and practice has failed to understand and affirm children's perspectives or to acknowledge the broadly defined (social, economic, physical, emotional, spiritual) conditions of their lives, ecofeminist philosophy runs the risk of perpetuating adultist assumptions toward children and the primary societal institutions which serve them. In this essay I build on the ecofeminist philosophy of Karen J. Warren and others to show how and why the inclusion of children's perspectives and issues within ecofeminist dialogue and activism is potentially liberating for children and deepens the significance and impact of the ecofeminist movement.

Ecological Feminism and the
Social Oppression of Children

Although empirical evidence documenting the decline of children's welfare in the United States and throughout the world continues to grow,[6] the social oppression of children is rarely acknowledged in either private or public forums. Perhaps this is because the social restrictions imposed on children's lives are often justified in terms of protection, affection, and assistance. Age-based discrimination can be subtle—difficult to name and therefore difficult to challenge. Or perhaps it is because most societies truly believe themselves to be dedicated to children's well-being that the social oppression of children is particularly painful to acknowledge and to own—the realities of children's lives are easily obscured by the uncritical assumption of adult goodwill. Whatever the reasons for this collective denial of the social injustices perpetuated against children, the lives of young people are diminished by our failure to acknowledge the broad social structures and belief systems which obstruct current attempts to create communities both responsive to children's needs and receptive to their contributions.

How then can ecological feminism help us to move beyond denial to understanding, commitment, and hope? As I will show, it does so by articulating a theoretical framework whereby the subordination of children can be conceptually and experientially linked to the more widely recognized systems of oppression affecting women and nonhuman nature. Ecofeminist philosophy provides a theoretical framework for seeing children's issues as centrally feminist issues—issues of oppression.

Oppressive Conceptual Frameworks

The theoretical position I draw from in defending my claim is well articulated in a series of works by Warren.[7] Warren explains that all systems of domination are justified and maintained by oppressive conceptual frameworks. An oppressive conceptual framework is defined by several significant features. First, it is centered in value hierarchical dualisms—"up-down disjunctive pairs in which the disjuncts are seen as oppositional (rather than complementary) and exclusive (rather than inclusive), and which place higher value (status, prestige) on one disjunct rather than the other."[8] Val Plumwood notes that the overall effect of adopting a value-laden, dichotomous world view is to alienate and to polarize, for "traits taken to be virtuous and defining for one side are those which maximize distance from the other side. The traits most highly regarded and treated as establishing what is 'authentically human,' for example, are those unshared by nonhuman nature."[9] Thus, rather than viewing humanity and elements of nonhuman nature as distinct yet related variations on a common evolutionary theme, they are perceived as isolated endpoints of a judgment-laden dichotomy privileging humans. Similarly, noted child psychologist Jerome Kagan identifies a cross-cultural tendency to ascribe categorically to adults those qualities valued by society and then to project onto children the opposite.[10]

Warren explains that the existence of value hierarchical dualism alone does not create an oppressive conceptual framework. This characteristic must be combined with a second distinguishing feature, a logic of domination—an argumentation structure which supplies the moral justification that sanctions subordination. To illustrate, the belief that adults generally possess more highly developed political awareness and political action skills than children is not necessarily oppressive vis-à-vis children. This stance is clearly oppressive, however, if one assumes that because adults possess political abilities children do not, adults are morally justified in exploiting the political process for their own purposes, without regard to the impact of their actions on children. For instance, the United States has witnessed a significant cross-generational shift in access to resources over the past several decades to the extent that today, for every dollar spent on federal support programs for children, eleven dollars are spent on programs for the aged.[11] Further, although this pattern of resource distribution clearly reflects the intensity and effectiveness of lobbying efforts on behalf of the elderly, we fail to acknowledge children's lack of political power as a significant impediment to their welfare and refrain from directly connecting children's losses to adults' gains.

Overall, the combination of value hierarchical dualism and the logic of domination creates a powerful conceptual dynamic which assures that children, by virtue of their position on the less-valued ("down") end of the adult/child dualism, will experience a parallel fate to women under patriarchy and will suffer disproportionately the effects of human exploitation of nonhuman nature. Consider why this is so.

Children, Adult Centrism, and Patriarchy

Children in adult-centered societies are subjected to forms of discrimination similar to those experienced by women under patriarchy—they are conceptually privatized, singularized, and stripped of their agency.[12] Perceived as subordinates, children, like women, are consigned to the margins of history, their activities restricted to the private domain (family, school, neighborhood) and their participation in public enterprises (knowledge creation, decision making) denied. Consequently, their social presence and social contributions remain largely unacknowledged. These are examples of adult centrism.

Adult centrism further tends to define children as a distinct social category or "singularity," thereby obscuring differences among children while emphasizing characteristics which supposedly separate or distinguish children from adults. In a society where traits associated with childhood are devalued, focusing on adult/child differences can perpetuate injustice. As John Holt noted, "When we say of children's needs, as of their virtues, that they belong only to children, we make them seem trivial, we invalidate them. What is more, we insure that they will not be met."[13]

Injustice is further perpetuated by this "politics of hierarchical difference" as children, stripped of their agency, become pawns of the political system rather than advocates on their own behalf.[14] Richard de Lone identifies a strong political tendency to use children to divert attention away from pressing and difficult social problems.[15] This is accomplished by promoting social policies designed to improve individual children rather than to directly address controversial issues deeply entrenched within the structure of our society. For example, although it is clear that low socioeconomic background plays a primary role in restricting educational opportunities,[16] we promote compensatory education programs for economically disadvantaged children rather than addressing the social, economic, and political inequities inherent in a free-market economy. In effect, we have adopted a child-deficit as opposed to a societal-deficit approach to resolving social conflict and promoting social reform. In this manner we maintain an unfortunate illusion whereby it is possible to create the appearance of working on behalf of children while maintaining adults' vested interest in children's powerlessness.

Children, Adult Centrism, and Environmental Degradation

Although the whole of humanity is diminished by global neglect and abuse of the biophysical world, the poor and the politically powerless suffer disproportionately. Increasingly it is children who bear the heaviest burden. Throughout the world the quality of children's lives (e.g., health, stability of family structure, nature of child labor) is repeatedly assaulted by failures to contain hazardous wastes and provide safe drinking water and by changes in soil, climate, and vegetation related to industrialization.[17] Children irradiated at Chernobyl, burned by toxic gases in Bhopal, and dying of starvation in Ethiopia are just a few of the examples that attest to the physical price that young ones pay. Examples such as these should be of primary concern to ecofeminists.

In addition to the highly visible negative impacts, perhaps as damaging and more pervasive are the "slow and silent killers," the hidden environmental toxins to which children are uniquely vulnerable. In a report entitled "What's Gotten into our Children?" published by the child advocacy organization Children Now, it is argued that although environmental pollutants create health problems for people of all ages, they pose a greater risk to children for several reasons.[18] First, children's developing bodies are more sensitive than adults' bodies to substances that interfere with growth processes and, being smaller, may be exposed to the same amount of toxin but acquire higher body concentrations. Second, children's playful, curious, exploratory behaviors, combined with limited experience as a basis for sound judgment, place them at greater risk. Third, children are likely to have more years of life ahead of them and are therefore more likely to experience continued exposure and eventually to manifest the disease states that develop over long periods (e.g., cancer-causing agents).

The report also suggests that the risks are magnified for poor children, who are most likely to be exposed and least likely to have access to health insurance and adequate health care. These concerns are well illustrated by Jonathan Kozol in his description of schooling in East St. Louis, where children study and play amid the fumes from two chemical plants, raw sewage released from antiquated waste-disposal systems, and severely contaminated soil poisoned by years of hazardous dumping. In this setting, children's opportunities to learn and to grow are severely constrained by levels of childhood asthma and lead poisoning among the highest in the United States.[19]

Children's lives are further diminished as environmental exploitation and militarism are locked together in a self-perpetuating cycle of destruction. Overconsumption of natural resources by citizens of industrialized nations and Third World elites results in growing militarization, which then requires increased consumption.[20] Tensions created by inequitable resource distribution are expected to grow as competition for limited commodities intensifies. Even now the lives of millions of children are ravaged by war.[21] Each day throughout the world children are killed, injured, orphaned, left hungry and homeless, conscripted, and held as political prisoners as a consequence of military activity. The amount of suffering imposed on children as a result of recent hostilities in the Middle East, Africa, and Eastern Europe has yet to be determined, and may never be fully acknowledged. In an essay entitled "If the Child is Safe," Marian Wright Edelman writes:

> In response to a distant tyrant, we [the United States] sent hundreds of Americans . . . to the Persian Gulf. According to Secretary of State James Baker, the Gulf War was fought to protect our "life style" and standard of living and the rights of the Kuwaiti people. No deficit or recession was allowed to stand in the way. How, then, can we reconcile our failure to engage equally the enemies of poverty and violence and family disintegration within our nation? When are we going to mobilize and send troops to fight for the "life style" of the 100,000 American children who are homeless each night? . . . Why are we able to put hundreds of thousands of troops and support personnel in Saudi Arabia within a few months to fight Saddam Hussein when we are unable to mobilize hundreds of teachers or doctors and social workers for desperately underserved inner cities and rural areas to fight the tyranny of poverty and ignorance and child neglect and abuse?[22]

To summarize, crippled by a world view that pits humanity against nature, male against female, adult against child, it is very difficult to make significant progress toward social and environmental justice in general or toward enhancing the quality of children's lives in particular. Exploitation of the biophysical world and the oppression of women, children, and others are intimately related and mutually reinforcing. Any attempt to radically challenge the social oppression of children must also challenge the oppression of women and human domination over the biophysical world.

Traditional Conceptualizations of a Child-Centered Social Ethic

In addition to helping to locate the social oppression of children in a more visible and prominent position alongside other more widely recognized systems of injustice and exploitation, Warren's ecofeminist analysis of oppressive conceptual frameworks provides insight into the relative ineffectiveness of traditional conceptualizations of a child-centered social ethic. A review of relevant literature, both scholarly and popular, reveals a strong societal tendency to adopt one of two contrasting positions: protectionism or liberationism. While protectionists attempt to promote children's interests by sheltering them from the perils of adult society, liberationists work to win for children the rights, responsibilities, and privileges traditionally reserved for adults. Because each position rests firmly on adult-centered dualistic assumptions, as I will show, neither represents the varied and complex experiences of youth. Consequently, neither can provide the conceptual and ethical framework necessary to create societies both responsive to children's needs *and* respectful of their aspirations and contributions.

The Protectionist Approach—Children without Competence

Protectionism is perhaps the most widely embraced ethical position on childhood. Protectionist themes are well represented in both academic and popular literature documenting the victimization of children in modern societies by physical, sexual, and emotional abuse, divorce, inadequate child care and educational practices, inadequate nutrition and health care, negative peer pressure, violent crime, drugs, television, sexually transmitted diseases, pregnancy, and parenthood.[23] The protectionist position rests on the assumption that children's needs, abilities, concerns, and aspirations are significantly different than those of adults. Children are weak, small, inexperienced, vulnerable. They are dependent upon adult attention, assistance, guidance, and support.

Though protectionist concerns merit serious consideration and large-scale response, protectionism cannot provide an adequate framework for a child-centered social ethic because it is so narrowly focused on children's vulnerability and incompetence. Protectionism is grounded in twentieth-

century models of child development, including socialization, encultura-
tion, and universal stage theories. These models project onto children
those qualities least prized in adults, remain largely uninformed by children's perspectives and interpretations, and systematically underestimate
and misrepresent children's capabilities.[24] Such criticisms reflect the extent
to which the conceptual roots of protectionism remain firmly grounded
in dualistic thought separating childhood from adulthood on the basis of
adult superiority or children's inferiority. Protectionist assumptions concerning the nature of childhood are further challenged by research documenting the ways in which children contribute to their own development
and work to enhance the quality of life for others.[25]

The Liberationist Approach—Children without Childhood

In sharp contrast to protectionists, liberationists contend that adult/child
distinctions are artificial, socially magnified, and politically motivated.[26]
Children, they contend, are basically the same as adults. Differential treatment is neither morally defensible nor relevant to children's needs. Rather
than contributing to their welfare, the protectionist approach is said by
liberationists to diminish children's dignity and their social status while
helping to justify and to perpetuate adult hegemony. Defined by adults as
innocent and vulnerable, children are forced to relinquish their rights to
freedom, autonomy, and participation. Thus liberationists contend that the
time has come to devote more attention to protecting children's rights than
to protecting children per se.

Based, however, upon the premise that children are essentially the same
as adults, liberationism as a framework for a child-centered social ethic is
also conceptually flawed. Although the adult/child dualism is abolished, it
is done so at the expense of children's very real and different-than-adult
needs for nurturance and protection. In focusing narrowly on children's
potentials to assume roles and responsibilities traditionally reserved for
adults, important areas of vulnerability are likely to remain unacknowledged and unaddressed.

It is true that children's dependency needs across the age spectrum
from early childhood through adolescence are generally greater than
adults'. Further, their needs for security and guidance are magnified in
rapidly changing, increasingly fragmented, pluralistic, and technologically
advanced societies.[27] Considering issues such as the rise of drug-related
violence, the AIDS epidemic, the impact of global recession, and the resurgence of political unrest and military activity, the world of the 1990s is
a more dangerous place than the world of the 1970s, when the most radical
of liberationist themes were promoted.

But special needs are not the only factors which distinguish children from adults. Traits such as rapid multidimensional growth, playfulness, spontaneity, conceptual and behavioral flexibility, unique insight, and energy are more easily accessed and frequently expressed in childhood.[28] Continued expression of these is at risk within the liberationist framework. In a critique of liberationist attempts to achieve social justice for women, Alison Jaggar suggests the goal of gender blindness is not particularly attractive: "Rather than appearing as the extension to women of the full human status enjoyed by men, sexual equality starts to look like an attempt to masculinize women and negate their special capacities. . . . Far from expressing the quintessence of feminism, the demand for equality with men in fact may negate feminism's most radical and distinctive vision."[29] Failure to acknowledge adult/child differences in an attempt to create an age-blind society could yield similar results. Important differences between children and adults *do* exist, differences that are obscured within a liberationist framework.

Social Justice for Children:
Through an Ecological Feminist Lens

In a series of related works, ecofeminist philosophers Karen J. Warren and Jim Cheney define a multidimensional system of social ethics centered in themes of relationship, pluralism, inclusion, and transformation.[30] I contend that these themes, taken together, provide a more appropriate conceptual and ethical framework for addressing the needs and interests of children than either protectionist or liberationist approaches permit. In the sections that follow, therefore, I adopt each theme as a primary criterion for a child-centered social ethic and attempt to outline in broad strokes the major implications of an ecofeminist ethic for youth and society.

Children and the Ethics of Relationship

From an ecological feminist perspective, most highly prized are values which stress the importance of beings-in-relationship—mutual care, friendship, reciprocity, diversity, and appropriate trust.[31] Weblike networks of care and responsibility help the individual to establish a strong sense of self while maintaining connection with others through mutually beneficial patterns of exchange. A child-centered social ethic therefore must promote interaction, interdependence, and collaboration rather than isolation, independence, and competition.

Networks of loving, reciprocal relationships are required if children are to develop a sense of security and confidence as well as an awareness of their value to the community. In a pioneering work, *The Ecology of Human Development*, Urie Bronfenbrenner makes explicit the multiple experiential settings which create for each child a unique developmental context. Home, school, place of worship, extended family, peer group, parent's place of employment, school board, political institutions, service agencies, and the quality of the relationships among these—all impinge on children's lives. Within the context of many diverse and mutually supportive social relationships, child development is motivated and sustained.[32]

Unfortunately, within the context of contemporary social structures, the relational worlds of children are strictly limited. In the United States, for example, access to adults is limited, as children are barred from the workplace and the responsibility for child rearing is delegated almost exclusively to parents (and often single ones at that). As noted by John Holt, the decline of the extended family has impoverished children's lives, leaving them to cope with too little variation in role models and with relationships that are too intense and too easily corrupted because there is always too much at stake.[33] Access to other children is limited, as young ones spend large amounts of time in large, geographically distant schools where it is commonly assumed that peer interaction interferes with the learning process and should therefore be restricted to the extent possible.[34]

Given these circumstances, the implications of an ethics of relationship for children are dramatic and far-reaching, though difficult to attain without a fundamental rethinking of the patterns of social exchange now prevalent within industrial and postindustrial societies. Cheney suggests that while "commodity exchange" in a market economy is not compatible with an ethics of relationship, an economy of "gift exchange" creates and sustains community.[35] In an economy of gift exchange, one's sense of self and social worth is developed through processes of giving and receiving rather than being measured in terms of one's ability to possess or accumulate. Reproductive processes—those activities which sustain the physical, emotional, social, and spiritual well-being of the community—are attributed importance equal to productive processes, or activities resulting in intellectual, material, or technological progress.[36] In this manner, the economic system is committed primarily to provide for basic human needs rather than to enlarge profit, to enhance the quality of lived experience rather than to increase the quantity of material wealth.

The roles and responsibilities assumed by children and adults and the relationships among them can be transformed as a market economy is replaced by a system emphasizing the reciprocal giving and receiving of gifts. For example, within an economy of gift exchange, special needs or areas of disadvantage are compensated for rather than being used as justification for limiting participation. The work of social cognitivists is instructive here. Vygotsky defines the "zone of proximal development" as the distance between the actual developmental level demonstrated through independent problem solving and the potential developmental level demonstrated through collaborative problem solving with adults or peers. Because cognitive development is inherently a social process, in collaborative situations performance can precede competence, learning can precede development.[37] Similarly, Howard Cohen suggests that when adults do not possess the skills necessary to address special needs, they "borrow" capacities from an "agent" (e.g., a lawyer, lobbyist, or financial adviser).[38] Rather than restricting children's autonomy rights on the basis of their incapacities, thereby restricting their opportunities to develop competence, in an economy of gift exchange, access to special forms of assistance now limited to adults would be extended to children.

Roles, responsibilities, and relationships can also be transformed as previously unacknowledged gifts are made visible. Children's contributions are easily obscured in societies narrowly focused on political and economic contributions that are provided almost exclusively by adults. In an economy of gift exchange a wide range of contributions are sought and valued. If the diverse needs of specific individuals are to be met and the quality of interpersonal relationships sustained, then a variety of gifts must circulate. Within this context, the social significance of children's contributions is more easily recognized.

What special gifts might young ones have to offer? In *Growing Young* Ashley Montagu provides an eloquent answer:

> Yet the truth about the human species is that in body, spirit, feeling, and conduct we are designed to grow and develop in ways that emphasize rather than minimize childlike traits. . . . What, precisely, are those traits of childhood behavior that are so valuable and that tend to disappear gradually as human beings grow older? . . . Curiosity . . . ; imaginativeness; playfulness; open-mindedness; willingness to experiment; flexibility; humor; energy; receptiveness to new ideas; honesty; eagerness to learn; and perhaps the most pervasive and the most valuable of all, the need to love.[39]

As these gifts are acknowledged as different but not less worthy than those more typically shared by adults (e.g., life experience, formal education, access to resources), children can be valued for their contributions as children rather than for their potential to contribute as adults.

In an economy of gift exchange, it is also possible that assets now stereotypically defined as age-specific would become more broadly dispersed across the age continuum to the benefit of both children and adults. As children's capacities to function as integral members of the gift community are acknowledged and valued, they are no longer restricted to assuming their socially assigned roles as continual dependents, learners, and recipients of protection and assistance. It then becomes possible to provide "adult" contributions without being dismissed as exceptional or deviant. Similarly, as adults are freed from their socially assigned roles as continual providers, teachers, and nurturers, they are freed to rediscover, and to share for the benefit of the community, the "child within." Eventually, then, the multiple roles and responsibilities required to sustain the community could be widely distributed and continually shifting, determined on the basis of individual interests, experiences, and abilities rather than age. In each of these ways, an ethics of relationship, operationalized through the metaphor of gift exchange, provides for children protection, attention, and loving response while addressing their needs to participate and contribute.

Children and the Ethics of Pluralism

There is no singular experience of childhood. Children are as varied in their needs, concerns, abilities, and aspirations as are adults. Grounded in ecofeminist theory, a child-centered social ethic will extend moral consideration to children not only as members of a broad social category but also as unique individuals. Just as "ecofeminism as a social movement resists social simplification through supporting the rich diversity of women the world over, and finding oneness in that diversity,"[40] so too must conceptions of childhood be pluralized.

Maintaining an ethical stance toward children poses a difficult societal challenge because the developmentally and culturally appropriate path toward nurturance and empowerment varies from child to child. To establish and sustain loving, reciprocal relationships requires specificity, intimacy, the ability to truly see the other—each child. Marilyn Frye's description of loving versus arrogant perception provides a guiding metaphor. While the arrogant eye seeks to control, conquer, assimilate, utilize, or erase difference, the loving eye seeks to acknowledge, sustain, and celebrate it. Frye explains:

> The loving eye knows the independence of the other. It is the eye of one who knows that to know the seen, one must consult something other than one's own will and interests and fears and imagination. . . . One must look and listen and check and question. . . . The loving eye does not have to simplify. It knows the complexity of the other as something which will forever present new things to be known.[41]

Which eye do we turn upon children in this society? Barrie Thorne contends that contemporary thought concerning the nature of childhood is dominated by three distinct images—the image of children as victims of adult society (children are vulnerable and in need of adult protection), as threats to adult society (youth are dangerous and in need of adult control), and as learners of adult society (children are incompetent and in need of adult guidance).[42] Although the images are quite different, each emerges from, then justifies and perpetuates, adult use of arrogant perception. Each clouds our vision, blinding us to the diversity and complexity of children's experience. Each blurs our perception of, or openly violates, the distinct boundaries and unique profile that each child struggles to establish within the context of a social reality largely defined by adults.

In contrast, the image of loving perception challenges us to throw aside preconceived notions of what it means to experience life as "a child" and to develop the motivation, openness, and flexibility required to gain awareness of an infinite variety of ways of being. To facilitate development of this loving eye, cross-age interaction should not be limited to traditional parent-related elder/child or teacher/student relationships. Adults from all walks of life are called upon to learn to relate to children in the egalitarian, mutually respectful, and supportive manner that hopefully characterizes their friendships with other adults. For it is through responding to the specific needs of others across domains of difference that moral sensitivity and creativity are developed and enriched.

Children and the Ethics of Inclusion

An ethics of relationship implies meaningful participation of all individuals in the life of the community. No one is to be relegated to the margins, allowed to participate only in subservient or inconsequential roles. A child-centered social ethic will encourage children—within the context of loving and reciprocal relationships and in the spirit of gift exchange—to bring their own special insights and talents to roles traditionally reserved for adults, including activities such as knowledge construction, policy design, and social governance. A child-centered social ethic will extend to children both conceptual and political power.

Conceptual power—the awareness of and ability to act upon one's capacities for constructing, validating, and disseminating knowledge—is central to an ethic of inclusion. Closely related is the concept of epistemic privilege. As explained by Warren, "those claims (voices, patterns of voices) are morally and epistemologically favored (better, preferred, less partial, less biased) which are more inclusive of the felt experiences and perspectives of oppressed persons."[43] The inclusion of children's voices is epistemologically necessary because children's voices offer corrective lenses against theory building concerning childhood that is inaccurate. Children can provide insights into their own constructions and interpretations of reality which are not readily accessible to adults.[44] Inclusion of children's voices is a moral imperative because they offer protection from theory building concerning childhood that is arrogant or harmful.[45] One striking example of the arrogance displayed by adults in studying children is the academic tendency to frame research questions almost exclusively in terms of the assumed inadequacies of youth rather than the potential shortcomings of adults.[46]

The concept of epistemic privilege further implies that children's perceptions of social ethics merit special attention. Because children have experienced discrimination, they, like members of other disenfranchised groups, possess a unique and valuable understanding of the structures and subtleties of their oppression and possibilities for reform.[47] It is essential, therefore, that children be encouraged to develop and to exercise their conceptual power by actively contributing to the process of defining a child-centered social ethic.

Conceptual power, however, is not enough. Inclusion also requires broad distribution of political power. Again returning to the concept of epistemic privilege, the welfare of children and their communities is promoted as all primary social institutions—family, church, school, state—are opened to accept guidance from children. But how can this be accomplished? Ecological approaches to problem solving provide no easy answers. Who will participate in social decision making and the level of influence afforded their wishes must be determined in context. At times it will be appropriate to assign equal value to the opinions of all members of a community, including children. In these situations, tools such as the delphi technique, designed to ensure anonymity while involving participants in an interactive decision-making process, can help to minimize the influence of traditional power differentials.[48] At other times it may be desirable for one population or a number of individuals from several populations to exercise greater control by virtue of special sensitivities or skills. Thus a pattern of multiple shifting hierarchies is established whereby all members of the community share according to their interests, abilities, and experiences in the design, implementation, and evaluation of social policy.

As an initial consequence of granting children full participation in political processes, young people will be called upon to assume roles and responsibilities with which they are unfamiliar and for which they are unprepared. Adults are therefore called upon to ensure that children's participation will be meaningful, empowering, and free from coercion. In other words, care must be taken to ensure that youth will not participate as tokens or pawns.

Uma Narayan's work is instructive here.[49] Narayan suggests that in working together across differences in the realm of political practice, goodwill is not enough. The risks of collaboration assumed by the disadvantaged are much greater than those assumed by the advantaged. For the disadvantaged—in this case, children—the consequences of failed efforts are more severe. Additionally they are especially vulnerable to insensitivities expressed by the advantaged—in this case, adults—whom they have begun to trust. For these reasons, adults are encouraged to proceed with "methodological humility," always assuming lack of complete understanding of the context of children's lives, and "methodological caution," taking care not to dismiss validity of children's points of view.

Children and the Ethics of Transformation

A social ethic centered in ecofeminist theory requires social transformation. New patterns of thought and behavior are necessary to liberate humanity and the biophysical world from all forms of oppression. We are challenged therefore to develop and to act in accordance with an "anticipatory utopian consciousness," one which embodies the desired future in the present.[50] To the extent that we work toward accomplishing this in collaboration with children, social and environmental justice and compassion are advanced.

Central to an ecofeminist consciousness is the development of a new way of being in relation to nonhuman nature. Ecofeminist ethical concerns extend beyond humanity to embrace all aspects of the biophysical world. The well-being, diversity, and continuity of nonhuman populations and ecosystems, as well as relationships between humans and nonhuman elements, are accepted as worthy of moral consideration.[51] Learning to respond to the biophysical world with responsibility and care becomes a moral imperative. Additionally, as I have argued, it is essential for children's welfare. Justice and compassion for children are advanced within a context of environmental responsiveness, not exploitation. Commitment to a child-centered social ethic requires intensive and ongoing efforts to conserve natural resources and curb pollution, develop environmentally responsive technologies, promote global redistribution of economic and political power, develop and utilize strategies for peaceful conflict resolution, and articulate and promote life-sustaining and life-enhancing spiritual and communal values.[52]

Cultivating a nonoppressive, socially and environmentally responsible utopian vision, however, is not an easy task. To what new horizons might we turn to catalyze social and moral imagination?

Woven throughout the literature of contemporary social and behavioral science is the assumption that children possess an unparalleled potential to generate utopian social and political imagery.[53] Studies of children's utopian future imagery also reveal intense interest, concern, and creativity regarding the status of the environment and the quality of human interaction with nonhuman nature.[54] These findings are reinforced by the growing participation of children around the world in efforts to protect endangered species, promote recycling and energy conservation, and save the rainforests.[55] The preceding suggests that exploring children's utopian images and strategies for social and environmental reform—while providing opportunities for young people to act on their commitments in meaningful ways—represents a major source of new challenges, choices, goals, and dreams for the future. Justice and compassion, grounded in an ethics of transformation, are advanced as children's efforts to reconceptualize and reconstruct the social order are acknowledged, encouraged, and sustained.

Children often entrust adults with the faith that their thoughts and intuitions will be respected and responded to. Their trust is betrayed when we accept adult-centered conceptions of childhood and derive from them approaches to social and environmental reform inadequate to the task. Ecological feminism provides an opportunity to regain children's trust while engaging their cooperation by defining an ethical framework on the basis of which to address the challenges and the complexities of children's lives. As concerns for nurturance and empowerment are woven through mutually supportive themes of relationship, pluralism, inclusion, and transformation, we are supported in our attempts to create a world both responsive to children's needs and receptive to their contributions. At the same time, to the extent that ecofeminist philosophy and activism engages in the mutually supportive projects of promoting just and compassionate relationships among children and adults, men and women, and humanity and nonhuman nature, the beauty and power of ecofeminist philosophy is enhanced.

Notes

1. M. Edelman, "Children at Risk," in *Caring for America's Children*, ed. F. Macciarola and A. Gartner (New York: Academy of Political Science, 1989), and *The Measure of Our Success* (Boston: Beacon Press, 1992); A. Bastian, N. Fruchter, M. Gittell, C. Greer, and K. Haskins, *Choosing Equality: The Case for Democratic Schooling* (Philadelphia: Temple University Press, 1986).

2. See, for example, K. J. Warren, chap. 1 in this volume; V. Sorokwu, "Africa's Children Caught in Crisis," *World View Press* (November 1992), 25–27.

3. For a review of the literature supporting these claims, see R. Kurth-Schai, "The Roles of Youth in Society: A Reconceptualization," *Educational Forum* 52 (1988): 113–32.

4. K. J. Warren. "The Power and Promise of Ecological Feminism," *Environmental Ethics* 12 (1990): 127–48.

5. B. Thorne, "Re-Visioning Women and Social Change: Where Are the Children?" *Gender and Society* 1 (March 1987): 86.

6. *Starting Points: Meeting the Needs of Our Youngest Children* (Carnegie Corporation of New York, 1994); S. Reed and R. C. Sautter, *Children of Poverty*, Kappan Special Report (Bloomington, Ind.: Phi Delta Kappa, 1990); S. Hewlett, *When the Bough Breaks* (New York: Harper Perennial, 1992); J. P. Grant, *The*

State of the World's Children (London: Oxford University Press, 1990); Select Committee on Children, Youth, and Families, "Children's Well-Being: An International Comparison" (Washington, D.C.: U.S. Government Printing Office, 1990).

7. Warren, "The Power and Promise of Ecological Feminism," and "Feminism and Ecology: Making Connections," *Environmental Ethics* 9 (1987): 3–20.

8. Warren, "The Power and Promise of Ecological Feminism," 128.

9. V. Plumwood, "Ecofeminism: An Overview and Discussion of Positions and Arguments," *Australasian Journal of Philosophy* 64 (1986): 132.

10. J. Kagan, *The Nature of the Child* (New York: Basic, 1984).

11. P. Taylor, "Like Taking Money from a Baby," *Washington Post Weekly*, March 4–10, 1991, 86–87.

12. Thorne.

13. J. Holt, *Escape from Childhood* (New York: Ballantine, 1974), 105.

14. J. Coons, "Law and the Sovereigns of Childhood," *Phi Delta Kappan*, September 1976, 19–24; H. Gideonse, "The Politics of Childhood," in *The Social Life of Children in a Changing Society*, ed. K. Borman (Norwood, N.J.: Ablex, 1982); Kagan.

15. R. de Lone, *Small Futures: Children, Inequality, and the Limits of Liberal Reform* (New York: Harcourt Brace Jovanovich, 1979).

16. J. S. Coleman, *Equality of Educational Opportunity* (Washington, D.C.: U.S. Department of Health, Education and Welfare, 1966); *Barriers to Excellence: Our Children at Risk* (Boston: National Coalition of Advocates for Students, 1985); D. Levine and R. Havighurst, *Society and Education*, 7th ed. (Needham Heights, Mass.: Allyn and Bacon, 1989).

17. Warren, chap. 1 in this volume.

18. D. Hughes, "What's Gotten Into Our Children?" (Los Angeles: Children Now, 1990).

19. J. Kozol, *Savage Inequalities: Children in America's Schools* (New York: Crown, 1991). See also N. S. Green, "America's Toxic Schools," *E: The Environmental Magazine* 3 (1992), no. 6: 30–37.

20. R. Guha, "Radical American Environmentalism and Wilderness Preservation: A Third World Critique," *Environmental Ethics* 11 (1989): 71–81.

21. See M. Jupp, "The International Year of the Child, Ten Years Later," in *Caring for America's Children*, ed. Macciarola and Gartner; R. Rosenblatt, *Children of War* (New York: Anchor/Doubleday, 1983); United Nations, "Condition of Women and Children in Emergency and Armed Conflict in the Struggle for Peace, Self-Determination, National Liberation and Independence," New York, 1988.

22. Edelman, *The Measure of Our Success*, 87–89.

23. See, for example, ibid.; Reed and Sautter; Hewlett; K. Zinsmeister, "Growing Up Scared," *Atlantic* 265, no. 6, 49–67; L. Schorr, *Within Our Reach: Breaking the Cycle of Disadvantage* (New York: Doubleday, 1988).

24. Thorne; Kagan; M. Goodman, *The Culture of Childhood* (Columbia University Teachers College Press, 1970); M. Speier, "The Adult Ideological Viewpoint in Studies of Childhood," in *Rethinking Childhood*, ed. A. Skolnick (Boston: Little, Brown, 1976), 168–86; F. Kessel and A. Siegel, eds., *The Child and Other Cultural Inventions* (New York: Praeger, 1983); V. Suransky, *The Erosion of Childhood* (Chicago: University of Chicago Press, 1982).

25. Kagan; Goodman; M. Richards and P. Light, eds., *Children of Social Worlds* (Cambridge: Harvard University Press, 1986); O. Stevens, *Children Talking Politics: Political Learning in Childhood* (Oxford: Martin Robinson, 1982); G. Matthews, *Dialogues with Children* (Cambridge, Mass.: Harvard University Press, 1984); M. Lipman, *Philosophy Goes to School* (Philadelphia: Temple University Press, 1988); R. Coles, *The Political Life of Children* (New York: Atlantic Monthly Press, 1986), and *The Moral Life of Children* (New York: Atlantic Monthly Press, 1986); J. Whiting and B. Whiting, *Children of Six Cultures* (Cambridge, Mass.: Harvard University Press, 1975); E. Boulding, *Children's Rights and the Wheel of Life* (New Brunswick, N.J.: Transaction, 1979); W. Corsaro, *Friendship and Peer Culture in the Early Years* (Norwood, N.J.: Ablex, 1985); J. Sommerville, *The Rise and Fall of Childhood* (Beverly Hills, Calif.: Sage, 1983).

26. Thorne; Holt; A. Jaggar, *Feminist Politics and Human Nature* (Totowa, N.J.: Rowman and Allanheld, 1983), 154; S. Firestone, *The Dialectic of Sex* (New York: Bantam, 1970); H. Cohen, *Equal Rights for Children* (Totowa, N.J.: Rowman and Littlefield, 1980).

27. L. Purdy, "Does Women's Liberation Imply Children's Liberation?" *Hypatia* 3 (1988): 49–62.

28. M. Dobbert and B. Cooke, "The Biological Foundations of Education: A Primate Based Perspective," *Educational Foundations* 1 (1987): 67–86; A. Montagu, *Growing Young* (New York: McGraw-Hill, 1981); E. Cobb, *The Ecology of Imagination in Childhood* (New York: Columbia University Press, 1977); Gideonse.

29. A. Jaggar, "Sexual Difference and Sexual Equality," in *Justice and Gender: Sex Discrimination and the Law*, ed. D. L. Rhode, (Cambridge, Mass.: Harvard University Press), 250.

30. Warren, "The Power and Promise," "Feminism and Ecology: Making Connections," and "Toward an Ecofeminist Ethic," *Studies in the Humanities*, December 1988, 140–56; J. Cheney, "Eco-feminism and Deep Ecology," *Environmental Ethics* 9 (1987): 116–45, and "Nature and the Theorizing of Difference," *Contemporary Philosophy* 13 (1990): 1–15; and K. J. Warren, *Quilting Ecofeminist Philosophy* (Boulder, Colo.: Westview, forthcoming).

31. Warren, "Feminism and Ecology."

32. U. Bronfenbrenner, *The Ecology of Human Development: Experiments by Nature and Design* (Cambridge, Mass.: Harvard University Press, 1979).

33. Holt.

34. D. Johnson, "Student-Student Interaction: The Neglected Variable in Education," *Educational Researcher*, January 1981, 5–10.

35. Cheney, "Eco-feminism and Deep Ecology."

36. J. R. Martin, *Reclaiming a Conversation: The Ideal of the Educated Woman* (New Haven, Conn.: Yale University Press, 1985).

37. L. Vygotsky, *Mind in Society: The Development of Higher Psychological Processes*, ed. M. Cole, V. John-Steiner, S. Scribner, and E. Souberman (Cambridge, Mass.: Harvard University Press, 1978).

38. Cohen.

39. Montagu, 2.

40. Warren, "Toward an Ecofeminist Ethic," 149.

41. Frye's metaphor as developed and quoted in Warren, "The Power and Promise," 136–37.

42. Thorne. For further discussion of societal images of children, see Kurth-Schai, "The Roles of Youth in Society."

43. Warren draws from U. Narayan's conception of epistemic privilege in "Toward an Ecofeminist Ethic," 149.

44. See, for example, Suransky; Gideonse; M. Wartofsky, "The Child's Construction of the World and the World's Construction of the Child: From Historical Epistemology to Historical Psychology," in *The Child and Other Cultural Inventions*, ed. Kessel and Siegel.

45. Cheney, "Nature and the Theorizing of Difference."

46. L. Sheleff, *Generations Apart: Adult Hostility to Youth* (New York: McGraw-Hill, 1981).

47. U. Narayan, "Working Together across Difference: Some Considerations on Emotions and Political Practice," *Hypatia* 3 (1988): 31–47; Marguerite K. Rivage-Suel, "Peace Education: Imagination and the Pedagogy of the Oppressed," *Harvard Educational Review* 57 (1987): 153–71.

48. For further description of the delphi technique and its adaptation for use with children and its use as a cross-generational decision-making technique, see R. Kurth-Schai, "Collecting the Thoughts of Children: A Delphic Approach," *Journal of Research and Development in Education* 21 (1988): 53–59, and "Educational Systems Design by Children for Children," *Educational Foundations* 5 (1991): 19–42.

49. Narayan.

50. "Ecological Feminism," *Zeta Magazine* 1(1988): 125.

51. This theme is woven through the works of Warren and Cheney previously cited.

52. For further discussion of environmentally responsive technology, see Rothschild; J. Smith, *Something Old, Something New, Something Borrowed, Something Due* (Missoula: Women and Technology Network, 1980). On strategies for peaceful conflict resolution, see E. Boulding, *Building a Global Civic Culture*; Rivage-Suel. On life-sustaining and life-enhancing spiritual and communal values, see chapters by C. Spretnak, R. Ruether, and Starhawk in *Healing the Wounds: The Promise of Ecofeminism*, ed. J. Plant (Philadelphia: New Society, 1989).

53. See, for example, Cobb; Stevens; R. Kurth-Schai, "Reflections from the Hearts and Minds of Children: Their Personal, Global, and Spiritual Images of the Future," Ph.D. dissertation, University of Minnesota, 1984; R. Lorenzo, "Emerging Utopian Sensibility in Children: Its Communication with Adults— Some Considerations," paper for discussion, United Nations Working Group on Household, Gender and Age Consultation, Rome, April 1982; E. Masini, "Women and Children as Builders of the Future," in *Education: A Time for Decisions*, ed. A. Harkins and K. Redd (Washington, D.C.: World Future Society, 1980).

54. Lorenzo; Masini; Kurth-Schai, 1984.

55. Examples include national organizations such as Kids for Saving Earth and numerous local programs and activities, such as those summarized by M. Weilbacher in "Earth Day: The New Children's Crusade," *E: The Environmental Magazine* 4, no. 2, 30–35.

Twelve

Ecofeminism and Meaning

Susan Griffin

In the last decade, a problem has threatened feminist theory. The crisis is in language. Questions have been raised about the word *woman*. On close examination, the word begins to dissolve. What is *she*? Who are *we*? And which *we* are we?

The use of this word opens up a series of chasms. By each of these descents one is led to a world of fiction. The term conjures up a creature who does not really exist, who is an absence, a social construct: the fantasy of cultural and political structures of power. Existing in and marked by these structures, the word *woman* is inseparable from them. And then there is the problem of nomination itself. How can one say anything *is* anything? For one defines words with other words, so by a tautological chase, the definitive meaning of meaning is deferred to a future that can never exist solely within language. Along with the word *woman*, language is doomed to failure.

But here is the core of the crisis. How can a feminist movement exist without the words, especially the word *woman*?

A regrettable and yet still predictable solution has been to create a divide. It is an old story. To survive internal crises, one creates enemies. Enter a new animal: essentialism, a category in thought by which some feminists are accused of using the word *woman*, as pure idea or pure matter without the more sophisticated knowledge that *woman* is a fiction of the social construction of gender. This creation becomes all the more possible since there is already a divide in language. Poststructural feminists have a unique vocabulary which other feminists do not understand.

Yet the solution to the problem has become in itself an even worse problem. No such animal as an *essentialist* really exists. Neither is this name one which any feminist theorist has chosen for herself, nor does *essentialism* accurately describe any major trend in feminist thought. It is instead a kind of *bête*, a creature of dreams who contains the fearsome thoughts and feelings which belong to the accuser.

Since feminism began in this century as an understanding of the social construction of gender, the idea of *essentialism* is, to borrow a phrase from Teresa de Lauretis, a "reductive opposition."[1] The word *woman* has not been used naively by feminist theorists but with the intention of transforming the constructions that define it within the Western philosophical tradition (what Derrida calls *logos*). To accuse early feminists of *essentialism* is oddly ahistorical, since the work of feminist thinkers in this century created the very ground on which gender is visible as a social construct. And if within this range a small number of women once put forward the possibility of a determining biological difference which makes women socially superior to men, or if some feminists still question whether or not biology may play a significant role along with socialization, even these notions (with which most feminist thinkers, myself included, disagree) sprang up, paradoxically, in the context of an understanding of the social construction of gender, which had created a fictional and derogatory notion of "woman."

Even the idea of a separate and different culture belonging to women was neither biologically determined nor metaphysically defined, but sprang again from the observation of the social construction of gender, which as part of that construction created separate spheres of labor, separate forms of schooling, of childrearing, so that girls were raised differently than boys, given different models of behavior, different sexual codes, different skills, crafts, even modes of knowledge, different ways of relating, roles within families, difference. That there is wide difference within that difference, small and extreme variations, does not contradict the observation that not only are women treated differently in society than men, but that women, by virtue of that different treatment, have different lives.

Finally this difference is not always regarded as negative. Escaping a dualistic (or binary) simplicity, difference can be predominantly negative and yet at the same time contain positive characteristics. As Angela Davis points out in her work on the role of African American women under slavery, forms of resistance, valuable not only to women, but for everyone's survival under slavery, could be found within that difference even in the ways that it constrained women under slavery.

And survival is significant in this discourse. Not the least of which is that now, when the word *essentialist* disappears, one is still left with the very crisis that the *bête* was created to contain. That is the crisis of the dissolving *woman*.

One might wish to hasten the death of this word.[2] The air around it is thin, its dimensions suffocating. It seems too narrow. What was once a liberation becomes a confinement. What was once a revelation becomes another form of silence. And yet with a premature death, we lose too much. We still need the word. And so the problem would appear to be insoluble. Except if one dives under it. Because to see other aspects of the construct, one must leave the interior to find a way to view language and culture from beneath.

If such is said to be impossible because of the power of language to enclose consciousness, the answer can only be that it is no less impossible for poststructuralism, postmodernism, and deconstruction, even *if* they place the focus inside, rather than outside, language. And what may be the only solution will be the recognition of many varieties of women within the word *woman* and at the same time the acceptance of various approaches, viewpoints, starting points, perspectives in discourse. So a problem raised by poststructuralist language philosophy might find the beginnings of an answer in ecofeminism.

But even to begin this beginning, one must correct a misreading of ecofeminism, which has at times also been accused of *essentialism*. Not wishing to revive this self-reflective beast, before using the approach of ecofeminism, it is important to clarify what ecofeminism is and what it is not.

What is critical in the emergence of ecofeminism is the meeting between ecology and feminism. Concepts of ecosystems, of natural processes which precede and yet also include human consciousness are at the heart of the ecofeminist approach. And these concepts accompany and illuminate the ecofeminist understanding of both the oppression of women and the social construction of gender.

This approach has been confused by both its detractors and some of its admirers with the very social construct it delineates: mainly the fiction that women are either biologically or metaphysically (if such is not an oxymoron) closer to nature.

The confusion becomes more complex when ecofeminist thinkers speak about traditional women's cultures which are in practice, in modes of consciousness, and also sometimes even in ideas of themselves, less alienated from nature and more in concert with the processes of ecosystems. This is quite another meaning of "closer to nature." If and when ecofeminism suggests that some women may at times be closer to nature than men, this closeness is understood as a result of the social construction of gender and of the socialization and division of labor which precede from those constructions.

Just as poststructural feminism has criticized the dominant culture's use of the words *woman* and *nature*, so ecofeminism criticizes those uses from another perspective. And like poststructuralism, ecofeminism sees both words as belonging to a system of thought in which hidden significance makes the meaning of the word *woman* dependent on a certain idea of nature. Like poststructuralists, ecofeminists argue that neither the word *woman* nor the word *nature* can be read apart from each other and both are shaped by, marked by, and contain traces of a larger system, a philosophy that is also a submerged psychology.

But where poststructural feminism chooses language as both its site and its focus, ecofeminism chooses the various ecological processes which make up the earth and its atmosphere as a source for knowledge. And so when the poststructural question about the meaning or meaninglessness of the word *woman* is encountered from an ecofeminist perspective, the ground shifts. Or rather, one might say, the ground appears.

Because when one keeps erasing the terms *woman* and, of course, *man* and, especially, *human*, where do we land?

Is the ground we now stand on a *tabula rasa*?

A white page, a spread sheet empty of lines, a field with no electromagnetic forces, no rules, no gravity? An openness with no necessity, no boundaries or membranes, no internal sense, no intrinsic meaning, nothing to be recognized, nothing that can be violated, nothing inviolate?

One can easily see the direction of the drift. It is not far from this philosophical non-ground, to genetic engineering, satellites in space which mechanically mimic ecosystems (and are proposed as a solution to the destruction of the biosphere), virtual reality replacing a reality grown too grim to face, cybernetic labor creating an even vaster unemployment, cloned cows, women as wombs as a kind of soil to breed children, radiated food, chemical food, the concept of mind over matter gone berserk, so that what is physical and of the earth seems infinitely malleable to purposes of power or even fantasy, and ultimately dispensable.

But another approach altogether from an ecofeminist perspective brings the ground into view once more. And yet one need not replace poststructuralism with ecofeminism. Attempts to establish a hegemony of ideas not only mirror Western *logos*, they also truncate the field of possible knowledge. Instead a shift can occur when insights from both approaches are held in mind. And these approaches are not as far apart as one might imagine.

Derrida's brilliant insight that neither meaning nor definition can reside in one word alone, that the sense of the word relies on other words, all containing histories, traces of a self-containing, self-sustaining system resembles the idea of an ecosystem. Within an ecosystem a tree is only provisionally a tree. Its root system cannot really be separated from the soil which nourishes it and which it shapes. It is constantly in an active exchange with the air whose very nature is defined by the leaves of the tree. Those same leaves fall and become part of a process of composting, and eventually become soil. Even the light by which one can see a tree is a crucial part of the tree's substance. The tree converts sunlight into wood, leaf, flower, shade, soil, bark. Not to speak of the process by which the tree affects the atmosphere which eventually determines how much light can fall to the surface of the earth.

There is however a singular difference between the two approaches. The closed system of language as described by deconstruction is a negation, a void, masquerading as meaning. But, of course, an ecosystem has no meaning outside of itself. It is meaning.

This argument is not meant, however, to privilege any culturally constructed idea of the meaning of nature over the meaning of language. Except in its own hubristic self-portrait, can language exist outside nature? Ecofeminism has this in common with deconstruction too, a critique of metaphysics, the idea that anything, any idea, or *essence* of being, precedes existence. But this is also true of language. The sounds of words have been determined thus by the shape of the human mouth, the capacities of the human tongue, and the range of the human ear. No words in any language contain sounds in the higher ranges that can be heard by other mammals.[3] Language is shaped to the human body. And because language arrives from and is part of nature, the meaning of ecosystems also belongs to language.

This is not to say that the problems of language disappear when language is applied to nature. Concepts of nature are many and various and have been used to justify the closed and totalitarian systems of political and social power (which also in turn create closed systems of language). There is of course the obvious discourse from the nineteenth century in which nature was evoked as the reason why women ought to remain in traditional roles, and African Americans in slavery. The derogation of homosexuality is also often based on a concept of nature. Lesbians or gay men are called "unnatural." In *Mein Kampf*, Adolf Hitler commandeered the power of nature, claiming at one and the same time that nature holds unfathomable secrets, and yet, that Nazism held the key to those secrets.

But these problems are not erased by erasing the word *nature* or any idea of nature from language. Though the separation of nature from language and culture is a fiction, it is one which culture and language have authored. In positing itself above nature, culture has created a separation and an alienation. If one can only refer to language but not to nature, this rift does not disappear, but deepens. In a civilization that pits culture against nature, if nature cannot be mentioned, it simply disappears.

In Western culture, language continually bears forth a conceit, sometimes hidden and sometimes not, that it can master nature. This is perhaps an early desire in the human psyche, at least within European culture. A desire and also a confusion. A child nearly three years old has a stomachache and tells her grandmother it must be from all the strawberries she ate. Her grandmother tells her that she ate those strawberries months ago. Yes, the child says, but I am telling you about it now. Elsewhere I have referred to Wittgenstein's observation that in language one can refer to an infinite line of trees when in nature such cannot exist. A wish exists within this culture, to erase the problems of nature, mortality, loss, loss of control, in and with language. This is not possible. And to erase the word *nature* from our vocabulary may be to eliminate the only way of knowing the limitations of language in language.

What remains then is the problematic nature of words, in particular, the nature of the word *nature* and of the word *woman*. But Derrida's description of the dependent nature of words in language provides a key, especially when one notices the similarity of this dependency to ecosystems. One cannot ultimately define a tree separately from its environment. So also, in language, one cannot understand the significance of a word separately from other words and the underlying social constructions which mark them. This negation of the definitive meaning of the word can be a tragedy leading to nihilism, but it can also be full of promise. Taken from a different perspective the dependency of words on each other, and finally the inability of language to determine truth, makes language dependent on other forms of knowledge, and other modes of existence; it signals an end to the only partly submerged goal of language to master reality, and it also sets language free from that goal. Language can then be explored as another mode of existence. Real in itself. A different territory. And this may be the most significant difference language can name.

Above all language has the capacity to portray various aspects and possibilities of human consciousness. Yes, language confines consciousness according to certain social constructs. But certain constructions begin to change when they are perceived as such, much the same way that certain confinements can become, temporarily, a means of liberation.

Certainly poststructural feminism as well as ecofeminism understands this. And both approaches also understand that the social construction of women cannot be understood without the social construction of men, and neither can be understood without the ideas of homosexuality and heterosexuality. Standing alone, the claim of each word on the truth is more forceful. But put side by side, explored as social constructions in tandem, the subtext of the fiction can more easily be revealed. Not just man and woman but a system of gender becomes visible in which man is the negation of woman and woman the negation of man. Depending on the angle of vision, both contain "the other half" of binary qualities in each other. If a man is courageous, a woman is vulnerable, if a man is strong, a woman is tender, if a man is intelligent and intellectual, a woman is emotional and sensual. These are all of course ideal qualities, themselves fictions, and insofar as they exist in real men and women are distortions of these ideals, even if the ideals were desirable.

This is the reason why the two halves of this bifurcated system cannot simply be patched together. Qualities in both halves are dependent on the system, a system of unequal power which demands domination and submission. When motivated by fear, vulnerability and tenderness become forms of submission. And the strength and courage supposed to be male, related to the requirements of armies and of men as participants in the growth of empire, are accompanied by a dissociation from emotions and from sensual knowledge. One is no more born a man than one is born a woman. A man learns to be tough, to dull his sensual perceptions and responses. And the making of boys into men belongs to the same habit of mind that uses the conquering of nature as a central metaphor.

But women do not escape this metaphor either. A woman may submit to a man because she can engage vicariously in his domination of the earth. Nor are women really connected with sensuality or emotions. The system requires women to be more connected with the body than are men, for whom this connection represents a threat. But first the realm of body and emotions must be designified, made meaningless. And dissociation is required for women too, as a way to survive many kinds of abuse.

Yet something is missing from this system. And that is another system, the ecosystem. Nature in fact is a hidden partner in the binary. This dyad is not possible, even in the discourse of *logos*, without the invocation of nature. Nature is used to justify the social construction of gender. And that it is a social construction of nature, an idea of nature that is used to justify an idea of gender and sexuality, makes this not less so but more the case.

In order to *reveal* the social construction of gender as a fiction, to understand its subtext, its goals of mastery and dominance, one must include the social construction of nature in this revelation. And the reverse is also true. The fictions made of nature cannot be understood apart from the fictions of gender.

And of course one other element might be said to be *essential*, one that must be said to *be*, and that is unconstructed nature. For in addition to the idea of the body there is a real body. And though this body varies enormously and appears to change radically depending on the perspective from which it is either viewed or experienced, and even though both view and experience are socially constrained, and distorted, still, like the bodies of other animals, and plants, like air or soil, the human body has a nature, even if unnamed and unnameable, one that can be violated, by pollution, by starvation, by chemical, nuclear or genetic manipulation, and by more subtle acts through which physical existence itself becomes invisible.

This is the grounding of ecofeminism. Ecofeminism begins with the fact of natural existence. Even if nature cannot be entirely nor accurately contained in language, ecofeminism aims toward the visibility of nature as a reality. With this approach one can begin to understand that the social construction (exploitation, destruction) of nature is implicit in and inseparable from the social construction of gender. The equation is not that women equal nature, but that by understanding how and why woman is associated with nature, one can decode many structures of injustice in Western society. The social construction of "race," for instance, which is also justified by an idea of nature, cannot be separated from ideas of gender. And the reverse is also true.

The inclusion in ecofeminism of many kinds of social constructions (oppressions) is not simply a loose coalition. Taken together, these social constructions define each other. The many fictions of women, of gender, of nature, of race, support and explain each other. And to a great extent these fictions are all bolstered and even stand upon a fiction of nature. But finally all of these categories also represent caesuras, pauses, sighs, a turning away, a blink, or even a forced blindness. What they claim to represent is designified, truncated, reduced, misread, diminished, derogated, left out of the equation altogether. One might say that to erase woman, or nature, would be like erasing homosexuality, or African American culture, which are already not only *sous rature*, under erasure, but nearly eliminated or eliminated entirely from *logos*. That all these are replaced by fictional or token representations does not make the erasure less complete. It merely hides the fact of the erasure. And it does something else, it hides the dependence of the entire social construction of *logos* on what it will not admit exists.

To give a simple example, thought relies on sensuality and on physicality to such a great degree that thought cannot be separated from what is called nature. The mind, which at one and the same time claims the power of nature as its own and places itself above nature in a sphere of pure ideas, falters without an adequate blood supply. One simply has to suffer a few days of mental confusion, names forgotten, a practical task unfathomable, to understand this. And *logos* itself, this particular, hubristic tradition of thought, is dependent too. For a speaker of language, consciousness cannot be separated from language, language cannot exist without consciousness. But it is also true that within language, the very vocabulary of thought relies on metaphors taken from nature, for instance the word *culture* has its roots in the act of cultivation, meaning to cultivate the soil.

And mental structures also mirror nature. Could it also be, for example, that binary systems reflect human physiology, when we say, for example, "on the one hand," and "on the other hand," and also the diurnal nature of time which is so dramatically marked by day and night? And certainly the fiction of immortality which in *logos* is metaphysical has been stolen from nature, the continuity and sustainability of life itself.

Designifying nature, the same *logos* which erases the necessity of blood, steals the meaning of blood, giving it a multitude of fictional meanings, not the least of which is "race," hides and shames menstrual blood and the blood of birth, elevates the blood of the soldier, and reduces the implicate meaning within blood, for example, by failing to note, or erasing the intelligence of blood cells. This is not a mystical concept. All cells possess a membrane which deciphers the chemical nature of what surrounds it, allowing some substances into the interior of the cell and keeping out other substances. Moreover the immune system, one aspect of which is located in blood cells, is infinitely more complex than the current models for scientific knowledge can even register, without being transformed. In other words, what we think of as transcendent thought is not only dependent on nature, but reshapes the very substance and manner of significance through an understanding of natural processes it nevertheless describes as separate from intelligence. And we are left by all this with a crisis not only in language but regarding the possibility of continued human intelligence. At this moment in history, while blood cells carry oxygen to the brain, a continued supply of oxygen on the earth is endangered by *logos*.

But if *logos* denies the dependency of human consciousness on nature, the traditional division of labor between men and women creates a similar hidden dependency and signification both in social practice and in social construct. Traditional women's labor—domestic work, childrearing, the growing of small amounts of food to sustain one family, the maintenance of emotional relatedness and connections—has been devalued. Such labor is not part of the Gross National Product in the United States. It is not paid. Eurocentric development in Africa, ignoring women's vital work in sustainability, has created starvation. The devaluation of childrearing and the education of children, a heedlessness about the needs of children, are crucial among other factors that have created an atmosphere of extreme violence in the lives of children in the United States today.

That masculine socialization also plays a crucial role in this violence is not contradictory. On the contrary, since fictional signification and designification work together in the same system, the devaluation of childraising and the idea of the masculine as dominate work hand in hand to create this violence.

But devaluation and designification, while similar, are not the same. The significance of domestic work, childbearing, childraising, making connections in family and community, growing and preparing food has also been erased and replaced with a fiction. And this fiction, the ideal family, in turn creates institutions. So one can speak of "the institution of motherhood" which Adrienne Rich so brilliantly separates from a possible experience of mothering, and from another meaning of that experience, which has been destroyed or distorted by the institution. One glimpses this existence, this meaning, and occasionally dwells within it, often desires it, yet even the desire is forbidden. That the knowledge of this meaning occurs in inarticulate patches, or only as potential, and is sometimes sentimentalized, should not be the pretext for joining with *logos* in the effort to hide it.

Moreover, actual domestic work and childrearing, even as institutionalized, contain knowledge, a valuable perspective, and an epistemology. The progression of empire is dependent on a home front not only to produce weapons, but also to preserve sanity. Biologically women are no closer to nature than men. And moreover both men and women live in a system that produces dissociation from natural processes, and from the body, or bodies. But within this system, and in order for it to survive, a place had to be created in which a closer meeting with nature could take place. So in the home food is gathered or grown, cleaned of earth (and now chemical pollutants), prepared, eaten, the waste of it handled, the waste from bodies handled. One is fed by this work in two ways, by the ingestion of food but also by the ingestion of knowledge. A knowledge of dependency. Of interdependency. This is evident, and yet it is not. The labor is hidden, in the "private" life. So along with this secret, the dependency of human life on the life of the biosphere is also hidden. And in the same way the dependence of anyone, including men, on traditional "women's work," is hidden too. It is transformed, distorted, and covered by the diminishment of this work and by the economic and social "dependency," of women on men.

And because dependency is demeaned within the system of *logos* in general, the meaning of "women's work" is made even less visible. Because there is meaning in dependence itself, or put another way, in the connectedness of all life. Despite the overuse and misuse of this word *connectedness*, this is no minor concept, no sentimental notion either. It includes a meeting with nature, the dissolution of the binary division between nature and culture, and the fall of *logos* from its pose of transcendence.

This is not to valorize housework, nor woman's traditional role within Eurocentric culture, but to discover what is buried beneath the disaster. Yet even if language begins to acknowledge women's work apart from the social construction of that work, and to allow this work to have meaning, the problem of categorization remains. Not all women do "women's work." And those who do, do it under different conditions. The category of woman in this sense creates silence.

Still, what may not be so evident is that all women, at least under contemporary conditions, are affected by the division of labor according to the social construction of gender. And we are affected in many ways, not the least of which is the idea of gender itself which is intertwined with and depends on this division. Anyone called a woman within Eurocentric culture is regarded in association with "woman's work." Moreover the association between a certain kind of work and nature makes the character of the derogation of women as a category clearer. And the fact of this association affects the entire culture and everyone in it. "Women's work" is part of an alienation from nature, and also from self, from the needs of and the life of the body, and one of the means through which both the social construction of woman and the social construction of nature is created.

This pattern, by which what exists in some women's lives affects all those who are traditionally called women, is true of all the socially significant differences between women. In this way a dependency exists which is also similar to an ecosystem. But the dependency is often hidden. And the claim to truth professed by various social constructs depends on the burial of the connections between them.

The paradox exists that in order to reveal the limitations of category one must name the category. Perhaps to describe the history of the feminist movement, and the atmosphere in which it arose, can shed some light here. What is called the second wave of feminism (but which is instead probably one of many successive waves) arose in the period when "black power" was an emerging concept. The word *black*, which had been derogatory, was seized, and this seizure was pivotal. It led to greater understanding not only regarding the social construct of "race," but for the potentiality of change. Many of us who were in the emerging feminist movement had also been part of and schooled by the civil rights movement. For myself, the very shape of social justice, the understanding of how culture affects lives, an understanding of internalized oppression, together with an awareness of the possibility of resistance, came from and through this movement.

The use of category makes oppression visible and though this may seem less urgent now, it could easily become urgent again for those who are called women. And when any category is either criticized or expanded other categories are used to question or correct it. Variation is one half of the binary system it forms with category. Both are necessary for discernment, and no discernment is ultimately either variation or category but is always both.

Nor does diversity obviate the social construction of a category by which anyone called by that name is oppressed, confined, and derogated. The term African American covers a wide variety of people who differ in class, gender, sexuality, country of birth (or ancestor's birth), culture, not to mention differences of temperament, inclination, idiosyncrasies. It is as much a fiction as any other noun. But there is common ground. And one meeting place is the place of oppression itself. Not the exact conditions of the oppression, nor the manner of suffering, or of bearing the suffering, but of suffering, of the fact of falling under this regard, the racist regard, the fact of being categorized and interpreted by a reigning *logos*, hostile to those it has named thus.

This in turn does not answer the problem of category that claims to be absolute in its definition, or that defines a more general condition according one narrow circumstance. Women are different, and the conditions we face are different. Yet cannot this problem be turned in another direction? This need not erase the word *woman* so much as simultaneously widen its meaning, and change the meaning of definition within language. If one possible reading of poststructuralism is that words do not have meaning out of the context of other words (of language and a consciousness formed by social constructs), one ecofeminist response is that meaning exists only in context, and that it even *is* context.

Both the word *woman* and the social construction of gender have meaning as they are perceived to be connected to a web of other meanings. The solution then is not to erase the words but to see how they change when concealed connections and differences are made evident.

This is clearer when a shared event or a condition, such as rape, is described and understood through this network of meanings. Since along with gay men (who among other things are accused of being "effeminate") women have in common that we are specified as targets of rape by virtue of the name *woman*, the nature of rape is made visible along with the word *woman*. That men more often commit rape than women contributes a key to the understanding of rape. Considered alongside the social construction of gender, a rape committed by a man against a woman can be understood more as an act of domination and aggression than as an expression of an irrepressible, uncensored sexuality. In fact rape becomes one effect (and also a cause) of another kind of censorship, the censorship of gender itself. That gay men are also raped by heterosexual men further reveals the construction of heterosexuality and of sexuality itself. In the same way, to ignore diversity among women, differences for instance in class, or culture, is to fail to understand the real nature of rape. Working women subjected to sexual harassment by their employers, Irish indentured servants raped, women working in factories raped by foremen and their bosses, African American women raped under slavery by plantation owners, and with greater impunity by white men today, calls into question the notion of rape as an exogenous activity, a taboo. The same men who protect some women, "their own" women, rape others. So one begins to understand that this protection does not exist for the sake of women, who ought to be inviolate, who have the right not to be violated, but for the sake of the man who is protecting she whom he also regards in some way as a possession and for the sake of his own pride. Rape then can be connected to lynching. And masculinity begins to reveal another aspect, that aspect which depends on the destruction of the pride (masculinity) of other men.

Again the meaning of rape, and also the word *woman*, changes when one understands that women called whores or who are prostitutes are not "protected" by other men from rape, and that rape has traditionally been acceptable in marriage. And all these understandings change once again when one adds nature to this web of connections. Is there a nature outside social construct? That men feel obliged to prove their masculinity, through rape for example, and the destruction of the masculinity of other men is a clue. Unless one is a philosopher trained in Western *logos*, why should one feel motivated to prove something that already exists naturally? The obligation to prove "masculinity" suggests that another masculine nature might exist, or at least its potential.

And finally the metaphorical use of the word *rape* to describe various kinds of ecological destruction, as in the rape of a forest, opens up another layer of meaning. Unwittingly this metaphor suggests a profound connection between the social construction of nature and the social construction of woman. And simultaneously, it describes the desire to conquer and violate woman and nature, and a less evident fear of both, since why does one have to conquer what is not challenging, fearsome, and in some way, wild, falling as it does outside the idea of mastery and control?

Neither rape, nor the word *woman* can be understood without an understanding of racism, nor can racism be understood without an understanding of the social construction of gender, nor can either be fully understood apart from ecology. The racist mind, the misogynist mind, the mind afraid of nature and which denies natural limitation and mortality are often the same mind. The historical convergence of these attitudes is not a coincidence. They share a pattern and a psychology. To name this pattern is not to wipe out the differences between women, but rather to clear a path for a clearer perception of those differences, and perhaps to leap over or dive under a false difference which alters every perception, the illusion that we who speak and write are not part of nature, not part of each other.

The question poststructural feminism asks about the word *woman* is important, and this essay is not meant to silence that question, but to continue it in still another direction. The intent of deconstruction has been to liberate consciousness from social constructions which favor dominant political structures of power. But even Derrida has noticed a tendency in the United States to use deconstruction for a nearly opposite purpose, to strengthen an "institutional closure."[4] One must use certain phrases, a certain vocabulary, a certain approach to be heard. This simply substitutes one *cul de sac* for another, one authority, or authorized set of texts, for another. (Especially when the *modus operandi* and goal of the discourse seems to be to invalidate other discourse and hence "conquer" the field.)

And what is equally crucial to see at this moment in history is that it is not only fictional meaning from which we suffer. We are also suffering from the lack of meaning altogether. This is not a new condition but it has intensified to the point of unbearableness. This state of mind does not confine itself to the privileged, many of whom are content with the false meaning of social fictions which give them power. On the contrary, as Cornel West writes, "The proper starting point for the crucial debate about the prospects for black America is an examination of the nihilism that increasingly pervades black communities. *Nihilism is to be understood here not as a philosophic doctrine that there are no grounds for legitimate standards or authority; it is far more the lived experience of coping with a life of horrifying meaninglessness, hopelessness and (most important) lovelessness."*

The question of meaning is vital. One of the bleakest consequences of the social system we share is that we cease to be able to experience the meaning of existence. Of what *is*. As Cornel West writes, this is not a philosophical problem. And yet philosophy can address it, and ceases to be relevant when it does not. Because there have been false meanings, does not require that meaning disappear. Western philosophy has been possessed by an obsessive desire to fix meaning. Now we see it cannot be fixed anywhere. Meaning, like life, is interdependent. Similar to the processes by which an ecosystem sustains itself, meaning arises from meeting and connection, from overlapping boundaries, shifting identities. No single perspective can reveal the truth of the whole. The truth exists in no particular site. No particular site can even be said to exist separately, or permanently. And perhaps no written or spoken meaning can ever subsume or confine the experience of meaning (or hope, or love.) But the relinquishment of this hubris may provide a beginning for the recognition of something, despite this, still wanting and wanted in our names.

Notes

1. Teresa de Lauretis, "Upping the Anti [*sic*] in Feminist Theory," in *Conflicts in Feminism*, ed. Marianne Hirsch and Evelyn Fox Keller (New York: Routledge, 1990), p. 261.

2. For a deeper discussion of this problem, see the work of Judith Butler, in particular *Gender Trouble, Feminism and the Subversions of Identity* (New York: Routledge, 1990).

3. In Hebrew spaces exist for what cannot or should not be pronounced but this too can be seen as admitting limitations of physical existence which also limit knowledge and the ability to articulate what is.

4. As cited by Madan Sarup, *An Introductory Guide to Post-Structuralism and Post-modernism* (Athens: University of Georgia Press, 1993), p. 55.

Thirteen

Ecofeminist Literary Criticism

Gretchen T. Legler

Ecofeminist literary criticism is a hybrid criticism, a combination of ecological or environmental criticism and feminist literary criticism. It offers
a unique combination of literary and philosophical perspectives that gives
literary and cultural critics a special lens through which they can investi-
gate the ways nature is represented in literature and the ways representations of nature are linked with representations of gender, race, class, and
sexuality. One of the primary projects of ecofeminist literary critics is
analysis of the cultural construction of nature, which also includes an analysis of language, desire, knowledge, and power.

Ecological literary critics argue that the English profession responded to
two of the most crucial movements of the 1960s and 1970s—the civil
rights and feminist movements—by changing hiring and promotion practices; by embracing race, gender, and class as part of literary theory and
criticism; and by engaging in a serious critique of the literary canon. But
the profession did not respond in the same way to the crucial issue of the
environment—a third major social movement of the last thirty years. Environmental concerns have mysteriously not made their way, until recently,
into the profession of literature. Ecocritics argue that what appears to be a
deepening global environmental crisis makes it necessary that the profession pay attention to environmental issues, specifically by addressing how
literature influences human behavior with regard to the natural world.[1]

Ecofeminists argue that dealing with practical environmental problems
(where to place nuclear waste dumps, where to build garbage incinerators,
how to design water systems in Latin American villages) is both an eco-

logical and a feminist task because the uses and abuses of the environment that have led to what they see as the potentially catastrophic present are largely due to a patriarchal environmental ethic that has conceptualized land as "woman." This patriarchal land ethic has been mostly uninformed and uninfluenced by the ways in which gender, race, and class come into play in the definition of nature and what is natural. Ecofeminists argue that unmasking the metaphorical, conceptual links between gender, race, class, and representations of nature in literature is an important part of forming a more viable environmental ethic.[2]

Ecofeminists also argue that constructions of nature as female (as mother/virgin) are essential to the maintenance of this harmful environmental ethic and are essential to the maintenance of hierarchical ways of thinking that justify the oppression of various "others" in patriarchal culture by ranking them "closer to nature" or by declaring their practices "natural" or "unnatural." Ecofeminists suggest that reimagining what nature is and what kinds of relationships can exist between humans and the nonhuman world is part of the elimination of institutionalized oppression on the basis of gender, race, class, and sexual preference and part of what may aid in changing abusive environmental practices.

Combining these two fields of knowledge—ecological literary criticism and ecofeminist criticism—allows us to ask important questions about literary texts. Some of the questions scholars in this growing field are asking include: What is nature writing? Does it include fiction, or does it only include nonfictional, pseudo-scientific essays, written by those who are already alienated from the natural world? What are the race, class, and gender politics of limiting the genre? What are the relationships between modernist/humanist concepts of the self and the body and representations of nature in literature? How can you reconceptualize human relationships with nature if nature is still regarded as "other" to humans/culture? In reconceptualizing human relationships with nature (granting nature "agency"), how do you avoid the Walt Disney syndrome (anthropomorphizing the natural world) or the pitfalls of the Romantic "perversion model" (we were all right until René Descartes and Francis Bacon came along and separated us from our "natural" harmony with the world)? How can developing an ecocritical literary theory help solve real environmental problems?

One important role ecofeminist literary criticism can play in this burgeoning field of inquiry is that it can serve as a kind of pivot from which scholars can critique the canon of nature literature—a position from which scholars can take another look at the nature writing of Ralph Waldo Emerson, Henry David Thoreau, John Muir, and others, whose works make up some of the first texts in the canon of traditional American nature literature.[3] Despite efforts to forge a new understanding of nature and a new relationship with it, many canonical authors still place nature "out there" as an "other."[4] Many canonical authors refine and entrench the notion of nature as a sacred place where only solitary, single, and chaste men go to cleanse their spirits and be one with God. Many canonical works also reinforce the humanist notion that the "authentic" self is necessarily dependent on the managing of spatial boundaries, especially the boundaries between nature and culture, between the me and not me, between the I and the other.[5]

Critiquing canonical works through an ecofeminist lens might include investigating the ways in which gender, race, and class are represented in and inform the writings of these "fathers" of American nature writing; deconstructing the canon of American nature writing by insisting that the definition of nature writing is too narrow, that it excludes, for instance, fiction, poetry, and personal narratives by Euro-American women, by women of color, by Native Americans, by colonized peoples, by nonwhite male writers; critiquing the very notion of "form" as a way to define a genre and insisting that genre or canon formation is a politicized process, and in the case of nature writing, that it has resulted in a canon that reflects masculinist values and assumptions about the natural world.

Last but perhaps most important, ecofeminist literary critics can engage in the process of "re-visioning" human relationships with the natural world by raising awareness about a whole range of alternative stories about landscape and the natural world that have heretofore been ignored as "nature writing."[6]

The work of contemporary women nature writers is an especially rich field for ecofeminist literary critics. Essayists, poets, and novelists including Gretel Ehrlich, Annie Dillard, Linda Hasselstrom, Sue Hubbell, Alice Walker, Josephine Johnson, Lucille Clifton, Joy Harjo, Mary Oliver, Ursula Le Guin, Leslie Silko, and Diane Ackerman are developing what could be called a "postmodern pastoral"—a posthumanist construction of human relationships with nature that makes more sense in a postmodern world; a vision that is informed by ecological and feminist theories, and one that images human/nature relationships as "conversations" between knowing subjects.

Many ecofeminists insist that how we act toward the material world—rocks, forests, rivers, wolves—is influenced by and influences our language, not only in terms of syntax and metaphor but also in terms of conceptual frameworks.[7] Donna Haraway notes in "Situated Knowledges" that central to the process of revising our actions and our language is a reconception of nature not as passive matter, as an object of study, but as an active subject.[8] This process of "embodying nature" involves writing nature out of a position as a passive mirror of culture into a position as actor or agent. Haraway notes that ecofeminists have been central in this movement, "insisting on some version of the world as active subject, not as a resource to be mapped and appropriated in bourgeois, Marxist or masculinist projects" (593). I argue that contemporary women nature writers are also central to this movement toward understanding human relationships with nature differently and that ecofeminist literary criticism can help us understand the richness of their work.

Ecofeminist critic Patrick Murphy suggests that an ecofeminist criticism might include the search for "emancipatory strategies" in ecological writing—the investigation of what ways and to what degrees a work challenges previous constructions of nature and human relationships with nature.[9] The "reconstruction of nature" is not possible without a widespread philosophical, ethical, conceptual shifting—a radical move away from patriarchal philosophy. I suggest that "emancipatory" stories produced by some contemporary authors coincide with, inform, and are informed by "emancipatory" projects being carried in other disciplines: French feminist efforts to revision phallic representations of female desire and sexuality, efforts by feminist scientists to develop a theory of "dynamic objectivity," and efforts by ecofeminist philosophers to develop an ecofeminist environmental ethic. Together these theories form a web within which the revision of nature is taking place.

Using the notion of "emancipatory strategies" as a point of departure, I would like to suggest that contemporary women writers whose subject is human relationships with the land might employ some of the following "emancipatory strategies" in their effort to reimagine nature and human relationships with the natural world:

1. "Re-mything" nature as a speaking, "bodied" subject.
2. Erasing or blurring of boundaries between inner (emotional, psychological, personal) and outer (geographic) landscapes, or the erasing or blurring of self-other (human/nonhuman, I/Thou) distinctions.
3. Re-eroticizing human relationships with a "bodied" landscape, or the introduction in Euro-American texts and the reconfiguration in some Native American texts of ritual sexual intercourse as a means of speaking with the land.
4. Historicizing and politicizing nature and the author as a participant in nature.
5. Expressing an ethic of caring friendship, or "a loving eye," as a principle for relationships with nature.
6. Attempting to unseat vision, or "mind" knowledge, from a privileged position as a way of knowing, or positing the notion that "bodies" know.

7. Affirming the value of partial views and perspectives, the importance of "bioregions," and the locatedness of human subjects.

Le Guin, in *Buffalo Gals and Other Animal Presences*, grants animals
individual subjecthood by allowing them to speak, to have voices and desires. She remarks in her introduction, "Animals don't talk—everybody
knows that" (9). She writes that in believing this, "civilized Man has gone
deaf. . . . He hears only his own words making up the world" (10). Talking
to animals seems naive and simplistic, but Le Guin's narrative of human/
animal community is not, as she points out, a simple harmony. She notes
that as much as the myth that animals can't talk is a "lie," so is the myth
of the peaceable kingdom—it denies wildness. The title story, "Buffalo
Gals, Won't You Come Out Tonight," is the story of a coyote, a slippery
trickster figure, who rescues a girl from a plane crash and brings her back
into a dreamtime animal community. Coyote is raunchy, sexual, crazy,
"sleeps around," has conversations with her turds, and travels back and
forth between "Their Town" (the human community) and the animal community. In the end coyote dies by eating poisoned salmon, and "Gal"
learns a lesson about relationships between human and nonhuman worlds.
In "The Direction of the Road," Le Guin comments on the perceived passivity of plants as she writes of a tree beside a highway whose job it has
always been to "loom and fade" as humans "appear," giving them the
impression that they are moving. The story culminates when the tree
"crashes into" a car, killing the driver. The driver looks up at the moment of his death and sees the tree. The tree complains that in that instant the driver "saw me under the aspect of eternity. He confused me with
eternity," with death, with fixity. "If they wish to see death visibly in the
world, that is their business, not mine," the tree says. "I will not act Eternity for them" (107–108).
In "Am I Blue," Walker writes about a white horse, Blue, whose initial
boredom and misery are relieved when a brown horse is "put with" him in
the pasture, only to be taken away after Blue impregnates her. Blue's look
of unabashed happiness turns to one of piercing grief. "If I had been born
into slavery and my partner had been sold or killed, my eyes would have
looked like that," Walker writes (7). It shocks Walker that she should know
how Blue feels. "I was shocked that I had forgotten that human animals
and nonhuman animals can communicate quite well" (5). Walker connects
this realization about our notion that "beasts" cannot feel grief or happiness with similar notions about women not being able to think, about
blacks being "naturally" lazy, about slavery being a "natural" institution, and children enjoying being frightened—about oppression justified
by "natural" fact (8).

What is partly at work in Le Guin's and Walker's revisions is what Haraway and Evelyn Fox Keller discuss in their critiques of modern science. Both make calls for a "dynamic objectivity" that would, in Haraway's words, "require that the object of knowledge be pictured as an actor, an agent, not as a screen or ground or a resource" (592). In other words, that "nature" be conceived of as more than inert matter that is probed and penetrated; that it have metaphorical status as a speaking, feeling, alive subject. What is also at work here is an important revision of the notion that nature is fixed. Diana Fuss, in *Essentially Speaking*, suggests that reconceiving of nature as a fluid, changing, historicized, constructed concept might be a way out of the essentialism/antiessentialism debate. Fuss suggests that the debate has always been grounded on the notion that appeals to "nature" are appeals to an oppressive, fixed, ahistorical concept. "It might be necessary to begin questioning the constructionist assumption that nature and fixity go together (naturally) just as sociality and change go together (naturally)," she writes (6). Also at work in these stories is the notion, which grows out of quantum physics, as explained by Elizabeth Dodson Gray in *Green Paradise Lost*, that "inert matter" is full of life, that objects are "patterns of energy," and that they participate in a continuous dance of energy (64).

Another way some contemporary women nature writers are articulating a "postmodern pastoral" is by imaging nature not only as a speaking subject but also as a desiring subject. In Emerson, Thoreau, and Muir we see sexual energy between "man" and nature channeled into a chaste, filial relationship; in Susan Griffin's words, "a silencing of eros." But in the work of some contemporary women nature writers we see this relationship imaged in a different way. Oliver, for instance, insists in her poetry not only upon the articulation of female desire but also upon imaging nature as desiring. In "Honey at the Table," "The Honey Tree," "Humpbacks," "Lightning," "Blossom," "The Plum Trees," and perhaps especially in "The Gardens," Oliver develops rich erotic relationships between the human female speaker and the landscape. While Patricia Yaeger suggests that the hunger of the speaker in "The Honey Tree" is for a language with which to express female sexual desire, I argue that, more explicitly and even more radically, the poem is about expressing lesbian desire in and through a relationship with the natural world. When Oliver writes, "Oh, anyone can see / how I love myself at last! / how I love the world! climbing / by day or night / in the wind, in the leaves, kneeling / at the secret rip, the cords / of my body stretching / and signing in the / heaven of appetite," the imagery seems to suggest the "secret rip" of a woman's body (81).

It is in this way that French feminist theories of writing the body come into play with ecofeminist ideas of reimaging nature. French feminist theory suggests that women's sexuality has been defined within phallic discourse as a mirror of and compliment to male desire. French feminists argue for a celebration of women, their bodies, their sexual pleasure, as erotically autonomous from male desire, and attempt to create a symbolic language that will speak women's sexuality, women's pleasure, or *jouissance*, outside of phallic discourse. This process of writing women's bodies they call *écriture féminine*. Nature, I argue, has been inscribed in the same way that women's bodies and sexual pleasure have been inscribed in patriarchal discourse, as passive, interceptive, docile, as mirror and complement. The conceptual links between women and nature suggested by ecofeminists make rewriting one part of rewriting the other.[10]

Another way some contemporary women authors are articulating a "postmodern pastoral" is by historicizing themselves as participants in a natural landscape and politicizing that participation. Part of what informs and illuminates these texts is the concept of human relationships with the natural world not as hierarchical and dominating but, as Karen Warren explains in "The Power and the Promise of Ecofeminism," as a relationship of friendship and care based on "loving perception." An example comes from Johnson's *The Inland Island*, a seasonal account of her life on an "island" of land in Ohio. The title suggests that Johnson's essays are not only investigations of ecological relationships on her small piece of wild land but are about inner landscapes as well. Especially important is her running commentary on the "progress" of the violence in Vietnam. She writes:

> I can't keep the horror of the burned children away. In April we will be presented with the bill for the burning of the children. And I can't separate the beauty of this place from the destruction of this place—the sewer water, the soapsuds, the hunters, the trappers, the dogs, the decay of the trees, the planes overhead. (26)

Johnson's is a bitter, ragged, emotional, and psychological journey through the seasons, but at the same time a celebration of her intimate relationship with "wild" things.

The works of Ackerman and Dillard, two very different "nature writers," suggest another aspect of a "postmodern pastoral." Both authors attempt to locate the creation of knowledge, i.e., the "knowing" of nature, in places other than the "mind." Ackerman, in *A Natural History of the Senses*, celebrates the idea that the body is endowed with multiple ways of knowing, none of which is located strictly in the mind. In fact, she suggests, modern science has been coming around to the idea that the mind does not dwell in the brain "but travels the whole body on caravans of hormone and enzyme, busily making sense of the compound wonders we catalogue as touch, taste, smell, hearing and vision" (xix). Dillard, considered by some to be America's premier "woman nature writer," writes in *Pilgrim at Tinker Creek* that the coded seeing of natural science may be faulty and she asks us to try to see nature in other ways, from the kind of "situated," "partial" positions that Haraway supports. Dillard asks in "Seeing" what it might be like not to have sight but hands and mouths and noses to "know" with. It would be like Eden before Adam named everything, she says. "The scales would drop my eyes; I'd see trees like men walking" (30).

While I do not wish to argue that it is the special task of ecofeminism or women writers alone to reimage nature, ecofeminists would argue that this is part of their philosophy and purpose, their specific subject being the interrelated dominations of women and nature. Warren insists that if we aim to undo the oppressive image of land-as-woman/woman-as-land, then feminism must include an ecological perspective and ecology must include a feminist perspective. She describes the task of ecofeminism as "making visible the various ways in which the dominations of women and nonhuman nature are sanctioned and perpetuated under patriarchy, and engaging in practices and developing analysis aimed at ending these dominations."[11]

The works cited here make up only a small sample of the stories by contemporary women authors that make visible, as Warren suggests, the intimate and intricate relationships between constructions of nature and constructions of knowledge, desire, power, language, race, gender, and sexuality. These stories suggest an alternative to the pastoral image of land-as-woman, positing instead an idea of nature as a nonfixed, bodied, subject that humans may "know" in multiple ways. By merging ecofeminist theory and ecological literary criticism, literary theorists and critics can assume a position from which to speak to and listen to these texts.

Notes

1. See Love; Murphy; Burgess.
2. Haraway's explanation of the conceptual relationship between nature and gender in *Primate Visions* is useful here. She writes, "Nature/culture and sex/gender are not loosely related pairs of terms; their specific form of relation is hierarchical appropriation, connected as Aristotle taught by the logic of active/passive, form/matter, achieved form/resource, man/animal, final/material cause. Symbolically, nature and culture, as well as sex and gender mutually (but not equally) construct each other; one pole of a dualism cannot exist without the other" (12). Also see Warren, "Feminism and Ecology," and the anthologies edited by Plant, and Diamond and Orenstein for more discussion of the conceptual link between women and nature. Griffin, in *Woman and Nature* and *Pornography and Silence*, makes clear the connections between the way a "split" culture (a culture that sees itself as disengaged from nature, that sees the mind as separate from the body) regards nature and the way gender, race, and class come to "justify" oppression in such a culture.

3. Use of the word *traditional* is problematic because it begs the question of whose tradition we mean. As I use the term here it means the tradition that originated with the writings of white male colonists, explorers, and settlers, later refined and "genrefied," taking shape as the American Nature Essay, whose "inventor" is considered to be Thoreau. *The Norton Book of Nature Writing* could be considered to exemplify this tradition, with its narrow view of what nature writing is: nonfiction travel, adventure, or natural history essays written by those who are sufficiently alienated from nature to gain perspective on it.

4. Many excellent studies exist that trace the historical construction of nature as "other" and suggest its links to sexism, racism, and classism. For example, see Griffin, Merchant, Bordo, Keller, Ruether, and Gray. All of these works offer accounts of the dissolution of an holistic world view which is replaced by a mechanistic view. The "death of nature" as a living subject and the separation of mind and body in Western philosophy is linked to the profound influence of Plato, Aristotle, and Descartes and the rise of modern science.

5. See Pratt, Mills, and Weisman for more on this. These authors discuss the idea that male subjecthood or identity is tied to the nature/culture dichotomy and that the dominating impulse of exploration narratives is an impulse toward ownership, mastery, and possession of the land, which consolidates and guarantees identity to the subject.

6. Central to this idea of redefining the boundaries of the genre is Haraway's notion in *Primate Visions* that science is one "story-telling practice" among many. Scientific stories are narratives with plots, heroes, obstacles, and achievements. Haraway suggests that what feminist revisionists must do is not simply trade masculinist stories for feminist stories but renegotiate the whole "story field." I see this as analogous to insisting that the genre American Nature Literature be renegotiated as a story field to include diverse storytelling practices. This is as crucial to Haraway's "successor science project" as it is to the creation of a new environmental ethic.

7. For more on conceptual frameworks, see Kolodny and Gray. Also see Warren, who makes this point in most of her work.

8. For more on conceiving of nature as an actor or agent, see Cheney, Campbell, Murphy, and Bookchin.

9. See Murphy, who borrows the notion of "emancipatory strategies" from Yaeger.

10. My understanding of French feminist theory comes from the work of Cixous, Irigaray, and Kristeva, and American critics of their work, including Dallery and Jones. French feminist theory is problematic for many American feminist constructionists (see, for example Moi's *Sexual/Textual Politics*) who argue that there can be no reality outside symbolic, or social, structures, i.e., that there can be no way to define women's sexual pleasure outside of phallic discourse. I do not want to suggest here that Oliver's work is a "perfect" example of *écriture féminine*. In fact, it is not. Instead it is an American feminist example of one aspect of French theories of writing the body.

11. Warren stresses the importance of an ecology informed by feminism and a feminism informed by ecology in most of her work. See, for example, "The

Power and the Promise of Ecological Feminism," "Feminism and Ecology: Making Connections," and (with Cheney) "Ecological Feminism and Ecosystem Ecology." Also see Warren, "The Quilt of Ecological Feminism." Warren makes clear in her work that ecofeminism is an "inclusive" philosophy, a "quilt," and that it aims to dismantle all "isms" of domination: racism, sexism, classism, heterosexism.

Works Cited

Ackerman, Diane. *A Natural History of the Senses*. New York: Random House, 1990.

Bacon, Francis. *The New Organon and Related Writings*. Fulton H. Anderson, ed. New York: Bobbs-Merrill, 1960.

Bookchin, Murray. *Remaking Society: Pathways to a Green Future*. Boston: South End Press, 1989.

Bordo, Susan. *The Flight to Objectivity: Essays on Cartesianism and Culture*. Albany: State University of New York Press, 1987.

Burgess, Cheryl. "Toward An Ecological Literary Criticism." Western American Literature Meeting, Coeur d'Alene, Idaho, October 13, 1988.

Campbell, Sue Ellen. "Land and the Language of Desire: Where Deep Ecology and Poststructuralism Meet." *Western American Literature* 24 (1989): 199–211.

Cheney, Jim. "Postmodern Environmental Ethics: Ethics as Bioregional Narrative." *Environmental Ethics* 11, no. 2 (1989): 117–34.

Cixous, Hélène, and Catherine Clément. *The Newly Born Woman*. Trans. Betsy Wing. Minneapolis: University of Minnesota Press, 1986.

Dallery, Arleen S. "The Politics of Writing (the) Body: *Ecriture Féminine*." *Gender/Body/Knowledge*, ed. Alison Jaggar and Susan Bordo. New Brunswick: Rutgers University Press, 1989, 52–67.

Daly, Mary. *Gyn/Ecology: The Metaethics of Radical Feminism*. Boston: Beacon Press, 1978.

Descartes, René. *Discourse on Method and The Meditations*. Trans. F. E. Sutcliffe. Hammondsworth, Middlesex: Penguin, 1968.

Diamond, Irene, and Gloria Feman Orenstein, eds. *Reweaving the World: The Emergence of Ecofeminism*. San Francisco: Sierra Club Books, 1990.

Dillard, Annie. *Pilgrim at Tinker Creek*. New York: Harper and Row, 1974.

Emerson, Ralph Waldo. *Nature: Addresses and Lectures*. Philadelphia: David McKay, 1892.

Finch, Robert, and John Elder, eds. *The Norton Book of Nature Writing*. New York: Norton, 1990.

Fuss, Diana. *Essentially Speaking: Feminism, Nature and Difference*. New York: Routledge, 1989.

Gray, Elizabeth Dodson. *Green Paradise Lost*. Wellesley: Roundtable Press, 1981.

Griffin, Susan. *Woman And Nature: The Roaring Inside Her*. New York: Harper and Row, 1978.

———. *Pornography and Silence: Culture's Revenge against Nature*. New York: Harper and Row, 1981.

Haraway, Donna. "Situated Knowledges: The Science Question in Feminism and the Privilege of Partial Perspective." *Feminist Studies* 14, no. 3 (Fall 1988): 575-99.

———. *Primate Visions: Gender, Race and Nature in the World of Modern Science.* New York: Routledge, 1989.

Harjo, Joy. *In Mad Love and War.* Middletown, Conn.: Wesleyan University Press, 1990.

Hasselstrom, Linda M. *Going Over East: Reflections of a Woman Rancher.* Golden, Colo.: Fulcrum, 1987.

———. *Windbreak: A Woman Rancher on the Northern Plains.* Berkeley: Barn Owl Books, 1987.

———. *Land Circle.* Golden, Colo.: Fulcrum, 1991.

Hubbell, Sue. *A Country Year.* New York: Harper and Row, 1987.

———. *A Book of Bees.* New York: Ballantine, 1988.

Johnson, Josephine. *The Inland Island.* New York: Simon and Schuster, 1969.

Jones, Ann Rosalind. "Writing the Body: Toward an Understanding of *l'Ecriture Féminine.*" *The New Feminist Criticism,* ed. Elaine Showalter. New York: Pantheon, 1985, 361-77.

Keller, Evelyn Fox. *Reflections on Gender and Science.* New Haven: Yale University Press, 1985.

Kolody, Annette. *The Lay of the Land: Metaphor as Experience and History in American Life and Letters.* Chapel Hill: University of North Carolina Press, 1975.

———. *The Land before Her: Fantasy and Experience of the American Frontiers, 1630-1860.* Chapel Hill: University of North Carolina Press, 1984.

Le Guin, Ursula. *Buffalo Gals and Other Animal Presences.* New York: Penguin, 1990.

Love, Glen. "Revaluing Nature: Toward An Ecological Criticism." *Western American Literature* 24, no. 5 (1990): 201-15.

Marks, Elaine, and Isabelle de Courtivron, eds. *New French Feminisms: An Anthology.* Amherst: University of Massachusetts Press, 1980.

Merchant, Carolyn. *The Death of Nature: Women, Ecology and the Scientific Revolution.* San Francisco: Harper and Row, 1980.

Mills, Sara. *Discourses of Difference: An Analysis of Women's Travel Writing and Colonialism.* New York: Routledge, 1991.

Moi, Toril. *Sexual/Textual Politics.* London: Methuen, 1985.

Muir, John. *The Wilderness World of John Muir.* Ed. Edwin Way Teale. Boston: Houghton Mifflin, 1954.

Murphy, Patrick. "Ground, Pivot, Motion: Ecofeminist Theory, Dialogics, and Literary Practice." *Hypatia* 6, no. 1 (Spring 1991): 146-61.

Plant, Judith, ed. *Healing the Wounds: The Promise of Ecofeminism.* Philadelphia: New Society, 1989.

Pratt, Mary Louise. *Imperial Eyes: Travel Writing and Transculturation.* New York: Routledge, 1992.

Ruether, Rosemary Radford. *New Woman/New Earth: Sexist Ideologies and Human Liberation.* New York: Seabury Press, 1975.

Silko, Leslie Marmon. "Yellow Woman." In *Spider Woman's Granddaughters: Traditional Tales and Contemporary Writing by Native American Women,* ed. Paula Gunn Allen. New York: Fawcett Columbine, 1989.

———. *Ceremony*. New York: Viking Press, 1977.

Thoreau, Henry David. *Walden and Civil Disobedience*. Boston: Houghton Mifflin, 1957.

Walker, Alice. *Living by the Word: Selected Writings 1973–1987*. San Diego: Harcourt Brace Jovanovich, 1988.

Warren, Karen J. "The Power and the Promise of Ecological Feminism." *Environmental Ethics* 12 (Summer 1990): 125–46.

———. "Feminism and Ecology: Making Connections." *Environmental Ethics* 9, no. 1 (1987): 3–20.

———. "Toward an Ecofeminist Ethic." *Studies in the Humanities* 15, no. 2 (1988): 140–56.

———. "The Quilt of Ecological Feminism. *Woman of Power* 20 (Spring 1991): 64–68.

———, and Jim Cheney. "Ecological Feminism and Ecosystem Ecology." *Hypatia* 6, no. 1 (Spring 1991): 179–97.

Weisman, Leslie Kanes. *Discrimination by Design: A Feminist Critique of the Man-Made Environment*. Urbana: University of Illinois Press, 1992.

Yaeger, Patricia. *Honey-Mad Women: Emancipatory Strategies in Women's Writing*. New York: Columbia University Press, 1988.

Fourteen

Rhetoric, Rape, and Ecowarfare in the Persian Gulf

Adrienne Elizabeth Christiansen

Beginning January 10, 1991, the United States Congress spent three days intensely debating several resolutions that would have either curtailed or authorized the use of military force against Iraq. Ultimately the Congress did authorize military force, and the Persian Gulf War ensued. One noteworthy aspect of the congressional debate is that there were almost no expressions of concern about women as a class, either as soldiers, civilians, or war casualties.[1] This near silence on the "women and war" question is remarkable given that the presence of 32,000 female soldiers in the Persian Gulf prompted several reporters to dub the conflict a "mommy's war" (Beck, 1990). In addition, the 102nd Congress had more female members (thirty) than at any other time in U.S. history. Nearly half of these members had identified themselves as feminists or as strong supporters of women's interests.[2]

The eight female legislators who were active environmentalists were similarly silent on how a Middle East war would affect the ecosystem. Of the more than fifty speeches given by women during the debate, only Representative Nancy Pelosi of California raised the subject of the Persian Gulf War's possible effect on the environment. The scenarios she outlined seem eerily prescient given the catastrophe that ensued.[3] Even though she merely described some of the devastation that would occur if Saddam Hussein fulfilled his public threat to blow up Kuwaiti oilfields, her speech prompted ridicule from her colleagues.[4]

Why was it that during the Persian Gulf War debates only two women in the House associated themselves with their longstanding political commitments to women and the environment? In contrast, the group of female legislators readily allied themselves with their family members who had served in the military, with reserve units from the states they represented, with their constituents, with President Bush, and with patriotic American fervor. Rather than depict the near silence merely as an example of wartime boosterism, political weakness, failure of nerve, or historical accident, I believe that this situation demonstrates the difficulty of raising feminist and environmental issues during times of heightened military activity, even when the consequences for women and the environment are enormous. The three-day televised debate in Congress provides a fascinating case study in the variety of communication barriers with which female legislators contend—barriers that are even more onerous when women must deal with the topics of war and peace. It also provides an opportunity to make a case for the important yet often overlooked relationship between rape/sexual assault, militarism, and environmental degradation.

A major tenet of ecofeminism is that seemingly disparate and unrelated entities are in fact connected, for example, that the treatment of women in this society is integrally related to the treatment of nonhuman nature. Ynestra King, in "The Ecofeminist Imperative," elaborates on this sense of "connection" and extends it to concerns about militarism:

Eco-feminism is about connectedness and wholeness of theory and practice. It asserts the special strength and integrity of every living thing. . . . We are a woman-identified movement, and we believe that we have special work to do in these imperilled times. We see the devastation of the earth and her beings by the corporate warriors, and the threat of nuclear annihilation by the military warriors, as feminist concerns. It is the same masculinist mentality which would deny us our right to our own bodies and our own sexuality, and which depends on multiple systems of dominance and state power to have its way. (1983: 10)

King is not alone in her belief that aggressive sexuality, militarism, and mistreatment of the environment are thematically united. A variety of writers have approached this question from different perspectives and with differing results.[5] Precisely articulating the nature of the relationship is a task for feminist scholars and is undertaken by Karen J. Warren and Duane Cady in an introductory essay to a special Feminism and Peace issue of *Hypatia*. In their article, "Feminism and Peace: Seeing Connections," they argue that these topics are connected by conceptual frameworks, empirical evidence, historical fact, political praxis, linguistic usage, and psychological systems (1994). In this chapter, I bring forth new evidence that demonstrates how the oppression of women, degradation of the environment, warfare, and "isms of domination" are integrally related.[6] In doing so, the project of ecofeminism is both strengthened and extended.

A case study of many wars could provide the evidence necessary to demonstrate ecofeminist issues. However, six qualities of the Persian Gulf War make it uniquely suited to show both the importance of ecofeminist concerns and how the expectations of contemporary public discourse maintain traditional relations between women, war, "isms of domination," and the environment. These six qualities are: (1) the Bush Administration's use of raped Kuwaiti women as a persuasive device to generate U.S. support for sending troops to the Persian Gulf. (2) Some 32,000 U.S. women served as soldiers in the war. They comprised approximately 11 percent of the U.S. troop strength (Beck, 1990). (3) The percentages of African-American women (and men) serving in the Gulf were far higher than what one might expect given their percentage in the general population.[7] (4) The House of Representatives had more female representation than at any other time in American history. All but six of the women spoke during the debate on whether or not to authorize military force against Iraq. Some women spoke many times. (5) Before it became unpopular to do so, President Bush argued that maintaining the flow of oil, what he called "the American way of life," justified military aggression against Iraq. (6) When retreating Iraqi forces burned more than seven hundred oil wells and dumped millions of barrels of crude oil into the Persian Gulf and onto the sand, their actions finally drew international attention to what many scientists and environmentalists have referred to as "ecocide" or "ecowarfare" and what the Bush Administration referred to as "ecoterrorism."

In the remainder of this chapter, I argue that the relative silence on the part of female legislators during the Persian Gulf War debates reflects their attempts to adapt to an extraordinarily problematic rhetorical situation. I first describe and analyze the three speeches in which concerns about women, war, and the environment were raised. I then enumerate the panoply of rhetorical obstacles that each female legislator had to overcome—regardless of whether or not she voted for the war resolution. The next section of the chapter describes the persuasive strategies used by many of the female legislators in their opposition to the war and discusses why these strategies actually reinforced the rhetorical obstacles rather than overcoming them. I conclude by arguing that the Persian Gulf War debates, the rape, sexual assault, and environmental devastation that took place, are thematically united by a conceptual framework that utilizes dominance as its central dynamo. The features of this framework are illuminated.

Women and the Environment
in the Gulf War Debates

If there ever is a time when the free and open exchange of argument and persuasion contribute to the health of a democracy, it is in deciding whether to wage war. Unfortunately, U.S. history is riddled with wars that were never declared (e.g., Vietnam War, Panamanian War); this made the 1991 congressional debate a rare and extraordinary opportunity to deliberate over the reasons for war or peace. For three days, Americans heard and watched their elected representatives somberly claim never to have voted on a more important resolution. The importance of their decision, it was repeated, necessitated an exploration of all the possible ramifications of a vote to go to war. There was much talk about "saving face," "having egg on our faces," the crisis being a "defining moment in history," "sending a message" to Saddam Hussein, the need to "stand firm with resolve and unity," and the upcoming war as the "last, best hope for peace." Many members of the House spoke briefly about the potential deaths of U.S. soldiers, but in general the debate was more a discussion of the economic, political, and geostrategic ramifications of a war with Iraq.[8]

In contrast to the lengthy speeches on how a Persian Gulf War might affect Middle Eastern stability, U.S. military might, the world economy, and the new world order, there was almost no discussion of war's effect on women or on the environment, even by staunch feminists and environmentalists. Representative Barbara Boxer of California was the only female legislator to discuss any aspect of women and war. Her comments on this topic were limited to two very brief statements, one in which she noted that female soldiers in Saudi Arabia were treated differently than their male comrades and one in which she decried the military's practice of sending single parents or both parents to the Gulf. Unfortunately, Boxer's examples of how the female soldiers were treated ultimately served to belittle their capabilities. She said:

> They are working very hard and they are explaining to us how it feels to have to go into the back door to use the gymnasium because the Saudis do not want them to come in the front door. They have to fight to get to have the use of the gymnasium, and then, once they are in there, being subjected to literature trying to convert them [to Islam]. It is tough for them to take. . . . In the rules our service people are told that women are not allowed to drive in Saudi Arabia. If they are in their military vehicle and in their military uniform, it is OK. However, I was informed that if they do that and they attempt to drive into town in their military car and in their uniforms, they are run off the road by the Saudis.

The problem with Boxer's statement is that it was not linked to any broader discussion of the justifications for or against going to war. She did not use these stories to raise her colleagues' consciousness about the morality of sending female soldiers to a war to reestablish nondemocratic monarchies, to defend societies where women's rights and movements are severely curtailed, or to talk about the environmental effects of war on women and other humans. By failing to link these anecdotes to a broader examination of the war's purpose, Boxer inadvertently reinforced the image of female soldiers as weak and incapable of enduring the rigors of war. Who would argue that the discomfort of going through back doors and having religious literature thrust upon them is in any way comparable to the discomfort of being on the "front line" in a desert combat zone? Ironically, Boxer did not discuss other issues about women and war that are serious and pervasive. Neither she nor her female colleagues discussed the likelihood of U.S., Iraqi, Kuwaiti, and Saudi Arabian women being raped and sexually assaulted during the war.[9] None of the women discussed the deleterious health effects of war on female munitions workers, especially those in the electronics industry.[10] No one addressed the limitations on U.S. military women's pay and career advancement due to congressional restrictions on women in combat positions. Only Representative Boxer mentioned the problem of minor children being left in the United States when parents were shipped to Saudi Arabia. To raise these issues, of course, would have held up the legislators to ridicule for paying attention to such picayune details when the important issues were about national humiliation, geopolitical strategy, and what George Bush called "a big idea—a new world order, where diverse nations are drawn together in common cause to achieve the universal aspirations of mankind: peace and security, freedom and the rule of law" (Bush, 1990).

Just as the female legislators did not raise issues typically thought of as important to women, most of them failed to articulate how a Middle East war might affect the environment. A claim of ignorance on the part of the legislators would be hard to sustain, given that prior to the congressional debate, Saddam Hussein had threatened to blow up the oil wells if he were attacked by coalition forces. He had already demonstrated his willingness to engage in ecowarfare when he blew up wells and dumped oil in the Persian Gulf in 1983 during the Iran-Iraq War. These actions were widely reported in the mass media and well known to the U.S. government.[11] In addition, the devastating effects of war on the environment have been a serious concern to scientists and environmentalists for at least fifteen years. The Stockholm International Peace Research Institute has been a leader in sponsoring extensive research on this topic (Westing, 1977, 1988). While it is unrealistic to expect legislators to be aware of scientific research studies on the subject of war and the environment, the mass media published a number of articles on this subject, specifically relating to a Persian Gulf War, prior to the congressional debate.

Representative Pelosi tried to warn her colleagues of the impending ecocatastrophe. Her remarks (January 12, 1991) were brief, vivid, and uncannily accurate:

> The war cloud that would result from exploding oil fields and large-scale bombing of Kuwait, Iraq, Saudi Arabia, and other countries in the Middle East would doom the environment for many years to come. . . . Let us focus on these images: Fires raging for weeks, or perhaps months, sending tons of smoke and debris into the Earth's atmosphere. Oil equal to a dozen Exxon Valdez spills coursing through Gulf waters. Millions of dolphins, fish, sea birds and other marine life washed onto Gulf shores. Smoke and debris blocking sunlight, causing temperatures to drop and altering crop seasons which would result in widespread famine. Toxic plumes ascending to the upper atmosphere and falling as acid rain. Chemical contamination of air, water and vegetation.

She urged the legislators to pay attention to concerns that would "affect human life and all of life on earth." In many ways, Pelosi had to contend with the opposite rhetorical problem that Boxer faced. Whereas Boxer failed to link her concerns about the treatment of U.S. female soldiers to any broader argument about why we should not go to war, Pelosi used many examples and linked them to worldwide harm as reasons why we should refrain from war. Where Boxer's examples seemed so minor that they could be shrugged off as irrelevant, Pelosi's case was so extensive that it apparently seemed fantastic and could be shrugged off as grandiose.

I would not expect elected representatives to be concerned with mangrove trees, cormorants, coral reefs, desert vegetation, or fish when U.S. troops and allies were about to face "weapons of mass destruction." Nevertheless, going to war to ensure the continuing flow of Middle Eastern oil had serious environmental consequences specific to the United States in the form of energy dependency, air pollution, and acid rain. Even on this myopic, self-centered point, only two female legislators spoke up. Representatives Marcy Kaptur and Mary Rose Oakar both made long, logical, well-supported cases in trying to dissuade their colleagues from voting for war. They described the "immorality" of going to war to protect a Middle East oil supply when we had had nearly twenty years since the 1973 OPEC oil embargo to fundamentally change our energy use. As Kaptur (1991) said, "America saw this crisis coming. This is not news to us." Both women strongly criticized the Bush Administration for its failure to provide an energy plan as required by the 1977 Energy Organization Act. Unlike Pelosi, who focused on environmental degradation, Kaptur and Oakar approached the subject as an issue of political independence from Middle East countries. Their solution was for us to develop new energy technologies. According to Oakar (1991), the United States has "centuries of unmined coal, shale oil, solar energy, synthetic fuel, unexcavated oil." Kaptur concurred:

"Let's spend those billions of dollars being wasted in the desert, let's spend them here in America to develop our clean coal technologies, our agriculture and alcohol fuels, hydrogen and solar power." Neither woman named continued or increasing pollution or environmental damage to the United States and its citizens as a reason to stay out of a war with Iraq, even though both women clearly believed that our energy use must change and that future energy technologies must be environmentally sound.

Why was it that during deliberations of the gravest importance to humans and to nonhuman nature, our legislators barely considered the environmental ramifications of our actions for ourselves, our allies, and our adversaries? Why did Pelosi's speech meet with derision? Was the near silence on the parts of the legislators an example of "selling out" politically, or part of some larger dynamic? The almost total lack of discussion about the environment during the congressional debate belies both an arrogance about the importance of humans over other kinds of nature and a remarkable shortsightedness about how the ecosystem and the earth's resources sustain human life. I believe that the sparse discussion of how the war would affect women and the environment was a result of their integral connection. To demonstrate this connection necessitates an examination of the rhetorical situation faced by the female legislators.

Analysis of Rhetorical Obstacles

Any female member of Congress who wanted to discuss how war would affect women or the environment would face a dizzying array of rhetorical barriers.[12] While none of these obstacles would be as blatant as eighteenth- and nineteenth-century prohibitions against women speaking in public, the obstacles would include social beliefs about what are the appropriate roles for men and women in times of war, the "feminine style" of rhetoric being at odds with the norms for "war talk" in deliberative bodies, and the general denigration of issues that challenge the premises of "power-over" political decision making.

Social attitudes and beliefs that men and women are fundamentally different create the most entrenched rhetorical obstacles that limit a woman's ability to discuss women and the environment in congressional debates about war. For centuries, women have been depicted as constitutionally peace loving where men are war loving.[13] Men fight one another at the war's front, but women are supposed to be passive, supportive observers on the home front. Women are supposed to abhor war because our procreative abilities make us "closer to nature." Since men cannot give birth to another human being, they are said to be "closer to culture," which includes the development of munitions and other technological advances.[14] In contrast to human procreation, men "give birth" to new social orders by creating and using sophisticated instruments of death and destruction. As William J. Broyles put it in an article entitled "Why Men Love War," "at some terrible level [it] is the closest thing to what childbirth is for women: the initiation into the power of life and death" (55). Carol Cohn (1987) also found a strong relationship between "giving birth" and creating atomic bombs in the language of the defense intellectuals she studied:

> The entire history of the bomb project, in fact, seems permeated with imagery that confounds humanity's overwhelming technological power to destroy nature with the power to create: imagery that converts men's destruction into their rebirth. Lawrence wrote of the Trinity test of the first atomic bomb: "One felt as though he had been privileged to witness the Birth of the World." In a 1985 interview, General Bruce K. Holloway, the commander in chief of the Strategic Air Command from 1968 to 1972, described a nuclear war as involving "a big bang, like the start of the universe."

In addition to having to deal with the illogic that equates human birth with wartime death and destruction, female members of Congress have little authority to speak about war—given longstanding attitudes that women are to be passive and silent during these times. Women's primary roles are restricted to being patriotic supporters, grief-stricken widows or family members, civilian casualties, or rape victims/war booty. Jean Bethke Elshtain has observed that the expectation that women are to fill passive roles during times of war even extends to passivity in articulating their concerns about war:

> In the matter of women and war we [women] are invited to turn away. War is men's: men are the historic authors of organized violence. Yes, women have been drawn in—and they have been required to observe, suffer, cope, mourn, honor, adore, witness, work. But men have done the describing and defining of war, and the women are "affected" by it: they mostly react. (1987: 164)

Another limitation on women's ability to speak authentically about war occurs because of their historic exclusion from military service and their continuing exclusion from combat positions. Since the earliest days of this country's existence, a powerful conceptual relationship has existed between military service and ideas about citizenship (Kerber 1990). This relationship is not unique to the United States and can be traced back to the beliefs and writings of the ancient Greeks (Segal, Kinzer and Woalfel, 1977).

Women's political ambitions have been thwarted by their inability to serve in military combat positions, resulting in obvious difficulties in speaking about war. The women who do get elected are unquestionably handicapped when their male colleagues use military service as an authorizing device for their political arguments. Sheila Tobias has established through historical example that during times when heroism in warfare and leadership in politics are strongly linked, women experience great difficulties in getting elected to public office. When military service is claimed to be a necessary precursor to public service, women lose out (Tobias, 1990). This was certainly the case during the 1988 presidential election between George Bush and Michael Dukakis. Bush repeatedly pointed to his military service as a Navy pilot to bolster his credentials for the presidency. He ridiculed Dukakis's well-known ride in an Army tank. Bush's derision stemmed not merely from the fact that the ride was an election-time publicity stunt but that it was obscene for Dukakis to take on the mantle and perquisites of soldiering when he had no previous military service. During the Persian Gulf War debates, female members of Congress were negatively affected by the attitude that prior military service was the only legitimate precursor for discussing war. Whereas their male counterparts repeatedly referred to their own military service and sacrifice, the women had to draw upon their connections to other people in the service. For example, several of the congresswomen mentioned their male family members who were servicemen or their congressional employees who were connected to the military. For some of the female representatives, their connection to the military was only that they were there to speak "on behalf" of their constituents who were in the Gulf or had family members in the Gulf.[15]

Elshtain claims that our society's belief that women ought always to remain in the "private sphere" of the home limits their ability to speak authentically about war in a deliberative body like Congress:

> Politics as policy formulation and implementation is not for amateurs. Women, too, are well advised to keep their noses out of this complex business unless they have learned not to think and speak "like women"—that is, like human beings picturing decimated homes and mangled bodies when strategies for nuclear or other war fighting are discussed. The worlds of "victims"—overwhelmingly one of women and children—and of "warriors" . . . have become nearly incommensurable universes to one another. (1987: 154)[16]

Had they wanted to discuss issues of women and the environment, the female members of Congress would have faced other restrictive obstacles—attitudes about the impropriety of women speaking in public. Prohibitions against women speaking in public have a long and well-documented history. Saint Paul's biblical edict for women to "remain silent" in church has been taken to mean that women should remain silent in *all* public spaces. By the very act of standing and addressing a group of people, a female speaker claims to have ideas worthy of an audience. She literally asserts her own authority and legitimacy. In part because of this powerful self-validating and self-authorizing action, women in the nineteenth century endured sanctions that included being criticized from the pulpit by clergy members, suffering ridicule in editorials and cartoons, being refused in their request to rent auditoriums, having to defend themselves from claims that they were sexual deviants and monsters, having to face angry mobs, and being repeatedly threatened with bodily harm (Campbell, 1990; Jamieson, 1988). Clearly, contemporary female members of Congress did not face these social sanctions when speaking during the Gulf War debates. However, each woman had to contend with the belief (reflected in numbers of women elected to the House) that the public sphere of government "belongs" to men and that she was usurping her socially defined position. Similarly, each woman had to face a prejudiced assumption that she was ignorant or incompetent about war simply because this culture defines war as a quintessentially masculine activity. Like contemporary female soldiers who are accused of being lesbians because they have violated assigned sex roles and have asserted their competence in military matters, female members of Congress risked having their qualifications as women called into question. Having to demonstrate their competence and authority while reassuring audiences that they are feminine women is an age-old dichotomy for female public speakers. Current examples of this phenomenon are provided by Geraldine Ferraro's unsuccessful run for the vice presidency (Campbell, 1988), the round of criticism Attorney General Janet Reno received when she was nominated for her cabinet post, and the ongoing, vitriolic criticism of Hillary Clinton's public policy roles.

The rhetorical obstacles to legitimacy that female members of Congress face as public speakers are quite daunting by themselves. When the subject is as significant and deadly as going to war, the rhetorical obstacles loom even larger for women. It is as if, in our fear and awe, we resort to our most ancient and entrenched beliefs about sex roles. In these times, female members of Congress face their greatest rhetorical challenges.

Counterproductive Responses
to Rhetorical Obstacles

Over time, seasoned female public speakers have drawn upon a set of rhetorical strategies designed to overcome their most prominent recurring obstacle: that the self-assurance, logic, and reason that our society expects of public speakers are fundamentally incompatible with traditional notions of femininity. Karlyn Kohrs Campbell argues that discourse that is adapted to the unique rhetorical situation faced by women often has several consistent qualities. This discourse she labels as the "feminine style" of rhetoric even though there is nothing essentially female about it and it has often been utilized by men. According to Campbell, the "feminine style" is characterized by a strong personal tone; it utilizes personal experience, anecdotes and examples; structurally, it is often inductive; the audience is addressed as peers and the speaker encourages them to test her claims of generality by comparing them to their own experiences (1990: 12–15).

The female members of Congress who spoke during the Persian Gulf War debates faced a rhetorical situation where masculine, gender-marked language and argument ruled the day.[17] Male members of Congress especially knew the political price they would have to pay if they were perceived to be "weak," "soft," or "appeasers." There was perhaps no better moment in recent congressional history where a situation was so thoroughly tied to maintaining images of traditional sex roles. Unfortunately, the "sexualized" and "gendered" nature of the war discussion put all congresswomen in an untenable rhetorical situation. If they used those strategies that demonstrated their traditional femininity, their arguments would be highly personal, singular, and particular. Their arguments would not be able to "engage," let alone challenge, the sweeping political, economic, and geostrategic arguments that dominated the discussion. If the congresswomen adopted deductive, abstract, and general arguments about whether to go to war, they risked sounding like most of their male colleagues and appearing to violate sex roles at a time when sex roles were being strongly enforced.

My analysis of the group of speeches given by the female members of Congress illuminates an interesting division. Those representatives who supported the resolution authorizing President Bush to use military force against Iraq utilized a language that was primarily devoid of those qualities that Campbell identifies as the feminine style. These speeches repeat militaristic jargon and "talking points" suggested by the Bush Administration. They are practically indistinguishable from the vast majority of speeches in favor of the war. For example, many in this group of speeches reasoned deductively—principles were laid out and the specific case of Iraq was judged by it. Remarks by Representative Olympia Snowe of Maine provides a good illustration:

> Tomorrow, I will vote to support the U.N. resolution and preserve all our options against Iraq. I will do so not because the military option is inevitable but in order not to undermine the President's efforts to achieve a peaceful outcome to this crisis—efforts which require that a credible military threat be maintained against a brutal aggressor who only understands the language of force. A credible threat is necessary against a man who has raised one of the world's largest armies, used chemical weapons against his own people, invaded two neighbors and is developing nuclear and biological capabilities. We are hardly dealing with a man of peace in Saddam Hussein. (1991)

In another respect, the language of the war's supporters was often abstract and generalized. References to American soldiers were almost always in terms of "American forces" or the "fine men and women of the military." In contrast, references to soldiers on the part of the war's opponents were couched in possessive terms like "our" and highlighted the soldiers' youth and vulnerability. Barbara Boxer repeatedly referred to soldiers as "our children" or "our kids." The war, she said, was "not about egg on our faces; it is about blood on our kids." Representative Patsy Mink's speech (1991) is also quite typical of this approach:

> Before we commit our children to this violence, I ask that Congress tell our children why declaring war against Iraq is necessary for peace in the world, and that Congress advise our children that they go to war because their Government has exhausted all other avenues to peace. I can say neither to my children nor to your children, and so I must vote no against war, and yes for a greater effort for peace.

This quotation aptly demonstrates the personal tone of the speaker. She invites audience members to consider their own offspring and to focus on themselves and their own families rather than generalized abstractions like the new world order.

The quality of abstraction versus concrete specificity is the single most defining difference between the speeches by the war's supporters and opponents. The female opponents tried to reduce the "distance" between war as a concept and war as a bloody reality. Utilizing the "feminine style," they took four rhetorical paths: (1) they discussed the potential war in familiar, highly personal terms; (2) they argued that the abstract logic used by the war's supporters was inappropriate; (3) they vividly depicted the war's violent outcome on human bodies and body parts; and (4) they tried to assert the primacy of domestic issues over foreign policy issues. A speech by Marcy Kaptur (1991) illustrates the personal tone taken by many of the war's opponents. She said, "Let me speak as one of the members of Congress who grew up during the Vietnam era, whose friends fought and died in that battle. . . . I speak on behalf of every mother, every wife, every father, every husband and relative who has a loved one serving our Nation in the U.S. military." Other representatives tried to deny the abstract logic of war that they heard during the debates. Boxer quipped that "this is not about . . . saving face. It is about saving lives. Peace through war makes about as much sense as health through sickness." Representative Cardiss Collins of Illinois made a similar argument when she noted that "there is not yet any reason good enough to die for. America should not be in the business of wasting our young lives for the sake of some oblique geopolitical strategy contrived on some chalkboard" (1991).

Whereas the war's supporters talked mostly about the political, economic, and strategic ramifications of going to war, several of the war's opponents reminded the country that Americans would not just be "lost" in battle but would be killing other people as well. The opponents stressed that war takes its toll on humans, especially human bodies. Representative

Jolene Unsoeld (1991) utilized this technique when she argued that "war is not a simple righting of wrongs. It is about tears and pain. It is about lost arms and legs. It is about paralyzed bodies lying inert in already overwhelmed veteran hospitals. It is about shattered dreams and shattered families and children losing their mothers and fathers. It is about sending America's children to kill and be killed." In similar fashion, Boxer drew upon the lyrics of a song popularized by Bette Midler called "From a Distance" in order to chastise the war's supporters. Although she was roundly ridiculed for employing such an unlikely and "inappropriate" source, the lyrics supported the point of her argument:

From a distance we all have enough, and no one is in need, and there are no guns, no bombs, and no disease, no hungry mouths to feed. From a distance you look like my friend, even though we are at war. From a distance I just can't comprehend what all this fighting is for. . . . Have you ever seen a body that is shot apart? Have you ever seen it up close? From a distance, from very far away, it may look still and peaceful. But up close you see the violence, the pain, the suffering, the horror.

The final way that the women who opposed the war dealt with the rhetorical obstacles they faced was by comparing foreign and domestic policy. In doing this, they attempted to speak about subjects that were properly thought of as belonging to women's "sphere." A number of female representatives made analogies between the expenses of running Operation Desert Storm and what that money might be used for in the United States. Representative Barbara-Rose Collins of Michigan, who had been sworn in only a week earlier, questioned why the Bush Administration was willing to spend so much money on a foreign monarchy "in a time of limited resources to rebuild our cities, feed and house our homeless, and educate our young" (1991). Mary Rose Oakar (1991) noted that the monthly price tag of more than two billion dollars "has led us into a recession which has seen a loss of almost a million jobs in the past five months." Representative Louise Slaughter (1991) asked a series of rhetorical questions about the costs of the war, including "What will be the cost, for example, of caring for a new generation of disabled veterans, who will require a lifetime of medical care as a result of a Persian Gulf War?" Finally, Boxer said in a very impassioned statement:

A robbery is taking place right here, right now. Billions of dollars out the door to pay for an operation called the World vs. Saddam Hussein. But the world does not pay. We do—Uncle Sugar Daddy. . . . We have spent more on Desert Shield so far than we spend in one year on Head Start, cancer research, AIDS research, Alzheimer's heart research, and childhood immunization, all combined.

Traditionally, the use of the "feminine style" of rhetoric is a helpful and appropriate way to deal with the competing demands that a female speaker be simultaneously logical and feminine. In this case, however, I believe that the rhetorical strategies that usually assuage an audience about a rhetor's femininity undermined the arguments that the women made in opposing the war. By discussing the effects of the war on human bodies, the women reinforced stereotypes that women cannot "reason" about war beyond the purely physical, emotional, and specific level. Those women who avoided the "feminine style" and spoke in an acceptably warriorlike language did not make themselves seem unfeminine as much as they made themselves invisible as women. They did not bring a "woman's perspective" to the debate. I leave to other writers the task of determining whether there are unique, "essential" female qualities. But in a warlike context where pressures to conform to the most rigid sex roles are in force, the breadth and diversity of human experience with war ought to be considered and discussed. In the case of the Persian Gulf War debates, female members of Congress ended up having to make one of two unsavory choices. On one hand, they could rhetorically adapt to the demands that they "be women" and provide an alternative voice to the war discourse. If they did this, their arguments would not be able to engage the "broader" issues of whether to go to war, and they would end up reinforcing stereotypes that women are mushy-headed thinkers. On the other hand, they could challenge prevailing norms about how women think and adopt the masculine language of war reasoning. In choosing this option, they would be entering the rhetorical and linguistic mainstream, but they would also be losing any advantage that their experiences as women might provide.

Interpretation and Discussion

The rhetorical strategies used by the female members of Congress who opposed the war clearly exemplified many of the elements of the "feminine style." As I have argued, these efforts not only failed to overcome all the persuasive barriers the women faced, but magnified them. I believe that short of a direct challenge to the underlying assumptions of the war discourse, no amount of rhetorical adaptation would have benefited the women. It is a vivid example of what Elshtain called the "incommensurable universes" between the language of military warriors and war victims. In addition, I believe that by failing to illuminate and attack the war's premise of "power-over" politics, no woman would have been able to credibly raise concerns about the war's effect on women and the environment. To support this claim requires a more thorough explanation of how and why war discourse is characterized by a distant stance and relies on abstraction.

The fundamental truth of war is that individuals are supposed to kill other human beings. To do otherwise is to not be engaged in war. Killing another human being is an act that relies on the highest form of abstract thinking—the mental transformation of oneself as a superior being whose lethal violence is justified and the transformation of one's enemy into a lesser "other" whose death is not only acceptable but morally inconsequential. The entire practice of war is predicated on the abstract concept of "exchangeability of human beings," including those in one's own military forces. By using this phrase, I mean to highlight the mental transformation that one must endure to continuously ignore one's ability to sense unending variations among people. Even among one's own troops, one tries to replace or exchange one fallen soldier for another, as if they were identical entities. The use of regulation haircuts, physical qualities, and military uniforms are all designed to reinforce the perception that one soldier is indistinguishable from another and therefore replaceable. The most important abstraction, however, is the one that transforms "equally created men" into superior and inferior men and thereby the justification for militarily dominating the inferiors. This form of thinking has been referred to as "power-over" politics (Warren and Cady 1994).

Beliefs in the justification of "power-over" politics served as the core assumption by both Iraq and the United States before and during the Persian Gulf War. Saddam Hussein obviously believed that it was appropriate for his troops to invade Kuwait, oppress the people through rapes, torture, and killing, and take the country's material goods. George Bush characterized the Iraqi actions as "naked aggression," and indeed they were. Nevertheless, his actions were predicated on the exact same set of operating assumptions that Saddam Hussein used—power-over.

The speeches given by the female opponents of the Gulf War were materially, argumentatively, and rhetorically ineffective because they did nothing to challenge "power-over" politics, or the use of force to make one's will manifest. No female legislator asked whether the United States had any right to compel another country to do its bidding, either through economic embargoes, United Nations sanction, or military aggression. In fact, many of the women affirmed that the United States "could not allow" Saddam Hussein's troops to stay in Kuwait. Thus the main question discussed during the congressional debate was not *if* the United States should force Iraq to do its will, but *how best* to force Iraq to do its will. In agreeing that the United States could force its will on Iraq, the female legislators ended up granting both the premise of "power-over" politics and the underlying justification for going to war.

When they accepted the underlying premise of the war—"power-over"—the congresswoman ensured that their arguments opposing the war would be unconvincing. In their speeches, Representatives Pelosi and Boxer attempted to make the concerns of women and the environment "count" in a context where domination of women and the ecosystem is part and parcel of "power-over" thinking. The rape of women by soldiers and the environmental degradation are an accepted reality (even perquisite) of war; they also symbolically represent the internal dynamic of war. During these times, women are not only secondary but also play a "background" role for the political and military action. We are supposed to eagerly support military aggression by laboring in munitions factories, raising children on our own, and providing "support services" to the men near the "front" as well as providing moral support, comfort, sexual release, and a rapt, listening audience for war stories when the fighting is over. The role of being a supportive backdrop is similar to the role played by the ecosystem during a war. The environment is perceived to be unimportant because it serves as background for the use and support of military action. It is supposed to easily give up its resources to the fighting forces without fail. Its well-being must not supplant the military objective.

The Persian Gulf War demonstrates not only the folly of using "scorched earth" tactics (e.g., dumping oil into the Gulf, destroying desalination plants, poisoning the land) as a military strategy but also the danger that every war poses to the ecosystem. The Gulf War brought into vivid relief the enormous devastation that war creates only because the Iraqi troops destroyed the very resource for which the United States was fighting. The Bush Administration's decrying of Iraqi "ecoterrorism" has a hollow ring to it. One need only look at how, during the Gulf War, the White House lifted the legal requirements for determining how military projects affect the environment (Schneider, 1991). One need only recall the environmental effects of nuclear fallout from test sites and the practice of deforesting the jungles of Vietnam and Cambodia with Agent Orange to recognize that the United States has no moral high ground upon which to criticize the Iraqi troops (Nietschmann, 1990; Pfeiffer, 1990). In the case of the Persian Gulf, the retreating forces devastated what the U.S. public perceived as "our" property (or that of our allies) rather than the economically "useless" islands in the Pacific or the jungles of Southeast Asia.

An analysis of the speeches given by female members of Congress during the Gulf War debates demonstrates that their relative silence about the war's effect on women and the environment was a product of social forces that narrowed the range of "acceptable" topics to military, economic, and geostrategic prudence. Their silence reflects the inability to make women and the environment "count" when the real issue of the debate was how best to overpower Iraq. The power-over politics that justified our involvement in the Persian Gulf War is the same dynamic that justifies using women as sexual war booty, destroying the environment in war, and denigrating women's concerns as unimportant in congressional debates.

The analysis provided in this chapter suggests that the conceptual framework which connects rhetoric, rape, and ecowarfare is typified by several faulty beliefs: (1) that humankind is independent of, not reliant upon, the nonhuman environment; (2) that the needs of nations and individuals are independent of the needs of other nations and individuals; (3) that our primary concerns are immediate rather than long-term, and instant gratification best solves our problems and meets our needs; (4) that our independence from one another also makes us better than one another. Thus to meet our own immediate needs or desires, we may engage in any form of behavior, including oppression, dominance, and destruction of those we identify as "other," even when in the process we destroy our own long-term self-interest and sustenance. The actions of both the United States and Iraq during the Persian Gulf War demonstrate that each country adheres to this conceptual framework. Until concerned men and women are able to directly challenge the underlying assumptions of power-over politics and this conceptual framework, wars will continue to be fought and the effect on women and the environment will continue to seem irrelevant. Unfortunately, if this patriarchal conceptual framework is not dismantled and our commitment falters in protecting the ecosystem that sustains us, our next war may be fought not over Middle Eastern oil, but "over water, forests, and fertile soil" (O'Riordan, 1990).

Notes

I wish to thank Melanie Hohertz for her invaluable research assistance and Debra L. Petersen for commenting on early drafts of this chapter.

1. Voting by female members of Congress fell along primarily partisan lines, with eight of nine Republican women voting to authorize force against Iraq and fifteen of eighteen Democratic women voting against authorizing force. For a breakdown of the voting records, see "Roll Call in House on Resolution Authorizing Use of Force."

2. See descriptions of the individual legislators in Duncan (1991).

3. In addition to the deaths of thousands of animals, birds, and marine life and the destruction of the Persian Gulf fishing industry, the damage to the environment and to human activities dependent upon it were enormous. One year after the war, a U.S. Senate committee concluded: "Kuwait's sewage treatment and drinking water supply systems were substantially damaged and harm to the desert ecosystem may be significant. Huge lakes of spilled oil remain and considerable oil fallout from the smoke plume has affected land and water areas. The enormous quantities of solid and hazardous waste generated by both the war and the cleanup are being landfilled in the desert, and may pose environmental problems in the future" (United States Senate Committee on Environment and Public Works, 1992, 4). For a scientist's perspective on the environmental effects of the Gulf War, see Cutter, 1991.

4. Hussein's threat was reported widely in the mass media. For an example of this reporting, see "War Could Ravage Environment, Scientists Say."

5. See, for example, Griffin, 1978; Brownmiller, 1986; Griffin, 1992; Diamond and Orenstein, 1990; Harris and King, 1989.

6. I borrow this term from Warren (1987), although many other ecofeminist writers echo this sentiment. For example, Ynestra King (1983: 7) writes: "In all our workings, we believe in the philosophy of nonviolence—that no person should be made into an 'other' to despise, dehumanise and exploit. . . . We are refusing to be the 'other' any longer and we will not make anyone else into an 'other.' Sexism, racism, class divisions, homophobia and the rape of nature depend on this process of objectification."

7. "Though black women comprise 12% of the general population in 1992, according to the Pentagon, they make up 48.7% of all women in the Army's enlisted ranks" (Enloe, 1993).

8. At least the legislators *did* talk about these subjects. According to Carol Cohn (1993: 237) the nuclear defense intellectuals and military strategists she was working with entirely failed to discuss the public policy ramifications of going to war. Instead, they challenged each other's masculinity and shut down discussion by referring to each other as "wimp," "pussy," and "fag." Their deliberations were reduced to pondering questions such as "Does George Bush have the stones for war?"

9. When George Bush discussed the attacks against Kuwaiti women by Iraqi soldiers, he highlighted a reality for women during war, regardless of their nationality, religion, or socioeconomic position—they are likely to be raped, often repeatedly. The phenomenon of seizing and raping women as war booty and a military strategy to demoralize a nation is not restricted to the well-documented cases in Bosnia or to the actions of the United States' enemies. According to Susan Brownmiller (1993), "sporadic cases of gang rape appear in the records of courts-martial for U.S. soldiers in Vietnam, and further accounts are contained in the Winter Soldier Investigation conducted by Vietnam Veterans against the War." Being a U.S. soldier also does little to protect women from rape. Prior to the Gulf War, a Pentagon study found that 5 percent of the respondents had reported a rape or attempted rape by their military comrades during the previous twelve months (Loubet, 1992). During the Persian Gulf War, U.S. female soldiers were taken as prisoners of war; two POWs, Rhonda Cornum and Melissa Coleman, were sexually assaulted by their Iraqi captors. Dozens of other U.S. female soldiers were sexually assaulted by their own military comrades while stationed in the Gulf. See Martz (1992) and Daniels (1992).

10. For a discussion of the kinds of dangers posed to women munitions workers, see Merryfinch.

11. For evidence that the government was aware that Hussein's troops had used ecowarfare as a military strategy, see United States Senate Committee on Environment and Public Works.

12. I do not mean to suggest that all female legislators agree on whether war is or is not justified in a given situation. Instead, I mean to draw attention to the generic, overarching rhetorical restrictions with which *all* women in Congress must contend. How women respond and adapt to these restrictions necessarily (and fortuitously) will vary.

13. This conception has been vigorously challenged by some ecofeminists. See, for example, Ruddick (1993), and Harris (1989).

14. Although Sherry B. Ortner (1974) does not agree with the perspective that women are "closer to nature," she provides a good discussion of this dichotomy.

15. This response was especially developed by Representatives Constance Morella of Maryland and Barbara Vucanovich of Nevada. Morella (1991) said, "As a mother of nine children, who has had family members who have served this country in combat, and who has a former staffer serving in Saudi Arabia, I believe that we must explore every possible alternative to war." Vucanovich (1991) went even further in trying to establish her credibility: "I come from a military family. Two of my brothers were West Point graduates. My dad, a career Army officer, taught at West Point, and my grandfather, also a career Army officer and a doctor, was in the medical corps. One of my brothers gave his life at Anzio, and I can remember the day my mother was notified of my brother's sacrifice."

16. For specific applications of how these attitudes restrict women's ability to talk about war and their war experiences, see Petersen (1990) and Corgan (1990).

17. For example, war discourse in the broader culture and on the floor of the House used imagery of masculine violence/sexual domination as a metaphor for what would happen to Iraq and to Saddam Hussein. George Bush was reported to have said that he wanted to "kick Saddam's ass." A popular bumper sticker in Texas echoed this sentiment: "Kick Their Ass, Then Take Their Gas"; reported by Molly Ivins (1991: 46). After the war began, Representative Gary Ackerman (1991) was prompted to exult on the floor of the House, "Slam, Bam, Thanks Saddam!"

Works Cited

Ackerman, Gary. "Slam, Bam, Thanks Saddam!" *Congressional Record*, January 17, 1991, H536.

Beck, Melinda. "Our Women in the Desert." *Newsweek*, September 10, 1990, 22–25.

Boxer, Barbara. "The Debate Will Strengthen Us." *Congressional Record*, January 10, 1991.

———. Remarks. *Congressional Record*, January 11, 1991.

———. Remarks. *Congressional Record*, January 12, 1991.

Brownmiller, Susan. "Making Female Bodies the Battlefield." *Newsweek*, January 4, 1993, 37.

———. *Rape: The Politics of Consciousness*. San Francisco: Harper and Row, 1986.

Broyles, William J., Jr. "Why Men Love War." *Esquire*, November 1984, 55–65.

Bush, George. Speech before the United Nations General Assembly. *Weekly Compilation of Presidential Documents*, October 1, 1990.

Caldecott, Leonie, and Stephanie Leland, eds. *Reclaim the Earth: Women Speak Out for Life on Earth*. London: Women's Press, 1983.

Campbell, Karlyn Kohrs. *Man Cannot Speak for Her*. New York: Praeger, 1990.

———, and E. Claire Jerry. "Woman and Speaker: A Conflict in Roles." In Sharon Brehm, ed., *Seeing Female: Social Roles and Personal Lives*. New York: Greenwood, 1988, 123–71.

Cohn, Carol. "Sex and Death in the Rational World of Defense Intellectuals." *Signs* 12 (Summer 1987), 687–718.

———. "Wars, Wimps, and Women." In Miriam Cooke and Angela Woollacott, eds., *Gendering War Talk*. Princeton, N.J.: Princeton University Press, 1993.

Collins, Barbara-Rose. Remarks. *Congressional Record*, January 12, 1991.

Collins, Cardiss. Remarks. *Congressional Record*, January 12, 1991.

Corgan, Verna. "Who Should Act, Who Should Talk: Women, War, and the Panamanian Invasion." Paper presented at the Speech Communication Association Convention, November 1990, Chicago.

Cutter, Susan L. "Ecocide in Babylonia." *Focus*, Summer 1991, 26–31.

Daniels, Mary. "Prisoner of War: Rhonda Cornum Talks about That 'One Bad Week' in the Persian Gulf." *Chicago Tribune*, September 6, 1992, 3.

Diamond, Irene, and Gloria Orenstein, eds. *Reweaving the World: The Emergence of Ecofeminism*. San Francisco: Sierra Club Books, 1990.

Duncan, Phil, ed. *Politics in America 1992: The 102nd Congress*. Washington, D.C.: Congressional Quarterly, 1991.

Elshtain, Jean Bethke. *Women and War*. New York: Basic, 1987.

Enloe, Cynthia. "The Right to Fight: A Feminist Catch 22." *Ms.*, July–August 1993, 84–87.

Griffin, Susan. *A Chorus of Stones*. New York: Doubleday, 1992.

———. *Woman and Nature: The Roaring Inside Her*. New York: Harper and Row, 1978.

Harris, Adrienne. "Bringing Artemis to Life: A Plea for Militance and Aggression in Feminist Peace Politics." In Adrienne Harris and Ynestra King, eds., *Rocking the Ship of State: Towards a Feminist Peace Politics*. Boulder, Colo.: Westview, 1989.

———, and Ynestra King, eds. *Rocking the Ship of State: Towards a Feminist Peace Politics*. Boulder, Colo.: Westview, 1989.

Ivins, Molly. "Happy Days for Armchair Rambos." *Progressive*, April 1991, 46.

Jamieson, Kathleen Hall. *Eloquence in an Electronic Age*. New York: Oxford University Press, 1988, 67–89.

Kaptur, Marcy. Remarks. *Congressional Record*, January 12, 1991.

Kerber, Linda. "May All Our Citizens Be Soldiers and All Our Soldiers Citizens: The Ambiguities of Female Citizenship in the New Nation." In Jean Bethke Elshtain and Sheila Tobias, eds., *Women, Militarism, and War*. New York: Rowman and Littlefield, 1990, 89–103.

King, Ynestra. "The Ecofeminist Imperative." In Caldecott and Leland, eds., *Reclaim the Earth*.

Loubet, Susan Thom. "A Soldier's Story: Fighting the Enemy in Her Own Camp," *Ms.*, November–December 1992, 88–89.

Martz, Ron. "Military Is Beginning to Change Attitudes." *Atlanta Constitution*, October 5, 1992, 4.

Merryfinch, Lesley. "Invisible Casualties." In Caldecott and Leland, eds., *Reclaim the Earth*.

Mink, Patsy. Remarks. *Congressional Record*, January 11, 1991.

Morella, Constance. Remarks. *Congressional Record*, January 12, 1991.

Nietschmann, Bernard. "Battlefields of Ashes and Mud." *Natural History*, November 1990, 35–57.

Oakar, Mary Rose. "The Persian Gulf Crisis." *Congressional Record*, January 11, 1991.

O'Riordan, Timothy. "The Environmental Consequences of a Gulf War." *Environment* 9 (November 1990).

Ortner, Sherry B. "Is Female to Male as Nature Is to Culture?" In Michelle Zimbalist Rosaldo and Louise Lamphere, eds., *Women, Culture and Society*. Stanford, Calif.: Stanford University Press, 1974, 67–87.

Pelosi, Nancy. Remarks. *Congressional Record*, January 12, 1991.

Petersen, Debra L. "Old Men Sending Young Men Off to War: The Exclusion of Women from Describing and Defining War." Paper presented at the Speech Communication Association Convention, November 1990, Chicago.

Pfeiffer, E. W. "Degreening Vietnam," *Natural History*, November 1990, 37–40.

"Roll Call in House on Resolution Authorizing Use of Force," *New York Times*, January 13, 1991, A8.

Ruddick, Sara. "Notes toward a Feminist Peace Politics." In Cooke and Woollacott, eds., *Gendering War Talk*.

Schneider, Keith. "Environmental Rule Is Waived for Pentagon." *New York Times*, January 30, 1991, A14.

Segal, David, Nora Kinzer, and John C. Woalfel, "The Concept of Citizenship and Attitudes toward Women in Combat." *Sex Roles*, 3 (1977), 469–77.

Slaughter, Mary Louise. Remarks. *Congressional Record*, January 12, 1991.

Snowe, Olympia. Remarks. *Congressional Record*, January 11, 1991.

Tobias, Sheila. "Shifting Heroisms: The Uses of Military Service in Politics." In Elshtain and Tobias, eds., *Women, Militarism, and War*.

United States Senate Committee on Environment and Public Works Gulf Pollution Task Force. *The Environmental Aftermath of the Gulf War: A Report*. Washington, D.C.: United States Congress, 1992.

Unsoeld, Jolene. Remarks. *Congressional Record*, January 10, 1991.

Vucanovich, Barbara. Remarks. *Congressional Record*, January 11, 1991.

"War Could Ravage Environment, Scientists Say." *Boston Globe*, January 4, 1991, 11.

Warren, Karen J. "Feminism and Ecology: Making Connections." *Environmental Ethics* 9 (Spring 1987).

———, and Duane L. Cady. "Feminism and Peace: Seeing Connections." *Hypatia* 9 (Spring 1994).

Westing, Arthur A. *Cultural Norms, War and the Environment*. Oxford: Oxford University Press, 1988.

———, and the Stockholm International Peace Research Institute. *Weapons of Mass Destruction and the Environment*. London: Taylor and Francis, 1977.

Fifteen

The Nature of Race
Discourses of Racial Difference in Ecofeminism

Noël Sturgeon

Ecofeminism is a contemporary political movement operating on the theory that the ideologies which authorize injustices based on gender, race, and class are related to the ideologies which sanction the exploitation and degradation of the environment.[1] Ynestra King, one of the founders of ecofeminism, has called it the "third wave of the women's movement," indicating her sense that this most recent manifestation of feminist activity is large and vital enough to parallel the first-wave nineteenth-century women's movement and the second-wave women's liberation movement of the 1960s and 1970s.[2] Given both its theory and its historical location as at least one of many third-wave women's movements, ecofeminism in the United States aims to be a multi-issue, globally oriented movement with a more diverse constituency than its predecessors. Assessing its claim to antiracism is the focus of this essay. In support of ecofeminists' desire to create an inclusive and antiracist movement, I identify several prevalent modes of discourse about racial difference which are problematic, however well-intentioned. This inquiry is crucial to understanding the ways in which racism has separated or united women in contemporary women's movements. Furthermore, I believe that without examining the ways in which conceptions of race as well as gender have influenced our ideas about nature, we cannot arrive at adequate solutions to environmental problems.

As a third-wave feminist movement, ecofeminism has had the benefit of arising in a context of widespread feminist critiques of the racism of the second-wave women's movement and, to a lesser extent, critiques of the racism of the U.S. environmental movement. I begin the essay with a short description and history of U.S. ecofeminism. Certainly its historical location has meant that ecofeminism has been better equipped to deal with questions of race than its parent movements. Still, many ecofeminists concentrate primarily on the part sexism plays in environmental crises, theorizing racism as analogous to sexism, or a subsidiary problem, rather than a problem which is *intertwined* with sexism, classism, heterosexism, or speciesism. Furthermore, in part because of its historical legacy, a binary conception of racial difference predominates in ecofeminist discourse. Using the example of an ecofeminist organization, WomanEarth Feminist Peace Institute, I identify problems with a binary conception of racial difference. Finally, I explore the extent to which, because of the particular project of theorizing the special relation between women and nature which is a central ecofeminist concern, Native American women have been characterized as the ultimate ecofeminists even in the face of the refusal of many of them to identify themselves as ecofeminists.[3] While this use of American Indian women by white ecofeminists has its origins in attempts by white ecofeminists to learn from and work in coalition with Native American feminist activists, I contend that it serves to merely paper over theoretical divisions within ecofeminism, as well as preventing an adequate ecofeminist analysis of environmental problems and envisioning of ecofeminist solutions. I stress that much of ecofeminist antiracism represents a positive example of third-wave feminism grappling with U.S. racism. Nevertheless, I will concentrate on the ways in which particular antiracist discourses may avoid direct confrontation with U.S. racism or conceptualize race in ultimately unhelpful ways. I hope that my effort here, besides constructively criticizing ecofeminism, will contribute to a more general project of better understanding of the processes by which race is socially constructed and what functions racism has in our culture, even in politically oppositional cultures.

An Ecofeminist Genealogy

A more detailed description of ecofeminism will provide a context for my analysis of discourses about racial difference. A name which can usefully if partially describe the work of Donna Haraway and Mary Daly, Alice Walker and Rachel Carson, Starhawk and Vandana Shiva,[4] ecofeminism is a shifting theoretical and political location which can be defined to serve various intentions. The present chaotic context of the relatively new and wildly diverse political positionings that go under the name of ecofeminism allows me to support my claims by constructing a definition of the movement which is interested and certainly contestable. Since part of my intention in this essay is to show that ecofeminism can *potentially* challenge racism, my description of ecofeminism is broad enough to include issues of race and the political action of antiracist women in several arenas. Others might not define ecofeminism in the same way.[5]

Both an activist and an academic movement, ecofeminism has grown rapidly since the early eighties and continues to do so in the nineties. As activists, ecofeminists have been involved in environmental and feminist lobbying efforts, in demonstrations and direct actions, in forming a political platform for a U.S. Green party, and in building various kinds of ecofeminist cultural projects (such as ecofeminist art, literature, and spirituality). Ecofeminist activists have taken up a wide variety of issues, such as toxic waste, deforestation, military and nuclear weapons policies, reproductive rights, and domestic and international agricultural development. In academic arenas, scholars who are either identified with or interested in ecofeminism have been active in creating and critiquing ecofeminist theories. A recent spate of publications in the area, including several special issues of journals, confirms research activity on ecofeminism in religious studies, philosophy, political science, art, biology, women studies, and many other disciplines.[6]

Ecofeminism in the United States arose primarily out of the nonviolent direct action movement against nuclear power and nuclear weapons. Its initiating event was the Women and Life on Earth: Ecofeminism in the 1980s Conference at Amherst in 1980, organized by Ynestra King (then of the Institute for Social Ecology), Anna Gyorgy (an organizer in the antinuclear Clamshell Alliance), Grace Paley, and other women from the antinuclear, environmental, and lesbian-feminist movements.[7] From this conference grew the organizing efforts for the Women's Pentagon Actions (WPA) of 1980 and 1981, in which large numbers of women demonstrated and practiced civil disobedience. As defined by the Unity Statement of the Women's Pentagon Actions,[8] the politics behind these early ecofeminist actions were based on making connections between militarism, sexism, racism, classism, and environmental destruction (however unevenly the action may have addressed these issues).[9] Influenced by the writings of Susan Griffin,[10] Charlene Spretnak,[11] Ynestra King,[12] and Starhawk, a set of political positions developed among women sympathetic to the politics of the WPA and other antimilitarist and environmental actions, which began to be called ecofeminism. Many women involved in later antimilitarist direct actions thus began to call themselves ecofeminists in the middle eighties as a way of describing their interlocking political concerns.[13] As the label became more common among feminist antimilitarist activists, a concomitant interest in ecofeminism was emerging in the academy. The two arenas were intertwined at the Ecofeminist Perspectives: Culture, Nature, Theory Conference in March 1987 at the University of Southern California, organized by Irene Diamond and Gloria Orenstein. This well-attended conference marked the beginning of a rapid flowering of ecofeminist art, political action, and theory which continues today.[14] The conference also marks the point where the word *ecofeminism* began to be widely used to describe a politics which attempted to combine feminism, environmentalism, antiracism, animal rights, anti-imperialism, antimilitarism, and nontraditional spiritualities. Which part of this politics is emphasized or even included varies widely and remains deeply contested among those who identify as ecofeminists.

Within this multivoiced and vibrant set of political positions were very different theorizations of the connections between the unequal status of women and the life-threatening destruction of the environment. A constant and ongoing focus of ecofeminist theorizing, as well as critiques of ecofeminism, has been how to conceptualize the special connection between women and nature presumed by the designation *ecofeminism*. I will summarize some of these theorizations here, as one of my contentions in this essay is that particular ecofeminist discourses of racial difference serve to sidestep the contradictions between particular theorizations of the connection between women and nature. Very briefly and generally, I will outline five ways this relation is described. Though I isolate these analyses as positions, in operation they are often combined and intertwined.

One position involves an argument that patriarchy equates women and nature, so that a feminist analysis is required to fully understand the genesis of environmental problems. In other words, where women are degraded, nature will be degraded, and where women are thought to be eternally giving and nurturing, nature will be thought of as endlessly fertile and exploitable.

Another position, which is really the other side of the position just described, argues that an effective understanding of women's subordination in Western cultures requires an environmentalist analysis, that in a culture which is in many ways antinature, which constructs meanings using a hierarchical binarism dependent on assumptions of culture's superiority to nature, understanding women as more "natural" or closer to "nature" dooms them to an inferior position. Furthermore, in a political economy dependent on the freedom to exploit the environment, a moral and ethical relation to nature is suspect. If women are equated with nature, their struggle for freedom represents a challenge to the idea of a passive, disembodied, and objectified nature.

A third position argues for a special relationship between women and nature using an historical, cross-cultural, and materialist analysis of women's work. By looking at women's dominant roles in agricultural production, the managing of productive resources for household economies, cooking, and child care, this position maintains that environmental problems are more quickly noticed by women and impact women's work more seriously.

A fourth position argues that women are biologically close to nature in that their reproductive characteristics (menstrual cycles, lactation, birth) keep them in touch with natural rhythms, both seasonal and cyclical, life- and death-giving. Ecofeminists who are comfortable with this position feel that women potentially have greater access than men do to sympathy with nature and will benefit themselves and the environment by identifying with nature.

A fifth position is taken by feminists who are interested in constructing resources for a feminist spirituality and have found these resources in nature-based religions: paganism, witchcraft, and Native American spiritual traditions. Because such religions historically contain strong images of female power and rank female deities at least equal to male deities, many persons who are searching for a feminist spirituality have felt comfortable with the appellation of "ecofeminist."

Before proceeding, I want to point to just one of the most obvious contradictions within ecofeminism: the serious lack of agreement between positions one and two and position four. The first two positions see the equation of women and nature as patriarchal; the fourth position sees this equation as empowering to women and as providing resources for a feminist environmentalism. Some variations of position five, concerned with feminist spirituality, also see the equation of women and nature as empowering. One of my contentions here is that white ecofeminist discourses about Native American women function to obscure this particular division within ecofeminism.[15] A more general critique of these positions is that the effort to make connections between women and nature rather than between feminism and environmentalism as political movements produces a theoretical context in which conceptions of both women and nature are frequently essentialist.

To construct these and other variations of the theoretical connections between women and nature, ecofeminists have drawn on feminist theories which, while not necessarily aimed at answering questions about the relation between feminist and environmental politics, provided crucial analytical tools. Feminist critiques of forms of abstract rationality which reified divisions between culture and nature, mind and emotion, objectivity and subjectivity; psychoanalytic theories of the ways in which male fears of women's reproductive capacities structured male-dominated political and economic institutions; a feminist rethinking of Christian theology; critiques of the patriarchal nature of militarism; feminist anthropological research; feminist critiques of science; analyses of the sexual objectification of women; feminist poststructuralist theories of constructed subjectivities are only a few of the vital feminist resources for ecofeminist theories.

Feminist antiracist theory was also an important resource for ecofeminists, providing a foundation from which to analyze the ways in which hierarchies were created and maintained and providing a guide to constructing a movement which was inclusive and antiracist. Antiracism was thus a political position apparent in the very beginnings of ecofeminism as theory and as practice, even though it has been a movement which is predominantly white. At the same time, there are many women of color who are either prominent in the movement or who serve as role models for white ecofeminists. To further complicate the picture, many environmental activists are women of color. Even though some white ecofeminists have wanted to claim these activists as part of an ecofeminist movement, most of these women do not identify as ecofeminists, given that the genealogy of the label arises from the white feminist, antimilitarist movement.[16]

Despite these complexities, antiracist analyses consistently appear in ecofeminist literature, and racism is usually counted as a factor in ecofeminist assessments of the production of environmental problems. Many of these antiracist analyses display the qualities of their origins. Political discourses in opposition to U.S. racism have followed particular histories constructed in the context of particular "racial formations."[17] Thus it is no surprise to find U.S. ecofeminism using discourses of racial difference relevant to its historical context or the social movements which have influenced it. Here I concentrate on two ways of dealing with racial difference that I see as problems for ecofeminism. In doing so, I am implicitly raising the question of whether and when an antiracist discourse deployed by a predominantly white movement is problematic.

The Race for Parity

The story of WomanEarth Feminist Peace Institute illustrates both the serious antiracist efforts of some ecofeminists and particular problems with a U.S. discourse on race which is prevalent within the movement. Stemming from the interaction of civil rights activists with feminist antimilitarists,[18] race appears in early ecofeminist analyses defined primarily as a dichotomy: white and black. During the middle 1980s, when women from a variety of racial and ethnic backgrounds finally were able to make visible a thoroughgoing critique of the racism of white feminists, the binary conception of race shifted to white and nonwhite, or white women and women of color.

Begun in 1985, WomanEarth Feminist Peace Institute was founded with the intention to establish an ecofeminist educational center, perhaps in the form of a summer institute, which would produce theory, teach classes, publish an ecofeminist newsletter or journal, and support political activities of various kinds. A long-term vision involved the creation of ecofeminist "locals," each with its own community project, connected in a national network by WomanEarth.

Following the advice of African-American feminist Barbara Smith, WomanEarth was founded on the principle of racial parity: there would always be an equal number of white women and women of color within the organization, particularly within its decision-making structures. Rachel Bagby, Gwyn Kirk, Ynestra King, Margy Mayman, Papusa Molina, Rachel Sierra, Starhawk, and Luisah Teish were founders and core members, and many other women were involved in various ways during the course of the organization's existence.[19] WomanEarth organized a successful ecofeminist conference in 1986 at Hampshire College, but by 1990 it had disbanded.

In the interviews I conducted with WomanEarth members, it was emphasized that there were many reasons why the organization did not continue besides difficulties with questions of race. Lack of funding after the conference, the geographical dispersal of the members, the amount of resources and energy depleted by organizing the Hampshire conference, and poor delegation of responsibility were probably the most important factors in WomanEarth's demise. But there were indeed problems accomplishing the goal of racial equality within the organization that racial parity was supposed to achieve. Meetings were difficult to arrange on a limited budget with a far-flung membership; and when they did occur, a great deal of time was occupied with sorting out issues stemming from racial difference.[20] Some of the white members I talked to had the sense that the agenda of WomanEarth was constantly shifting because of the attempt to construct an organization based on racial parity. This did not necessarily mean, for them, that antiracist work was not on the ecofeminist agenda but that the need to constantly address racism within the group caused organizing efforts, in the words of one member, to unravel "at the same time (they) were put together . . . nothing could be assumed." For all members, there was clearly a great deal of pain associated with the memory of these discussions, as well as a sense of having learned a great deal.

The women in WomanEarth were on the whole powerful, experienced feminists with long histories of activism and antiracist work. Why did they run into so much difficulty operating under the requirement of racial parity? One answer is that working in coalition, as Bernice Johnson Reagon has pointed out,[21] is difficult, painful work and cannot be expected to be otherwise. Taking this to heart means understanding that the difficulties experienced in WomanEarth were a sign that its members were practicing serious antiracist politics. But I would like to suggest that another factor increasing the difficulty could be the way in which racial difference was defined by WomanEarth: in terms of white women and women of color. This dualistic conception of race gave the women involved only two choices of racial subjectivity and thus impoverished the conversations among the members, continually returning them to only one axis (white and nonwhite) along which to conceive of the social construction of race and the operations of racism.

When binary rather than multiple subject positions are emphasized, racialized identities appear to inhere only in the nonwhite women, as opposed to multiple categories which complexify identities beyond simple racial categories, and which point to the fact that it is racism itself which insists on the conceptualization of "white" and "nonwhite." Antiracist work, according to a dualistic way of thinking, can only be done with those who are "raced." Thus antiracist practice appears to be appropriately conducted between differently raced individuals, rather than being a practice which targets the consequences of U.S. racism. In this way, a dualistic conception of race leads white people to believe that the best way to work against racism is to find some way to get people of color to join white organizations. It does not lead white people to examine the way in which they are "raced" themselves, that is, the way in which they are carriers of racial identities constructed by structural racism.

This dualistic conception of race does not encourage discussions of the way in which U.S. racism affects various women of color differently. A nuanced, historical analysis of the way in which racism is reproduced and maintained is thus difficult to achieve. "Women of color," as Chela Sandoval, among others, has argued, must be seen as a "tactical subjectivity," an "oppositional consciousness" of a social movement formed from the ongoing political and strategic negotiations for and against power carried on within feminist and antiracist circles.[22] As an oppositional category, it is useful inasmuch as it is understood not to be an essential category. That is, "women of color" are not in some biological or unchangeable way alike. They share a struggle against racism *because* of the way in which U.S. racism only allows two racial categories of importance: white and nonwhite. Both a historical perspective of the variable ways in which racism has operated and a focus on the consequences of racism rather than raced individuals would put white ecofeminists in a position to form coalitions with the movement against environmental racism, which grounds its analysis on both of these elements.[23] To fully understand U.S. racism, however, dualistic conceptualizations must be resisted and the flexibility and historical variation of racism must be fully confronted.

What Sandoval does not emphasize, although it is implied by her work, is the way in which the political construction of the category "women of color" reflects and maintains the processes of the construction of the category "white women." As the marked category in this kind of antiracist discourse, *white* is defined as "not colored"; defined as lack from the point of view of the category "women of color," the category "white" nevertheless operates within a context of racial privilege and power. While the category "women of color" is a political coalition masquerading as an identity, the category "white women" remains a monolithic "personal" identity.

Ironically for the members of WomanEarth, trying to achieve racial parity using a dualistic conception of race ensured that white women, as half of the oppositional pairing, would retain a dominant position within the organization. Simply from a numerical point of view, giving an entire half of WomanEarth to white women increased their numbers (assuming they occupied one political position on a racial continuum) relative to other variations within the category "women of color" (i.e., African-American, Chicano, Native American, Asian-American, and other "racial" pluralities). Furthermore, used to thinking of "white" as unproblematically unified, a given racial location, white women can more easily occupy this position without the kind of historical and critical analysis which would uncover its instability.[24] What is lost to ecofeminism by the unproblematic use of a dualistic conception of racial difference is the kind of nuanced, complex analysis of power found in theories of simultaneous oppressions, which present racial identity as a problem, as both an achieved and a compulsory political location.[25] Fixed by a dualistic conception of racial parity, women of color are located on one side of the racial divide, forced to minimize their differences and ironically solidify the racist category "nonwhite" as an antiracist political strategy.

My interviews with WomanEarth members showed clearly that the emphasis on racial parity served to obscure or trivialize many other differences which turned out to have almost equal force in the meetings and at the conference: differences in religious or spiritual orientation, sexual orientation, economic privilege, and national backgrounds. These differences would often arise with great force, unanticipated because of the focus on racial differences. Or, just as problematically, these differences would be retranslated into "racial" differences and thus left unanalyzed. Ultimately, the focus on racial parity became a goal for the organization rather than just an operating principle. Racial parity resulted in antiracist work taking place between individuals (not entirely a useless practice) to the detriment of a focus on environmental and feminist problems caused or exacerbated by structural racism.

Naturalizing the Natives

In this section, I want to look specifically at the relation of American Indian women to a movement which so far has had predominantly white participants. To say this is not to make invisible all of the feminist environmental activists who are American Indians, several of whom are prominent ecofeminist activists and theorists. But ecofeminism has been primarily a white women's political identification. As I have implied, it does not necessarily follow that the movement cannot be antiracist because it has mostly white participants. It is an important and encouraging phenomenon that white activists take on the responsibility of analyzing racism and acting against it without first requiring that people of color be present in a movement. But much of ecofeminist discourse about Native American women silences their voices even while idealizing them. This process, besides supporting racism, prevents ecofeminists from effectively envisioning solutions to environmental problems.

To give a few examples of this discourse, I will use as representative artifacts of U.S. ecofeminism two anthologies, *Healing the Wounds: The Promise of Ecofeminism*, edited by Judith Plant and published by New Society Publishers in 1989 (hereafter *HTW*); and *Reweaving the World: The Emergence of Ecofemism*, edited by Irene Diamond and Gloria Orenstein and published by Sierra Club Books in 1990 (hereafter *RTW*). While there are other important ecofeminist books, and at least two more anthologies recently published, these books are exemplary representatives of the diversity within ecofeminism, the many voices staking out the territory.

However, in terms of racial or ethnic identification, this diversity is represented in some problematic ways. *HTW* has twenty-seven articles whose authors' racial or ethnic identification is as follows: two Native American, one African-American, four Indian (Asian), twenty European-American. *RTW* has twenty-six articles: one Native American, three African-American, one Indian (Asian), and twenty-one European-American.[26] Again, the fact that European-American women are the most represented authors is not necessarily problematic in itself. But it brings up a question. Why should American Indian cultures, their rituals, beliefs, and practices, be so frequently referenced in the articles written by the European-American women?

Native American cultures appear so often in ecofeminist writings because they represent ecological cultures that in some instances can also make claims to relative equality between men and women. The combination seems to be ecofeminist by definition. Furthermore, imagining that American Indian women embody the "special relation" between women and nature at the same time that they are portrayed as representing nonpatriarchal cultures achieves an apparent resolution to one of the major contradictions within ecofeminism which I identified at the start of this chapter. The figure of the Native American woman as the "ultimate ecofeminist" mediates, for white ecofeminists, the conflict between the critique of the patriarchal connection between women and nature and the desire for that very connection.

But there has been resistance among American Indian women to being identified as ecofeminist. Winona LaDuke, an Anishinabeg feminist and environmental activist, when asked if she called herself an ecofeminist, stated that while she was glad there was an ecofeminist movement developing, she thought of her activism as stemming from her acculturation as a member of her people.[27] Marie Wilson, a Gitksan woman who is interviewed in *HTW*, expresses a similar isolation from ecofeminism: "Though I agree with the analysis, the differences must be because of where I come from. In my mind, when I speak about women, I speak about humanity because there is equality in the Gitksan belief: the human is one species broken into two necessary parts, and they are equal."[28]

Another uneasiness expressed by Native American women concerns the use of their spirituality within ecofeminism, stemming from the intersection of ecofeminism and New Age feminist spirituality. Though this is only one strand within ecofeminism as a political movement, the use of American Indian rituals and the symbolic positioning of Native American women as white ecofeminists' spiritual teachers comes close to what Andy Smith, a Cherokee woman, has characterized as "spiritual abuse."[29] Smith has argued that the use of American Indian spirituality in the New Age movement without a concomitant willingness to get to know Native American communities and become allies of American Indian political struggles constitutes a silencing of Native Americans. Furthermore, generalizing American Indian spirituality to apply it to white ecofeminist concerns violates the very embedment, of spirituality in land and tribe that attracts white ecofeminists. As Smith says, "Indian religions are community-based, not proselytizing religions. For this reason, there is no *one* Indian religion."[30]

Given that there are these problems in asking Native American women to identify as ecofeminists, does this mean that ecofeminism cannot learn from American Indians a concept of nature and perhaps, in some cases, examples of more equal relationships between women and men? Why shouldn't ecofeminists, as long as they participate in Native American movements and treat Native American culture with respect, continue to point to the more ecological cosmology, economic practices, and equal social relationships developed by some American Indians? Can ecofeminists use Native American philosophy and practice as resources for constructing theory and creating strategies for action?

The problem here lies in the characterization of indigenous people as the "ultimate ecologists," to use Calvin Martin's phrase.[31] This is a common feature of European-American environmentalism and a legacy of that movement for ecofeminists. Certainly, many Native American conceptions of nature seem to lend themselves to environmentalism in that they generally don't make adversarial distinctions between humans and animals or humans and nature. The sense that life involves constant change within a balanced system and that the interdependence of all living and nonliving beings constitutes the environment seems, in comparison with Western beliefs, to be not only more ecological but also (at least potentially) more feminist. But there are several problems with the valorization of Native American conceptualizations of nature.

First, the idea that it is possible to borrow from Native American culture without practicing an American Indian way of life once again does not respect the way in which Native American concepts of nature are embedded in Native American cultural practice. Furthermore, such a conceptualization places American Indians closer to nature in ways which some ecofeminists analyze as being negative for women. To me, these problems are amusingly brought home by a remark made by a Native American man to Judith Plant, who quotes him in her article in *HTW*. "You and us, we're different," this unnamed Indian man said to Plant, "but we're sort of the same, too. You want to learn to live off this place, we can already do this. You value the salmon, we value the salmon. You don't trust the government, neither do we. Not all Indian people are like us. Not all white people are like you. We're the natives and you're the naturals." At which point, according to Plant, "he roared with laughter."[32] This labeling, this distinction between "natives" and "naturals," is very telling. A "native" is primarily identified with a very specific and fixed area of land; a "natural" must have a preexisting distinction between culture and nature, and perhaps between civilization and primitivism, in order to "return" to "nature." As long as ecofeminists rely on notions of Native Americans as more naturally ecological, they will present access into Native American cultural practices only through a logic of rejecting culture for nature. Ironically, this theoretical move contains notions of separation between the two concepts which are radically different from much American Indian philosophy.

A second problem lies in the dehistoricizing and stereotypical results of the ecofeminist idealization of Native American culture. As the man in Plant's article says, "Not all Indians are like us. Not all white people are like you." Discussions of American Indians as the "ultimate ecologists" tend to generalize across tribal cultures and obscure the specific problems and varied solutions which compound Indian struggles for cultural survival. What happens when Native Americans choose strategies for their struggles which go against ecofeminist political theory and practice? Will they then become "bad Indians" instead of "noble savages"? Marie Wilson expresses this fear when she says: "I have had the awful feeling that when we are finished dealing with the courts and our land claims, we will then have to battle the environmentalists and they will not understand why. I feel quite sick at this prospect because the environmentalists want these beautiful places kept in a state of perfection. . . . In a way this is like denying that life is happening constantly in these wild places, that change is always occurring. Human life must be there too. Humans have requirements and they are going to have to use some of the life in these places."[33]

Valorization of the ecological and feminist elements of Native American culture reinvigorates a noble savage stereotype with a dangerous history in this country. Furthermore, the return of the this stereotype creates a conceptual paradox in which ecological and feminist solutions are seen to reside in tribal hunting-and-gathering societies. Because of the way in which the stereotyping of Indian culture prevents knowledge and analysis of the various ways in which Native American tribal cultures have changed, have been both resistant and accommodating to the dominant European-American culture, the noble-savage stereotype brings with it the myth of the "vanished Indian." The "ecological" tribal cultures held up for imitation are thus characterized as either disappearing or preserved in some ideal state. Besides preventing white ecofeminists from really hearing what Native American women think are serious issues in their communities, this characterization creates a stumbling block for ecofeminists trying to imagine solutions to the complexity of contemporary ecological problems. If the only way we can live as ecofeminists is to "return" to a hunting-gathering culture, we cannot begin to inspire people to take action now in the middle of their urban, industrialized, global, environments. If white ecofeminists stopped ideologically separating nature from culture, they would not become tribal peoples—rather, they would be challenged to creatively deal with the politics of their daily technology, their cyborg natures.[34] Ecofeminists would have to start imagining nature as including the urban and constructed landscapes in which many of us live. This would put ecofeminists in a position, once again, to ally themselves with antiracist environmental movements that are concentrated on urban problems. Ecofeminists could then share in developing activist strategies that could provide the basis for an effective coalition politics, not just between white ecofeminists and Native American women environmentalists but across the multitude of differences that divide women.

Earlier, I suggested that it is useful to think of the task of ecofeminist theory as developing strategic connections between feminism and environmentalism, rather than between women and nature. The antiracist theories we use are one important link between these political movements. I have argued that ecofeminism inherits a legacy of discourses about racial difference from feminist antimilitarism and white environmentalism that needs to be critically examined if ecofeminism is to be able to create an effective antiracist political strategy. I have identified problems with a binary conception of race and with a valorization of Native American women as the "ultimate ecofeminists." In both cases, I suggest two intertwined approaches to these problems. First, we need to acknowledge and analyze the ways in which U.S. racism operates in multiple arenas, developing a historical understanding of the ways in which racism is reproduced and maintained. Second, I believe that we need to use the antiracist theory developed by people of color to examine the ways in which racism constructs white as well as nonwhite subjects. Otherwise, "women of color" will remain "natural resources" for white ecofeminists rather than feminist environmentalists with whom we can have solidarity in political struggles. These suggestions do not, of course, exhaust the elements necessary for a successful antiracist ecofeminist agenda.[35] But they are one place to start.

Notes

I appreciate the critical readings given to different versions of this chapter by Karen J. Warren, Sue Armitage, and T. V. Reed, as well as members of the panels and audiences at various conferences where I've presented portions. Thanks also to Kari Norgaard, my research assistant.

1. This definition paraphrases Greta Gaard, "Living Interconnections with Animals and Nature," in Greta Gaard, ed., *Ecofeminism: Women, Animals, Nature* (Philadelphia: Temple University Press, 1993), 1.

2. Ynestra King, personal communication, May 1990, repeated in several public speeches.

3. At present, I find that many U.S. women of indigenous heritage use either *Native American* or *American Indian*. Thus in this chapter I will alternate between the two.

4. Donna Haraway, a white socialist feminist deeply influenced by poststructuralism, explicitly calls herself an ecofeminist in "Situated Knowledges: The Science Question in Feminism and the Privilege of Partial Perspective," *Simians, Cyborgs, and Women: The Reinvention of Nature* (New York: Routledge, 1991), 201. Mary Daly's radical feminist classic, *Gyn-Ecology* (Boston: Beacon Press, 1978, 1990), is now considered by many to be a foundation for ecofeminist theory. Alice Walker, a prominent best-selling African-American writer, has contributed explicitly to ecofeminist antimilitarist and animal liberationist concerns, most clearly through her pieces "Only Justice Can Stop a Curse," *In Search of Our Mother's Gardens* (San Diego: Harcourt Brace Jovanovich, 1983), 338–42, and "Am I Blue?" *Living by The Word* (San Diego: Harcourt Brace Jovanovich, 1988), 3–8. Rachel Carson, a natural scientist who was not an explicit feminist, is claimed as an ecofeminist foremother because of her book *Silent Spring*, which arguably intitiated the first nonconservationist environmental movement in the United States (see Grace Paley's dedication to Carson in Irene Diamond and Gloria Feman Orenstein, eds., *Reweaving the World: The Emergence of Ecofeminism* [San Francisco: Sierra Club Books, 1990], p. ii). Starhawk, a pagan, witch, activist in the nonviolent antimilitarist direct action

movement, writer, and theorist, has had an important influence on ecofeminism; see her *Dreaming the Dark* (Boston: Beacon Press, 1982), *The Spiral Dance: A Rebirth of the Ancient Religion of the Great Goddess* (San Francisco: Harper and Row, 1988), and *Truth or Dare* (San Francisco: Harper and Row, 1985). Vandana Shiva is a theoretical physicist who is also the director of an environmental research institute in Dehra Dun, India; her book *Staying Alive: Women, Ecology and Development in India* (London: Zed Press, 1988) is an important ecofeminist text.

5. However, my description is not simply an arbitrary construction. Both my own participation in the ecofeminist movement as an activist and theorist since 1984 and my experience as editor of the *Ecofeminist Newsletter* (published annually since 1990) give me a broad and immediate sense of the movement and ongoing personal contact with a wide variety of people who call themselves ecofeminists. For an excellent history and overview of ecofeminism, see Carolyn Merchant, "Ecofeminism," *Radical Ecology* (New York: Routledge, 1992), 183–210.

6. The last few years have seen a rapid increase in literature on ecofeminism in the context of a growing body of environmental literature. An analysis of the publication history of ecofeminist literature indicates a trend from marginal, movement-oriented publications to scholarly journals and university presses. Journals which have devoted special issues to the topic are *Heresies* 13 (1981), *New Catalyst* 10 (Winter 1987–88); *Woman of Power* (Spring 1988); *Studies in the Humanities* 15, no. 2 (1988); *Hypatia: Journal of Women and Philosophy* 6, no. 1 (1991); the American Philosophical Assocation's *Newsletter on Feminism and Philosophy* (Fall 1991, Spring 1992); and *Society and Nature* 2, no. 1 (1993). Journals which have published numerous articles on ecofeminism are *Environmental Ethics, Contemporary Philosophy, Environmental Review, National Women Studies Association Journal*, and *Woman Studies International Forum*. A sampling of recent and forthcoming books on ecofeminism includes Shiva, *Staying Alive*; Irene Dankelman and Joan Davidson, *Women and Environment in the Third World* (London: Earthscan, 1988); Judith Plant, ed., *Healing the Wounds: The Promise of Ecofeminism* (Philadelphia: New Society, 1989); Carolyn Merchant, *Ecological Revolutions: Nature, Gender and Science in New England* (Chapel Hill: University of North Carolina Press, 1989); Janet Biehl, *Finding Our Way: Rethinking Ecofeminism Politics* (Boston: South End Press, 1991); Diamond and Orenstein, *Reweaving the World*; Stephanie Lahar, *Ecofeminist Roots: Foundations for a New Psychology* (Boston: South End Press, 1991); Rosemary Radford Reuther, *Gaia and God: An Ecofeminist Theology of Earth Healing* (San Francisco: Harper and Row, 1992); Carol Adams, ed. *Ecofeminism and the Sacred* (New York: Continuum Press, 1993); Val Plumwood, *Feminism and the Mastery of Nature* (New York: Routledge, 1993); Maria Mies and Vandana Shiva, *Ecofeminism* (London: Zed Press, 1993); Karen J. Warren, ed., *Ecological Feminism* (New York: Routledge, 1994); Irene Diamond, *Fertile Ground: Women, Earth, and the Limits of Control* (Boston: Beacon Press, 1994); and Ynestra King, *Ecofeminism: The Reenchantment of Nature* (Boston: Beacon Press, forthcoming). A popular interest in ecofeminism is indicated by special issues of the *Utne Reader* 36 (November–December 1989) and *Ms.* (1991).

7. See Barbara Epstein, *Political Protest and Cultural Revolution: Nonviolent Direct Action in the 1970s and 1980s* (Berkeley: University of California Press, 1991), 161.

8. The Unity Statement, including its original illustrations depicting women of all races and ages, has been reprinted in Lynne Jones, ed., *Keeping the Peace* (London: Women's Press, 1983), 42–43.

9. For a discussion of the complex political agenda of the WPA, see T. V. Reed, "Dramatic Ecofeminism: The Women's Pentagon Action as Theater and Theory," *Fifteen Jugglers, Five Believers: Literary Politics and the Poetics of American Social Movements* (Berkeley: University of California Press, 1992), 120–41. In particular, the WPA actions were criticized for the "essentialism" of their rhetoric connecting women and nature. See Ellen Willis's columns in the *Village Voice* 25, no. 25 (June 18–24, 1980), 28, and 25, no. 29 (July 16–22, 1980), 34. Additionally, and more relevant to my argument here, many feminist activists of color identified the feminist antimilitarist movement as a white-dominated movement.

10. Particularly Susan Griffin, *Women and Nature: The Roaring Inside Her* (New York: Harper and Row, 1978).

11. Especially Charlene Spretnak, ed., *The Politics of Women's Spirituality: Essays on the Rise of Spiritual Power within the Feminist Movement* (New York: Anchor, 1982).

12. A prolific and extremely important ecofeminist theorist, King has collected many of her classic essays in *What Is Ecofeminism?* (New York: Ecofeminist Resources, 1990), available from Women's Studies Program, Antioch College, Yellow Springs, OH, 45387 for US $3.50.

13. See Judith McDaniel, ed., *Reweaving the Web of Life: Feminism and Nonviolence* (Philadelphia: New Society, 1982), for several early formulations of the connections between feminism and environmentalism stemming from feminist antimilitarism. Note the reworking of this title in Diamond and Orenstein's explicitly ecofeminist anthology *Reweaving the World*.

14. See Diamond and Orenstein's description of the conference and its importance in their "Ecofeminism: Weaving the Worlds Together," *Feminist Studies* 14 (Summer 1988): 368–70. There have been a number of important ecofeminist conferences since.

15. Elsewhere I discuss other political dangers as well as advantages inherent in the essentialism of some ecofeminist formulations of the connection between women and nature. See Noël Sturgeon, "Positional Feminism, Ecofeminism, and Radical Feminism Revisited," *Newsletter on Feminism and Philosophy* 93, no. 1 (Spring 1994): 41–47.

16. Gwyn Kirk, "Blood, Bones, and Connective Tissue: Grassroots Women Resist Ecological Destruction," paper presented at the National Women Studies Association, Austin, June 1992.

17. The term is used by Michael Omi and Howard Winant in their *Racial Formations in the United States* (New York: Routledge, 1988).

18. The representative figure here is Barbara Deming, a lesbian-feminist whose career as a nonviolent activist spanned the civil rights movement, feminist antimilitarism, and early ecofeminism. Indeed, Deming had a direct influence on WomanEarth. During her last illness, she spoke with Ynestra King about the importance of forming interracial organizations and sent King to Barbara Smith to talk about how to do this. Smith then suggested to King the principle of racial parity upon which WomanEarth was based, and Smith became involved in an early meeting of the organization. Interview with King, October 1993.

19. My information about WomanEarth comes from literature I received from the group during 1987–89, two articles (Rachel Bagby, "The Power of Numbers," in Plant, *Healing the Wounds*, 91–95, and Lindsy Van Gelder, "It's Not Nice to Mess with Mother Nature," *Ms.*, January–February 1989, 60–63), and interviews with Ynestra King, Gwyn Kirk, Rachel Bagby, Starhawk, Luisah Teish, Rachel Sierra, Margy Mayman-Park, Papusa Molina, and Margo Adair in 1992–94. I cover the history of WomanEarth and the issues I touch on here in more detail in Noël Sturgeon, *Ecofeminist Natures: Race, Gender and Transnational Environmental Politics* (New York: Routledge, forthcoming).

20. A WomanEarth flyer distributed at the 1989 Greens Conference in Eugene, Oregon, described a meeting of the group in which most of the time and energy was consumed by adjusting an imbalance of numbers between white women and women of color.

21. Bernice Johnson Reagon, "Coalition Politics: Turning the Century," in Barbara Smith, ed., *Home Girls: A Black Feminist Anthology* (New York: Women of Color Press, 1983), 356–69.

22. See Chela Sandoval, "Feminism and Racism: A Report on the 1981 National Women's Studies Association Conference," in Gloria Anzaldua, ed., *Making Face, Making Soul: Haciendo Caras* (San Francisco: Aunt Lute Foundation, 1990), 55–71, and "U.S. Third World Feminism: The Theory and Method of Oppositional Consciousness in the Postmodern World," *Genders* 10 (Spring 1991): 1–24.

23. For examples of analyses arising from the movement against environmental racism, see Robert D. Bullard, ed., *Confronting Environmental Racism: Voices from the Grassroots* (Boston: South End Press, 1993), Richard Hofrichter, ed., *Toxic Struggles: The Theory and Practice of Environmental Justice* (Philadelphia: New Society Publishers, 1993), Andrew Szasz, *EcoPopulism: Toxic Waste and the Movement for Environmental Justice* (Minneapolis: University of Minnesota Press, 1994), and the journal *Race, Poverty and the Environment*.

24. For just two examples of analyses of the construction of "whiteness" which question the unity of the category, see Biddy Martin's and Chandra Talpade Mohanty's discussion of Minnie Bruce Pratt's autobiographical essay in their "Feminist Politics: What's Home Got to Do with It?" in Teresa de Lauretis, ed., *Feminist Studies/Critical Studies* (Bloomington: Indiana University Press, 1986), 191–212, and Ruth Frankenberg, *White Women, Race Matters: The Social Construction of Whiteness* (Minneapolis: University of Minnesota Press, 1993).

25. For a few examples of this theorization of the politics of racial identity, see Combahee River Collective, "The Combahee River Collective Statement," in Barbara Smith, ed., *Home Girls: A Black Feminist Anthology* (New York: Women of Color Press, 1983), 272–82; Gloria Anzaldua, *Borderlands/La Frontera: The New Metiza* (San Francisco: Aunt Lute Foundation, 1987), which, by the way, is considered by some to be an ecofeminist text; and Sandra Harding, "Reinventing Ourselves as Other: More New Agents of History and Knowledge," in Linda S. Kaufmann, ed., *American Feminist Thought at Century's End* (Cambridge: Blackwell, 1993).

26. I have established the racial or ethnic identities of these authors in a very non-systematic way: through paying attention to self-identifications and comparing other writings of these authors. I fully expect to have made several errors in this process. In my forthcoming *Ecofeminist Natures*, I identify another problematic discourse of racial difference in U.S. ecofeminism, one which sidesteps questions of the specific interrelation of U.S. racism and environmental problems by the use of non-U.S. ecofeminists to represent "racial diversity." The breakdown of the authors in these two anthologies demonstrates this particular problem; in the book, I analyze in a similar vein the makeup of participants in the World Women's Congress for a Healthy Planet in Miami, 1992. Ecofeminists who are not from the United States, who are an important part of ecofeminism as an international movement, do not generally engage in the particular discourses about racial difference I criticize in this essay.

27. Personal communication, Winona LaDuke, during a question-and-answer period for her lecture "The Legacy of Columbus: What It Means for Women and the Environment," Washington State University, 1992. The tendency for women environmental activists of color to identify their politics as stemming from community membership rather than as women and the implications of this for a redefinition of "motherist" or "maternalist" politics is discussed by Giovanna Di Chiro in "Defining Environmental Justice: Women's Voices and Grassroots Politics," *Socialist Review* 22, no. 4 (October–December 1992): 93–130.

28. Marie Wilson, "Wings of the Eagle: A Conversation with Marie Wilson," in *Healing the Wounds*, 212.

29. Andy Smith, "For All Those Who Were Indian in a Former Life," in Adams, ed., *Ecofeminism and the Sacred*, 168–71.

30. Ibid., 169. Greta Gaard also argues that using portions of Native American philosophy, spirituality, and culture outside the context of Native American life is a form of imperialism on the part of ecofeminists. See Gaard, "Ecofeminism and Native American Cultures: Pushing the Limits of Cultural Imperialism?" in Gaard, ed., *Ecofeminism*, 295–314.

31. For two interesting treatments of the problems which inhere in this characterization of Native Americans, see Calvin Martin, "The American Indian as Miscast Ecologist," in Robert C. Schultz and T. Donald Hughes, eds., *Ecological Consciousness* (Lanham, Md.: University Press of America, 1981), and Tom Regan, "Environmental Ethics and the Ambiguity of the Native American's Re-

lationship with Nature," *All That Dwell Therein: Animal Rights and Environmental Ethics* (Berkeley: University of California Press, 1982), 206–39.

32. Judith Plant, "The Circle is Gathering . . . " in *Healing the Wounds*, 250.

33. Wilson, "The Wings of the Eagle," 217.

34. Using the cyborg as a useful and explicitly ecofeminist identity is advocated by Donna Haraway in "A Cyborg Manifesto: Science, Technology and Socialist-Feminism in the Late Twentieth Century," *Simians, Cyborgs, and Women: The Reinvention of Nature* (New York: Routledge, 1991), 149–82.

35. Another area of necessary work for ecofeminists is to develop other analyses of ideological conceptions of women and nature than those they presently use. In *Ecofeminist Natures*, I undertake an ecofeminist analysis that examines the mutual construction of images and ideologies of race, gender, and nature. We have not just myths of gendered nature which shape our environmental practices but myths about gendered and *raced* nature.

Sixteen

Ecofeminism in Kenya
A Chemical Engineer's Perspective

Joseph R. Loer

There is reason to suspect the assumptions of the human
brain when it becomes too elevated from the earth that nurtured it.

—John Hay

When men are oppressed, it's tragedy. When women are oppressed, it's tradition.

—Bernadette Mosala

When I was offered a position in Kenya, I didn't know what to expect,
other than the endless terrain captured on film in *Out of Africa*. But
though Kenya is much more developed overall than I had assumed, the remote region in which I lived, Tharaka, is considered backward by Kenyans
themselves. Hot and dry, without such proofs of progress as electricity and
plumbed water, it seemed a good place to send this American engineer.

I recall sitting on a huge rock looking out over this land, toward Somalia
on the horizon. The human inroads were barely visible: little mud-and-
thatch huts, bare dirt roads narrowing to paths before disappearing, an oc-
casional acre of cultivated hillside. The landscape—acacia trees and thick
plant life covering rocky hills—dwarfed the recognizably human part. This
landscape, it seems now, was indeed the vast ruggedness I imagined existed
everywhere in Africa. Calling this land the "bush" made perfect sense. It's
not just that the human hold there was tiny and fragile but that the bush
seemed to be patiently waiting, without any notion of time or acknowledge-
ment of human effort, to reconsume what it had once covered if this human effort receded.

The rock I sat on was part of a water-supply project undertaken jointly
by our Ministry of Water Development staff and the people of a village
called Kondo. Three years earlier, a rock rainwater-catchment system had
been built. The idea behind the system was to find a vast rock surface high-

est at the center. A foot-high concrete wall had then been built around the lower base of the rock to collect rainwater by gravity at the lowest point along the wall. At this point a concrete collection box was built, with screens of decreasing size to keep out everything from branches to small snakes. A pipe led from the box to metal-reinforced concrete storage tanks farther downhill. The system had worked for one season but had since sat unused and empty, in disrepair. The bush had done well in the three years: climbing up to my lookout I was scratched a dozen times by the resettled, thorny bushes.

Technically, our water-supply project was straightforward. We planned to rehabilitate the system's existing structures and add a pipeline running half a mile from the tanks to two taps, one in the village and one at the primary school. The technical work required the creation of engineering designs, the drafting of blueprints, and the surveying of pipeline routes, along with the laying of masonry, pipefitting, and construction—work similar to the previous effort.

The previous effort, though, had relied exclusively on a technology-based approach used for decades by Westerners in development work. But for decades these projects had had high failure rates because of their Band-Aid approach and the dependency it fostered. Most projects had failed because the outsiders who came in to build the systems had left, something simple like a pipe or a valve had broken, and everyone in the village had waited in vain for the white men to return and fix the problem. Before the projects were built, these communities had never had potable water; when the systems failed, their only recourse was subsistence methods, such as gathering from streams. The recipients of such projects appreciated the outsiders' coming in to provide clean water: the kids were healthier, the women didn't spend half their days carrying water, and animals drank all they wanted. But when the system wasn't maintained properly and broke and no one in the community knew how to make the necessary repairs, the year or two of easy water was simply forgotten. Not until members of a community believed something to be theirs and were given the necessary knowledge would they protect, maintain, and repair the system.

At Kondo, the technical work alone would have taken just three weeks, but we used a multidisciplinary approach that took four months—*and* had a realistic chance of long-term success. First, I was one of only two Westerners in a hundred-member water development team. The rest were Kenyans. Even so, because "outsider" equates to "expert" in that remote area, we Westerners quickly realized that our opinions carried a great deal of weight and would overwhelm the local voices if we weren't careful. Our approach, which I learned there, was to go to the village with an engineer, a translator, and a sociologist. Past lessons indicated the need to explain the technical aspects of our project clearly and, more important, to integrate the villagers into the project.

Using this approach, we made allowances for cultural factors. We let the villagers know up front that we wanted a community effort, that women would have to be integrally involved, and that no, we wouldn't put in an extra tap at the chief's house. Our second meeting with the whole village allowed us to explain that we would provide the pipes, cement, and skilled workers while villagers would provide large rocks for construction of the walls and would break rock into gravel and haul sand for concrete. They would also have to pay a fourth of the material costs.

The community agreed to do the project only after discussion of the considerable burden these obligations placed on them. But though the Kondo people acted in good faith, three more meetings and six weeks passed before they were ready for what seemed small steps. One week we arrived in Kondo to find that our meeting had been canceled because all the men had gone off to pay their respects for a death in another community. We understood, of course, but it meant that we had to return another day just to reschedule the meeting for the following week. All of the leaders in this culture, from the chief on down, were men. The children and women who had stayed behind the first day had no authority to do the rescheduling.

At first I felt that such delays were totally unnecessary. The people of Kondo had the harshest life I had ever seen. Their water came from muddy, seasonal streams or hand-dug wells easily contaminated by livestock, and they usually walked a mile to get it. Their livestock was decimated regularly by disease, and even in good times the animals were scrawny. Pupils at the primary school had the worst grades in the district—most likely because of ill health. So why didn't these subsistence farmers rush to embrace the technological help we offered? Not until I had spent time in this place did I begin to sense the villagers' understanding of time and of progress. It wasn't that they didn't view the project as beneficial, but their lives revolved around what was cyclical, not progressive: crops, rains, traditions, heat. Progress might be good, but it had to come at their pace or not at all. They had, after all, watched the last best attempt to use modern technology in their village get swallowed up by the bush.

Coming into such a situation was difficult in part because, in bringing along my Western values and my rational baggage, I was easily annoyed and distracted. But over the long haul I learned this lesson: as an outsider, I needed to give up the assumption that the outsider knows best and to learn to respect other people's ways of life. I began to accept the Kondo villagers' notion that a delay of a few weeks was insignificant. Similarly, I learned to shrink my notion of progress to a basic level. In truth, our fancy new tanks, even if they worked properly for decades, wouldn't significantly change the Kondo villagers' lives. Yes, cleaner water would improve things, but only marginally. Especially the women, who I think viewed the project suspiciously all along, knew that the fabric of their lives would remain the same long after the tanks' installation, because change didn't come miraculously in their world. The overwhelming tendency of persons living so basically, so tied to the land, was toward constancy. And for the people in Kondo, constancy meant that the men assumed the male roles, such as thinkers and decision makers, while the women remained responsible for the caretaking female roles, such as gathering and distributing water. Though the men of Kondo seemed to view the tanks, and technology itself, as good, the women's lack of enthusiasm was understandable. For them, what would actually change?

Thinking Ecofeminist

I have since learned of an alternative ecological perspective called ecological feminism (ecofeminism) that would clearly have helped my understanding of our efforts at Kondo. The essay "Taking Empirical Data Seriously: An Ecofeminist Philosophical Perspective" by Karen J. Warren (chapter 1 in this volume) discusses how such a project must be understood as involving three key factors: technology, local community life, and feminism. When considering the ideal way to approach the ecological question of humans and our environment, in this case how to get cleaner water for an improved life, we must use the complementary and supportive insights of these three fields, specifically where they overlap each other. Warren visually presents the section where ecofeminist philosophy lies as at *:

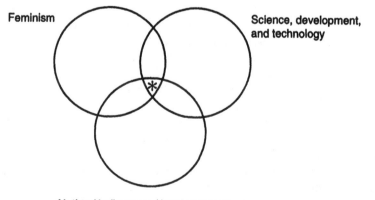

Feminism

Science, development, and technology

Native / indigenous / local perspectives

At Kondo, the first attempt to provide water focused exclusively on the use of science and technology in the role of development. I've shown how that first attempt failed. When our staff became involved we understood that until we combined our technology with the cultural perspective of the people there—of what they needed and wanted—the project would simply fail again. Understanding how these two perspectives could combine with feminism (*), or why they needed to, is most difficult.

Feminism can be expressed in many ways, but certainly one way is to realize that the Kenyan society separates male values such as reason and mind and female values such as emotion and body, then assumes men should act like "males" and women should act like "females." Men should discuss and think in the public realm, and women should tend fields and children in the private realm. Furthermore, the male roles aren't seen simply as different but as somehow morally superior. Feminism—which involves the recognition of such realities—needed to be integrated into our water project because the nature of the society directly affected the project.

For example, when it came time for training, the males would step forward because they believed that as the thinkers they were the most capable of being trained. But the maintenance itself would be a job for the women. If the knowledge was with the males and the women were responsible for implementation of the knowledge—the work—the necessary upkeep wouldn't get done. The reality was that women were integrally necessary for long-term worthiness of the project, because in the course of their daily lives they'd simply be more involved with the whole system. Unless that was understood by us all, a flaw as harmful as an unsound engineering design doomed the overall effort.

We succeeded to some degree in integrating these insights of feminism into our recognition that local voices must be integrated with the technological concerns by insisting that women participate on the water committee to make decisions and to receive the necessary training. Where we didn't succeed was in shifting the emphasis of the project far and clearly enough so that the project was viewed by the women of Kondo as truly reflecting their needs—as the direct users and maintainers of the system. For example, the location of the village tap was chosen by their water committee, but the women's preference on locale based on the shortest distance for them to carry water did not prevail. The male chief influenced the location of the tap to reflect his prestige. Also, though we tried to get a local storeowner to carry spare parts for the system, he didn't see that any real profit incentive existed—which was accurate—so we had to stock spare parts in a bigger city forty miles away from Kondo. But the women weren't likely to travel forty miles to get spare parts, even though they *were* more likely to regularly see the need for them.

While at Kondo, we didn't use ecofeminist theory to make our decisions. We didn't debate changes in gender roles in relation to the effect of imposing an outsider's values, specifically where technology is involved. None of the issues were ever that clear, so practical considerations prevailed. We knew the project wouldn't even last two years if there weren't such moves, so we insisted on them. And as any engineer knows, when practical considerations in the field follow a theory, this says a lot for the theory.

Ecofeminism and Science

Although some of the science- and technology-related issues faced here at home may be more complicated, the problems created by our level of progress and the resulting impact on the environment may still require that this marriage (section *) work to solve them. Jacques Cousteau (1981) has written:

> Born of the legitimate struggle for survival, ironically, the pursuit of technology and progress may today endanger the very survival of the human species, as well as that of practically all life on earth and in the ocean. However, those who would denounce technology and progress altogether in an attempt to solve the problem have only a limited vision; and limited vision is sometimes more dangerous than blindness. We must not forget that the same civilization that has clouded our view with toxic smog has also given us the satellite to help us view the planet from high above. The technology that we use to abuse the planet is the same technology that can help us to heal it. (xviii)

Technology's role in change is to push us along, to show what is possible—as a stimulus, an illuminator of the path ahead. However, technology isn't magical and doesn't hold any meaning or value until it impacts our lives.

The ecology movement has raised and debated the issue of science, technology, and society for decades. In "The Death of Nature" Carolyn Merchant (1993) discusses how feminism and the ecology movement could naturally combine:

> Juxtaposing the goals of the two movements can suggest new values and social structures, based not on the domination of women and nature as resources but on the full expression of both male and female talent and on the maintenance of environmental integrity. (268)

An ecofeminist position is one that seeks to help us create options for our own progress and development by recognizing that the way dominators view nature—as a resource and as inferior morally to human culture and reason—is fundamentally connected to, and indeed caused by, the way a male-dominated society views female values. Ecological feminism fits into this essay with science because it "is a feminism which attempts to unite the demands of the women's movement with those of the ecological movement" (Warren and Cheney 1991, 179). And the ecological movement isn't fully valid unless it rests on good science. Ecofeminism, as one type of feminism, has as a fundamental tenet the belief that our conceptual world views are shaped by our social structure. Though perhaps less extreme than in Kenya, our social structure is also patriarchy, "an oppressive, male-gender privileged conceptual framework and the sorts of power relations and behaviors it legitimizes" (Warren 1991, 87). Only if we perceive and acknowledge harmful practices can we then empower ourselves to positive change, to creation of alternatives like integration of science and technology with our own "local" voices to take realistic looks at our notions of progress. Though new ecological directions devoid of scientific understanding are limited, perhaps even threatening, in their narrow-mindedness, a larger vision is also impossible through a narrow scientific approach. None of us can be so well educated and experienced as to have an expert's depth of understanding of enough individual disciplines to truly see a whole picture. Which makes seeing the connections across disciplines and to our everyday lives—which only the local voice can do—and acknowledging them as legitimate all the more important. Here the insights of feminists, local people, and science become equally important (section *).

Now, what does this have to do with scientific ecology? The "way" in which we conduct scientific observation of our environment is dependent upon our world view and will affect the outcome of that observation. Ecofeminist philosophers have not only incorporated the role of science as vital to their philosophy but have also shown that the ideology of particular researchers and the choice of "scientific method" in itself influences the science. One observes based partly on the way one observes. In "Ecosystem Ecology and Metaphysical Ecology," Warren and Jim Cheney (1993) discuss viewing the varieties of scientific ecological methods along a continuum, with the two extremes being the population-community and process-functional approaches:

> The population-community approach focuses on the growth of populations, the structure and composition of communities of organisms, and the interactions among individual organisms. It is grounded in Darwinian theory of natural selection. . . . In contrast, the process-functional approach is based on a quantitative, mathematical, thermodynamic, biophysical model which emphasizes energy flows and nutrient cycling. (179)

Working scientists utilize approaches along the continuum, depending on what they're studying. And they disagree over exactly what approach is correct. These two approaches don't need to be opposites, though, according to "hierarchy theory," which is a way of viewing ecosystem ecology that "provides a framework for understanding the relationship between organisms in a system and the functions of the system without reducing one to the other" (102). Hierarchy theory focuses on the observation set used, thereby acknowledging that the way an ecosystem is observed, with regard to spatiotemporal scale and the measurements taken and techniques used, will intrinsically affect the outcome. No single methodology is therefore correct but must be determined instead based on circumstance. In short, the scientific ecological methodology appropriate to studying the rain forest is not the same as that for studying ozone-layer depletion.

Modern science and technology, like a powerful tool, is extremely important in development work in the southern hemisphere (the south). But when applying knowledge to a different society than the one which shaped it, a contextual understanding is required for guidance. Another example comes from my work as a water engineer in Kenya. Many of the projects we built were hand pumps installed over drilled boreholes. Because these hand pumps were usually the only clean, available sources of water for miles around, people brought their livestock herds from miles around to water them there. And hundreds of hungry cattle and goats trodding every day on the semiarid land around these water pumps wiped out every trace of vegetation. Which left sand. The slide into desertification that threatens so much of the south—which we in the north should be concerned about beyond compassion (we *are* on the same planet, connected by global cycles and a single atmosphere)—occurred there because we had maldeveloped those areas. That is, the development was not sustainable. Yes, there was clean water that improved life, but that led also to ecologically unsound changes in habits. Additional strife occurred because the loss of vegetation destroyed the field of someone who had to be coaxed into allowing the land to be used by the whole community in the first place.

Two issues are relevant here: this effect wasn't considered before building the pumps, and we had no good ideas about what to do once it had occurred. Even these simple hand pumps were therefore inappropriate uses of technology. I, as a chemical engineer, and my Kenyan engineer colleagues didn't know the first thing about approaching ecology from a population-community perspective. Water-flow equations and chemical analyses that helped us design, build, and test water projects were pretty much useless when a herd of goats were stepping out the last few blades of grass holding the soil down. Though there are ecologists who have been trained to approach such problems, the point is that my scientific and engineering skills simply couldn't extend to that situation. But if we had sought out more local voices beforehand, they might have been able to help us think of better approaches, such as draining water away from the pump to a better spot for the animals. More than a single viewpoint is necessary, depending upon the circumstances.

While the role of the Western-trained scientist/engineer is necessary in sustainable development of the south, because such tremendous knowledge is beneficial, it's also important to realize that maldevelopment occurs through inappropriate uses of science and technology. Many small and large engineering projects have failed because they were not well-informed or thought-out with regard to the surrounding cultural context. What these examples haven't shown, because it's more difficult than contrasting my culture to life and work in another, is that the cultural context is still as crucial but is just as rarely acknowledged in our own development (in part because we generally perceive ourselves as "developed" and don't think that we're just at a different point in a never-ending process). Utilization of the scientist/engineer, among others, here at home is necessary to determine appropriate uses of technology for our own continual but sustainable development. The scientific voice is vital for philosophers, feminists, policymakers, environmentalists, or anyone else seeking ecologically sound theories and practices.

However, central to the environmental philosophy of ecofeminism is the necessity of inclusion of all approaches and voices only if they contribute positively to the dialogue. The scientist's voice isn't more important than the local voice but equally necessary for an overall view. My voice as an engineer is that of an "Up" (outsider become expert), but when I acknowledge this bias it's a positive contribution. My use of narrative in an essay is another way I enlarge my perspective and acknowledge a bias, by being purposefully subjective. This voice allows me to consider and relate personal experience and tie it into the overall discussion.

Ecofeminists address cultural issues because they see these relations as intrinsic to our basing of ecological world views. Consider this notion from "The Power and Promise of Ecological Feminism":

> Relationships are not something extrinsic to who we are, not an "add on" feature of human nature; they play an essential role in shaping what it is to be human. Relationships of humans to the nonhuman environment are, in part, constitutive of what it is to be human. (Warren 1990, 335)

All relationships, and therefore by extension nature, are, in a sense, social constructions. To get better definitions of the relationships is to look to those constructions. Ecological solutions rely on understanding ourselves socially and how those defined relationships extend to the natural world. Ecofeminism offers insights into the dysfunctional social structures that lead to these relationships and how we might address them.

As I allow other voices into my perspective, I do so largely in relation to science because I'm rooted there, but also because changes there will eventually flow back to society. And it's a two-way street, one affecting the other. In *Gaia, a Way of Knowing: Political Implications of the New Biology*, William Irwin Thompson writes:

> the observer of the scientific observer changes the science of the scientist. The literary writer, the poet, becomes possessed by science, and in reflecting the work back to the scientist, the scientist sees his image transformed. Over his shoulder in the mirror he sees himself involved in a cultural landscape he had not noticed before. He or she sees the mythic structures of the imagination and discovers the science and the humanities are moving into a postmodernist world in which neither one is what it was before. This is not a case of an easily split world, with soft subjectivity to one side and hard objectivity on the other, with humanities here and science there; it is a new condition of biology and the way of knowing. (10)

Ecofeminist philosophy, calling for that merger of the voices of feminism, science, and the subjective individual (the "local" or artistic voice), offers the same new insights, this new "way of knowing."

Though I've taken many steps to achieve a world view that draws from a blend of the sciences and humanities, quite honestly I still have to leap a bit to believe our ecologically dysfunctional social structures are fully caused by patriarchy. But I do agree with two things: science needs to be integrally involved in helping us to a more sound ecological world view, and science itself could benefit from feminism. As explained in a recent article in *Utne Reader* reviewing work done to examine new approaches to science by Evelyn Fox Keller, a theoretical physicist and molecular biologist,

> Keller in no way discounts the achievements of science. Rather, she appeals to scientists to expand the range of thinking styles they employ, in order to achieve the "reclamation, from within science, of science as a human instead of a masculine project." Keller does not imply that the objective method is inherently bad. On the contrary, she finds objectivity essential, but suggests that science might also benefit from encouraging subjectivity, feeling, intuition, and other traits that traditionally have been ascribed to women. (Morse 1993, 26)

The article also points out that Barbara McClintock, a geneticist, conducted her work showing genes in corn jumping from one chromosomal site to another by having a "feeling for the organism," by being intuitive. She was ostracized for this unorthodox thinking, then, nineteen years later, awarded a Nobel Prize once her work's importance was finally understood.

When I consider my own career, I realize that engineering knowledge is enhanced by an understanding of the cultural context of any project, in any place. For this reason, I've become more of a humanist. The connections aren't obvious and certainly not easy to search for, but if I want to believe in ecological solutions, if I want to avoid the pessimism and despair that so many with ecological understanding (or misunderstanding) seem to fall into, then I need this humanist, interdisciplinary perspective. Having said this, though, I still agree strongly with what scientist Paul Ehrlich wrote:

> But agreeing that science, even the science of ecology, cannot answer all questions—that there are "other ways of knowing"—does not diminish the absolutely crucial role that good science must play if our overextended civilization is to save itself. Values must not be based on scientific nonsense. (1986, 18)

Even as a humanist and a interdisciplinarian, I'll always think like an engineer. But the additional insight provided by ecofeminist thinking is invaluable, indeed indispensable. What a career move!

Works Cited

Cousteau, Jean Jacques. 1981. *The Cousteau Almanac*. Garden City: Doubleday.

Ehrlich, Paul. 1986. *The Machinery of Nature*. New York: Simon and Schuster.

Merchant, Carolyn. 1993. "The Death of Nature." In *Environmental Philosophy: From Animal Rights to Radical Ecology*, ed. Michael Zimmerman et al. Englewood Cliffs, N.J.: Prentice Hall, 268–83.

Morse, Mary. 1993. "Women in Lab Coats." *Utne Reader*, May–June.

Thompson, William Irwin, ed. 1987. *Gaia, a Way of Knowing: Political Implications of the New Biology*. Great Barrington: Lindisfarne Press.

Warren, Karen J. 1993. "The Power and Promise of Ecological Feminism." In *Environmental Philosophy*, ed. Zimmerman et al., 320–42.

——. 1991. "Toward a Feminist Peace Politics." *Journal of Peace and Justice Studies*, 87–102.

——, and Jim Cheney. 1993. "Ecosystem Ecology and Metaphysical Ecology." *Environmental Ethics* 15, no. 2 (Summer): 99–116.

——. 1991. "Ecological Feminism and Ecosystem Ecology," *Hypatia* 6, no. 1: 179–97.

Seventeen

Keeping the Soil
in Good Heart

Women Weeders, the Environment,
and Ecofeminism

Candice Bradley

The thesis of this chapter is that weeds, as well as women weeders, are victims of a sixteenth-century world view in which man dominates nature (Griffin 1989). The destruction of weeds for purely human, utilitarian purposes reflects a lack of perception of the interconnectedness of nature that ecological feminism calls attention to (Warren 1991, Warren and Cheney 1991). Women weeders are custodians of wild plants temporarily out of place in an anthropocentric ecosystem, preserving their spot in the larger ecosystem while utilizing their soil-enriching qualities.

The displacement of women as weeders is an example of what Shiva (1989, 82) calls maldevelopment, "a development bereft of the feminine, the conservation, the ecological principal." The process of intensification, as an outgrowth of agricultural development, displaces the productive labors of women as weeders and replaces them with plows, chemicals, and genetic engineering. As such, the responsibility of weed control moves from the hands, hoes, and digging sticks wielded primarily by women to the destructive and polluting weed-killing technology used mainly by men and corporations. The displacement of women from the field, along with their transformation into low-paid wage laborers, coincides with the denuding of the soil, the destruction of wildflowers, and the pollution of the surrounding area with chemicals. As such, both weeds and weeding are concerns of ecological feminism.

Few academics have written seriously about weeds and weeding. Trade books about weeds on bookstore shelves are either cute or sentimental.

Chapters about weeds sometimes appear in artistic little gardening diaries, punctuated by detailed ink drawings of plants with tiny yellow or blue flowers, washed in watercolors. The jacket flaps sport the inevitable photo of a gray-haired woman in a straw hat. To be interested in weeds in this way is to be white, Western, and leisured.

Men also write eccentric books about weeds. These books are usually compendia, or lists of weeds, which include their scientific names, habitats, and historical origins. Much like birdwatcher's guides, these are usually books by biologists written for the elite. They are reminiscent of the amateur naturalism of nineteenth-century Europe.

Though these books are authored by men, the drawings are often done by women. The small, detailed work of drawing wildflowers, as well as shells, insects, and birds, became an acceptable role for women during the second half of the nineteenth century. Some of these women artists made major contributions to U.S. government botanical surveys, working for such institutions as the National Herbarium. Women began to work as scientific illustrators at a time when basic concepts of women's roles were changing, and now women dominate the field (Norwood 1993). This fine, meticulous work, though highly skilled, represents an arena in which women are valued for detail-oriented work, reproducing existing gender stereotypes.

Not even an essay about weeds by Wisconsin naturalist Aldo Leopold was received with total seriousness. To talk about weeds is to be playful, ironic, and humorous. Note this recent editors' comment on Leopold's 1943 essay "What Is a Weed?" (Flader and Callicott 1991, 306): "this is a fine example of Leopold's wry, ironic humor in service of a deeply serious concern as anything he wrote . . . "

Weeding is not grand theory. Yet Leopold acknowledges this by recognizing that weeds are, by definition, undervalued. Leopold argues on behalf of the weed, supporting his argument from other essays that wildflowers, like wildlife, must be conserved. The process of obliterating weeds denies us and the environment their beneficial qualities.

How the weed is defined reflects its ambiguous position as a marginal inhabitant of a garden or farm. Like the weed itself, the activity of weeding is also marginalized in the farming cycle. Not surprisingly, weeding is an activity dominated by women in 60 percent of the world's agricultural societies.

There is a sort of hierarchy of weed control, which in the simplest forms of agriculture are the least damaging to the environment. In these horticultural societies, weed control is dominated by women. As agriculture becomes more complex, forms of weed control evolve and change. When irrigation and plowing become important, men begin to take over weeding from women and women's agricultural roles diminish. The most complex forms of agriculture use chemical herbicides rather than human labor, and tillage becomes unnecessary. This type of weed control destroys weeds and is the most poisonous to human beings and the environment.

This chapter explores the relationship between the undervaluation of the wildflowers we call weeds and the undervaluation of the roles of women weeders in most of the world's farming societies.

What Is a Weed?

Weeds are commonly defined as "plants out of place" (Martin 1987). Anthropologists recognize this as a slightly altered version of Mary Douglas's definition of pollution. Douglas defines pollution as "matter out of place" (1966, 35–36). In cross-cultural perspective, *pollution*, the symbolic opposite of purity, refers to beliefs in the dangers of such things as menstrual blood, dead bodies, pork, lepers, and epileptics. Pollution is dirt, the opposite of order and classification. Indeed, it is the opposite of *culture*, a word which has the same Latin root as *cultivate*.

Weeds are identified contextually, by the company they keep. This is an anthropocentric definition. Leopold argues that the monolithic utilitarian perspective of the agriculturalist or gardener defines weeds as something to be rid of. From this anthropocentric position, they are troublesome intruders, pests, difficult to exterminate and useless.

Paul Crosby has a chapter titled "Weeds" in his book *Ecological Imperialism*, in which he discusses the intrusion of weeds into North America through the expansion of the world system. One plant Crosby describes is the peach tree, a weed transported from Europe. Peaches eventually grew in abundance all over North America, and one of the earliest beneficiaries of this "ecological imperialism" was the American Indian (Crosby 1986).

A peach is not a weed if you are interested in the fruit. A violet is not a weed if you want to enjoy its flowers. To define something as a weed means that you must be rid of it to restore order, to ensure the fertility of the soil, to protect the growth of the plants you cultivate versus the plants that are uninvited.

Weeds are sometimes defined by how they look. Their flowers are often small, their leaves often ragged or toothed, like the ubiquitous dandelion, the weediest of weeds. Yet even the lowly dandelion has medicinal properties. Indeed, weeds have many valuable qualities. They may be food for other species or have important nitrogen-fixing qualities. In horticultural systems, the burning of undergrowth fertilizes the soil and makes it ready for planting.

There is nothing inherent in the weed itself which makes it a weed. Crosby (1986) writes: "Weeds are not good or bad; they are simply the plants that tempt the botanist to use such anthropomorphic terms as aggressive and opportunistic." Leopold argues that no plant is inherently good or bad, but some, "occasionally harmful to agriculture," are incorrectly regarded as worthless in all settings. Thus the notion of weed is a cultural construction. Symbolically, weeds are a form of pollution. Even our use of the word *weed* denies for us their other identities as indigenous plants, wildflowers, grasses, hedges, fodder, and salad ingredients.

This construction of weeds extends to our notions of weeders. For those of us who think of weeds as something to be rid of, weeders are the "others." For chemical corporations and industrial agriculturalists, women weeders in Africa, Asia, and South America are othered as useless parts of the process that will drop away once proper technology is available. As we will see, the undervaluation of weeds, and consequently of those who weed, results in an underestimation of the importance of women's contributions to agriculture cross-culturally.

Labor-Intensive Weeding

Horticulture is the least intensive form of farming. There are few inputs other than human labor. The tools of horticulture usually include a digging stick, a machete, and a hoe. In horticultural societies, there is usually a long fallow period when the land is not used. The trees are then chopped, the large debris removed, and the field burned. Many kinds of plants are sown, sometimes reproducing the structure of the forest in the cultivated field. The field is good for two or three years, during which time it is usually the women who weed (Boserup 1970). This is hard labor. Women in Kenya bend at the waist for long hours, sometimes with babies on their backs, digging the weeds out of the ground with a hoe and tossing them aside. In a few horticultural societies it is the men who do this work. In all cases, the quality of weeding and the number of times one weeds determine the length of time one can use the field. The quality of the weeding also determines how well the sown plants will thrive.

The most labor-intensive form of weed control, hoeing, has the fewest implications for the environment. In addition, the weeds that are burned contribute to the quality of the soil. The unwanted plants benefit from the same conditions that allow the sown plants to grow. After two or three years, the weeds become unmanageable and the field is abandoned and allowed to rest. The weeds are the first to return, and the forest's secondary growth will be chopped again years or decades later.

In the permanent horticultural fields of western Kenya, men do not consider weeding to be an important activity. On funeral days, when work is prohibited, women still weed the fields and gardens. A Logoli man once told me that this is because "weeding isn't work," but his wife, weeding a few feet away, shook her head in dismay. Since weeding is the responsibility of women in western Kenya, the onus of a poorly weeded garden or farm falls on her shoulders. The neighbors can be very critical: "Did you see Anne's *shamba* (farm)? It is overrun with weeds, and the maize and beans are not thriving." In societies where men weed, they are also subject to criticism from their peers. It is shameful to have a polluted field.

Weeding with Plows

As new technology is added to fields, weeding becomes more of a men's task. Irrigation and plowing are the two most important additions to agriculture, and with both of these inputs, men weed more (Bradley n.d.). Plowing is dominated by men in nearly all the world's agricultural societies. Women do the plowing only if men are not available. This is as true in the North American Midwest as it is in Ireland and Africa. The fact that men plow is less a matter of upper body strength than it is a combination of other factors, including control over important technology and the workload women carry in other arenas (Bradley n.d., Boserup 1970, Ember 1983).

Plows control weeds in two ways. First, they turn the weeds under. Weeds that are either hoed or plowed help build the soil. The protoplasm of decaying weeds is then available to the nitrogen-fixing microorganisms in the soil. Without a fresh supply of dead weeds, the humus in the soil decreases. Plowing or hoeing weeds under keeps the soil "in good heart" (Spencer 1940, 314).

Second, plows can be used to weed fields that are planted in rows. Weeding and plowing become parts of the same process, "cultivation." A crop that is weeded is cultivated, and a cultivator is a machine that both breaks up the soil and uproots weeds.

If men wield plows, this kind of weeding is a man's job. But plowing does not reduce the number of weedings needed to keep the fields in shape (Bradley n.d.). Indeed, weeding may increase because of the animals used in plowing. They carry weeds in their intestines and on their fur, sometimes importing new weeds into the system if the animal is brought from elsewhere. Purchased seeds also contain new weeds, and when agriculture is changed by increased inputs from overseas, these new weeds become a part of the local ecosystem.

Men are more likely to weed in societies with irrigation. This is probably because irrigation involves control of important water resources. Again, the crops are planted in rows, and plows are used in most of the societies that irrigate. Water brings new weeds with it, so weeding becomes a more arduous task with irrigation (Bradley n.d.).

Industrial Farming in Kenya

Industrial farming in western Kenya is often combined with a horticultural system in which women do the bulk of the work. The sugar factories contract, usually with male household heads, to plant sugar on private farms. Tractors come in to plow the fields, taking over a job that traditionally belonged to men, and then the sugar is planted. Sugar requires several weedings, and this task falls to the women who are responsible for the upkeep of the fields. The sugar companies provide men and trucks to do the harvesting, and the money for the sugar returns to the male household head. The women may see none of it.

People also grow tea on their private plots. The tea is weeded by day workers, commonly women who need the money to pay school fees for their children. When I was in Kenya, the daily rate for weeding tea was less than one U.S. dollar. A taxi driver in Nairobi earns the equivalent of three dollars for a short ride across town. When this inequitability is pointed out to men, they laugh, and do not answer. Weeding is the poorest-paying day labor job in western Kenya.

The undervaluation of weeding in Kenya is not merely a problem of the international corporations that contract with private farmers. It is also a problem rooted in western Kenya itself. In this farming region, men do not seem to realize how arduous and demanding weeding can be. But the corporations do not think about who the weeders are; or perhaps they know and choose to ignore it. They benefit from the knowledge and labor of women, as well as an ideology which lays the blame for a poorly weeded field on the woman. Smallholders also choose to devalue weeding, paying women far less than they are worth for a backbreaking task that consumes entire days.

Weed Killers

Organic herbicides led to the development of no-till cultivation. With no-till cultivation, fields are first sprayed to eliminate weeds. Thus there is no longer a need to plow. Crops that are not plowed do not have to be planted in rows. For the individual farmer, labor and energy costs are lower.[1]

For the wildflowers we call weeds, the cost of no-till cultivation is high. Under no-till cultivation, the weeds are destroyed and their valuable food-supplying and nitrogen-fixing qualities are lost. General chemical herbicides are nonselective and therefore must be used before crops are planted. Although land under no-till cultivation has fewer problems with soil run-off because the need to plow has been eliminated, under no-till cultivation the soil is kept "in good heart" through artificial means. Their nonselective weed-killing power also kills the other plants in the field.

Herbicide use has increased phenomenally. Between 1972 and 1987, the dollar value of herbicides shipped by the U.S. chemical industry increased 700 percent. In 1992, U.S. firms shipped nearly $11 billion worth of herbicides. More money was spent on herbicides in 1987 than on any other agricultural chemical, including insecticides and fungicides. Over 70 million acres of corn, 36 million acres of wheat, and 58 million acres of soybeans were treated with herbicides. Ninety-seven percent of corn and soybean crops in the United States were treated. More than $1 billion in annual sales came from a single herbicide, Roundup (glyphosate). Roundup, manufactured by Monsanto, is sold to 120 countries worldwide and used on a wide range of crops, including coffee, soybeans, grapes, and Christmas trees.

Many herbicides are known chemical pollutants, associated with skin disorders, genetic mutations, cancer, premature births, and birth defects. Home herbicide users, a fraction of the $630-million home pesticide market, are generally sold herbicides that agricultural markets no longer receive. One common home herbicide is 2,4-dichlorophenoxy acetic acid (2,4-D). 2,4-D causes plants to die by swelling plant cells, stopping root growth, thickening leaves, and harming photosynthesis. 2,4-D has been linked to a rare form of cancer. Herbicides have been used in warfare to defoliate crops and forests, as well as to destroy coca in the war on drugs. Agent Orange, or tetrachlorodibenzo-p-dioxin (2,4,5-T), was used in South Vietnam by the U.S. military and is believed to have caused premature births and birth defects in Vietnamese children as well as many animal deaths. Vietnam veterans have blamed Agent Orange for various cancers and genetic disorders, though links have been difficult to demonstrate. Agent Orange was banned in 1979. Roundup has been around for twenty years and is considered relatively safe; it decomposes quickly and, because it facilitates no-till cultivation, helps farmers avoid topsoil runoff. Monsanto claims Roundup is harmless to the nervous system, but there have been questions about its safety to human beings.

Herbicides and other pesticides are used by more affluent farmers in western Kenya. I have seen boys, barechested in shorts, spraying fields with tanks strapped to their backs. No precautions are taken to protect the boys from the chemicals. Inevitably, when the rains come, the chemicals wash into the river along with seas of red mud. Some people draw water from the river to feed their cattle, wash their clothes, or water their vegetable gardens on the river's edge. The milk from the cows is put in tea and given to small children to drink. Sometimes cows are sold to butchers, and women purchase small amounts of beef from the butcher to accompany the *ugali* (a maize dish). Drinking water is taken from wells in ravines at the bottom of the fields.

Control of weeds with herbicides means that there is little or no weeding. In farming systems where women's major contributions once came from crop-tending activities, women are turned away from the farm. Men who once weeded continue to work in other farming activities. In the hierarchy of weed control, the use of herbicides, particularly in no-till cultivation, is the most wasteful form of weed control. It is also the most exclusionary of women's labor and the most costly to the environment.

Biological herbicides will be the next step in "weed control." Genetic engineering firms such as Crop Genetics International (CGI) are testing bioherbicides that will turn "naturally occurring bacterial weed pathogens" against specific weeds. Since bioherbicides will be plant-specific, they will eliminate some of the nonselectivity associated with the chemical herbicides. Thus fewer chemicals will be needed. CGI (1992) argues that bioherbicides "promise to be more attractive than chemical herbicides due to their benign effects on the environment and wildlife." Weeds, thus defined as external to the environment and wildlife, will weaken and then succumb to "bacterial agents."

Chemical and biological herbicides can reduce the genetic diversity of the local ecosystem in two ways. Most obviously, many chemical herbicides destroy the wildflowers directly as well as other plants in the surrounding area. Biological herbicides cause an added problem. When unleashed on a field, they result in the destruction of some, but not all, of the plants. The plants that remain, although hardier in the face of these products, contain a narrower spectrum of the gene pool. Because they are immune, these plants then fill the niche, including the field where they are no longer destroyed by the old herbicides. The genetic engineers will need to return to the drawing board to come up with a new weed killer. The genetic diversity of the field is thus narrowed, and new weed killers are introduced at a later point.

Weeding, like plowing, is an activity that turns a disorderly field into an orderly one. Both activities bring culture to the field. But it is weeding alone that is degraded. Weeds, a kind of pollution of the field, are the responsibility of women in many cross-cultural settings. The undervaluation of weeding is like the undervaluation of housework. Indeed, weeding is housework—cleaning up—in the fields. Yet weeders, as custodians of the field, conserve the weeds as a by-product of their cleaning up. The weeds, the weeders, and the crops are linked in a generative cycle of production and reproduction.

In horticultural systems, where weeding is accomplished with human labor, weeds and cultivated plants exist side by side. The weeds are removed but meanwhile provide nourishment for the fields. Even when a plow is pulled by an ox, the weeds are merely turned under. They appear again later, and in the meantime keep the soil "in good heart." Herbicides, which circumvent the need for human labor in tillage, both destroy weeds and harm the environment. Industrial agriculture disconnects the weeders, usually women, from the agricultural process, thereby losing their knowledge. Alternatively, industrial agriculture exploits the labor of women by employing them at incredibly low wages as weeders in monocultured crops. Industrial agriculture brings in new varieties of weeds, increasing the workloads of weeders around the globe and decreasing the genetic diversity of the existing wildflowers in that ecosystem. In this sense, industrial agriculture and chemical or biological herbicides represent a form of maldevelopment.

I have seen the subject of weeds approached in two ways in our culture. On the one hand, they are interesting little wildflowers to be documented and painted, the subject matter of a leisured elite. On the other hand, we will do anything to eradicate weeds from our gardens and our fields. We invest billions of dollars in weed killers, using them in our own backyards and selling them around the world. These two views of weeds are disconnected, in the same way that a person who lives in the city might disconnect a clucking chicken from the roasted breast on a plate.

Ecofeminism calls attention to the rift between the self and the environment, as well as the connection between the domination of the environment and the domination of women. Weeds, so small and insignificant, are a poignant metaphor for that domination. To define weeds as wildflowers is to begin to "heal the wounds" (Plant 1989, 4). To acknowledge the ecological benefits of low-technology weeding would mean turning away from agricultural maldevelopment, including the multibillion-dollar international herbicide industry, and advocating nondestructive forms of weed control that take more time. It would mean paying women weeders in agricultural development schemes what they are worth for their work. And it would mean recognizing and celebrating women who keep the soil "in good heart"—particularly women of color at the edge of the world system—as the guardians of fields and wildflowers.

Note

1. Information on no-till farming, chemical herbicides, and bioherbicides came from several sources, including *The Encyclopedia Americana, International Edition* (Danbury, Conn.: Grolier, 1993); *Academic American Encyclopedia*, online edition (Danbury: Grolier Electronic, 1993); A. Kimery, "Weed Killer," *Progres-*

sive, July 1987; U.S. Department of Commerce, *Statistical Abstracts of the United States*, Washington, D.C., 1991; U.S. Bureau of Statistics, U.S. Department of Commerce, *Census of Manufacturers, Industrial Series: Agricultural Chemicals*, Washington, D.C., 1987; Monsanto Company Annual Report, Form 10-K (Washington, D.C.: Securities and Exchange Commission, 1992); H. F. Holman and D. C. Swindell, Crop Genetics International Corporation, 1992. Thanks to William J. Boehme of Piper Jaffray, Appleton, Wisc., for generously providing me with SEC and annual reports for a dozen herbicide manufacturers.

References

Boserup, E. 1970. *Women's Roles in Economic Development*. London: Allen & Unwin.

Bradley, C. n.d. Weeds, Field and Metaphors: Gender and Weeding in Cross-Cultural Perspective. Unpublished manuscript.

Crop Genetics International (CGI). 1992. Annual Report. Columbia, Md.: Crop Genetics International.

Crosby, P. 1986. *Ecological Imperialism: The Biological Expansion of Europe, 900–1900*. Cambridge: Cambridge University Press.

Douglas, M. 1966. *Purity and Danger: An Analysis of Concepts of Pollution and Taboo*. London: Routledge and Kegan Paul.

Ember, C. R. 1983. The Relative Decline in Women's Contribution to Agriculture with Intensification. *American Anthropologist* 85: 285–304.

Flader, S. L., and J. B. Callicott (eds.). 1991. *The River of the Mother of God and Other Essays by Aldo Leopold*. Madison: University of Wisconsin Press.

Griffin, S. 1989. Split Culture. In J. Plant, ed., *Healing the Wounds: The Promise of Ecofeminism*. Philadelphia: New Society.

Leopold, A. 1943. What Is a Weed? In Flader and Callicott, *The River of the Mother of God*, 306–309.

Martin, A. C. 1987. *Weeds*. New York: Golden Press.

Norwood, V. 1993. *Made From This Earth: American Women and Nature*. Chapel Hill: University of North Carolina Press.

Plant, J. 1989. Toward a New World: An Introduction. In Plant, *Healing the Wounds*.

Shiva, V. 1989. Development, Ecology, and Women. In Plant, *Healing the Wounds*.

Spencer, E. R. 1974 (originally 1940). *All about Weeds*. New York: Dover.

Warren, K. J. 1991. Introduction. *Hypatia* 6, no. 1.

——, and J. Cheney. 1991. Ecological Feminism and Ecosystem Ecology. *Hypatia* 6, no. 1: 179–97.

Eighteen

Remediating Development through an Ecofeminist Lens

Betty Wells and Danielle Wirth

Many of the inconsistencies and inequities of international development arise from the world view of the developer. Today's dominant world view accords neither respect nor reciprocity to women, nor to the earth. To cast development in more inclusive terms and processes requires that developers sensitize their world view as they apply their interventions. To this end, we begin by addressing three voids in development as conventionally practiced: nature, local culture, and women (and other oppressed people). We offer ecological feminism as a counterbalance to today's dominant world view.

Nature: Can There Be Renewal in Development?

The deterioration of the world's environment, primarily the result of human activities, has been accelerated by development. The pursuit of development through colonialism, industrialization, and urbanization has extracted a huge cost from the environment. Unsound agricultural practices typify the exploitation of natural resources. Conventional Western agriculture is imposed on the land in a seeming effort to control and subdue nature with the monoculture crop—in contrast to integrated multicrop, multilevel family and community farming systems which work in partnership with the land and natural cycles.

The failure of development programs as guided by the dominant world

300

view has led to a revised paradigm, called sustainable development. Sustainable development seeks a balance between resource use and the satisfaction of human needs based on continuing and renewable processes, not on the exploitation and exhaustion of the principal or the capital of the living resource base (Loening, 1990). The World Commission on the Environment and Development (1987, 43) stresses meeting "the needs of the present without compromising the ability of future generations to meet their own needs." Sustainable development requires living within our physical and biological carrying capacity.

Sustainable development, although generally conceptualized in natural science terms of environment and natural resources, increasingly encompasses social, political, and economic elements (such as social justice and economic viability) because to live within our carrying capacity requires new ways of thinking, leading, solving problems, organizing and doing business. Old approaches will further abuse our diminishing, fragile resource base.

The concept, although resonating with apparent good intention, is not easily operationalized at the local, perhaps most significant, level. Is sustainable development a contradiction in terms? If not, can the same be said of sustainable economic development? That this new discourse for development can be so readily appropriated into the mainstream vernacular offers little compelling hope that it will in practice be more respectful of nature, indigenous cultures, and women and children.

Local Culture: Can Diversity Be Protected?

The imposition of external systems through development damages cultural as well as natural diversity. The globalization and dominance of Western intellectual epistemology (and scientific and technical knowledge) erases history and cultural distinctiveness. Why, asks Easton (1991, 27), would Western experience lead to universal criteria for the production of reliable knowledge more so than the divergent experience of other cultures? If our conceptions of method and knowledge are products of a unique historical experience, considerable cultural bias will be reflected in our ways of learning and organizing knowledge.

The recent movement to preserve or blend indigenous knowledge with other forms of knowledge is a significant effort to counter the hegemony of Western influence. Indigenous knowledge refers to the system by which members of a given community define and classify phenomena in the physical/natural, social, and ideational environments. According to Michael Warren (Mathias-Mundy 1993, 3-4), this traditional local knowledge is distinct from the international knowledge system (what we call Western) generated through universities, government research centers, and private industry. The indigenous knowledge approach encourages the two-way flow of information, promoting indigenous scholarship as a counterpart or counterpoint to what the developer has to offer.

The documentation of a knowledge domain is incomplete without identifying gender variations. These differences are manifest in several ways (Norem et al., 1989). Women and men may have different knowledge about different things or different knowledge about similar things. Women and men may acquire knowledge from different sources and have different ways of communicating knowledge from person to person or transferring it from one generation to the next. They perceive risk differently. Some types of knowledge are primarily the domain of women; some tasks are typically performed by women, and some decisions are made by women.

Women and men may have different ways of organizing knowledge. For example, in an agrarian society, both may have extensive knowledge about a particular crop and sophisticated systems of classifying crop varieties, but one system may be based on the suitability for soil types or growing seasons and the other on nutritional content, modes of preparation, and storing qualities.

Questions remain. Whose priorities are driving development programs? Will indigenous knowledge be appropriated without benefit to indigenous peoples in the same way that other resources are appropriated? After documenting the knowledge systems of women and men in distinct typologies, what mechanisms will be used to communicate concepts across the boundaries of the knowledge domains, e.g., between researchers and female producers and between scientific and indigenous classification systems (Jiggins, 1986, 57)?

Women: Can Difference Be Valued?

Women by and large have been denied the benefits of development, and some projects have worsened their situations. The big picture is clear: women represent half of the world's population, put in nearly two-thirds of all working hours, receive only one-tenth of the world income and own less than one percent of the world's property (United Nations, 1980b). They comprise a growing proportion of heads of households. Women provide care for the young, old, and sick, and process and prepare food for home consumption. They produce over 50 percent of the food in some parts of the developing world. When women are excluded from development and denied equitable access to resources, the effects reach far beyond women.

How can this invisibility be explained? Gender, along with age, is the most salient marker of human beings in virtually all societies (Chafetz, 1990, 14). Gender is a universal system of stratification which patterns all thought, structures, and processes (Lengermann and Niebrugge-Brantley, 1990). These patterned differences usually involve the real or symbolic subordination of women. Advantage and disadvantage are patterned through, and in terms of a distinction between, male and female, masculine and feminine (Acker, 1992, 250).

The publication in 1970 of Ester Boserup's *Woman's Role in Economic Development* unleashed a flood of attention to the problems of women in development. Yet progress has been meager in integrating women as participants in programs and projects (Staudt, 1990, 9). Separate women's divisions and ministries have been established but are hard pressed to influence government and, worse, may allow other agencies to shift their responsibility for women's programs to the underresourced women's unit (ibid., 8). The extension of female political rights has made dents in the institutional superstructure, but at higher levels the key players remain mostly male. Gender-based domination is maintained by all social institutions, perhaps most tellingly in the knowledge and political institutions toward which we look for solutions.

The focus is now shifting from "women as a problem in development" to "development as a problem for women" and from "women-in-development" to "gendered development" (Ferguson, 1990). This shift, from biological differences to social relationships, to what both women and men do, is as much strategic as conceptual (Moser, 1993).

Because the exclusion of women from development cross-cuts theory, empirical inquiry, and practice, and because there are few incentives for the dominant scientific enterprise to consider viewpoints representing other social realities, valid constructs are likely to emerge only by challenge from competing paradigms (Levy, 1988, 145). Indeed, the sustainable development, indigenous knowledge, and women-in-development initiatives challenge the status quo and contribute to a positive development dialogue. The ecofeminist perspective, to be articulated next, draws from the complementary ecological underpinnings of sustainable development, the documentation of indigenous (and gendered) knowledge systems, and feminist theories toward the end of a more inclusive praxis.

Ecofeminism: New Development Discourse

Ecological feminism, an emerging minority tradition and praxis within Western philosophy, is a world view with potential to positively influence the course of development. To Jim Cheney (1987), concerns for the environment and women's concerns may be parallel, bound up with one another, perhaps even one and the same, since both women and the environment have been treated with ambivalence and disrespect by the dominant culture.

Ecological feminism is a feminism[1] which attempts to bring about a world and a world view that are not based on socioeconomic and conceptual structures of domination (Warren and Cheney, 1991). According to Karen J. Warren (1989), oppressive conceptual frameworks share at least the following characteristics:

1. Value hierarchies—(up-down) thinking; ranking diversity.
2. Value dualisms—a set of paired disjuncts in which one disjunct is valued more than the other. Examples: male/female where males are always valued more; nature/culture where human culture is valued more.
3. A logic of domination—where differences justify oppression.

While there are many varieties of ecofeminism, "all ecofeminists agree that the wrongful and inter-connected dominations of women and nature exist and must be eliminated" (Warren, 1991, 1).

Warren (1989) also provides a useful schematic for conceptualizing ecological feminism. The intersecting and complementary spheres of feminism, indigenous knowledge, and appropriate science, development, and technology create an ecofeminist development rationale which takes seriously epistemic privilege, women's issues, and technologies which work in partnership with natural systems.

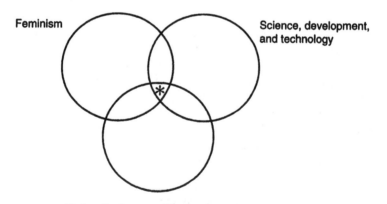

Science and technology are needed to solve environmental problems. Ecofeminism not only welcomes appropriate science and technology but, as an ecological feminism, requires the inclusion of appropriate insights and data of scientific ecology (Warren and Cheney, 1991, 190–93). However, as a feminism, ecofeminism also insists that data about the historical and interconnected exploitations of nature and women and other oppressed peoples (including their perspectives) be recognized and brought to bear in solutions. Ecological feminism and the science of ecology are engaged in complementary, mutually supportive projects; ecological feminism opposes the practice of one without the other.

Integrating a feminist perspective requires identifying gender-centered biases in theory, methods of empirical inquiry, and practice and making appropriate corrections or substitutions (Levy, 1988, 143). Gender bias enters during the selection of research topics, extends to the specification of variables and domain assumptions that form the theoretical constructs, and continues throughout research operations and the application of the research results.

Men have traditionally defined knowledge and constructed reality by virtue of having their theories accepted as legitimate (Smith, 1974; Spender, 1983; Gray, 1992). The male-dominated scientific enterprise has limited inquiry to the study of what males do and what men value and dismissed as trivial scholarship by women and about women (Levy, 1988, 143). As we come to understand theoretical constructs as social products which reflect the scientific training and the personal biases of their creators, we must question whether the social and symbolic worlds of women can be understood using the theories and methods that explain the social relations of males (Levy, 1988,146).

Reliance on Western males as categorizers of social phenomena and normative proxies for most categories of people restricts exploration of the private, unofficial, informal world that exists outside a male-defined division of labor and produces invalid constructs that perpetuate many common gender stereotypes (Levy, 1988, 146). Two examples come to mind: gross national product and bureaucracy.

As a measure of a nation's productivity, the economic construct "gross national product" is inaccurate and misleading because it excludes the productive, nonpaid labor that women typically perform in, for example, the home (Levy, 1988, 144). The food women produce for home consumption is not counted in agricultural statistics even though it subsidizes visible agricultural development. We lack a construct that adequately values women's labor in terms of time and economic return, although Sivard (1985, 5) estimates that if given economic value, the unpaid labor of women in the household would add one-third to the world's annual economic product.

Similarly, the construct of bureaucracy involves the rationalization of labor in a work sphere only incidentally populated by women (Levy, 1988, 144). In the bureaucratic structures of the state, women are governed by the public framework but are rarely official actors or direct beneficiaries (Staudt, 1990, 10). A body of knowledge that adequately reflects women's experiences and represents female participation within the formal organization of work or in the structuring of the state has yet to be produced (Mills and Tancred, 1992; Levy, 1988).

Research methods, relying on biased theoretical constructs, are also flawed. To account for the less obvious, less direct, and less easy to access lives and outlooks of females may require the regrounding of research processes.

Ecofeminist Development

The ecofeminist effort to free women and nature from domination is informed by feminist and ecological theory, systematic inquiry, and commitment to action in a context of ethics and responsibility. Theory, methods and practice, treated separately in the following discussion, are in fact inseparable.

Theory

Ecofeminist theory is situated, meaning that it emerges historically and socially from people's different experiences and observations and changes over time (Warren and Cheney, 1991, 191). Situated knowledge requires that the object of knowledge be actor and agent, not merely screen or ground or resource (Haraway, 1988). Women's experiences, voices, perceptions, and knowledge ground the rewriting and recreating of the world. The world, too, is active subject in the construction of knowledge.

Methods

There is not one ecofeminist method. Praxis is practice achieved through the conscious commitment to methodological inquiry and informed by theory (Bawden, 1991, 28). The ecofeminist developer-as-researcher conducts participatory action research to elicit the shifts in thinking and action among developers and local people. The researcher, along with her perception of the situation and system being studied, becomes part of what is studied.

The feminist methodology of consciousness raising as a method of analysis and practice reconstitutes the meaning of women's social experience as lived by individual women and accords respect to women's convictions and knowledge (Sherwin, 1989). Dialogue begins with concrete personal experience. Molina (1994) suggests talking first about the material conditions of life so that each individual in the group dialogue realizes that "I'm not the only one." One then moves to broader analysis and generalization. Molina recommends determining who is ultimately responsible for the material conditions of one's life and, relatedly, whose interests one is serving and where one's values lie. The third, indispensable step is taking direct action to influence one's situation.

The ecofeminist method of analysis may be characterized as pattern discovery (Frye, 1990, 177–80). Ecofeminist as researcher can help uncover, articulate, and assess patterns. Pattern discovery requires encounters with difference—understanding how experience may vary from patterns, how differences of experience are necessary to perceive the patterns. Generality of pattern is not defeated by variety. Meaning and understanding are produced as patterns are evaluated in light of diverse experiences.

Consider the patterns in the United States by which farm women are stereotyped. Stereotypical roles are enforced through familial, religious, economic, educational, and regulatory institutions and facilitated by relative isolation, strong-tie networks, and powerful sanctions (Wells and Tanner, 1994). Farm women are stereotyped as helpers although most are partners. Categories which structure the responses to the U.S. census of agriculture do not even include "farm partner" as an option, forcing women to chose between farm operator and farm spouse. A male bias in research and practice further affects this process of exclusion. The Iowa Agricultural and Home Economics Experiment Station in 1992 included only one woman on its eighteen-member advisory board. Such differences matter because research priorities set and policies created without the input of women reinforce stereotypes and perpetuate discrimination.

How might such patterns play out in local contexts? On September 17, 1993, Izola Crispin of Madrid, Iowa, read in her local paper about a new Iowa State University project supported by the U.S. Department of Agriculture to site the National Swine Research Center near her home. As she read the site description, she realized that the six-hundred-sow facility would be her new neighbor. Izola and her husband, Charles, had farmed the same seven hundred acres since 1955. They made their living by hard work and avoided costly inputs of pesticides and chemicals. The Crispin family had raised hogs in the past, but not on the scale proposed by the USDA and Iowa State University.

As the scale of the project became clearer to the Crispins, they alerted their neighbors. Izola, along with Mary Todd, also of Madrid, organized the first meeting of the Big Creek Watershed Protection Committee to oppose the project. Izola and Mary began to gather information from around the country about large-scale livestock operations and how citizens of local communities were banding together to prevent large facilities from entering their communities. PrairieFire, a family farm activist group, is assisting this grassroots group with information and encouragement. PrairieFire planned to introduce legislation in the Iowa legislature to require stricter guidelines for manure management and groundwater protection. It was feared that injection of pig manure into the soil, one of the standard ways of dealing with livestock waste, may contaminate the groundwater, since the area is full of artesian wells and the topography is hilly. These physical characteristics of the site were actually preferred over a flat area so that the research might show that it is possible to manage intensive livestock operations even in sensitive drainages.

What are the costs? Iowa's farming families have struggled since the early 1970s with escalating costs, lower farm prices, and the encroachment of multinational agribusiness into local communities. Local communities forced to "host" large-scale livestock confinement operations find themselves faced with more than economic competition. Depending on the size, confinement operations can produce the raw-sewage equivalent of cities of fifteen thousand or more. Improper management of livestock waste from some facilities has impacted local stream and river systems, damaged wildlife resources in terms of fishkills from ammonia pollution, impaired aesthetic qualities of recreational resources, and posed hazards to local drinking water supplies.

Over half of the drinking water wells on Iowa farms are contaminated with nitrates, thus requiring farm families to use bottled water. An outbreak of illness in Milwaukee was due to contaminated water (King, 1993). The culprit was a microscopic organism called Cryptosporidium, often associated with fecal material. Local municipalities across the nation are now advocating watershed protection in order to maintain drinking water quality. Living next to a large-scale hog operation several years ago caused Izola Crispin to develop respiratory problems. She believes her immune system has been impaired, and she remains on antibiotics. Residents are worried that the cultural environment will also be harmed. The farrowing house will be built across from a 125-year-old community church, a place in Iowa where community is generated and maintained.

We are beginning to cast situations such as these in an ecofeminist framework. This work will challenge us to define the feminist components of grassroots efforts such as this and to explore the patriarchical connections between the increasing corporate control of agriculture and the patriarchial domination of the institutions failing Iowa's farm families and rural communities.

Practice

Practical work is an important component of a feminist's contribution to theory. This is consistent with the concept of praxis (the integration of theory and action) put forth by the Brazilian popular educator Paulo Freire (1968): the educational process is not considered complete until learners take concrete steps to apply what is learned for change. Action is an educational process, an opportunity to test and develop theory. It is praxis because the practitioner elevates her methods of practice into a critical framework which embraces wisdom, ethics, and responsibility. The ecofeminist developer-as-practitioner helps local people further their own development by supporting their agendas and facilitating the two-way flow of information.

The ecofeminist-as-developer is thus variously theorist, researcher, and practitioner. Bawden (1991) suggests that participatory action research leads to an improved situation in which the practice is practiced and to improved practice by the practitioner-researcher, improved understanding of the practice by the practitioner, and improved understanding by the practitioner of the situation in which the practice was practiced, thus eliciting the shift in thinking and action among researchers, practitioner-developers, and local people needed to transform development programs.

Ecofeminist Interventions/Implications

To use the term *international development* to refer to doing development in communities other than one's own perpetuates the illusion (or perhaps even worse, the reality) that it is the international system that is being developed. We choose to reconceptualize international development as it must be done in today's world as remediation. The consequences of past abuse must be remediated in the same way that ecologists remediate damaged ecosystems. Remediation means to go back to predamaged conditions, for example, restoring potholes in Iowa's prairies. By protecting biodiversity, storing floodwaters, and providing a natural filter for cleaning polluting water, this action benefits human life, not only wildlife. This ecological praxis of remediation must be feminist to ensure the incorporation of the very perspectives and actions upon which such remediation is predicated, for example, the recognition that while we are different from wildlife, we are not separate.

We cannot remediate ecological messes without reconsidering our purpose, analyzing the results of our past actions, and sensitizing our world view. We must recast our research and praxis as conversation with a world only partially known (Haraway, 1988), drawing upon detailed and nuanced localized knowledge to add essential substance and texture to this conversation.

Changing the patterns of actions that are embedded in and reinforce gender stereotypes requires developing the language framework for naming what is happening (Gray, 1992) and making taken-for-granted patterns explicit (Frye, 1990). Careful observation and documentation of patterns of interaction can make visible patterns which are invisible to the person who lives them everyday.

We must examine both theory and methods of dominant science to identify gender-centered biases and to make appropriate substitutes.

When organizations and institutions are part of the problem rather than part of the solution (as they increasingly are), we must change, redesign, or create them anew. Institutions—the embodiments of the belief systems and technologies prevailing at the time of their origin—are unlikely to re-form themselves. Change is likely to come slowly as the numbers of women in decision-making positions reach a critical proportion. Because women as a social category are unique both in quantity and in dispersion through society (Verba, 1990, 560), multiple-sector and multilevel strategies are essential (Chafetz, 1990, 108).

Spretnak (1990, 14) suggests that the most effective, though not the easiest, strategy is to lead by example: "to contribute to the new philosophical base and to work in its new ecopolitics and ecoeconomics; to organize around the concrete issues of suffering and exploitation; to speak out clearly but without malice against those who further policies of injustice and ecological ignorance." The struggle against a science that does not respect nature and a development that does not respect people requires challenging fundamental conceptions of nature and women and of science and development. An ecofeminist effort to free nature from ceaseless exploitation and women from limitless marginalization transcends gender. Its praxis is humanly inclusive, replacing ideological claims to universalism with diversity (Vandana Shiva, cited in Rodda, 1991, 5).

Note

1. Merchant (1990) articulates the place of ecofeminism among several strands of feminist thought.

References

Acker, Joan
    1992   Gendering organizational theory. Pp. 248–60 in A. Mills and P. Tancred (eds.), *Gendering Organizational Analysis*. Newbury Park, CA: Sage.

Bawden, Richard
    1991   Towards action research systems. Pp. 10–35 in O. Zuber-Skeritt (ed.). *Action Research for Change and Development*. Brookfield, VT: Avebury.

Boserup, Ester
    1970   *Woman's role in economic development*. New York: St. Martin's Press.

Chafetz, J. S.
1990   *Gender Equity: An Integrated Theory of Stability and Change.* Newbury Park, CA: Sage.

Cheney, Jim
1987   Eco-feminism and deep ecology. *Environmental Ethics* 9 (Summer): 115–45.

Easton, David
1991   The division, integration, and transfer of knowledge. Pp. 7–36 in David Easton and Corinne S. Schelling, *Divided Knowledge: Across Disciplines, Across Cultures.* Newbury Park, CA: Sage.

Ferguson, Kathy
1990   Women, Feminism and Development. Pp. 291–303 in Kathleen Staudt (ed.), *Women, International Development and Politics.* Philadelphia: Temple University Press.

Freire, P.
1968   *The Pedagogy of the Oppressed.* New York: Seabury Press.

Frye, Marilyn
1990   The possibility of feminist theory. Pp. 174–84 in Deborah L. Rhode (ed.), *Theoretical Perspectives on Sexual Difference.* New Haven: Yale University Press.

Gray, Elizabeth Dodson
1992   *A Feminist Analysis of Power.* Manuscript.

Haraway, Donna
1988   Situated knowledges: the science question in feminism and the privilege of partial perspective. *Feminist Studies* 14 (3): 575–99.

Jiggins, Janice
1986   *Gender-related impacts and the work of the international agriculture research centers.* Washington, DC: World Bank.

King, Jonathan
1993   Something in the water: you are what you drink, more than you think. *Amicus Journal* (Fall): 20–28.

Lengermann, Patricia M., and Jill Niebrugge-Brantley
1990   Feminist sociological theory: the near-future prospects. Pp. 316–44 in George Ritzer (ed.), *Frontiers of Social Theory.* New York: Columbia University Press.

Levy, Judith A.
1988   Gender bias as a threat to construct validity in research design. Pp. 139–57 in *A Feminist Ethic for Social Science Research: Nebraska Sociological Feminist Collective.* Women's Studies. Vol. 1. Lewiston/Queenston: Edwin Mellen Press.

Loening, U. E.
1990   The challenge for the future. Pp. 11–15 in A. J. Gilbert and L. C. Braat (eds.), *Modeling for Population and Sustainable Development.* New York: Routledge.

Mathias-Mundy, Evelyn
1993   Background to the International Symposium of Indigenous Knowledge
        and Sustainable Development. *Indigenous Knowledge and Development
        Monitor* 1 (2): 2–3.

Merchant, Carolyn
1990   Ecofeminism and feminist theory. Pp. 100–105 in Irene Diamond and
        Gloria Feman Orenstein (eds.), *Reweaving the World: The Emergence of
        Ecofeminism.* San Francisco: Sierra Club Books.

Mills, Albert J., and Peta Tancred (eds.)
1992   *Gendering Organizational Analysis.* Newbury Park, CA: Sage.

Molina, Papusa
1994   Presentation at session on "Consciousness and Community: Neglected
        Dimensions in Contemporary Approaches to Women and Economic
        Development." National Women's Studies Association. Ames, IA.

Moser, Caroline
1993   *Gender Planning and Development: Theory, Practice and Training.* New
        York: Routledge.

Norem, Rosalie H., Rhonda Yoder, and Yolanda Martin
1989   Indigenous agricultural knowledge and gender issues in third world ag-
        ricultural development. Pp. 91–100 in D. Warren, L. Slikkerveer
        and S. Titiola (eds.), *Indigenous Knowledge Systems: Implications for Ag-
        riculture and International Development. Studies in Technology and So-
        cial Change*, Monograph 11, Iowa State University, Ames.

Rodda, Annabel
1991   *Women and the Environment.* Atlantic Highlands, NJ: Zed Books.

Sherwin, Susan
1989   Philosophical methodology and feminist methodology: are they com-
        patible? Pp. 21–35 in A. Garry and M. Pearsall (eds.), *Women, Knowl-
        edge, and Reality: Explorations in Feminist Philosophy.* Boston: Unwin
        Hyman.

Sivard, Ruth Leger
1985   *Women . . . A World Survey.* Washington, DC: World Priorities.

Smith, D.
1974   Women's perspective as a radical critique of sociology. *Sociological In-
        quiry* 44 (1): 7–13.

Spender, D.
1983   Introduction. Pp. 1–7 in D. Spender (ed.), *Feminist Theorists: Three
        Centuries of Women's Intellectual Tradition.* London: Women's Press.

Spretnak, Charlene
1990   Ecofeminism: our roots and our flowering. Pp. 3–14 in Irene Diamond
        and Gloria Feman Orenstein (eds.), *Reweaving the World: The Emer-
        gence of Ecofeminism.* San Francisco: Sierra Club Books.

Staudt, Kathleen
1990   Gender politics in bureaucracy: theoretical issues in comparative per-

spective. Pp. 3–34 in Kathleen Staudt (ed.), *Women, International Development and Politics*. Philadelphia: Temple University Press.

United Nations
1980   *Report of the World Conference of the UN Decade for Women: Equality, Development and Peace*. New York, UN.

Verba, S.
1990   Women in American politics. Pp. 555–72 in L. Tilly and P. Gurin (eds.), *Women, Politics and Change*. New York: Sage.

Warren, Karen J.
1991   Introduction. *Hypatia* 6 (1): 1–2.
1990   The power and promise of ecological feminism. *Environmental Ethics* 12 (Summer): 125–46.
1989   Environmental ethics for environmental educators. Presented at Environmental Ethics Conference, Springbrook Conservation Center.

Warren, Karen J., and Jim Cheney
1991   Ecological feminism and ecosystem ecology. *Hypatia* 6 (1): 179–97.

Wells, Betty L., and Bonnie O. Tanner
1994   The organizational potential of women in agriculture to sustain rural communities. *Journal of the Community Development Society* 5 (2): 246–58.

World Commission on the Environment and Development
1987   *Our Common Future*. Oxford: Oxford University Press.

Nineteen

Scientific Ecology and Ecological Feminism

The Potential for Dialogue

Catherine Zabinski

Although it has been suggested that ecological science and ecofeminism are supportive fields (Warren and Cheney 1991), joined together (King 1989), or in some way inextricably linked (Collard and Contrucci 1988), scientific ecology is a reluctant or oblivious partner in this symbiosis.[1] In this chapter I discuss the relationship between scientific ecology and ecological feminism in light of recent work by Karen J. Warren and Jim Cheney (1991), who consider ways in which the two programs are complementary and mutually supportive. They focus on the two fields' parallel endeavors to integrate a diversity of voices and rely on ecosystem hierarchy theory to identify common ground between the two fields. I begin with a brief definition of ecological science and ecofeminism, continue with a critique of the use of hierarchy theory to function as a bridge between the two, and close with a discussion, from an ecologist's perspective, of the potential for a more extensive dialogue between ecofeminists and ecologists.

Scientific Ecology

Scientific ecology is the study of nature, specifically the interaction of organisms with their living and nonliving environment. It is a science with a broad vision of nature—ranging from the microscopic to the global—and with an equally broad perspective of time—from prehistoric to future events. Scientific ecology recognizes the complexity and diversity of nature and looks for patterns and their causes within that complexity. And like other sciences, it relies on observation, hypothesis testing, and experimentation to advance our understanding.

The focus of ecological research questions is also diverse: physiological adaptations that enable plants or animals to thrive in their environment; the causes of changes in size and geographic extent of populations; interactions among species, including predation, herbivory, mutualism, and competition; the organization of biological communities—why some are more species-rich than others, for example; and the cycles and flows of matter and energy in ecosystems. The techniques used to collect data range from simple observations to the use of technologically sophisticated equipment.[2]

Confusion about scientific ecology exists in part because the word *ecology* is commonly used to refer to the environmental movement in general; hence the assumption that scientific ecology is a scientific study of environmental issues such as pollution, recycling, and human population growth. Furthermore, the ecologists closest to being household names—Aldo Leopold, Rachel Carson, Paul Ehrlich—have stepped outside the narrow range of traditional scientific activities and have entered the public arena by applying ecological principles to social or environmental problems. If the primary goal of science is to further scientific knowledge, then the application of such knowledge to societal issues is outside the realm of science—applied as opposed to pure science. The study of nature, using scientific methodology, is considered science, but the communication of that information to nonscientists, while possibly a duty, is not a primary goal of science. Hence the distinction between *pure* and *applied* science, terms heavy with connotations.

Ecofeminism

The voices of ecofeminism are diverse, but their common thread is the recognition of the relationship between the domination of nature and the domination of women. In patriarchal societies, culture and reason are perceived as male attributes, in opposition to the female attributes of nature and emotion. Traits associated with male are valued over those associated with female.

Ecofeminists are working to create a consciousness that goes beyond nature/culture and male/female dualisms toward a consciousness of peoples living with the earth, valuing both biological and cultural diversity (Diamond and Orenstein 1990). To do this requires the unraveling of the conceptual framework that justifies the logic of domination, a logic that makes one set of traits—i.e., male attributes—morally superior to a second set of traits—female attributes (Warren 1987). Value-hierarchical thinking within oppressive contexts maintains the domination of the superior group over the inferior group. Warren's expansive definition of *ecofeminism* goes beyond the analysis of male/female and nature/culture dualisms to oppose value-hierarchical thinking based on class, race, age, sexual preference, or any trait used to perpetuate a power-over relationship (Warren 1990).

Mutually Supportive Fields?

While ecofeminism and scientific ecology both endeavor to understand nature, ecofeminists work toward an understanding of the social context of nature—the metaphors used to describe nature, society's attitudes toward nature, the relationship between nature and women, and how that relationship has been exploited to subordinate nature and women. Ecology as a science embraces a mechanistic, materialist, reductionist approach to studying nature. The questions asked and the methods of answering them fall within standards set by the scientific community. And as with most sciences, self-reflection and an understanding of its social context are not goals of traditional ecological science. This leaves little inherent overlap in the two fields' goals and approaches to studying nature.

Warren and Cheney's analysis of the meeting point of ecofeminism and ecology delves deeper than my analysis, and they find as common ground for these two disparate fields the ideology expressed in ecosystem hierarchy theory (as outlined by O'Neill et al., 1986). Simply put, both ecofeminism and ecosystem hierarchy theory are engaged in the challenge of valuing multiple voices to inform their projects. With feminism, the goal is to incorporate the diversity of women's voices into a richly textured tapestry. Likewise in scientific ecology, the complexity of interactions and processes presents the ecologist with the challenge of integrating "voices" from multiple data sets.

More specifically, Warren and Cheney identify ten similarities between the goals of hierarchy theory and those of ecofeminism, including the understanding of context-dependent reference points; an appreciation of alternative reference points and alternative data sets; an antireductionist, inclusivist approach that centralizes diversity by recognizing and appreciating the unique contributions of alternative data sets; and a recognition of the autonomous and relational existence of individuals. Warren and Cheney draw parallels between the recognition by O'Neill et al. that alternative spatial and temporal scales yield different data sets and the ecofeminist goal of integrating multiple perspectives on ecological and feminist issues.

While I appreciate Warren and Cheney's point that feminist studies and scientific ecology have, from at least one perspective, parallel endeavors, I question their use of hierarchy theory to make their point. First, I fail to see that hierarchy theory is more sensitive than scientific ecology in general to what I have understood to be one of the commonsense conclusions of ecology: the context-dependent conclusions of alternative data sets. Hierarchy theory does not need to be invoked to argue for the appreciation by ecologists of alternative data sets. Second, I argue that when you look beyond the *claims* of hierarchy theory to its actual mechanics and assumptions, what you find is an approach to studying nature that is not very consistent with ecofeminist goals. This is not to belittle the need or value of a dialogue between ecofeminism and scientific ecology, but merely to point out that one need not adopt all of the baggage that comes with a complex scientific theory in order to argue for such a dialogue.

Warren and Cheney state that the "basic contribution of hierarchy theory is to call attention to the importance of observation sets and spatiotemporal scales" to ecological study. But such an appreciation for alternative reference points is not limited to, and did not originate with, ecosystem hierarchy theory. In an anthology entitled *Community Ecology* published in 1986, the same year as O'Neill et al., six of the thirty-three contributed chapters address directly the importance of spatial or temporal scale in ecology.[3] In a discussion of different temporal and spatial scales, Wiens et al. (1986, 153) state that "none of these approaches yielded the same answer as any other approach. . . . The most useful choice of scale will depend on the species studied, the question asked, and logistical constraints." That different "observation sets" are valid and appropriate and contribute to an understanding and appreciation of the complexity of nature is a conclusion found throughout scientific ecology; it is not limited to hierarchy theory.

Consider, for example, the effect on sugar maple trees of a single aspect of the physical environment—climate. We know that climate varies on a localized spatial scale (moving from a sunny spot to a shady spot) or on a short temporal scale (with daily temperature changes). As we expand the scale, either spatially or temporally, we pick up different patterns relevant to different ecological questions. A focus on microclimate is appropriate for asking why sugar maple seedlings germinate successfully at one site and not another within a forest, but a focus on larger-scale climate patterns is appropriate for asking why no sugar maple trees grow north of the Hudson Bay. Neither the micro- nor the macroclimatic data set is inherently better.

Adherents of ecosystem hierarchy theory claim not only an appreciation of alternative observation sets but also an approach that incorporates alternative data sets to yield a new view of ecosystems. O'Neill et al. claim to bridge two approaches to studying ecosystems. The population-community approach views ecosystems as populations and communities of plants and animals living within a matrix of the physical and chemical environment. The process-functional approach considers primarily matter and energy flow through an ecosystem, lumping plants and animals into "black boxes," the components of which function enough alike as to make them indistinguishable. O'Neill et al. admit early on that

> the distinction we have drawn between biotic and functional views has been exaggerated for the sake of presentation. For some ecologists, ecosystems are either biotic assemblages or functional systems. For most, the ecosystem concept contains elements of both. (12)

But even if the dichotomy that hierarchy theory claims to dissolve is largely artificial, the theory needs to be examined more carefully to learn how alternative data sets are incorporated into a more complex view of ecosystems. If hierarchy theory is to meaningfully inform ecofeminist studies, it deserves a close scrutiny.

Hierarchy theory derives from the study of systems, defined as large or small groups of interacting units which may or may not interact with their environment. Systems are classified as small-number, medium-number, or large-number systems. Small-number systems have few enough subunits to be described fairly easily by mathematical equations. Likewise, large-number systems are composed of enough subunits to allow for abstraction of large patterns, ignoring the deviations within the data. The gas laws describe the large-number system of molecules of gas at different pressures and temperatures (O'Neill et al., 42–43).

Ecosystems (unfortunately for mathematical ecologists) fall into the category of medium-number systems, difficult or impossible to analyze mathematically. Hierarchy theory of ecosystem ecology simplifies ecosystems into small-number systems by classifying subunits of ecosystems into groups, or holons. Components of holons interact frequently with each other and less frequently with members of other holons. Such groups have traditionally been defined as tangible units: levels in a food chain (plants, herbivores, carnivores, etc.), or physical strata (forest canopy, subcanopy, shrub layer, herb layer, litter layer, below-ground), for example. O'Neill et al. advocate the definition of holons based on differences in rates of physiological processes.[4] In hierarchy theory, each level of the system controls the levels below it.

The justification for the application of hierarchical structure to nature is supported primarily by mathematical models, with only "some" empirical evidence. Reliance on models to advance our understanding of nature requires a careful assessment of whether we are learning more about theoretical ecology or nature.[5] The need for mathematical tractability in theoretical models dictates the simplification of nature into ideal units. Such simplification eliminates intragroup diversity; every member of a population or species is identical to every other member. In addition, many of the parameters central to theoretical models are impossible to measure in the real world of nature. These parameters include variables quantifying the effect of competition by a species on a second species or the intrinsic rate of increase of a population, for example. For those few instances where such parameters can be measured, the values are specific to the environmental conditions of that field season.

With the use of hierarchical structure in theoretical models and of matrix algebra, O'Neill et al. show that ecosystems can be viewed as a dualistic hierarchy, with constraints operating in either the process-functional plane or the population-community plane. Applying Ockham's razor—things should not be multiplied without good reason—leads one to ask why the assumptions of hierarchy theory need to be invoked in order to argue for the benefits of and need for a dialogue between ecofeminism and scientific ecology. One can argue for such a dialogue without invoking the matrix-algebra-dependent conclusions of hierarchy theory. The conclusion that alternative data sets provide unique information is prevalent throughout ecology. One can glean from the first several pages of virtually any ecology textbook that ecology addresses scientific questions beginning at the simplest level of individual organisms in their environment and progressing through the population, community, and ecosystem levels. That the texts are divided into sections addressing each of these levels implies that the information from any given level cannot be subsumed into that of a higher or lower level, and that insights from each level of study are unique and important.

A Dialogue between Scientific Ecology and Ecofeminism

A dialogue between ecologists and ecofeminists would be beneficial for both groups, if for no other reason than to increase our understanding of each other's endeavors. But more important, there are definite contributions that an ecofeminist perspective could make in ecologists' thinking about nature and about the way nature is studied.

The first benefit of a dialogue between ecofeminists and scientific ecologists is a greater understanding of the social context of scientists' views of nature.[6] It is essential to understand how the assumptions ecologists make about nature (hierarchical structure, for example) affect the questions we ask and the conclusions we draw. For example, within scientific ecology, competition is generally considered to be much more important than mutualism in structuring biological communities.[7] Over the six-year period of 1987 through 1992, 132 papers were published in the journal *Ecology* on the subject of competition and only seventeen on mutualism. For a better understanding of community ecology, one would want to know if the disparity in numbers of papers published reflects patterns in nature or a socially determined view of nature. There is a striking similarity between the published perception of the natural world and the structure of academic communities, with tenure-track positions, research funding, and space in scientific publications being highly competitive.

Unfortunately, scientists are often less interested in questioning the social context of their science than are historians and philosophers of science. Many scientists talk about scientific knowledge as though it emerges from data sets. One of the strongest beliefs in science, passed down through introductory science courses, is the sanctity of the scientific method and the objectivity that it confers on the body of knowledge that accumulates under its auspices. With objectivity as one's guide, scientists and the scientific process become the conduit through which truth is revealed. If you assume this, then you can also believe that scientists function free of a social context. Then there is little need to examine the assumptions that we make as ecologists about the organization of nature.

A convincing argument for examining hidden assumptions comes from Helen Longino (1990), who argues that the same data set can be used to support contrasting hypotheses. The choice of hypothesis is determined by the background assumptions or beliefs of the scientist. What confers objectivity to science, she claims, is the social structure of science. Peer review serves to identify biases in interpretation through "the subjection of hypotheses and the background assumptions . . . to varieties of conceptual criticism" (75). This self-imposed system of objectivity fails when the background assumptions are hidden, as in the case of cultural biases, or become invisible, when scientists deny their existence. Feminist critique of science has illuminated biases and hidden assumptions, mostly about gender issues in scientific practice.[8] A continuation of this work, examining how the assumptions scientists make about nature affect their conclusions and our management plans of nature, would be a worthy goal of a dialogue between ecologists and ecofeminists.

Such a dialogue could also address the domination of nature and how science in general and scientific ecology specifically contribute to that domination. One of the best known ecosystem studies is the landmark research conducted at Hubbard Brook Forest beginning in the 1960s.[9] In a comparison of nutrient dynamics in forested watersheds, a 15.6-hectare section of the forest was clearcut, with the logs and branches left lying. The forest was sprayed with herbicides for the following three years to kill understory plants and delay regrowth. Nutrient output was measured and compared with that in unlogged patches of forest. The results showed that nutrient losses in stream runoff increase significantly after a clearcut, then decline once plants regrow. Similar results have been obtained from measurements in nearby commercially logged forest stands.

What can an ecofeminist perspective on the domination of nature tell us about clearcutting and herbiciding a forest? Is clearcutting in and of itself an act of domination? Does the increase in scientific knowledge justify such an act? Such questions have never arisen in the numerous scientific discussions I have heard of the Hubbard Brook study, and I'm not prepared to answer them here. The point is that within the context of ecological science, nature is the data set, or holons in the words of hierarchy theory, and manipulations are a necessary part of experimental design. Scientific ecology does not address the domination of nature and can be as easily used to perpetuate domination as to construct new ways of living with nature. The benefit to ecologists and ecofeminists of a dialogue would be to increase our understanding of how the practice and theories of ecology perpetuate the dominator ideology.

Warren and Cheney argue that appreciation for multiple data sets leaves open the door for inclusion into the solution of environmental problems data originating from women and indigenous peoples (presumably nonscientists). They state that "ecofeminism welcomes appropriate ecological science and technology" (190), but to my knowledge, no reciprocal acknowledgment of ecofeminist goals has appeared in a scientific publication. While ecofeminists are advocating the inclusion of previously silenced voices in the discussion of environmental issues, ecologists (with some notable exceptions such as Oldfield and Acorn, 1991) are not generally advocating the inclusion of nonscientific data into natural resource management decisions.

The Ecological Society of America (ESA), a professional society founded in 1915, published a report, "The Sustainable Biosphere Initiative: An Ecological Research Agenda" (Lubchenco et al., 1991), that was generated by a sixteen-member committee and presented to about a thousand members for their comments at the ESA's 1990 annual meeting. The report emphasizes the importance of ecological science for solving environmental problems and calls for "basic research for the acquisition of ecological knowledge, communication of that knowledge to citizens, and incorporation of that knowledge into policy and management decisions" (373). Unlike Warren and Cheney's request that "the perspectives of women and indigenous peoples with regard to the natural environment also be recognized as relevant 'data' " for environmental problem solving, the ESA's thirty-eight-page initiative never mentions women or indigenous knowledge systems. The role envisioned by the ESA for ecological science in the context of sustainable development is "to prescribe restoration and management strategies that would enhance the sustainability of the Earth's ecological systems" (374).

A Format for Dialogue

Assuming we can agree that a dialogue would benefit both fields, there remains the question of the format in which to dialogue. The first prerequisite for a dialogue is a shared vocabulary. I venture that most nonscientists who try to read the journal *Ecology* will have as much difficulty as most nonphilosophers have reading philosophical discourses. The long years of training in our respective fields have left us with terminology and ways of structuring arguments that are unique to each field and often render our fields inacessible to others. We need to find a common ground on which we can anchor our discussions.

Warren and Cheney suggest that the similar endeavors between ecosystem hierarchy theory and ecological feminism are sufficient common ground. I have argued in this chapter against the invocation of hierarchy theory as a basis for a dialogue, and I do not support an alternative ecological theory as the foundation. What I suggest as a worthy common endeavor is a study of the social context of our assumptions of nature, which can only improve our understanding of ecological science and methodology, and a review of the ways in which scientific ecology can contribute to or work against the domination of nature and women. I do not envision that all scientific ecologists or their representative organizations are going to embrace this dialogue but suggest that some ecologists and ecofeminists share common goals of understanding nature and its social context.

Warren and Cheney have initiated the dialogue between ecofeminists and ecologists. While I suggest a change in the direction of the dialogue, I support their intent. The next step in this pursuit might be for philosophers and ecologists, instead of dialoguing in separate chapters, to collaborate in joint efforts to understand our common ground.

Notes

1. Thanks to Wayne Schwartz for careful readings and discussions of this chapter in its various stages and to Karen J. Warren, Steve Fifield, and Beth Lynch for comments on an earlier version.

2. The December 1991 issue of *Ecology* includes a special feature on remote sensing data in ecological studies. Computer simulations, statistical analyses, and techniques originally developed for molecular biology are standard tools in scientific ecology.

3. Diamond and Case (1986).

4. Dividing ecosystems into tangible units such as plant, herbivore, carnivore versus dividing ecosystems into units with equivalent rates of physiological processes is not a subtle distinction. One needs little expertise or equipment to identify plants, herbivores, and carnivores. To measure rates of metabolism or respiration, one needs more extensive training and scientific machinery. The difference is between a low-tech, accessible approach to classifying nature and a high-tech, high-expertise approach.

5. Evelyn Fox Keller (1985), in her discussion of the pacemaker theory as applied to slime molds, states, "In our zealous desire for familiar models of explanation, we risk not noticing the discrepancies between our own predispositions and the range of possibilities inherent in natural phenomena" (157). See also the discussion of mathematical theory in Hairston (1989, 11–12).

6. Philosophers of science, including but not limited to feminist philosophers of science, have artfully analyzed many cases of the influence of social context on scientific theory. A critique of the assumptions that ecologists bring to their study of nature is not limited to ecofeminist ideology, but it is consistent with ecofeminist's goal of understanding the relationship between the domination of nature and the domination of women.

7. See especially Boucher et al. 1982, Schoener 1983, and Connell 1983.

8. See Hrdy 1981, Keller 1983 and 1985, Bleier 1984, Fausto-Sterling 1985, Haraway 1989 and 1991.

9. A discussion of Hubbard Brook can be found in most ecology texts.

Bibliography

Bleier, Ruth. 1984. *Science and Gender: A Critique of Biology and Its Theories on Women*. Oxford: Pergamon Press.

Boucher, Douglas H., Sam James, and Kathleen H. Keeler. 1982. The ecology of mutualism. *Annual Review of Ecology and Systematics* 13: 315–47.

Collard, Andrée, with Joyce Contrucci. 1989. *Rape of the Wild: Man's Violence against Animals and the Earth*. Bloomington: Indiana University Press.

Connell, Joseph H. 1983. On the prevalence and relative importance of interspecific competition: Evidence from field experiments. *American Naturalist* 122: 661–96.

Diamond, Irene, and Gloria Feman Orenstein, eds. 1990. *Reweaving the World: The Emergence of Ecofeminism*. San Francisco: Sierra Club Press.

Diamond, Jared, and Ted J. Case. 1986. *Community Ecology*. New York: Harper and Row.

Fausto-Sterling, Anne. 1985. *Myths of Gender: Biological Theories about Women and Men*. New York: Basic.

Hairston, Nelson G., Sr. 1989. *Ecological Experiments: Purpose, Design and Execution*. Cambridge: Cambridge University Press.

Haraway, Donna. 1989. *Primate Visions: Gender, Race and Nature in the World of Modern Science*. New York: Routledge.

——. 1991. *Simians, Cyborgs, and Women*. New York: Routledge.

Hrdy, Sarah Blaffer. 1981. *The Woman That Never Evolved*. Cambridge: Harvard University Press.

Hunter, A. F., and L. W. Aarssen. 1988. Plants helping plants. *Bioscience* 38: 34–40.

Keller, Evelyn Fox. 1983. *A Feeling for the Organism: The Life and Work of Barbara McClintock*. New York: W. H. Freeman.

——. 1985. *Reflections on Gender and Science*. New Haven: Yale University Press.

King, Ynestra. 1989. The ecology of feminism and the feminism of ecology. In

Healing the Wounds: The Promise of Ecofeminism, ed. Judith Plant. Philadelphia: New Society.

Longino, Helen E. 1990. *Science as Social Knowledge*. Princeton: Princeton University Press.

Lubchenco, Jane, et al. 1991. The Sustainable Biosphere Initiative: An ecological research agenda. *Ecology* 72: 371–412.

Oldfield, Margery L., and Janis B. Alcorn, eds. 1991. *Biodiversity: Culture, Conservation and Ecodevelopment*. Boulder: Westview.

O'Neill, R. V., D. L. DeAngelis, J. B. Waide, and T. F. H. Allen. 1986. *A Hierarchical Concept of Ecosystems*. Princeton: Princeton University Press.

Schoener, Thomas W. 1983. Field experiments on interspecific competition. *American Naturalist* 122: 240–85.

Warren, Karen J. 1987. Feminism and ecology: Making connections. *Environmental Ethics* 9: 3–21.

———. 1990. The power and promise of ecological feminism. *Environmental Ethics* 12: 125–46.

———, and Jim Cheney. 1991. Ecological feminism and ecosystem ecology. *Hypatia* 6, no. 1: 179–97.

Wiens, John A., John F. Addicott, Ted J. Case, and Jared Diamond. 1986. Overview: The importance of spatial and temporal scale in ecological investigations. In *Community Ecology*, ed. Jared Diamond and Ted Case. New York: Harper and Row.

PART III:
PHILOSOPHICAL PERSPECTIVES

Twenty

Androcentrism and Anthropocentrism
Parallels and Politics

Val Plumwood

Feminist and ecofeminist exposure of masculinism in environmental thinking is sometimes portrayed as carping, purely critical and negative. This portrait overlooks not only the role of feminist criticism in developing a better theory but also the positive theoretical improvements feminist theory can bring to environmental thought as it applies feminist models and understandings to the core concepts of environmental philosophy. In this chapter I argue that the sophisticated understanding of androcentrism which has emerged from feminism can help resolve some problems with the key concept of anthropocentrism which threaten the foundations of environmental philosophy. Since women differ from individual to individual and are oppressed in multiple ways, a commitment to ending the subordination of all women implies that feminism must address itself to many forms of oppression and attempt to theorize some of the connections between them (Jaggar 1994). Consequently some forms of feminist theory have been led to develop a more general account of what I will call centrism, which discerns a common centric structure underlying different forms of oppression (Hartsock 1990). Since ecofeminism insists that feminism must address not only the forms of oppression which afflict humans but also those that afflict nature, the extension of feminist insights and models of centrism to illuminate problems in the concept of anthropocentrism is a core concern of the ecofeminist theoretical project. These insights from a feminist account of centrism can also, as I argue in the last

327

part of this chapter, cast some valuable light on how we are able, as eco-feminists, to speak for nature.

Concepts of centrism have been at the heart of modern liberation politics and theory. Feminism has focused on androcentrism, phallocentrism, and phallogocentrism as theoretical refinements of its central concept of sexism; it has also focused on the connection between these and other forms of centrism. Antiracist theory critiques ethnocentrism, movements against European colonization critique Eurocentrism, gay and lesbian activists critique heterocentrism, and so on. The Green movement's flagship in this liberation armada has been the notion of anthropocentrism, or human-centeredness. The critique of anthropocentrism, however, unlike the other critiques of centrism, continues to be denied legitimacy in many quarters, including some Green quarters, and its usefulness to the Green movement is under challenge. After two decades of intensive debate in ecophilosophy over the concept, the discussion seems to be irretrievably bogged down in largely repetitious argument between two opposing camps. The concept of anthropocentrism, which is so powerfully defended by some as the heart of environmental philosophy, continues to be seen by others as subject to fatal objection and fit only for the dustbin. William Grey (1993) is just the latest of those who declare the search for a nonanthropocentric ethic to be "a hopeless quest."

The critique of anthropocentrism has been almost the defining task of ecophilosophy, whose characteristic general thesis has been that our frameworks of morality and rationality must be expanded to include the welfare of at least certain categories of nonhumans; stopping these frameworks at the human species boundary is considered anthropocentric. But beyond this point of agreement, ecophilosophy is deeply divided as to how best to accomplish this expansion and how far it should go; according to its critics, it is suffering from what Andrew Dobson has called "the failure to make itself practical" (1990, 70). What Dobson means by this is that ecophilosophy, as articulated by the thinkers he considers—mainly deep ecologists—may give personal uplift but appears to provide little help with practical Green action, strategy, or politics. To the extent that the theory it has developed proscribes as anthropocentric all prudential types of argument which adduce ill consequences for humans from current environmental practices and attitudes, it seems to run counter to the practical politics of environmental activism. But abandonment of the critique of anthropocentrism is also problematic, since its demise not only threatens the loss of the major revolutionary insights of environmental thought but also appears to threaten the claim to autonomy of the Green movement and the independence of its intellectual critique. So a major impasse seems to confront the foundations of environmental philosophy—abandon the core critique and risk absorption and co-optation into other movements (such as ecosocialism, which is waiting in the wings) or try to struggle on with an embattled central concept which seems to be finding little support.

Those who continue to believe that the concept of anthropocentrism is fundamental to the Green critique (and I count myself among them) have a number of alternatives open to them in the face of this seemingly implacable resistance to its core concept. We could interpret the embattled nature of this core concept as showing that this form of centrism is more fiercely defended and perhaps deeper and more resistant to change than the other forms. We could point to its far-reaching implications and note that those who fail to see its relevance, and indeed those to whom the case must be put as well as those who must articulate it, are from the group which, in terms of other liberatory critiques, corresponds to the oppressor class. But an alternative (or additional) hypothesis which I shall explore here is that the apparent failure of the critique of anthropocentrism to carry the same conviction as other liberatory critiques may reflect problems and limitations not only in the understanding of its critics but also in the way the concept of anthropocentrism has been developed by its major exponents in ecophilosophy. In what follows, I attempt to resolve the dilemma outlined above by showing how certain difficulties for the critique arise out of a specific, problematic understanding of anthropocentrism which I will call cosmic anthropocentrism. Using concepts and models originating in feminine theory and other liberation critiques, I will outline an alternative, feminist rereading of the concept of human-centeredness which is theoretically illuminating, of practical value to the Green movement, and capable of showing why anthropocentrism might be a serious problem in contemporary life. I shall argue that it is this problematic understanding of anthropocentrism as cosmic anthropocentrism which has invited the kinds of criticisms which have been widely seen as fatal to the concept.

The Cosmic Concept of Anthropocentrism

To see how the understanding of anthropocentrism has arisen and how it has led both critics and supporters into a problematic relationship with the characteristic insights of ecological thought and action, I will examine what is perhaps the strongest rejection of these insights, by Grey (1993). Grey rejects any need for a concept of anthropocentrism, declaring robustly that anthropocentric perspectives are benign, natural, inevitable, and quite adequate for an environmental ethic. Grey asserts indeed without any qualification the even stronger thesis that nature itself is not something which can intelligibly be valued independently of human interests (470), or what he evidently takes to be the same, that constraints on human conduct can take into consideration only human interests (464), that only humans can be morally considerable.[1] The latter thesis, dubbed anthroposcopism by Ted Benton (1993), implies that even highly conscious animals have no right to moral consideration. Although this is certainly a much stronger thesis than most critics of anthropocentrism and environmental ethics have wanted to assert and its implications for animals are widely rejected by theorists from many different ethical and political positions, Grey gives this extraordinarily counterintuitive consequence of his claims no attention. One's first question, of course, is benign for whom? Grey does not explain how a position which so downgrades the claims and visibility of animals and nature can possibly be benign for them, especially in the present circumstances.

Grey offers no argumentation for his remarkable claim that anthropocentrism is benign, other than the failure of the concept of anthropocentrism he discusses. Grey's argument for the failure of this concept treats as unproblematic, as univocal and universal,[2] an account of anthropocentrism which has been extensively problematized over the last two decades by a number of philosophers who have distinguished different senses or grades of it.[3] Yet Gray focuses on one sense only of *anthropocentrism*, which he does not explicitly define but which on examination turns out to be indistinguishable from the one which has been widely rejected as trivial and perverse. In this cosmic sense of anthropocentrism, a judgment can be claimed to be anthropocentric if it can be made to reveal any evidence of dependency on a human location in the cosmos, on human scale or "human values, interests and preferences" (473). Grey motivates this cosmic reading of the key concept of environmental ethics in his opening paragraphs by setting anthropocentrism up as an error of location and partiality, invoking a central contrast of anthropocentric world views with the Copernican revolution and the defeat of geocentrism as a displacement of humanity from the center of the stage. Just as the sun was assumed to revolve around the earth, so, before the Copernican revolution, the universe was assumed to revolve around the human. We can overcome this epistemological limitation, the contrast suggests, by taking a larger, less located, and more impartial and modern view of the universe. In the same way that Copernicus overcame parochialism by moving to a less limited, less earth-centered viewpoint, overcoming anthropocentrism requires a move away from human locality and human perspective to a view of the world *sub specie aeternitatis*, through cosmic rather than human spectacles. According to Grey's account, to defeat anthropocentrism we must distribute our preferences with detachment and perfect impartiality of concern across humans and nonhumans, to achieve at last a view-from-nowhere which abandons all specifically human viewpoints on, or preferences about, the world. It is no surprise that this turns out to be impossible, and Grey then proceeds to the conclusion that anthropocentrism is vindicated and environmental philosophy in general shown to be misguided.[4]

As Grey sets them out, the basic steps in the argument for the inevitability of cosmic anthropocentrism are these: (1) To avoid anthropocentrism we must avoid any reliance on human location or bearings in the world, any taint of human interest, perception, values or preferences, human standards of appropriateness, human concerns, and signs of human origin in these, such as "recognisably human scale." Thus, Grey writes, "we [must] eschew all human values, interests and preferences" (473). We must view the world austerely and impartially, *sub specie aeternitatis*, without parochialism, interpreted as distributing our concern impartially over time and species. (2) But this task of removing all traces of self is impossible, as demonstrated by obvious examples of absurd results, the discovery of obvious human reference, and by general argument. For example, in support of step 2, Grey argues that we cannot adopt a completely impartial time scale without losing "recognisably human scale" and that when we lose this, there is no ground for preferring any one geostate over another. (3) Therefore anthropocentrism is unavoidable, and the demand for its avoidance is evidence of conceptual confusion. From this, Grey assumes he is entitled to go on to draw the anthroposcopic conclusion (4), that only human interests are morally considerable, can count in determining moral action.

I will discuss some problems in this cosmic account of anthropocentrism briefly before turning to the main question of why anthropocentrism should be interpreted along these lines. I think it can be conceded that it is impossible to avoid a certain kind of locatedness, but Grey's argument equivocates and ignores complexities about what kind of location is presupposed in ethical judgment and about how we are tied to our own location. Ethical consideration, to the extent that it involves treating others with sensitivity, sympathy, and consideration for their welfare, often seems to require some version of putting ourselves in the other's place, seeing the world from the perspective of a creature with its own needs and experiences rather than our own. This may be said to involve some form of transcendence of our own location, but it does not require us to eliminate our own location, rooting out any trace of our own experience and concern for our own needs; otherwise moral consideration for others would be just as impossible as the avoidance of anthropocentrism is said to be. If moral consideration is assumed to require eliminating our own location, the argument would seem to lead toward ethical solipsism or egoism in the human case just as much as in the nonhuman. But the account of cosmic anthropocentrism given by Grey assumes that moral consideration involves the strong sense of total elimination of our own location, not merely some form of transcendence of it or escape from confinement to it. Thus intermediate conclusion 3 and the final conclusion 4 seem to require this second stronger sense, since in order to claim that you cannot consider another's welfare as in conclusion 4, you would need to know that you cannot transcend your own location. Therefore the argument for 2 in the strong sense has by no means established its case, showing only that we cannot eliminate our own location. I will return to these points below.

There are, as this shows, complexities and ambiguities in 1 and 2. However, even if we concede 2 without clearing these up, we cannot proceed to 3 or superstrong 4 because of another crucial ambiguity. First, 3's claim that the rejection of anthropocentrism is confused requires a meta-assumption that cosmic anthropocentrism is the only sense of anthropocentrism relevant to determining the morality of action, and this is another key place where the argument fails. The cosmic sense of anthropocentrism in which a judgment is anthropocentric if it depends on human "bearings" is one of *several* accounts or senses of anthropocentrism. 1 and 2 require that by anthropocentrism we mean "cosmic anthropocentrism," and so 1 and 2 only support 3 if *anthropocentrism* in 3 means "cosmic anthropocentrism." But then we cannot get to the anthroposcopic conclusion 4, since the unavoidability of cosmic anthropocentrism does not support the conclusion that only human interests can count. Nor does it support the second half of 3, the intermediate conclusion that the demand to eliminate anthropocentrism is confused, since it is only the demand to eliminate cosmic anthropocentrism or locatedness which has been shown to be confused. But this intermediate conclusion and the anthroposcopic conclusion 4 require that all reasonable senses of anthropocentrism are unviable. Alternatively, one might say that the step from 3 to 4 is invalid, since to follow from 3, 4 would have to use *anthropocentrism* in a universal sense which is quite different from the way it is used in 1 and 2. In short, the argument assumes that cosmic anthropocentrism is the only relevant or possible sense of anthropocentrism, since the claim about conceptual confusion and the anthroposcopic conclusion assume that all demands for avoidance of anthropocentrism are demands for the avoidance of cosmic anthropocentrism. This, as I shall show and as the literature demonstrates, is false.

Cosmic Irrelevance

There is, as Grey's list of what must be avoided illustrates, an interest version as well as a locatedness version of this same cosmic argument. The cosmic argument is one of a family of arguments which depend on an ambiguity like the one above between transcendence and elimination of base class interest or location in order to provide a general justification for restricting consideration to that base class. That is, they are arguments for some version of psychological egoism where the crucial equivocation between locatedness and restriction of interest to the self lies buried in the concept of "selfish interest."[5] Without some assumption which equates transcending own interest or location with completely eliminating own interest (or location) and demonstrates the impossibility of the latter, the fact of locatedness can do nothing to establish the egoistic equivalent of the anthroposcopic thesis that human judgments can consider only the interests of human beings. The perennial appeal of this argument deriving human selfishness from locatedness can be seen to derive from its status as a species version of psychological egoism. But it is this very same complex which gives rise to the reading of anthropocentrism as the product of human location, and the idea that escaping it involves adopting a view-from-nowhere perspective which eliminates all human bearings. The result is a concept of anthropocentrism which draws a contrast different from the ones needed for the purposes of the Green critique, is irrelevant to the main purposes of environmental concern, and is unable to show us why anthropocentrism is a problem for contemporary society.

Environmental critiques usually ask for more weight to be given to the needs of nature and more attention paid to our own relations of dependency on nature, usually supporting this by pointing to the ill effects for humans or for some other parts of the biosystem of ignoring these needs. To see why and how cosmic anthropocentrism misses the point of such environmental critiques, I shall model the debate between the Green critic of anthropocentrism and the cosmic anthropocentrist in terms of the following marital dialogue between A and B, in which Ann accuses Bruce not of being human-centered but of being self-centered, of giving insufficient weight to her needs.

Ann: "I think you ought to do a bit more of the housework around here. I'd like a chance to write some philosophy too. I think you're really self-centered; you only think about your own interests; you never think about my needs at all."

Bruce: "I see you're being emotional and confused again, darling. Don't you know everybody's self-centered? There's absolutely no way to avoid it. We all give weight just to our own interest. That's what you're doing too. We're all located in space and time. We all see the world from that perspective of the self. Inevitably our own experiences, interests, values and preferences, standards of appropriateness must color and shape our universe, underlie everything we do."

The dialogue is interrupted as Ann throws the dishmop at Bruce and adds some remarks suggesting he is too smart for his own good. "What's all that rubbish got to do with it!" she says. "I'm asking you to take over some more of the housework!"

"But I can't," says Bruce. "That's what I'm trying to explain to you! I can't because I can only really consider my own interests. Yours don't count at all, unless I choose to give them some weight. I could do that if it was in my interest, but you'll have to show me how it is—how you might try to please me better if I did, for example. But you haven't done that yet, have you? You've just got angry, and—"

The dialogue closes with some more frustrated remarks from Ann, which I won't repeat in detail, but which are to the effect that Bruce is a narcissistic idiot unable to consider others. Divorce follows shortly after. It was plainly inevitable: Ann and Bruce are not on the same wavelength at all. Ann asks for more weight to be given to her interests. Bruce responds with an epistemological locatedness argument that self-centeredness is inevitable, so he can't do what she asks. He gives such unreasonable weight to this abstract argument over his clear options for practical action that it is reasonable to suspect that he is using it as a rationalization for his self-centeredness. Bruce's ultimate hint of a concession indicates he will agree to Ann's request, if he does, only in expectation of something she shouldn't be required to give, that is, for the wrong sorts of reasons, out of concern for his interest, not out of respect and consideration for hers. This will tell on their relationship in the long run, even if they reach a temporary compromise. The main point I want to draw out of this dialogue for now, though, is that Bruce's response is totally inappropriate to Ann's request. Ann asks for fairness and consideration; Bruce meets her with philosophical cant about locatedness and psychological egoism. His and Ann's positions appear to meet, but actually they do not. That is why Ann, in the same situation as the critic of human-centeredness, believes she has been fobbed off. Her respondent has not caught the sense of her claim, has the wrong kind of self-centeredness in mind, perhaps because he has been badly educated, or perhaps because he is in bad faith. There is certainly some reason to suspect the latter, since he is using his argument to refuse to do something we know perfectly well he could do: give more weight to Ann's needs.

Now in just the same way, it seems to me, the response of the defender of cosmic anthropocentrism completely misses the point of the Green critic of human-centeredness and misinterprets the sorts of demands that are being made in terms of it. Interpreting the Green critic as asking for a better deal for nature, a larger share, more concern, more respect, more awareness, gives a rather better reading of the basic thrust of Green activism than the idea of viewing the world *sub specie aeternitatis*, which has little to offer either ecological politics or activism. The critic of human-centeredness is making a prudential or a justice claim for better consideration for nature, and the cosmic anthropocentrist, for motives which may similarly include giving an undue priority to the dictates of abstract argument over options for practical action, responds by making an epistemologically grounded point about the inevitability of human locatedness and ultimately human self-centeredness and psychological egoism. I want to use this example to show that the cosmic anthropocentrist has, for the purposes of the debate over how to reconstruct the culture in more ecologically sensitive terms, got hold of an inappropriate model of anthropocentrism. That, I suggest, is one of the main reasons why the ecological philosophy based on this cosmic concept is out of kilter with ecological politics and ecological activism.

An Alternative to Cosmic Anthropocentrism

Psychological egoism is a remarkably persistent, widespread, and socially fostered fallacy, but if the persistence of the argument from cosmic anthropocentrism was only due to the logical confusions and equivocations of psychological egoism, it is unlikely that the defenders of anthropocentrism would have raised the cosmic argument so persistently.[6] What complicates the issue further is that the cosmic sense of anthropocentrism is not entirely a straw man but has been given sustenance by the accounts of anthropocentrism found in major Green philosophers, as well as by the opponents of environmental ethics. The reasons for its appeal to opponents of the Green critique are obvious—cosmic anthropocentrism is a reading of the concept which holds out the prospect of an easy victory over the Green critic of anthropocentrism. Its use by ecophilosophers is harder to understand but can be explained in terms of a failure to distinguish between two crucially different models of anthropocentrism which are based on different contrasts, comparisons, and extensions. These are, first, cosmic anthropocentrism based on the Copernican model of detachment from a human location, and second, what I will call the liberation model of anthropocentrism, based on extending to the human/nature case the understanding of centrism drawn from liberation concepts such as androcentrism, ethnocentrism, and Eurocentrism. Many ecophilosophers appeal to both senses as suits their argument—inconsistently, since the models are incompatible. For example, deep ecologists such as Arne Naess and Warwick Fox both call on the liberation sense from time to time,[7] but the model which is developed in detail and relied on primarily in deep ecology is the cosmic model or transpersonal reading which treats overcoming anthropocentrism in terms of the overcoming of personal attachment. Thus Fox, in the most thorough treatment of anthropocentrism in the ecophilosophical literature, establishes the basis for his subsequent treatment of it in cosmic terms by an early appeal to the Copernican model and glosses anthropocentrism repeatedly as "human self-importance," which leads on to the idea of detachment from self. It is a short step from the accounts of the ecological self as the overcoming of attachment and particularity, the accounts which characterize deep ecology, to demanding detachment from epistemological location. Feminist thinkers have pointed out that this understanding of the key concepts involves a masculinist and rationalist demand for absence of emotional attachment and discarding of particular ties (Kheel 1990; Plumwood 1993). Deep ecology has therefore helped to generate the cosmic understanding of anthropocentrism, which in turn invites the sort of argument advanced by Grey. Although the view that avoiding anthropocentrism demands eliminating all human bearings and extending concern impartially to all times and species is attributed by Grey to a group specified vaguely as "environmental philosophers,"[8] this attribution not only buries a major area of contest but obscures the fact that concern with cosmic anthropocentrism is closely associated with one particular group of environmental philosophers—deep ecologists—and reflects their orientation to transpersonal and transcendence-of-self philosophies. The alternative liberation model of anthropocentrism I now sketch constructs a "human-centered" parallel to the sophisticated tribe of liberation concepts I outlined initially, concepts such as androcentrism, Eurocentrism, and ethnocentrism. Not only is this liberation model not subject to objections like Grey's and Thompson's which the cosmic model invites, but it can give a much more sensible and politically useful reading of the Green critique than does the account in terms of cosmic anthropocentrism, enabling us to draw on many of the well-elaborated political insights of these liberation models in developing an account of human-centeredness.[9] I shall argue in a later section that this alternative model does not suffer from the irrelevance and impracticality of cosmic anthropocentrism.

First let us note that we cannot understand these liberation concepts along the lines of the cosmic model as requiring detachment from location or elimination of bearings. As many feminists have argued, we cannot understand overcoming androcentric bias in our culture as the development of gender neutrality, the abandonment of all gender location or perspective (either male or female) to achieve the gender equivalent of a view-from-nowhere (Mackinnon 1987). Neither does overcoming Eurocentrism and ethnocentrism require us to detach ourselves from or abandon all cultural location—on the contrary, it may require a stronger assertion of certain locations and their admission in explicit terms, as also in the case of gender. Rather, overcoming these forms of centrism requires attention to a certain sort of nexus of political relationships which exhibit a centric structure. This centric structure, which Nancy Hartsock (1990) has described as one which "puts an omnipotent subject at the centre and constructs others as sets of negative qualities," is held in common, she suggests, between the different forms of centrism which underlie racism, sexism, and colonialism.[10] The shared logical characteristics of the structure enable us to think of centrism as a determinable with the specific varieties as determinates,[11] and much room for political inflection and cultural variation. I don't want to suggest that this structure gives a complete account of oppression or of the concept of the other, to deny that there may be other kinds of oppression or features specific to particular kinds of oppression, or claim that race, class, gender, and nature centrism constitute a complete list.[12] In the case of androcentrism, the chief features of this centric structure between the masculine Center and the feminine Other are as follows:

1. Radical exclusion marks out the Otherized group as both inferior and radically separate. Any institutionalized system of domination that aims to avoid arbitrary elements and take full advantage of cultural potential for its reproduction must aim to mark out clearly the dominating group from the others, usually by cultural means which define the identity of the Center (cast as reason) by exclusion of the inferiorized qualities of the periphery. The woman is set apart as having a different nature, is seen as part of a different, lower order of being lesser or lacking in reason. This separation denies or minimizes continuity and shared qualities and justifies assigning women inferior access to cultural goods. Separate "natures" explain, justify, and naturalize widely different privileges and fates between men and women, block identification and sympathy, tendencies to question. A sharp boundary and maximum distance enables the male beneficiary of these arrangements to both justify and reassure himself.

2. Homogenization allows differences within an Otherized group to be disregarded (Hartsock 1990). The Other is stereotyped as interchangeable, replaceable, all alike, homogeneous. To the one at the center, such differences are of little importance unless they affect his own welfare. Diversity which is surplus to the center's desire and need does not require respect or recognition. The Other is not an individual but is related to as a member of a class of interchangeable items which are treated as resources to be managed to satisfy the center's need. Hence essential female nature is uniform and unalterable. "Women are all alike," the "experienced" man advises the inexperienced. "They all want a good—" (fill in the blank yourself). 1 and 2 work together to set up a polarized structure, described by Marilyn Frye: "To make domination seem natural, it will help if it seems to all concerned that the two groups are very different from each other and . . . that within each group, the members are very like one another. The appearance of the naturalness of dominance of man and subordination of women is supported by the appearance that . . . men are very like other men and very unlike women, and women are very like other women and very unlike men" (1983, 32). Breaking the polarized structure is strongly discouraged for both parties. This polarized structure itself is often thought of as dualism, but dualism usually involves also the further features of centrism set out below.

3. Denial, backgrounding. Once the Other is marked in these ways as separate and inferior, there is a strong motivation (explained in part by the

dynamic set out in Hegel's Master-Slave Dialectic) to represent them as inessential. Dependency on the Other cannot be acknowledged. In an androcentric context, the contribution of women to any collective undertaking will be denied, treated as background, as inessential, or as not worth noticing. "Women's tasks" will be background to the aspects of life considered important or significant, often classified as natural in involving no special skill or care. This feature facilitates exploitation of the denied class via expropriation of what members of the class help to produce, but carries the usual problems and contradictions of denial: "Women's existence is both absolutely necessary and irresolubly problematic for phallocratic reality" (Frye 1983). Denial is often accomplished via a perceptual politics of what is worth noticing and what can be acknowledged, but fear and anxiety remain when the Other threatens to return.

4. Incorporation. The woman is defined in relation to the man as central, often conceived as a lack in relation to him, sometimes crudely as in Aristotle's account of reproduction, sometimes more subtly. In Simone de Beauvoir's classic statement, "humanity is male and man defines woman not in herself but as relative to him; she is not regarded as an autonomous being . . . she is defined and differentiated with reference to man and not he with reference to her; she is the incidental, the inessential as opposed to the essential. He is the Subject, he is the Absolute, she is the Other" (1965, 8). His features are set up as culturally universal; she is then the exception, negation, or lack of the virtue of the Center. Her difference thus represented as lack is not just diversity but the basis of hierarchy, inferiority, exclusion.

5. Instrumentalism.[13] The Other's independent agency is downgraded or denied. Traditionally, she is conceived as "passive" and her agency is subsumed within the agency of the male who is her "protector." She is valued as a means to ends rather than accorded value in her own right, deriving her social worth instrumentally, from service to others, as the producer of sons, etc. "Woman's nature" or woman's virtue is defined instrumentally, as being a good wife or mother, classically as "silence and good weaving," romantically as being there to please. The main sphere of her efforts, that of domestic care, may be accorded a similarly instrumental status.

A similar structure of Otherization can be extracted from the analysis of theorists of colonization.[14] My examples will be drawn mainly from the colonization of indigenous peoples in Australia, which combines elements of both ethnocentrism and Eurocentrism.

1. Radical exclusion, hyperseparated identity. The colonized Other is set apart as having a totally different and inferior nature lacking in the defining feature of the colonizer—usually reason-as-civilization—which justifies the Other's devaluation and conquest. Others are described as "stone

age," "primitive," "uncivilized"; Aborigines are like "beasts of the forest," they are nature, while the colonizer in contrast is "rational" or "civilized." Continuity is denied, relationship ignored (they are not really human). Differences are exaggerated (for example, via "civilized or refined manners") to fit a model of virtue defined by exclusion of the Other's supposed traits. Identification and sympathy are canceled by this denial of continuity and kinship, and a separate code of conduct which inferiorizes or punishes is judged appropriate for "them." The colonized are deprived of or accorded lesser political rights, social consideration, and access to voice.

2. Homogenization. The colonized are seen as interchangeable and replaceable units and appear in stereotypical terms as "all the same" in their deficiency; diversity surplus to the colonizer's need and desire is ignored, for example, tribal or group cultural, linguistic, and religious diversity is discounted, people are thrown in together indiscriminately in reserves, and so on. 1 and 2 together result in a polarized structure of opposed communities, one inferiorized and excluded by the other whose attributes, languages, and so on are inscribed as culturally central.

3. Backgrounding, denial. The colonized are denied as the unconsidered background to "civilization," the Other whose prior ownership of the land and whose dispossession and murder is never spoken, admitted. These people's trace in the land is denied, and they are represented as inessential as their land and their labor embodied in it is taken over as "nature." The Others' agency and resistance are denied (they did not fight or win any battles in the colonizer's history), as is the originating cause of conflict in exclusion or dispossession. They are perceived as threatening to the established order, especially as unassimilated speakers.

4. Incorporation. The colonized are judged as lacking in relation to the colonizer, as negativity (Memmi 1965), devalued as an absence of the colonizer's chief qualities ("backward, lack of civilization"), usually represented as reason. Differences are judged as grounds of inferiority. The order which the colonized possess is represented as disorder or unreason. The colonized with their "disorderly" space are available for use without limit, and the assimilating project of the colonizer is to remake the colonized and their space in the image of the colonizer's own self-space, own culture or land, which is represented as the paradigm of reason, beauty, and order. The speech or voice of the colonized is recognized only to the extent that it is assimilated to that of the colonizer.

5. Instrumentalism. The Other is reduced to a means to the colonizer's ends. The colonizer denies the colonized's agency and independence of ends and subsumes them under his own. The extent to which Aboriginal people actively managed the land, for example, is denied, and they are presented as largely passive in the face of nature. Since the colonized's own agency is denied, it is appropriate that the colonizer impose his own, and

the colonized are made to serve the colonizer as a means to his ends (for example, as servants, as "boys").

The commonality of this centric structure helps to explain the transfer of metaphors between different kinds of centric oppression and the reinforcement of the ideologies which support one kind of centric oppression by the ideologies for another (Radford Ruether 1975, Warren 1990). Conversely, it helps explain the way liberation perspectives and insights have historically supported one another and been transferred from one area of oppression to another and back again, for example, in the nineteenth century between women's oppression and slavery and in the mid-twentieth century from antiracist movements to second-wave feminist movements. Since the critique of the human/nature relationship too has exhibited this pattern of political transfer from other liberation perspectives in an especially striking way, it should not be surprising that the same pattern of centricity can be discerned in certain cultural treatments of the human/nature boundary.

Nature as (Colonized) Other

We can now characterize as anthropocentric those patterns of belief and treatment of the human/nature relationship which exhibit this same kind of structure, and by extension categorize as anthropocentric certain cultures and groups which typically host such patterns.

1. Radical exclusion. An anthropocentric viewpoint treats nature as radically other and humans as hyperseparated from nature and from animals. It treats nature as lacking continuity with the human and stresses the features which make humans different from nature, rather than those they share, as constitutive of human identity. It leads to a view of the human as outside of and apart from a nature which is conceived as lacking human qualities such as mind and agency, these being appropriated exclusively to the human. Human virtue is often defined in terms of the exclusion of what is assimilated to nature or animality in the human self, and in culture and society, and those inferiorized social groups associated with nature. Identification and sympathy are blocked for those classed as nature, as Other.

2. Homogenization. The famous presidential remark, "You've seen one redwood, you've seen them all," was quite consciously based on a racist analogy. Nature and animals may be seen as all alike in their absence of consciousness, for example, which is assumed to be exclusive to the human, and the diversity of mindlike qualities found in nature and animals is ignored. Differences in nature are attended to only if they are likely to be of use or contribute in some other way to human welfare. The difference of nature is a ground of inferiority, not just of difference. Nature is conceived

in terms of interchangeable and replaceable units (as "resources" or standing reserve) rather than as infinitely diverse and always in excess of classification. Homogenization leads to a serious underestimation of the complexity of nature and is implicated in mechanism. These two features work together to produce a polarized understanding in which there are two quite different substances or orders of being in the world.

3. Backgrounding, denial. Nature is massively denied as the unconsidered background to technological society, represented as inessential. Since it is seen as an inessential constituent of the universe, its needs are systematically omitted from account and consideration in distributive decision making. Dependency on nature is denied systematically, so that nature's resistance and needs are not perceived as imposing a limit on human goals or enterprises. Attention to them is ameliorative, after disaster occurs. Where consciousness of the dependency on nature cannot quite be banished, it remains a source of anxiety and threat.

4. Incorporation. Nature is judged as lacking in relation to the human colonizer, as negativity, devalued as an absence of qualities appropriated for the human ("rationality"). Differences, for example in the case of animals, are judged as grounds of inferiority. The intricate order of nature is perceived as disorder, as unreason, to be replaced where possible by human order in development, an assimilating project of colonization. The preservation of the order of nature is not perceived as representing a limit, so once again nature is available for use without restriction.

5. Instrumentalism. Nature's agency and independence of ends are denied and are subsumed in, or remade to coincide with, those of the human. Mechanistic world views especially deny nature any form of agency. Since it has no agency of its own and is empty of purpose, it is appropriate that the colonizer impose his own, and nature can only have purpose and value when it is made to serve the human colonizer as a means to his ends. Since there are no moral limits, expediency is the appropriate morality.

The Liberation Model as a Practical Model

This structure has deep roots in the West and does, I think, correspond approximately to the dominant Western outlook on nature (Plumwood 1993). But the main points I want to stress here concern the liberation model of human-centeredness: first, that it captures many of those elements of the dominant technological world view which make it so profoundly hostile to an ecological world view and therefore so profoundly dangerous; and second, that since liberation models do have a practical orientation (after all, they have mostly emerged from the reflection of people involved in active social change in liberation movements), the model can close the gap between ecophilosophy and ecopolitics to validate and theoretically illuminate the sorts of practical responses adopted in Green activism. This is not the source, however, from which ecophilosophy has tended to seek its wisdom, preferring instead various sources which promise to provide an uplifting alternative religion of cosmic character. In contrast, the liberation model does seem to have considerable practical force and suggests ways in which this human-centered structure can be countered through appropriate social change and what really amounts to a good ecological education.

Thus the Green movement, ecological thinkers and activists, can try to counter radical exclusion by an emphasis on human continuity with nonhuman nature and by bringing about an understanding of human embedment in nature. They can contest dualized conceptions of the human and challenge conceptions of human virtue based on exclusion of characteristics classed as natural, stressing instead ones which acknowledge human care for and relatedness to the natural world. In the crucial area of countering backgrounding and denial, ecological thinkers and Green activists can try to raise people's awareness of how much they depend on nature and of how this denial is expressed, for example, by critiquing relentlessly institutions and forms of rationality which fail to recognize this dependency on nature, such as conventional economics. They can stress the importance and value of nature in practical exchanges and education and work to change systems of distribution, accounting, perception, and planning so as to acknowledge and allow for nature's needs. Bringing about such changes is what political action for ecological sustainability is all about. Activists can aim to counter homogenization by bringing about an ecological understanding of nature's diversity and of its own complex order, and they can counter incorporation by creating an understanding of the developmental story of nature. They can try to counter instrumentalism and human claims to control by establishing some humility, by stressing uncertainty, the extent of what we don't know, alternative caring models of relationship to the land, by learning about other culture's noninstrumental relations with nature, and by generating a local earth story so as to place local relationships with nature in a different, less instrumental framework.

Now this list, of course, is very much what ecological education and nitty-gritty grassroots Green activism is all about. Much of it may seem disappointingly ordinary—there is nothing obviously cosmic in it, although there is certainly a lot that is difficult and demanding of care, commitment, and perseverance. The point is not only that the model can deepen and help explain the basis for activist practice but that in doing this range of practical things, ecological activists are already doing precisely what is necessary to counter the historical legacy of human-centeredness; their practice "walks the talk" of the critique of human-centeredness. The situation is misdescribed in terms of a choice between a shallow ecology movement concerned with practical activism and a deep movement concerned with philosophical and spiritual growth which challenges anthropocentrism. Working against the rationality of human-centeredness is not a matter of attaining depth by adding a spiritual ingredient as an optional extra onto an otherwise instrumentally based, "shallow" practical activism (as in the cosmic account); rather it is an implicit but integral part of the politics of ecological activism and of ecological education once these are understood in sufficiently thorough ways.

Another important feature of the liberation model of human-centeredness is that it can validate the ecological insight that the dominance of such a framework is a serious problem, and it does so in a far clearer way than the cosmic model. Proponents of the cosmic model sometimes assert that anthropocentrism is a problem, but they do nothing at all to show how and why it is a problem, and the cosmic account is, I think, quite unable to provide an adequate explanation of this key point.[15] (Another reason I discuss below for the inability of the cosmic model to develop an account of the hazards of anthropocentrism is that it sees such arguments about danger as instrumental and therefore proscribes them as "shallow.") Since a concern with the danger of neglecting or mistreating the environment is the most fundamental of modern environmental intuitions and motivations, the inability to confirm or explain such concern is another reason why the cosmic model fails to make a good connection to environmental politics and activism, and why, in its version, ecophilosophy appears to be no more than the optional spiritual icing on the Green cake, something of no real practical importance or value a Green activist can take or leave alone according to taste. In contrast, the liberation model can, I think, explain why human-centeredness must be addressed in the politics of any serious ecological movement, whether it does so consciously or not. It can also explain why, if such human-centeredness is indeed the dominant framework of the present, the current situation is one of extreme danger and urgency. To show this, I will again make use of parallels from liberation politics to show that such a framework of beliefs leads to dangerous perceptual distortion and blind spots.

The centric structure provides a form of rationality, a framework for beliefs, which naturalizes and justifies a certain sort of self-imposition and dispossession, which is what Eurocentric and ethnocentric colonization frameworks as well as androcentric frameworks involve. The centric structure accomplishes this justification by promoting insensitivity to the Other's needs, agency, and prior claims as well as a belief in the colonizer's apartness, superiority, and right to conquer or master the Other. Thus it provides a distorted framework for perception of the Other, and the project of mastery it gives rise to involves dangerous forms of denial, perception, and belief which can put the centric perceiver out of touch with reality about the Other. The framework of mastery does not provide a basis for sensitive, sympathetic, or reliable understanding and observation of either the Other or of the self; mastery is (it would be nice to say "was") a framework of moral and cultural blindness. Think, for example, of what such a Eurocentric framework led Australians to believe about Aboriginal people: that they were semi-animals without worthwhile knowledge, agriculture, culture, or *techne*, that they were wandering nomads with no ties to the land, were without religion, were all basically the same, and so on. It told white Australians that the Aboriginal presence in this land imposed no limits on their actions, that the land was *terra nullius*, simply "available for settlement." In all that, it created a belief system which was the very opposite of the truth, and evidence to the contrary was simply not observed, was discounted or denied. As a number of feminist thinkers have noted in the case of scientific observation, a framework of perception and reason designed for subjugating and denying the other is not a good framework for attentive observation and careful understanding of that other, and even less is it one for evolving life strategies of mutual benefit based on mutual need satisfaction.

If human-centeredness similarly structures our beliefs and perceptions about the other which is nature, it is a framework for generating ecological denial and ecological blindness in just the same way that ethnocentrism is a framework for generating moral blindness. The upshot of such a structure in the case of nature is a perceptual framework and form of rationality which fosters insensitivity to the intricate patterns and workings of nature, encouraging those who hold it to see only a disorderly other in need of the imposition of rational order via development. Through radical exclusion of mindlike qualities appropriated for the human, such a human-centered framework generates a mechanistic conception of the world which is unable to see in nature other centers of striving and needs for Earth resources. The human-centered framework is insensitive to the other's needs and ignores the other's limits in favor of an aggressive self-maximization. It tends through incorporation to view the other of nature entirely in terms of human needs, through homogenization to treat this other as involving replaceable and interchangeable units answering to these needs, and hence to treat nature as an infinitely manipulable and inexhaustible resource. If this is beginning to sound like the dominant economic system, you are on the right track. Both liberal capitalism and the Marxist productivist model (Benton 1989) fall in with this framework of ecological denial, the latter denying the agency of nature by treating it as the passive object of labor, the former by leaving out of account its irreplaceability, nonexchangeability, and limits.

What makes this human-centered framework of rationality especially dangerous, though, in the case of nature is that it encourages a massive denial of dependency, fostering the illusion of nature as inessential and encouraging through radical exclusion the illusion of the human as outside nature, invulnerable to its woes. A framework which is unable to recognize in biospheric nature a unique, nontradable, and irreplaceable sustaining other on which all life on the planet depends is deeply antiecological. That is why the development of ecological world views has been so profoundly revolutionary. Now, let us put this distorting framework of ecological denial beside the reality of our total dependency on the biosphere and the reality of the present human level of resource use, in which human activity consumes as much as 40 percent of the net photosynthetic product of the earth, in a pattern which has been doubling every twenty-five to thirty years (George 1993). This figure is a good indication of the extent to which the intentional structure of those systemic processes oriented to maintaining planetary biospheric systems is being rapidly and indiscriminately overridden by the very different intentional structures of human society, foremost among which in the present global political context is the exchange value maximizing intentional structure of the market. The juxtaposition of these two features, the dominant rational framework which denies dependency and the reality of our ever-increasing threat to the natural systems on which we depend, is little short of alarming. In the present context in which human activity increasingly requisitions the resources the biospheric other needs to survive, such a rationality of human-centeredness I have sketched must plainly involve, just as Greens and ecologists have urged, a recipe for disaster.

The Dangers of Instrumentalism

The liberation model of human-centeredness, unlike the cosmic model, has little difficulty in explaining why human-centeredness is a problem, why it is not, as Grey claims, benign. However, this raises a new problem of justification, now at a higher level, because although the considerations of danger from ecological denial I've outlined figure very large in the thinking and practice of Green activists, conventional ecophilosophy seems to cut the ground from under their feet by casting doubt on whether truly Green thinkers are entitled to make use of them. Reasons invoking human survival and damage are often said to be merely instrumental and therefore "shallow." By providing such human-providential reasons for considering nature, some ecophilosophers suggest, we may win some battles but lose the war, because we are perpetuating the very instrumentalism a good Green theorist should seek to combat (Fox 1990, 11).

Here again I think there is a major difference between the cosmic model urging elimination of human bearings and the liberation model of human-centeredness of the sort I've given. Only in the account of anthropocentrism as cosmic anthropocentrism is it essential to avoid anything which smacks of human bearings and preferences in the interests of pursuing superhuman detachment. On the liberation account of human-centeredness, there is no problem or inconsistency in introducing some prudential considerations to motivate change or to show why, for example, the sort of mastery framework I've outlined (often conceived narrowly as instrumentalism) must lead to bad consequences for humankind. To see why, I'll return to the marital example of Bruce, whose relationship with Ann exhibits a self-centered structure which somewhat resembles that of the centeredness structure I've set out above and appears to have a distinctly instrumental cast (that is, reducing the other to a means to self's ends). Thus Bruce seems to see his interests as radically separate from and exclusive of Ann's, so that he is prepared to act on her request for more consideration only if she can show it is in his own self-contained interest to do so. It is a reasonable guess, too, that he denies his dependency on Ann and is unaware of the extent to which he will suffer when the relationship he is abusing breaks down.

Now a third party thoroughly critical of instrumental relationships, a counselor perhaps, could take on the task of pointing out to Bruce that his continued self-centeredness and instrumental treatment of Ann would be likely to lead in short order to the breakdown and loss of his relationship, a relationship whose sustaining character he may have underestimated. There is no inconsistency here; the counselor can point out these consequences of instrumental relationship without in any way endorsing or encouraging instrumental relationships. In the same way, the critic of the regime of mastery can say with perfect consistency to a society caught in the rationality of mastery that unless it is willing to give enough consideration to nature's needs, it too could lose a relationship whose importance it has failed to understand, has systematically devalued and denied (with, perhaps, rather more serious consequences for survival than in Bruce's case). The account of human-centeredness I have given, then, unlike the cosmic account demanding self-transcending detachment, does not proscribe the use of human-prudential types of ecological argument, although it does suggest several important qualifications with respect to their use. Confusion on this issue arises in part from the failure to distinguish the use of prudential reasons from instrumentalism.[16]

The qualification is that while prudential reasons for treating someone or something with respect are a part of the picture and have a place, often an important place, at certain stages of creating awareness of the need for change, they are inadequate and incomplete on their own. In the case of personal relationships, prudential arguments for respect are the kinds of arguments one would tend to use in a context where there is a rather elementary understanding of the dynamics of relationships. In the same way, the exclusive use of prudential ecological considerations tends to be appropriate where there is a less sophisticated understanding of ecological dependencies and relationships. In most contexts it is worthwhile placing such prudential arguments into a larger critical, noninstrumental framework to promote the higher-order, reflective understanding of the need to transcend the instrumental mode, in the relationship case, for example, the insight that those who treat their friends instrumentally do not keep their friends. Although there is a basic opposition between the exclusively instrumental mode which reduces the other to a means to the self's ends and the care mode which respects the other's difference and agency (Plumwood 1993), prudential reasons can quite properly supplement a care perspective, and care itself has prudential aspects. For example, Ann probably wants to know that consideration of her needs will be a settled feature of Bruce's behavior toward her, to ask for some dispositional security that he is likely to continue considering her needs. So she will probably want to be sure he is acting out of the right reasons of care which support counterfactual and dispositional consideration, rather than the sorts of narrowly instrumental and ephemeral ones that Bruce puts up.[17] In the same way, the Green critic will aim through ecological education and institutional change to generate the right sorts of reasons for considering nature's interests, supporting counterfactual and dispositional bases for concern of the sort care can provide.

While the idea that eliminating centrism involves eliminating location and concern for self is misconceived in the cosmic account of anthropocentrism, there is an important point in the idea of certain kinds of transcendence of limitation in location. Cross-species exchanges of perspective with nonhumans can enlarge the understanding of the other and burst the confines of a centric world view in the same way that similar exchanges with humans can do.[18] But there are two important qualifications here which are relevant to the cosmic detachment interpretation. First, while this sort of exchange with an inferiorized or instrumentalized other can be important as a source of individual change, it is not a substitute for changing institutions which embody the centric logic. And second, in such transcendence of our location, it is not to a view-from-nowhere detachment that we transfer in a misguided attempt to eliminate all trace of our own origins, but another perspective-haver's view that we briefly share, come to terms with, or remain untouched by. And the liberation account will give a rather different account not only of what such a transcendence of location is but also of what works against it, pointing to dualistic features such as radical exclusion as blocking the ability to transpose one's self into another's place.

Of course, reasons which invoke threat or danger from ecological denial are by no means the only kinds of reasons the liberation model suggests for regarding human-centeredness as a problem. Another important set of reasons why human-centeredness cannot be tolerated derives not from its effect on the oppressed, animals, and nature itself, but from its distorting effect on the oppressors, on human identity and human society. The structure of human-centeredness distorts and limits the possibilities for who we are and what we can become as humans in much the same way that the structures of racism and sexism do for colonizer identities and for masculinist identities. The structure of human-centeredness not only constructs nature as subordinate and as denied self; it constructs dominant human identity and virtue in those cultures which endorse it as the identity and virtue of the master. The effect on these cultures is enormously damaging, and the dualized treatment of those social groups and aspects of the culture which are associated with nature and the body undermines all ideals of equality, democracy, and freedom. Explaining this effect on the master culture has also been an important part of the ecofeminist and Green philosophical critique (Radford Ruether 1975; Dodson Gray 1979; Griffin 1978, 1982; Bookchin 1982; Plumwood 1993).

There are also, of course, moral and political reasons of the same general kind as in the human case for respecting animals and nature; one of the corollaries of the liberation model is that our relations with nature have a political aspect, not only the ethical aspect philosophers have attended to. Some of these ethical parallels are not always suitable to extension to certain types of nonhuman cases; for example, rights views entailing intervention to secure justice in the lives of wild animals are often of doubtful application, if only because of the information problems encountered for humans about relationships in communities of wild animals (Plumwood 1991a). But we can try to balance this out by laying stress on other dimensions of moral assessment, for example, virtue ethics,[19] which give a type of ethical guidance more applicable to these cases. To sum up, then, the liberation account of human-centeredness seems to be able to show us what the essentials of the dominant human-centered view of nature are, what we can do about it, and why it is a problem. You can't get much more practical than that.

Liberation Speech and the Limitations of the Model

Some of the political advantages of integrating an account of human-centeredness with accounts of other forms of centrism are discussed in Plumwood (1993). The model enables us to appropriate much of the liberation critique for nature, but there are limitations in its application and not all aspects of the human liberation critiques may transfer. With the area of voice and representation, there are, as might be expected, major divergences, but also some helpful parallels. Foucault speaks of "the indignity of being spoken for by another," and this is usually considered an important liberation principle. However, a major difference between the liberation of nature and the other liberation critiques then seems to be that ecophilosophers and Green activists do speak for the other; nature does not speak for its own liberation. Some commentators have considered this objection so crippling as to rule out any transfer of the liberation concept (Rodman 1977). This is not the conclusion I will draw here. There are some crucial differences between the speaking position of those who speak for nature and other kinds of liberation speech, but they are not such as to completely invalidate the model. In fact, the liberation model can help to resolve some problems for ecofeminism on the implications of our speaking for nature. Even if few of us can claim to speak as identical with the oppressed group in the way we can in the case of other liberation struggles, it is still important to be clear who we are in this speech and who we are not, as well as what our identity and positioning entitles us to say and do.

Several positions, including some forms of ecofeminism and of deep ecology, try to get over this problem of speaking for the other by representing their speech as based on identity, assuming that they can speak as nature. Thus Susan Griffin, in a powerfully written passage which seeks to remind us of our denied identity as nature, materiality, and animality, suggests that women can speak *as* nature (Griffin 1978). Many critics have seen elements of reversal, of acceptance of women's exclusion from nature, here, but other interpretations which deny the opposition between nature and culture seem truer to Griffin's themes. Western culture has typically denied that humanity is included in nature, and combating this denial, based on human-centeredness, is at the heart of the ecological challenge. Nevertheless, the assumption that we as humans can therefore speak *as* nonhuman nature seems to play on inclusive and exclusive senses of "nature," and also to assume that we can somehow completely eliminate the nature/culture divide, not merely overcome its dualistic construction. Other ecofeminist analyses also suggest that women can speak as nature, in virtue of the close identification of their interests, especially in Third World and subsistence contexts (Shiva 1988; Hallen 1994), their exemplary activism, or their historical construction as nature which gives them a special and unique relationship to it (Merchant 1981; Hallen 1994). This relationship is sometimes assumed to be such that empowering women will also empower nature (Mies and Shiva 1994).

Several of these arguments for women speaking as nature seem to me problematic. For example, we cannot honestly extend to all women, including to elite Third World and to First World women, a set of concerns identified with nature which is clearly specific to the situation of certain groups of Third World women in subsistence economies. And even in the case of these Third World women, it is usually only certain interests, agricultural health for example, which are shared with nature. The construction as nature is something that was and is shared between a number of oppressed groups, for example, both women and indigenous groups, and their voices are not always in agreement. Deep ecology often seems also to assume that we can speak as the other, or at least that we are entitled to speak as the other if we have performed the requisite self-enlargement, part of the point of which is to explain our right to speak. There is often a certain arrogance in this identity assumption, which does not allow us to adequately acknowledge or take responsibility for reconstructing our oppressor identity. I think we need to acknowledge and envisage a plurality of bases for speech for nature, which can be multiple and conflicting even for a single speaker, and that not all acceptable bases for speech are based on claims to some sort of identity with nature.

How then can we, as ecofeminists, ecological activists, and ecophilosophers, justify our speech for nature? Can it ever be acceptable to speak for the other? Some postmodernist sources (for example, Yeatman 1993) seem to suggest that this is never acceptable. But there are surely situations where speaking in defense of the other is not only permissible but necessary. It is essential to distinguish cases here. Taking the place of others and speaking instead of them when the others are perfectly capable of and best placed to speak for and about themselves is, of course, insufferably arrogant, and is typical of the mindset of the colonizing groups. This form of "speech for the other" is actually a form of silencing or assimilation. But this case should be distinguished from the different case where we speak for others, by taking the part of others when they are prevented from speaking for themselves—or, on a closer analogy to the case of nature, when they do speak but are not heard. This kind of speech, the speech of the liberation supporter, such as the white antiracist or the male feminist, has always been an essential part of effective liberation politics, and is the kind of speech in defense of the other it is not only permissible but often necessary for those aware of the other's plight to make.

Those of us who speak from this position, and this includes, I think, many First World ecofeminists, have to speak from two sides, as does the "outsider within" who speaks with bifurcated consciousness (Harding 1991). As reformed colonizers, as the oppressors who have begun to decolonize our minds, we speak as critics of our own culture or group and as supporters of the other, in the same way as the white antiracist or the male feminist. Our speech for the other is made possible by the commonality of the centric structure, for as ecofeminists we speak as those who are ourselves oppressed in a different area, as women, and we are able to transfer our understanding to the other's oppression. The common centric structure plays an important role here in enabling us to grasp the situation of the other, to see the human/nature relationship from both sides, as it were. This is a speaking position with its own special ethics and requirements of humility (Harding 1991). As supporters of non-human nature we take the part of the other, but we are not that other and will never enter fully into its situation. So we speak not instead of, or in the place of, nature but as interpreters of its distress and joy, for those who, often because of the human-centered framework I have sketched, are unable to see or hear these things for themselves.

Notes

1. Grey seems to want to assert the even stronger thesis that the universe of moral discourse is confined to humans. Thus Grey rejects my proposal (Plumwood 1991b) to take the possession of an independent teleology as a criterion for moral considerability. I take this principle of teleology as expressing our need to come to terms with and recognize purposes and projects in the world other than our own. The principle of moral recognition for other purposes marks out the area which must be taken into account in moral theory (the universe of discourse). It is not that these purposes must always be acceded to. I do not propose passivity in the face of these other purposes, which do not always override one's own in the way Grey seems to assume with his examples of the HIV and smallpox viruses. Where the goal of an organism is the destruction of other lives and goals, these purposes may well be resisted.

2. Thus Grey asserts that "my concern is with anthropocentrism in general and not just its manifestation in deep ecology" (464).

3. The obvious point that there are weaker and stronger senses of anthropocentrism has been made often and widely by environmental philosophers. Those who have distinguished different senses include Plumwood and Routley (1979); Goodpaster (1979); Callicott (1984); Elliott (1985, 1989); Hanson (1986); Dobson (1990); Fox (1990); Plumwood (1991b); Williams (1992).

4. Grey's argument here is similar to, and refers to, that of Thompson (1990).

5. For a detailed analysis, see Plumwood and Routley (1979) and Plumwood (1993).

6. Novice environmental philosophers almost invariably object that anthropocentrism is inevitable because of locatedness, that is, they implicitly appeal to the cosmic model. Philosophers who have appealed to the cosmic sense to discredit anthropocentrism include Mannison (1980) and Thompson (1990) as well as Grey.

7. See, for example, Fox (1990, 20–21).

8. Despite his footnote noting that viewing all environmental philosophers as deep ecologists is wrong, Grey insists on going on to do exactly that, labeling all environmental philosophers who query anthropocentrism "deep ecologists" re-

gardless of whether they have accepted the label or not. This mislabeling is not just a matter of convenience; it facilitates Grey's attribution of concern with cosmic anthropocentrism to environmental philosophers in general and his failure to consider other possible models of the concept.

9. Contrary to the claims in Goodin (1992, 74) that such concepts drawn from liberation theory have little to offer an account of Green value and Green politics except rhetoric.

10. This structure goes under a number of names, and its basic features have been independently identified by several authors, for example, Benton (1993). The structure may be thought of also as that of dualism (Plumwood 1993) or as giving an account of the concept of the other. My account here follows that of Hartsock (1990) at a number of points.

11. The features outlined should be considered as marks, or as a cluster, rather than a set of necessary and sufficient conditions.

12. Elsewhere I argue that these forms of centrism acquire cultural centrality in the specific political system of liberalism as the major exclusions of the liberal master subject. See Plumwood (1994).

13. Although I use the expression *instrumentalism* here to name this specific feature of denial of agency and the use of the periphery as the means to the center's ends, the term is often used to designate something like this entire complex of thought, for example, as "instrumental rationality."

14. For example, Said (1979), Memmi (1965), Freire (1972), Hartsock (1990), Frye (1983), Beauvoir (1965), hooks (1989).

15. See, for example, Fox, who claims that anthropocentrism is "a dangerous orientation toward the world" (1990, 13) but does nothing at all in his extensive account to back up this claim. It is true that deep ecology and transpersonal ecology stress relationship and therefore dependency, but the understanding of the self which is the basis of this claim is so indiscriminate in its validation of relationship that it is hard to see how it can discriminate between ecologically sound relationships and relationships based on denial or oppression.

16. Prudential reasons consider the self's ends and the consequences of actions on the self, but without implying, as instrumentalism does, that this self is self-contained, that these kinds of reasons are exhaustive, or that the other is reducible to a means to the self's ends. Thus prudential reasons and nonprudential reasons for action are not, as the critics and the cosmic account both assume, mutually exclusive; prudential and nonprudential reasons can combine and reinforce one another, do not need to be kept sharply separate, and any normal situation of choice will always involve a mixture. Similarly for self and other orientation: avoiding self-centeredness does not imply self-sacrifice or self-neglect, a Kantian-style obsessive purity which scours the conscience for signs of corrupting self-concern in "some secret impulse of self-love" (Kant 1981, 19). The process of considering others is not adequately conceived as a process of substituting their interests for yours, other concern for self-concern, and only on a cosmic account with its demand for abandonment of the self does such purity have any relevance as an aim. Care must involve concern for self as well

as for other, although it is important to avoid a simple additive model here to take account of relationality of interest and higher-order interest. Here we meet again the ambiguity of transcending versus eliminating self-concern, of being located versus being confined to that location; there may be a need to go beyond concern for the self's needs to avoid instrumentalism, but there is no need to eliminate it.

17. So-called enlightened self-interest, often appealed to as the saviour here, is only as good as the assurance that the actor will remain enlightened, and the question of what guarantees that in the absence of a dispositional base such as care is not addressed.

18. For example, a change from everyday "human scale," such as exchanging a human-located perspective with a nonhuman perspective in a play of recognition, can, but need not, involve two reciprocal exchanging consciousnesses, one human and one nonhuman. Such exchanges can take a number of forms, all only possible because the nonhuman perspective-haver has its own intentional capacity in the first place; for example, two human consciousness reflecting on a third nonhuman perspective-haver's consciousness, and an exchange of intentionality expressed via intentional action rather than in symbolic or linguistic mode. And such exchanges may take place between the nonhuman perspective-havers or between them and other species of nonhuman perspective-havers; this should be able to count just as well, because no principle which was not blatantly anthropocentric could insist that only human perspective-havers could start the exchange of recognition or that they had a favored place in it.

19. As I argue in Plumwood (1993).

Bibliography

Beauvoir, S. de (1965). *The Second Sex*. London: Foursquare Books.

Benton, T. (1989). "Marxism and Natural Limits: An Ecological Critique and Reconstruction," *New Left Review* 178, 51–86.

———. (1993). *Natural Relations*. London: Verso.

Bookchin, M. 1982. *The Ecology of Freedom*. Palo Alto, Calif.: Cheshire Books.

Callicott, J. (1984). "Non-anthropocentric Value Theory and Environmental Ethics," *American Philosophical Quarterly* 21, 299–309.

Dobson, A. (1990). *Green Political Thought*. London: Routledge.

Dodson Gray, E. (1979). *Green Paradise Lost*. Wellesley, Mass.: Roundtable.

Elliott, R. (1985). "Meta-ethics and Environmental Ethics." *Metaphilosophy* 16, 103–17.

———. (1989). "Environmental Degradation, Vandalism and the Aesthetic Object Argument." *Australasian Journal of Philosophy* 67, 191–204.

Fox, W. (1990). *Toward a Transpersonal Ecology*. Boston: Shambala.

Freire, P. (1972). *Pedagogy of the Oppressed*. Harmondsworth: Penguin.

Frye, M. (1983). *The Politics of Reality*. New York: Crossing Press.

George, S. (1993). *The Debt Boomerang*. London: Pluto.

Goodin, R. (1992). *Green Political Theory*. Cambridge: Polity.

Goodpaster, K. (1979). "From Egoism to Environmentalism." In K. E. Goodpaster and K. M. Sayre, eds., *Ethics and Problems of the Twenty-First Century*. Notre Dame: University of Notre Dame Press.

Grey, W. (1993). "Anthropocentrism and Deep Ecology." *Australasian Journal of Philosophy* 71, no. 4, 463-75.

Griffin, S. (1978). *Women and Nature*. New York: Harper and Row.

———. (1982). "The Way of All Ideology." *Made from This Earth*. London: Women's Press.

Hallen, P. (1994). "Reawakening the Erotic: Why the Conservation Movement Needs Ecofeminism." *Habitat Australia*, February, 18-21.

Hanson, P. (1986). "Morality, Posterity and Nature." *Environmental Ethics: Philosophical and Policy Perspectives*. Burnaby: Simon Fraser University.

Harding, S. (1991). *Whose Science? Whose Knowledge?* Ithaca: Cornell University Press.

Hartsock, N. (1990). "Foucault on Power: A Theory for Women?" In L. Nicholson, ed., *Feminism/Postmodernism*. New York: Routledge.

hooks, bell. (1989). *Talking Back*. Boston: South End Press.

Jaggar, A., ed. (1994). *Living with Contradictions: Controversies in Feminist Social Ethics*. Boulder: Westview.

Kant, I. (1981). *Observations on the Feeling of the Beautiful and Sublime*. Trans. Goldthwait. Berkeley: University of California Press.

Kheel, Marti. (1990). "Ecofeminism and Deep Ecology." In I. Diamond and G. Orenstein, eds., *Reweaving the World*. San Francisco: Sierra Club Books.

MacKinnon, C. (1987). *Feminism Unmodified*. Cambridge: Harvard University Press.

Mannison, D. (1980). "What's Wrong with the Concrete Jungle?" In D. Mannison et al., eds., *Environmental Philosophy*. Canberra: Australia National University.

Memmi, A. (1965). *The Coloniser and the Colonised*. New York: Orion Press.

Merchant, C. (1980). *The Death of Nature*. London: Wildwood House.

Mies, M., and V. Shiva. (1993). *Ecofeminism*. London: Zed.

Plumwood, V. (1991a). "Nature, Self and Gender: Feminism, Environmental Philosophy and the Critique of Rationalism." *Hypatia* 6, no. 1, 3-27.

———. (1991b). "Ethics and Instrumentalism: A Response to Janna Thompson." *Environmental Ethics* 13, 139-50.

———. (1993). *Feminism and the Mastery of Nature*. London: Routledge.

———. (1994). "Feminism, Liberalism & Radical Democracy." *Anarchist Studies*, forthcoming.

———, and R. Routley. (1979). "Against the Inevitability of Human Chauvinism." In Goodpaster and Sayre, *Ethics and Problems of the Twenty-First Century*.

Radford Ruether, R. (1975). *New Woman/New Earth*. Minneapolis: Seabury.

Rodman, J. (1977). "The Liberation of Nature?" *Inquiry* 20, 83-131.

Said, E. (1979). *Orientalism*. New York: Vintage.

Shiva, V. (1988). *Staying Alive*. London: Zed.

Thompson, J. (1990). "A Refutation of Environmental Ethics." *Environmental Ethics* 12, 147-60.

Warren, K. (1990). "The Power and Promise of Ecological Feminism." *Environmental Ethics* 12, no. 2, 121-46.

Williams, B. (1992). "Must a Concern for the Environment Be Centred on Human Beings?" In C. Taylor, ed., *Ethics and the Environment*. Oxford: Corpus Christi College.

Yeatman, A. (1993). "Voice and Representation in the Politics of Difference." In S. Gunew and A. Yeatman, eds., *The Politics of Difference*. Sydney: Allen and Unwin.

Twenty-one

Revaluing Nature

Lori Gruen

As our knowledge of environmental devastation and the global consequences of this devastation grows, so do questions about how we ought to
think about and act toward the natural world.[1] Initially such questions were
left to economists and policymakers; more recently these questions have
been dealt with, although not answered, by politicians and government bu-
reaucrats. Philosophers too have played an important role in the global environmental debate. Philosophical reflection has done a great deal to clarify and illuminate useful strategies for dealing with our global ecological
crises. Here I will examine contributions to environmental ethics through
an ecofeminist lens. Specifically I will look at how an ecofeminist might
begin to answer these two questions: How do we justify our moral claims
about human interactions with nature? Does this justification provide motivating reasons for acting morally toward nature?

Intrinsic Value and
Ecological Moral Ontologies

Insofar as there is something that can be called a philosophical tradition in
environmental ethics, it is a tradition which often attempts to answer questions of justification by drawing on the notion of intrinsic value. An examination of two prominent strains of thinking about the construction of
an environmental ethic, namely social ecology and deep ecology, illustrates
the central role intrinsic value plays. While there are significant differences
between these two positions,[2] I want to suggest that they both attempt to

justify moral claims about the environment by appealing to a particular conception of intrinsic value.

This conception of intrinsic value comes out of an ontological doctrine of objectivism about value. Those theorists who adopt this conception of intrinsic value are moral realists who argue that intrinsic value is part of the fabric of the universe. They maintain that there are values that exist independently of our conceptual schemes and linguistic frameworks and that these values can be determined not only independently of the usefulness of a particular entity but also independently of our feelings or attitudes about it. On this view, minds discover values; they do not create them. The intrinsic value that I will be discussing is what Holmes Rolston has called "non-instrumental, non-anthropogenic" value.[3]

I will look first at what is called social ecology, a theory most commonly associated with the work of Murray Bookchin which finds some of its roots in the writing of the early Frankfurt School.[4] Simply put, social ecology sees the problem of environmental destruction as emerging from a number of social structures, most fundamentally capitalism and the centralized state. In order to address global environmental problems, social ecologists argue that we must engage in complete analyses of advanced capitalist societies and ultimately recognize how the social structures within these societies are antithetical to both humans' and nonhumans' free nature or *telos*.[5]

According to social ecologists, "values are implicit in the natural world."[6] Bookchin claims that "mutualism is an intrinsic good by virtue of its function in fostering the evolution of natural variety and complexity . . . similarly freedom is an intrinsic good."[7] They are not, he suggests, simply human values but are apparent "in larger cosmic or organic processes."[8] Social ecologists adhere to a type of naturalistic moral realism which suggests that values can be located in "the latent potentialities" and "essences" inherent in the natural world. This naturalistic theory is characterized by a strict objectivism. For example, Janet Biehl claims that "the ecology question thus raises once again the need for an objective ethics. . . . We must once again find an ethics somehow grounded in objectivity."[9] Following Bookchin, she maintains that there is an inherent logic in nature that can serve as the foundation for a "dialectically naturalist ethic."[10] Such an approach is important and necessary according to the social ecologists because "obviously, the ground of an ecological ethic must be ontological: it cannot be grounded on the vagaries of social constructions, public opinion, or tradition."[11] While the ontological complexities that these assertions involve require more analysis, for present purposes suffice it to say that social ecologists believe that our moral claims about the environment can be grounded by appeals to natural properties. For this sort of theorist, to say that x is intrinsically valuable is to say that x has some particular natural property y instantiated in it.

A problem which has always plagued naturalistic views is that of determining which natural properties make a thing "good" or "intrinsically valuable" and what the relationship is between the two. Bookchin and others talk of latent potentialities, but what are these? It seems that defining inherent value in terms of such intangible natural properties doesn't help much. Social ecologists talk about self-organization and natural evolution, but this too leads to problems. If, as Bookchin and many others suggest, humans are part of nature, then their destruction of nature can be seen as a function of natural evolution. If what accords with natural evolution is right, then the destruction of the environment is right. A social ecologist would undoubtedly respond that it is the social institutions in capitalist societies which have thwarted natural evolution, that humans are thus separated from their true self-organization which they must regain in order to fulfill their natural ethical mandate. While it is difficult to dispute the claim that humans are influenced by the social conditions in which they may find themselves, it is harder to substantiate the claim that there is some objective mutualist human nature that lies beneath the social conditioning. However, even if such an argument were available, there is the difficulty of determining how these moral facts would motivate moral behavior. If the motivation is thought to be natural or unavoidable, then it is hard to figure out how we as a species have gotten ourselves into the current ecological predicament. Unsurprisingly, naturalistic environmental ethical theories, though initially attractive, run into the same problems that naturalistic ethical theories do.

Perhaps the justification can be found in a nonnaturalistic theory of value. This is the approach that the deep ecologists have embraced. When these theorists suggest that nature has intrinsic value, which is the first basic principle of deep ecology, they adopt a realist moral ontology that suggests there are knower-independent, nonnatural values that exist in the world. Tom Regan claims that "the presence of inherent value in a natural object is independent of any awareness, interest or appreciation of it by a conscious being."[12] One is forced to ask how we discover this value, a question that many have posed for the nonnaturalist theories, and Regan's only response is, "I wish I knew." Others have answered the question by suggesting that objective, nonnatural moral values are discovered by some special faculty or by intuition. This answer, however, seems to imply that only those specially trained or gifted can know what is intrinsically valuable, and thus they may be the only ones motivated to act accordingly.[13] In addition, some have suggested that such odd values and such utterly unique ways of knowing them make a mockery of moral thinking. Others have argued that such questionable ontological commitments cut certain kinds of values off from others and from the very process of valuing itself.[14]

The objectivist ontologies that ground these approaches to environmental ethics are problematic in a number of ways. They do not appear to provide particularly defensible or coherent ways of justifying moral claims about our environmental concerns. Moreover, even if such claims could be justified by appeals to objective, nonanthropogenic intrinsic value, it is not at all clear that such claims provide compelling reasons for acting morally. Yet if we reject such a foundation for environmental value, we may be left unable to justify our moral claims. I want to suggest that there may be a way to justify such claims without appeals to an objectivist moral ontology and that such justification could provide direct motivation for acting morally.[15]

Valuing in Community

In recent years there has been a resurgence of communitarian philosophy, which includes a range of views all maintaining that moral claims can be justified in community.[16] The growing popularity of communitarian views can be attributed in part to the problems associated with objectivist approaches to justifying values, and perhaps to a rejection of the underlying presuppositions of liberalism as well.[17] For communitarian theorists, the values arrived at in community serve as the foundations for our moral knowledge. But here too there are problems.

Specifically, the concern with many standard formulations of communitarianism is their focus on tradition and their potential legitimation of a merely conventional morality. Many communitarian notions of community are based on national identities or the family and neighborhood into which one is born. These communities are nonvoluntary; they are communities in which we simply find ourselves and discover relationships rather than ones in which we create ourselves and our relationships. And as Marilyn Friedman has suggested in a feminist analysis of communitarianism, "communities of origin may harbor ambiguities, ambivalences, contradictions, and oppressions."[18] One needs only to think of the inferior status of women in virtually all countries in the world or of our conventional attitudes toward nonhuman animals in order to recognize how values originating in these communities will be problematic.

In order to avoid these dangers, a richer theory of community must be developed. The meaning of community must be more than simply a place where intersubjective agreement determines value. For a community-based justification of value to be defensible and to motivate moral behavior, the proper conditions of dialogic communication and evaluation must be clarified.

Friedman recommends that the focus be placed on communities of choice and uses the example of modern friendships to illustrate the importance of this enhanced notion of community. Friendship, as we commonly understand it, can serve as a model for communities of choice, as it is within friendships that support, respect, and mutual growth most readily occur. However, while friendship is indeed a central feature of building community and may be a necessary relationship for building a respectful appreciation of difference,[19] friendship itself is not enough. Often our friendships are strained by political affiliations and motivations. Consider how friendships can be destroyed when one person becomes a vegetarian while the other continues to eat meat; or when the lesbian one came out with begins sleeping with a man; or when a pacifist's friend joins the military; or when a friend's racism becomes overt. Communities of choice based on friendship may serve as one model, but contemporary individuals are rarely, if ever, constituted (or reconstituted) by a singular community. Chosen political affiliations must also play a significant role.

Ann Ferguson's notion of "oppositional" communities is particularly appropriate in this regard. "An oppositional community involves a network of actual and imagined others which one voluntarily commits oneself to, and in so doing, re-defines one's personal identity." These oppositional communities move beyond friendship in that they provide a central place from which to challenge the racist, sexist, classist, heterosexist, and other biases our friends have. Communities of opposition, while created due to certain shared interests, allow for the important recognition of differences between members of the community. Such communities are committed to "revolutionary love or caring that requires that those feminists with race, class and national privilege accept an ethic of radical justice which continually challenges and attempts to dismantle the effects of such privilege, particularly in our relations with others in our intentional communities."[20] Thus oppositional communities provide room not only for challenging our friends but also for challenging our selves.

Chosen oppositional communities are places in which status quo interests can be reconstituted.[21] The process of reconstituting our interests may come about due to concerns community members express about one's status quo interests or through the recognition and reconciliation of particular contradictions in one's self, contradictions which are made clear because of the way the self is situated. It is important to note that the contradictions that exist within a self are contradictions that stem not from a clash between essential components and something outside of the self, but rather from the self in different aspects.[22] As Ferguson writes, "Each aspect of self is defined by its relation to a different set of social practices with different built-in norms and expectations, and therefore different meaning-relations with others. The self is a multi-faceted conscious and unconscious process."[23] A central feature of the process of defining self in community is experience.

In her recent work, Alison Jaggar highlights the importance of experience not only for self-construction but as a way of knowing and valuing in community. Her work, drawing on the practice of feminist dialogue, provides a starting point for a feminist moral epistemology.

> . . . feminist practical dialogue continues to assume that personal experience is indispensable to moral and political knowledge and that every woman's experience is equally important, both morally and epistemically. It also continues to assume that the ideal context for revealing personal experience is a nurturing and supportive environment.[24]

The practice of feminist dialogue is more than just a way of reaching knowledge; it is also an important moral experience in itself, in that it cultivates "not only the values of mutual equality and respect but also virtues such as courage, caring, trust, sensitivity, self-discipline, and so on." Jaggar, like Ferguson, recognizes the crucial role that challenges within community play in creating better knowledge and value claims, and to that end suggests that the dialogic community be made up of people with very different lives and experiences. Both suggest that we should always seek to make our chosen communities as inclusive as possible.

Clearly, the central role that experience plays in the process of generating moral claims is an advantage to this approach. Community becomes more than just a place where values are created; it also encourages participants to take seriously the moral imperatives that are reached. In this way, the generation of moral claims and the motivations to act according to them are inseparable. An answer to the question "why should I do X?" is simply that "you were part of the evaluative process that arrived at X as the right thing to do."

The process of generating values in community can only occur between those willing to engage in a self-reflective way. Valuing in community is predicated upon the desire to communicate, not the desire to talk at or dictate to other members of the community. Those persons who are unable or unwilling to enter into the democratic process that leads to value claims—persons who hate, for example—can legitimately be excluded from the community. As concentration camp survivor Elie Wiesel wrote,

> I believe in dialogue, even when the dialogue is difficult. But I would never dialogue with one who hates. I would never dialogue with a Nazi. . . . A hater doesn't listen. You may speak to the hater, but you will never convince him because he doesn't listen. A hater doesn't remember. A hater doesn't live except with the framework of his or her hatred.[25]

But in a world that seems hopelessly incapable of engaging in such a process, won't those who do be marginalized and won't their value claims be invalidated if not ignored? While this may be the case among those persons who refuse to evaluate their own perspectives, I would suggest that the simple moral subjectivism of these very persons can be revealed and challenged. Because of their refusal to engage honestly in the process of value generation, the values that they represent, values based on unchallenged subjective beliefs, can rightly be rejected.

The process of generating value in chosen communities requires that individuals and communities themselves always seek to expand their moral experience by including those who may not initially be friends but who nonetheless deserve respect. In this way we can begin building a community of communities and avoid the parochialism that plagues traditional communitarian notions. This inclusive process allows for a broader base on which to build knowledge and at the same time allows those in community to reconstitute their selves. In addition, the process of feminist dialogue, which encourages the cultivation of values of care, courage, and cooperation, also strengthens the community. Valuing in community allows for the creation of more self-reflective individuals and more complete, fulfilling, and just communities.

While I believe these insights are tremendously important for the creation of a feminist moral epistemology, how do they help with the creation of an ecofeminist theory of moral justification and motivation? Jaggar, for example, suggests that feminist community be based on actual dialogue, which "presupposes that the speakers are members at least of a linguistic community."[26] Ferguson notes that community must be a "group of real or imagined humans through which an individual identifies an aspect of self."[27] Other feminist theorists, such as Marilyn Friedman and Iris Young, look to urban cities as possible models for community. All of these feminist theories, like all constructivist or contractual approaches to valuing, are human-centered and thus run into the problem of exclusion. Even when the communities are committed to including as many individuals and other communities as possible, how can nature fit in?

Community with Nature

I believe the feminist articulation of valuing in community can provide insight into building community with nature. Including nature in community is not inconsistent with at least some of the views expressed by feminist theorists, as there are a number of common features of feminist theory which can be used to justify a place in community for the natural world. The concern with empathic identification with the oppressed and the focus on the direct experience of actual dialogue are good places to start.

The ability to empathize does not seem to require that the community be only human. The ability to empathize with nonhuman animals, for example, is not only possible but widely practiced. Our ability to empathize with other beings need not be based solely on anthropomorphic projection.[28] That is to say, empathy does not require that our response rests solely on a being's likeness to us. This way of understanding empathy suggests that we can empathize with animals that are not close to us, either in their physical makeup or in their relational proximity. An aardvark, for example, with whom I have no relationship and from whom I consider myself very different, may nonetheless be a being I can empathize with.

An additional possibility for building community with nature may be found in Jaggar's work, albeit indirectly. One of the adequacy conditions of her theory of feminist practical dialogue is that such dialogue be actual. This requirement is emphasized because it is only through the actual experience of others in community (and the process of dialogue that ensues) that strong value claims can be generated. Talking *about* the lives and experiences of women in the "Third World," for example, and talking *with* women who have lived experiences in the "Third World" will generate different sorts of knowledge. The former is apt to carry a certain amount of imperialist bias as well as being prone to ethnocentric distortion. Direct experience in conversations with these women will serve to eliminate (or at least mitigate) these problems. Clearly it is not possible for the nonhuman world to engage directly in the process of practical dialogue, but the underlying motivation for actual dialogue—direct experience—can serve as a guide for including nature in community.

For example, just as it is better to talk with women from other cultures about their lives rather than guess what their lives might be like, so too is it better to directly experience nature rather than guess what such an experience might be like. Much of the problem with the attitudes many have toward animals and the rest of the nonhuman world stems from a removal from them. Our experience of the consequences of these attitudes have been mediated. Consider how most Western people obtain the meat they eat. Most do not think to ask, "Who are these animals who suffer and die so that I can eat pot roast?" I do not deprive them of movement and comfort; I do not take their young from them; I do not have to look into their eyes as I cut their throats.[29] Similarly, few people from the industrialized world have experienced the barrenness of a clear-cut forest and thus are not compelled to think about the vast destructiveness that accompanies the consumption of large quantities of paper, overpackaged products, redwood decks, and the like. Direct experiences of the nonhuman world will create better knowledge of nature and can only help us make more informed judgments about our relation to it.

In addition, direct experiences of nature can provide us with challenges that provide significant opportunities for the reconstitution of our selves. Valuing in community requires diversity of both lives and experiences. Such diversity allows for significant moral challenges. A community which includes the natural world can be challenging in a variety of ways. In addition to the aforementioned experiences and the challenges these experiences evoke, one can look to the positive experiences people have in the natural world and the effect they have on different aspects of our selves. For example, I found living in an intentional rural community designed to create more harmonious relations between humans and nature to radically alter the way I think of my self in the world. The series of experiences I had in this community posed difficult questions (how were we humans to coexist with the woodchucks who persistently ate the bean crop? how could we ensure the growth of the cornstalks in a drought? if we rescued the crippled duck whose wing was frozen to the river, would it be possible to preserve her wildness while at the same time protecting her from predators?) and the process of answering them reshaped my knowledge and values. Hiking among thousand-year-old trees, revitalizing a polluted lake, rock climbing,[30] any such encounter with the natural world or those people for whom nature is an integral part of their community,[31] can only add to a reconstitution of self and increase the diversity of experience that makes community-based values solid.

At this point, it might be suggested that it is precisely this ability to work nature into community-based valuing that is objectionable. This objection may be raised by some feminists or by some environmentalists. Some feminists have devoted much energy to arguments insisting that women are just as much a part of culture as men and therefore should be accorded the respect that they deserve as full participants in human cultural activities.[32] For too long, these theorists argue, women have been relegated to the undervalued realm of nonculture or at best thought to be the bridge between culture and nature. Some might suggest that if we allow nature into the moral community—if, that is, we start valuing nature seriously and start seeing the nonhuman world as providing us with challenges that can influence not only our selves but our values—aren't we thereby devaluing what is distinctly human?[33] Wouldn't this inclusion of nature, and the arguments for such an inclusion made by women, legitimate the subservient position reserved for women in patriarchal cultures, a position that feminists have struggled so hard to leave behind? Isn't this expansion of community to include nature just regressive and ultimately harmful for women?

I think not. As many feminists, ecofeminists, and others have suggested, the distinction between culture and nature or between the social and the biological is problematic, not only because it is conceptually difficult to maintain[34] but also because it provides the groundwork for a system of domination. "Nature" and "culture" are categories that humans have created to help us understand and order the world. Like all categories, one is not better than the other until humans make it so. Because it is thought that reason, culture, and all that is distinctively human emerges from nature and then transcends it, the two categories are indelibly cast in opposition to one another. As long as this model of distinction and transcendence shapes our understanding of nature and our human place in it, the relationship between humans and the nonhuman world will be shaped by what Karen J. Warren has called the logic of domination.[35] In working to eliminate domination, whether it be the domination of women, people of color, working-class people, lesbians, bisexuals, or gays, or the nonhuman world, the logic that separates and subjugates must be exposed and rejected. The division between nature and culture is based on such logic. It seems that some feminists' objection to the inclusion of nature in communities is based on a dangerous dichotomy. As some have suggested, feminist thinking, rather than being antithetical to nature, is in fact continuous with ecological perspectives.[36]

The environmentalists' objection to my argument may take different forms. The first may be that we cannot base our commitment to nature on our subjective experiences of it. There must be some other reason for including the nonhuman world into our communities because positive experiences of nature may not be had by everyone. Eric Katz argues in this way and suggests that we must have an ethical obligation to protect nature that is not based on experience.

> some people do not care at all about the experience of nature. . . . The ethical obligation to tell the truth is not based on the subjective experience of truth telling, nor on the avoidance of the experience of lying. One need not experience adultery to know that it is ethically incorrect. . . . If some people do not respond to nature in a "positive" environmentalist way, that is no excuse for them to violate the obligation to protect the environment.[37]

There are a number of responses to this sort of concern. As I suggested earlier, the views that maintain that there are intrinsic values to which we can appeal in order to ground an environmental ethic have serious problems. Insofar as this is what Katz is advocating, I believe the burden of proof lies with him, and those like him, to show how the problems associated with intrinsic value can be overcome. However, if the concern is rather that even within the framework of communitarian valuing it is not going to be possible to have every community include nature because certain communities may consist entirely of people who do not have positive experiences of nature, then there is something to say.

First, it is not only positive experiences that are going to provide the challenges to selves, communities, and the knowledge claims they generate. Direct experience is what is important. And the direct experience need not exactly correspond to any particular moral dilemma. For example, if a community is entrusted with making a decision about whether to dam a river, it will be enough if one member of that community has experienced a canyon before and after the river that ran through it was dammed. She needn't experience the canyon and river in question, although that would be desirable. In addition, it is not only direct experience that guides the decision. Direct experience can be thought of as a necessary but not always sufficient condition for valuing.

Second, given that more inclusive, more diverse communities will tend to generate more complete knowledge claims, it seems that a community that has no experiences of nature will strive to incorporate such experiences. For this reason, I believe it will not be possible for such a community to arrive at the conclusion that there is no basis for valuing, and thus protecting, nature. It might be suggested that it is mere optimism that leads me to believe that such a conclusion would not be reached. However, given that community-based knowing and valuing is understood as a process and that the community of knowers and valuers will be shifting to include more people and experiences over time, perhaps including future generations, it seems a well-supported optimism.

The objection that Katz raises is partially directed at the underlying fear that community-based valuing condemns us "to the swamp of subjective relativism."[38] I would argue that to accept community-based valuing does not commit one to accepting arbitrariness, chaos, emotionalism, or any relativistic notion. To conceptualize in this fashion is to reduce and oversimplify an issue that is far more complex than many believe. The problem is not between objectivism and what Sandra Harding calls its "mirror-linked twin, judgmental relativism."[39] Indeed, many have argued that the issue is not strictly polar.[40] As the early Frankfurt School theorists argued, this sort of false dichotomization is a

> characteristic of the sickness that even the best-intentioned reformer who uses an impoverished and debased language to recommend renewal, by his adoption of the insidious mode of categorization and the bad philosophy it conceals, strengthens the very power of the established order he is trying to break.[41]

For many, relativism only makes sense "from the biased assumption of a static ontology."[42] When we recognize the dialectical nature of the process of valuing in the world, the concerns that are generated by the oversimplified conception of relativism should be minimized. The choices that we seem to be presented with presuppose an illusory structure. If we recognize that values are central features of our conceptual schemes and theoretical frameworks, we can begin to feel less worried that there is no order. In structuring our beliefs, we can do better or worse. As Nelson Goodman suggests,

> Willingness to accept countless alternative true or right world-versions does not mean that everything goes, that tall stories are as good as short ones, that truths are no longer distinguished from falsehoods. . . . Though we make worlds

by making versions, we no more make a world by putting symbols together at random than a carpenter makes a chair by putting pieces of wood together at random.[43]

Positing objective, nonanthropogenic intrinsic value is but one way of ordering the world; it is neither the best nor the only way.

Furthermore, by accepting community-based valuing we are not forced to choose between rationalism and emotionalism. The very distinction that is made between reason and emotion must be challenged.[44] Morwenna Griffiths suggests that

> in effect, feelings are a route to truth: they both provide us with our beliefs about the world and also provide a basis for assessing beliefs. . . . it appears that the place of feelings in human conduct has not been properly understood. Attention to its significance is important because any proper running of private and public life depends on it.[45]

I would suggest that just as we can alter and critically reflect on our commonly held beliefs and "cultivate" tastes, we can be reasonable about creating our versions of reality. The interactive process of reason and emotion, of feeling and contemplation, allows us to set limits on what is acceptable. Ruth Anna Putnam argues that

> (1) we are constrained by the actual sensory inputs we receive; (2) we are constrained by what we have made of our sensory inputs in the past, the conceptual framework embodied in our prior beliefs, what we have taken to be facts so far; (3) we are constrained by the insistent demand for coherence and consistency.[46]

Far too often the concern about relativism stems from the belief that without objective values we will have no way to resolve disagreement. Once we start recognizing that reason and desire are not entirely separate and can be the objects of critical reflection, then we have at least one way to approach resolutions. However, it is important to note that this particular concern presupposes that there is a great deal of fundamental disagreement, and I want to suggest that such a focus comes from a fixed and negative conception of human nature. When living in a society which is structured in an atomistic and competitive fashion, it is not surprising that individuals find it difficult to recognize the widespread agreement and fundamental similarity in belief that structure a common world. If relativism was as troublesome as people often make it out to be, then we should find virtually complete epistemic disorder in areas that one might call "common space."[47] Consider the experiences of travelers who come together from various cultures and find themselves in another culture with which they are unfamiliar. Even when language and custom are not shared, it is often the case that individuals from very different backgrounds can successfully engage in activities that require considerable negotiating. I am not suggesting that problems don't arise or that conflicts and disagreements don't exist but rather that the problem of value relativism is not as severe as some would make it.

If we view valuing as a communitarian process, then we must also recognize and learn to be comfortable with the trial and error that any such process entails. Making a commitment to the process is a sure way to avoid most of the pitfalls associated with relativism, and this commitment must come from a blend of reason and emotion. As Adorno said, seemingly anticipating the work of recent feminist philosophers of science,

> I have never really understood the so-called problem of relativism. My experience was that whoever gave himself over in earnest to the discipline of a particular subject learned to distinguish very precisely between true and false, and that in contrast to such experience the assertion of general insecurity as to what is known had something abstract and unconvincing about it.[48]

This process can work particularly well when the concept of community is taken seriously.

Another environmentalist objection is that valuing based on community is basically human-centered and thus anthropocentric. The debate about anthropocentrism has permeated the environmental ethics literature for years.[49] As the debate became more sophisticated, distinctions started to be made between what we might call pernicious anthropocentrism, the view that humans are all that matter, and inevitable anthropocentrism,[50] the view that while values are created by humans, nature nonetheless has a place in this process. It should be clear that it is the latter view to which I have been appealing. Without getting too far into the debate, as that would surely be beyond the scope of this discussion, there are two arguments in favor of inevitable anthropocentrism that must be mentioned.

If we are to accept something like the framework provided by community valuing, then a rejection of inevitable anthropocentrism would entail one of two views. First, it could mean the acceptance of pernicious anthropocentrism, which is unacceptable in itself and which, in combination with the justificatory framework being suggested here, becomes inconsistent. As I have briefly suggested, the community that provides the most compelling value claims will be one which seeks diversity of experience. A disregard for the natural world would deny relevance and value to all such experiences.

The second view that a rejection of inevitable anthropocentrism might imply is one in which nature is itself seen as possessing a kind of subjectivity. This approach requires positing consciousness or intentionality within the natural world. Some theorists have attempted to develop the notion of nature as a knowing, speaking subject. Linda Holler, for example, suggests that the world is always part of the evaluative dialogue. While

I appreciate the notion that we all need air to breathe in order to even engage in community activities, I worry about the idea that "we can find support in the voice of the earth, long silenced but now crying loudly and tragically in its refusal to absorb the by-products of our denial of being in the world."[51] Similarly, I do not know how to understand the questions Elizabeth Dodson Gray asks: "What language do mountains speak to tell of the grandeurs of time so vast we can scarcely imagine it? Do you begin to sense the nonverbal language of the Earth as a living organism? . . . Can we hear the plant calling out to us just before the bulldozers reach it?"[52] While it may be useful in certain instances to speak metaphorically of the subjectivity of nature, the literal suggestion to "think like a mountain" only serves to obfuscate and confuse.[53]

While feminist practical dialogue stresses the importance of trying to take another's point of view, it is difficult to imagine what point of view nature might have. Even with nonhuman animals, who possess consciousness, what is assumed to be their points of view is actually but nontrivially the animals' point of view from a human point of view.[54] It is presumptuous and misleading to think that we can actually achieve the particular perspective of another. We are always restricted by the resources of our own minds and the experiences that we have had. These resources and experiences may be inadequate for understanding the experiences of those persons who are significantly different from us, whether in ethnicity, sexual orientation, gender, or species. This position does not imply, however, that the perspective of an other does not count. Quite the contrary. But when it is unclear whether or not an entity has a perspective, that is, when the entity in question does not have at least the minimal characteristics needed for the formulation of a perspective, a different approach is necessary.

Inevitable anthropocentrism avoids the unintelligible suggestion that nature is intentional, yet when combined with an inclusive conception of dialogic communities can provide a meaningful way to know and value the nonhuman world. The approach I am suggesting, rather than stretching the notions of consciousness and volition, stretches human imagination and perception in ways that provide challenges not only to our selves but also to our very ways of living on the planet. It is consistent with the suggestion made by Patrick Murphy, that "the point is not to speak for nature but to work to render the signification presented us by nature into a verbal depiction by means of speaking subjects, whether this is through characterization in the arts or through discursive prose."[55] Including nature in community requires that we learn to comprehend nature's signs, some of which are relatively obvious, for example, the "jelly-fish" babies born of Bikini Island women, the mass death of dolphins in the North Sea, the contamination of southern California groundwater that has caused deformities in animals and congenital diseases in humans, the thinning of the ozone layer, and the like. In communities that are voluntary, empathetic, inclusive, and actual, we can give these signs meaning and act accordingly; we can thus value the natural world.

I have suggested that an ecofeminist theory of moral justification and motivation—an ecofeminist answer to the questions, "How can we justify our moral claims about human interactions with nature, and can this justification provide motivating reasons for acting morally toward nature?"— should not be grounded in traditional objectivist notions of intrinsic value. A rejection of this sort of foundation for valuing does not, however, leave one in a relativist abyss. I have tried to show that a conceptualization of values which focuses on chosen communities, direct experience, and inclusivity is a starting point from which to build an ecofeminist moral theory. Furthermore, I have suggested that the inclusion of nature is not only possible but also desirable in terms of the criteria of adequacy for communitarian philosophy itself. What I have not done is address the practical difficulties that must be overcome in order to make this kind of theory a reality. Obviously, progress toward the ideals of ecofeminist communitarian philosophy depends upon progress in the conditions of democracy itself.[56]

Notes

1. When I speak of nature I am not necessarily speaking of wilderness, wild areas, etc. Rather I am speaking of all that is nonhuman. This way of understanding the term *nature* is meant to include nonhuman animals, ecosystems (urban and otherwise), and nonsentient natural things. The distinction between human and nature is not meant to be the same as the distinction between culture and nature; it is not meant to imply that humans are not a part of nature nor to capture any normative dualism. It is a constructed distinction which I hope will allow for clarity; nothing beyond clarity is implied.

2. For an interesting, albeit at times ideological, look at the differences, see Murray Bookchin and Dave Foreman, *Defending the Earth* (Boston: South End, 1991).

3. There has been an interesting discussion about the meaning of intrinsic value, and not all environmental philosophers view intrinsic value in the same way. See, for example, J. B. Callicott, "Intrinsic Value, Quantum Theory, and Environmental Ethics," *Environmental Ethics* 7 (1985), and Robin Attfield, *The Ethics of Environmental Concern* (New York: Columbia University Press, 1983). Some philosophers use the term *intrinsic value* to mean something other than instrumental value. Others have made distinctions between inherent value and intrinsic value. See my "Intrinsic Value Theories and Environmental Ethics" (forth-

coming). For present purposes, intrinisic value is objective value—value that a being or thing has in and of itself, independent of human valuation.

4. Particularly Max Horkheimer and Theodore Adorno, *Dialectic of Enlightenment* (New York: Continuum, 1987), and Horkheimer, *Eclipse of Reason* (New York: Columbia University Press, 1974).

5. Janet Biehl, *Rethinking Ecofeminist Politics* (Boston: South End, 1991), 127.

6. "Recovering Evolution: A Reply to Eckersley and Fox," *Environmental Ethics* 12 (Fall 1990), 255.

7. Murray Bookchin, *The Philosophy of Social Ecology* (Montreal: Black Rose, 1990), 83.

8. Ibid., 85.

9. Biehl, *Rethinking Ecofeminist Politics*, 21.

10. Biehl writes, "Education, writes Bookchin, is directed 'toward an exploration of [a potentiality's] latent and implicit possibilities.' It aims to understand the inherent logic of a thing's development"; ibid, 123.

11. Ibid., 124.

12. Tom Regan, in Bill Devall and George Sessions, *Deep Ecology* (Salt Lake City: Gibbs M. Smith, 1985), 71. In appendix D, Sessions goes on to develop the deep ecologists' nonnaturalistic intuitionism by drawing on such traditional philosophers as Spinoza.

13. Or worse, the motivation for those that don't share the intuition might be coercion or fear of retribution from those who do see the flashing light of intrinsic value, assuming those specially trained or gifted are in a position of power over those who aren't.

14. See, for example, J. L. Mackie, *Ethics: Inventing Right and Wrong* (New York: Penguin, 1977), chap. 1, and Anthony Weston, "Beyond Intrinsic Value: Pragmatism in Environmental Ethics," *Environmental Ethics* 7 (1985).

15. To avoid appealing to an objectivist moral ontology for the justification of moral value is not to deny the possibility that there may be objective moral values. This sort of claim would require further argument and is beyond the scope of the present discussion. Here I want to assume a certain agnosticism about objective value and proceed from there.

16. See, for example, Alisdair MacIntyre, *After Virtue* (Notre Dame: University of Notre Dame Press, 1981); Michael Sandel, *Liberalism and the Limits of Justice* (New York: Cambridge University Press, 1982); and Michael Walzer, *Spheres of Justice* (New York: Basic, 1983).

17. Communitarians are apt to note that the liberal notion of the abstract individual whose identity can be understood apart from her place in community is flawed. For a review essay of the communitarian critiques of liberalism, see Amy Gutmann, "Communitarian Critics of Liberalism," *Philosophy and Public Affairs* 14 (1985). Gutman suggests (310) that Sandel's criticism, for example, is that "liberalism rests on a series of mistaken metaphysical and metaethical views: for example, that the claims of justice are absolute and universal; that we cannot

know each other well enough to share common ends; and that we can define our personal identity independently of socially given ends."

18. Marilyn Friedman, "Feminism and Modern Friendship: Dislocating the Community," *Ethics* 99 (1989), 285.

19. María Lugones and Vicki Spelman argue that it is only through friendship that women of privilege can begin to respect and understand the experiences of nonprivileged women, and that this understanding is essential in order to build a nonimperialistic, nonethnocentric, and respectful feminist theory. See Lugones and Spelman, "Have We Got a Theory for You! Feminist Theory, Cultural Imperialism and the Demand for 'The Woman's Voice,'" in Marilyn Pearsall, *Women and Values* (Belmont, Calif.: Wadsworth, 1986). While I agree that friendship is an important first step for bridging gaps and working across differences, I believe that it mustn't be the last step.

20. References to Ann Ferguson's work on oppositional communities come from her paper, "Constructing Ourselves through Community: Feminism and Moral Revolution," presented at the Morris Colloquium on Feminist Ethics, held in Boulder in November 1991; hereafter, AF manuscript.

21. AF manuscript, 17

22. See Ann Ferguson, "Feminist Aspect Theory of the Self," in Marsha Hansen and Kai Nielsen, eds., *Science, Morality, and Feminist Theory* (Calgary: University of Calgary Press, 1987).

23. AF manuscript, 15

24. References to Alison Jaggar's theory of feminist practical dialogue are from her work in progress, *Telling Right from Wrong: Feminism and Moral Epistemology*; AJ manuscript, 19.

25. "Education against Hatred: A Conversation with Elie Wiesel," *AAHE Bulletin*, June 1991, 10.

26. AJ manuscript, 32.

27. AF manuscript, 17.

28. John Fisher notes two features of our ability to empathize with other creatures: "The first is that our lives are part of a larger biological life full of common characteristics and needs. Animals have needs for nourishment, water, air; they have life cycles, a sort of family life, a sort of social life with other members of their species; they suffer and flourish; many of them engage in exploratory and playful behavior. . . . The second mitigating feature [is that] we frequently feel sympathy for a creature when we believe it to be suffering. . . . Although I may have it wrong when I think that a penguin suffers to hatch its egg, I plausibly have it right when I think that a young ape is suffering if it appears to pine over its mother's death and dies a few days later"; Fisher, "Taking Sympathy Seriously," *Environmental Ethics* 9 (1987): 203.

29. I briefly discuss this problem in my piece "Animals" in Peter Singer, ed., *A Companion to Ethics* (Oxford: Blackwell, 1991), 350–52.

30. For a discussion of the latter, see Karen J. Warren, "The Power and the Promise of Ecological Feminism," *Environmental Ethics* 12 (Summer 1990), 134–38.

31. For a discussion of how Western views about nature differ from indigenous people's, see, for example, J. Baird Callicott, "Traditional American Indian and Western European Attitudes toward Nature: An Overview," and the citations therein; *In Defense of the Land Ethics* (Albany: State University of New York Press, 1989), 177–202.

32. See, for example, Simone de Beauvoir, *The Second Sex* (New York: Bantam, 1953), or Sherry Ortner, "Is Female to Male as Nature is to Culture?" reprinted in Pearsall, *Women and Values*.

33. Virginia Held, for example, argues this way in her article "Birth and Death," *Ethics* 99 (1989), 362–89.

34. Alison Jaggar suggests that "we cannot identify a clear, nonsocial sense of 'biology,' nor a clear, nonbiological sense of 'society' "; cited in ibid., 374.

35. Warren, "The Power and the Promise of Ecological Feminism."

36. See Lorraine Code's discussion of community and ecology in "Second Persons," in Hansen and Nielsen, *Science, Morality and Feminist Theory*, 371–74. See also Karen J. Warren and Jim Cheney, "Ecological feminism and ecosystem ecology," *Hypatia* 6 (1991), 179–97.

37. Eric Katz, "Searching for Intrinsic Value," *Environmental Ethics* 9 (Fall 1987), 238–39.

38. This ironic and ill-chosen phrase seems to represent not just fear but terror. Subjectivism is, of course, quite different from relativism, and it should be clear that it is not really the problem with community valuing, given the emphasis on community. Simple relativism, however, is a concern. (It is ironic because while arguing for the value of nature, even what we find unpleasant, he ends up devaluing swamps.) Katz, "Searching for Intrinsic Value," 239.

39. Sandra Harding, *Whose Science? Whose Knowledge?* (Ithaca: Cornell University Press, 1991), 142.

40. Donna Haraway, in "Situated Knowledges," *Feminist Studies* 14 (1988), also argues against viewing the problem in polar extremes.

41. Horkheimer and Adorno, *Dialectic of Enlightenment*, xiv. Adorno also writes: "The problem of relativism exists only so long as one discusses the relation of a supposed 'consciousness in general' to a supposed 'object in general.' It disappears in the concrete process in which subject and object mutually determine and alter each other"; quoted in Susan Buck-Morss, *The Origin of Negative Dialectics* (New York: Free Press, 1977), 53.

42. Buck-Morss, *The Origin of Negative Dialectics*, 225.

43. Nelson Goodman, *Ways of World Making* (Indianapolis: Hackett, 1978), 94.

44. See Alison Jaggar, "Love and Knowledge," in A. Jaggar and S. Bordo, eds., *Gender/Body/Knowledge* (New Brunswick: Rutgers University Press, 1989).

45. Morwenna Griffiths, "Feminism, Feeling and Philosophy," in M. Griffiths and M. Whitford, eds., *Feminist Perspectives in Philosophy* (Bloomington: Indiana University Press, 1988), 148–49.

46. Ruth Anna Putnam, "Creating Facts and Values," *Philosophy* 60 (1985), 198.

47. I owe this insight to Nancy (Ann) Davis.

48. Quoted in Buck-Morss, *The Origin of Negative Dialectics*, 53.

49. Donald Scherer, "Anthropocentrism, Atomism, and Environmental Ethics," *Environmental Ethics* 4 (Summer 1982), 115–24; W. H. Murdy, "Anthropocentrism: A Modern Version," in Donald Scherer and Thomas Attig, eds., *Ethics and the Environment* (Englewood Cliffs: Prentice-Hall, 1983), 12–21; Richard Watson, "A Critique of Anti-Anthropocentric Biocentrism," *Environmental Ethics* 5 (Fall 1983), 245–56; Bryan Norton, "Environmental Ethics and Weak Anthropocentrism," *Environmental Ethics* 6 (Summer 1984), 131–48; and Warwick Fox, *Toward a Transpersonal Ecology* (Boston: Shambhala, 1990), 3–40.

50. Inevitable anthropocentrism should not be confused with inevitable human chauvinism, which Richard and Val Routley argued against in "Against the Inevitability of Human Chauvinism," in Kenneth Goodpaster and K. Sayre, eds., *Ethics and Problems of the Twenty-First Century* (Notre Dame: University of Notre Dame Press, 1979), 36–59. It is rather like the view articulated by J. Baird Callicott, that "there can be no value apart from an evaluator, that all value is as it were in the eye of the beholder. The value that is attributed to the ecosystem, therefore, is humanly dependent or at least dependent upon some variety of morally and aesthetically sensitive consciousness"; *In Defense of the Land Ethic*, 26.

51. "Thinking with the Weight of the Earth: Feminist Contributions to an Epistemology of Concreteness," *Hypatia* 5 (Spring 1990), 19.

52. Elizabeth Dodson Gray, "Seeing and Hearing the Living Earth," *Woman of Power* 20 (Spring 1991), 21.

53. There is a trend among feminist theorists to reappropriate terms, and this may be what is going on with the suggestion that nature is intentional. Many feminist theorists, for example, are disinclined to give up terms such as *autonomy* and *objectivity* and choose instead to redefine them. I tend to think that creating new terms, such as *autokeonony*, coined by Sarah Hoagland in *Lesbian Ethics: Toward New Value* (Palo Alto: Institute for Lesbian Ethics, 1988), is not only a clearer strategy but also marks the significant differences from traditional usage that such theories suggest. That is not to say, however, that the reappropriation of certain normative terms, such as *dyke*, with the corresponding shift in value is not appropriate or liberatory.

54. For a discussion of this claim, see my work with Marc Bekoff et al., "Animals in Science: Some Areas Revisited," in *Animal Behaviour* (in press).

55. Patrick Murphy, "Ground, Pivot, Motion: Ecofeminist Theory, Dialogics, and Literary Practice," *Hypatia* 6 (Spring 1991), 152.

56. I would like to express my gratitude to the following persons who read or heard versions of this chapter and provided useful commentary: Ann Ferguson, Alison Jaggar, Ken Knowles, Earl Winkler, and participants in the Center for Values and Social Policy discussion, March 1992.

Twenty-two

Self and Community in Environmental Ethics

Wendy Donner

Ecofeminism has already shown itself to be an environmental theory of considerable power and illumination. Inevitably, however, it has also undergone critical scrutiny. For example, social ecologist Janet Biehl challenges this theory's claim to speak for almost all feminists and ecologists. One of her central points is that this theory "largely ignores or rejects legacies of democracy, of reason . . . as part of a radical liberatory movement" and thus has elements that are regressive (Biehl 1991, 1). She further claims that "as a woman and a feminist, I deeply value my power of rationality and seek to expand the full range of women's faculties" (7). Women's "minds are part of their human nature . . . the capacities of reason, language, culture, and consocation for choice and decision-making, for ethical and political behaviour, as well as for affection and nurture—all are capacities that people have as human beings, whether they are women or men" (155–56).

My concerns are more modest. In this chapter I want to take up questions about the tendency of some proponents of ecofeminism to repudiate or undervalue all forms of such human capacities as reason, autonomy, and a strong sense of self. The model of human nature and human well-being I operate with was put forward by John Stuart Mill, among others (Donner 1991, 1993). This model is based on the view that all humans have a variety of generic human capacities which can appropriately manifest in many different forms. It is crucial to our human well-being, however, that these human capacities be developed, exercised, and balanced against each other and that none be allowed either to atrophy or to take over. Thus reason and

375

emotion, individuality, autonomy and sociality, care and connectedness must all find their appropriate balance within each individual self. Reason and emotion, as generic capacities, can be out of balance or in harmony with other capacities; they can be used for good or for ill, for oppressive and tyrannical purposes as well as for liberatory ends. It makes no more sense to condemn rationality in general because it has been ill used to attempt to justify domination and oppression than it makes sense to condemn emotion in general because rage and hatred have been the impetus for genocide and torture.

Reason and Universal Principles

The critique of reason, rationality, and universal principles as male concepts is a familiar theme in many environmentalist, feminist, and ecofeminist writings. This critique rarely sorts out the forms of rationality and universalizability that are of legitimate concern for feminists and environmentalists from those forms that are valuable or essential to retain. Ecofeminist Val Plumwood, in an overview, writes that "there are major gaps in the arguments for the position, a need to clarify many of the key concepts and to distinguish more carefully between quite different positions which have been lumped together under the 'ecofeminism' label" (Plumwood 1986, 120).

When Plumwood turns to a discussion of rationality in a later article, she thus takes care to explore which forms of rationality she disputes, and she does not completely dismiss the value of reason. Plumwood does indeed take issue with "the rationalist tradition, which has been inimical to both women and nature" (Plumwood 1991, 3). She also disclaims "rationalist-inspired accounts of the self" (3). She argues that this rationalist account has "denied possession of a reason" to women and "the earth's wild living things" (5). Rationalism creates a split between humans and the nonhuman world and a similar split within the human self. She opposes such an "oppositionally construed" reason (6).

So what Plumwood thinks is problematic is instrumental reason, egoistic reason, oppositional reason, abstract, disconnected, and universal reason. Oppositional reason creates splits in denying emotion an equal place and in denying women reason. Since Plumwood complains that women have been denied possession of reason, she cannot be denying the value of reason in all its manifestations, but only reason as construed above, as out of balance with, and demanding a place superior to, other human capacities. I am in agreement with much of her critique of rationalism as specified.

There is one aspect of her critique which I find troubling, however: her concept of universal reason and her construal of the universal as being in opposition to the particular. Here she does not take the care she exhibits in the rest of her argument and fails to distinguish Kantian universalization from a moderate universalization. This latter form, I argue, is essential to all moral thinking and decision making.

Ethical universalization, in Plumwood's account, is part of the process of "abstraction and generalization, part of the move away from the merely particular—*my* self, *my* family, *my* tribe—the discarding of the merely personal and, by implication, the merely selfish" (6). She reiterates that universal, abstract, general reason (all closely linked and sometimes treated as synonymous) are in opposition to particularity. She says that "special relationships . . . are treated by universalizing positions as at best morally irrelevant and at worst a positive hindrance to the moral life" (7). Universalizing rationality is tied to a "failure to deal adequately with particularity." She concludes that "concern for nature, then, should not be viewed as the completion of a process of (masculine) universalization, moral abstraction, and disconnection, discarding . . . special ties" (7). Reason is out of place in making moral judgments about particulars; particular others and particular relations and special ties can only be accommodated in ethics via a route of an emotion-based ethic of care.

I accord a central place in ethical life to care, emotion, and connection. But I think that Plumwood has not given reason its due here. She argues as though Kantian universalization were the only form, and in ignoring the moderate form she blocks off a crucial route of argumentation. Furthermore, her view of particularity and special relationships as solely the jurisdiction of caring and emotion, as shut off from the realm of universal reason, along with her connection of this view to other tenets of environmental and feminist theories having to do with contextualization and narratives, has potentially unsettling and unpalatable implications.

The moderate account of universalization in ethics is quite widely held, but its implications for issues of context are not so widely noted. The account given by Tom Beauchamp is standard. He takes up the question of "universalizability" as a "criterion of moral judgments, principles, and ideals" (Beauchamp 1991, 18). He notes that Kantian universalizability, with its "unconditional, categorical demands on all alike, without regard to individual differences," can rake a "hornet's nest," but that in a more moderate form it "seems to capture a necessary condition of morality" (18). The moderate formulation is that "a moral judgment must, for any person who accepts the judgment, apply to all *relevantly similar circumstances*. The principle itself does not say *what is to count* as a relevantly similar circumstance" (19).

It is clear that on the basis of the moderate account of universalizability, universal principles or judgments about particular relations or special ties can be quite readily constructed. For example, whenever any parent must choose between saving her or his child from a fire or saving ten strangers, the parent is permitted or entitled or obliged to save his or her child and allow ten strangers to die. This meets the logical requirements of the moderate form of universalizability, and it takes full account of the special ties of parents and children. The sort of judgment that is ruled out is the following: whenever Rachel Kline must choose between saving her child, Amanda, or saving ten strangers, she is obliged to save Amanda, but whenever Dave Clermont must choose between saving his child, Marcia, or ten strangers, one of whom is Amanda Kline, Dave Clermont is not obliged to save his child but is obliged to save Amanda Kline. This does make a special case for Amanda Kline and thus violates moderate universalizability. It goes far beyond the acknowledgment that all persons are entitled to take special note of their own particular attachments (which may be to especially loved trees, rivers, or places as well as kin).

What perhaps needs emphasis is that this moderate universalizability does not detach or distance from particularity, but it in fact invites and requires agents to look at the context and the details of the moral situation in order to come to a judgment. This moderate form is simply a requirement of logical consistency and its rejection leads to judgments that are arbitrary and indefensible. It is a distortion to claim that this form of universalizability is detached from context. Agents are required, in light of this model, to get as much detail and information about the circumstances and to scrutinize the context with great attention in order to make a judgment about which features of the situation are relevant to its rightness or permissibility. Having made this judgment about the right-making features of the situation, they must be prepared to come to the same judgment in all other situations which they judge to exhibit relevantly similar right-making features. If two circumstances do appear to be similar but the agent forms different moral judgments, then reason requires that a relevant difference must be present to support these conflicting claims. Agents who reject this demand for basic consistency are heading down a dangerous path of arbitrariness and lack of moral accountability.

If we examine the alternative often presented by philosophers who reject moderate universalizability and substitute a purely care- or emotion-based appeal to context, the unacceptable implications become even clearer. I use Jim Cheney's discussion as my example, but the approach he sets out is widely propounded. Cheney explains the pure-care-context approach as a "tendency to get as detailed as possible until (if possible) the solution emerges from a compelling representation of the situation" (Cheney 1987, 143). Tying this in to the narrative approach, he says that "to contextualize ethical deliberation is, in some sense, to provide a narrative, a story, from which the solution to the ethical dilemma emerges as the fitting conclusion" (144). Notice that no grounds are given for accepting that what "emerges" from the situation is indeed the "fitting conclusion" rather than an arbitrary prejudice. No explanation is given as to what we are to look for and how we are to know when we are face to face with it. This is an abdication of justification or accountability, and it is the predictable result when reason is labeled as "abstract" or "universal" and abandoned. The proper approach will bring both care and reason to bear in moral deliberation.

When agents explore circumstances for relevantly similar features, this deliberation encourages the very drawing of connections and relations which ecofeminism rightly insists upon. Such an exploration reinforces our common human experience by inviting us to see the relevant similarity between, for example, the suffering of a Canadian mother whose child has died in a fire and the suffering of a Somali mother whose child has died of starvation. But Cheney's alternative conception of context, where a solution emerges like a creature from a bog, severed in principle from connection to other moral situations, encourages isolation and encourages people to believe that they do not have to bother trying to draw connections between their experiences and those of others.

Self and Other

One major question in environmental ethics, emphasized by both deep ecology and ecological feminism, is the appropriate account of the self in ethical and environmental theories and the appropriate relation of self and other—self and intimates, self and community, self and nature. These environmental theories rightly point out that in many ethical and environmental theories, the self posited is an egoistic self, a self split off from or alienated from others. These theories attempt to overcome these alienations by offering what they see as more appropriate accounts of the self and its relations. Questions about the nature of the self are also bound up with questions about the value of autonomy in feminist and environmental theories.

I begin my examination of this cluster of issues by taking up Plumwood's account, because, I claim, her view of the self-in-relation is most promising. She arrives at her own account after working through and rejecting several alternative accounts of the self offered by deep ecologists who also wish to overcome the alienation of the self. Plumwood looks at three different versions of the self: the indistinguishable self, the expanded self, and the transcendent self. Her critiques of all three are compelling, but I have space here to examine only the indistinguishability account of identification of self with nature. "The indistinguishability account rejects boundaries between self and nature," Plumwood states (1991, 12). To resolve the problem of discontinuity between humans and nature, this deep ecology thesis "proposes to heal this division by a 'unifying process,' a metaphysics that insists that everything is really part of and indistinguishable from everything else" (13). But this move to resolve the problem by "obliterating all distinction" is much too drastic (13). It does not leave room to scrutinize the kind of relation of humans to nature. It holds to a view of the self that has clear dangers, which have been pointed out in the context of feminist care ethics by Jean Grimshaw and Sarah Hoagland (Grimshaw 1986; Hoagland 1991).

Plumwood stresses that "we need to recognize not only our human continuity with the natural world but also its distinctness and independence from us and the distinctness of the needs of things in nature from ours" (13). She refers to Grimshaw, who makes the same point about the question as it recurs in feminist ethics. But Grimshaw goes much further than Plumwood and refers back to R. D. Laing's work on family dynamics in *Sanity, Madness and the Family* and *The Politics of the Family* (Laing and Esterson 1970; Laing 1976). She explores Laing's theories of insanity, which hold that the self of the child who cannot distinguish itself from others in the family drama is the schizophrenic self that had become simply a role or relation in the "family phantasy" (Grimshaw 1986, 177). These daughters (they were all female) had had their basic experiences systematically invalidated to such an extent that "they often felt unable to trust their own judgments in any way, or distinguish between appearance and reality. It also led to severe confusions about self, in the sense that they did not know sometimes whether they thought or wanted something or *if it was they* who thought or wanted it" (177–78). They became insane, according to Laing, because "absolutely any attempts to achieve any form of independence from parental control or wishes were interpreted as 'bad'; all attempts at autonomy were blocked. The progression from 'badness' to 'madness' was a result of the *failure* to achieve any sort of autonomy" (176–77). This autonomy was blocked by the parents in the name of the need "to preserve 'the family' " (177). The daughters were told repeatedly that "they could not, or did not, think, perceive, remember, do, or want what they did, in fact, think, perceive, remember, do and want" (177). This is what Laing calls the invalidation of experience which leads to insanity. Their resulting confusion is accurately described "by the idea that they felt themselves to be 'essentially indistinct as persons' " (178). "Laing often describes them as lacking a sense of 'agency,' of being uncertain whether it was they who actually did or thought things" (178). This is a clear example of the lack of distinctness and autonomy leading to schizophrenia. Grimshaw concludes that "it would clearly be wrong to see this sort of 'indistinctness of persons' as something that feminism ought to applaud or to suppose that the rejection of certain individualistic and egoistic doctrines implies any such thing" (178). I heartily concur with her conclusion, and I think that such clearheaded and commonsensical discussion about what it means to lack autonomy should lead to a strong endorsement of autonomy as an essential feminist value.

From this extremely damaging example of lack of distinctness of self, Grimshaw moves to the example which is taken up by Plumwood. Distinct selves are necessary in situations of care for others, particularly the parent-child relationship. Grimshaw points to the tendency of some feminist theorists (Chodorow and Scheman) to write as if human relationships can be described in terms of two "poles." On the one hand, there is something called "connectedness," which involves being in some way "less distinct from" or "more continuous with" other people; and this is seen as related to the capacity for "empathy" or for the imaginative understanding of others. On the other hand, there is something called "separateness," which involves a lack of this understanding (181–82).

But the mothers in *Sanity, Madness and the Family* "are 'connected' to their daughters in that they see them simply as a projection of a family 'phantasy' of their own beliefs and desires." They can't "conceive of the 'separateness' of their daughters" (182). So Grimshaw's point, quoted by Plumwood, is that

> certain forms of symbiosis or "connection" with others can lead to damaging failures of personal development . . . care for others, understanding of them, are only possible if one can adequately distinguish oneself *from* others. If I see myself as "indistinct" from you, or you as not having your own being that is not merged with mine, then I cannot preserve a real sense of your well-being as opposed to mine. Care and understanding require the sort of distance that is needed in order not to see the other as a projection of self, or self as a continuation of the other. (Grimshaw 1986, 182–83)

The questions that arise here about the theoretical tools needed to analyze and evaluate relationships are myriad. There are enough issues about autonomy and separateness to occupy oneself for quite some time in analyzing even a loving, caring mother-daughter relation; when we turn to cases of schizophrenia and multiple personalities which are linked with severe childhood abuse, the complexities multiply. The need for and value of autonomy for women is so strong, particularly in cases of female survivors of abuse, that feminists should make it a priority to dissolve this dichotomy and restore autonomy to its rightfully valued place in feminist theory.

Since Plumwood fully understands the importance of avoiding the "identification" approach of deep ecology, she argues for a "nonholistic but relational account of the self" which does not deny the "independence or distinguishability of the other," whether the other is another human, the community, or nature (Plumwood 1991, 14). She focuses on the problem of instrumental reason. The solution to the problem is the self-in-relation.

We require a theory that "enables us to stress continuity without drowning in a sea of indistinguishability" (19).

But when Plumwood explains the instrumentalism which is diagnosed as the problem, there seems to be trouble looming for her argument. Having just exhibited considerable skill in her argument that a distinct and independent self is crucial, she seems to undermine her argument by explaining the *problem* in just these terms. She says that "the self that complements the instrumental treatment of the other is one that stresses sharply defined ego boundaries, distinctness, autonomy, and separation from others"; it is a self that "is defined against others, and lacks essential connections to them" (19).

At first glance, it seems as though Plumwood is contradicting herself and undermining the case that she has carefully built. She has taken great pains to establish that a distinct and independent self is of crucial importance; now she seems to be saying that a distinct self is a key part of the problem. One way of looking at her remarks to limit the damage is to interpret her, when she says that the self is one that is distinct but that does not *stress* distinctness, as claiming that the distinctness should not be too pronounced or too strongly emphasized. But then the question is—as against what? The most promising interpretation is that she is claiming that this distinctness must be balanced by other properties having to do with connectedness. So she is not questioning the need for distinctness of selves; she is simply claiming that these distinct selves must have other properties of connectedness as the appropriate balance. This view of the argument is supported by some of her further comments. She says that her "view of self-in-relationship . . . enables a recognition of interdependence and relationship without falling into the problems of indistinguishability, that acknowledges both continuity and difference" (20). So the problem that seemed to loom may have dissipated.

It may be useful at this point to set out what I think is the most helpful view of the self-in-relation at the core of many ethical and environmental theories. I am not claiming that this is the account held by Plumwood or others, but I think that it is the most defensible account.

What do we mean by the notion of a self-in-relation? This notion is nonholistic; that is, it focuses on individual selves. Furthermore, these are distinct selves, so they are not fused with or merged with the other—the individual other, the community, the cosmic whole, and so on. These selves have solid, though not impermeable, boundaries. These selves are not shattered or fragmented selves. They have a core unity which holds their parts together. Though they have many aspects, parts, dimensions, and levels, they are a unity, a unity in diversity. They are autonomous selves, and so they have the ability to rationally scrutinize their different aspects as well as their relations and connections and to endorse, commit to, or reject and repudiate those aspects and relations. They have relations and connections with many things outside of their boundaries—other selves, communities, systems, institutions, projects, goals, and values. This may be described in metaphysical terms by saying that selves have both intrinsic and relational properties. This does not imply that relational properties are extrinsic, in Karen J. Warren's sense of "add on." Relational properties, on the contrary, do indeed play an "essential role" in defining "who we are" (Warren 1990, 143). The intrinsic properties are about that distinct bounded self in itself, not as relating to others. Relational properties are what tie or connect that self to the other—that self's relation to friend, family, community, nature. Relational properties, by definition, are properties of at least two things (thing being construed broadly to include individual things, holistic things, abstract things). But these relational properties of the self are at least the property of this self, anchored in this self, and joining this self to the other. A relation, being a property or attribute, must be a property or quality of some thing(s)—in this case, at least this one self, and at least one other thing. Relations are anchored in things and cannot exist apart from, or be defined apart from, the things they relate.

On this view, a self-in-relation cannot, logically, become fused with another thing, because in order for there to be a relation there must be at least two things which are related, and if two things become fused then there are not two things but one. So not only must there be at least two things for there to be a relation, but a relation is logically and metaphysically dependent upon the two things it relates.

Applying these considerations to the question of self-in-relation, I argue, shows that the self in the self-in-relation is logically, axiologically, and metaphysically prior to its relations, those properties of itself that connect it to others. This is not to deny, however, what is clearly true, that selves are fundamentally affected by and shaped by their relational properties—but there must be something to be shaped or constituted.

In the light of this analysis of self-in-relation, it is instructive to look at Karen J. Warren's theory, as Warren appears to reject some of these elements. She is in agreement with the need for a distinct self. She claims that an ecofeminist perspective "presupposes and maintains difference—a distinction between the self and other. . . . One knows 'the boundary of self,' where the self—the 'I' . . . leaves off. . . . There is no fusion of two into one, but a complement of two entities acknowledged as separate, different, independent, yet in relationship" (Warren 1990, 137).

But I am puzzled by some of Warren's further comments about relations of the self-in-relation. She states that we need "a sensitivity to conceiving of oneself as fundamentally 'in relationship with' others. . . . It is a modality which takes relationships themselves seriously. It thereby stands in contrast to a strictly reductionist modality that takes relationships seriously only or primarily because of the nature of the relators or parties to those relationships" (135). She adds that "recognition of the relationships themselves as a locus of value is a recognition of a source of value that is different from and not reducible to the values of the 'moral beings' in those relationships" (135). If these comments mean that relational properties are important attributes or aspects of the relators, then their meaning is clear. But Warren appears to make a stronger claim, and if this is the case, more clarification and defense are called for.

I can understand quite a few ways in which relations are important to relators. Relations are crucial to defining a self, both in the sense of how others see the self and how the self perceives itself, which may not at all come down to the same thing. Relations are critical to the constitution of the identity of the self. When asked "Who are you?" much of the answer comes in the form of naming our relations. Our relations are clearly critical to our sense of self-worth and to our well-being. While many communitarians greatly overstate the degree to which identity and well-being depend upon such relations of the self, nevertheless it is the case that such relations are essential to identity, well-being, and self-esteem. But these considerations must be balanced by liberal insights that selves have the ability, and must, if well-being is to be enhanced, have the ability, to scrutinize, to accept or reject, these relations. What seems to be too often overlooked in the overvaluing and glorification of connectedness, community, and relation is just how many of our relations could use a healthy dose of autonomous scrutiny. Abusive relations are horrifyingly sustainable and horrifying in their power to construct, define, and maintain a self's identity and undermine the well-being of that self through the power of the defining abusive relations.

But the fundamental theoretical point is this puzzling question: how do any of Warren's claims show that relations are important in themselves apart from their effect on the relators? Take, for example, the relation of being a sister. Suppose that Angela and Ruth are sisters. Suppose that Angela's primary identity is that of being Ruth's sister and that the primary source of her well-being derives from this relation, which she perceives to be loving and supportive. Wherein lies the value of the relation of being a sister in itself, apart from its impact on Angela and Ruth? Suppose further that Ruth, although she consciously feels herself as loving toward Angela, in fact has repressed and denied her rage toward Angela deriving from buried childhood memories. Suppose this buried rage leads Ruth not to intervene when Ruth's husband sexually assaults Angela. Perhaps it even leads Ruth to collaborate in setting up the situation which allows the assault. What sort of value or importance does the relation of being a sister have in itself, not reducible to the effects upon these two individual sisters? It remains, for me, a mystery.

Feminist theory, I argue, badly needs to return to insights achieved early in the wave of feminism of the 1960s. Few seemed to doubt at that time that equality and the end of oppression and domination of women called for an end to the damaging stereotypes of women as self-sacrificing and as especially capable as care givers and nurturers. Few seemed to doubt the value of self-affirmation, strength, independence, and autonomy as indispensable and valuable tools for the emancipation of women. While the breakthroughs of more recent feminism are also, in many cases, of great value, I argue that much has been lost and some theories are actually regressive rather than liberatory in undervaluing reason and autonomy for women (Biehl 1991, 128–30, 133–59). A strong sense of self, a unity of self, a self-affirming, autonomous self are essential.

In "Sisterhood," bell hooks insightfully notes the effect of certain trends within feminist theory:

> Sexist ideology teaches women that to be female is to be a victim. Rather than repudiate this . . . women's liberationists embraced it, making shared victimization the basis for woman bonding. . . . Bonding as victims created a situation in which assertive, self-affirming women were often seen as having no place in feminist movement. . . . Ironically, the women who were most eager to be seen as "victims" . . . were more privileged and powerful than the vast majority of women in our society. An example of this tendency is some writing about violence against women. Women who are exploited and oppressed daily cannot afford to relinquish the belief that they exercise some measure of control, however relative, over their lives. They cannot afford to see themselves solely as "victims" because their survival depends on continued exercise of whatever personal powers they possess. (1992, 392)

What hooks highlights is that some feminist theories have excluded or undermined the position of two groups of women, neither of whom deserves to be abandoned. Both strong, self-affirming women and abused and battered women have been left to one side. (These groups can overlap, because many women are strong and self-affirming because they are survivors of abuse who have healed themselves.) To illustrate the importance of these capacities, it is instructive to look at cases of women who are survivors of severe childhood sexual abuse. While there is little dispute among feminists about the causes of these problems in the most extreme manifestation of tyrannical patriarchy and domination of female children by their fathers, brothers, and other relatives, the dispute lies in issues of the survival, healing, and recovery process. I argue that autonomy and strongly bounded selves are crucially valuable for these recovery processes and that feminist theories should not disown or undervalue these. In fact, it is axiomatic among those who work on these processes that boundary issues are central to the recovery process, and yet many feminist theories overlook this when they devalue strong boundaries and autonomy.

James Glass's *Shattered Selves: Multiple Personality in a Postmodern World* is a critique of postmodernist theories' celebration of multiple and fragmented selves. Many of Glass's arguments are illuminating for my concerns. Glass examines the narratives of women diagnosed as having multiple personality disorder and argues that the postmodernist theories' insensitivity to their extreme suffering reveals the limitations of this approach. These women's situations underscore the importance of cohesive selves and a firm sense of identity for human well-being. Glass explores these examples of incest as a form of tyranny. His view of the self is a psychoanalytic rather than a postmodern one. He says that the stories of these women "of physical abuse and indifference to suffering portray the grimmest aspects of human desire: fathers renting their daughters to other men to satisfy gambling debts, using their daughters as private preserves for the exercise of erotic power . . . mothers refusing to believe their daughters' stories or sitting silently, blindly, while Daddy raped his little girl in the next room" (1993, xviii). To escape the horror and trauma, these girls' identities were split among various alter personalities produced by different trauma experiences. These were isolated and split off from each other, so that the "host" personality, who experienced blackout in periods when other personalities took over, was spared the full horror and suffering held by each alter. The healing process consists of reacquainting these selves with each other and reintegrating and consolidating the multiple personality into a unified whole.

> When the Other in the form of the father as terrorist invades the self's being, the personality responds not as a rational instrument but as a terrorized presence. To keep terror from literally imploding consciousness, the process of dissociation produces an alter personality to live through the force of the father's invasion. (55)

Glass highlights what the psychoanalytic approach can bring to the healing and recovery process, and its insights are those repudiated by some postmodernist perspectives.

> Psychoanalytic views of what the self is depend on clinical observations that describe conditions of real distress. The experiences of selves in pain demonstrate how important it is to think of the self as a malleable structure . . . free to change and choose, but nonetheless a self distinguished not by its fragmentation but by the need to live and survive with fixed points of reference, stable boundaries between self and other, and a firm sense of one's identity as an active agent in the world. (100)

Significant numbers of female survivors of childhood abuse are being diagnosed as multiple personalities, but most victims of abuse do not become multiple personalities. However, these survivors share the multiple personalities' need for strong and secure boundaries and a sense of their own inner healing strength. I now want to outline the case of Elly Danica, who healed herself in part by writing of her experiences in a book called *Don't: A Woman's Word* (1990). This anguishing case study helps me to crystallize the value for women of liberal autonomy and a personal search for self, apart from community constructions and definitions of the self. And it illuminates what I see as some of the dangers of placing too much emphasis on the relational aspects of the self. It also illustrates why I see some dangers in Cheney's rejection of "defining the self by means of individual achievement" and his endorsement of "a relational definition of the self" (Cheney 1987, 130).

From the time she was four years old, Elly Danica was sexually assaulted in the most terrorizing and brutalizing manner by her father. When she was eight her father began taking pornographic photographs of her in a basement room he had arranged as a setting for his assaults. When she was nine her father began selling her to be raped by the judges, farmers, and businessmen of their Saskatchewan community. When she reached out for help to her aunt she was defined as "a bad and dirty child. . . . Filthy kid. Rotten kid. Ugly kid" (Danica 1990, 14). She writes that "at home I am the child who stands apart. The watcher" (25). Her mother tells her she "was mixed up in my mind. She would never be able to trust me again. Once a liar, always a liar" (26). Her sister tells her "she is a liar. She tells terrible lies about daddy. . . . You always lie. . . . You hate him because you are an evil and obnoxious bitch" (28). This is how she is defined by her family. These are her defining relations. "Daddy said you are bad. So you are bad" (29). "Forty. Still bad. Still telling lies. . . . How could I be such a mean and awful bitch." "Forty. A trouble maker. . . . No wonder he hates you. How did you ever get to be so evil? . . . Troublemaker. Man hater. . . . What did any man ever do to you? They can't stand you. It's no wonder" (30–31). "Another sister: learn to be a lady. Keep your mouth shut. He hates you because you provoke him. . . . He doesn't hate me. Only you, because you never learned to keep your mouth shut" (31). Elly writes, "Nothing is as I think it ought to be. Silence. Fear. It is hopeless. A loathing of self without reason. . . . There is something wrong with me. Everyone tells me. The world is not how you imagine it to be. You've imagined everything. Your pain is imaginary. You are imaginary. You are crazy." "My mother dismisses me. I am not significant. . . . She says that I was always an evil child and I am an obnoxious bitch as a woman" (68–69).

Elly marries and leaves home at eighteen. She is sent to a psychiatrist, who says she would get better if she took her pills. Both her husband and her doctor think she would be better if she had a baby. She is forced into pregnancy and motherhood and experiences this as being trapped in a box with the lid nailed down. "Trapped forever." She decides to leave. "I will not stay to have more children. To die in the box" (81–82). Then she is further defined by her community. "What a dangerous bitch. Only a monster would leave her child, her son, not yet two years old" (83). "I stop telling people I have a son. They are too quick with their judgment. Women call me monster, unnatural. No one offers support or understanding. It was beyond reason. My selfishness. You must be crazy. Again. . . . No compassion" (88–89).

Elly moved into an abandoned church on the Saskatchewan prairie, which she called her sanctuary. It did not have plumbing or heat, and she had to cut wood. She lived there for ten years. She made paintings and weavings and bartered them for food and books. She healed herself, finding her self though her own achievement and without the aid of relations or rescue.

> Here is my dream: to live alone in a big house in the country. . . . My dream. Alone. . . . My dream does not include anyone else. I have no energy to bring anyone with me. No energy for relationships, not even with a cat or a goldfish. Alone. A dream to stand alone and tall in sunlight. (92–93)

> Light. A crack in the wall of darkness. . . . No rescuer. No mother wisdom. Fingernails. Teeth. Determination. . . . Soul dwelling: found. Self: found. Heart: found. Life: found. Wisdom: found. Hope, once lost: found. . . . The mind. Free. Freedom. Bestowed from within. Self. . . . I am. (94–95)

Elly affirmed her own inner self, a self achieved and defined from within through personal determination. She rejected all of the devastating defining relations that had been imposed on her by her family and community and redefined herself as someone who was free and capable of love. Her narrative is a moving reminder of the indispensability of reason and autonomy for feminism and ecofeminism.

Note

I presented an earlier version of the second half of this chapter at the Tenth International Social Philosophy Conference, Helsinki, in August 1993. I would like to thank the members of the audience on that occasion for their questions and comments.

References

Beauchamp, Tom, *Philosophical Ethics*, 2d ed., New York: McGraw-Hill, 1991.
Biehl, Janet, *Finding Our Way: Rethinking Ecofeminist Politics*, Boston: South End Press, 1991.

Cheney, Jim, "Eco-Feminism and Deep Ecology," *Environmental Ethics*, 9, Summer 1987, 115–45.

Danica, Elly, *Don't: A Woman's Word*, Toronto: McClelland & Stewart, 1990.

Donner, Wendy, *The Liberal Self: John Stuart Mill's Moral and Political Philosophy*, Ithaca: Cornell University Press, 1991.

——. "John Stuart Mill's Liberal Feminism," *Philosophical Studies* 69, 1993, 155–66.

Glass, James, *Shattered Selves: Multiple Personality in a Postmodern World*, Ithaca: Cornell University Press, 1993.

Grimshaw, Jean, *Philosophy and Feminist Thinking*, Minneapolis: University of Minnesota Press, 1986.

Hoagland, Sarah Lucia, "Some Thoughts about 'Caring,' " in *Feminist Ethics*, ed. Claudia Card, Lawrence: University of Kansas Press, 1991, 246–63.

hooks, bell, "Sisterhood: Political Solidarity between Women," in Janet Kourany, James Sterba, and Rosemarie Tong, eds., *Feminist Philosophies*, Englewood Cliffs: Prentice-Hall, 1992.

Laing, R. D., *The Politics of the Family*, Harmondsworth: Pelican, 1976.

——, and A. Esterson, *Sanity, Madness and the Family*, Harmondsworth: Pelican, 1970.

Plumwood, Val, "Ecofeminism: An Overview and Discussion of Positions and Arguments," *Australasian Journal of Philosophy*, Supplement to Vol. 64, June 1986, 120–38.

——. "Nature, Self, and Gender: Feminism, Environmental Philosophy, and the Critique of Rationalism," *Hypatia* 6, no. 1, Spring 1991, Special Issue on Ecological Feminism, ed. Karen J. Warren, 3–27.

Warren, Karen J., "The Power and the Promise of Ecological Feminism," *Environmental Ethics*, 12, Summer 1990, 121–46.

Twenty-three

Kant and Ecofeminism

Holyn Wilson

Little has been made of Kant's contributions to a theory of anthropology
and environment, and it appears timely now to reconsider the possible interest of his lifelong work in this area.[1] Unlike some of the standard versions of feminism, liberal, Marxist, radical, postmodern, and socialist,
ecofeminism provides an opportunity for reflecting on whether Kant's theory of anthropology might be more consistent with a feminist position than
his ethics is thought to be.[2] Ecofeminist philosopher Karen J. Warren
maintains that human beings must be understood nonoppositionally and
nonhierarchically in the context of their ecosystems, and yet at the same
time she does not want a reductionist account which would (1) eliminate
all differences between human beings and animals, (2) entail biological de-
terminism (Darwinism), or (3) undercut the thesis of the social construction of knowledge and biology.[3] In "Feminism and Ecology: Making Connections," Warren argues that none of the standard versions of feminism
can form an adequate basis for an ecofeminist perspective because none
of them make the connection between nature and women. Thus what is
needed is a transformative feminism which would integrate the positive
insights and contributions of the standard versions while including centrally the ecofeminist insight that naturism is just as much at the root of
patriarchy as are classism, racism, and sexism.[4]

A transformative feminism, Warren writes, "would involve a rethinking
of what it is to be human, especially as the conception of human nature
becomes informed by a nonpatriarchal conception of the interconnections
between human and nonhuman nature . . . that we see ourselves as both
co-members of an ecological community and yet different from other
members of it."[5] A transformative feminism, she argues further, would

390

preserve the socialist feminist acknowledgment of the interconnection of all systems of oppression, the moral theorist's recognition of women's distinct ethical orientation toward care, and the feminist critique of science as socially constructed knowledge. Eliminating patriarchal bias, then, entails most urgently a rethinking of our ethical and scientific relationship to the earth and to nature. In other words, we have to reconceive nature and human nature in order to have a more complete account of what is needed to overcome women's oppression.

I believe Kant's understanding of the human being as *animal rationabile* (animal capable of rationality) rather than as *animal rationale* (rational animal) reflects a point of view on human nature that ecofeminism might find helpful. Other strands of the philosophical tradition (Aristotelian and Cartesian) have located reason as the specific difference in human beings and have thereby hierarchically opposed human beings to animals and the whole natural realm.[6] As opposed to this essentialist tradition, Kant is offering a subtle alternative. Human beings are naturally (essentially) different from other animals, but this is not the basis for any claim to natural superiority. Any claim to superiority can only be imputed to human beings in terms of moral worthiness. Technical and pragmatic uses of reason, which in part differentiate human animality from other animality, do not elevate human beings, unless these uses are in the service of morally worthy action.[7]

When Kant characterizes the human species as the animal capable of rationality, he means that (1) the human species, in distinction to other animals, is capable of moral action and deliberation; (2) the human being is an animal, but with the difference that it has to be educated through concepts and narrative to its destiny,[8] and (3) it is through human judgment that the natural realm can be understood as an organized whole, i.e., as an ecosystem. It is through narratives of the organization of the ecosystem that human beings manage the ecosystem according to arbitrary or nonarbitrary goals.

Ecofeminists believe first of all that there are better ways to relate to women and to nature, and there are also worse ways. The better ways take women's voices and their concerns seriously. Even if Kant did not draw the conclusion that women's humanity is deserving of respect, his theory calls for such a conclusion.[9] Second, ecofeminists want to understand women's concrete involvement with the ecosystem in which they are living; women's narrative of the environment ought to count in the calculus and deliberation on the means for making use of natural resources.[10] Kant's theory of human nature places the human being in its natural environment. Concrete human beings are not isolated, unattached rational beings but are found in groups, whose character as a whole is partially determined by the regional conditions in which they live. Third, Kant argued that we understand human beings as living, organized beings when we judge them purposively, that is, in terms of the general purposes they pursue. Judgment of purpose necessarily gives us a variety of human narratives of the ecosystem, because the narrative will vary according to the purpose pursued. Hence one narrative will never be methodologically adequate to the whole of the ecosystem. Ecofeminism presupposes such a perspective when it argues for the importance of indigenous women's narrative for gaining a better picture of regional ecosystems.[11] Neither scientific nor economic narratives are sufficient if they have not been informed by the feminist perspective and women's regional narratives.

The first part of this chapter will present the argument that Kant had an intense interest in the concrete conditions in which human beings flourish. It is widely known that Kant never traveled from Königsberg in order to gain regional knowledge, but he was well read in the travel journals and reports from those who did travel. His extensive interests in regional conditions elsewhere is amply proved in his physical geography lectures, his anthropology lecture notes, his works on race and physical anthropology. Although these works have obvious implications for issues in social justice, they have, nonetheless, been marginalized by Kantians.

Next I will concentrate on Kant's works on anthropology and teleological (purposive) judgment in order to show Kant's methodological relevance for ecofeminism and ecological premises in general.[12] Much of the secondary literature on Kant and hence much of the feminist critique of Kant centers on his critical works. Much of the feminist critique depends on establishing that Kant's theory of the rational subject is defective in a number of ways, but most primarily because the rational subject is isolated (autonomous) and rational (nonemotional) and has a fetish with objectivity or control.[13] In stark contrast to his critical works, Kant's *Anthropology from a Pragmatic Point of View*, though little mentioned in the English secondary literature, has established that the human species has an animal as well as a rational destiny, and that this latter destiny is a developmental process rather than a given fact that determines human evolution. Human beings are concrete, are attached to each other in purposive ways, and ought to pursue objectivity as part of their technical predisposition, not as part of their pragmatic predisposition. The pragmatic predisposition is developed in skills that harmonize one's activities with those of others. By making these kinds of distinctions based on Kant's theory of anthropology, I hope to show that some of the obvious binary oppositions believed to be guiding Kant's positions are not characteristic of his theory of human nature.

Finally, I will argue that Kant's *Critique of Teleological Judgment* establishes the methodological necessity of teleological judgment for understanding human destiny, natural organisms, and especially the interrelation of organisms in whole systems, i.e., ecosystems. Contemporary biological science excludes teleological judgment and final causality because of its attempt to limit its region of knowledge to the integrity of the organism; as a result, naturalists and ecologists are marginalized as biological scientists, since they require a concept of final causality in order to discuss the interrelations of species.[14] This limitation needs to be critiqued by feminist philosophy of science. In addition, feminist reconsideration of Kant needs to critique the dominant interpretative strategy among Kantians who privilege his transcendental and critical works over his works dealing with the concrete human subject.

Kant and the Alleged
Superiority of Human Beings

It is often pointed out that Kant maintained in his *Lectures on Ethics* that our duties to animals are derivative from our duties to humanity, which seems to imply that human beings are superior to animals. Tom Regan has argued that this is not an adequate ethical basis for our relationship to other beings or, by implication, to the environment and the earth. He suspects that if animals have no independent moral worth or rights, there will be no constraints to commercial, private, and scientific exploitation.[15] The argument generally proceeds as follows: (A) "animals are not persons or human beings," therefore (B) "we do not have direct duties toward them," because (C) "only human beings are ends in themselves." Yet a small detail is continually overlooked by Kant interpreters, and that is that it does not follow even if we accept (A), "animals are not persons or human beings," that (D), "persons or human beings are not animals, i.e., a type of mammal." If we add the premise from Kant's *Critique of Teleological Judgment* and his *Anthropology*, that human beings are animals, then it is not hard to follow Kant's conclusion: cruelty to one type of animal might well lead to the willingness to be cruel to other types of animals, including the human animal.[16] Kant's argument is much more complex than he is given credit for by Kant interpreters.[17] The significant issue here for ecofeminism is whether Kant's commitment to premise (C), "only human beings are ends in themselves," necessarily entails that Kant believed that (1) human beings are superior to animals and that (2) humans are to be understood in opposition to animals, and thereby to the environment.

I take it that ecofeminism is concerned about the presumption of the superiority of human beings insofar as it is propitious to the conclusion often drawn: that it is therefore permissible to dominate other animals and other nature.[18] So the question, as I see it, is whether premise (C) necessarily entails that human beings are opposed to their environments by virtue of their reason and therefore that "humans are morally justified in subordinating plants and rocks."[19] To answer this question in the negative I am not going to speculate about how Kant's theory of morality, i.e., the categorical imperative and the perfect and imperfect duties, can give rise to a duty to animals and to the earth, but rather I am going to turn to Kant's explicit works on the environment and human beings' relationship to it, in order to establish that Kant considered human beings to be a type of animal, whose moral destiny has to be worked out in the natural realm, on the earth, in conjunction with other organic beings. I believe this perspective makes the presumption of the superiority of human beings problematic. Human beings thus cannot simply oppose themselves to the environment and other animals and then unproblematically justify strategies of domination. We too are animals that are dependent on ecosystems. To dominate animals and ecosystems indiscriminately is to dominate ourselves. Kant rejects the simple dichotomy between humans and animals when he writes that human beings are "so dependent on the other creatures on earth, . . . even though his understanding was able to rescue him (for the most part at least) from these devastations."[20]

Kant as Ecologist

Kant's earliest text on the human being's role in the cosmos and on the earth can be found in the *Universal Natural History and Theory of the Heavens*, which appeared anonymously in March 1755. Here Kant articulates for the first time human co-membership in the natural realm:

> Human beings, standing immensely removed from the uppermost rank of beings, are indeed bold to flatter themselves in a similar delusion about the necessity of their own existence. [But] the infinity of nature includes within herself with the same necessity all beings which display her overwhelming richness.[21]

In the natural realm, human beings have no more worth than animals, even if human beings want to accord themselves more importance. In early 1756, Kant expressed a similar thought in his three articles on the Lisbon earthquake. Earthquakes, he argues, point to human powerlessness in the face of natural disasters, and this should not be an occasion to renew our efforts of control and domination, but rather to rethink our relationship to the natural realm. He argues that we demand inappropriately that the ground be so constituted that

> one could wish to live on it forever. With this we flatter ourselves that we could manage everything better to our advantage, if providence had asked our opinion. Thus we wish, for example, to have the rain in our power, so that we could apportion the year according to our comfort, and could always have pleasant days between the overcast ones.[22]

Human beings imagine their reason raises them so far above the natural realm that they believe they could organize nature better, but Kant denies any legitimacy to this presumption. Instead, the very fact that the complexity of nature is beyond human powers gives us cause to rethink our relationship to it. In 1757 Kant introduced his lectures on physical geography, which he continued nearly every year for the next forty years. In the announcement Kant proposes that the character of peoples arises out of their locality:

> The animal kingdom, in which human beings will be viewed comparatively with regard to the differences of their natural form and color in different regions of the earth . . . I shall lecture on this first of all in the natural order of classes and finally cover in geographic survey all the countries of the earth, in order to display *the inclinations of human beings as they grow out of the particular region in which they live*; the variety of their prejudices and types of thinking, insofar as all of this can serve to make human beings more intimately acquainted with themselves; and in order to give a brief idea of their arts, commerce, and science, an enumeration of the . . . products of the various regions, their atmospheric conditions, etc.: in a word, everything which belongs to physical geography [emphasis added].[23]

Human beings are first of all natural beings, with a natural character grounded in regional existence. In a second announcement of these lectures, Kant explains that "the second section considers human beings according to the manifold of their natural characteristics and the differences among them, what is moral about them, *in the whole earth; . . . a very important consideration* [emphasis added]."[24] Kant acknowledges human natural difference, and he believes this gives rise to questions concerning the status of those differences, whether there is something moral about it or not. In his *Anthropology*, Kant maintains that human natural differences do give rise to quasi-moral issues, since difference is purposive for the development toward morality in the human species.[25] Nonetheless, these differences are not themselves moral differences.

In 1771, for the *Königsbergerischen gelehrten und politisehen Zeitungen* (Königsberger Scholarly and Political Newspaper), Kant reviewed an article, "The Essential Bodily Difference in Structure Between Human Beings and Animals," written by the Italian anatomy professor Peter Moscati and published the same year in Göttingen. Kant wonders whether the fact that human beings stand upright can be a basis for elevating human beings above animals. He concludes that uprightness strengthens and weakens human beings in the natural realm, and therefore the physiological differences between human beings and other animals does not give rise to any superiority.

In 1775, in *On the Different Human Races*, Kant introduced his lectures on anthropology, which he was going to hold in conjunction with the physical geography lectures. This publication instigated a dispute between Kant and the naturalist Georg Forster concerning the concept of race.[26] Kant published two more essays (*Determination of the Concept of a Human Race*, and *On the Use of Teleological Principles in Philosophy*) defending the oneness of the human species against racists such as Forster who wanted to see the white race as the original and true form of the human species. In the *Use of Teleological Principles*, Kant began a careful account of the method and principles that should be applied in the organic realm. He was convinced that bias of the type Forster fell prey to could be eliminated by the correct use of appropriate scientific concepts and principles. In other words, proper methodology can eliminate bias. As a conclusion to his entire critical framework, Kant included the *Critique of Teleological Judgment* in the *Critique of Judgment* (1790), which lays out decisively how Kant believed we ought to approach our understanding of organic nature. Then, in 1797, he published *Anthropology from a Pragmatic Point of View*, which was based on his lectures on anthropology. This text lays out Kant's theory of the concrete human subject and presupposes the conclusions of the *Critique of Teleological Judgment*, since it concerns the human being as its "own final purpose."[27]

One common theme running through all these works is that human beings are first of all animals in the system of nature: they are referred to as living earth dwellers or beings (*lebenden Erdbewohner, Erdwesen*)[28] in terms of their animality (*Tierheit*),[29] human species (*Menschengattung*), human being in the system of organic nature (*Mensch im System der lebenden Natur*),[30] and as having natural predispositions (*Naturanlagen*)[31] and temperaments which can be developed toward the human natural destiny (*Naturbestimmung*).[32]

Common to all these works is the theme of the human being as an organic being. Nowhere does Kant assume the superiority of the human species or advocate it; rather he finds he has to struggle in some way to justify distinguishing the human species from other species, since in the system of nature the human species is not marked out for special treatment but must suffer natural disasters and natural laws like any other species. He maintains that the human species has racial characteristics because of environmental factors (climate),[33] national character because of local conditions (mountains, water, trade possibilities due to local resources, etc.), gender difference,[34] and a unique species characteristic that it can make of itself the rational animal through education and the development of its natural predispositions (animal, technical, pragmatic, and moral).[35] What makes the human being different, however, is its ability to conceive of ends through reason and propose the means toward achieving those ends through judgment. In comparison to animals, it turns out that the human species can indeed set arbitrary (survival nonspecific) ends and choose the means toward those ends, which is why human beings can attempt to dominate nature. Yet it is judgment that determines the means for pursuing our ends. The same ends may well be achieved through less violent means.

The four natural predispositions are all teleological in nature. All require the development of skills (means) which help achieve their ends.[36] The end (intent) of becoming an environmental philosopher requires knowledge of organic and natural systems. The end of happiness requires a certain amount of social skill that allows one to harmonize with other human beings. Achieving moral ends requires the development of skills in judgment and the recognition of the equal moral worth of all human beings. No human being has special status with respect to other human beings, but the human being has special status in nature because she or he is the only being "on earth who can form a concept of purposes and use his reason to turn an aggregate of purposively structured things into a system of purposes."[37] Only human beings can cultivate ecosystems, because only they can form the concept of a system. However, their privilege is justified only insofar as they cultivate ecosystems in ways which are consistent with all human beings being treated as ends and never as means only. Human beings are not unproblematically superior; their status calls forth a special responsibility:

> The human being is indeed the only being on earth that has understanding and hence an ability to set himself purposes of his own choice, and in this respect he holds the title of lord of nature; and if we regard nature as a teleological system, then it is the human being's vocation to be the ultimate purpose of nature, *but always subject to the condition*: he must have the understanding and the will to give both nature and himself reference to a purpose that can be independent of nature, self-sufficient, and a final purpose [emphasis added].[38]

The final purpose of all ecosystem stewardship has to be the point of view of finding human beings as subject to moral laws.[39] All other ends will simply be contingent ends that presuppose some self-interest.

Kant's Anthropology

That the human being is an animal is not the complete story. That human beings are guided not merely by instinct[40] but also by reason, which is capable of setting ends, and judgment, which evaluates the worth of those ends, entails that we must inquire deeper into human nature in order to discover why human beings can and do tend toward strategies of domination rather than strategies of living in and with the natural realm. The tendency to dominate nature does not appear to be universal and a result of instinct, since some cultures have organized their society around living in and with ecoenvironmental patterns.[41] Reason also guides and can guide human action, even if not always in a "rational" or productive manner. That is, reason guides human action even when human beings don't do what they believe they ought to. Part of the reason why individual human beings fail to follow through on the rules they hold themselves to is that it is part of the character of the human species that individual human beings find it hard to behave morally when they can anticipate that other human beings are not going to behave morally.[42]

Human beings, according to Kant, unlike other species, have a conflicting internal character of being "unable to do without associating peacefully," as well as being "unable to constantly avoid offending one another."[43] The social motive gives rise to harmony and civilization, refined feelings of sympathy and empathy, tact, decency, manners, aesthetic sensibilities, dispositions of benevolence, etc., which would give us a tendency to live in harmony with other human beings on the earth, and the asocial motive gives rise to tensions and dominating strategies. Kant's works on history and anthropology show us that the ineradicable tension of unsociable-sociability in the individual human being cannot be mediated without the increasing progress of the entire human species toward the development of better civil institutions and world government, i.e., in the universal recognition of the mutual interdependence of human beings.[44]

Kantian anthropology gives us an account of the four natural predispositions which we share in common with all human beings. It also explains why human beings tend toward strategies of domination, since we have the inherent character of unsocial-sociability. Finally, it forecasts the hope of betterment of the current situation in the realization that human destiny is interconnected. Environmental philosophy teaches us that our ecosystems are interconnected and what happens in one region affects other regions. Senators Timothy E. Wirth and John Heinz concluded in their public policy study on ozone: "Like the greenhouse effect, stratospheric ozone depletion is a true global commons problem. POD emissions from any nation eventually affect the ozone layer everywhere. International cooperation in limiting ozone depletion is therefore essential."[45] Kant teaches us that the only resolution of this problem has to lie in the realization of the mutual interdependence of all human beings. In order for all human beings to realize the greatest development of their natural predispositions, the civil condition has to be achieved whereby the "mutually conflicting freedom [of the individuals] is countered by lawful authority."[46] Yet civil society is not enough to resolve environmental regional conflicts. More is needed, and that is "a cosmopolitan whole, a system of all states that are in danger of affecting one another detrimentally."[47] Kant anticipated the development of the United Nations, and he could do so because he recognized that conflicting nations were very much like conflicting individuals. Yet he is wisely skeptical, as feminists are today, of the ability of constitutional and institutional structures to eliminate "people's ambition, lust for power, and greed, especially on the part of those in authority. . . . "[48]

In the logic of this story, however, as it is presented in the *Critique of Teleological Judgment*, Kant has failed to recognize a possibility for the resolution of the conflict of freedoms among people and nations. In paragraph 83, Kant glibly suggests that war is not only inevitable but also a useful incentive for developing talents and skills that contribute to culture. Two centuries later we have experienced and witnessed the utmost devastating power of nuclear war and economic war. These advents are completely self-defeating with respect to the utmost development of the skills of all people. Although Kant opposes the culture of discipline to the culture of skill even in the *Critique of Teleological Judgment*, he fails to articulate an insight he later maintains in the *Anthropology*. Another possibility for overcoming the conflict of freedom is simply for human beings to recognize their mutual interdependence and restrain their actions on the basis of this affirmative interdependence that arises out of social feelings and ideals:

> As culture advances they feel ever more keenly the injuries their egoism inflicts on one another; and since they see no other remedy for it than to subject the private interest (of the individual) to the public interest (of all united), they submit, though reluctantly, to a discipline (of civil constraint). But in doing this they subject themselves only to constraint according to laws they themselves have given, and feel themselves ennobled by their consciousness of it: namely, by their awareness of belonging to a species that lives up to man's vocation, as reason represents it to him in the ideal.[49]

Ecofeminists such as Karen Warren and Vandana Shiva are carrying out this type of response. In thinking through environmental problems, feminists extend the calculus of costs beyond the economic survival of multinational corporations that are often the culprits of environmental exploitation to include the costs and injuries of this exploitation on women and children.[50]

The ethic of care when applied in this context is not a mere paternalism but rather a responsible taking up of the point of view that all human beings ought to count in the calculus of interest and that some human beings, namely enterprisers, ought not to count more. Warren's type of ecofeminism does not emphasize the rights orientation as a response to the conflict of freedoms, because that leads to opposing rights and setting up dualisms and dichotomies. The rights of women and children and the rights of enterprising business appear to be mutually exclusive rights. The care orientation seeks to find a perspective in which such mutually exclusive dichotomies do not arise. One inclusive perspective might be that these women and children are the wives, mothers, sisters, and children of these enterprisers.

Ecofeminism's Critique of
Patriarchal Domination of Nature

Kant defended the rights neither of animals nor of the environment, and with respect to ecofeminism that is a point in his favor, since the justice tradition, with its overemphasis on rights, has come under criticism from the care orientation.[51] With ecofeminism, Kant places the human species on the earth, in its locality, and that is the context in which the human species has to understand itself. Neither Kant nor ecofeminism wants to oppose human beings and the organic realm and then set up their conflicting claims against each other. Ecofeminism sees the tendency toward domination of the environment as an extension of the logic of patriarchy. There is a long sedimented history of thought which has opposed human culture to the natural world.[52] Women have been associated with nature and have been judged to be inferior in this logic of privileging culture over nature. Kant does not reverse this logic but rather supplants it with a rather complicated dialectical logic. Nature is not inferior to culture, because natural talents give rise to the skills of culture.[53] Yet the more culture progresses, the greater the challenge to human freedom and happiness. Kant agrees with Rousseau on this point, but he goes beyond Rousseau in proposing increasing civilization, lawful relations between individuals and nations, as the solution to the conflict of freedoms.[54]

Patriarchal strategies of domination are real, and global laws need to be established in order to curb self-interest. Multinational corporations use rhetoric to convince indigenous people to sell their rights to their own natural resources, without informing these people that the next generation will have no natural resources with which to develop and use their skills. The rhetoric emphasizes participation in the free market but fails to recognize the possibility of sustainable regional economies, which would allow indigenous people both to participate in the free market and to maintain autonomous regional economies. A recent Kant interpreter, Onora O'Neill, argues persuasively that the respect for humanity that Kant is advocating means primarily obtaining consent for action in a context in which dissent is genuinely possible.[55] Indigenous people do not have the possibility of dissent unless they are fully informed of the far-reaching consequences of selling off their rights to their resources. Laws should be introduced to ensure that indigenous people are fully informed, just as patients have rights to be fully informed as to the effects of medical procedures. Until these laws are introduced we can count on the narrow self-interest of multinational corporations to use rhetoric which preempts consent and dissent.

In lieu of adequate global laws, we will have to depend on persuasion to convince the narrowly self-interested. Neither the interests of multinational corporations nor the interests of the human beings who operate them will be served by long-term exploitation of global resources. Kant was right in believing that nature has its own way of educating the human species to the self-defeating consequences of its massive strategies of domination.[56] We now know that the preservation of regional natural resources is essential to the preservation of global natural resources. Nature as a whole is not as vulnerable to exploitation as we think, because we are dependent on nature. Self-interested exploitation will inevitably have consequences that hit home in some other way.

Today we could understand the organization of nature as a whole as the power of nature in the face of the human species' tendency toward self-destruction through technology and overpopulation. These advents ought to lead us to reconsider our strategies of relating to the earth. Domination is one such strategy, but it is a crude and massive strategy that is blind to the complexity of nature. The disastrous results of monoculture agricultural policies indicate the self-defeating consequences of attempting to make nature conform to limited technological ends. The overuse of antibiotics in microbial ecology succeeded in weeding out non-resistant bacteria while increasing the survival capacity of resistant strains. Our experience tells us we are simply up against something much more complex than we know. Just as the organization in the body, according to Kant, eludes all mechanistic explanation, control, and reduction, so the organization in ecosystems and the whole of nature eludes domination.[57] The human species must learn new strategies.

Feminism is articulating some of these new strategies when an ethic of care, reciprocity, diversity, pluralism, and attunement to complexity and context is advocated. This new articulation calls for restraint toward nature as opposed to the unrestrained use of our skills for the purpose of dominating nature. This is consistent with Kant's insight in the *Critique of Teleological Judgment*, that it is the culture of civil discipline and civilization, not the culture of skill, that "furthers the will in the determination and selection of its purposes."[58] Restraint toward nature requires a reflection on which strategies are more appropriate and thus not inherently self-defeating. Greater civilization and greater global regulation are required to restrain selfish exploitation. Methodologically speaking, any environmental ethics has to have some notion of final causality as well as efficient causality in order to bring into consideration the kinds of ends human beings can and ought to pursue in relation to the environment. Patriarchal logic not only constructs social reality by artificial constructions of difference (gender, race, class) and thereby creates artificial boundaries between people, but it also constructs artificial boundaries between the disciplines of knowledge, expertise, and authority. This fragmentation of our knowledge needs to be ameliorated by concepts which mediate between the various disciplines (in this case, between biology and ethics).[59] While environmental ethicists argue about which ethical theory should be embraced and then "applied" to the environment, biologists continue to fragment their discipline (biochemistry, molecular biology, etc.) by devising new methodologies which establish new fields of knowledge.[60] What occurs is a dichotomy between theory and practice which paralyzes us. We need concepts which mediate the various levels of knowledge and discourse.

The Social Construction of Knowledge and Regulative Judgment

In general feminist consensus, ethics and political discourse as well as scientific discourse are socially constructed. Universalism, formalism, objectivity, and neutrality as regulative ideals are themselves social constructs. Yet a critique of the various disciplines which asserts that they are socially constructed is not enough. What is at stake is the purpose for which they are constructed in the way that they are. What is the purpose of trying to understand biological reality on the basis of computer models? What purpose might a formalistic ethics serve? If the disciplines of knowledge are constructed in such a way as to perpetuate patriarchy, then some new methodology needs to be proposed. And we need to know what ends can be served by this new scientific methodology.

Kant's work on regulative judgment, I argue, can offer a way of conceptualizing the relationship between scientific statements based on models and the human dimension of ethical and political discourse. In the *Critique of Teleological Judgment*, Kant argues effectively and influentially for the developing science of biology,[61] that organic nature requires another type of judgment than the mechanistic one required by the mathematical sciences such as physics and mechanics. Kant referred to the latter type of judgment as mechanistic, but he makes it clear that it is any type of judgment that depends on an artificial model, that is, a model of human art or artifacts. The computer models we use today present an alternative model to mechanism but do not differ insofar as computers too are human artifacts, devised to serve some purpose.

The living organism's organization, on the other hand, cannot be sufficiently explained in mechanistic causal terms, since the parts are reciprocally means and ends to one another. In fact, it turns out that we can only judge, not explain, the organization, and that is why teleological judgment must supplement mechanistic judgment. Teleological judgment simply evaluates the purposes of organs with respect to the whole organic being and can evaluate the purposiveness of species for one another. The latter type of judgment represents a type of causal connection grounded in concepts of reason (*nexus finalis*) rather than in concepts of the understanding (*nexus effectivus*), as does the former type of judgment.[62] Teleological judgment, since it is always concerned with ends and purposes, can mediate between biological functionalism and human interests. Using teleological judgment, we judge the purpose of various organs with respect to their place in the whole of the organism. We can legitimately extend that kind of judging to the whole of nature or ecosystems, because what we find in the part we ought to expect in the whole, but in the whole of nature we can judge the purpose of various organisms with respect to one another only on the criterion of each organism's usefulness to other organisms.[63] Consistent with the ecosystem insight into the mutual interdependence of species, Kant claims that no one species, including the human species, can claim unconditionally to be the last purpose or greatest purpose of nature. Finally, as I have already argued, stewardship or cultivation of ecosystems can only be done with respect to some purpose suggested by the stewards.

The human species plays a special role in the living system of nature in that it is only through human narrative that the ecological organization can be seen as a whole. The fact that it is some sort of narrative which organizes our knowledge of the environment is what gives rise to the debate concerning methodology in the social sciences. Evelyn Fox Keller has pointed out that alleged "objective" knowledge is nonetheless related to certain strategies and projects (the project of patriarchy and domination).[64] Standpoint feminists, as Hartsock argues, recognize that taking the standpoint of women tends to give scientific outcomes more favorable to women.[65] Harding has refined the standpoint feminist position and has argued, appealing to the perspective of postmodern feminism, that there can be no one standpoint of women, since there is only a plurality of women's voices.[66] Yet to say that women's various voices, narratives, and experiences have equal legitimacy is to presuppose that it is through human narrative that the environment becomes accessible to us. To the point that women deserve to be heard through their own voices must be added the point that male narratives (science) have been misguided. The initial stance of scientific methodology, then, is that of a critique of patriarchy, a critique of a system of knowledge, ethics, and strategies that privileges and empowers white Western males and conveys the impression that this class of human beings is morally superior to any other class of human beings and deserves therefore to be heard. The second stance will be that women's narratives will be heard and given weight. Many women's narratives of their own regional ecosystems can help give us a fuller picture of the complexity of organic nature. The ends these women pursue give them an access to knowledge of sustainable plant and animal life in their own regions.

One thing is clear: our information concerning animals, sustainable plant life, and the ecosystem will have to be organized through human narrative and judgment, whether through the medium of human scientific or that of human personal narrative. We have no direct access to animal or environmental narrative apart from human narrative. This is another way of saying that human beings are ends in themselves, and other animals are not. Again, I will emphasize that taking human beings as ends in themselves does not necessitate the conclusion that human beings are morally superior to animals and thus may or should dominate the environment. What we do have to conclude, however, is that there is no one right way to cultivate ecosystems, except to say that it should be a responsible cultivation which allows for the greatest possibility that all human beings, including women and children, will be treated as ends in themselves. In order to do that, their perceptions and narratives of the environment have to be heard. Women and children should be able to become an integral part of the ongoing dialogue and be able to promote the direction of the discourse.

The primary contribution Kant can make to environmental ethics, it seems to me, lies in his insight that the organization in organic beings and in the whole of nature exceeds any model presupposing human artifact. The concept of organic organization was intended to defeat the type of mind/body dualism Descartes initiated. Kant was well informed of the debates by the naturalists (Georg Forster), medical anthropologists (Ernst Platner), and physiologists and medical doctors (Samuel Thomas Sömmering, Albrecht von Haller, Georg Ernst Stahl) of his day as they argued for the merits of animism or mechanism or attempted to describe the effects of the soul on the body or the body on the soul.[67] Kant disputed that the soul could be a genuine concept in science, and therefore he maintained that it belonged only in metaphysics. At the same time, he saw the limits of mechanism.[68] The concepts of organization, self-organizing, and reciprocally means and ends were devised by Kant to give biological science critical concepts with which to approach organic nature. Kant and ecofeminism agree that mind/body dualism is inherently misguided when applied to the organic realm. Human knowledge is socially constructed, and that implies that we cannot ignore human intentionality or purposiveness, i.e., human narrative. Computer models are not sufficient for understanding nature; they may be necessary, but they are not sufficient. Teleological judgment needs to supplement knowledge gained on the basis of artificial constructs and models. The kinds of purposes involved in wood gathering by women lead to a kind of knowledge of the ecosystem that is just as legitimate as the kind of knowledge which results from purposes a scientist pursues in trying to understand the greater relationships in the ecosystem. Yet because of patriarchy, environmental strategies have been developed which privilege the scientific and technological domination of the environment without regard for indigenous strategies of living with the complex organization of a regional ecosystem.[69]

Pluralism, Difference, and Human Nature

Current trends in postmodernism and feminism have argued that difference and diversity should be recognized and celebrated. This move is crucial for ecofeminism, since women's experiences vary in different regions of the world. Patriarchy may be pervasive and pernicious, but it is experienced differently, as bell hooks puts it, when one is also a victim of racism or classism.[70] Vandana Shiva argues that Third World women are also victims of "maldevelopment": the resource exploitation of intensive production increases the work for women. She writes, "In Garhawl, for example, I have seen women who originally collected fodder and fuel in a few hours, now traveling long distances by truck to collect grass and leaves in a task that might take two days."[71] European-American women have demanded recognition for their experiences in their own voices, and women of color have also demanded recognition of their experiences in their own voices. Any policies and strategies being advocated for the environment must then be in touch with local perceptions and narratives of experience and understanding of the ecosystem in that region. From the perspective of Western industrialization, indigenous technologies may be viewed as backward, but from the perspective of autonomous sustainable development, these technologies appear appropriate and adequate to fulfill the needs of indigenous people.[72]

The restraint involved in this perspective implies that we live in a pluralistic world, not an individualistic world in which one would be free to pursue one's ends oblivious of the effects of those actions on other human beings. Ecofeminism, then, has a great interest in a pluralistic perception of the world. Practical reason, for Kant, is more fundamental than theoretical reason, and practical reason has to be established publicly among a plurality of voices and agents who share a world.[73] Pluralism makes sense morally, but it also makes sense methodologically. The more narratives we have, the better we are able to perceive the complex organization in the environment. The more we perceive the world through the eyes of others, the more complete our vision becomes.

Kant's lifetime interest in the organic natural world and his interest in the concrete human subject need to be taken more seriously if we are to make a fair assessment of Kant's contribution to patriarchal thinking.

There can be no disputing that Kant interpreters have privileged his critical works over his works on the concrete human subject. Thus his epistemology and his theory of ethics have been assessed apart from his more
embracing view of human life. It may be time to reconsider the relation
between Kant's moral theory and concrete human subjects from this wider
and more complete perspective. As well, the claims that ecofeminism
makes about the relevance of women's narratives and judgment about ecosystems can be justified scientifically as well as morally, if we view nature
methodologically through teleological judgment. Scientific method has
privileged the model of mechanism over the purposive organic model for
the past two hundred years, and the result has been an "objective" view of
nature, a fragmentation of our knowledge, a view of nature that opposes it
to human reason (binary oppositions). Ecofeminism can make its strongest
claim if it attempts to bring scientific discourse and women's narratives
into dialogue with each other on common ground.

Notes

1. I am grateful to the National Endowment for the Humanities for a travel grant
   (1991) awarded to research the influence of the German Enlightenment (biological and pedagogical) on Kant. I became more aware of the importance of
   Kant's works in physical geography and biology through my research. I am
   grateful to Werner Flach of the University of Würzburg for his guidance in
   interpreting these works scientifically. I am also thankful for the helpful comments, critiques, and encouragement I received from the women attending the
   Midwest Society for Women in Philosophy (Washington University, April 9,
   1993). Also, special thanks to Kari Anderson.

2. See Waters (1994).

3. Warren (1987).

4. Naturism assumes that human beings are unproblematically and naturally superior to nature or other organisms and that human beings may then dominate
   nature.

5. Warren (1987, 19).

6. Kant, *Anthropologie im pragmatischer Hinsicht*, 119 and 321 (*Anthropology from
   a Pragmatic Point of View*, 3 and 183).

7. Kant, *Grundlegung zur Metaphysik der Sitten*, 396 (*Fundamental Principles of the
   Metaphysics of Morals*, 14). Kant writes, "For as reason is not competent to
   guide the will with certainty in regard to its objects and the satisfaction of all
   our wants . . . this being an end to which an implanted instinct would have led
   with much greater certainty. . . . " In other words, humans are naturally handicapped by reason, and therefore have a claim to inferiority.

8. Kant, *Anthropologie*, 325 (*Anthropology*, 186).

9. See Waters (1994, 122).

10. Shiva (1993a).

11. Shiva (1993b).

12. Teleology does not mean "goal-directedness" for Kant. This type of Aristotelian understanding of teleology is often what is presupposed in most uses of the word *teleology*. See, for example, Cahen (1988).

13. Schott (1993), in particular chaps. 8–10. Schott gives a type of Freudian-Marxist analysis of underlying themes in Kant and maintains that he has a fetishism with objectivity. My way of characterizing some of these same themes in a different light is made by interpreting them as Kant's concern with a type of self-discipline indispensable for morally worthy action. Nonetheless, Schott's critique of "objectivity" in Kant represents a venerable and central element of feminist critique, which I cannot address in this essay.

14. Atlan (1987).

15. Regan (1983).

16. Kant, *Lectures on Ethics*, 239–41.

17. One major mistake made by Kant scholars is failure to distinguish when Kant is speaking of the transcendental world-purified subject that grounds critical philosophy and when he is speaking of the concrete human subject. Any concrete ethics must include an account of anthropology. See Firla (1981) and Gregor (1963), who argue that Kant's *Doctrine of Virtues* presupposes his anthropology. Some more recent interpreters are beginning to see this as well: O'Neill (1989) and Wood (1991).

18. This is a rather odd proposition simply because it presupposes that human beings are not animals and have no nature.

19. Warren (1990, 129).

20. Kant, *Kritik der Urteilskraft*, 428 (*Critique of Judgment*, 316).

21. Kant, *Allgemeine Naturgeschichte und Theorie des Himmels*, 353–54 (*Universal Natural History and Theory of the Heavens*, 185).

22. Kant, "Geschichte und naturbeschreibung der merkwürdigsten Vorfälle des Erdbebens, welches an dem Ende des 1755sten Jahres einen großen Theil der Erde erschüttert hat," 454.

23. Kant, "Entwürf und Ankündigung eines Collegii der physischen Geographie nebst dem Anhange einer kurzen Betrachtung über die Frage: Ob die Westwinde in unsern Gegenden darum feucht seien, weil sie über ein großes Meer streichen," 9 (trans. in Schilpp [1938, 20]. Schilpp believes that "nearly all of Kant's writings of the sixties show a decided undertone of moral interest," in contrast to the thesis that Kant's interests changed radically from scientific ones with the advent of the critical era (21). This is in line with the thesis developed here that the critical era did not usher in a whole new direction but rather only a critical support of his already well-established interests.

24. Kant, "Nachricht von der Einrichtung seiner Vorlesungen in dem Winterhalbenjahre von 1765–1766," 312.

25. Gender difference, for example, is relevant to the civilization of the human species and thus also for the moralization of the human species.

26. For an account of this dispute, see Fischer (1883, 221–33) and Riedel (1989).

27. Kant, *Anthropologie*, 119 (*Anthropology*, 3).

28. Ibid., 322, 331 (183, 191).

29. Ibid., 327f (188f).

30. Ibid., 321 (183).

31. Ibid., 285, 321–27, 329 (151, 182–87, 189).

32. Ibid., 285, 324 (151, 185).

33. Kant, *Bestimmung des Begriffs einer Menschenrace*, 98, 103.

34. Kant, *Anthropologie*, 303ff (*Anthropology*, 166ff).

35. In the *Anthropologie*, 322ff (183ff), Kant lists the predispositions as the technical, the pragmatic, and the moral. In *Die Religion innerhalb der Grenzen der bloßen Vernunft*, 26 (*Religion within the Limits of Reason Alone*, 21), the three predispositions discussed are the predispositions to animality, humanity, and personality. The account of the predisposition to animality is missing in the *Anthropologie*. In the *Religion*, the account of the technical predisposition is missing. This does not necessarily represent a conflicting account of the four original predispositions, since the descriptions are given with respect to different purposes.

36. Kant, *Anthropologie*, 322–25.

37. Kant, *Kritik der Urteilskraft*, 427 (*Critique of Judgment*, 314).

38. Ibid., 445 (334).

40. Kant, *Anthropologie*, 325 (186).

41. See Momaday (1994).

42. Kant, *Religion*, 27 (22).

43. Kant, *Anthropologie*, 331.

44. Kant, *Kritik der Urteilskraft*, 432 (320), and *Anthropologie*, 329 (190).

45. Wirth and Heinz (1994).

46. Kant, *Kritik der Urteilskraft*, 432 (320).

47. Ibid.

48. Ibid., 433 (320).

49. Kant, *Anthropologie*, 329 (190).

50. I am referring to a presentation Karen Warren made at the 1993 Chicago meeting of the International Society for Environmental Ethics.

51. Gilligan (1987).

52. Griffin (1989).

53. Immanuel Kant, *Tugendlehre*, in *Kants Gesammelte Schriften*, vol. 6, 444.

54. Kant, *Anthropologie*, 326–27 (187–88).

55. O'Neill (1989, 105–25).

56. Kant, *Anthropologie*, 328 (188–89).

57. Kant, *Kritik der Urteilskraft*, § 78.

58. Ibid., 431–32 (318–19).

59. One way in which patriarchal logic prevails is in isolating and fragmenting not only women but also experience itself.

60. Atlan (1987, 121).

61. See Lenoir (1989).

62. Kant, *Kritik der Urteilskraft*, 409 (294).

63. Ibid., 380–81 (260–61).

64. Keller (1984).

65. Hartsock (1983).

66. Harding (1987, "Conclusion").

67. Among the animists, one can count Georg Ernst Stahl (see Stahl, 1961), whom Kant mentions in the preface of the *Critique of Pure Reason*. For discussion see King (1964) and Lenoir (1989). For a medical anthropologist, see Ernst Platner (1772); see also Mclaughlin (1985).

68. Kant, *Kritik der Urteilskraft*, 410–11 (295).

69. Warren (1990, 143).

70. See hooks (1984).

71. Shiva (1989, 85–86.)

72. Ibid., 88.

73. See O'Neill's impressive argument (1989, 3–27). Kant uses the word *pluralism* (even in the German) to characterize those people who are not egotists but rather have a type of thinking in which they perceive themselves as world citizens and behave in a like fashion (*Anthropologie*, 130).

References

Atlan, Henri. "Unconscious Finalities," in *Gaia, a Way of Knowing: Political Implications of the New Biology*, pp. 110–127. Ed. William Irwin Thompson. Hudson, N.Y.: Lindisfarne Press, 1987.

Cahen, Harley. "Against the Moral Considerability of Ecosystems." *Environmental Ethics*, Fall 1988, 195–216.

Firla, Monika. *Untersuchungen zum Verhältnis von Anthropologie und Moralphilosophie bei Kant*. Frankfurt/Bern: Peter Lang, 1981.

Fischer, K. *Immanuel Kant und seine Lehre*. Vol. 2. Munich, 1883.

Gilligan, Carol. "Moral Orientation and Moral Development," in *Women and Moral Theory*, pp. 19–33. Ed. Eva Feder Kittay and Diana T. Meyers. New York: Rowman & Littlefield, 1987.

Gregor, Mary J. *Laws of Freedom*. Oxford: Blackwell, 1963.

Griffin, Susan. "Split Culture," in *Healing the Wounds: The Promise of Ecofeminism*. Ed. Judith Plant. Philadelphia: New Society, 1989.

Harding, Sandra. *Feminism and Methodology*. Bloomington: Indiana University Press, 1987.

Hartsock, Nancy. "The Feminist Standpoint: Developing the Ground for a Specifically Feminist Historical Materialism," in *Discovering Reality: Feminist Perspectives on Epistemology, Metaphysics, Methodology and Philosophy of Science*, pp. 283–310. Ed. S. Harding and M. Hintikka. Dordrecht: Reidel, 1983.

hooks, bell. *Feminist Theory: From Margin to Center*. Boston: South End, 1984.

Kant, Immanuel. *Kants Gesammelte Schriften*. Ed. Königlich Preußische [now Deutsche] Akademie der Wissenschaft. Vols. 1–29. Berlin: G. Reimer [now de Gruyter], 1902– .

———. *Allgemeine Naturgeschichte und Theorie des Himmels*, in *Kants Gesammelte Schriften*, vol. 1, 215–368. Translation: *Universal Natural History and Theory of the Heavens*. Trans. and intro. Stanley L. Jaki. Edinburgh: Scottish Academic Press, 1981.

———. *Anthropologie im pragmatischer Hinischt*, in *Kants Gesammelte Schriften*, vol. 7, 117–333. Translation: *Anthropology from a Pragmatic Point of View*. Trans. Mary Gregor. The Hague: Martinus Nijhoff, 1974.

———. *Bestimmung des Begriffs einer Menschenrace*, in *Kants Gesammelte Schriften*, vol. 8, 89–106.

———. "Entwürf und Ankündigung eines Collegii der physischen Geographie nebst dem Anhange einer kurzen Betrachtung über die Frage: Ob die Westwinde in unsern Gegenden darum feucht seien, weil sie über ein großes Meer streichen," in *Kants Gesammelte Schriften*, vol. 2, pp. 1–12.

———. "Geschichte und naturbeschreibung der merkwürdigsten Vorfälle des Erdbebens, welches an dem Ende des 1755sten Jahres einen großen Theil der Erde erschüttert hat," in *Kants Gesammelte Schriften*, vol. 1, pp. 429–62.

———. *Grundlegung zur Metaphysik der Sitten*, in *Kants Gesammelte Schriften*, vol. 4, 385–464. Translation: *Fundamental Principles of the Metaphysics of Morals*. Trans. Thomas K. Abbot. Indianapolis: Bobbs-Merrill, 1949.

———. *Kritik der Urteilskraft*, in *Kants Gesammelte Schriften*, vol. 5, 165–485. Translation: *Critique of Judgement*. Trans. Werner S. Pluhar. Indianapolis: Hackett, 1987.

———. *Lectures on Ethics*. Trans. Louis Infield. Indianapolis: Hackett, 1963.

———. *Die Metaphysik der Sitten*, in *Kants Gesammelte Schriften*, vol. 6, 203–493. Translation: *The Metaphysics of Morals*. Trans. Mary Gregor. New York: Cambridge University Press, 1991.

———. "Nachricht von der Einrichtung seiner Vorlesungen in dem Winterhalbenjahre von 1765–1766," in *Kants Gesammelte Schriften*, vol. 2, pp. 303–14.

———. *Die Religion innerhalb der Grenzen der bloßen Vernunft*, in *Kants Gesammelte Schriften*, vol. 6, pp. 1–202. Translation: *Religion within the Limits of Reason Alone*. Trans. Theodore M. Greene and Hoyte H. Hudson. New York: Harper & Row, 1960.

Keller, Evelyn Fox. *Reflections on Gender and Science*. New Haven, Conn.: Yale University Press, 1984.

King, Lester Snow. "Stahl and Hoffmann: A Study in Eighteenth Century Animism." *Journal of the History of Medicine and Allied Sciences* 19 (1964): 118–30.

Lenoir, Timothy. *The Strategy of Life*. Chicago: University of Chicago Press, 1989.

Mclaughlin, Peter. "Sömmering und Kant: Über das Organ der Seele und den Streit der Fakultäten," in *Samuel Thomas Sömmering und die Gelehrten der Goethezeit*. Stuttgart: Fischer, 1985.

Mies, Maria, and Vandana Shiva. *Ecofeminism.* London: Zed, 1993.

Momaday, N. Scott. "Native American Attitudes to the Environment," in *The Environmental Ethics and Policy Book: Philosophy, Ecology, and Economics,* pp. 102–5. Ed. Donald VanDeVeer and Christine Pierce. Belmont, Calif.: Wadsworth, 1994.

O'Neill, Onora. *Constructions of Reason: Explorations of Kant's Practical Philosophy.* Cambridge: Cambridge University Press, 1989.

Platner, Ernst. *Anthropologie für Aerzte und Weltweise* (1772).

Regan, Tom. *The Case for Animal Rights.* Berkeley: University of California Press, 1983.

Riedel, Manfred. "Historizismus und Kritizismus. Kants Streit mit G. Forster und J. G. Herder," in *Urteilskraft und Vernunft: Kants ursprüngliche Fragestellung,* pp. 148–70. Frankfurt: Suhrkamp, 1989.

Schilpp, Paul Arthur. *Kant's Pre-Critical Ethics.* Evanston: Northwestern University, 1938.

Schott, Robin May. *Cognition and Eros: A Critique of the Kantian Paradigm.* College Park: Pennsylvania State University Press, 1993.

Shiva, Vandana. "Development, Ecology, and Women," in *Healing the Wounds: The Promise of Ecofeminism.* Ed. Plant. 1989.

———. "The impoverishment of the environment: Women and children last," in *Ecofeminism,* pp. 70–90. Ed. Maria Mies and Vandana Shiva. London: Zed, 1993a.

———. "Women's indigenous knowledge and biodiversity conversation," in *Ecofeminism,* pp. 164–73. Ed. Mies and Shiva. London: Zed, 1993b.

Stahl, Georg Ernst. *Über den Unterschied zwischen Organismus und Mechanismus.* Trans. B. J. Gottlieb. Leipzig, 1961.

Warren, Karen J. "The Power and the Promise of Ecological Feminism," *Environmental Ethics* 12, no. 2 (Summer 1990): 125–46.

———. "Feminism and Ecology: Making Connections," *Environmental Ethics* 9, no. 3 (Winter 1987) 3–20.

Waters, Kristin. "Women in Kantian Ethics: A Failure in Universality," in *Modern Engendering: Critical Feminist Readings in Modern Western Philosophy,* pp. 117–25. Ed. Bat-Ami Bar On. Albany: State University of New York Press, 1994.

Wirth, Timothy E., and John Heinz. "Ozone Depletion," in *The Environmental Ethics and Policy Book,* pp. 589–92. Ed. VanDeVeer and Pierce. 1994.

Wood, Allen W. "Unsociable Sociability: The Anthropological Basis of Kantian Ethics," *Philosophical Topics* 19, no. 1 (Spring 1991): 325–51.

Twenty-four

Women–Animals–Machines
A Grammar for a
Wittgensteinian Ecofeminism

Wendy Lee-Lampshire

Autonomy, Anatomy, Anonymity from
Descartes to Churchland

Among the most common political objections raised by feminists to the articulation of a uniquely feminist standpoint is that it is destined to essentialize the experiences and perspectives of some women (usually white, educated, heterosexual women) at the expense of others. Whether any such things can exist as *the* feminist standpoint, *the* standpoint of marginalization, or *the* standpoint of the oppressed invites questions which go to the very heart of dissent among black, Hispanic, radical, lesbian, Jewish, Third World, and many other underrepresented feminists.[1] I suggest, however, that political objections to the articulation of a feminist standpoint are the least of its problems; *its philosophical troubles run much deeper.*

One such trouble is that the notion of a single unified standpoint able to represent the experiences of all women tacitly presupposes the same model of epistemic privilege utilized to underwrite the oppression of women throughout post-Enlightenment Western history: Cartesian introspection.[2] A common criticism aimed at the analyses of oppression by Betty Friedan and Dorothy Dinnerstein, for instance, is that in their attempt to be inclusive they tacitly assume that their experience *as women* gives them privileged insight into the experience of all women. As Susan Bordo and Sandra Harding point out, however, such analyses fail the moment we re-

412

alize that inclusivity requires an epistemology as much rooted in Cartesian dualism as that which has served so well to identify women with the bodily, the irrational, and the passive.[3]

Harding and Bordo argue that to universalize all of women's experience on the basis of one individual's or even one group's experience is to sever the conceiving mind from the experiencing body as inexorably as Descartes did. For nothing could guarantee the universality required to achieve inclusivity other than some form of introspective transcendence, that is, introspectively generated knowledge that one's own experience as a woman represents that of all women in a way which transcends cultural or other differences. This transcendence, however, is itself rooted in the same mind-body dualism that, insofar as women have been traditionally identified with the body conceived as inferior and irrational, has served to legitimate oppression. Thus, because Friedan's and Dinnerstein's conception of women's experience tacitly endorses this dualism, it is ill-suited to found an emancipatory feminist standpoint.

However important and well-documented, this criticism is rapidly becoming overshadowed by a far more serious threat from a quarter seemingly remote to feminist theory and politics: the eliminativist trend in contemporary philosophy of mind-brain. According to eliminativists such as Paul Churchland, Patricia Smith-Churchland, and Steven Stich, recent advances in genetics, neurophysiology, and evolutionary theory may well be antiquating the use of such so-called psychology terms as *mind, self, intention, subject, autonomy*, and *I*, by showing how these terms have no physical analogues.[4] In short, since words like *mind* do not name anything, we have no justification for their continued use in the explanation of behavior; a naturalistically conceived world fully explicable in terms of physical laws has no room for occult objects like "minds." Eliminativists predict that just as the term *phlogiston* was replaced by *oxygen*, so the terms we use to describe mental events will inevitably be replaced by terms that more accurately describe physical processes; in effect, anatomy will replace autonomy just as surely as the discovery of the earth's rotation around the sun displaced human beings from the universe's conceptual center to the sun's anonymous periphery.

Any standpoint which presupposes a subject whom the standpoint represents is endangered by eliminativism, particularly if the subject's autonomy is a necessary condition for critique. When this subject is a woman, an especially ironic situation ensues, for the autonomy presupposed as a necessary condition for critique has little precedent in traditional historical accounts of women. That is, since historical accounts of women have rarely been treated as accounts of autonomous subjects, what could become antiquated on an eliminativist program is at best unclear.[5] Doubly ironic is that just as women have begun to achieve political autonomy in some parts of the world, philosophers, principally male (Derrida, for instance) have undertaken to challenge the notion of "subject." Yet the eliminativists are correct about at least one thing: the scientific evidence antiquating notions like "mind" is becoming more compelling. The task, then, for anyone attempting to articulate a feminist standpoint is not only to reconceptualize subjecthood but also to reconceptualize a *naturalist* alternative of "subject" able to account for women's historiographical absence.

Another Kind of Naturalism: What Wittgenstein Does

The alternative to the eliminativist's bleak scenario is to be found in the remarks of the later Wittgenstein. Through his *experimental style*, that is, his use of example, portrayal, and question, Wittgenstein exemplifies the myriad ways that psychological terms are used not as names for occult entities such as minds but as ways of describing the relationship between something and its bio-psycho-social and historical context. In *Philosophical Investigations*, paragraph 282, Wittgenstein remarks:

"But in a fairy tale the pot too can see and hear!"
(Certainly; but it *can* also talk.)
"But the fairy tale only invents what is not the case; it does not talk *nonsense*."—it is not as simple as that. Is it false or nonsensical to say that a pot talks? Have we a clear picture of the circumstances in which we say of a pot that it talked? (Even a nonsense-poem is not nonsense in the same way as the babbling of a child.) We do indeed say of an inanimate thing that it is in pain; when playing with dolls for example.[6]

And further, at paragraph 283:

What gives us *so much as the idea* that living beings, things, can feel? Is it that my education has led me to it by drawing my attention to feelings in myself, and now I transfer the idea to objects outside myself? That I recognize that there is something here (in me) which I call "pain" without getting into conflict with the way other people use this word? I do not transfer my idea to stones, plants, etc. Couldn't I imagine having frightful pains and turning to stone while they lasted? Well, how do I know, if I shut my eyes, whether I have not turned to stone? And if that has happened, in what sense will *the stone* have the pains? In what sense will they be ascribable to the stone? And why need the pain have a bearer here?! And can one say of the stone that it has a soul and *that* is what has the pain? What has a soul or pain to do with the stone? Only of what behaves like a human being can one say that it *has* pains. For one has to say it of a body, or, if you like, of a soul which somebody *has*. And how can a body have a soul?[7]

These passages portray several ways in which psychological terms like *pain* or *soul* are used. However, much more is going on here than revelation of variety in language use. For through the use of psychological terms Wittgenstein effectively treats things—human and nonhuman—*as if* they were subjects, and in so doing shows the following: first, how the meaning of a term *is* its use; second, what little sense it makes to say that psychological terms are names for mental entities; third, how critical the use of psychological terms is for understanding the behavior and actions of things.[8]

When we say that a pot, a doll, a stone, or a human being has pain or a soul, how are we using the terms *pain* and *soul* in each instance? What does each use tell us about the relationship between that thing and its context? What sense does it make to treat each of these things as subjects, that is, as things which warrant the application of psychological terms? Where is the line to be drawn between a descriptively useful and a nonuseful application (between animate and inanimate, neurologically complex or simple, things that look human and things that do not)? Among the many questions the passages evoke, these suggest not only that the ordinary use of psychological terms is not reducible to the naming of mental entities but that variety of usage provides a basis for understanding the relationship of a thing to its context. Treating the pot as animate *may* turn out to be uninformative, but, as Wittgenstein's example suggests, this depends upon the circumstances in which such an application is made.

The question "Where is the line to be drawn between descriptively useful and nonuseful?" is difficult to answer. A nonsense poem in which a pot is said to talk is by no means senseless; it is not, as Wittgenstein points out, like the babbling of a child (which itself is not necessarily senseless but is differently sensible from a talking pot). Perhaps the circumstances under which the pot is said to talk are strictly fictional, given its inanimacy. But what if, instead of a talking pot, the nonsense poem portrayed a talking computer? What if we say of the pot we just dropped, "Oh! I bet that hurt!"? Wittgenstein asks us to imagine turning into stone while we are experiencing pain. When does the application of the word *pain* no longer make sense? When we could no longer be said to have a soul? What sorts of objects can be described as having a soul?

As opposed to names for mental entities, Wittgenstein treats psychological terms as *metaphors or descriptive heuristics* for the complex system-context relationship expressed in something's behavior. We can imagine cases like the following where the application of the word *pain* is best understood as a metaphor which describes something's behavior in a way that no purely physical description could. In *Philosophical Investigations*, paragraph 284, Wittgenstein remarks:

Look at the stone and imagine it having sensations.—One says to oneself: How could one so much as get the idea of ascribing a *sensation* to a *thing*? One might as well ascribe it to a number!—And now we look at a wriggling fly and at once these difficulties vanish and pain seems to get a foothold here, where before everything was, so to speak, too smooth for it.[9]

What is the difference between a stone's rolling down a hill and a wriggling fly's sliding down a window pane to a window ledge? It's not that one behaves while the other does not; they both behave. However, the rock's behavior is fully explicable in terms of physical concepts, such as gravity, angle, and momentum, whereas, although such concepts apply to the fly's behavior as well, they do not exhaust that behavior. But does "pain get a foothold here" simply because we say that one is animate while the other is not? This is strange, considering that such a criterion is as trivial as it is true; we would not attribute any more sentience about this fact to the fly than to the stone. Yet the fly *wriggles*. Its behavior exhibits some unspecified minimum of behavioral indeterminacy, and this is enough like those things that we say "have" mental states to attribute pain to it.

I believe Wittgenstein's point is twofold. First, no unambiguous transition occurs between such cases; to say that one thing exhibits mental states and one thing does not is uninformative with respect to explaining their behavior. Second, although attributing mental states to the fly does sound strange, describing the fly's behavior via the use of words like *pain* is not uninformative. For on a Wittgensteinian account to say that something believes or has pain is to treat that something *as a subject*; this is to treat it as an entity whose relationship to and within a context is of sufficient complexity that to use psychological terms to describe its behavior is warranted on the ground that such an application helps make sense of this complexity. To say that the fly wriggles because it *wants* to live or because it *knows* that it is injured tells us something about the fly regardless of its sentience, for it gives us a framework within which the fly's behavior makes sense.

On a Wittgensteinian account we neither need nor can mark any point of transition whereby the use of psychological terms becomes appropriate; instead, we ask whether treating something as a subject is informative. What we discover is not only that answers to this question are as various as the circumstances in which we use such terms, but that under some circumstances the use of psychological terms offers the most viable route toward understanding the relationship between something and its context.

Wittgenstein offers a viable, naturalist alternative to eliminativism. For while he agrees with eliminativists that no such things as mental entities exist, Wittgenstein shows that the use of psychological terms to describe behavior in no way depends on the existence of such entities. Wittgenstein's portrayals and examples effectively discredit the analogy that psychological terms stand to behavior as nouns stand to objects in the world, as names, and he does so in a way that is fully consistent with a naturalist framework. For conceived as metaphors or descriptive heuristics, psychological terms apply not to an entity alone but to an entity's *relationship* to all of the myriad factors which inform a context. The applicability of a term thus depends upon how much more sense can be made of something's behavior within this context, a simplistic-sounding criterion that nevertheless contains everything essential to its adequacy. For this criterion is firmly tethered not only to the assumption that the application of a psychological term must allow us to explain more than its eliminativist rival, but to a naturalist framework within which we can assess empirical evidence.

Dissonance: Another Kind of Information

Just as the use of terms such as *belief* or *intention* to describe complex behavior need not commit us to the view that an organism or system really has such mental objects, so could feminists appropriate terms common to feminist discourse without making essentialistic assumptions about what all women's experience really has in common. This is not to suggest that any particular vocabulary unique to feminism exists; instead, a Wittgensteinian strategy offers a radically novel way of using terms common to feminist discourse—*mother, dyke, virgin, body, whore, blood, marginality, woman, emancipation*—as *metaphors* for the complex bio-psycho-social and historical positions that women occupy.

Instead of attempting to articulate the nature of women's experience or compensate for a globally conceived subordination under patriarchy, such a strategy suggests that to attribute subjecthood to women (as to anything else) is to treat women as the occupants of complex psychosocial positions. No different in principle from the application of psychological terms to the fly or the teapot, this strategy asks how much more sense could be made of women's experiences were we to treat terms common to the feminist lexicon heuristically, as ways of describing the contexts which imbue experience.

If treating flies and teapots as if they were subjects is informative under some circumstances, treating women as historical subjects—as thinking and feeling beings within an historical locale—ought surely to prove that much more informative about women. This, however, is not the case. Indeed, rather than the rich pool of information hoped for by the compensatory historian, reconceiving women as historical subjects produces nothing less than a resounding dissonance between the complex positions that women occupy in the present and the lack of subjecthood that characterizes typical representations of women in the past.[10]

This dissonance is captured by terms critical to the feminist vocabulary. For whether elevated or denigrated, dominating or dominated, typical historical stereotypes of women as whore, other, hysteric, tomboy, dyke, coquette, dutiful daughter, or heroine hold one thing in common *cross-cultur-*

ally—lack of subjecthood. Note that we do not need to be able to characterize all historical representations of women in terms of this lack, nor need we be able to exhaustively define what each stereotype means or includes. We need only be able to show that portrayals of women bear enough of a "family resemblance" cross-culturally with respect to lack of subjecthood that to treat women as historical subjects fails; and this claim is well borne out by the many failed attempts at writing compensatory history.[11]

The failure of compensatory history, however, justifies conceiving dissonance as a kind of information. Dissonance is information about the gaps, incongruities, continuities, in short, the relationship between women and their historical representations. How much more sense the metaphorical application of a "feminist" term makes of this relationship depends upon the dissonance the application produces. For the *differences* between women's historical portrayals and the self-conceptions we have striven to articulate are themselves something shared among women. Dissonance provides an interstice for the critical evolution of historical stereotypes in that the lack of subjecthood which characterizes these stereotypes is not only an obstacle to universalizing claims, but a vehicle by which to make sense out of this lack. Dissonance describes an interstice between positions that women *have* occupied and those that women *do* occupy, between images of past and present.

Dissonance characterizes the relationship between stereotypes of the past and complexities of the present; however, it also characterizes the relationship between these same psychosocial positions and current images of women. Little more than a glance at a Budweiser, Barbie, Windex, or Rice-a-Roni commercial, a glimpse of an Indian movie advertisement or Japanese corporate roster, or a peek at U.N. labor statistics is needed to convince you that many current images of women are not images which warrant the attribution of psychosocial complexity. For example, a recent commercial for Diet Pepsi opens with several women swaying and stroking themselves to the piano rhythm of a male celebrity. The camera then pans back to reveal a perspiring, musically engaged all-male band. For just a second, the camera focuses on the face of one band member and then follows his line of vision forward toward the swaying women's breasts. The camera then pans down to the celebrity, who is thirstily consuming the contents of a bottle of Diet Pepsi, and then up just in time to glimpse the women's collective "Uh Huh!" The message is subtle but clear. The celebrity is already a subject for the viewing audience; so too his band, who, by association, share the same status as active engaged musicians. The women's status as subjects, however, is lacking, since their role in the commercial is defined not by their musical contribution or even their thirst but rather by their ability to elicit images of consumption, sexual or otherwise.

Like Diet Pepsi, women are things to be consumed by subjects but are not subjects themselves.

For whatever their cultural differences, images of rental wombs, dumb blondes, "Stepford wives," super moms, sexual disposables, veils, "hospitality" girls, even feminists provide precisely the interstice—the discursive space—which makes the articulation of a feminist standpoint possible. For these images, like their historical predecessors, share one common characteristic: lack of subjecthood. Just as we may reconceive historical stereotypes as metaphors for the contexts which produced and maintained them, so we may reconceive present images of women as metaphors for the contexts which make women so different from each other. Our criterion here is the same as above: how much more sense can we make of the psychosocial positions women occupy via such a strategy?

The answer is striking. For the dissonance produced by the heuristic application of a flat image onto the context of a complex life exposes what I take to be at the heart of feminism's internal struggle to articulate a standpoint, namely, further dissonance between being a subject and being a woman, between being something which warrants attribution of psychosocial complexity and being classified as female.

The implicit denial of subjecthood which characterizes images of "Stepford wives" and welfare queens, the denial that allows some antiabortion activists to justify their position by characterizing women as incapable of making moral decisions, the denial that fuels Camille Paglia's reinvigoration of the slogan "no means yes," stand in stark contrast to the complexity of experience which differentiates, for instance, bell hooks from Judith Butler, Mary Daly from Donna Haraway.[12] As I will show, the very acts of self-reference which serve to differentiate women from each other are acts that contravene these images and thus heighten the dissonance. For regardless of other differences, women share this much in common: in no clear sense are being-a-subject and being-a-woman compatible.

The notion of *speaking* woman, of the act of self-reference contained in the word *I*, generates dissonance.[13] For this act tacitly contains the subjecthood that both past and present images of women deny. To speak "I" is to implicitly *be* that position from which a given utterance takes place; it is to claim to be what women, given these images, cannot be, namely, subjects. Given this denial, it's no wonder that the articulation of a feminist standpoint should be so difficult; it's only a wonder that women from cultures so different and differently oppressive should find enough in common to make the dispute over what a feminist standpoint represents worthwhile. Self-referential acts provide the needed key for overcoming this denial, for through such acts we can reconceive the psychosocial position from which such words are uttered. That is, we may reconceive the self-reference embodied in the attribution of subjecthood as a metaphor for psychosocial complexity.

This reconceptualization is wholly consistent with the Wittgensteinian strategy exemplified thus far in that "I" is paradigmatic of the kinds of psychological terms which are indispensable to the description of complex organisms. By this same token, the application of "I" as a metaphor to some human individuals (some white men), well describes the complexities that differentiate their experience. Applied to women, however, "I" serves to expose what women and all oppressed persons share—the denial of subjecthood expressed in the dissonance produced by acts of self-reference. Conceived as a metaphor for the relationship between women and their bio-psycho-social contexts, and given the dissonance this produces, acts of self-reference by women are as ambiguous as those of animals and machines; yet it is here that a feminist standpoint becomes articulable as a Wittgensteinian ecofeminism.

Sketching a Wittgensteinian Ecofeminism: Women, Animals, Machines

In "A Manifesto for Cyborgs" Donna Haraway argues that trends in contemporary science and technology have rendered traditional grounds for distinguishing between human beings, animals, and machines thoroughly ambiguous if not obsolete.[14] She argues that advances in neurophysiology, cybernetics, and evolutionary theory are bound to be followed by a "confusion of boundaries" with respect to what counts as a subject. For Haraway, this confusion is epitomized in the image of the cyborg. Neither wholly biological nor wholly artificial, its possibility poses a threat to traditionally drawn distinctions between natural-artificial, observer-observed, real-fake, agent-patient, rational-irrational-nonrational, mind-body.[15]

Haraway's confusion of boundaries is relevant for feminists in that, as a wealth of feminist scholarship demonstrates, each of these distinctions is reflected in historical portrayals of women as nonsubjects. In fact, boundary confusion is much of a piece with the notion of dissonance discussed above. For within the interstice or boundary between representations of past women as bodies, patients, the nonrational, and the struggle to articulate women's present experience is engendered the dissonance and confusion that frustrates attempts to develop critical postures. This confusion is further reflected by the insight that the desire to politically unify women by universalizing women's nature and experience requires the maintenance of these same distinctions—distinctions traditionally used to justify human enslavement, animal abuse, and other forms of inferiorization.

For Haraway this confusion will not be resolved, as eliminativists might have it, by scientific discovery, but rather through the adoption of a standpoint which allows us to take responsibility for the evolving world in which we find ourselves:

> From one perspective, a cyborg world is about the final imposition of a grid of control on the planet, about the final abstraction embodied in a Star Wars apocalypse waged in the name of defense, about the final appropration of women's bodies in a masculinist orgy of war. From another perspective, a cyborg world might be about lived social and bodily realities in which people are not afraid of their joint kinship with animals and machines, not afraid of permanently partial identities and contradictory standpoints.[16]

We may conceive the Wittgensteinian strategy as the standpoint Haraway has in mind; that is, we may conceive the application of psychological terms such as *subject* or *I* as an act of taking responsibility for the evolving and complex world described by such an application. For to treat the cyborg as a subject is no different in principle than to so treat teapots, flies, women—or men. The question is in every case the same: how much more sense can be made of something's behavior by treating it/her/him as a subject?

An ecofeminist standpoint modeled after a Wittgensteinian approach to the use of psychological terms offers us Haraway's second scenario, namely, a way to explicitly subvert the devaluation which attends identification with the bodily, not by "merely" revaluing the bodily but by revaluing subjecthood as a metaphor for bio-psycho-social complexity. As a metaphor for complexity, the notion of subjecthood captures the interstice between mind-body, subject-object, agent-patient. For on this account what warrants ascribing subjecthood to something blurs all such distinctions, namely, the complexity of the relationship between something and its context.

Acts of self-reference are a crucial part of this strategy in that they epitomize Haraway's insistence that we as feminists take responsibility for the way we conceive what counts as a subject. If *I* is itself best conceived as a metaphor for the complexity of the position from which it is uttered, then *every* utterance of *I* exposes the dissonance between women's lives and images. Such acts make a claim to precisely what the images deny: subjecthood. To acknowledge the dissonance is to take responsibility for it, for it is to recognize how such acts blur the distinctions that separate human beings from animals and machines, as well as men from women. To speak "I" on this account is to engage in an act of ecological conscience, for by the same token that you take responsibility for the complexity of the bio-psycho-social and historical position which you uniquely occupy, you also include yourself among others whose positions are sufficiently complex that, as Wittgenstein suggests, we cannot describe them but for the use of psychological terms.

A working definition of a Wittgensteinian ecofeminism, then, is that standpoint which takes as its point of departure the complexities and dissonances which characterize the bio-psycho-social positions occupied by things. Such a standpoint is neither essentialist nor eliminativist but endeavors to articulate a radical alternative to the oppressive Cartesianism of the essentialist as well as the antiquation of psychological terms by the eliminativist by enlisting the use of psychological terms as heuristics which describe the relationships between things and their contexts. Such a standpoint treats subjecthood as a descriptive or explanatory term applicable to anything whose behavior is rendered more informative by so doing. The extent to which distinctions between rational-nonrational, agent-patient, etc. are preserved in such applications is itself the product of what may be warranted given the complexity of particular cases.

The crucial advantage of such a standpoint is that the metaphorical use of psychological terms enjoins us to take responsibility for differences among feminists. Moreover, it enjoins us to face squarely what we share in common with animals, machines, and men, namely, the complex positions that we are as evolved, inculturated, and physical things. For difference is the product of this commonality. This recognition is fundamentally political as well as ethical in that, as Wittgenstein points out, however we conceive a being affects our view of it as slave or citizen, resource or user.[17]

A Wittgensteinian ecofeminism makes us responsible for our conceptions by exposing the lack of an essence which underlies them, a lack made acute in women's utterance of "I" because it asserts the subjecthood denied by the philosophical tradition and, given this denial, the ambiguous but fruitful relation between women, animals, and machines. As Haraway puts it, "A cyborg body is not innocent; it was not born in a garden; it does not seek unitary identity and so generates antagonistic dualisms without end (or until the world ends); it takes irony for granted."[18] So too an ecofeminist standpoint which takes as its point of departure Wittgenstein's insight that the meaning of a term is its use. For far from unitary identity such a standpoint is grounded in the interstice, in the irony and dissonance that have exiled women from the garden, an exile that founds discourse in the multiple possible applications of subjecthood to human beings, animals, and machines.

Notes

1. E.g., bell hooks (Gloria Watkins), "Sisterhood" (27–41); Charlotte Bunch, "Not for Lesbians Only" (319–25); Janice Raymond, "The Visionary Task" (342–54), collected in *A Reader in Feminist Knowledge*, ed. Sneja Gunew (New York: Routledge, 1991). Also see Susan Bordo, "Feminism, Postmod-

ernism, and Gender Scepticism," *Feminism/Postmodernism*, ed. Linda J. Nicholson (New York: Routledge, 1990), 133–56.

2. E.g., Sandra Harding, "Why Is the Sex/Gender System Visible Only Now?" or E. F. Keller, "Gender and Science," collected in *Discovering Reality: Feminist Perspectives on Epistemology, Metaphysics, Methodology, and Philosophy of Science*, ed. Sandra Harding and Merrill B. Hintikka (Dordrecht: Reidel, 1983). Also see Carolyn Merchant, *The Death of Nature* (San Francisco: Harper and Row, 1980).

3. Susan Bordo, *Flight to Objectivity* (New York: State University of New York Press, 1987).

4. E.g., Paul Churchland, "Eliminative Materialism and Propositional Attitudes" (206–23); Patricia Smith-Churchland and T. J. Sejnowski, "Neurophilosophy and Connectionism" (224–52), collected in *Mind and Cognition: A Reader*, ed. William Lycan (Cambridge, England: Basil Blackwell, 1990). Also see Steven Stich, *From Folk Psychology to Cognitive Science* (Cambridge, Mass.: MIT Press, 1983).

5. See Sandra Harding, "Is Gender a Variable in Conceptions of Rationality?" *Dialectica* 36, nos. 2–3 (1982): 226–42; Susan Hekman, "Reconstituting the Subject: Feminism, Modernism, and Postmodernism," *Hypatia* 6, no. 2 (Summer 1991), 44–63; Gerda Lerner, *The Creation of Patriarchy* (New York: Oxford University Press, 1986); Wendy Lee-Lampshire, "Absence: The Deconstruction of Woman in the History of Man," *American Philosophical Association Newsletter on Feminism* (March 1989); and Jane Tibbitts Schulenberg, "Clio's European Daughters: Myopic Modes of Perception," *The Prism of Sex* (Madison, Wisc.: University of Wisconsin Press, 1979).

6. Ludwig Wittgenstein, *Philosophical Investigations* (hereafter cited as PI), trans. and ed. G. E. M. Anscombe (New York: Macmillan, 1958), para. 282.

7. PI, para. 283.

8. For an expansion of this notion specific to philosophy of mind-brain, see Daniel Dennett, *Brainstorms* and *The Intentional Stance* (Cambridge, Mass.: MIT Press, 1981 and 1987). For a fuller account of Dennett and Wittgenstein on the notion of metaphor as a way of describing complexity, see Wendy Lee-Lampshire, "A Grammar of Subjecthood: Wittgenstein, Deconstruction, and Dennett's Intentional Stance," Ph.D. dissertation, Marquette University, 1992.

9. PI, para. 284.

10. Harding, "Is Gender a Variable in Conceptions of Rationality?" 228–31.

11. Wendy Lee-Lampshire, "History as Genealogy," *Philosophy and Theology* 5, no. 4 (Summer 1991): 314–27.

12. E.g., Camille Paglia, "Interview with *Spin* Magazine on Date Rape," *Spin* 7, no. 6 (1991); bell hooks, "Challenging Patriarchy Means Challenging Men to Change," *Z Magazine* (February 1991); Judith Butler, *Gender Trouble: Feminism and the Subversion of Identity* (New York: Routledge, 1990); Mary Daly, *Gyn/ecology: The Metaethics of Radical Feminism* (Boston: Beacon Press, 1978); Donna Haraway, "A Manifesto for Cyborgs," in *Feminism/Postmodernism*, ed.

Linda Nicholson (New York: Routledge, 1990), 190–233. Speaking from very different perspectives and experience, each of these feminists arrives at a radically different answer to questions such as "What is gender?" An inevitable social construct with a biological basis for Paglia is for hooks the product of sexual, racial, and economic convenience for white men. For Butler, gender is the product of a mother-infant psychological dynamic, whereas for Daly gender defines a patriarchal conspiracy to guarantee the continued subservience of women. Haraway, however, makes this question particularly difficult to answer because of the blurring effect that the notion of a cyborg has on the attempt to differentiate mind and body—sex and gender.

13. Wendy Lee-Lampshire, "Moral 'I': The Feminist Subject and the Grammar of Self-Reference," *Hypatia* 7, no. 1 (Winter 1992): 34–51. Also see Linda Alcoff, "Cultural Feminism versus Poststructuralism: The Identity Crisis in Feminist Theory," *Signs* 13, no. 3 (Spring 1988), 405–36.

14. Haraway, "A Manifesto for Cyborgs," 190–233.

15. Ibid., 192–225.

16. Ibid., 196. Also see Ludwig Wittgenstein, *Zettel* (Berkeley: University of California Press, 1967), para. 528.

17. Ibid., para. 528–30.

18. Haraway, "A Manifesto for Cyborgs," 222.

Twenty-five

Radical Nonduality in Ecofeminist Philosophy

Charlene Spretnak

The majority of books, articles, and lectures on ecofeminism have included the now-familiar litany of dualistic constructs to be rejected: femininity/ nature/body/emotion/connectedness/receptivity/the-private-sphere are devalued in Western societies and considered to exist in service to their "superior" counterparts in the dualistic world view, masculinity/culture/ mind(spirit)/reason/autonomy/aggressiveness/the-public-sphere. Hence it seems appropriate to focus attention on ecofeminist alternatives to a dualistic interpretation of the world. Although various conceptualizations of a relational, interdependent understanding of reality have been put forth by ecofeminist philosophers, they generally stop far short of accepting a radical nonduality and, indeed, tend to dismiss it as disreputable, for reasons I shall cite presently.

A minimalist sense of nonduality accepts that persons and other entities in nature are autonomous subjects that exist in some sort of interdependent relationship with other subjects. Radical nonduality goes further and asserts the existence of unitive dimensions of being, a gestalt of a subtle, unitary field of form, motion, space, and time. My purpose in this chapter is to encourage ecofeminist philosophical consideration of radical nonduality.

I begin by examining the context for this discussion: the resistance among many ecofeminist philosophers to acknowledging unitive dimensions of being, which are denied by both modern and deconstructive-postmodern world views. In the second section, I suggest a phenomenological appreciation of experiential knowledge of unitive dimensions of being. In the final section, I discuss ontological implications of an orientation I call "ecological postmodernism" that are relevant to ecofeminist philosophy, radical nonduality, and the concerns cited in the first section of this article.

There Goes the Neighborhood

An ecofeminist philosopher whose work I respect read an early version of this chapter and sent me a friendly but quite alarmed letter, peppered with capitalized phrases and much underlining. If I would just drop any mention of unitive dimensions of being in discussing alternatives to dualism, she painstakingly explained, I would be accepted by academic ecofeminist philosophers! Alas, I cannot do that and remain true to my experience, but the incident did serve to highlight the current restrictions on acceptable philosophical orientations.

There are three major obstacles to moving radical nonduality into the neighborhood of respectable philosophy: (1) the pervasive scientistic and objectivist dismissal in modern Western cultures of that which cannot be quantified and is more subtle than matter, (2) the grip of deconstructive postmodernism on much contemporary intellectual (particularly academic) thought, and (3) feminist suspicions of nonduality based on patriarchal interpretations of it.

Prejudices of Modern Western Philosophy

The cultural inheritance from the modern Western tradition clearly predisposes most contemporary philosophers to devalue organicism and nonduality as a rather immature and primal clinging to a failed romanticism that was properly displaced by various analytical orientations. The alternative of deconstructive postmodernism, while claiming to constitute a radical break from Western tradition, continues the habit of antipathy toward nondualistic apprehensions and generally dismisses them as "magical thinking." The deconstructionist orientation in philosophy champions a neorationalism that has merely been refocused in scale from the "universal" to the local, particular context; many of the familiar prejudices of Enlightenment rationalism remain intact.

A second cultural objection to nonduality stems from the modern Western enthronement of the individual. Within that orientation, the perception of an essential, protective separation between the self and the rest of the world—a radical discontinuity—is of paramount importance. Hence the self is felt to be threatened with obliteration if unitive dimensions of being are recognized. This rejection of nonduality—that is, the defense of the core Western dualism of self versus world—is often expressed with intense emotion. Clearly, nonduality is misconstrued as an annihilating monism. I and others, however, understand *nonduality* to mean a dynamic system of relations wherein any particular manifestation functions simultaneously as a distinct part and the unbroken whole. The parts are not derivative of the whole, nor vice versa. Each aspect constitutes the other. Metaphors of a web or a net are often used by nondualists, but they seem to me not quite dynamic enough to convey subtle processes of wholeness and diversity, of nonduality and particularity.

Deconstructive-Postmodernist Attitudes

This orientation emphasizes the social construction of knowledge and asserts that conceptual traditions of knowledge ("discourses") are framed and elaborated to serve the controlling forces in a culture or subculture. If the deconstructive project involved solely a massive challenge to conceptual modes of domination throughout the status quo, what feminist could object? Indeed, similar analytical work by feminists and other activists long predates the emergence of deconstructive postmodernism. The expansion of such work is a welcome development.

Of great concern to me, however, is the ideological baggage that comes with the world view of deconstructive postmodernism. Deconstructionists (also called "constructivists") make a leap from noting that concepts are socially constructed to concluding that there is *nothing but* social construction in human experience. Every human perception appears to them to be socially invented in a particular time and place—*except* perceptions of difference, particularity, and inherent autonomy. The perception of "nothing but difference" is believed by deconstructionists to be the sole island of neutrality from which one can scan social construction for 360 degrees.

To this orientation, the most offensive perceptions are those that are opposite of supposedly pure difference and autonomy: any recognition of a unitive dimension of being. Perceptions of difference are accepted as obvious truth, while perceptions of an inherent continuity are dismissed as "a fictive unity." Investing perceptions of difference and particularity with the conceptual weight of being *the fundamental reality* is most certainly not a neutral position; it is an ideological choice. What proof exists within the epistemic grasp of humans that there is "nothing but difference" in human society, the earth community, and the cosmos? Their a priori categorical denial of the possibility of any inherent unity in the cosmos and human affairs must necessarily sweep under the rug a wide range of perceptions to the contrary, as I shall discuss. Most ecofeminist philosophers who subscribe to the assumptions of deconstructive postmodernism, however, stop far short of the extreme "Lone Cowboy ethos" that informs many of the works by the founding fathers of that movement.

The widespread insistence by deconstructionists that all relationships are political, that is, constructed of power relations, influences the ways in which ecofeminist philosophers may interpret attention to a unitive dimension of being. They point out correctly that idealist constructions of unity and organicism have been used politically to oppress people in several historical contexts. From such examples they deduce that *solidarity* (of thoroughly discrete beings) is an acceptable concept, but *unity* is not.[1] I feel that their extension of political philosophy to all ontological apprehensions of the cosmos is quite limiting. It is based on the deconstructionist belief that *all* relationship is inherently power-laden, or "political." Even the myriad subtle relationships that are other than human-to-human?

For some ecofeminist philosophers influenced by this orientation, the cosmological processes explored in contemporary physics are distrusted as being the construction of "a dubious metaphysical holism," while certain observations from field ecology that emphasize the importance of "discrete and relatively disconnected or autonomous holons and hierarchical levels of organization" are embraced as the "informed" version of ecological theory. The latter body of data is valued far more highly than either postmodern physics or holistic ecological observations for being relevant to evolving theories of ecosocial ethics and morality because the antiholistic perspective is believed to protect one from arriving at supposedly false perceptions of organicism.[2]

Feminist Concerns

Ecofeminist philosophers also find expressions of a holistic identification of self with nature, as put forth by various male philosophers, to be problematic for reasons that are rooted in gender politics. For example, deep ecology's sense of the expanded self, or "ecological self," is immensely unappealing if it can be construed to mean the expansion of the male ego to cosmic proportions ("Le cosmos, c'est moi!").[3] I personally do not read that meaning in Arne Naess's coining of the term *ecological self*; certain other male deep ecologists, however, give good cause for concern. A related feminist criticism of deep ecology's recommendation of a gender-neutral, expanded, ecological self is based on recognition that "the self" is socialized quite differently in men and women. Since men in modern-Western-patriarchal cultures derive social status from being culturally elevated above the natural world while women in those societies are devalued as part of the natural realm, the two sexes cannot very well pursue the same path to an enriched sense of self in an ecological age.[4]

A second area of feminist concern focuses on the fact that Western women in general have traditionally been socialized to cultivate a sense of permeable, loosely defined boundaries of their self-identity *in order to* put themselves in malleable service to the needs and demands of others around them. Hence the idealizing—by male ecophilosophers who are often dismissive of ecofeminism—of expansive, arbitrary boundaries of the self calls forth concerns about female exploitation.

Experiential Knowledge of Radical Nonduality

The chilly reception accorded to recognition of unitive dimensions of being in most contemporary philosophical circles warms somewhat, especially among ecophilosophers, if the concept of nonduality is limited to meaning "interdependence" or "interrelatedness" of autonomous entities. Such an alternative to dualistic thinking is acceptable to many ecofeminist philosophers who reject any stronger, or more radical, sense of nonduality. I believe, however, that paying attention to the evidence for a radical nonduality—which is located largely in types of knowledge that have been marginalized and devalued by the modern, objectivist orientation—yields ample cause to reconsider the dominant conceptualizations of acceptable epistemology.

In a variety of circumstances, humans have perceived an inherent and continuous systemicity within the unfolding universe, a constitutive unity that exists *along with*, not instead of, manifestations of particularity and subjectivity. Ecophilosophy would be enriched by recognizing that human perception can be polyvalent, that different kinds of perception can occur, many of them nonlinguistic. Moreover, it is necessary to acknowledge *scale* in perception: discontinuity may seem obvious at one level of perception but absent at other levels.

Female Body Parables

To discuss experience rooted in female physicality in ecofeminist philosophical circles today, one must first respond to the ready charge of "essentialism," the deconstructionist insistence that "woman" is entirely a social construction and that any assertion of women's experience is "totalizing" and oppressive to the individual. I feel that the essentialist debate has been framed too crudely: the issue is not a universal, essential feminine personality structure but, rather, the question of whether the fact that females, in all our particular and cultural diversity, bleed in rhythm with the moon and have the capability to grow people from our flesh, as well as transform food into milk for the young, has any effect on the ways in which we experience life. Deconstructive "antiessentialism" slams the door on that question—viewing gender as noteworthy social construction drawn from the dumb body, just as culture is usually understood to be constructed from dumb nature—but I feel that ecofeminism should explore it.

The erotic processes of the female body-mind often yield states of consciousness that can be appreciated as "body parables," expressions and reminders of unitive dimensions of being that underlie the supposedly fixed delineations of separateness. In the postorgasmic state many women experience a peaceful, expansive mind state of free-floating boundarylessness. Indeed, the clitoris seems to exist for no other purpose than erotic pleasure, an experience that can be the passage to expanded consciousness during and shortly after orgasm. On the first day of menstruation a woman sometimes experiences a sense of soft boundaries of her body-space. In pregnancy and childbirth, the delineation between me and not-me can seem blurred and somewhat elusive. In nursing, while cradling the extension of her flesh to her breast, a woman again may experience a dreamy sense of soft boundaries. All of these greater or lesser immersions into experiencing nonduality teach one that although separateness and discrete boundaries can be important in this life, they are not absolute. Rather, other perceptions of the world are just as real, even though they receive almost no validation in official modern Western culture.

Perceived Unity with Nature

A second mode of experiencing nonduality can occur through immersion in natural surroundings, such as the deep silence one can encounter on wilderness trips when the dualistic habit of perceiving self apart from nature gradually loses its grip and the apparently fixed boundary between inner and outer seems to become permeable and gives way, at times, to a palpable sense of being at one with the surroundings. People often experience less intense versions of the same phenomenon at the seashore, in a large park, or in a backyard garden.

The Magical, Unitive World of Young Children

A third type of experiencing nonduality reportedly occurs cross-culturally among young children. Many of them commonly perceive a magical, felt connection with their world in general or with particular objects such as a tree or an animal. Their organic orientation is generally suppressed and denied by socialization in Western cultures, yet a great many adults remember at least an impression of that mode of being in which boundaries were quite permeable and the world was perceived as being vividly alive and unified.

Sudden, Unexpected Apprehensions of Nonduality

Experiencing awareness of a unitive dimension of being can also occur at quite unexpected moments, not necessarily connected to particular settings or activities. Describing such experiences in retrospect, people often report that their consciousness was grasped, suddenly and usually fleetingly, by an intense awareness of the unity of all being. A biologist at Oxford University established a research project during the 1970s in which he and his staff gathered and classified over four thousand accounts of such experiences. A typical account of a unitive experience was related by an individual who was walking down Marylebone Road in London and "was suddenly seized with an extraordinary sense of great joy and exhultation. . . . all things living, all time fused in a brief second."[5] Such revelatory encounters with a unitary dimension of being may be *extra*ordinary, but they are not *super*natural. They would more accurately be labeled *ultra*natural, a journey into the cosmological nature that lies within the world that Westerners tend to perceive as an aggregate of discrete fragments bound by such forces as gravity and electromagnetism.

The Unitive World Views of Indigenous Peoples

Throughout much of the complex cultural diversity of native nations runs a commonly expressed perception that the earth is alive and humans are not separate from it or from the rest of the cosmos. Traditional native peoples generally apprehend the Great Family of All Beings as consisting of forms that are diverse manifestations of the boundless Great Holy, or Great Mysterious. As ecofeminists have come to learn more about native cultures, many have experienced a resonance in the native holistic orientation, which finds countless assumptions of Western epistemology to be absurdly discontinuous.

Meditation and Related Practices

In numerous cultures, both Eastern and Western, traditions of mental practices have been passed down through generations because they preserve efficacious techniques whereby one can experience nonduality. Such practices include various forms of Buddhist meditation, raja and bhakti yoga, Sufi dancing, and contemplative exercises in Christianity. The specific techniques vary a great deal, but the fact that an organic and unitive perception emerged in so many different cultural contexts indicates the presence of something more than mere social construction.[6]

Holistic Perceptions in Contemporary Science

The mechanistic and objectivist orientations in Western cultures have not yielded to the considerable scientific evidence for a holistic world view. Many scientists are coming to realize that we can no longer make sense of reality except as an evolving whole in which we ourselves are situated.[7] In cosmological terms, the perceptual shift is moving from the modern sense of our surroundings as a collection of discrete objects undergoing events that are unconnected except for the effects of local forces to a sense that all interactions are manifestations of unified primordial "universe activity."[8] That is, the universe is not just a thing but also a mode of being that has been continually unfolding since the time of the primordial fireball. Every being has its particular mode of existence (informed by events and relationships in its immediate context) and its universe mode of existence (informed by cosmological events and relationships)—or its microphase mode and its macrophase mode. Hence several physics experiments during the past twenty years, such as those establishing Bell's theorem of nonlocal causality, have demonstrated that it is not viable to think of a subatomic particle or event as being completely determined by its local circumstances; events taking place elsewhere in the universe are directly, instantaneously, and inherently involved. Focusing solely on the microphase mode of being yields a partially valid but limited understanding.[9]

The major shift in contemporary science is a movement from viewing nature as "a mechanics" (as did Descartes, Newton, and Bacon) not only to recognizing subjectivity in the natural world but also to recognizing immensely complex capabilities for self-organization and self-regulation in vast systems, or communities. The notion of "mind" is no longer limited strictly to an individual organism. Self-regulating "decisions," for instance, are apparently made continuously by the great biocybernetic system that has been called Gaia, our planetary home.[10]

Central to each type of observation of nonduality in the above list, which is by no means comprehensive, is the recognition of a continuous dimension of being that unites seemingly separate, discrete entities. Since recent discoveries in Western science are focusing attention on various examples of nonduality, perhaps a reconsideration will occur in Western philosophy, which has largely delegitimized discussion of the phenomenon.[11] Ecofeminist philosophy, with its particular interest in relational aspects of being (a focus shared by both feminism and ecology), might logically become a site of development—one among many—of the meanings and implications of acknowledging nonduality.

Ontological Implications of Ecological Postmodernism

I have proposed elsewhere a version of postmodernism that seeks transformation beyond the failed assumptions of modernity and focuses attention on the social construction of concepts—but does not make the leap to insisting that there is *nothing but* difference and social construction in human experience.[12] What I call ecological (or ecological/cosmological) postmodernism acknowledges *both* the enormous role of social construction in human experience *and* our constitutive embeddedness in subtle biological, ecological, cosmological, and quantum processes about which contemporary Western society has only an extremely rudimentary level of understanding. When deconstructive postmodernists conclude that there is nothing to life but arbitrary social construction and utter groundlessness, they continue and intensify the diminished conceptualization of the human that was begun by Renaissance humanism, the scientific revolution, and the Enlightenment. These foundational movements of modernity cumulatively framed the human story apart from the larger unfolding story of the earth community. Deconstructive postmodernists shrink the human story even further, insisting that it is entirely a matter of power plays and language games. What is needed, *in addition to* exposing the power dynamics inherent in the "metanarratives" of the modern world view, is to break out of the conceptual box that keeps modern society self-identified apart from nature and to reconnect with a fuller, richer awareness of the human as an integral and dynamic manifestation of the subjectivity of the universe.

Ecological postmodernism asserts that there *is* a grounding for social construction and all other human endeavors. The human species does not conceptualize in pure autonomy, masterfully existing on top of nature. Yet even to discuss "grounding" or "autonomy" with relation to ecological postmodernism reveals the poverty of our inherited vocabulary. The "grounding" so central to ecological postmodernism does not refer to a foundational quantum field from which all physicality emerges as derivative manifestations. Rather, the vibratory field of matter/energy does not exist apart from its manifestations of form, which arise and pass away at the quantum level trillions of times per second. The "quantum soup" is not a base, or source, but part of the play of matter/energy. The grounding of human agency and subjectivity lies in a multiplicity of processes, such as one's genetic inheritance of behavioral predispositions; one's cognitive functions, which include the continuous resculpting of neuronal groups and pathways near synaptic interactions; the influence of bodily experience on metaphor, by which most conceptual thought is organized; the influences of landscape, weather, and other dynamics of one's bioregion on imagination and mood; the self-regulating dynamics of the body-mind; the effect of daily exposures to strong and weak electromagnetic fields; and the subtle manifestations of nonlocal causality and other relational dynamics that lace the universe.

If these aspects of human experience are acknowledged, one can accurately speak of the "autonomy" of an individual only by incorporating a sense of the dynamic web of relationships that are *constitutive* for that being at a given moment. We need new words—or, at the very least, some means of distinguishing between the old "Lone Cowboy" sense of autonomy and the ecological/cosmological sense of uniqueness coupled with intersubjectivity and interbeing. The objectivist, mechanistic, and arrogant framing of a number of core concepts in the Western philosophical tradition inhibits the development of a deeply relational sensibility that is attentive to contextual dynamics of great subtlety.

Ecological postmodernism offers a conceptual framework with which ecofeminist philosophy might accept radical nonduality as a dimension of relational ontology. This orientation addresses the objections cited earlier from the deconstructionist, feminist, and modern perspectives. First, ecological postmodernism challenges the deconstructionist insistence that all relationship in human experience is inherently repressive with respect to (an idealized) autonomy. Cosmological, ecological, biological, and historically generated social relationships in and around an individual can *evoke* the unfolding of profound subjectivity, or interiority.

To the deconstructionist objection that any universal frame of reference is merely "substitutionalist universalizing" and is inherently "totalizing," ecological postmodernism responds that the universal, or cosmological, gestalt does not obliterate the gestalt of an atom, a cell, an organism, or a holonic subsystem within an ecosystem. Any particular level of focus will always yield partial knowledge and involve a larger context.

Regarding the feminist concern about the "ecological self" being interpreted by male ecophilosophers as an expansion of the masculine ego, one cannot rule out that sort of projection on the part of some, but ego aggrandizement is contraindicated by the appreciation in ecological postmodernism for the astounding diversity and profound *difference* in the universe.

The feminist concern that loosely defined boundaries of self have historically been encouraged for women in order to exploit them and the related fear that the modern construction of the individual would be annihilated by acknowledging radical nonduality are both addressed by the honoring of polyvalent perception in ecological postmodernism: the subjectivity of every manifestation in the universe is as real and precious as its far-reaching participation in systems of vast proportion.

Perhaps the most compelling reason for ecofeminist philosophy to look favorably on ecological postmodernism and its inclusion of radical nonduality in the search for alternatives to dualistic thinking is that humility and attentive engagement are called for in acknowledging the complex processual grounding of human existence. It is quite possible and even probable that human apprehension of the countless modes of dynamic relation will always be decidedly incomplete. Yet the perceptual habits of absolutist delineation and overbearing reductionism long imbued by dualistic thinking haunt contemporary efforts to move beyond patriarchal, authoritarian, exploitative societies to new possibilities. The ecofeminist critique of dualism needs to be joined not only with an appreciation of pluralism but also with an open-minded consideration of unitive dimensions of being. An ontology based on dynamic and admittedly partial knowledge *as well as* awe toward the complexity of embodied and embedded existence would contribute substantially to the profound social transformation that is needed.

Notes

I would like to thank Carol Adams, Greta Gaard, Linda Holler, Charles Jencks, Mara Keller, Daniel Moses, Brian Swimme, Karen J. Warren, and Michael Zimmerman for helpful comments on an earlier draft of this article.

1. See, for example, Christine J. Cuomo, "Unraveling the Problems in Ecofeminism," *Environmental Ethics* 14, Winter 1992, 358–59.

   In a related vein, see Karl Popper, *The Open Society* (Princeton: Princeton U. Press, 1991), although his alternative to idealist versions of holism, which he sees as the roots of fascism, is a scientistic objectivism that would appeal to few ecofeminists.

2. See, for example, Karen J. Warren and Jim Cheney, "Ecosystem Ecology and Metaphysical Ecology: A Case Study," *Environmental Ethics* 15, no. 2, Summer 1993, 99–116.

3. See Val Plumwood, "Nature, Self, and Gender: Feminism, Environmental Philosophy, and the Critique of Rationalism," *Hypatia: A Journal of Feminist Philosophy* 6, no. 1, Spring 1991, 13–15.

4. See Marti Kheel, "Ecofeminism and Deep Ecology: Reflections on Identity and Difference," in *Reweaving the World: The Emergence of Ecofeminism* (San Francisco: Sierra Club Books, 1990), 129–32.

5. Alister Hardy, *The Spiritual Nature of Man* (Oxford: Oxford University Press, 1979), 1.

6. A number of constructivist positions are presented in Steven Katz, ed., *Mysticism and Philosophical Analysis* (Oxford: Oxford University Press, 1978); rebuttals are presented in Robert K. C. Forman, ed., *The Problem of Pure Consciousness: Mysticism and Philosophy* (Oxford: Oxford University Press, 1990).

7. Wan Ho, "Evolution in Action and Action in Evolution," *Gaia and Evolution*, ed. Peter Bunyard and Edward Goldsmith (Camelford, Cornwall, England: Wadebridge Ecological Centre, 1989).

8. See Brian Swimme and Thomas Berry, *The Universe Story* (San Francisco: HarperCollins, 1992), chap. 1.

   Also see Erich Jantsch, *The Self-Organizing Universe: Scientific and Human Implications of the Emerging Paradigm of Evolution* (New York: Pergamon Press, 1980); David Bohm, *Wholeness and the Implicate Order* (London: Routledge and Kegan Paul, 1980); and John Briggs and F. David Peat, *Turbulent Mirror* (New York: Harper & Row, 1989).

9. Ibid. Also see F. David Peat, *Einstein's Moon: Bell's Theorem and the Curious Quest for Quantum Reality* (Chicago: Contemporary Books, 1990).

10. James Lovelock, *Gaia: A New Look at Life on Earth* (Oxford: Oxford University Press, 1979), and *The Ages of Gaia: A Biography of Our Living Earth* (New York: Norton, 1988).

11. As for the question of whether various kinds of perception of nonduality reveal various aspects of a *sole* unitive dimension of being or whether they reveal several *different* unitive dimensions of being, I do not know.

12. Charlene Spretnak, *States of Grace: The Recovery of Meaning in the Postmodern Age* (San Francisco: HarperCollins, 1991).

Contributors

Candice Bradley is Associate Professor of Anthropology at Lawrence University. She has done cross-cultural research on agriculture and the world system and is the author of essays appearing in the journals *American Anthropologist* and *Cross-Cultural Research* and in the edited volume *Situating Fertility: Anthropology and Demographic Inquiry.*

Douglas J. Buege is an environmental philosopher and an avid backpacker, canoeist, and bicyclist.

Adrienne Elizabeth Christiansen is Associate Professor of Communication Studies at Macalester College. Her writings focus on the rhetoric of social movements and of war. She is working on a book about sexualized discourse and the Persian Gulf War.

Deane Curtin is Professor of Philosophy at Gustavus Adolphus College, where he directs Community Development in India, a program for college students based in Madras. His essays have appeared in *Hypatia, Environmental Ethics,* and *Philosophy East and West.* He is coeditor of *Cooking, Eating, Thinking: Transformative Philosophies of Food* and is at work on a book titled *Ethics and the Margins,* on the ethics of environmental conflicts between the First and Third Worlds.

Wendy Donner, Associate Professor of Philosophy at Carleton University in Ottawa, is the author of *The Liberal Self: John Stuart Mill's Moral and Political Philosophy* and articles on environmental ethics, ethics, and political philosophy.

437

Karen M. Fox is Associate Professor at the University of Manitoba and a Research Associate of the Health, Leisure and Human Performance Research Institute. Her essays have appeared in the *Journal of Leisure Research* and other publications.

Susan Griffin is the author of numerous books, including *Woman and Nature: The Roaring Inside Her* and, most recently, *A Chorus of Stones: The Private Life of War*. She is at work on a collection of essays, *The Eros of Everyday Life*, and on *Knowledge of the Body*, a book about illness and society.

Lori Gruen teaches philosophy at Lafayette College where she is also Associate Director of the Ethics Project. She has published on the topics of ethics and animals, ecofeminist theory, and environmental philosophy. She is coeditor of two books, *Reflecting on Nature* and *Sex, Morality, and the Law*. She is working on a book-length project, tentatively titled *Overcoming Moral Alienation*.

Leland Robert Guyer, Associate Professor of Spanish and Portuguese at Macalester College, has published articles on Hispanic and Luso-Brazilian literature as well as a book on the poetry of the Portuguese Fernando Pessoa. He has translated extensively from both Spanish and Portuguese, including *Dirty Poem / Poema Sujo* by the Brazilian Ferreira Gullar.

Petra Kelly (1947–1993?) was a grassroots activist, a leading figure in global peace and human rights campaigns, and a cofounder of the German Green party. In 1982 she was one of twenty-seven Green party members elected to the German Parliament. Kelly served as a member of Parliament for eight years, and her work there and in the peace and human rights movements helped shift national and international debates to include many "Green issues" and a new kind of grassroots democracy. She wrote several books and many articles in English and German on subjects including ecology, feminism, children's cancer, disarmament, and Hiroshima. She coedited *The Anguish of Tibet*.

Ruthanne Kurth-Schai is Associate Professor of Education at Macalester College. Her articles have appeared in journals including *Educational Theory, Education Foundations, Journal of Teacher Education*, and *New Designs for Youth Development*, as well as in the edited volume *The Handbook of Qualitative Research in Education*.

Wendy Lee-Lampshire is Assistant Professor of Philosophy at Bloomsburg University. Working principally from the fields of philosophy of mind and philosophy of language, over the past several years she has been attempting to craft a viable Wittgensteinian feminism applicable to issues in feminist standpoint theory, ecofeminism, and lesbian philosophy.

Gretchen T. Legler is Assistant Professor of Creative Writing and English at the University of Alaska-Anchorage. Her work has appeared in *Studies in the Humanities, Western American Literature, ISLE*, the *Indiana Review*, and anthologies including *Uncommon Waters, Another Wilderness, The House on Via Gombita*, and the *1992/1993 Pushcart Prize* collection. Her first collection of essays, *All the Powerful Invisible Things: A Sportswoman's Notebook*, was published in 1995.

Joseph R. Loer has worked as a chemist, engineer, teacher, and analyst in the environmental field. His current work focuses on the remediation of contaminated soil and groundwater and the incorporation of waste-reduction techniques into business operatives.

Christy Elizabeth Newman painted the cover illustration "Ecofeminist" as her creative project for the ecofeminism seminar taught by Karen J. Warren at Murdoch University, Perth, Western Australia, in 1995. She is currently completing a degree in communication studies and English and comparative literature at Murdoch University.

Judith Plant is coeditor of *The New Catalyst* magazine. She has edited *Healing the Wounds: The Promise of Ecofeminism* and coedited several books on bioregionalism, including *Home! A Bioregional Reader* and *Turtle Talk: Voices for a Sustainable Future*.

Val Plumwood is a forest activist, forest dweller, bushwalker, crocodile survivor, and wombat mother. (The Plumwood is a beautiful local rainforest tree.) She is part of a green women's network in Canberra.

Robert Alan Sessions, Professor of Philosophy at Kirkwood Community College in Cedar Rapids, Iowa, is editor of *Working in America*. He has published articles on environmental philosophy and the philosophy of education.

Andy Smith is Cherokee and a member of Women of All Red Nations as well as other feminist and social justice organizations.

Charlene Spretnak is Visiting Professor on Philosophy and Religion at the California Institute of Integral Studies. She is the author of *States of*

Grace: The Recovery of Meaning in the Postmodern Age, coauthor of *Green Politics*, and editor of *The Politics of Women's Spirituality*.

Noël Sturgeon, Assistant Professor of Women's Studies at Washington State University, edits the *Ecofeminist Newsletter*. She has written on the nonviolent direct-action movement and is completing a book entitled *Ecofeminist Natures: Race, Gender, Feminist Theory, and Political Action*.

Dorceta E. Taylor is Assistant Professor of Environmental Sociology in the School of Natural Resources and Environment and the Center for Afro-American and African Studies, University of Michigan. She has written extensively on environmental activism (particularly the participation of people of color) in the United States and Britain. She is researching a book on the representations of people of color in the writings of John Muir.

Karen J. Warren is Associate Professor of Philosophy at Macalester College. The author of many articles on environmental philosophy, she is also the editor of *Ecological Feminism, Ecological Feminist Philosophies*, and *Feminism and Peace* and author of *Quilting Ecofeminist Philosophy*.

Betty Wells, Associate Professor of Sociology/Extensions at the Iowa State University Extension to Community Program, is the author of *A Myth for Modern Times: A Curriculum Package for Coalition Building / Community Development*. In addition to exploring the application of ecofeminist perspectives in community and international development, she helps facilitate a network of the women leaders of a dozen agricultural and rural organizations and is conducting research on the position of women in agricultural organizations and institutions.

Holyn Wilson is Assistant Professor of Philosophy at Marquette University. Her articles on Kant have appeared in several journals, including *Kant-Studien*. She is translating essays by Kant for *Kant in Translation*.

Danielle Wirth is an instructor in Environmental Studies at Iowa State University. She has worked as a professional naturalist, park ranger, natural resource manager, environmental education specialist, and restoration ecologist for county, state, and federal agencies.

Catherine Zabinski is Adjunct Research Assistant Professor in the Division of Biological Science at the University of Montana. Her research interests include restoration ecology and plants' ability to adapt to their environment. She is the author of articles on eastern hemlock genetics and the impacts of global climate change on the forests of the Great Lakes.

Index

Abbott, Sally, 30–31, 37*n*43, 74*n*54
Abercrombie, Nicholas, 72*n*12
Ackerman, Diane, 229, 233
Ackerman, Gary, 257*n*17
Acorn, Janis B., 321
Activism: and ecofeminist theory, 33; and
    Women of All Red Nations, 33–34; and en-
    vironmental justice movement, 69–70; and
    indigenous peoples of Brazil, 149–50. *See
    also* Politics
Adair, Margo, 276*n*19
Adams, Carol J., 14*n*2, 274*n*6
Adorno, Theodore, 368, 371*n*4, 373*n*41
Ageism, environmental: and children as
    ecofeminist issue, 11–12. *See also* Centrism
Agent Orange, 296
Agriculture: as ecofeminist issue, 8–9;
    women's practices and knowledge, 84, 85,
    88–90; soil depletion and industrialized in
    Iowa, 177–80; industrialization of and rural
    culture, 189*nn*7–12; weeds and women as
    weeders, 290–98
Alcoff, Linda, 424*n*13
Alienation: ecofeminism as response to, 126–
    31; nature/culture dualism and work sys-
    tems, 186–87
Allaby, Michael, 71*n*2
Allen, Paula Gunn, 22, 35*n*9
Allison, M. T., 163
Alpine Club of Canada, 161
Andrews, Lynn, 31–32

Androcentrism: ecofeminist philosophy on an-
    thropocentrism and, 327–51
Anthropocentrism: ecofeminist philosophy on
    androcentrism and, 327–51; and commu-
    nity-based valuing, 368, 369
Anzaldua, Gloria, 277*n*25
Arctic Wildlife Refuge, 26–27, 67
Aristotle, 157, 162, 234*n*2, 235*n*4, 338
Atlan, Henri, 407*n*14, 409*n*60
Attfield, Robin, 370*n*3
Australia: colonization of indigenous peoples
    of, 338–40
Autonomy: and feminist theory, 380–81, 385;
    and oppression of women, 412; and decon-
    structive postmodernism, 427; and ecologi-
    cal postmodernism, 433–34

Bacon, Francis, 228, 432
Bagny, Rachel, 266, 276*n*19
Bandyopadhyay, Jayanta, 15*n*6
Bastian, A., 208*n*1
Bawden, Richard, 309
Beasly, Conger, 36*n*17
Beauchamp, Tom, 377
Beauvoir, Simone de, 62, 73*n*37, 338, 373*n*32
Beckers, T., 168
Behaviors: leisure and ethical, 169–70; work
    systems and dysfunctional, 188
Bekoff, Marc, 374*n*54
Benton, Ted, 330, 352*n*10
Bergmann, Frithjof, 190*n*24

441

Berkshire Farm Preserve Notes, 136
Berry, Thomas, 435n8
Berry, Wendell, 177, 188n4
Biehl, Janet, 73n36, 74nn51,55,59, 274n6, 357, 371nn5,9–10, 375
Big Creek Watershed Protection Committee, 307
Bioregionalism: relationship of to ecofeminism, 131–34
Blacks: ecological differentials between whites and, 18n45; nihilism in communities of, 226. *See also* Race; Racism, environmental
Blauner, Robert, 73n45
Blumberg, Louis, 71n11, 72n24
Body: and women's knowledge, 90–91; language and meaning, 219; and social construction of gender, 429–30
Bohm, David, 435n8
Bookchin, Murray, 133, 235n8, 357, 358, 370n2, 371nn7,10
Bordo, Susan, 235n4, 412–13, 422n1, 423n3
Boserup, Ester, 94n5, 189nn6,12, 303
Boulding, E., 210n25, 211n52
Boxer, Barbara, 242–43, 244, 250, 251, 253
Bradley, Candice, xiv
Bramwell, Anna, 71n2
Brazil: colonialism and indigenous peoples of, 140–51
Briggs, John, 435n8
British Columbia: Native Americans and forest management in, 137–38
Brody, Hugh, 99–100, 104, 109n4
Bronfenbrenner, Urie, 201–202, 210n32
Brownmiller, Susan, 256nn5,9
Broyles, William J., 246
Bryant, B., 45, 46
Bryant, Pat, 67
Buck-Morss, Susan, 373nn41–42, 374n48
Buege, Douglas J., xii
Bullard, Linda, 47
Bullard, Robert D., 45, 46, 71nn4,7,10–11, 276n23
Bunch, Charlotte, 422n1
Burgess, Cheryl, 234n1
Burwell, Dollie, 56
Bush, George, 110n8, 125, 241, 243, 247, 253–54, 256n9, 257n17
Butler, Judith, 226n2, 419, 423n12
Buttel, Frederick H., 71nn2,5
Buvinic, Mayra, 8, 17nn30–32

Cady, Duane, 240
Calabrese, Edward, 10, 18n39
Callicott, J. Baird, 351n3, 370n3, 373n31, 374n50
Calvin, John, 157, 171n4
Campbell, Karlyn Kohrs, 248–49
Campbell, Sue Ellen, 235n8
Canada: policies toward Native Americans, 124–25; and free trade, 126; Native Americans and forest management, 137–38. *See also* Inuit (Canada)
Cannon, Shilela, 56
Capitalism: anthropocentrism and view of nature, 344
Caring: development and women in Third World, 91–92
Carson, Rachel, 39, 55–56, 261, 273n4, 315
Case, Ted J., 322n3
Cashman, Kristin, 94n1
Cassava: women and cultivation of, 8, 17n31
Caste system: and diversity of women's lives in India, 82–83
Catton, W. R., Jr., 71n2
Center for Third World Organizing, 45
Centrism: patriarchy and oppression of children, 196–99; ecofeminist philosophy on androcentrism and anthropocentrism, 327–51
Cerrel Associates, 71n11, 72n24
Charleton, Sue Ellen M., 189nn6,12
Chavis, Ben, 67
Cheney, Jim, 106–107, 110n9, 201, 202, 210n30, 211nn35,45, 235n8, 285, 303, 314, 316–17, 321, 373n36, 378–79, 435n2
Children: as ecofeminist issue, 11–12, 19n47, 193–208; indigenous peoples of Brazil and education of, 144; and experience of nonduality, 430
Children Now (child advocacy organization), 197
Chipko movement (India), 5, 6, 7, 15n6, 85–86, 89
Christ, Carol P., 31, 37n45, 73nn30–31
Christianity: and spirituality, 31; and environmentalism, 190n15
Christiansen, Adrienne, xiv
Chrystos, 32, 37n47
Churchill, Ward, 35nn10–12, 36n29
Churchland, Paul, 413, 423n4
Civil rights: and environmental justice movement, 55–56

Index

443

Civil War (American): and industrialization of agriculture, 189n7
Cixous, Hélène, 235n10
Clarke, J., 169
Class: and population control, 29; and environmental justice movement, 64–65
Clean Air Act, 44
Clifton, Lucille, 229
Clinton, President Bill, 28
Cobb, E., 210n28, 212n53
Cochrane, Willard, 189n7
Code, Lorraine, 103, 373n36
Cohen, Howard, 203, 210n26, 211n38
Cohn, Carol, 12–13, 19n51, 246, 256n8
Coleman, J. S., 209n16
Coles, R., 210n24
Collette, Will, 71n7
Collins, Barbara-Rose, 251
Collins, Cardiss, 250
Colonialism: ecofeminist analysis of environmental racism and, 21–34; and Inuit of Canada's Eastern Arctic, 99–109; and indigenous peoples of Brazil, 140–51; and indigenous peoples of Australia, 338–40; and speaking for the Other, 350
Colorado, Pam, 25, 36n24
Commoner, Barry B., 71n2
Communication: and environmental justice movement, 48–49. *See also* Language
Communitarianism: and concept of community, 359; critique of liberalism, 371n17
Community: and responsible knowing, 106; differences and ecofeminist, 120–39; and industrialization of agriculture, 178–79, 189nn7–12; valuing in, 359–62; and nature, 362–70; and self in environmental ethics, 375–88
Conceptual frameworks: patriarchy as oppressive, 19n52; and oppression of children, 195–96, 199–201; characteristics of oppressive, 304; ecological postmodernism as, 434. *See also* Ideology
Constitution (U.S.): Native American influence on, 122
Consumerism, and leisure, 169
Cook, Karen S., 72n12
Cooke, B., 210n28
Coons, J., 209n14
Cope-Kasten, Vance, 19n52
Copernicus, 330

Corgan, Verna, 257n16
Corsaro, W., 210n25
Cousteau, Jacques, 284
Crawford, Mary E., 161–62
Creevey, Lucy E., 189nn6,12
Crenson, M. A., 71n2
Crispin, Izola, 307, 308
Critcher, C., 169
Crosby, Paul, 292–93
Culture: nature/culture dualism and development strategies, 87–93; and concepts of freedom of choice, 158–59; industrialized agriculture and decline of rural, 178–80, 189nn7–12; nature/culture dualism and alienation in work systems, 186–87; and social construction of gender, 215; development programs and local, 301–302; and value relativism, 367–68
Cuomo, Christine J., 73nn36,42, 74nn55,57, 435n1
Curtin, Deane, xii, 94n3

Dallery, Arleen S., 235n10
Daly, Mary, 73n36, 261, 273n4, 419, 423n12
Danica, Elly, 387–88
Daniels, Mary, 256n9
Dankelman, Irene, 274n6
Davidson, Joan, 274n6
Davis, Angela, 214
Deconstruction: and social construction of meaning, 217, 225; and radical nonduality, 426, 427–28
Deep ecology: and anthropocentrism, 335–36; and speaking as Other, 350; and relationship, 352n15; intrinsic value and ecological moral ontologies, 356–59; and concept of self, 428
DeerInWater, Jessie, 24, 36n22
de Lauretis, Teresa, 214, 226n1, 276n24
Deming, Barbara, 276n18
Dennett, Daniel, 423n8
Derrida, Jacques, 214, 216, 218, 225, 414
Descartes, René, 228, 235n4, 404, 413, 432
Devall, Bill, 71nn2,5, 371n12
Development: and women's knowledge in India, 82–93; sexism in programs of international, 116; politics of in Brazil, 147–49; ecofeminist analysis of water project in Kenya, 279–89; ecofeminism and new strategies of, 300–10

Development Alternatives with Women for a New Era (DAWN), 89
DeVore, Irven, 190*n*23
Dewer, J., 168
Diamond, Irene, 74*n*52, 256*n*5, 263, 269–72, 273*n*4, 274*n*6, 275*n*14
Diamond, Jared, 322*n*3
Diamond, Stanley, 190*n*23
Di Chiro, Giovanni, 277*n*27
Dickerson, Janice, 44
Difference: and ecofeminist community, 120–39; leisure and value of, 163–64; ecofeminist discourse on racial, 260–73; and deconstructive postmodernism, 427
Dillard, Annie, 229, 233–34
Dinnerstein, Dorothy, 74*n*47, 412
Dissonance: and feminist vocabulary, 417–20
Dobbert, M., 210*n*28
Dobson, Andrew, 328, 351*n*3
Dolin, Eric J., 71*n*2
Domination: patriarchy and logic of, 20*n*52, 184; and race in ecofeminist analysis, 63; gender and issues of power, 112–19; Kant on nature and, 400–402
Donner, Wendy, xv
Dorsey, Michael, 10, 18*n*39
Doubiago, S., 74*n*56
Douglas, Mary, 292
Dualisms: development schemes and nature/ culture distinction, 87–93; and patriarchy, 184; and concepts of race, 266–68; oppressive conceptual frameworks and, 304; and androcentrism, 337; ecofeminist philosophy and radical nonduality, 425–35. *See also* Culture; Nature
Dukakis, Michael, 247
Duncan, Phil, 255*n*2
Dunlap, Riley E., 71*n*2
Durning, Alan Thein, 169, 185–86, 190*n*18
Dustin, D., 170

Eckhoff, T., 72*n*12
Ecofeminism: definitions and descriptions of, xi, 4, 261–65, 304, 315–16; and empirical data, 3–14; colonialism and environmental racism, 21–34; and environmental justice movement, 38–70; women's knowledge and ecodevelopment in India, 82–93; Inuit and epistemic responsibility, 99–109; women and power, 112–19; differences and community of, 120–39; colonialism and indigenous peoples of Brazil, 140–51; and leisure, 155–71; and work, 176–88; and children, 193–208; language and meaning, 213–26; and literary criticism, 227–34; gender and militarism in Congressional debates on Gulf War, 239–55; discourse on racial difference, 260–73; and development in Kenya, 279–89; agriculture and women weeders, 290–98; and alternative strategies of development, 300–10; and scientific ecology, 314–22; and revaluing of nature, 356–70; self and community in environmental ethics, 375–88; and Kant, 390–406; development of Wittgensteinian, 412–22; and radical nonduality, 425–35. *See also* Empirical data, and ecofeminism; Interdisciplinary perspectives, in ecofeminism; Philosophy, ecofeminist
Ecological literary criticism, 227, 228
Ecological Society of America (ESA), 321
Ecology: ecofeminism and scientific, 314–22. *See also* Deep ecology; Ecosystems
Economics: and environmental issues in politics, 176–85; and ethics of relationship, 202–204. *See also* Development; Labor
Ecosystems: herbicides and diversity of, 297; Kant's theory of, 392, 394, 397. *See also* Ecology
Ecotourism, 169, 190
Edelman, Marian Wright, 198, 208*n*1, 209*n*22
Education: and indigenous peoples of Brazil, 144, 149
Edwards, Clive A., 189*n*7
Egoism: anthropocentrism and psychological, 333–34, 335
Ehrlich, Gretel, 229
Ehrlich, Paul, 289, 315
Eisler, Riane, 35*n*7, 73*n*31, 74*nn*48,54
Elliott, R., 351*n*3
Elshtain, Jean Bethke, 246, 247, 252
Emerson, Ralph Waldo, 228, 232
Emotions: and responsible knowing, 104
Empirical data, and ecofeminism: ecofeminist philosophical perspective on, 3–14; colonialism and environmental racism, 21–34; and environmental justice movement, 38–70; women's knowledge and ecodevelopment in India, 82–93; colonialism and Inuit of Canada's Eastern Arctic, 99–109; women

and power, 112–19; differences and ecofeminist community, 120–39; colonialism
and indigenous peoples of Brazil, 140–51
Energy: and politics of development in Brazil,
147–49
Energy Organization Act (1977), 244
Environmental justice movement: ecofeminist analysis of environmental racism and,
38–70
Environmental organizations: and environmental justice movement, 40–41, 50–51, 52–
53; gender and leadership of, 60–61
Environmental Protection Agency (EPA), 44,
47–48, 72n22
Environmental racism. *See* Racism, environmental
Epstein, Barbara, 275n7
Equality: sexual and racial in ecofeminist
thought, 63–64
Eskimo: use of term, 109n5
Esquivel, Julia, 164–67
Essentialism: and definition of "woman," 213–
14; and Wittgensteinian ecofeminism, 422;
and deconstructive postmodernism, 429
Ethics: and child welfare, 199–200, 201–205;
intrinsic value and ecological moral ontologies, 356–59; self and community in environmental, 375–88. *See also* Values
Ethnicity: leisure and ethnic identity, 163. *See
also* Race
European Economic Community, 100, 104
Evans, Sarah, 73n36
Evidence: and environmental justice movement, 44–48. *See also* Empirical data, and
ecofeminism
Experience: and valuing in community, 360–
61; insanity and invalidation of women's,
380, 387–88; knowledge and radical nonduality, 429–32

Faich, Ronald G., 71n5
Fairfax, Sally K., 6, 7, 16nn13–15
Fanon, Frantz, 73n45
Fear: ecofeminism as response to, 126–31
Feminism and feminist theory: scope of is-
sues in, 3–4; and ecofeminist philosophy, 4;
and relations between First and Third
Worlds, 82; standpoint theory, 94n6; chil-
dren and agenda of, 194; and definition of
"woman," 213–14; language and meaning

in poststructuralist, 215–16, 218, 225; cri-
tique of androcentrism, 327; reappropria-
tion of terms, 374n53; and concept of self,
385, 428–29; critique of Kant, 392; disso-
nance and vocabulary of, 417–20
Ferguson, Ann, 360, 362, 372nn20,22
Ferraro, Geraldine, 248
Ferree, Myra Marx, 73n36
Fink, Deborah, 189nn5,7,11
Firestone, S., 210n26
Firla, Monika, 407n17
Fischer, K., 408n26
Fischer, Michael, 26
Fisher, John, 372n28
Flaherty, Robert Joseph, 101
Flannery, D., 163
Flinn, W. L., 71nn2,5
Flynn, John, 35n13
Food: control of supply, 136–37. *See also* Agri-
culture
Foreman, Dave, 131–32, 370n2
Forestry: as ecofeminist issue, 5–7; women's
knowledge and development in India, 84–
86; clear-cutting of rain forests in British
Columbia, 130, 133; innovative strategies
for sustainability, 137–38; and conflict be-
tween jobs and environment, 188n2; Hub-
bard Brook Forest Study, 320–21
Forman, Robert K. C., 435n6
Forster, Georg, 396, 404
Fortmann, Louise P., 6, 7, 16nn11,13–15
Foucault, Michel, 73nn29,33, 74n57, 349
Fox, Karen M., xiii, 182, 183, 190n19
Fox, Stephen, 71nn2,5
Fox, Warwick, 335, 351nn3,7, 352n15, 374n49
Frankenberg, Ruth, 276n24
Fraternidad de Mujeres Salvador, 156
Freeman, Jo, 73n36
Freeman, Minnie Aodla, 105, 107, 108, 109
Freire, Paulo, 308, 352n14
Freudenberg, Nicholas, 17n27, 18n41
Freysinger, V. J., 163
Friedan, Betty, 412, 413
Friedman, Marilyn, 359–60, 362, 372n18
Friendship: and community, 359–60; in femi-
nist theory, 372. *See also* Relationships
Fruchter, N., 208n1
Frye, Marilyn, 100, 109n6, 204, 211n41, 337,
338, 352n14
Fuss, Diane, 232

Gaard, Greta, 64, 68, 73n38, 46, 273n1, 277n30

Gale, Richard P., 71n5

Geisler, C. C., 71n2

Gelb, Joyce, 73n36

Gelobter, Michael, 44, 71n3

Gender: and leadership of environmental justice movement, 58–70; and sustainable development programs, 87–88, 302–303; social construction of, 214, 215, 219, 221–23, 224–25, 429–30

General Accounting Office, 45

Genetic engineering, 297

Germany: conscription of women into military, 118

Gideonse, H., 209n14

Giles, R. H., Jr., 71n2

Gilligan, Carol, 408n51

Gitskan (British Columbia), 123, 137–38

Gittell, M., 208n1

Glass, James, 386

Goddess worship: and environmental justice movement, 66–67. See also Spirituality

Goldman, Emma, 112, 119n1

Goodin, R., 352n9

Goodman, M., 210nn24–25

Goodman, Nelson, 366–67, 373n43

Goodpasture, K., 351n3

Gorz, Andre, 181

Gottlieb, Robert, 71n11, 72n24

Grant, J. P., 208n6

Gray, Elizabeth Dodson, 16n19, 232, 235nn4,7, 369, 374n52

Green, N. S., 209n19

Green Belt movement (Kenya), 89

Greenberg, J., 72n12

Greenpeace, 71n9

Greer, C., 208n1

Gregor, Mary J., 407n17

Grey, William, 328, 329–32, 336, 345, 351nn1–2,4–6,8

Griffin, Susan, xiii–xiv, 73nn30–31,36,38, 127, 232, 234n2, 235n4, 256n5, 262, 275n10, 349, 408n52

Griffiths, Morwenna, 367, 373n45

Grimshaw, Jean, 380–81

Gruen, Lori, xv, 73nn36,41, 372n29

GRUMIN (Women's Group for Indigenous Education), 140–41, 149, 150, 152

Guarani (Brazil), 145, 150–51

Guatemala: and poetry of Julia Esquivel, 164–67

Guha, R., 209n20

Gulf War: as environmental catastrophe, 17n26, 255n3; and children, 198; gender and militarism in Congressional debates on, 239–55

Gutierrez, Juana, 56

Gutmann, Amy, 371n17

Guyer, Leland, 152

Gwich'in (Alaska), 26

Gyorgy, Anna, 262

Hamilton, Cynthia, 11, 19n46, 48, 71n3, 74n60

Hanson, P., 351n3

Haraway, Donna, 229–30, 232, 234, 235n6, 261, 273n4, 278n35, 373n40, 419, 420–21, 422, 423nn12,14,18

Harden, Lakota, 35n15

Harding, Sandra, 277n25, 366, 373n39, 409n66, 412–13, 423nn2,5,10

Hardy, Alister, 435n5

Hare, Nathan, 18n45

Harjo, Joy, 229

Harris, Adrienne, 256n5, 257n13

Harry, J., 71n5

Hartmann, Betsy, 27, 36nn33,37

Hartmann, Heidi, 73n44

Hartsock, Nancy, 336, 352nn10,14, 403, 409n65

Haskins, K., 208n1

Hasselstrom, Linda, 229

Haudenosaunee, 124

Havighurst, R., 209n16

Hawkins, Howard, 74n57

Hazard Ranking System (EPA), 47, 72n22

Hazardous wastes: and contamination of water supplies, 8; Native American lands and disposal of, 23; and children, 197–98. See also Pollution; Toxins

Health: and water supplies, 7–8; women and environmental hazards in household, 10, 18n37

Hegel, Georg W. F., 190n17

Heinz, John, 398, 408n45

Hekman, Susan, 423n5

Held, Virginia, 373n33

Hendee, J. C., 71n5

Herbicides, 292, 295–97

Heron, R. P., 168

Hershey, M. R., 71n2
Hewlett, S., 208n6, 209n23
Hierarchy: Native Americans and European concept of, 123–24; and patriarchy, 184; oppressive conceptual frameworks and, 304; scientific ecology and theory of, 316–19
Hill, D. B., 71n2
Hillman, James, 185, 190n24
History: leisure and periods of, 171n4; Kant's works on, 398
Hitler, Adolf, 217
Ho, Wan, 435n7
Hoagland, Sarah, 374n53, 380
Hoexter, Michael, 74n57
Hofrichter, Richard, 71n10, 276n23
Hogan, Linda, 128
Hohn, C. F., 71n2
Hole, Judith, 73n36
Holler, Linda, 368
Holt, John, 196, 202, 209n13, 210nn26,33
hooks, bell, 73n39, 385, 409n70, 419, 422n1, 423n12
Horkheimer, Max, 371n4, 373n41
Horticulture: labor and weeding, 293–94
Horvat, R. E., 71n2
Hoskins, Marilyn, 16n16
Household: environmental health hazards in, 10, 18n37
Hubbard Brook Forest Study, 320–21
Hubbel, Sue, 229
Hughes, D., 209n18
Hughes, Lance, 10, 18n40, 19n49
Human nature: Kant's theory of, 391–92, 397–400
Hunnicutt, Benjamin, 190n26
Hussein, Saddam, 243
Hynes, H. Patricia, 74n52

Identity: leisure and ethnic, 163
Ideology: and indigenous people's knowledge in ecofeminist theory, 101–103; of economics vs. environment in politics, 177–85. See also Conceptual frameworks
Inclusion and inclusivity: women and leisure, 168–69; children and ethics of, 205–207
India: rate of deforestation in, 15n7; replacement of natural forests in, 15n8; women's knowledge and ecodevelopment, 82–93. See also Chipko movement (India)
Indian Reorganization Act of 1934, 35n16

Industrial Revolution: and domination of nature, 128–29
Industrialization. See Agriculture
Instrumentalism: and androcentrism, 338; and anthropocentrism, 339–40, 341, 345–48; use of term, 352n13; and self-concern, 352n16; and concept of self, 381–82
Interdisciplinary perspectives, in ecofeminism: and leisure, 155–71; and work, 176–88; and children, 193–208; language and meaning, 213–26; and literary criticism, 227–34; gender and militarism in Congressional debates on Gulf War, 239–55; discourse on racial difference, 260–73; and development project in Kenya, 279–89; weeds and women as weeders, 290–98; and new strategies of development, 300–10; and scientific ecology, 314–22
International Development Ethics Association (IDEA), 94
International Fund for Animal Welfare, 100
Inuit (Canada): military exercises over lands of, 23; and colonialism, 99–109; use of term, 109n5; patriarchy and traditional culture of, 110n11
Inukpuk, Peter, 106
Iowa: industrialized agriculture in, 177–80, 307–308
Ippellie, Alootook, 105–106
Iran-Iraq War (1983), 243
Irigaray, Luce, 235n10
Iroquois (New York), 122–23
Ivans, Molly, 257n17

Jackson, Jesse, 67
Jagger, Alison M., 73n36, 171n3, 201, 210nn26,29, 360–61, 362, 363, 372n24, 373nn34,44
Jaimes, M. Annette, 22, 35nn5–6,8
Jantsch, Erich, 435n8
Johnson, D., 210n34
Johnson, Ernestine, 44
Johnson, Hazel, 69–70
Johnson, Josephine, 229, 233
Johnson, Sonia, 129
Jones, Ann Rosalind, 235n10
Jones, Lynne, 275n8
Joseph, Ammu, 36n38
Judaism: and environmentalism, 190n15
Jupp, M., 209n21

Kagan, Jerome, 195, 209n10, 210nn24–25
Kaibab Paiute, 18n42
Kaigang (indigenous chief, Brazil), 152n2
Kant, Immanuel, 390–406, 406nn6–8,
    407nn12,16–17,20–24, 408nn27–38,42–
    44,46–49,53–54,56–57, 409nn62–63,67–68
Kaptur, Marcy, 244–45, 250
Katz, Eric, 365, 366, 373n37
Katz, Steven, 435n6
Kaufmann, Linda S., 277n25
Keller, Evelyn Fox, 232, 235n4, 288, 403,
    409n64, 423n2
Keller, Helen, 112
Keller, Mara L., 74n54
Kellert, S. R., 71n2
Kelly, J. R., 160, 171
Kelly, Petra, xii
Kenya: ecofeminist analysis of development
    project in, 279–89; women and weeding,
    293–94, 295
Kerr-McGee uranium processing plant, 24
Kheel, Marti, 74n52, 435n4
King, Lester Snow, 409n67
King, Ynestra, 21–22, 34n2, 35n4, 73nn36,42,
    74nn54 ?. 128, 240, 256nn5–6, 260, 262,
    266, 2? , 274n6, 275n12, 276nn18–19
Kirk, Gw⌣, ⌣, 266, 275nn16,19
Knowledge: of indigenous peoples, 6, 99–109,
    301–302; Indian women and ecodevelop-
    ment, 82–93; ecofeminism and science- and
    technology-related issues, 284–89; and alter-
    native strategies of development, 301–302;
    and feminist critiques of science, 320; Kant
    on regulative judgment and, 402–405; and
    radical nonduality, 429–32
Kollontai, Alexandra, 112
Kolodny, Annette, 235n7
Kope-Kastin, Vance, 13
Kozol, Jonathan, 198, 209n19
Kramer, Mark, 189n7
Kreger, Janet, 71n2
Kristeva, Julia, 235n10
!Kung, 120
Kuper, Adam, and Jessica Kuper, 72n12
Kurth-Schai, Ruthanne, xiii, 208n3,
    211nn42,48, 212nn53–54

LaBalme, Jenny, 71n11, 72nn14,18, 73n34
Labor: organization of workers' groups by in-
    digenous peoples of Brazil, 149–50; and so-
    cial construction of gender, 221–23; horti-

culture and weeding, 293–94; development
    programs and value of women's, 305–306.
    See also Work
LaDuke, Winona, 22, 269–70, 277n27
Lahar, Stephanie, 274n6
LaHart, D. E., 71n2
Laing, R. D., 380
Language: sexist-naturist as ecofeminist issue,
    12–13; and community, 106; ecofeminist
    analysis of meaning and, 213–16; gender
    and militarism in Congressional debates on
    Gulf War, 239–55; feminist theory and re-
    appropriation of terms, 374n53; Wittgen-
    stein's analysis of, 414–17. See also Commu-
    nication
Lavelle, Marianne, 47–48, 72nn20–21, 74n61
Lee, Dorothy, 190n23
Lee, Pam Tau, 53–54
Lee, Richard B., 190n23
Lee-Lampshire, Wendy, xv–xvi, 423nn5,8,11,
    424n13
Legler, Gretchen T., xiv
LeGuin, Ursula, 126–27, 128, 229, 231, 232
Lehrman, Karen, 32–33, 37n48
Leisure: ecofeminist analysis of, 155–71; and
    patriarchal labor system, 182, 183; and con-
    sumerism, 190n19
Lenoir, Timothy, 409nn61,67
Leopold, Aldo, 292, 293, 315
Lerner, Gerda, 423n5
Lerner, M. J., and S. C. Lerner, 72n12
Lester, S. V., 71n7
Lévi-Strauss, Claude, 190n23
Levine, D., 209n16
Levine, Ellen, 73n36
Liberalism and liberationism: and children's
    issues, 200–201; model of androcentrism
    and anthropocentrism, 341–45, 348–51;
    communitarian critique of, 371n17
Lipman, M., 210n25
Literary criticism: and ecofeminism, 227–34
Locke, John, 184
Loer, Joseph R., xiv
Logan, Josephine, 171n3
Lone, Richard de, 197, 209n15
Long, Gretchen, 36n39
Longino, Helen, 320
Lorenzo, R., 212nn53–54
Love, Glen, 234n1
Lovelock, James, 436n10
Lowe, G. D., 71nn2,5

Lugones, María, 91, 171n3, 372n19
Luther, Martin, 157, 171n4
Luxemburg, Rosa, 112

McAvoy, L., 170
McClintock, Barbara, 288
McDaniel, Judith, 275n13
McGaw, Judith, 182–83, 189nn11,13
McIntyre, Alisdair, 371n16
Mackie, J. L., 371n14
MacKinnon, Catharine, 74n50
McLaughlin, Peter, 409n67
Mann, Eric, 45, 71nn3–4,11
Mannison, D., 351n6
Martin, Biddy, 276n24
Martin, Calvin, 270, 277n31
Martin, J. R., 211n36
Martz, Ron, 256n9
Marx, Karl, 63–64, 177, 186, 190n21
Marxism: anthropocentrism and view of nature, 344
Masini, E., 212nn53–54
Matthews, G., 210n25
Matz, Michael, 36n28
Mayman-Park, Margy, 266, 276n19
Meaning: ecofeminist analysis of language and, 213–26
Means, Lorelei DeCora, 22, 35n5
Media: women's power and hostility of male-dominated, 117–18
Medicine: and women's knowledge, 86, 89
Memmi, A., 352n14
Merchant, Carolyn, 73nn36,38, 74nn52,54, 235n4, 274nn5,6, 284, 310n1, 423n2
Merryfinch, Lesley, 256n10
Metzger, Deena, 130
Mies, Maria, 274n6
Militarism: and oppression of children, 198; and gender in Congressional debates on Gulf War, 239–55
Military: Native Americans and weapons testing/war exercises, 23–24. See also Gulf War; Militarism; Vietnam War
Mill, John Stuart, 375
Miller, Frederick D., 73n36
Miller, Jean Baker, 114, 119n2
Mills, Sara, 235n5
Mills, Stephanie, 132
Mink, Patsy, 250
Mitchell, Robert C., 71n2
Mohai, Paul, 45, 46, 71n5

Mohanty, Chandra Talpade, 276n24
Mohawk (Canada), 124–25
Moi, Toril, 235n10
Molina, Papusa, 266, 276n19, 306–307
Momaday, N. Scott, 408n41
Monson, Jamie, 189n6
Montagu, Ashley, 203, 210n28, 211n39
Mor, Barbara, 74n54
Morast, Daniel, 109n3
Morella, Constance, 257n15
Morgan, Robin, 115, 119n3
Morrison, Denton E., 71n5
Moser, Caroline, 44, 71n11
Mother: indigenous peoples of Brazil and Earth as, 140, 150
Muir, John, 228, 232
Murdy, W. H., 374n49
Murphy, Patrick, 230, 234n1, 235nn8–9, 369, 374n55
Mylenbusch, Helmut, 17n34

Naess, Arne, 335, 428
Nanook of the North (film, 1920s), 101–102
Narayan, Uma, 104, 206–207, 211nn43,47,49
Nash, Roderick, 71n2
National Indigenous Union, 149
National Resources Defense Council, 11
Native Americans: and ecofeminist analysis of environmental racism, 10, 11, 18n42, 22–34; world views of precontact, 122–23; and European concept of hierarchy, 123–24; Canada's policies toward, 124–25; and forest management in British Columbia, 137–38; women and ecofeminist movement, 261, 268–72
Native Americans for a Clean Environment, 10
Nature: as ecofeminist issue, 4, 5; nature/culture dualism and development strategies, 87–93; and Industrial Revolution, 128–29; women and leisure, 161–62, 172n7; and women in conceptual framework of patriarchy, 184–85; nature/culture dualism and alienation of work, 186–87; language and concepts of, 217–18, 219; and social construction of gender, 219; and ecofeminist literary criticism, 228–34; and alternative strategies of development, 300–301; and scientific ecology, 314–15; anthropocentrism and Other, 340–41; and problem of speaking for Other, 349–51; ecofeminist philosophy and revaluing of, 356–70; use of

term, 370n1; Kant on humans and, 393–402; definition of naturism, 406n4; and experience of nonduality, 430

Navajo, 23

Nelson, Lin, 74nn51,52,60

Newton, Isaac, 432

Nhandewa (Guarani chief, Brazil), 150–51

Nihilism: in black communities, 226

NIMBYism: and environmental justice movement, 49–50

Nollman, Jim, 120

Norplant devices, 28–29

Northwest Territories (Canada): and Nunavut agreement, 108

Norton, Bryan, 374n49

Nozick, Robert, 72n12

Nuclear Regulatory Commission, 24

Nunavut agreement (Canada), 108

Nussbaum, Marta, 94n2

Oakar, Mary Rose, 244–45, 251

Objectivity: and feminist critiques of science, 320; and intrinsic value, 357–59

Oelschlaeger, Max, 187, 188n3, 189n14

Oldfield, Margery L., 321

Oliver, Mary, 229, 232, 235n10

Olson, Ann, 17n25, 19n50

Omi, Michael, 275n17

O'Neill, Onora, 400, 407n17, 408n55, 409n73

O'Neill, R. V., 316, 317–18, 319

Oppression: ecofeminist analysis of in anticolonial framework, 22–34; and power, 112–19; of women and nature through leisure, 168–69; of children, 194–99; and social construction of gender, nature, and race, 220, 223–24. See also Domination; Patriarchy

Orenstein, Gloria, 256n5, 263, 269–72, 273n4, 274n6, 275n14

Organization of Indigenous Movements, 149

Ortner, Sherry B., 257n14, 373n32

Ostheimer, J. M., 71n2

Other: androcentrism and the feminine as, 337–40; anthropocentrism and nature as, 340–41; and liberation model of anthropocentrism, 343–44; problem of speaking for, 349–51; and self in environmental ethics, 379–88

Paehlke, Robert, 71nn2,5

Paglia, Camille, 419, 423n12

Paley, Grace, 262, 273n4

Palley, Marian L., 73n36

Palmer, Parker, 190n25

Patriarchy: as oppressive conceptual framework, 19n52; and traditional Inuit culture, 110n11; gender and domination, 113–14, 115, 118–19; as dysfunctional system, 180–81, 184; and oppression of children, 196–97; Kant and, 400–402, 405–406

Peat, F. David, 435nn8–9

Pelosi, Nancy, 239, 243–44, 245, 253

People of Color Environmental Summit (Washington, D.C., 1991), 23, 26, 42–44, 54, 58, 67

Pepper, David, 71n2

Perfecto, Ivette, 71n11, 72n26

Perictione II, 162

Petersen, Debra L., 257n16

Philosophy, ecofeminist: on empirical data, 3–14; on androcentrism and anthropocentrism, 327–51; and revaluation of nature, 356–70; self and community in environmental ethics, 375–88; and Kant, 390–406; and Wittgenstein, 412–22; radical nonduality in, 425–35

Pieper, Joseph, 160

Pinhey, T. K., 71n2

Planned Parenthood, 27

Plant, Judith, xii–xiii, 30, 37n42, 269–72, 271, 274n6, 278n32

Platner, Ernst, 404, 409n67

Plato, 157, 162, 235n4

Play: and leisure, 169–70

Plumwood, Val, xv, 195, 209n9, 274n6, 348, 351nn3,5, 352n12, 353n19, 376–77, 379–80, 381–82, 435n3

Pluralism: children and ethics of, 204–205; and difference in ecofeminist theory, 405; Kant's use of term, 409n73

Poincelot, Raymond, 189n7

Politics: of environmental racism, 35n16; and environmental justice movement, 56–58, 69–70; personal and political values in leftist, 133; of development in Brazil, 147–49; environment vs. economics in, 176–85; and oppression of children, 196, 197, 205–207; gender and militarism in Congressional debates on Gulf War, 239–55; and liberation model of anthropocentrism, 341–43. See also Activism

Pollution: adult centrism and oppression of children, 197–99; definition of, 292. See also

Hazardous wastes; Racism, environmental; Toxins; Water

Popper, Karl, 435n1

Population control: and environmental racism, 27–29

Population-Environment Balance, 28

Population Institute, 27

Postmodernism: on speaking for Other, 350; and concept of self, 386; radical nonduality and deconstructive, 426, 427–28; ontological implications of ecological, 432–35

Poststructuralism: language and meaning in feminist theory, 213, 215–16, 218, 225

Potiguara, Eliane, xiii, 151–52

Poverty: gender and age as factors in, 12. *See also* Children; Development

Power: gender and ecofeminist analysis of, 112–19; and children, 205–207

Prabha, Sasi, 95n7

PrairieFire, 307

Pratt, Mary Louise, 235n5

Privilege: patriarchy and concepts of, 184

Protectionism: as ethical position on childhood, 199–200

Proudhon, Pierre-Joseph, 190n21

Psychology: leisure as state of mind, 159–60; egoism and anthropocentrism, 333–34, 335

Purdy, L., 210n27

Pursell, Carroll, 71n2

Putnam, Ruth Anna, 367, 373n46

Quebec: separatism as environmental issue, 125

Quilt: metaphor of ecofeminist, 155–56, 160, 170–71

Quinby, Lee, 73n42, 74nn50,57,60

Race: women of color and environmental justice movement, 58–70; use of term *women of color*, 70n1; social construction of, 220; and discourse on difference in ecofeminism, 260–73; Kant on, 396. *See also* Ethnicity; Native Americans; Racism, environmental

Racism, environmental: as ecofeminist issue, 10–11; ecological differentials between blacks and whites, 18n45; colonialism and ecofeminism analysis of, 21–34; and environmental justice movement, 38–70; and social construction of gender, 225

Radiation poisoning: and Native Americans, 24

Radical feminism: and ecofeminism, 62

Rajaratnam, Dr. K., 95n7

Rancourt, A. M., 159

Rape: and social construction of gender, 224–25; and militarism, 256n9

Rationality and reason: and critique of universal principles in ecofeminist philosophy, 376–79; Kant on, 391–93

Rawls, John, 72nn12–13

Raymond, Janice, 74n52, 422n1

Razak, Arisika, 74n52

Reagon, Bernice Johnson, 266, 276n21

Realism: responsible knowing and normative, 105–106

Redford, K., 110n7

Reed, S., 208n6, 209n23

Reed, T. V., 275n9

Regan, Tom, 277n31, 358, 371n12, 393, 407n15

Reid, Richard, 17n26

Relationships: and concept of leisure, 162–63; and work systems, 185–88; children and ethics of, 201–204; and deep ecology, 352n15; and concept of self, 382–84

Relativism: and community-based valuing, 366, 367–68; and subjectivism, 373n38

Reno, Janet, 248

Research: and environmental justice movement, 44–48

Resource Conservation and Recovery Act, 48

Rich, Adrienne, 221

Riedel, Manfred, 408n26

Ritt, L. G., 71n2

Rivage-Suel, Marguerite K., 211nn47,52

Robbins, Rebecca, 36n16

Robinson, W. Paul, 71n11

Rocheleau, Dianne, 16nn11,14

Rolston, Holmes, 357

Rose, Hilary, 94n6

Rosenberg, Harriet, 18n37

Rosenblatt, R., 209n21

Rosenzweig, R., 168

Routley, R., and V. Routley, 351nn3,5, 374n50

Ruddick, Sara, 257n13

Ruether, Rosemary Radford, 73n36, 211n52, 235n4, 274n6

Russell, Franklin, 71n2

Sabuco, Oliva de, 162

Sachs, Carolyn E., 189nn7,12

Sahlins, Marshall, 185, 190n23

Index

Said, E., 352n14
Salleh, Ariel, 74n56
Samdahl, D. M., 159
Sand, George, 112
Sandel, Michael, 371nn16–17
Sandoval, Chela, 267, 276n22
Sarup, Madan, 226n4
Sauter, R. C., 208n6, 209n23
Schapiro, Mark, 72n26
Scherer, Donald, 374n49
Schiller, Herbert, 190n18
Schilpp, Paul Arthur, 407n23
Schor, Juliet, 190nn19,26
Schorr, L., 209n23
Schott, Robin May, 407n13
Schulenberg, Jane Tibbitts, 423n5
Science: ecofeminism and knowledge, 284–89;
    ecofeminism and ecology, 314–22; and holis-
    tic perceptions, 431–32
Seager, Joni, 17n25, 19n50
Sejnowski, T. J., 423n4
Self: leisure and concept of, 159, 172n5; and
    community in environmental ethics, 375–
    88; feminism and concept of, 428–29
Sen, Amartya, 94n2
Sessions, George, 71n2, 371n12
Sessions, Robert, xiii, 190n24
Sexism: and oppression in ecofeminist analy-
    sis, 22; in international programs of devel-
    opment, 116
SHARE (Self Help Association for a Re-
    gional Economy), 135–36
Sheleff, L., 211n46
Shiva, Vandana, 15n6, 84, 117, 119n4, 261,
    274nn4,6, 290, 399, 405, 407nn10–11,
    409nn71–72
Shotter, John, 171n3
Sierra, Rachel, 266, 276n19
Sierra Club, 26, 29
Silko, Leslie, 229
Sivard, Ruth Leger, 305
Sjöö, Monica, 74n54
Slaughter, Louise, 251
Slavery: resistance of indigenous peoples of
    Brazil to, 145, 146
Slayton, Christa D., 68, 74n57
Smiley, Jane, 189n9
Smith, Adam, 183, 184, 188
Smith, Andy, xii, 37n44, 270, 277n29
Smith, Barbara, 21, 34n1, 266, 276n18, 277n25
Smith, J., 211n52

Smith-Churchland, Patricia, 413, 423n4
Snowe, Olympia, 249
Social ecology: and concept of "home," 133;
    intrinsic value and ecological moral ontolo-
    gies, 356–59
Social justice: environmental racism and envi-
    ronmental justice movement, 38–70; and
    children, 201–208
Social movements: and environmental justice
    activism, 65–66; male-led as exchanges of
    power, 118
Social responsibility: women and leisure,
    168–69
Socialist feminism, and ecofeminism, 62
Sommerville, J., 210n25
Sorokwu, V., 208n2
Sosa, Marie, 69
Speier, M., 210n24
Spelman, Vicki, 372n19
Spinoza, Baruch, 371n12
Spirituality: Native American traditions and
    ecofeminist, 30–32, 270; Goddess worship
    and environmental justice movement, 66–
    67; ecofeminism and search for, 264
Spivak, Gayatri, 73n42
Spretnak, Charlene, xvi, 73nn36,44, 74n54,
    211n52, 262, 275n11, 310, 436n12
Stahl, Georg Ernst, 409n67
Stanley, Autumn, 88–89
Starhawk, 36n26, 74n54, 211n52, 261, 262,
    266, 273n4, 276n19
Stevens, O., 210n25, 212n53
Stich, Steven, 413, 423n4
Stockholm International Peace Research Insti-
    tute, 243
Stone, Merlin, 74n54
Struhl, Paula R., 73n36
Sturgeon, Noël, xiv, 275n15, 276n19, 277n26,
    278n35
Subjectivity: and relativism, 373n38; and
    Wittgensteinian ecofeminism, 412–22
Suro, R., 71n7
Swimme, Brian, 73n31, 435n8
Szasz, Andrew, 276n23

Tallman, Valerie, 35n14, 36nn8–10,23
Tamoio Confederation (Brazil), 146
Taylor, Dorceta E., xii, 71nn2,5,8, 72n25
Taylor, P., 209n11
Taylor, Verta, 73n36
Technology: as ecofeminist issue, 9; gender

and Green Revolution, 85; and ecofeminist analysis of development project in Kenya, 279–89

Teen pregnancy: political scapegoating of, 29–30

Teish, Luisah, 266, 276n19

Thatcher, Margaret, 114

Theano II, 162

Third World: and population control, 27–29; diversity of women's lives in, 82. See also Development; India

Third World Network (Malaysia), 89

Thomas, Laura, 17n23

Thompson, J., 351nn4,6

Thompson, William Irwin, 288

Thoreau, Henry David, 228, 232, 235n3

Thorne, Barrie, 194, 204, 208n5, 209n12, 210nn24,25, 211n42

Timberlake, Lloyd, 17n23

Tinker, Irene, 16n14

Tobias, Sheila, 246–47

Todd, Mary, 307

Torgovnick, Marianna, 102

Toxins: as ecofeminist issue, 10; herbicides as, 296. See also Hazardous wastes; Pollution

Toyucas (Brazil), 141–42

Trimble, Lillie C., 71n11, 72n24

United Church of Christ, 11, 45, 55

United Farm Workers, 51, 53

United States: resource consumption and over-population, 28

Unsoeld, Jolene, 251

Urban Environment Conference, 45

Values: personal and political in politics of Left, 133; and leisure, 169–70; and community, 359–62; use of term intrinsic value, 370n3; objectivism and moral, 371n15. See also Ethics

Van Ardsol, Maurice D., Jr., 71n2

Van Gelder, Lindsy, 276n19

Van Liere, K. D., 71n2

Vietnam War, 296

Violence: against indigenous peoples in Brazil, 146–47

Vucanovich, Barbara, 257n15

Vygotsky, L., 202, 211n37

Walker, Alice, 167–68, 229, 261, 273n4

Walzer, Michael, 371n16

Waring, Marilyn, 16nn12,22, 17nn23,28

Warren, Karen J., xii, 14nn2–3, 19n52, 21, 34n3, 73nn36,38,41,46, 74nn47,53,60, 101, 103, 107, 108, 109n6, 110n9, 155, 161, 171nn1,3, 172n6, 180–81, 184–85, 189n6, 190nn16,22, 195–96, 199, 201, 205, 208nn2,4, 209nn7–8,17, 210nn30–31, 211n40, 231, 232, 233, 234, 235nn7,11, 240, 256n6, 274n6, 282, 285, 287, 304, 314, 315–17, 321, 365, 372n30, 373nn35–36, 383–84, 390–91, 399, 406nn3,5, 407n19, 409n69, 435n2

Water: as ecofeminist issue, 7–8; women's time spent in collecting, 17n24, 85; energy industries and contamination of in Brazil, 148; ecofeminist analysis of development project in Kenya, 279–89; and manure management in Iowa, 307–308. See also Pollution

Waters, Kristin, 406n2, 407n9

Watson, Richard, 374n49

Watts, George, 138, 139

Weeds and weeding: and ecofeminist analysis of agriculture, 290–98

Weilbacher, M., 212n55

Weir, David, 72n26

Weisman, Leslie Kanes, 235n5

Welch, Sharon D., 163–64, 171n3

Wells, Betty, xiv–xv

Wenzel, G., 109n3

West, Cornel, 73n39, 225–26

Westerfelt, M. O., 71n2

Weston, Anthony, 371n14

Wetsuwet'en (British Columbia), 123, 137–38

Whitbeck, Caroline, 104

White, Harvey, 71n11

Whiting, J. and B. Whiting, 210n25

Whittier, Nancy, 73n36

WIDA (Integrated Rural Development of Weaker Sections in India), 95n7

Wiens, John A., 317

Wiesel, Elie, 361

Wilkinson, Merv, 137

Williams, B., 351n3

Willis, Ellen, 275n9

Wilson, Holly L., xv

Wilson, Marie, 270, 271–72, 277n28, 278n33

Winant, Howard, 275n17

Wirth, Danielle, xiv–xv

Wirth, Timothy E., 398, 408n45

Witt, Susan, 135

Wittgenstein, Ludwig, 218, 414–17, 420–22, 423n6, 424n16

Woman: feminist theory and definition of, 213–14

WomanEarth Feminist Peace Institute, 261, 265–68

Women of All Red Nations (WARN), 33–34, 89

Women's Pentagon Actions (WPA, 1980, 1981), 262

Wood, Allen W., 407n17

Work: difference between leisure and, 157–58; ecofeminist analysis of, 176–88. *See also* Labor

World Commission on the Environment and Development, 301

Wortman, Jack, 190n24

Wyden, P., 74n52

Yaeger, Patricia, 232, 235n9

Yakima (Washington), 23

Yanomami (Brazil), 152n1

Yeo, E., and S. Yeo, 169

Young, Iris, 362

Yucca Mountain nuclear waste site, 23, 24

Yudelman, Sally, 8, 17nn30–32

Zabinski, Catherine, xv

Zalzberg, Ellen, 17n27, 18n41

Zimmerman, Michael E., 25, 36n25, 74n54

Zinsmeister, K., 209n23

CPSIA information can be obtained
at www.ICGtesting.com
Printed in the USA
JSHW030247230922
30824JS00002B/16

9 780253 210579